AN ARISTOTELIAN ACCOUNT OF INDUCTION

McGILL-QUEEN'S STUDIES IN THE HISTORY OF IDEAS
Series Editor: Philip J. Cercone

1 Problems of Cartesianism
Edited by Thomas M. Lennon, John M. Nicholas, and John W. Davis

2 The Development of the Idea of History in Antiquity
Gerald A. Press

3 Claude Buffier and Thomas Reid: Two Common-Sense Philosophers
Louise Marcil-Lacoste

4 Schiller, Hegel, and Marx: State, Society, and the Aesthetic Ideal of Ancient Greece
Philip J. Kain

5 John Case and Aristotelianism in Renaissance England
Charles B. Schmitt

6 Beyond Liberty and Property: The Process of Self-Recognition in Eighteenth-Century Political Thought
J.A.W. Gunn

7 John Toland: His Methods, Manners, and Mind
Stephen H. Daniel

8 Coleridge and the Inspired Word
Anthony John Harding

9 The Jena System, 1804–5: Logic and Metaphysics
G.W.F. Hegel
Translation edited by John W. Burbidge and George di Giovanni
Introduction and notes by H.S. Harris

10 Consent, Coercion, and Limit: The Medieval Origins of Parliamentary Democracy
Arthur P. Monahan

11 Scottish Common Sense in Germany, 1768–1800: A Contribution to the History of Critical Philosophy
Manfred Kuehn

12 Paine and Cobbett: The Transatlantic Connection
David A. Wilson

13 Descartes and the Enlightenment
Peter A. Schouls

14 Greek Scepticism: Anti-Realist Trends in Ancient Thought
Leo Groarke

15 The Irony of Theology and the Nature of Religious Thought
Donald Wiebe

16 Form and Transformation: A Study in the Philosophy of Plotinus
Frederic M. Schroeder

17 From Personal Duties towards Personal Rights: Late Medieval and Early Modern Political Thought, c. 1300–c. 1650
Arthur P. Monahan

18 The Main Philosophical Writings and the Novel *Allwill*
Friedrich Heinrich Jacobi
Translated and edited by George di Giovanni

19 Kierkegaard as Humanist: Discovering My Self
Arnold B. Come

20 Durkheim, Morals, and Modernity
W. Watts Miller

21 The Career of Toleration: John Locke, Jonas Proast, and After
Richard Vernon

22 Dialectic of Love: Platonism in Schiller's Aesthetics
David Pugh

23 History and Memory in Ancient Greece
Gordon Shrimpton

24 Kierkegaard as Theologian: Recovering My Self
Arnold B. Come

25 Enlightenment and Conservatism in Victorian Scotland: The Career of Sir Archibald Alison
Michael Michie

26 The Road to Egdon Heath: The Aesthetics of the Great in Nature
Richard Bevis

27 Jena Romanticism and Its Appropriation of Jakob Böhme: Theosophy – Hagiography – Literature
Paolo Mayer

28 Enlightenment and Community: Lessing, Abbt, Herder, and the Quest for a German Public
Benjamin W. Redekop

29 Jacob Burckhardt and the Crisis of Modernity
John R. Hinde

30 The Distant Relation: Time and Identity in Spanish-American Fiction
Eoin S. Thomson

31 Mr Simson's Knotty Case: Divinity, Politics, and Due Process in Early Eighteenth-Century Scotland
Anne Skoczylas

32 Orthodoxy and Enlightenment: George Campbell in the Eighteenth Century
Jeffrey M. Suderman

33 Contemplation and Incarnation: The Theology of Marie-Dominique Chenu
Christophe F. Potworowski

34 Democratic Legitimacy: Plural Values and Political Power
F.M. Barnard

35 Herder on Nationality, Humanity, and History
F.M. Barnard

36 Labeling People: French Scholars on Society, Race, and Empire, 1815–1849
Martin S. Staum

37 The Subaltern Appeal to Experience: Self-Identity, Late Modernity, and the Politics of Immediacy
Craig Ireland

38 The Invention of Journalism Ethics: The Path to Objectivity and Beyond
Stephen J.A. Ward

39 The Recovery of Wonder: The New Freedom and the Asceticism of Power
Kenneth L. Schmitz

40 Reason and Self-Enactment in History and Politics: Themes and Voices of Modernity
F.M. Barnard

41 The More Moderate Side of Joseph de Maistre: Views on Political Liberty and Political Economy
Cara Camcastle

42 Democratic Society and Human Needs
Jeff Noonan

43 The Circle of Rights Expands: Modern Political Thought after the Reformation, 1521 (Luther) to 1762 (Rousseau)
Arthur P. Monahan

44 The Canadian Founding: John Locke and Parliament
Janet Ajzenstat

45 Finding Freedom: Hegel's Philosophy and the Emancipation of Women
Sara MacDonald

46 When the French Tried to Be British: Party, Opposition, and the Quest for the Civil Disagreement, 1814–1848
J.A.W. Gunn

47 Under Conrad's Eyes: The Novel as Criticism
Michael John DiSanto

48 Media, Memory, and the First World War
David Williams

49 An Aristotelian Account of Induction: Creating Something from Nothing
Louis Groarke

AN ARISTOTELIAN ACCOUNT OF INDUCTION

Creating Something from Nothing

Louis Groarke

McGill-Queen's University Press
Montreal & Kingston · London · Ithaca

ISBN 978-0-7735-3595-4 (cloth)
ISBN 978-0-7735-3596-1 (paper)

Legal deposit second quarter 2009
Bibliothèque nationale du Québec

Printed in Canada on acid-free paper that is 100% ancient forest free (100% post-consumer recycled), processed chlorine free.

This book has been published with the help of a grant from the Canadian Federation for the Humanities and Social Sciences, through the Aid to Scholarly Publications Programme, using funds provided by the Social Sciences and Humanities Research Council of Canada. Funding has also been received from St Francis Xavier University.

McGill-Queen's University Press acknowledges the support of the Canada Council for the Arts for our publishing program. We also acknowledge the financial support of the Government of Canada through the Book Publishing Industry Development Program (BPIDP) for our publishing activities.

Library and Archives Canada Cataloguing in Publication

Groarke, Louis
An Aristotelian account of induction: creating something from nothing / Louis Groarke.

(McGill-Queen's studies in the history of ideas; 49)
Includes bibliographical references and index.
ISBN 978-0-7735-3595-4 (bnd)
ISBN 978-0-7735-3596-1 (pbk)

1. Aristotle. 2. Induction (Logic). I. Title. II. Series: McGill-Queen's studies in the history of ideas; 49

B491.L8G76 2009 161 C2009-902359-8

Le Nouveau-né (*The Newborn*) by Georges de la Tour (1593–1652) was perhaps intended as a nativity scene. It depicts a midwife holding a candle in front of a mother holding a newborn in surrounding darkness. The pictorial elements of la Tour's painting provide a physical parallel to the mental acts of creativity discussed in this book. Ancient and medieval authors compared human intelligence to a mental light that, proceeding from an unseen source, illuminated the darkness of ignorance. And Socrates, of course, thought of the philosopher as a midwife who attends to the student as he or she gives birth to a new understanding. To think is to conceive. Just as the mother in the painting grasps her newborn child, so the mind, in an act of immediate intellection or insight, *without logic*, brings into the world something new and wondrous. (Image courtesy of Musée des beaux-arts de Rennes.)

This book was typeset by Interscript in 10/12 Baskerville.

For Joseph A. Novak

οἱ δὲ παιδεύοντες καὶ ἰατρεύοντες καὶ διδάσκοντες ἀγαθόν τι,
οὗτοι δὲ ταῖς ἐπιστήμαις εὐεργετοῦσιν.

Diogenes Laertius, *Lives of the Eminent Philosophers*, "Plato," bk 3, ch. 96

Contents

Figures and Tables

FIGURES

TABLES

Acknowledgments

LET ME START THEN, BY THANKING JOSEPH NOVAK, to whom this book is dedicated. Professor Novak ("Joe" to friends) has been an unassuming mentor, teacher, and friend to successive waves of graduate students as they passed through the University of Waterloo philosophy department. A genuinely thoughtful presence, a polyglot, an excellent classicist, with impeccable taste in music, chocolate, and science fiction, he is also a man with sincere religious convictions who, despite his invariably courteous and unflappable nature, does not retreat from taking unpopular positions and standing up for what he believes in. Joe taught me ancient philosophy and is, in some sort, responsible for initiating the unlikely chain of events leading to this book. I speak on behalf of many former students when I say that it is a pleasure and an honour to count him as a friend and a colleague.

I want to acknowledge the assistance of two anonymous referees who made helpful and incisive comments on an earlier version of the manuscript. In different ways, they were both open-minded and generous in their support and yet fairly took me to task on a number of precise points. I have incorporated many of their suggestions in the final text of the book. A more balanced and thorough treatment is the result.

I have had many useful conversations with different members of my department. In particular, I must mention Christopher Byrne, a specialist in Aristotle who has challenged my understanding of material cause; Steve Baldner, a reliable source on all things Thomistic; Ed Carty, an expert in classical languages and modern empiricism; Laura Byrne, who repeatedly directed me to important historical sources on the early modern period; and last but not least, William Sweet, who has always been a mentor in all things philosophical and professional.

I would also like to thank two close colleagues and friends: Professor Jonathan Lavery (Wilfrid Laurier, Brantford) and Professor Jason West (Newman Theological College) for constant advice and helpful support.

My brothers Leo (principal of the Brantford Campus of Wilfrid Laurier University) and Paul (presently in the Department of Criminal Justice and Criminology at Saint Thomas University) have always been an email or a phone call away. And two young scholars, Paolo Biondi (University of Sudbury) and Dwayne Raymond (University of Texas, Austin), make me believe that there is a new Aristotelianism on the rise in Canada.

In this day and age, academic life is sometimes a transient affair. A number of colleagues have befriended me in the course of several years work only to move on to other universities or positions. I remember them fondly. Joseph Khoury, from our English Department, has been a brother and a friend. De plus, je n'aurais pu accomplir ce travail sans le soutien constant de mon épouse Marie-Andrée et de mes enfants. Je tiens à les remercier sincèrement.

Philosophers are not always known for their business sense. Marcy Baker, our secretary, who has been invariably patient in putting up with my foibles, has managed to rescue me from more than one practical disaster.

I am also grateful for funding provided through the Aid to Scholarly Publications Program from the Social Sciences and Humanities Research Council of Canada. Dr Mary McGillivray, Academic Vice-President at St Francis Xavier University, and Dr Steve Baldner, in his role as dean of Arts, also provided helpful financial aid.

Finally, let me personally thank Philip Cercone, Executive director and senior editor at McGill-Queen's Press, Brenda Prince, editorial assistant, and Joan McGilvray, coordinating editor, for their professional support and understanding. Jim Thomas did a masterful and meticulous job of copy-editing; the result is a better book. Through its excellent reputation and hard-working staff, the Press continues to provide an essential service to Canadian scholars.

1

A New (Old) Theory of Induction

The theory of induction is the despair of philosophy – and yet all our activities are based upon it.

Alfred North Whitehead[1]

Western culture – any hopeful, humanitarian, knowledgeable, and right culture – depends on induction not merely in its parts, to justify its particular scientific inquiries and political inventions. It depends on induction altogether and in principle. *Spes est una in inductione vera* [Our only hope is in true induction].

Donald Carey Williams[2]

PROLEGOMENON

THIS IS A BOOK ABOUT INDUCTION. Contemporary philosophers, almost universally, understand induction as the form of logical argument that allows us to infer universals from particulars: I see one black crow, two black crows, three, four, etc., and I conclude "all crows are black." Or, more carefully, that "most crows are black."

As anyone familiar with present-day philosophy will know, the established view holds that there is a logical problem with induction. Because I observe a hundred black crows I cannot logically infer that the next crow I observe will be black. The next crow may be an albino one, for all we know.

This general view that there is an unsolvable problem with induction has been embraced by most philosophers. It risks precipitating, however, an all-out scepticism. Donald Carey Williams, who links a loss of faith in science with a loss of confidence in inductive argument, goes so far as to make dire predications for the future of Western civilization. Williams cites Alfred North Whitehead: "the theory of induction is the despair of

1 *Science and the Modern World*, 35.

2 *Ground of Induction*, 16. The Latin phrase is from Francis Bacon, *Novum Organum*, bk 1, aphorism 14 (in Bacon, various documents).

philosophy – and yet all our activities are based upon it."[3] Without an adequate basis for induction we cannot account for knowledge, for science, or for morality.

Williams, who has a penchant for embellished prose, proclaims,

> so prodigious a theoretical contretemps cannot remain a tempest in the professors' teapot. The news that no foundation is discoverable for the procedures of empirical intelligence, and still more the proclaimed discovery that there is no foundation, and still more the complacency which recommends that we … proceed by irrational faith or pragmatic postulate, will slowly shatter civilized life and thought, to a degree which will make the modernist's loss of confidence in Christian supernaturalism, so often cited as the ultimate in spiritual cataclysms, seem a minor vicissitude … To dispute the rational validity of induction … is to deny that reason and good-will have a purchase on reality, to deny mind's hope of acclimating itself to any world whatever, natural or supernatural.[4]

Williams' alarmist stance may overstate the degree of importance which ordinary people attach to theoretical problems in modern epistemology. I will argue, however, that scepticism regarding inductive reasoning does undermine knowledge in a radical and wholesale way. This book presents a response to scepticism about induction, a positive response, one that has been overlooked by modern authors such as Williams.[5] It attempts to reconstruct and argue for an account of induction that originates in the ancient Greek author Aristotle. Aristotle's views clash with the modern consensus on this issue. He and his followers in the tradition provide a very different answer to the alleged problem of induction, an answer worth examining seriously.

Contemporary debates about inductive reasoning have pushed Aristotle's comments on this issue to the margins of mainstream intellectual inquiry. Very able scholars have both interpreted and commented on Aristotle's logical works, but this is a discourse of specialists focusing on historical concerns. Contemporary accounts of induction largely bypass Aristotle. I want to reintroduce Aristotle's ideas on induction to the general philosophical

3 Whitehead, *Science and the Modern World*, 35.

4 Williams, *Ground of Induction*, 15–16.

5 Williams does provide an answer to the problem of induction, based on the probability calculus.

reader, to students of Aristotle, and to specialists in philosophy of science and in argumentation theory.

The course of intellectual history has served to obscure Aristotle's ideas. The rise of empiricism, the triumph of the Enlightenment, the short-lived victory of positivism, and the supremacy of what has come to be known as analytical philosophy has changed the direction of philosophy. Aristotle's sophisticated but commonsense realism and, in particular, his account of induction has been buried under misunderstanding after misunderstanding. Modern scholars have variously overlooked, dismissed, or misinterpreted his views. This is unfortunate. The aim of the present book is to systematize and explain in a straightforward and accessible way Aristotle's somewhat scattered and abbreviated remarks on induction. The project is not antiquarian but critical. I will argue that Aristotle's account, properly understood, provides, at the very least, a cogent competitor to its modern empiricist rival.

Aristotle was a serious logician and provided a detailed and explicit theory of deduction in his account of the syllogism. This pioneering work, after passing through modifications, has given rise to a standardized theory of syllogistic that is still taught in undergraduate critical-thinking courses to this very day. Unfortunately, Aristotle never systematized his understanding of induction or ἐπαγωγή (*epagoge*) in any parallel way. What we have instead are brief and often obscure remarks scattered here and there throughout his *Organon* (the six books on logic) and elsewhere. There are at least three major kinds of problems.

Firstly, Aristotle's style of writing (if it is really *his* writing) poses serious problems. It may seem scandalous to begin a book on Aristotle with such a frank admission, but the difficulties posed by his prose cannot be passed over or attributed to a mere absence of literary style.[6] Aristotle's prose is laborious and less than felicitous. The texts that have come down to us belong, for the most part, to his pedagogical or acroamatic works, originally published, catalogued, and edited by Andronicus of Rhodes.[7] These texts, which represent private lectures given to advanced students at the Lyceum, are only compilations and notes – one translator speaks of "*rough* notes" – collated, at a later date, by members of Aristotle's school.[8]

6 This is the traditional suggestion. See, for example, Jaeger, *Aristotle*, 6; Bambrough, in Aristotle, *Philosophy of Aristotle*, 18; Copleston, *Greece and Rome*, pt 2, 12 – and so on.

7 For an accessible discussion of the provenance of the actual texts, see Guthrie, *History of Greek Philosophy*, "Aristotle: The Written Remains," vol. 6, 49–65.

8 E.S. Forester, introduction to the *Topics*, 206 (in Aristotle, *Aristotle in 23 Volumes*).

Although the ideas expressed are both insightful and compelling, the prose is repetitious, elliptical, disconnected, broad-ranging, technical, and highly obscure. The logical works especially are largely impenetrable to the causal modern reader.

Richard McKirahan describes the text of the *Posterior Analytics,* a key source for Aristotle's thought about induction. "As usual," McKirahan writes, "we find obscure arguments, unclear transitions and cross-references, and inadequate examples, all of which place stringent demands on the reader. But in addition the work seems rough and unfinished, a series of jottings on different aspects of its subject matter ... It does not read like a finished treatise, making definitive statements, but like an inchoate collection of thoughts, some worked out more thoroughly than others."[9] This list of problems is emblematic of the textual difficulties Aristotelian scholars must face. The philosopher's tortuous prose has limited his influence among a broader, educated public and fostered fractious and sometimes fruitless debates among scholars.

Some historical commentators have gone so far as to claim that Aristotle consciously chose to write in a challenging style. Contemporary specialist Lambertus Marie de Rijk relates an amusing story about Ammonius, an early commentator, who compares Aristotle's inscrutable prose to a curtain in a religious temple used to shield the most sacred objects from the eyes of the unwashed multitudes. Ammonius explains, "Just as in temples curtains are used to prevent everyone, and particularly the impure, from encountering things they are not worthy of meeting, so Aristotle uses the obscurity of his philosophy as a veil, so that good people may stretch their minds even more, and bad people can be deterred."[10] Keeping to the spirit of the metaphor, I want to pull back the temple curtain, so to speak, to open wide a window on Aristotle, to explain and elucidate his thoughts in a way that renders his account of induction intelligible to anyone who takes the trouble to wrestle with his challenging ideas. I believe that Aristotle's ideas are eminently understandable. In my own teaching, I have found that his commonsense realism strikes a sympathetic cord even with students. (And if nonspecialists can understand his general drift, so much the worse for the distinction between the academically pure and the unwashed multitudes!)

The second type of problem facing anyone searching into Aristotle's account of induction is that the philosopher clearly believes that the process of induction is, to some degree, self-explanatory. In the *Topics,* he goes so

9 McKirahan, *Principles and Proofs,* 3.

10 De Rijk, *Aristotle,* vol. 1, §22, 18. De Rijk's source is *Ammonius in Aristotelis Categorias commentarius.*

far as to remark, "What induction is, is obvious."[11] Such comments are less than helpful! And yet, they do illustrate a general attitude. Unlike modern philosophers of more sceptical or suspicious bent, Aristotle is not in the business of justifying or defending induction. He simply accepts that we can derive knowledge of universals from specific sense perceptions and proceeds accordingly. Perhaps this is why, although he touches on important points here and there, he does not feel the need to provide any exhaustive, detailed justification of the subject.

Thirdly, I will argue that induction itself is an elusive process. Although Aristotle explicitly comments on the leap of mental cognition that initiates induction, he does not consistently explore the ramifications of his own theory. This has lead to considerable misunderstanding. Insomuch as induction is a creative act that produces new knowledge, it relies crucially on a moment of mental insight or inspiration. An attentive survey of empirical data is not enough. Sense perception must be illuminated by mind or νοῦς (*nous*), a mental capacity allowing us to leap from the individual to the universal. Aristotelean induction is, then, fundamentally and inevitably creative. His theory borrows more from Plato's philosophy than is commonly recognized.

Aristotle's view of induction sharply contrasts with what has become the received modern view. Contemporary accounts of induction can be traced back to David Hume, who is well-known for having brought the incomplete nature of the inductive process into clear light with his trenchant critique of metaphysical theories of induction. Hume's account has, over time, established itself as the new orthodoxy. I will argue that considered as a criticism of Aristotle, the Humean account is seriously inadequate. Although the Humean model has provided the impetus for a much more sophisticated account of probabilistic reasoning, Aristotle's account more closely mirrors the most familiar form of induction that ordinary people regularly resort to in everyday discourse. His lost perspective better illuminates the inductive method of science and more deftly captures the heuristic insight that makes inductive reasoning possible.

Aristotle's explanation of induction may, paradoxically, strike the contemporary reader as iconoclastic. If the critic complains that the arguments elaborated here clash with the received wisdom of the present age, this is, of course, true. But such complaints are misguided. In fact, the Aristotelian stance I defend is the traditional point of view; it has been defended and elaborated by a long line of important historical authors. Situated within the history of Western philosophy, it is the majority view.

11 *Topics* (Forester), pt 8, ch. 1, 157a8.

Although it has been vilified, caricatured, or, most often, simply forgotten in the present age, this is a fairly recent phenomenon. In any case, the Aristotelian stance is not wrong because it has fallen out of favour. As an account of inductive reasoning, it must be judged on its own merits.

In this book, I approach traditional philosophy with respect but not with uncritical devotion. Earlier authors, Aristotle included, made mistakes, sometimes serious mistakes. I try to present an original synthesis of the best that has been said before. I am indebted both to traditional philosophy and to contemporary scholarship. While delving into exegetical and historical issues, I want, first and foremost, though, to present a critical account of induction, one that can rival predominant trends in contemporary argumentation theory, ethics, and modern philosophy of science. The account I elaborate may, as a minority view, serve to illuminate contemporary debates from a neglected perspective.

FIRST PRINCIPLES

The content of this volume may be described in another way. Although it is principally a book about induction, it is equally one about first principles. Greek philosophers from the Presocratics onward searched into the ἀρχαί (*archai*), the roots or origins of the cosmos. Aristotle was not content to limit his investigations to the deep nature of the physical world. In his study of the human person, he turned the inquiry inward, searching into the roots or origins of human thought. As we shall see, he believed that induction supplies first principles, the most basic building blocks, the *archai* of human knowledge.

We must begin by clearing up a misunderstanding. Contemporary thinkers view induction primarily as an argument form that, in the paradigm case, moves from incomplete premises dealing with particular instances to a conclusion that makes a universal claim. For Aristotle, induction is not, first and foremost, a form of argument, but a kind of intelligent grasping that allows the knower to move from a more restricted to a more general understanding. The human mind is somehow able to synthesize experience, to bring together within a single concept or claim what is uniform, constant, or necessary about the world. The same basic process of mental illumination produces individual concepts, general rules about mathematics and logic, and universal claims about the empirical world. At the deepest level, induction produces the first principles of knowledge.

Aristotle proposes, then, a much broader account of inductive reason than those we find in circulation at present. The conclusion of the inductive argument (above) that "all crows are black" is a product of induction. But even the concept "crow," or the concept "black," is a product of induction. These concepts materialize in the mind because we can somehow seize on an underlying similarity that brings together a number of otherwise divergent experiences. Inductive arguments are, then, an expression of a deeper, more comprehensive mental process. Aristotle uses the Greek term for induction, *epagoge*, to refer, in the first instance, to this process, and only secondarily, to induction understood as an argument form.

One might argue that Aristotelian induction is, at its origins, a form of intuition, except that the debased, vernacular use of the word "intuition" sends the wrong message. The modern English term "insight" better captures Aristotle's basic attitude. We *see* what must be true. Reasoning begins in the mental activity of induction, understood not as an argument form, but as a mental realization triggered by sense perception. Earlier authors in general distinguish between discursive and inductive reason. Discursive reason moves from claim, to claim, to a conclusion. Inductive reason, understood as an initial capacity for intelligent discovery, provides the immovable starting points for intelligible discourse. There is often a powerful psychological side to this inductive process – grasping a universal truth may, for example, be accompanied by an aha! experience. Nonetheless, Aristotelian induction is a properly epistemological mechanism. It is not a matter of mere feeling.

A contemporary rationalism demands a reason for everything. But thought does not begin in argument. The goal of intellectual inquiry is ultimately knowledge; however, we cannot argue, let alone think, unless we have something to think with. On the Aristotelian account, induction, understood as a capacity for accurate mental insight, supplies us with a wide assortment of concepts, definitions, universals, logical and metaphysical laws, the most basic natural facts of science, and moral principles. This is where thought begins, with induction understood as an intuitive cognitive capacity, not with argument. Consider an analogy.

Suppose George, an engineer, is an expert bridge-builder. And suppose we take away the tools and materials he needs to build bridges. Suppose we confiscate every bit of wood, metal, plastic, brick, and cement. We remove all aids: his calculator, his pencil and paper. What can George use to build bridges with? Perhaps, the sly will respond, he can build imaginary bridges inside his mind. But suppose we could somehow take away the tools and the materials he needs to think with. Eliminate all concepts, definitions, rules of grammar, laws of logic and mathematics, all knowledge of physics or chemistry, and so forth. At the end of the day George will be left with nothing to build bridges with. It does not matter if he has the talent to be a superior bridge-builder; without the necessary tools and materials, he will be unable to build bridges.

Traditional authors such as Aristotle conceived of the activity of first thought in a similar way. Thought presupposes certain tools and raw materials. It presupposes the requisite immaterial objects: concepts, definitions, the rules of logic and grammar, the first principles of the physical sciences, and so on. Intuitive induction supplies these first principles. Although ancient and medieval philosophers believed that induction could be formalized as an argument (i.e., as a syllogism), they would never have supposed that we could *prove* the soundness of the mental activity of induction. They would instead have dismissed any such demand for proof as misguided. This is to get the epistemological process backward. We do not use propositions to prove first principles; rather, we use first principles to prove propositions. If, however, we do not prove first principles, it does not follow that they are arbitrary. First principles force themselves on us. Our rational understanding hits on them in a momentous and necessary insight. We derive them, not out of thin air, but from an intelligent – even cunning – analysis of experience.

In the present climate, any talk of first principles may summon up images of old-fashioned claims to absolute truth. But Aristotle never makes claim to the kind of absolute infallible knowledge commonly reviled in contemporary philosophy. Indeed, the fashionable myth that earlier authors were well-meaning but gullible sorts who uncritically assumed that their own opinions were true without qualification is a conspicuous caricature perpetrated by philosophical pundits who, apparently, do not bother to read primary sources. In his *Metaphysics*, Aristotle complains about people who demand a reason for everything. This is, he says, impossible. We simply cannot come up with a reason for everything, for human finitude is an unbreachable obstacle.

Aristotle's epistemological stance balances between two extremes. On the one hand, he is, in contemporary terms, a fallibilist. (One might be so bold as to call him a pragmatist, but a pragmatist who still believes in metaphysics.) He makes no claims to providing an absolute proof for the veracity of first principles, and he seems entirely aware of sceptical challenges. On the other hand, he insists that first principles are, properly understood, infallible. *Seen from a human perspective*, certain beliefs are inescapable. They cannot be doubted. They must be accepted as true.

The ancients and medievals in general did not believe that we could make knowledge claims from the omniscient perspective of a perfect God. Aristotle makes no claims as to the noumenal (or superhuman) validity of knowledgeable assertion. In a pre-Kantian world, this is not at issue. Along with other authors in the mainstream historical tradition, Aristotle adopts a sophisticated (not a naive) commonsense realism. All that we can surmise from the evidence we are presented with is that any intelligent attempt to understand the world must embrace specific claims, concepts, definitions, rules, and so on. These cannot be consistently doubted. This is what Aristotle (and other early authors) meant by the infallibility of first principles. We shall investigate this issue further in a later chapter.

While, then, this is a book about induction, it is also about the first principles produced by induction and, inevitably, about the limits of philosophy. Human reasoning must begin somewhere, and it must end somewhere. Beginning in induction, it ends in the ineffable, in mysticism if you will. A contemporary rationalism raises suspicions about induction and it denies, of course, anything resembling mysticism. This is not a book about what, if anything, lies beyond philosophy. An attentive study of the history of ideas reveals a (sometimes misguided) striving toward transcendence. If the human mind strains skyward, toward ultimate and universal explanations, this may, among other things, tell us something important about the indomitable human spirit, about the existence of God, or about the human need for overcoming. Whatever our account of the *au delà,* Aristotle insists that philosophy, science, and morality originate in induction, in a non-discursive but epistemologically authoritative moment of intellectual understanding or insight.

METHODOLOGY

This book is driven by several methodological convictions. The approach can be described as synoptic, historical, critical, informal (or semantic), positive and negative, and self-contained.

As Jon Moline observes, Plato coins the Greek term συνοπτικός (*synoptikos*), which means "seeing the whole together" or "taking a comprehensive view[12]" – hence, we have the modern English equivalent "synoptic." Aristotle is a synoptic philosopher in that he devotes himself to elaborating a comprehensive world view, rather than exclusively developing one, specialized branch of learning. The general reader may find Aristotle's synoptic propensities a refreshing relief from the overly technical discourses of much current work, but even when it comes to the exploration of more specialized topics, the synoptic method is itself a useful exegetical tool. We cannot understand Aristotle's account of induction by focusing on isolated passages. It is a mistake to focus exclusively on familiar sections from the

12 Moline, *Plato's Theory of Understanding*, xi.

Prior Analytics, the *Posterior Analytics,* the *Metaphysics,* or the *Nicomachean Ethics.* Puzzling passages need to be examined in light of other passages, and still others, and ultimately in the light of a general, overarching world view. The best guide to Aristotle is Aristotle himself. The approach adopted here is *synoptic* in that it tries to bring together in one coherent account the notion of inductive reasoning implicit in Aristotle's logic, metaphysics, natural philosophy, psychology, and moral philosophy. When we focus on the philosopher's overall ideas and how they link together, details often felicitously fall into place.

Distinguished scholars such as D.W. Graham, G.E.L. Owen, and Terence Irwin distinguish sharply between the young, anti-Platonic Aristotle of the *Organon* and the more mature, reconciliatory Aristotle of the *Metaphysics*.[13] Although I dispute their specific account, no one who seriously reads Aristotle could overlook many apparent inconsistencies in the text. Jonathan Barnes cites two quick examples: the differing accounts of pleasure in the *Nicomachean Ethics* and his contradictory comments about the provability (or unprovability) of definitions in the *Topics* and *Posterior Analytics.*[14] I deal with the latter issue directly, but the more general point is well taken. A detailed analysis of Aristotle's original corpus is a risky and sometimes inconclusive business.

When it comes to interpretative details, Aristotle specialists and classicists do not agree among themselves. Still, many apparent inconsistencies resolve themselves when his comments are seen for what they are, scattered notes and remarks, composed on various occasions, for various purposes, by a subtle thinker who must have modified his general philosophical world view over time.[15] While some details remain obscure, we can nevertheless distil a relatively uncontroversial description of Aristotle's general philosophical approach or world view. Using the principle of charity, we can follow through the ramifications of his thought to their logical conclusion.

If the present volume is intended as a contribution to contemporary debate on induction, the method is *historical.* J.R. Milton writes, "Many philosophers in the analytic tradition have professed a conception of the nature of their subject which makes the history of philosophy almost completely irrelevant; the occasional remarks and discussions about historical figures are as perfunctory as those which appear in scientific textbooks,

13 See Graham, *Aristotle's Two Systems*; Owen, "Tithenai ta Phainomena"; and Irwin, *Aristotle's First Principles.*

14 Barnes, "Life and Work," 15.

15 For the classical statement of the chronology and development of Aristotle's ideas see Jaeger, *Aristotle.*

and indeed have a similar function."[16] Someone who wants to learn about chemistry does not devote much time to the study of medieval alchemy. The history of philosophy is a history of past mistakes; not much is to be gained from the perusal of ancient or medieval sources.

This kind of triumphalism is on the wane, but it has not been completely extinguished. One champion of the modern mindset explains that contemporary logicians and philosophers of language, unlike ethicists, have little, if anything, to learn from history. As he puts it,

> Twentieth Century, Logic and Philosophy of Language are two of the few areas of philosophy in which philosophers made indisputable progress. For example, even now many of the foremost living ethicists present their theories as somewhat more explicit versions of the ideas of Kant, Mill, or Aristotle. In contrast, it would be patently absurd for a contemporary philosopher of language or logician to think of herself as working in the shadow of any figure who died before the Twentieth Century began. Advances in these disciplines make even the most unaccomplished of its practitioners vastly more sophisticated than Kant. There were previous periods in which the problems of language and logic were studied extensively (e.g., the medieval period). But from the perspective of the progress made in the last 120 years, previous work is at most a source of interesting data or occasional insight. All systematic theorizing about content that meets contemporary standards of rigor has been done subsequently.[17]

This is, to say the least, a little rich. There are, no doubt, more people who share this view than those few who are foolhardy enough to say so in print. The present book, needless to say, is motivated by a different mindset. I argue that modern logicians ignore what ancient and medieval philosophers had to say about induction at their peril. The blanket rejection of past philosophy as a comedy of errors does not withstand scholarly scrutiny. Indeed, modern accounts of induction are defective, in large part, because we have forgotten or misunderstood the work of earlier authors. If, however, we are to profit from our acquaintance with earlier philosophers such as Aristotle, we must work at developing a historically precise interpretation of his works. This is an arduous task. Our own assumptions and prejudices do not fit the assumptions and prejudices of earlier ages. What comes naturally to us is not necessarily what earlier authors had in mind.

16 Milton, "Induction before Hume," 49.

17 Stanley, "Philosophy of Language," 1 (online).

It would be self-defeating to remake Aristotle in our own image. Reading him is a salutary philosophical exercise precisely because his views are radically different from the assumptions that underlie so much of contemporary philosophy. He offers modern readers a refreshingly novel perspective on the problem of induction. All too often we are subjected to an anachronistic reading of earlier authors. Such efforts seem, from both a historical and a critical perspective, a sheer waste of time. They subvert the originality of their subject matter and block access to a larger world of ideas outside our own epoch and more comfortable ways of thinking.

We can study history for history's sake, to better grasp what earlier individuals were doing and thinking. But we can also study history in order to access the knowledge and wisdom that has been obscured by contemporary prejudices. In the later case, historical research becomes a tool to a better philosophical understanding. The study of the history of ideas advances hand in hand with critical philosophy. The present project has two goals: to secure an accurate historical interpretation of Aristotle's philosophy and to develop a modern theory of induction *ad mentum* Aristotle. These twin goals are necessarily connected. Looking at Aristotle through the lens of history produces a philosophically defensible understanding of induction.

Historical awareness is an aid to philosophical understanding. We must not lose sight of the bigger picture. Contemporary philosophy, like all important intellectual traditions, is a product of historical development. To make a long story much too short: Aristotle's empiricism was reworked by medieval authors and eventually supplanted by the ideological empiricism of early modern authors such as Locke and Hume. This new scientific philosophy of the Enlightenment, adopted and adapted by Kant, gave rise, in turn, to contemporary schools of Continental and Anglo-American philosophy. I offer a historical analysis of this development as it relates to the problem of induction, paying special attention to authors who preserved and developed the Aristotelian synthesis such as Thomas Aquinas and some of his more recent disciples.

We should have the greatest respect for Aristotle's prodigious intellectual achievement, and for the wonderfully patient work of succeeding generations of commentators. Still, the man the medievals called "the philosopher" did not say all there is to say. Indeed, his formulation of his own position is not without its shortcomings. There are gaps in his account. What he merely hints at must be elaborated at length; scattered observations, systematized; his assumptions rigorously argued for, in light of modern challenges; and his (and others') confusions, cleared away. Aristotle does not always acknowledge the implications of his own stance or the radical nature of some of his suggestions. He could not have foreseen the development of competing schools of modern philosophy, but the appearance of these rivals provides an opportunity for a more balanced elucidation and evaluation of points of view he sometimes takes for granted.

We need to approach Aristotle's comments *critically*. It is not that he completed the specific philosophical project he began. It is rather that he initiated a certain philosophical approach, a commonsense realism that stands in need of further elucidation and continued development. The point is not to rely on mere argument from authority. A certain theory of induction is not correct because it originates in Aristotle, who is after all, a fallible thinker like the rest of us. An Aristotelian theory of induction must, in the end, stand on its own two feet. This book aims to capture all that is best in Aristotle's understanding of induction, without refraining from necessary criticism and amendment.

This is not a book on formal logic. I do briefly consider some formal aspects of the syllogism in chapter 6, but in a short-hand way that should be accessible to the uninitiated. The approach I adopt borrows heavily from contemporary argumentation theory, what is familiarly but somewhat misleadingly called "informal logic." Argumentation theory began, in large part, as an attempt to open up the study of argument to wider concerns than those privileged in modern courses on formal logic.[18] Contemporary philosophers such as Stephen Toulmin, Ralph Johnson and Tony Blair, Douglas Walton, Leo Groarke, and representatives of the Dutch "pragma-dialectic" school, such as Frans H. van Eemeren and Rob Grootendorst, have pushed the study of logic and persuasion in a unique direction.[19] Without eschewing a legitimate preoccupation with issues of logical form and deductive validity, argumentation theorists turn their attention to the study and evaluation of concrete "real-life" examples, to natural-language arguments, and to rhetoric and dialectic. While this is a book on inductive reasoning, there is nothing exotic about the process. We all induce conclusions on a regular basis, in both academic and casual contexts. I want to study Aristotle's account, in part because of the light it sheds on this everyday argument form.

Of course, this kind of *informal* approach includes consideration of the formal issues. Most importantly perhaps, I will argue that Aristotle, in

18 For a brief introduction to contemporary argumentation theory see *Stanford Encyclopedia of Philosophy*, s.v. "Informal Logic" (by Leo Groarke).

19 Authors such as Chaim Perelman and Lucy O'lbrecht-Tyteca have done similar work in the field of contemporary rhetoric, and overall the list should include further authors, such as John Woods, Paul Schollmeier, Trudy Govier, Robert Pinto, Christopher Tindale, Michael Gilbert, and Hans Hansen.

complete contrast to most modern authors, presents inductive arguments as deductively valid. There is a deep epistemological puzzle about the success of inductive reasoning, but this relates to the issue of creativity not to issues of logical form. I will argue that Aristotle's attitude toward inductive inference mirrors, more or less, that of deductivists, as they are called, in argumentation theory.[20] Although the modern-day deductivist account needs to be carefully qualified, I will show that Aristotle maintains that all good arguments have a valid form. It follows that inductive syllogisms are amenable to symbolic treatment and that we can elaborate a deductively valid account of the inductive syllogism using elementary notation.

The notion of a more informal approach to logic has not always been welcomed by theoreticians. The early Rudolf Carnap famously (or infamously) wrote, "All questions in the field of logic can be formally expressed and are, then, resolved into syntactical questions. A special logic of meaning is superfluous; 'non-formal logic' is a contradiction *in adjecto.* Logic is syntax."[21] Carnap here appeals to a common distinction between syntax and semantics. Many argumentation theorists are uncomfortable with this distinction (in ways too complicated to describe or evaluate in any detail here). According to this way of thinking, those who study argument can move in two directions. Those who study syntax (ways of putting properly formulated assertions together regardless of meaning) focus on proof. The basic goal is to show, by means of a series of well-formed statements, that if something is true, something else can be logically derived from it. On the semantic side of things, the focus is on the meaning and reference of concepts and statements, on issues of truth, and on validity or weaker (inductive) versions of logical cogency. The basic goal is the construction of arguments, often in natural language, that move from meaningful premises to meaningful conclusions while communicating or preserving (as much as possible) truth. (Questions naturally arise as to the relationship between the semantic and the syntactic side of things. Does validity always lead to provability, and does provability always lead to validity? Etc.)

Insomuch as we want to rely on this terminology, this project moves toward the semantic side of things. The focus is squarely on inductive reasoning understood in the context of scientific discovery, on substantive (not mathematical) reasoning, on natural-language arguments, on validity understood as a kind of truth preservation or entailment, on issues having to do with the definition and content of concepts, and even on

20 See Louis Groarke, "Deductive Account of Induction."

21 Carnap, *Logical Syntax of Language,* 259.

direct intellection as a "formless" (or "method-less") conduit to truth. The focus is not on the construction of logical proofs or derivability. Clearly, Aristotle is very proud (excessively proud perhaps) of the syllogism, but his theory of logic, as we shall see, has both formal and semantic elements. On an Aristotelian account, they cannot be definitively separated, for the precise meaning of terms and propositions has an important bearing on the degree to which a given argument has logical force. It is the combination of logical form *and* the content in terms of meaning (and reference) that determines the kind of argument we are dealing with. In chapter 6, I do introduce a very simple formalism for inductive syllogisms (what might be loosely called an arithmetic of syllogisms), but even here the focus is on validity and entailment rather than on what modern specialists conceive of as formal proof.

There are inevitably two sides to any controversial treatment of contemporary issues. My method has a *negative* and a *positive* aspect. I criticize the orthodox empiricist account of induction, and I elaborate a competing theory. My critique is not intended as an assault on any one author or identifiable school, but as a protest against a widespread dogma that often functions as an unassailable presumption, a self-evident axiom contemporary thinkers often take for granted. I mean to challenge the usual view of induction and present, in a more constructive light, a very different explanation of its logical persuasiveness.

Taken as a whole, this book captures the development of my thought as the project progressed. The finished product preserves, I hope, something of the sense of intellectual discovery I experienced over years of close acquaintance with Aristotle. It is humbling to find at least hints of solutions to contemporary philosophical problems already laid out in an ancient author. Although the book as a whole looks at inductive reasoning from a wide-ranging perspective, individual chapters are largely *self-contained*. They can, for the most part, be read on their own. Each chapter focuses on a different issue, and each issue is, insomuch as that is possible, considered in its own right and in as accessible and as jargon free a manner as possible.

A word about Greek terminology. This is a work of contemporary critical philosophy rather than a study in classics. I want to elaborate on the importance of Aristotle's ideas for contemporary philosophers. It is necessary, nonetheless, to review Aristotle's exact terminology, for the Greek terms he employs do not always map neatly onto their contemporary English counterparts. Etymology is, at times, a crucial aid to understanding. I will, then, refer to Aristotle's technical nomenclature where appropriate. Any standard ancient Greek dictionary would provide additional help with the common Greek terms referred to here.

As this is a work directed toward a wide audience, readability is an important concern. Clearly, many translations of Aristotle's works are available. To cite only one example, the *Posterior Analytics*, an especially important work for any investigation into Aristotle's attitudes about induction, has been wholly or partly translated by such eminent classical scholars as W.D. Ross, Jonathan Barnes, Hugh Tredennick, Hippocrates Apostle, Renford Bambrough, G.R.C. Mure, W.K.C. Guthrie, G.E.L. Owen, Terrence Irwin, Richard McKirahan, Robin Smith, Paolo Biondi, and so on. I try to introduce and explain Aristotle's technical terminology, while citing from translations that are accessible to modern-day readers with only a modicum of classical learning. One inevitably prefers some translations to others, but nothing in my argument hinges on one precise translation. Understanding the Stagirite is not a matter of literal translation, but of understanding the systematic orientation of his thought, the overall structure of his arguments, the historical context of his writing, and the general thrust of his ideas. (Aristotle was traditionally dubbed "the Stagirite" because he was born in the northern Greek colony of Stagira.)

PLAN OF THE BOOK

Turn now to the plan of the book. Chapter 1 is, of course, this introduction. Chapter 2 begins by briefly describing induction as an argument form. I consider, in some detail, the standard modern view of induction and particularly Hume's famous attack on the validity of inductive reasoning. This enormously influential historical landmark has set the tone for a certain type of discussion. Modern authors of all colours and stripes have commented on the problem of induction, variously attempting either to secure the validity of inductive reasoning or to show that all such attempts are doomed to failure. I argue that the familiar Humean critique of traditional accounts of induction depends crucially on a caricature of the metaphysical notion of substance. The Humean critique conflates "Cartesian" with evidence-based scepticism. It mistakes a dogmatic uncertainty, deriving from inevitable human fallibility, for an evidence-based uncertainty that motivates reasonable doubt.

In chapter 3, I go on to explore Aristotle's basic approach to inductive argument as a response to the Humean puzzle. In contrast to many recent commentators, I argue that Aristotle's famous example of an inductive syllogism in *Prior Analytics*, book 2, chapters 23–4, does not refer to an instance of so-called "perfect induction." This widespread interpretation rests on a misunderstanding. On Aristotle's account, inductive arguments are *valid* syllogisms that depend on a presumed resemblance and, more fundamentally, on a notion of identity. His approach resembles that of a largely neglected school of older textbook authors, including "traditional logicians" such as Richard Clarke, Peter Coffey, Ralph Eaton, George H. Joyce, and Jacques Maritain.

In his discussion of the inductive syllogism, Aristotle appeals to the key concept of "convertibility" or "counter-predication." I investigate this forgotten logical relation in some detail. Although Aristotle's understanding resembles that of the deductivists in contemporary argumentation theory, we can reformulate his account, using modern propositional logic and the argumentation-theory device of hidden or implicit premises. As we shall see, Aristotelian induction applies to both natural and artificial kinds. It is the identification of an underlying similarity that binds individuals together within a specific species or genus, securing a form of logical necessity.

In chapter 4, I argue that Aristotle's theory of induction is more finely structured than in the prevailing account. I identify five main levels of induction. The first two involve a non-discursive mode of intuitive insight or intellection. The first, which I call "true induction" or "induction proper," is more rigorous than the second, which is merely a generalized sensitivity to resemblance. The first level begets the concepts, definitions, universals, laws, and natural facts acting as the starting points for the activity of rigorous science. In a practical vein, it also produces the first principles of morality. It operates by means of contemplative thought or νόησις (*noesis*). The second level involves the way we identify a contingent likeness. It operates by a less reliable form of inductive insight that I will call "recognition."

The remaining three levels involve actual arguments. We can, then, distinguish between three types of inductive argument. What I call "true inductive syllogism" makes inferences about the necessary or essential properties of things; it produces universal knowledge or ἐπιστήμη (*episteme*). It can be described as an unorthodox or imperfect type of demonstrative syllogism or ἀπόδειξις (*apodeixis*). Rhetorical (or dialectical) induction produces general but not necessarily universal or necessary knowledge. Aristotle identifies two kinds of rhetorical induction: what he calls arguments from likeness (ὅμοιος) and arguments from example (παράδειγμα). Both these arguments produce probable or plausible conclusions. The third type of inductive argument involves modern treatments of mathematical probability. Aristotle overlooks this last category of statistical inference. Given his biological view of science, it seems safe to say that he would have considered it the least important form of induction.

In chapter 5, I consider Aristotle's account of the role of inductive reasoning in moral philosophy as elucidated in texts such as *Nicomachean Ethics*. I argue that Aristotle's account of moral deliberation echoes his inductive-deductive model of theoretical science. It can be divided into stages: moral induction and practical syllogism. Morality involves practical reason or φρόνησις (*phronesis*). Science is logically a more rigorous form of intellectual inquiry. Nonetheless, the first principles of science and morality are equally fallible (or equally authoritative) in that they both spring from the same ultimate source in inductive reason.

In chapter 6, I propose a formal account of the inductive syllogism. George Englebretsen has shown how Fred Sommers' account of the syllogism can be used to formulate a term logic that can replace or supersede more popular mathematical accounts of sentential logic.[22] My goals are more modest. I revisit, in passing, the historical controversy that swirled around William Hamilton's suggestion that the predicate term in a categorical statement be quantified along with the subject term. Reworking Hamilton's proposal, I develop an elementary formalism based on a parallel form of double quantification. One can use the very same formalism to evaluate deductive and inductive syllogisms. It could easily be used to teach Aristotelian logic to undergraduates. The notation (overlooked by Aristotle and his later medieval commentators) is, in effect, a formal expression of his somewhat hasty treatment of the key concept of convertibility.

Aristotle, like other traditional philosophers, situates the beginning of reason in induction. In chapter 7, I offer a historical overview of the way several important philosophers account for our ability to recover first principles. I begin with the Presocratics, Plato, and Aristotle. As it turns out, the Aristotelian concept of *epagoge* or induction closely parallels the Platonic concept of ἀνάμνησις (*anamnesis*) or recollection, in that both processes depend on some mysterious capacity for creative intuition or νόησις (*noesis*). I go on to briefly examine Neoplatonic notions of *noesis*, Thomas Aquinas' doctrine of *intellectus*, René Descartes' account of the natural light of reason (*lumine naturali*), and Blaise Pascal's description of "knowledge from the heart," and, in a turn to contemporary philosophy, Bernard Lonergan's understanding of "insight." I claim that earlier accounts share a common understanding that more recent authors misconstrue. Representatives of the modern view such as Descartes and Lonergan embrace, wittingly or unwittingly, an eliminative rationalism that leads inevitably to the dead end of scepticism.

22 See Englebretsen, *Three Logicians*. Other logicians have busied themselves translating Aristotle's syllogistic into a propositional calculus. Cf. J. Lukasiewicz, *Aristotle's Syllogistic from the Standpoint of Modern Formal Logic*. Or see the scholarly apparatus in Jonathan Barne's translation of the *Posterior Analytics*.

In chapter 8, I focus the creative aspects of induction. In the Greek mind, inductive inference is not irrational, but it is quasi-divine, for it involves, in a way to be explained, the creation of more from less. It is the creative leap at the heart of induction that rankles modern empiricists. Mathematical or computational attempts to reproduce or represent the inductive insight in cognitive science fail. In some important sense, they miss the point. I argue that art provides a more instructive analogy. Indeed, the way Renaissance sculptor Michelangelo Buonarroti describes artistic inspiration closely parallels Aristotle's account of inductive insight. Induction is, in some qualified sense, a τέχνη (*techne*), a kind of making. It *makes* first principles. If, however, this is a creative endeavour, it does not follow that first principles are purely subjective or arbitrary.

In chapter 9, I consider the epistemological status of induction and the role it plays in modern science. Ancient and medieval authors claimed that first principles are infallible. In an age of philosophy still marked by a lingering Cartesian doubt, these claims have been misunderstood. I elucidate and defend the traditional point of view. First principles are infallible insomuch as they cannot, *from a human perspective*, be meaningfully challenged. They are, so to speak, immovable. To eliminate them is to undermine our very sanity. In the course of my argument, I consider modern and not-so-modern attempts to undermine perhaps the most celebrated first principle of all, the law of non-contradiction. I provide an Aristotelian solution to the liar's paradox and critique the narrow formalism of modern treatments. Though first principles are authoritative expressions of human intelligence, we can, of course, still make mistakes in inductive reasoning. I examine Thomas Aquinas' explanation of intuitive error and Aristotle's use of ᾗ (*qua*) as method for resolving inductive ambiguity.

Although modern scientific philosophers have been, at times, hostile to Aristotelian metaphysics, this attitude is far from universal. Contemporary philosophers of science such as Hilary Kornblith, Brian Ellis, Howard Sankey, and James Freeman argue for a "new essentialism," which they allege is necessitated by the discoveries of modern science. I give this new essentialism and the associated attempt to recover a notion of *a posteriori* necessity a sympathetic reading. I do, however, argue that Aristotle's original account of induction is superior to modern notions of abduction or "inference to the best explanation." I also argue that we cannot consistently embrace the new essentialism and reject metaphysical realism. I finish the chapter by showing that the alleged logical incompatibility of Aristotle's metaphysics with modern theories of evolution is largely based on a misunderstanding.

2

Before and after Hume

Like every other innovator of modern times, [Darwin] had to combat the authority of Aristotle. Aristotle ... has been one of the great misfortunes of the human race. To this day the teaching of logic in most universities is full of nonsense for which he is responsible.

Bertrand Russell[1]

I doubt, therefore I exist.

René Descartes[2]

THE POPULAR SCIENCE-FICTION WRITER ISAAC ASIMOV, in *The Intelligent Man's Guide to Science*, tells an all-too-familiar tale about the triumph of modern science over earlier natural philosophy. Asimov presents Galileo Galilei (1564–1642) as a kind of rebel hero who courageously rejected the narrowly deductive methods of traditional ancient thinkers. "Galileo's general viewpoint," we are told, "was just the reverse of the Greeks." If "the Greeks minimized the role played by induction, Galileo looked upon induction as the essential process of gaining knowledge, the only way of justifying generalizations."[3] Galileo, on this account, turned ancient philosophy upside down, ushering in a new scientific world view. His revolutionary insight "consisted in elevating induction above deduction."[4]

Since Asimov's version of intellectual history is only a popular account, it seems less than charitable to labour over obvious inaccuracies. Even from a book directed at the educated layperson, however, the quoted passage is illuminating as a not-too-distant echo of a ubiquitous attitude and conspicuous foil to the view to be developed here. Asimov, the amateur philosopher, confuses Greek philosophy as a whole with the schools of Plato and

1 *Scientific Outlook*, 15.

2 *Recherche de la verité*, 1135–6 (my translation throughout).

3 Asimov, *Intelligent Man's Guide to Science*, 17.

4 Ibid., 16.

Pythagoras. Ancient Greek thinkers were, he thinks, abstract thinkers, in love with mathematics and formal geometry. They were impressed "with the beauty of pure deduction."[5] In their enthusiasm for the spiritual purity of immaterial mathematical forms, they did not deign to observe attentively the physical world around them. This "worship of deduction from self-evident axioms" brought Western civilization to "the edge of a precipice with no place to go."[6] It was, in other words, an intellectual dead end. As Asimov describes the history of Western civilization, the ancient and mediaeval world was left wallowing in a sea of ignorance and unscientific superstition until Galileo and his followers came to the rescue with their invention of "the inductive method [that] starts with observations and derives generalizations ... from them."[7] Modern science went on to save the modern Western world from the sterility of abstract philosophy.

If popular culture lacks philosophical sophistication, it is, for that very reason, unable to wrestle itself free from the reigning orthodoxy. This misinterpretation of Western intellectual history is not unprecedented. Asimov is not a trained philosopher, but what are we to think of Bertrand Russell's comments on the "deductive attitude of the Greeks," which, according to Russell, "made the experimental method scarcely possible."[8] Russell attributes the Greeks' aversion to science to two factors: their poetic temperament and their aristocratic ways. In his words, "the Greek genius was deductive rather than inductive" because they "observed the world as poets rather than as men of science ... [and] because all manual activity was ungentlemanly, so that any study which required experiment seemed a little vulgar."[9]

Russell's text is the probable source of Asimov's caricature. But this deductive account of the Greek mind has historical roots.[10] Henry Tappan, in the introduction to an important logic textbook published in 1856, grandly asserts, "The work undertaken here differs ... from the systems of logic which have hitherto been given to the world. The Aristotelian logic is simply the method of deduction; and as such, it is complete. Subsequent works ... have closely copied the great master [confining] themselves to an exhibition of deductive principles and processes."[11] Tappan, in elaborating

5 Ibid., 15.

6 Ibid., 13.

7 Ibid., 16.

8 Russell, *Scientific Outlook*, 20.

9 Ibid., 18.

10 Ibid.

11 Tappan, *Elements of Logic*, 3.

his own account of induction, believes that he is filling a vacuum, that he is doing something never done before. He dismisses or ignores the inductive theories of the ancients. It is as if the ancient Greek philosophers had no grasp of the inductive method whatsoever.

Whereas Asimov points to Galileo as the modern champion of the empirical method, one could better award that distinction to Francis Bacon, in many ways, the founder of British empiricism. J.R. Milton, in an informative paper on the history of induction, writes, "Francis Bacon appears, as he would have wished, as the first really systematic thinker about induction."[12] But Bacon, like Asimov, Russell, and Tappan, overlooks (and misunderstands) the ancient doctrine of induction. In the *Novum Organum* (1620), Bacon lumps together under the pejorative rubric of "Sophist" almost all ancient philosophers, including, "Gorgias, Protagoras, Hippias, Polus … Plato, Aristotle, Zeno, Epicurus, Theophrastus, and their successors Chrysippus, Carneades, and the rest."[13] Bacon believes that all these philosophers force nature into the straitjacket of their own abstract, *a priori* philosophical conceptions. In a passage remarkable for its historical inaccuracy, Bacon complains that even Aristotle, the empiricist student of Plato, does "not consult experience … but having first determined the question according to his will, he then resorts to experience, and bending her into conformity with his placets, leads her about like a captive in a procession."[14] And so it is for Greek philosophers generally. "All is tainted and corrupted," Bacon laments, "in Aristotle's school by logic; in Plato's by natural theology; in the second school of Platonists … by mathematics."[15]

The attitudes of thinkers like Asimov, Russell, Tappan, and Bacon notwithstanding, the empirical method of scientific observation is not, needless to say, a modern innovation. Long before the advent of modern Renaissance science, Aristotle recognized and discussed, in some detail, the momentous nature of the inductive method. This book attempts to elucidate and extend his thought. I will argue that Bacon and succeeding generations of modern philosophers advance a misleading caricature that has little to do with what the real, historical Aristotle or his later followers taught or believed. If we cut through layer upon layer of caricature and return instead to the actual texts (or to enlightened commentary), we will discover an

12 Milton, "Induction before Hume," 49. Milton is describing the received view, not his own idiosyncratic but helpful account.

13 Bacon, *Novum Organum*, bk 1, aphorism 71 (in Bacon, various documents).

14 Ibid., bk 1, aphorism 63.

15 Ibid., bk 1, aphorism 96.

account of induction that makes sense even today. Aristotle's account needs to be refined and expanded, no doubt, but it is, in the main, correct.

An early modern thinker such as Bacon was not in a position to fairly evaluate or even understand earlier theories of induction. His patience tried by generations of scholastic commentary, Bacon goes so far as to assert that the authority of Aristotle is an obstacle to intellectual and scientific progress. We must reject Aristotle if we wish to move forward. He peevishly observes, "Knowledge is like a water that will never arise again higher than the level from which it fell; and therefore to go beyond Aristotle by the light of Aristotle is to think that a borrowed light can increase the original light from whom it is taken."[16] But the simile is doubly incorrect. Firstly, Aristotle would undoubtedly think of his own philosophy, not as the source of light, but as a lens through which the light shines. Aristotle is not worthy of critical scrutiny because he is Aristotle but because his doctrines capture something true about the facts of human experience and our relationship to the world. It is the penetration and scope of his thought that interests the philosophically minded reader.

Secondly, it is a mistake to think of Aristotle's corpus as the idiosyncratic work of an aloof, lonely genius. Aristotle was, of course, Plato's pupil, was well-traveled, had connections in high places, ran his own school, taught many students, and was wholly familiar with the thought of other Greek philosophers. His encyclopaedic oeuvre is, in part, a compendium of philosophical opinions from diverse sources. I will approach Aristotle, not as I would a solitary genius, but as a representative of an ongoing tradition that captures something true and deep about the inductive method. His position on induction is articulated, at least in part, by groups of thinkers, both before and after him. Aristotle, however, expresses this view in a particularly forceful and comprehensive way.

The present chapter begins with a brief introduction to Aristotle's view. I will then move on to consider contemporary theories of inductive reasoning and their historical antecedents. David Hume's famous critique of induction successfully shifted the focus of philosophical attention and set the scene for modern empiricist treatments of the "problem of induction." I revisit and re-evaluate Hume's influential argument, which derives ultimately from John Locke and is reiterated by a host of early modern philosophers. Despite Hume's undeniable eloquence, I claim that his account depends crucially on an epistemological attitude I call "Cartesian scepticism." Consistently applied, Cartesian scepticism undermines, not only induction, but

16 Bacon, *Valerius Terminus*, ch. 4, "Of the Impediments of Knowledge, Being the Fourth Chapter, the Preface Only of It."

every other kind knowledge. I will elaborate a more detailed treatment of Aristotle's ideas in chapter 3, "A 'Deductive' Account of Induction," chapter 4, "Five Levels of Induction," and chapter 5, "Moral Induction."

WHAT IS ARISTOTELIAN INDUCTION?

Begin with Aristotle who distinguishes, in various places, between two different ways of knowing.[17] In deduction or συλλογισμός (*sullogismos*), we move from previously established propositions to a conclusion that follows necessarily; in induction or ἐπαγωγή (*epagoge*), we move from the observation of particular instances to general claims about the nature of the kind of thing in question. Deduction involves an inference from previous statements, whereas induction requires a cognitive "progress from [observed] particulars to universals."[18] Consider a simple example of induction Aristotle himself refers to.

Sometime, at the dawn of geometry, someone or some group of people must have examined one or two or however many triangles and come to understand that the interior angles of *any* triangle add up to 180 degrees. These individuals were led from the observation of *some* triangles to the recognition of an abstract principle that applies to *all* triangles.[19] They could somehow leap to "the universal from ... the particular."[20] This is, for Aristotle, what induction is all about. Induction supplies "proof from a number of particular cases that such is the rule."[21] We *observe* particulars and somehow arrive at an overarching principle applicable to every case.

Aristotle gives divergent examples of inductive arguments. Some are explicitly stated; some are implicitly referred to in the text. In a frequently discussed example explaining the difference between "knowledge of the fact" and "knowledge of the reasoned fact," Aristotle demonstrates that planets, unlike stars, do not twinkle (undergo intermittent variation in luminosity), because they are closer to us.[22] He claims that the universal

17 See, for example, *Prior Analytics*, bk 1, ch. 2, 24b18–20; *Posterior Analytics*, bk 1, ch. 1, 71a1–10; *Topics*, bk 1, ch. 1, 105a11–20; and *Rhetoric*, bk 1, ch. 2, 1356b. We will return to these passages later.

18 *Topics* (Forester), bk 1, ch. 14, 105a10–15 (in Aristotle, *Aristotle in 23 Volumes*).

19 See *Posterior Analytics*, bk 1, ch. 1, 71a20–25, where the process is reversed.

20 *Posterior Analytics* (Tredennick), bk 1, ch. 1, 71a5–10 (in Aristotle, *Aristotle in 23 Volumes*).

21 *Rhetoric* (Freese), bk 1, ch. 2, 1356b10–16 (in Aristotle, *Aristotle in 23 Volumes*).

22 *Posterior Analytics*, bk 1, ch. 13, 78a20 ff.

principle that nearby light sources do not twinkle has to be established "by induction or sense perception." This rather bald textbook example can be read in two ways.

We might, at first, jump to the universal conclusion that nearby light sources do not twinkle, by observing that nearby light sources – i.e., those here on earth – do not (as a rule) twinkle. But this kind of mechanical conclusion begs the question. Why should what happens in the heavens be the same as what happens on earth? Aristotelian induction is more than a matter of thoughtlessly jumping to a conclusion that what we are used to (on earth) is what must be the case (in the heavens). Something more complicated is going on here. Why should we, on seeing that the stars twinkle and the planets do not, come to the conclusion that the latter are *necessarily* closer? Think of what twinkling involves. To twinkle is to intermittently undergo something close to extinction. It is to give off an intensity of light that is continually interrupted by moments of dimness. Hence the key insight: sources very far away, being much weaker, are subject to intermittent dimness, i.e., they twinkle. Whatever physics of light we adopt, the farther a source is away from us, the more tenuous its effect on us. Hence the (correct) conclusion that twinkling is (in the case of the stars) a function of their great distance from us. Once we know this, we can go on to conclude that the planets, which do not twinkle, are closer than the stars.

Scientific induction is, for Aristotle, a matter of understanding what must be the case; it is the capacity of insight (not argument) that allows us to make logical sense of observation. We can (as we shall see) turn an inductive insight into an argument. Indeed, Aristotle gives precise instructions as to how we are to do this. But, for Aristotle, induction, in its purest sense, begins in an intelligent leap that grasps what is going on. This mental quickness supplies us with the first principles of science. Confronted with repeated instances of a phenomenon; human reason arrives at a universal principle, and then goes on to use this universal principle in scientific argument.

In the *Topics*, a sometimes neglected book about strategies of dialectical (as opposed to scientific) reasoning, Aristotle supplies a string of inductive examples. Some of these are rather trite textbook cases, but the general theme is unmistakable. Debaters may secure their conclusions by deduction or induction, by referring to previously established propositions or by examining concrete cases illustrating a general principle. Induction is presented as an important source of general knowledge. Aristotle suggests, for example, that we "try to obtain knowledge" of ethics, logic, and cosmology "by the habitual practice of induction, examining [each subject matter] in the light of ... examples."[23] If we wish to debate about morality, we should examine particular examples of moral and immoral acts. If we wish to debate about logic, we should examine particular examples of good and bad arguments. And if we wish to debate about astronomy, we should examine particular examples of individual planets, stars, or constellations. In each case, an investigation of particular instances provides insight into the general principles underlying the corresponding subject matter.

Consider another example of inductive reasoning. Aristotle enunciates a basic metaphysical principle: "If the increase of the accident follows the increase of the subject ... it is obvious that it is really an accident of the subject, but if it does not follow it, it is not an accident of it." He concludes, "This result must be obtained by induction."[24] What does Aristotle have in mind? There is no need to be intimidated by this metaphysical terminology. Consider a modern example. A child is blowing up a balloon. And suppose the expression, "New York," is written on the balloon. As the balloon increases in size, the letters in the expression, "New York," also increase in size. The balloon is "the subject"; the lettering is "the accident." So the increase in the size of the lettering, the accident, follows upon the increase in the size of the subject, the balloon. We can then conclude that the lettering is a genuine part of the balloon. Suppose, however, there is a paper tag with the words, "New York," attached to the end of the balloon. As the balloon increases in size, the words, "New York," on the tag do not increase in size. So we can conclude that the tag is not a genuine part of the balloon. The general point is clear: when the accidental attribute genuinely belongs to the subject, an increase in a subject must be accompanied by an increase in the accident.[25] There are possible counter-examples, but Aristotle does not, in any case, intend this as an instance of foolproof metaphysical reasoning.[26] Dialectical reasoning deals with "generally accepted opinions" rather

23 *Topics* (Forester), bk 1, ch. 14, 105b25–30. Aristotle had earlier suggested that debaters make up lists of examples about "the good" or about "animal life," etc. (bk 1, ch. 14, 105b12–16).

24 Ibid., bk 2, ch. 10, 115a1–6.

25 There are other examples of this kind of induction-based debating exercise. See, for example, ibid., bk 4, ch. 2, 22b15–20; bk 4, ch. 3, 123b1–10; and bk 8, ch. 1, 155b30–35.

26 One might complain, for example, that the hair, fingernails, and toenails are parts of the subject that continue to grow long after the latter's growth stops, except that hair and nails are made up of dead tissue and are not literally part of the living organism. But we need not investigate such details here.

than scientific truth.[27] What is important is that we can establish, through an induction from observations, a plausible metaphysical principle.

Aristotle writes that induction is "the way in which general concepts are conveyed to us by sense perception."[28] Sense perception accesses particular things in the world: this chair, that tree, this sunset, that falling object. Induction turns this limited experience of particular things in the world into knowledge of the general case. It is the mental ability to somehow "jump" from an experience of particular things to concepts, rules and principles covering a wide variety of cases. We can, then, define Aristotelian induction in two different ways. If induction is, as traditionally understood, an inference from particular to the universal, it is also, in its most basic form, an inference from sense perception to knowledge. We begin in perception and we end up with words or symbols: with propositions made out of some kind of language, with verbal or linguistic claims that ultimately affirm what is true, in a general way, about the world.

Aristotle writes, "We cannot employ induction if we lack sense perception, because it is sense perception that apprehends particulars."[29] Sense perception is, so to speak, the ground floor of knowledge. All knowledge ultimately arises out of sense perception, and therefore, out of induction. For Aristotle, we do not learn by accessing inborn ideas ready made inside our heads or by moving, in the first instance, from one state of knowledge to another. Aristotle writes, "States of knowledge are neither innate in a determinate form, nor developed from higher states of knowledge, but [developed] from sense perception."[30] In other words, we learn, in the first instance, through an induction from observation. Clearly, induction is crucial to knowledge. Indeed, it is, for Aristotle, the ultimate source of all knowledge.

In contrast to Plato, Aristotle privileges the essential role of observation in learning.[31] At the beginning of the *Metaphysics*, he points out that we naturally revere the senses because they help us to know.[32] Again, in the *Posterior Analytics*, he remarks that "if any sense-faculty has been lost, some knowledge must be lost with it."[33] Those who go blind or deaf, those who lose their sense touch or taste or smell, lose their access to a realm of

27 Ibid., bk 1, ch. 1, 100b18–25.

28 *Posterior Analytics* (Tredennick), bk 2, ch. 19, 100b1–5.

29 Ibid., bk 1, ch. 18, 81b5–10.

30 *Posterior Analytics* (Mure), bk 1, ch. 1, 100a10 (in Aristotle, *Works of Aristotle*).

31 It is not, as some seem to think, that Plato left no room for sense perception, but Aristotle came to *privilege* its role in a way foreign to Plato.

32 The sense of sight, especially, *Metaphysics*, bk 1, ch. 1, 980a22–30.

33 *Posterior Analytics* (Tredennick), bk 1, ch. 18, 80b15–20.

human experience that plays a role in knowledge formation. This point of contact between the human being and the surrounding world is where knowledge starts. On Aristotle's account, someone who lacked all sense perception to begin with, someone born totally devoid of all five senses could never learn. Knowledge would be inaccessible to them.

Although this picture of Aristotelian induction is, in the main, true, it is admittedly overly simple. Aristotle's use of the term *epagoge* is multi-layered. Depending upon the context, the term may refer to the method of observation, to a cognitive process of illumination, or to various types of syllogisms. If induction begins in a bout of illumination that is more than merely psychological (it is not a matter of mere feeling), this direct insight gives rise to concepts, to propositions, and ultimately to arguments describing reality in general terms. When it comes to the kind of inductive arguments contemporary logicians place at the center of their investigations, we can make an induction from particular instances. To use the old saw, "Socrates, Plato and Aristotle are men. Socrates, Plato, and Aristotle are mortal. Therefore, all men are mortal." Or we can make an induction from smaller groups to larger groups, i.e., from species to genus or from genus to larger genus. For example, we can argue: "All human beings are animals. All human beings are mortal. Therefore, all animals are mortal." Overlook, for the moment, issues about the logical validity of such arguments. Clearly, the conclusion, "all animals are mortal," includes animals other than human beings. Because this argument entails a movement from a smaller to a larger group, it counts as an instance of induction. As Robin Smith points out, Aristotle considers individual and group predications as formally equivalent.[34] When it comes to rigorous science, however, Aristotle privileges arguments having to do with species and genera.

And there are other variations in Aristotle's theory of inductive inference. In *Topics*, for example, he recommends its use to deliberately arrive at a generalization to be subsequently shown to be false.[35] This is a kind of *reductio ad absurdum* reasoning. Again, the Philosopher refers to a rhetorical kind of induction he calls "argument from example." Here the movement is not from "part to whole ... but [from] part to part, or like to like."[36] This is, in the modern idiom, reasoning from analogy. And so on. We shall explore all these different levels of Aristotelian induction in a future chapter. The

34 *Stanford Encyclopedia of Philosophy*, s.v. "Aristotle's Logic" (by Robin Smith) (an excellent general introduction).

35 *Topics*, bk 2, ch. 5, 111b37–112a1.

36 *Rhetoric* (Freese), bk 1, ch. 2, 1357b (in Aristotle, *Aristotle in 23 Volumes*).

present discussion is only meant as a brief introduction. Nonetheless, the general picture is clear. Induction involves a mental leap from particular to general. It begins with an intelligent movement of understanding giving rise to concepts, propositions, and arguments. At the most basic level, it is the bridge between sense perception and knowledge; it somehow penetrates concrete, particular experience to produce a general understanding of a nature.

MODERN DOGMA

There is an approach to induction that is distinctly modern. Most contemporary commentators question the authority, the reliability, or at least the logical rigor of inductive reasoning. As *The Oxford Companion to Philosophy* declares "most philosophers hold that there is a problem about induction."[37] On this pervasive view, induction usually involves an attempt to predict something about the future, but we can never be sure that the future will conform to past experience. In Bertrand Russell's colourful words, "All [our] rather crude expectations ... are liable to be misleading. The man who has fed the chicken every day throughout its life at last wrings its neck instead." If inductive reasoning assumes that the future will resemble the past, we may, philosophically, "be in no better position than the chicken which unexpectedly has its neck rung."[38]

Norman Campbell describes induction as "the process of arguing from the particular to the general, or from the small portion of our experience of which we have knowledge ... to the much greater portion which is at the time wholly unknown to us."[39] It is this movement from what is known to what is unknown (or from past to future) that disturbs the modern mind. Consider our original example about black crows. We observe that this crow, that crow, and that other crow are black. We see hundreds of black crows. We conclude, "all crows are black." The problem is, of course, that not all crows are black. There are rare albino crows and crows with spots of white on their wing, toes, bills, or other parts of their bodies. So the generalization "all crows are black," understood as a blanket statement about what must be the case about crows, turns out to false, even though it may conform to our own everyday experience.

The abstruse qualifications of analytical philosophy notwithstanding, knowledge still tends to be associated in some way with empirical verifiability.

37 *Oxford Companion to Philosophy*, s.v. "Induction" (by Michael Collins).

38 Russell, *Problems of Philosophy*, 63.

39 Campbell, *Foundations of Science*, 89.

Hence the so-called problem of induction. Induction entails a movement "from the observed to the unobserved."[40] We observe *these* particular crows and are led to a generalization that pertains to *all* crows. But how can we have conclusive or necessary or authoritative knowledge about crows that have not been and never will be observed? We can explain the problem in the following way.

Translate every observation of a black crow into a premise, "this crow at this time at this place was observed to be black." Gather these premises together in support of the conclusion, "all crows are black." The conclusion of this argument applies to all crows at all times in all places. In Brian Skyrms' words, it "asserts more than the premises."[41] Even if all observed crows are black, it is still possible that some unobserved crows are not black. It does not matter how many observations we collect. The premises of the argument (in Richard Feldman's words) "always leave some room for the falsity of the conclusion." So the conclusion of an inductive argument does not follow necessarily from the premises. Inductive inference "is not conclusive."[42]

A standard textbook neatly lists the alleged differences between deductive and inductive reasoning.[43] Firstly, the truth of the premises in a (properly constructed) deductive argument guarantees the truth of the conclusion, whereas the truth of the premises in a (properly constructed) inductive argument does not guarantee the truth of the conclusion. Secondly, all the content of the conclusion in a deductive argument is implicitly present in the premises; whereas the conclusion of an inductive argument has content that goes beyond the content of its premises. (Deduction is "non-ampliative," indeed tautologous, whereas induction is "ampliative" and non-tautologous.) Thirdly, although the addition of new premises cannot undermine the formal validity of a properly constructed deductive argument, it may completely undermine even a strong inductive argument (deduction is, and induction is not, "erosion proof"). And fourthly, all valid deductive arguments are equally valid, whereas properly constructed inductive arguments may be stronger or weaker, depending upon the amount of evidence amassed in support of each conclusion.

40 This is an echo of Aristotle and Mill; *Routledge Encyclopedia of Philosophy*, s.v. "Inductive Inference" (by Patrick Mayer), 756.

41 Skyrms, *Choice and Chance*, p. 8.

42 Feldman, *Reason and Argument*, 104.

43 This list has been adapted from Salmon et al., *Introduction*, 11.

(Deductive validity is held to be all or nothing, whereas inductive arguments come in various degrees of probability or strength.)[44]

This overview may seem to throw a rather worrisome light on the soundness of inductive reasoning. But we need induction. As John Kemeny comments, induction is "a much more useful kind of thing than deduction. Induction tells us things we did not know before, whereas deduction only tells us things we knew already but did not realize we knew."[45] Indeed, we need induction, not just for science, but in order to survive. As Kemeny drily observes, "If nature was designed so that plausible inductions invariably turn out to be wrong, the human race would be wiped out soon."[46] If we could not make accurate generalizations, if we could not accurately predict the future, science – indeed, human life – would utterly fail. We are left with a pressing philosophical problem: How can we justify a "logical" procedure that we must, and indeed we do, use?

Mark Kaplan states that "the problem of induction" is that we must be able "to show how we can be justified in regarding one [statement] as evidence for the truth of another when the first does not logically imply the second."[47] Contemporary logicians, with few exceptions, accept that inductive arguments are *invalid*: the premises do not, in any strict sense, entail the conclusion. This problem has haunted modern philosophy. In a valid argument, the conclusion follows necessarily from the premises. It is impossible for the premises to be true and the conclusion to be false. Validity does not, of course, guarantee the truth of premises or conclusion. *If*, however, the premises in a valid argument are true, the conclusion *must* be true. It should be clear from the preceding discussion, however, that inductive arguments are not (at least not in this precise sense) valid. Even if we have observed innumerable black crows, it does not follow, *as a matter of necessity*, that all crows are black. Because the conclusion covers more cases than the premises, the truth of the premises about our previous observations of black crows cannot guarantee the truth of the conclusion. Even if the premises are true, it is at least possible that the conclusion is false.

44 Hence Williams, in an unusual passage, argues that inductive arguments invoke "a degree of implicative connection intermediate between strict entailment and inconsistency" (Williams, *Ground of Induction*, 47).

45 Kemeny, *Philosopher Looks at Science*, 113.

46 Ibid., 121.

47 *Shorter Routledge Encyclopedia of Philosophy*, s.v. "Epistemic Issues in Induction" (by Mark Kaplin), 748.

On the modern view, even a *good* inductive argument will be invalid. Wesley Salmon writes, "a logically correct inductive argument may have true premises and a false conclusion."[48] John Vickers concurs: "good inductions may lead from true premises to false conclusions."[49] In other words, even the best inductive arguments are uncertain. As John Hospers explains to introductory-level students, "inductive arguments are not deductively valid and the conclusion [of an inductive argument] does not logically follow from the premises."[50]

Albert Blumberg summarizes the difference between deductive and inductive arguments. "It is *impossible* for the conclusion [of a deductive argument] to be false if the premises are true," whereas "it is [only] *improbable* that the conclusion [of an inductive argument] is false, given that the premises are all true."[51] We are left with a twofold division in modern logic. S.F. Barker notes that inductive conclusions are only "supported or confirmed or made probable," whereas deductive conclusions are logically "implied or entailed."[52] Richard Feldman informs us that inductive arguments are characterized by mere "cogency," whereas deductive arguments are characterized by logical "validity."[53] Merrie Bergmann, James Moor, and Jack Nelson observe that inductive arguments are "weak" or "strong," whereas deductive arguments are "valid" or "invalid."[54] P.F. Strawson carefully distinguishes between inductive "support" and deductive "entailment."[55] And so on. If a properly constructed deductive argument with true premises guarantees the truth of the conclusion, the best we can say of a properly constructed inductive argument is that it inspires (in Tom Tymoczko and Jim Henle's phrase) "some degree of confidence."[56]

The contemporary view establishes, in effect, two independent standards for good reasoning. Good deduction must conform to a strict standard of validity. Good induction must satisfy a weaker standard; it must establish that the conclusion is more *likely* than not, that it is *probably* true,

48 Salmon, *Logic*, 53 (1984 edition).

49 Vickers, "Problem of Induction" (online).

50 Hospers, *Introduction to Philosophical Analysis*, 122.

51 Blumberg, *Logic*, 10.

52 S. Barker, *Induction and Hypothesis*, 3.

53 Feldman, *Reason and Argument*, 102–7.

54 Bergmann, Moor, and Nelson, *Logic Book*, 10–12.

55 Strawson also distinguishes between "premises" that prove a deductive conclusion and mere "evidence for an inductive conclusion" (*Introduction to Logical Theory*, 237).

56 Tymoczko and Henle, *Sweet Reason*, 358.

that we have *some* reason to believe it. Clearly, some inductive arguments seem strong; some seem middling; some seem weak. None of this is intended to suggest that all inductive arguments inspire the same degree of confidence. The question is whether the modern (non-Aristotelian) account gives us adequate grounds to accept the logical authority of inductive reason.

Since Aristotle's time, one may chronicle a major shift in philosophical conceptions of induction. Whereas Aristotle defined induction as an argument that moves from particular to universal, as up to date an authority as the *Stanford Encyclopedia of Philosophy* dismisses this idea as "outdated and too narrow."[57] *The Philosopher's Dictionary* reports as follows: "In an outdated way of speaking, deduction is reasoning from the general to the particular, and induction is reasoning from the particular to the general. Nowadays, this distinction between kinds of reasoning is made as follows: correct deductive reasoning is reasoning of a sort that if the premises are true, the conclusion must be true; whereas correct inductive reasoning supports the conclusion by showing that it's more probably true."[58] But this is only to say that correct deduction is, and correct induction is not, valid. It seems, then, that philosophers have moved away from traditional conceptions of induction privileging the movement from the particular to the universal, in favour of an account privileging the idea that induction is, unlike deduction, invalid. This is not a trivial shift. Compare briefly the Aristotelian with the contemporary account.

ARISTOTELIAN AND CONTEMPORARY DESCRIPTIONS OF INDUCTIVE ARGUMENT

On the older view, deduction is a logical movement from more general to more specific; induction, from more specific to more general. The argument, "All human beings are mortal; Socrates is a human being; therefore Socrates is mortal," is a deduction. The "reverse argument, "Socrates is a human being; Socrates is mortal; therefore all human beings are mortal," is an induction. Vickers, who summarizes a wide swath of opinion, complains, however, that the old view that induction moves from specific to general, and deduction from general to specific, falls apart under more rigorous inspection. He presents three short arguments that are supposed to explode the traditional account. Consider his arguments briefly. As we shall see, they are quickly disposed of.

57 Vickers, "Problem of Induction" (online).

58 Martin, *Philosopher's Dictionary*, s.v. "Deduction/Induction."

(1) First, in direct opposition to the traditional view, Vickers contends that there are *deductions* that move from specific to general. He cites as proof the following argument: "New York is east of the Mississippi. Delaware is east of the Mississippi. Therefore, everything that is either New York or Delaware is east of the Mississippi."[59] This is a deductively valid argument: the truth of the premises guarantees the truth of the conclusion. But as we discuss below, Aristotle believes that properly constructed inductive arguments are deductively valid. So the mere fact that this argument is deductively valid does not show that it is not an inductive argument. A deeper question is whether it really does represent a movement from more specific to more general. If I insist, "Gorgi is tall; Yannick is tall; therefore Gorgi and Yannick are tall" – does this really count as a logical inference? A careful Aristotelian would probably claim that this is mere repetition. Logical inference must arrive at a new understanding. So either the argument is a deductively valid induction or it does no logical work. One way or another, the intelligent traditionalist will not be shaken by Vicker's counter-example. Nothing here shows that the traditional view is wrong.

(2) Vickers argues next that there are inductive arguments that from general to specific. He offers the following (famous) example: "All observed emeralds have been green. Therefore, the next emerald to be observed will be green."[60] The point is supposed to be that this inductive argument moves from a larger group, "all emeralds observed in the past" to a smaller group, "the next observed emerald." So we move from a group made up of many exemplars to a group made up of only one. Yet this reading is little more than verbal slight of hand. In fact, the argument about the next green emerald presupposes a hidden subconclusion that "all emeralds are green." At least, this is the most natural reading of what is going on.

Vicker's example (which he borrows from Nelson Goodman) is not essentially different than the extended argument, "all observed crows have been black; so all crows are black; so the next crow will be black." There is a hidden inductive step here; we move from observed emeralds in the past to the universal conclusion, "all emeralds are green," and only then to an implicit deduction, "because all emeralds are green, the next one will be green as well." Vicker's treatment glosses over these details. But we cannot *logically* conclude that the next emerald will be green without assuming that all, most, many, or at least the majority of emeralds (including those which are unobserved) are green. Otherwise, we would have no rational basis for adopting this conclusion. So this kind of argument inevitably includes an

59 Vickers, "Problem of Induction" (online).
60 Ibid. (online).

inductive step or stage. As we shall see in a future chapter, Aristotle rigorously examines such arguments. The intelligent traditionalist will, once again, have no problem dealing with this alleged counter-example.

(3) Vickers argues, finally, that some inductions involve a movement from an individual case to another individual case without any kind of generalization. Vickers claims that this kind of "singular predictive inference" (what is essentially an argument from analogy) does not involve a movement from less to more. But here again, this seems hasty. In fact, Aristotle gives a detailed account of such arguments, claiming that they always involve an implicit movement up from one individual case to a larger generalization and then back down to the next individual. We discuss the issue below. For the moment, simply note that there is nothing here that defeats the traditional account of induction as a movement from specific to general. (In fact, the traditional view is more complicated than Vickers realizes. Some traditional authors do argue that some inductive arguments involve a movement from general to specific, but that is a special case we discuss in a future chapter.)

Champions of the contemporary view reject the older view of induction as a movement from less to more. One sometimes gets the impression that they understand induction in opposition to deduction as that argument form that, *unlike deduction*, is invalid. Robert Baum goes so far as to define inductive reasoning as "any argument which is not deductively valid."[61] Skyrms concurs.[62] If this seems extreme, it is arguably the end the modern account logically tends toward. Traditional authors point to the mental movement from particular to universal as the defining property. But once we reject this description, what are we left with? Vickers argues that "inductive inferences are contingent, deductive inferences are necessary."[63] In other words, inductive inferences may or may not turn out to be reliable. But this seems to be just another way of saying that inductive arguments are invalid. On the modern account, it seems that invalidity is not just a necessary property of inductive arguments: it seems, indeed, to operate as the defining property.

But perhaps this is too negative. After all, most modern logicians acknowledge that there are good inductive arguments. It is not just that proper inductive arguments are invalid; in the best case scenario, they are *invalid and strong* at the very same time. The question is, of course, whether we can make sense of this in-between status. Broach the problem through a

61 Baum, *Logic*, 22.

62 Skyrms, *Choice and Chance*, 8–9.

63 Vickers, "Problem of Induction" (online).

quick example. Consider the previously mentioned argument: "all observed crows have been black; therefore, the next crow will be black." Do these premises in this inductive argument provide at least some support for the conclusion? Vickers mistakenly suggests that "until the middle of the previous century induction was understood to be what we now know as enumerative induction."[64] Although thinking about induction as a kind of enumerating or tabulating has older antecedents, it is, in fact, a fairly late development in mainstream Western philosophy. Here lies the problem. As we shall see in subsequent chapters, Aristotelian induction is about causality. The main focus is not, as in the modern philosophy, on predicting when (or how often) something will occur. The focus is squarely on understanding what is happening. This is where induction derives its logical force. Once we understand what exactly is happening, we can, for example, know how and when something will occur.

The modern account, furthermore, predicts what will happen by analyzing the frequency of past occurrences. But without knowing why something occurs, we cannot know when it will happen again. This is Russell's point about the chicken: several hundred times in a row the farmer comes in and feeds it until the absolutely last time, when he comes in and abruptly cuts off its head. Admittedly, once we know *what* is going on – the farmer is fattening the chicken in order to eat it – we can easily predict what will eventually happen. When we focus solely on the frequency of past events without understanding what the farmer is doing, we misconstrue what is going to happen. It is not, then, the number of times that the farmer feeds the chickens that is the key to this situation; it is the rationale behind the farmer's actions. This is why modern accounts of induction are inherently problematic, because they rely on mere counting rather than on explanatory inference.

It does not matter how sophisticated our mathematical apparatus is, a reliance on sheer number is not enough to distinguish a random string of happenings from a law-like sequence that follows in some orderly fashion. Consider the every-crow-is-black argument. We are asked to conclude that because the last one hundred crows were black, the next crow will be black. But one hundred black crows, evaluated solely in terms of frequency, do not provide sufficient evidence for determining that the next crow will be black. Numbers are just numbers. Suppose that the difference between the next crow being white or black is like flipping a coin. We could, in principle, flip a coin one hundred times and always get heads. And we could flip it one more time and get tails. Every time we flip the coin, there is an equal

64 Ibid. (online).

possibility of heads or tails. (To think that the previous sequence of coin flips somehow influence future flips is in fact a well-known fallacy.) If, then, crow colour is like a random coin-flipping, we have no way of knowing what the colour of the next crow will be. Black or white is equally likely, regardless of the previous sequence of all black crows.

This is not a book about probability. Still, we should note that the probability of randomly flipping a coin and getting one hundred heads in a row, followed by a one hundred tails in a row, is no smaller than that of any other sequence of results. (In fact, the probability for any fixed set of two hundred outcomes is the same: $(\frac{1}{2})^{200}$.) If then, the possibility of a black or white crow is like the possibility of heads or tails, it does not matter how many black crows we have already seen in the past. This does not (contrary to popular belief) make it any more likely that the next crow will be black. So there is a serious problem with induction.

But in fact the situation may be even worse than first appears. A definite probability is associated with coin-flipping, precisely because a coin has a definite nature, because the force of gravity does not change, the laws of physics regulating quantities such as velocity, acceleration, momentum, and work are orderly and predictable, and so on. In a purely random world, we would have nothing to base probability calculations on. Anything could happen. But how do we know that we are not in a purely random world? The numbers themselves do not rule out this possibility. They are equally open to any interpretation. In a purely coincidental world, we could observe one hundred black crows, followed by a white crow, or three thousand black crows, followed by fourteen white crows, or any other combination. Everything is just coincidence. So the inductive conclusion that the next crow is likely to be black does not follow logically in a purely coincidental world.

Of course, we all believe that it cannot be a coincidence that we have observed one hundred black crows in a row. But it is not the numbers that matter; it is the numbers combined with an unprovable metaphysical belief that the world is regular, orderly, and composed of things with definite natures. This metaphysical belief is what makes us accept the probability calculus as a good predictor of what will happen in the future. We believe the world must have something non-random about it that makes the previous one hundred crows black and that this feature – whatever it is – must operate somehow consistently. We interpret numerical frequency, then, as an expression of a deeper, ordered causality and logically conclude that the frequency of events puts on display some kind of (often complicated) metaphysical design. But ultimately it is not the numbers but the metaphysical belief in an underlying order that makes even numerical induction work.

Seen from an Aristotelian perspective, numerical accounts of induction, considered on their own, miss the point. Induction is about understanding why crows are black, which has something to do with understanding the physical anatomy of feathers, the chemical composition of pigment, the biological mechanism of sexual reproduction, and so on. Aristotle believes that we can go some way to understanding what is going on. And once we understand what is going on, we will have some reason for believing – although this is not the main purpose behind induction – we can make a good case that the next crow will probably be black.

THE WHITE-SHOE PARADOX

Numerical accounts of induction have more than one strange consequence. Let us briefly examine a logical puzzle Carl Hempel is thought to have solved, which I will call the white-shoe paradox.[65] Because the numerical account understands induction as a matter of probability and the Aristotelian one defines it as a matter of explanatory causality, they view the problem Hempel raises in a different light. Focusing briefly on this issue should help to elucidate the basic difference between the two views.

Begin with the inductive generalization, "all crows are black." On the numerical account, every time I see a black crow, this further supports the claim (assuming the world is regular) that all crows are black. This much, at least, seems intuitive. But suppose I observe that a white shoe is not a crow. Oddly enough, this observation also supports the claim that all crows are black. Why? To say that all crows are black is logically equivalent to saying that anything that is not black is not a crow. A white shoe is obviously not black and is not a crow. So the observation that a white shoe is not a crow lends some support to the claim that all crows are black.

But this seems counterintuitive. How could the obvious fact that white shoes are not crows have anything to do with proving the claim that "all crows are black?" And yet, if induction is a kind of tabulating, this makes perfect sense. Consider an altogether simple thought experiment. Suppose the universe contained only four objects: a black crow, a white shoe, a red scarf, and a blue marble. And suppose we have already observed the black crow. In this four-object universe, the individual observation of the white shoe removes one possible counter-example from the list. It significantly increases the probability that all non-black things (in this universe) are not crows. And suppose we go on to observe that the red scarf and the blue marble are not crows. This clinches the case. Taken together, these

65 Hempel, "Studies," pts 1 and 2.

individual observations prove that all non-black things in this universe are not crows. It *must* follow that all crows – only one exists here – are black. So the seemingly irrelevant observation that a white shoe is not a crow can, in this universe, add further support to the claim that all crows are black. Of course, the universe we live in is filled with a limitless number of many-coloured objects. So the knowledge that a white shoe is not a crow is (in our universe) a trivial advance in knowledge; indeed, it represents such a slight increase in knowledge as to be entirely inconsequential. Still, as Hempel suggests, the white-shoe inference is not so much wrong as trivial.

On an Aristotelian account, by contrast, the observation that a white shoe is not a crow is truly a non sequitur. It has nothing to do with what induction and science generally are about. If we observe the world carefully, we can use our intelligence to see *what* must be case. This is, in the first instance, what induction is about. When we understand *what* things are, we can understand why things are the way they are. The all-important question is, "What?" Observing that a white shoe is not a crow cannot help us to understand *what* a crow is. It cannot help us understand *what* makes the crow's feathers black. It cannot help us understand *what* accounts for the transmission of colour traits from parents to fledgling. So this true observation has no inductive value. It has no inductive value, not because it is false, but because it is beside the point.

Return to the four-object universe. Aristotle would think that the observation that the white shoe is not a crow is unhelpful even in this kind of universe. It would not constitute a momentous advance in knowledge. Adding up samples may be a prelude to scientific discovery, but it is not what science is really about. The point is not to determine how many crows are black but to *understand* why crows are black. Realizing that the white shoe, the red scarf, and the blue marble are not crows does not do any inductive work. Induction is about discovering *what* it is that makes crows black. It is hard to see how the mere observation that this white shoe is not a crow could trigger this kind of understanding.

But this is not all. Aristotle believes that we do not have to rely on mere counting, for thorough observation can uncover the nature of things in a non-random world. Before dismissing this "naive" confidence, note that the argument from "all crows (or ravens) are black," repeated *ad nauseam* in the literature, is *wildly* misleading. This would be, from the perspective of real biology, an altogether suspect assumption. As it turns out, many members of the crow family (the family Corvidae in the genus *Corvus*) have white feathers. Hooded crows (*Corvus cornix*) have large amounts of white or grey on their bodies; the thick-billed raven (*Corvus crassirostris*) has a large, distinctive patch of white on its neck and a spot of white on its bill;

the pied crow (*Corvus albus*) has a large white region ranging from shoulders to its lower breast – and so on. Even the familiar American crow (*Corvus brachyrhynchos*) is not always black. According to one report from the field, about 4 per cent of nestlings have white spots on their bills, toes or other non-feathered parts, whereas about 1 per cent have some white feathers.[66] Add to this the well-known phenomenon of albinism and the regularly reported observance of albino crows. A thorough biologist is hardly going to jump to the conclusion that a white crow is an impossibility. They will, on the basis of adequate observation, arrive at the correct conclusion that non-black crows are a definite possibility. Good induction begins with observation, not stereotypes.

The Aristotelian account of induction is close to the commonsense view. There are different kinds of things in the world. Because things possess a certain kind of nature, they act and react in specific ways. Once we ascertain their nature, we can know something about when they occur, although this is not the main point about induction. Modern numerical induction has its place. In some cases, we simply cannot know the complicated and contingent causes of things (in many public opinion polls, for example). In other cases, numerical induction is really a kind of observation. It is the first step in understanding what is going on. But this is not a book about numerical induction (a topic which is more than adequately treated by many contemporary logicians). This is a book about the mental faculty that makes various types of induction – including numerical induction – possible.

When we add our belief in the regular nature of the world to an understanding of probability, we can make sense of the modern account of induction. We cannot believe that it is just a coincidence that so many crows are black, because we do not believe in a purely coincidental world. It is our commitment to an ordered world that makes statistical induction persuasive. It is this metaphysical supposition that things in the world have a predictable nature (despite whatever appearances to the contrary) that gives numerical induction its logical force. Frequency is, so to speak, an expression of some deep order; it is not just a random by-product of something that can change without rhyme or reason. Even if the frequency model has, in light of this (unprovable) metaphysical assumption, considerable logical force, it is not what Aristotle is about. Put a little too strongly, numerical induction would be a minor subset of a minor subset of Aristotelian-type induction. Although we can use Aristotle's model to explain numerical induction, we need, first and foremost, to explain the basic orientation of earlier generations of philosophers toward inductive reasoning. Induction is

66 McGowan, "White Crows?"

not, for Aristotle, an issue of mere counting. What makes an inductive argument a good one is its explanatory power.

Aristotle, in direct opposition to the usual modern view, believes that inductive arguments are valid (though not necessarily sound). In his formulation of the syllogistic, true premises in a properly constructed inductive argument *guarantee* the truth of the conclusion. But his basic approach can be symbolized by means of other formal techniques. The deeper issue is that Aristotle believes that inductive reasoning is logically compelling because there are natural kinds in the world and because we have the intelligence needed to recognize and explain them. (This power of explanation is, in some sense, what Aristotle thinks intelligence is.) The modern approach has forced philosophers to ask deep questions about the epistemological justification of inductive reasoning. Aristotle, who is not uncritical or absolutist, offers a sensible and thoroughly pragmatic answer to such doubts. But before engaging in the Aristotelian account in more detail in later chapters, we must turn back to the origins of the modern view of induction in Locke and Hume. If Aristotle needs to be consulted, it is because of problems inherent in the modern, post-Enlightenment account of induction.

HUME: SLICES OF BREAD

Ludwig Wittgenstein, in the *Tractatus*, observes that induction "has no logical justification but only a psychological one."[67] This is a paraphrase of David Hume. As Hume is widely recognized as having discovered the modern view of induction, we need to examine his account closely.

The usual focus on Hume's scepticism regarding induction is historically misleading. John Haldane ventures the opinion that "inductive scepticism of the type associated with Hume predates him by at least four centuries."[68] Haldane points to medieval authors such as Nicholas of Autrecourt, Al-Ghazali, and Nicholas of Cusa as representatives of a similar school of thought. Hume's own views derive, more immediately, from Locke. And even Locke's views are similar to those found in contemporary authorities such as Pierre Gassendi (1592–1655), the authors of the *Port Royal Logic* (Antione Arnauld, 1612–1694, and Pierre Nicole, 1625–1695), Thomas Hobbes (1588–1679), and at least the early Gottfried Wilhelm Leibniz (1646–1716).[69] Still, the relevant passage in Hume's *An Enquiry Concerning Human Understanding* contains what is probably the most influential

67 Wittgenstein, *Tractatus Logico-Philosophicus*, §6.3631.

68 Haldane, "Insight, Inference, and Intellection," 34.

69 See Milton, "Induction before Hume," for an excellent review of sources.

account of induction in the entire history of philosophy.[70] As such, it deserves close scrutiny.

Hume, following after Locke, sees himself as an Enlightenment empiricist and a fierce opponent of an outmoded Aristotelianism. Neither a rigorous technician nor an assiduous student of the history of philosophy, he associated traditional metaphysics with religion and superstition. Metaphysics is "not properly a science," but "an inevitable source of uncertainty and error." Metaphysical distinctions arise "either from the fruitless efforts of human vanity, which would penetrate into subjects utterly inaccessible to the understanding, or from the craft of popular superstitions, which, being unable to defend themselves on fair ground, raise these intangling brambles to cover and protect their weakness."[71] In contrast to the metaphysician, who would penetrate the world of appearances to gaze upon a truer reality composed of naked substances, occult causes, and ghostly essences, Hume claims that the only thing we can know is sensation.

Hume, like Locke, was deeply influenced by Robert Boyle's corpuscularism, the forerunner to modern atomic theory that supplanted a more traditional Aristotelianism. On this scientific account, the activity of an underlying realm of unobservable particles or corpuscles determines the surface appearances of things. Hume assumes, quite naively, that the precise nature of this substratum, the residuum that underlies empirical experience, is thoroughly unknowable. So the real, true nature of things is – like Kant's *noumenon* – inaccessible. This opens the door to a general suspicion about induction. We can set out Hume's position on induction in a few steps:

(1) Nature is secretive. As Hume explains, "Nature has kept us at a great distance from all her secrets, and has afforded us only knowledge of a few superficial qualities of objects; while she conceals from us those powers and principles, on which the influence of these objects entirely depends."[72]

(2) Because nature is secretive, when we perceive objects or events in the world, we do not perceive the true causes which regulate and constitute the objects or events in question. Hume assures us that "the particular powers, by which all natural operations are performed,

70 Hume, *Enquiry*, §4, pt 2. See also *Treatise*, bk 1, pt 3, §6.

71 Hume, *Enquiry* (Selby-Bigge, Nidditch), §1, para. 6, 11 (in Hume, *Enquiries*).

72 Ibid., §4, pt 2, para. 29, 32–3.

never appear to the senses."[73] We only perceive the exterior aspect, the surface appearances of things, the outer shell so to speak. In other words, we do not perceive the cause, only the effect.

(3) When we make generalizations about similar sensible objects, we inevitably *assume* that they are always produced by the same secret powers and principles. We assume that the same observable effect is produced by the same underlying cause. Hume writes, "Notwithstanding this ignorance of natural powers and principles, we always presume, when we see like sensible qualities, that they have like secret powers, and expect that effects, similar to those which we have experienced, will follow from them."[74]

(4) But different causes may produce the same effect. I may, for example, feel hot, either because (1) it is a sweltering summer day or because (2) I have a fever. The same effect, the feeling of being physically hot, has a different cause in each case. This obvious truth undermines our previous assumption (3), above.

(5) It follows from (4) that similar objects or properties or events may have different – indeed, very different – causes. Suppose object *A* and *B* resemble one another. We cannot assume, despite the observed resemblance, that similar objects *A* and *B* will be alike in all respects, for these objects may have different secret causes.

(6) It follows that induction, which is based on the assumption that similar effects derives from similar causes, is inevitably an inconclusive form of reasoning.

Hume illustrates his meaning with the example of slices of bread. When I have a piece of toast in the morning, I assume that this slice of bread will be like other slices I have eaten, and consume it without any compunction. As Hume puts it, "If a body of like colour and consistence with that bread, which we have formerly eat, be presented to us, we make no scruple of repeating the experiment, and foresee, with certainty, like nourishment and support."[75] But Hume thinks that the implicit induction, "other slices of bread were nourishing, therefore this one will be nourishing," is logically suspect. He asks a rhetorical question: "The bread, which I formerly eat, nourished me; that is, a body of such sensible qualities was, at that time, endued with such secret powers: but does it follow, that other bread must also nourish me at another time, and that like sensible qualities must always be

73 Ibid., §5, pt 1, para. 35, 42.

74 Ibid., §4, pt 2, para. 29, 33.

75 Ibid.

attended with like secret powers?" And he responds, "The consequence seems nowise necessary."[76]

Induction is, for Hume, an argument from ignorance. Our knowledge is limited to what we perceive. We never come into direct contact with the secret corpuscular powers that underlie the sensible characteristics of the world. Although we can see and touch and taste and smell each slice of bread, we cannot perceive or even understand the secret metaphysical nature causing its nourishing properties. Induction is based then, not on certain knowledge, but on a lack of knowledge. It is an argument from presumption. We do not move from knowledge of the cause to knowledge of the effect. We move from knowledge of the effect to a guess or a presumption about an inaccessible cause. But guesses or presumptions are, in a logical sense, inconclusive.

Hume writes, "It is allowed on all hands that there is no known connexion between the sensible qualities and the secret powers; and consequently, that the mind is not led to form such a conclusion concerning their constant and regular conjunction, by anything which it knows of their nature."[77] Because we have no insight into the relationship between the secret causes that determine the nature of objects and the sensory appearances we actually perceive, we cannot assume that we are, in similar situations, dealing with the same thing. We cannot even be certain that the same secret cause will always produce the same effect. Even if two sensible objects had (unknown to us) the same cause, we cannot be certain that they would have the same properties.

Hume's attack on induction might be described in the following way. Suppose Aunt Mary were to give me a tin box with a picture of a cake on the lid. And suppose I open the box and, indeed, find a freshly baked cake inside. Further suppose Mary (being a most generous aunt) gives me a similar tin box with a similar cake inside it every morning. Does it logically follow that the box must contain another cake when I open it tomorrow? Surely not. A box with a picture of a cake on the lid could, without contradiction, contain a completely different object the next time around – an orange, an old shoe, a golf ball. This is how Hume envisages induction. Because objects with the outside appearance of bread have been edible and nourishing in the past, this does not guarantee that they will enclose the same secret powers of nourishment in the future. The outside impression may be completely misleading. Whatever it is that provides nourishment in the case of a slice of bread may or may not be

76 Ibid., §4, pt 2, para. 29, p. 34.

77 Ibid., §4, pt 2, para. 29, 33.

present underneath the sensible appearances of this new slice of bread. So we are not, in a strict logical sense, justified in generalizing from one slice of bread to another.

It is important to remember that Hume is writing before modern advances in medicine, physiology, and biochemistry. He assumes, wrongly as it turns out, that the power in bread which causes human nourishment is eternally hidden from our understanding. Hume states, "Our senses inform us of the colour, weight and consistence of bread, but neither sense nor reason can ever inform us of those qualities, which fit it for nourishment and support of a human body."[78] Nourishment, he assumes, derives from the secret underlying substance. This imperceptible substance, Hume insists, is beyond human understanding.

In effect, Hume spins out three separate arguments in support of his basic position on induction. Firstly, as we have seen, he argues that because we have no knowledge of the secret causes of things, we cannot be certain that similar objects have similar causes and therefore similar properties. Secondly, he argues that even if similar objects have similar causes, similar causes could have different effects, and so the objects produced by these similar causes may have different properties. And thirdly, he argues that all inductive arguments "proceed upon the supposition, that the future will be conformable to the past."[79] Because we cannot know the secret powers that regulate the properties in things, we cannot know if or how or when the sensible objects they give rise to will change. "It implies no contradiction," he claims, "that the course of nature may change, and that an object, seemingly like those which we have experienced, may [in the future] be attended with different or contrary effects."[80]

Induction is, in Hume's eyes, without logical rigor. It is not a matter of logical necessity but of habit or custom. For example, we become accustomed to the fact that flames are regularly accompanied by heat, and so when we encounter a flame we naturally expect heat. Hume writes, "When we assert ... the constant conjunction of two objects – heat and flame, for instance ... we are determined *by custom alone* to expect the one from the appearance of the other."[81]

Our familiarity with Hume's critique may obscure the radical nature of his account. If induction is a matter of mere custom or habit, it is not, properly speaking, a species of *logical* argument. Custom has little or no

78 Ibid.
79 Ibid., §4, pt 2, para. 30, 35.
80 Ibid.
81 Ibid., §5, pt 1, para. 36, 43 (original italics).

epistemological force. Suppose that in my village no one has a beard. I become accustomed to beardless men. I assume, without really thinking about it, that bearded men do not exist. I associate "men" with "beardlessness." This is more habit than logical inference. Hume suggests that something analogous happens every time we perform an induction.

We respond to Hume's account in more detail below. For the moment, simply note that his account seems counterintuitive. He himself cites the example of an open flame that gives off heat. When I conclude, from my previous experience of open flames, that any flame will throw off heat, is this a matter of mere habit or custom? Could it be the case that in some households or neighbourhoods or countries flames are hot and that in others they are cold? Surely, flames (if they really are flames) are hot everywhere. They *must* throw off heat because of their chemical and physical nature. Customs may change, but a flame that does not give off heat would be impossible chemically.

Hume, in appealing to habit or custom, presents induction as a disastrously weak form of inference. As contemporary philosophers such as Hilary Kornblith, Brian Ellis, Howard Sankey, and James Freeman intimate, his account clashes with the contemporary scientific world view. Science purports to discover the deepest regularities inherent in nature. On a truly scientific view, induction cannot be a matter of convention. It must be, instead, one of φύσις (*physis*) or nature, as Aristotle argues.

LOCKE AND INDUCTION

Hume's general position on induction derives historically from Locke. Locke, like Hume, sees himself as a champion of the modern scientific method against an outdated metaphysical Aristotelianism. A great devotee of Boyle's corpuscularism, Locke divides reality into two spheres or levels of existence: a microscopic realm composed of unseeable corpuscles (or atoms) and the macroscopic world we experience. Locke believes that the behaviour of these invisible corpuscles determines the nature of the physical objects and events we perceive. The observable depends, then, on the unobservable. This is the crucial premise in both Locke's and Hume's arguments against induction. What we perceive is only the tip of the iceberg. The true corpuscular cause of things is below the surface, out of reach, and unknowable. This is why induction has no logical force. As we have seen, induction is an argument from ignorance, an argument about surface appearances.

Locke views any claim that we can see into the secret causes behind things as unscientific, even superstitious. This is why induction is irredeemably inconclusive. As Locke puts it, "Of the truth of general propositions …

we cannot be sure."[82] Locke does not shy away from specific examples. "We cannot with certainty affirm," he claims, "that all men sleep by intervals; that no man can be nourished by wood or stones; that all men will be poisoned by hemlock."[83] We cannot have such general knowledge. Locke writes, "Possibly inquisitive and observing men may ... often guess right at what experience has not yet discovered to them. But this is but guessing still; it amounts only to opinion, and has not that certainty which is requisite to knowledge."[84] Induction deals, at best, with probable conjecture, and that in no way constitutes knowledge.

As someone interested in the new chemistry, Locke seemed remarkably pessimistic about the possibility of acquiring genuine scientific knowledge. He writes, "And thus, speaking of a man, or gold, or any other species of natural substances ... we cannot be certain of the truth of any affirmation or negation made of it. For man or gold ... stand for we know not what; and the extent of these species, with such boundaries, are so unknown and undetermined, that it is impossible with any certainty to affirm, that all men are rational, or that all gold is yellow."[85] According to Locke, we cannot even begin to study a chemical substance like gold, for we cannot determine where a true instance of gold might exist in the world. He writes, "[we] cannot be sure that any parcel of matter in the world is ... gold; being incurably ignorant whether it has ... that real essence of gold whereof we have no idea at all. This being as impossible for us to know as it is for a blind man to [know] in what flower the colour of a pansy is ... to be found."[86]

Locke distinguishes between nominal and metaphysical knowledge. When it comes to science, we can know the meanings of words; we can have nominal knowledge; but we cannot have metaphysical knowledge, knowledge about the nature of what really exists. Induction, insomuch as it deals with general concepts, is only a report on the way we use words. Nothing more. Locke explains, "General certainty is never to be found but in our ideas. Whenever we go to seek it elsewhere, in experiment or observations without us, our knowledge goes not beyond particulars. It is the contemplation of our own abstract ideas that alone is able to afford us general knowledge."[87] If, however, induction is limited to universal statements

82 Locke, *Essay*, bk 6, ch. 4, §5, 581.

83 Ibid., bk 6, ch. 4, §15, 590.

84 Ibid., bk 4, ch. 4, §13, 588.

85 Ibid., bk 5, ch. 4, §4, 580.

86 Ibid., bk 6, ch. 4, §5, 581.

87 Ibid., bk 6, ch. 4, §16, 590–1.

about our own ideas, it is not of much use as a scientific tool; it cannot penetrate or describe the deep structure of physical reality.

A SECOND LOCKE?

Hilary Kornblith, a student of W.V.O. Quine and an ardent champion of inductive reasoning, identifies himself as a modern Lockean.[88] This may seem more than odd, given Locke's pessimistic remarks about the impossibility of inductive knowledge. Kornblith claims, however, that we can discern a second line of reasoning in some of Locke's less familiar remarks. (His interpretation derives perhaps from Mackie.[89]) Consider, then, Kornblith's gloss on Locke.

As we have seen, Locke argues that the real nature of the physical world is "entirely unknowable by us." This is, as Kornblith admits, "a theme which [Locke] repeats many times and quite emphatically."[90] However, Locke also seems to suggest, in a discussion of chemistry, that the hidden essence of a thing is causally linked directly to its observable features. Because the secret corpuscular essence determines the exact chemical properties of things, "it is ... impossible that two Things partaking exactly the same real Essence, should have different Properties."[91] In other words, Locke rejects Hume's claim that the same cause can produce different effects. In contrast to the later Hume, he posits a basic one-to-one correspondence between the observable properties of chemical substances, like minerals, and the secret corpuscular essences or powers causing these minerals to exist. Minerals produced by the same secret objects or powers must possess the same observable properties. It follows, in direct opposition to Locke's earlier claim, that we can divide the world into natural kinds. As Kornblith comments, "There is an easy way to determine that two things do not belong to the same natural kind: all we need do is determine that they differ in some property or other."[92] Minerals that possess the same observable

88 See Kornblith, *Inductive Inference*, ch. 2, "Locke and Natural Kinds," 13–34.

89 Mackie, *Problems from Locke*. See the discussion of substance below.

90 Kornblith, *Inductive Inference*, 24.

91 Locke, *Essay*, bk 3, ch. 3, §17, cited in Kornblith, *Inductive Inference*, 26. Locke goes on to relate "the sad experience of Chymists" who, more often than not, find that "bodies of the same *Species*, having the same nominal *Essence*, under the same name; yet ... upon severe ways of examination betray Qualities so different from one another, as to frustrate the Expectation and Labor of very wary Chymists" (Locke, *Essay*, bk 3, ch. 6, §8).

92 Kornblith, *Inductive Inference*, 26–7.

properties must possess the same secret essence; that is, they must belong to the same natural kind. Minerals possessing different observable properties cannot possess the same secret essence, that is, they must belong to different natural kinds.

Kornblith goes on to argue that early empiricists such as Locke underestimated the future success of modern science. As it turns out, using the basic principle that observable properties must be a precise reflection of unobservable ones, we can delve into the corpuscular reality underlying things and, as a result, rigorously sort things in the world into their basic categories (or natural kinds). Hence the development, for example, of a definitive taxonomy for chemists, i.e., the periodic table. As I discuss in the last chapter of this book, Kornblith, in effect, tries to use Locke to defeat Locke; that is, he uses the Lockean suggestion of a one-to-one correspondence between observable and unobservable properties to defeat Locke's scepticism about scientific knowledge and inductive reasoning in general. While Kornblith's approach has something to recommend it, I will argue, first, that Locke's philosophical work is in large part motivated by a kind of systematic philosophical scepticism that is impervious to correction; and second, that it overlooks a much lengthier and more robust source of similar ideas, namely, the Aristotelian tradition. The principle Kornblith attributes to Locke – that two things that possess the same real nature must possess the same properties – is in fact the hidden premise in Aristotle's account of inductive reason. Although Kornblith sees himself, then, as a robust champion of modern empiricism, the essential tenet in his defence of induction is already present in Aristotle.

DISPUTING HUME

Hume's argument against the logic of induction, however influential, is not above criticism. The easiest way to undermine his stance is to simply point out that although he correctly believed that the physical world we interact with is determined by a corpuscular substratum (molecules, atoms, elementary particles, etc.), he was wrong to assume we could never come to know anything about the nature of that corpuscular realm. Indeed, the history of modern science seems to suggest just the opposite. Contemporary physicists, equipped with high-speed particle accelerators, lasers, electron microscopes, spectroscopes, computers, and a whole panoply of technical and mathematical aids are arguably able to test and probe the nature of atomic and even subatomic events. We can thus know the "secret powers" or "hidden essences" that cause the properties of things we actually perceive, and Hume's take on induction is therefore factually wrong. His argument goes from the premise "we cannot know what these powers and causes are," to the conclusion, "therefore induction is wrong." But modern science demonstrates the falsehood of the premise. So the argument does not provide us with any adequate reason for believing its conclusion.

Hume's argument about slices of bread is a case in point. He contends that we cannot come to the conclusion that the next slice of bread is nourishing, for we cannot have any knowledge of the secret nourishing powers of bread. He wrongly assumed, however, that we cannot know anything about the secret nourishing powers of bread. Modern chemistry tells us, unambiguously, that bread is nourishing because it is made of starches the body can break down by precise enzymatic and mechanical processes to supply the energy it needs. If something is really bread – i.e., if it is composed of these very same starchy substances – it must (depending, of course, on how we define the word) be nourishing. (Leave out anomalous cases such as those involving bread laced with arsenic, people with digestive disorders, and such like for the moment.) And the same point could be made with reference to countless other natural processes. Hume complains that we cannot generalize about the kinds of things and, by extension, about the events that compose the world. But the fact is that modern science has been able to explore and explain many of the hidden mechanisms that regulate and determine the nature of observable events and objects. Hume, at least on this point, is simply wrong.

For all the seemingly endless discussion, it is possible that Hume's original objection to induction was much simpler and more modest than conventionally thought. On this reading, Hume is not questioning science in principle; he simply cannot comprehend how far science could go in unpacking the mysteries of the corpuscular world. He lacks, so to speak, imagination. Consider Hume's famous claim that we cannot predict future events. Some commentators enthusiastically argue that Hume, in doing away with induction, deliberately and knowingly undermined our confidence in future prediction. J.J.C. Smart writes, "Hume showed conclusively that our belief that all past, present, and future A's are B's cannot depend on a valid deductive argument from the fact that all hitherto A's have been B's. We cannot even deduce the much weaker proposition that the next observed A will be a B. His reason is a very simple one: There is no contradiction in asserting the proposition 'All A's have been B's but some not yet observed A's are not B's'."[93] Smart is simply rehashing arguments discussed above. But in fact, Hume's position on induction seems more complicated

93 Smart, *Between Science and Philosophy*, 177.

than this; Smart's reading (the standard interpretation) seems, at the very least, to clash with Hume's stated position on science and miracles.

Before reconsidering how to interpret Hume, an important qualification is necessary. He does indeed argue that all inductive arguments "suppose, as their foundation, that the future will resemble the past."[94] But this attribution of the features of past experience to future experience is not an indispensable aspect of induction. Suppose I am struck by the thought, "I am a living human being and I have a beating heart. So Socrates must have had a beating heart." This case of induction involves a leap backwards into the past. Or suppose I think, "I am a living human being with a beating heart, so everyone in Sri Lanka must have a beating heart." This induction involves a leap from one place to another in the present. Induction does not require a mental leap from past to future. It is rather the movement from examined to unexamined instances that is crucial. As John Stuart Mill explains, "It is not from the past to the future ... that we infer, but from the known to the unknown; from facts observed to facts unobserved; from what we have perceived, or been directly conscious of, to what has not come within our experience."[95]

Obviously, we cannot observe the future. Future events are, in some definitive sense, empirically unverifiable. Knowledge of them must rely on inductive reasoning in a particularly conspicuous way. (In some brutal sense, that is all it can rely on.) Does it follow from this that anything can happen in the future? Consider an example from chemistry. When aqueous solutions of silver nitrate ($AgNO_3$) and salt ($NaCl$) are mixed, the silver (Ag^+) and chlorine (Cl^-) ions combine to yield a white precipitate of silver chloride ($AgCl$) – formally, $Ag^+(aq) + Cl^-(aq) \rightarrow AgCl(s)$. Suppose we perform this experiment several times and induce the following conclusion: "Whenever someone adds aqueous solutions of silver nitrate and salt (under the same conditions), they will obtain a solid white precipitate." Is it plausible or even rational to claim that someone will get a different result if they perform the same experiment at a different time (tomorrow, next week, three years from now, or a hundred years from now)? How could the mere passing of time change the results? The experimenter might make a mistake and employ the wrong chemicals or measure incorrectly or change the procedure in some significant way, but this would be tantamount to performing a different experiment. Chemistry stipulates that if we perform the experiment correctly, this *must* happen. We cannot empirically verify

94 Hume, *Enquiry* (Selby-Bigge, Nidditch), §4, pt 2, para. 32, 37.

95 Mill, *System of Logic*, bk 3, ch. 3, §1, 201.

future cases, but this is irrelevant. Our observations do not determine the nature of the chemical reaction. They only reveal a pattern already at work.

Chemistry has its laws. If someone were to mix an aqueous solution of silver nitrate and salt and obtain a different result, this would require a momentary suspension of the laws of chemistry. In short, it would require a "miracle."[96] But Hume himself dismisses any belief in miracles as preposterous. "Uniform experience," he writes, "amounts to a proof … a direct and full proof … against the existence of any miracle."[97] According to Hume, the sane person expects the non-miraculous event "with the last degree of assurance, and regards his past experience as a full *proof* of the future existence of that event."[98] If, therefore, past experience provides a "full proof" of future events, inductive reasoning must provide "full proof" of its conclusions. When we compare Hume's position on miracles with his stance on induction, it reveals an obvious conflict, not to say a contradiction, defying resolution.

Hume asks a rhetorical question, "Why is it *more than probable*, that all men must die; that lead cannot, of itself, remain suspended in the air; that fire consumes wood, and is extinguished by water; unless it be, that these events are found agreeable to the laws of nature, and there is required a violation of these laws, or in other words, a miracle to prevent them?"[99] But these laws of nature are, of course, the product of inductive reasoning. When Hume says that they are *more than probable*, he seems to suggest they are authoritative. Indeed, they are remarkably authoritative. They cannot be broken without a miracle. (Knowing Hume's position on miracles, that seems tantamount to saying that they can't be broken.) If, however, the laws of nature cannot be broken, then we *can* predict the future (given adequate knowledge) and induction is, at least in principle, sound.

Hume seems to paint himself into a corner. On the one hand, he wants us – in good Enlightenment form – to accept the authority of science. On the other hand, he argues against the reliability of induction. One cannot have it both ways. To believe in science is to believe in induction. Surely, we do not want to argue that the laws of physics are based on mere habit or custom. The universal law of gravitation is not like the social custom of holding your fork in the right or left hand. You can do either. Gravitation is, in contrast, something logically or at least metaphysically necessary. (At least, this is what most scientists claim.) We can perhaps make better sense

96 This is how Hume defines miracles. This is, rigorously speaking, not a proper religious definition.

97 Hume, *Enquiry* (Selby-Bigge, Nidditch), §10, pt 1, para. 90, 115.

98 Ibid., §10, pt 1, para. 87, 110 (original italics).

99 Ibid., §10, pt 1, para. 90, 114–15.

of Hume's position if we take him to be arguing, not that induction is, in principle, illogical, but that *based on insufficient evidence* it is illogical – except, of course, that Hume, with his penchant for making bold claims, does seem to suggest the former.

It may be helpful to distinguish here between inductive logic and inductive reasoning. The ardent inductive sceptic might argue (like Karl Popper) that neither works. But a more mitigated sceptic (like Hume) may contend that although *inductive reasoning* is (pragmatically) a successful practice, *inductive logic* is problematic. This would amount to saying that while we can successfully induce general conclusions such as "*all* men must die," "lead *never* suspends itself in thin air," "fire *inevitably* (or even *usually*) burns wood," we cannot logically explain why or how this knowledge comes about. Hume, who styled himself a mitigated sceptic, might be attracted to this kind of pragmatic point of view. If we (properly) rely on induction to our great benefit in daily life, we could perhaps insist that no equivalent argument could satisfactorily account for or illustrate this process. This would mean that we are left with a kind of bare inference when it comes to induction, a bare inference that, however successful, cannot be derived, through logical steps, from previous premises in a proper argument.

If this is a fair description of what Hume is about, Aristotle's approach to inductive reasoning is both the same and dissimilar. Consider Aristotle's approach to ethics. Aristotle does not begin with *a priori* moral ideas that he then imposes on humanity. No; he observes what people do and then develops a theory to explain and evaluate what he observes. Likewise for induction. People use induction on a regular basis, often with great success. Despite all kinds of mistakes (which Aristotle readily acknowledges), we can often induce accurate generalizations about the world. Up to this point Aristotle's approach is not unlike Hume's more sceptical methodology. But then, so to speak, everything changes. Aristotle, unlike Hume, thinks that we can have an inductive *logic*. We can, in the fullest sense of the word, elaborate an explanation, not only of inductive argument, but of induction generally. This explanation can go some way to accounting for the origin of the inductive impetus, as well as supplying a taxonomy of the various types of inductive argument. Once we come to understand the deep nature of inductive reasoning, we can better distinguish between good and bad inductive arguments.

POST-CARTESIAN SCEPTICISM

It is not easy to know what a historical figure such as Hume thought he was arguing. Suppose we take Hume's admonitions about induction as a moderate warning against relying on inductive arguments based on insufficient evidence. Now that science has given us additional knowledge about the deeper corpuscular levels of reality, does it follow that we have sufficient knowledge to reason inductively? Is scepticism of the Humean (and Lockean) sort no longer warranted? Can science pull itself up by its bootstraps and resolve lingering philosophical doubts about induction, simply by on the basis of further scientific evidence.

Any validation of science by science seems *prima facie* viciously circular. And there is an additional problem. The corpuscular mode of explanation these authors favour would, in principle, never come to an end. Whatever level of explanation we achieve, someone can always demand a further, deeper one. How do we know that there is a bottom floor to existence? Perhaps (as Anaxagoras thought) it has infinitely many further levels of more finely grained explanation. We cannot prove this is not the case. Indeed, it could be argued that modern physics has always progressed by moving one level further down on the grid of explanation: from elements, to molecules, to elementary particles, to sub-elementary particles, to the objects of field theory, to those of superstring theory, and so on. But this leaves open the possibility of another, deeper level of secret essences and powers that remains beyond the range of present theory. The mere possibility of another level of explanation overthrows, on Hume's argument, the logical merit of inductive reasoning. We can always argue, along the lines of Hume and Locke, that the available scientific evidence is inconclusive. Any inductive reasoning will be, on these grounds, an argument from ignorance. Any inductive generalization will be open to doubt. The Humean/Lockean model appears to offer no way to resolve this dilemma.

The pragmatically minded might feel some impatience with this philosopher's caveat. What – they might ask – do philosophers want? Complete certainty? Arguably, this is, indeed, what a certain coalition of modern and contemporary philosophers has demanded. Much of the contemporary scepticism about inductive reasoning derives from a more generalized attitude of epistemological doubt that can be traced back at least as far as René Descartes. As everyone knows, Descartes posits the possible existence of an evil demon who, with God-like power, tricks us into accepting falsehood as fundamental truth. Descartes uses this literary conceit in the *Meditations* as a device for clearing away old beliefs and prejudices. The problem is that this demon, once unleashed (like the evil demons inside Pandora's box), undermines, not just inductive reasoning, but our idea of knowledge generally.

Charles Sanders Peirce writes, "Descartes is the father of modern philosophy, and the spirit of Cartesianism ... teaches that philosophy must begin with universal doubt."[100] Peirce contrasts a medieval scholasticism that was acquiescent to the authority of the Church and tradition with a bold Cartesian spirit setting out to question everything. Descartes is clearly not a sceptic. He proposes comprehensive, radical doubt as a method, not as the aim, of rigorous philosophy. If, however, he firmly believed that he could respond to his own sceptical puzzle, his solution is highly questionable. The image of Descartes bequeathed by history to future generations is – rightly or wrongly – not that of someone who rescued knowledge from the jaws of scepticism but that of someone who set knowledge on fire with an unquenchable scepticism.

Although the *Meditations* is his most famous work, Descartes systematically broached the theme of comprehensive, methodological doubt in a lesser known and now incomplete manuscript, *La recherche de la verité par la lumière naturelle* (*The Search for the Truth by the Natural Light* [of Reason]). This text relates a dialogue between the protagonist Eudoxe (Greek, meaning "good opinion"), his pupil Poliandre (Greek, meaning "many men," so the "plain man" or "everyman"), and a meddling scholar, Epistémon (Greek, meaning "knowledge"). Eudoxe, who argues on behalf of Descartes, tells his interlocutors that they must begin their quest for knowledge by doubting everything: sense perception, whatever they have a natural inclination to believe, all they have been taught. Epistémon, the meddling scholar, protests, "It is very dangerous to advance too far ahead on this path. Such general doubts will lead us straight to the ignorance of Socrates, or to the uncertainty of the followers of Phyrro [the ancient sceptic]; and this is deep water, where we may not find a footing."[101] But Eudoxe reassures him, "Let me inform you that these doubts that first frightened you are like ghosts and useless images that appear at night thanks to an uncertain and crazy light; if you flee, your fear will follow you; but if you approach as if to touch them, you will discover that they're nothing, only shadow and air, and will be more confident when you meet them again in the future."[102]

Descartes believed we could use universal doubt to elaborate a complete system of knowledge. Eudoxe tells the assembled company, "Just lend me your attention and I will lead you further than you think. Because, from out of this universal doubt, like a fixed and unmovable point, I am planning to derive knowledge of God, of yourself, and finally of all things that exist in

100 Peirce, "Some Consequences of Four Incapacities," 211.

101 Less literally, "this is deep water, we are in over our heads" (Descartes, *Recherche de la verité*, 1120).

102 Ibid., 1121.

nature."[103] Absolute doubt is, then, the "Archimedean point," that fixed and solid fulcrum, on which we can rest a lever to lift up the entire world.

Poliandre, the earnest student, immediately endeavours to put the sceptical method into practice. "[I will] contemplate," he says,

> the biggest difficulties that I can imagine, and ... employ my powers of concentration to doubt things such as whether all my life has been a dream, or if all [my] ideas ... are not formed in the mind by themselves, just as similar ones materialize every time I sleep, when I know perfectly well that my eyes are closed, my ears plugged, and, in short, that none of my senses contributes to their appearance. Consequently, I will not know, not only if there are other people in the world, if there is a planet Earth, if there is a sun; but still, even further if I have eyes, if I have ears, if I have a body, and even if I am presently speaking to you, if you are speaking to me, in short, I will be uncertain of everything.[104]

This point of absolute uncertainty is, according to Descartes, the place from which to start philosophy.

Descartes approach is, at the very least, counterintuitive. Pretending that we are deaf, blind, dumb, dreaming, alone, uncertain about anything at all, is an odd starting place for knowledge. We might argue that we should start with what knowledge we have and improve on it. But what Descartes wants, above all, is a new beginning. He thinks that beginning our philosophical investigations from the standpoint of universal doubt will force us to throw away what is questionable in our starting presumptions and retain only what is unshakeably true. He is confident, of course, that some of our beliefs are so self-evidently true they could resist absolute doubt. He begins of course with his *cogito*. You cannot, after all, doubt that you are doubting. Eudoxe asks Poliandre, "Can you doubt your doubt, and remain uncertain whether you doubt or not?"[105] And the surprised student is forced to conclude that doubting his own existence is impossible, "because if I did not exist, I could not doubt." Eudoxe triumphantly observes, "You exist then, and you know that you exist, and you know it because you doubt."[106] He goes on to elaborate a second version of Descartes' famous *cogito*: "Je doute, donc j'existe; ou, ce qui est la même chose: Je pense, donc, j'existe

103 Ibid., 1122.
104 Ibid., 1121.
105 Ibid., 1122.
106 Ibid., 1132.

[I doubt, therefore I exist, or, which is the same thing, I think therefore I exist]."[107]

Descartes commitment to systematic doubt is unswerving. Persistent, relentless, intransigent doubting is the road to self-knowledge and to knowledge of the entire world. Poliandre remarks, "I can thus affirm that I began to know myself as soon as I began to doubt"[108] – except that Descartes' optimistic belief that such doubt defeats itself and that reason turns, through some kind of magical alchemy, the base metal of scepticism into the gold of certain belief, seems, in retrospect, remarkably naive. His own logical system certainly did not satisfy later philosophers. Indeed, his response to doubt faded away (becoming, in the minds of most philosophers, a historical curiosity), and the method of relentless, unstoppable doubt became instead his legacy.

At least two problems affect universal Cartesian doubt. First, we can question whether comprehensive doubt is even possible. Peirce writes, "most modern philosophers have been, in effect, Cartesians ... [But] we cannot begin with complete doubt. We must begin with all the prejudices which we actually have when we enter upon the study of philosophy."[109] Peirce thinks that Cartesian doubt is pantomime, mere pretending. He explains,

> [Our] prejudices are not to be dispelled by a maxim, for they are things which it does not occur to us can be questioned. Hence this initial skepticism will be a mere self-deception, and not real doubt; and no one who follows the Cartesian method will ever be satisfied until he has formally recovered all those beliefs which in form he has given up. It is, therefore, as useless a preliminary as going to the North Pole would be in order to get to Constantinople by coming down regularly upon a meridian ... Let us not pretend to doubt in philosophy what we do not doubt in our hearts.

Peirce does, of course, leave plenty of room for doubt; but authentic doubt arises when a rigorous thinker is presented with counter-evidence to claims, not from a wilful disposition to doubt. Peirce comments, "A person may, it is true, in the course of his studies, find reason to doubt what he began by believing; but in that case he doubts because he has a positive reason for it, and not on account of the Cartesian maxim."[110]

107 Ibid., 1135–6.
108 Ibid., 1137.
109 Peirce, "Some Consequences of Four Incapacities," 212.
110 Ibid.

The second problem with Cartesian doubt is that any attempt to consistently apply universal doubt erodes away our belief in anything. Methodological scepticism cannot be contained. Like watercolour, it bleeds across boundaries. Descartes' optimism, his belief that we can defeat universal doubt, was dashed on the rocks of later philosophy. Even the *cogito* can be doubted. Nietzsche, writing at the end of the nineteenth century in a hasty note to himself, lambastes Descartes: "Along the lines followed by Descartes one does not come upon something absolutely certain but only upon the fact of a very strong belief." If we believe something strongly, it does not *prove* that it is true. Nietzsche believes that the most that Descartes can show is that *the way we use language* seems to indicate there is a thinking subject. We cannot prove, however, that the way we use language corresponds to reality. Nietzsche comments, "'There is thinking: therefore there is something that thinks', this [claim] is the upshot of all Descartes' argumentation. But that means positing as 'true *a priori*' our belief ... that when there is thought there has to be something 'that thinks' [and that] is simply a formulation of our grammatical custom that adds a doer to every deed."[111]

Nietzsche is, in the true modern spirit, a consummate doubter. He uses Descartes' method against himself. What was unthinkable to Descartes, that one could even doubt the *cogito*, is, in Nietzsche's mind, mere child's play. With a little scribble on a piece of paper, with hardly a blink of an eye, he thinks he can overthrow what was for Descartes the most secure foundation of all knowledge. We do not have to agree with Nietzsche – that is not the point. It is not that Nietzsche's position can be properly defended. The point is that Nietzsche's ability to question even the most basic beliefs was an inevitable development of the wholesale doubt Descartes champions.

Søren Kierkegaard, in *Fear and Trembling*, describes the doubting disease that infects the would-be modern philosopher. He sardonically observes, "Every speculative monitor who conscientiously signals important trends in modern philosophy, every assistant professor, tutor and student, every rival outsider and tenant incumbent in philosophy is unwilling to stop with doubting everything but goes further ... What those ancient Greeks ... assumed to be a task for a whole lifetime, because proficiency in doubting is not acquired in days or weeks ... with that everyone *begins* in our age."[112]

Kierkegaard is not far off the mark. The idea that we can doubt absolutely everything has become universal coin in modern philosophy. In every

111 Nietzsche, *Will to Power*, §484, 268.

112 Kierkegaard, *Fear and Trembling* (Howard and Edna Hong), 57–8 (my italics) (in Kierkegaard, *Fear and Trembling / Repetition*).

contemporary university, one can hear philosophers and students of philosophy boldly and brazenly doubting just about everything. But Cartesian doubt is an expression of will rather than understanding. It is not truly epistemological but dispositional. As Peirce suggests, we need to distinguish between Cartesian doubt and evidence-based doubt. In the case of evidence-based thought, we accept the truth of some evidence. Indeed, it is our acceptance of *this* evidence that leads us to question *that* evidence. Descartes, however, would have us doubt all evidence; we are to wipe the slate clean and start all over again. In the first case, we have epistemological doubt, scepticism raised by a careful weighing of evidence. In the second case, we have wilful doubt, scepticism embracing a complete disregard of evidence. Thomas, somewhere in his commentary on Aristotle's *Metaphysics*, advises the reader that the important thing is not to doubt but to doubt well. If an objective, thorough examination of issues may lead us to doubt specific claims, a stubborn, persistent desire to doubt anything is not epistemologically compelling. Yes, post-Cartesian scepticism undermines inductive reasoning, but it also undermines deduction and everything else. This kind of absolute doubt, consistently practiced, makes genuine knowledge impossible.

Like other practitioners of the same methodology, Descartes wants to use radical doubt to undermine his opponents' position. He does not see that the comprehensive doubt he uses to undermine natural belief and traditional philosophy can, in turn, be used to undermine his own philosophy. As the history of modern philosophy demonstrates, we can never satisfy those who feel entitled to question everything. Cartesian doubt can be used to question first principles, concepts, sense perception, logic, metaphysics, science, religion, morality – in short, it can be used to question anything. We have no way of restraining or limiting Cartesian doubt. Once let out of its box, it eats up and erodes everything.

The argument we use to justify the Cartesian stance is not that important. In the *Meditations*, Descartes raises the spectre of an evil genius with supernatural powers who deceives us into believing that the world is different than it really is. He does not use this device in *La recherche de la verité*, which suggests that it is not this trope but the method of comprehensive doubt that interests him. Later authors such as Locke and Hume went on to argue that the true natures of things are inaccessible to human perception, or, as with Kant, that human cognition may divide the world into categories that mask the true nature of the world, or again, more recently, that language is inevitably deceitful, or more simply, that human fallibility is a barrier to reliable knowledge. We have made mistakes in the past, so we may be making them now. And so on.

None of these arguments prove their point. They are transcendental arguments; they raise an unverifiable possibility that disqualifies an entire category of confident belief; they question the possibility of knowledge itself. These kinds of arguments do not supply a criterion for distinguishing between what counts and what does not count as knowledge. They do not provide us with a method for sorting through true and false, justified and unjustified claims; instead, they undermine this kind of distinction altogether. Although philosophy has a place for discussion of this transcendental sort, to place it at the centre of epistemology is to misconstrue what epistemology is about. Comprehensive, radical scepticism is impervious to correction. It is an invulnerable philosophical stance; it cannot be defeated – not because it has epistemological merit, but because it is a determined expression of wilful doubt. To make positive epistemology dependent on the defeat of Cartesian scepticism is to ensure the defeat of epistemology.

The Cartesian approach sanctions a method of recurrent objection: just be persistent, keep raising difficulties. This can be a legitimate method, depending on the circumstances. But any approach that demands a complete proof of knowledge ends in scepticism for (as I shall discuss further) a complete proof of anything is impossible. How, then, do we stop the everlasting downward spiral from objection to objection? How do we put an end to Cartesian doubt? We begin by recognizing the limits of epistemologically responsible doubt. Aristotle (somewhat bluntly) advises, "It is not necessary to examine every problem and every thesis but only one about which doubt might be felt by the kind of person who requires to be argued with and does not need castigation [or] lack perception. For those who feel doubt whether or not the gods ought to be honored and parents loved, need castigation, while those who doubt whether snow is white or not, lack perception."[113] Obviously, human knowledge is finite. It begins and ends somewhere. Recognizing this means that we simply accept that some objections are not worth answering; some disputes, frivolous; some claims, as far as we can tell, unassailable. We will discuss these issues at much greater length throughout this book. If human beings are clearly fallible, it does not follow that knowledge of any sort is impossible.

To argue that inductive reasoning is flawed because it is susceptible to Cartesian doubt is not very convincing. We can, of course, find a way to doubt inductive reasoning. This book discusses specific arguments in more detail below. But the mere fact that we can doubt something (in the

113 These comments are offered within the context of dialectical reasoning, but they can be taken as emblematic of a larger attitude (*Topics* [Forester], bk 1, ch. 11, 105a1–10).

Cartesian sense) is not necessarily momentous. Many authors assume, for example, that deduction is logically unassailable whereas induction is suspect. But Cartesian doubt, *consistently applied*, does not allow for such distinctions. Deductive reasoning, like inductive reasoning, is an expression of the fallible human mind. It is based on strong beliefs about what is true, consistent, sound, or valid. If, however, we set out to doubt everything and anything, it is hard to see how deduction can escape rigorous questioning. The point is not simply that inductions are not deductions; seen from a Cartesian point of view, all logic, inductive and deductive, is equally open to doubt.

And there is a deeper issue. In the present book, we are not just interested in logic understood as a mere formalism. We are interested in science. But science, which has an inductive and a deductive side, makes claims about what is true about the world. It is not enough to argue that deductive reasoning is formally correct (which can be doubted). If science is to make any sense, any use the scientist makes of deductive reasoning must provide a reliable model of the nature of the world. But whether our thought, in any manifestation, corresponds to what is really out there is precisely what Descartes and legions after him throw into question.

GOODMAN'S NEW RIDDLE OF INDUCTION

Many modern arguments against induction are little more than an expression of radical Cartesian doubt. In the literature, one encounters a prominent attitude: induction somehow has to be proved. If we are going to be epistemologically rigorous, we must first doubt everything; we must begin without epistemological convictions and then somehow prove that induction is a legitimate species of cogent thought. The onus of proof is on those who would defend induction, not on those who would undermine it. The tendency is to discredit induction as an entire category of inference, not to discredit this or that instance or kind of induction. Appeals by authors in the history of philosophy such as Locke, Hume, and Kant to ideas of invisible substance, occult essence, or the noumenon largely supply the rationale for doubting induction. As I discuss below and in the following chapters, these arguments are demonstrably all instances of Cartesian doubt. But Cartesian doubt is not a purely historical phenomenon. It pervades present-day discussion. Consider, briefly, a contemporary argument directed against induction: Nelson Goodman's so-called "new riddle of induction."[114]

114 See Goodman, *Fact, Fiction, and Forecast.*

At least from an Aristotelian perspective, Goodman's celebrated puzzle is hardly momentous. Goodman invents an artificial property he calls "grue." Something is grue if it fills one of two criteria: if it is green and first observed before time *t*, or if it is blue and only observed after time *t*. Suppose we arbitrarily set time *t* to 1 January 2010. If *x* is a green piece of moss first observed *before* that date and *y* is a blue stone first observed *after* that date, then both *x* and *y* qualify as grue. But neither qualifies as grue if *x* happens to be a green piece of moss first observed *after* 1 January 2010 and *y* is a blue stone first observed *before* that date. Once an object is described as possessing (or not possessing) the property of grue, it can always be described as having (or not having) that property. All that matters is that the requisite colour is FIRST observed before or after the required date.

Goodman thinks that the possibility of a predicate such as "grue" explodes the reliability of inductive reasoning. Suppose one examines a number of emeralds before 1 January 2010. Emeralds are, of course, green. But because these emeralds are observed before 1 January 2010, they can be described as either green or as grue. We can, then, produce parallel inductive arguments. We can argue (1) "This, this, and this emerald is green; therefore all emeralds are green." Or we can argue (2) "This, this, this emerald is grue; therefore all emeralds are grue." These arguments possess the same logical form and both possess true premises. It must follow that they are equally strong. But any such suggestion seems problematic. Suppose that after 1 January 2010, we observe a new emerald. The two previous inductions indicate that the emerald will be green and grue. But this is impossible. Now that the date has passed, the emerald will have to be blue to qualify as grue. To say that induction shows that the same emerald must be green and grue is (in this case) to say that induction shows that the same emerald will be green and blue – i.e., green and "not green" – at the exact same time. But this is a contradiction. Hence (by *reductio ad absurdum*) induction is illogical, incoherent, unreliable, or useless.

Goodman believes that he has shown that a particular inductive inference is no more *confirmed* (that is, supported by the data) than any number of contradictory inferences. Even if induction could be justified through non-circular reasoning, we have no way of determining what makes one given application of it better than another. Goodman (who is much closer to Hume than he admits) goes on to argue that induction is a matter of social custom; it is not, properly speaking, a species of *logical* argument. He weakly asserts that "entrenched" predicates are "projectible," that we can legitimately make future predications about emeralds being green because this squares with human convention. Correct induction becomes, on this model, a product of collective habit; we are used to thinking that emeralds are green, and so we can sanction this induction. If, however, I grew up in a society with people in the habit of thinking that emeralds are grue, then that would count as a correct induction. On Goodman's account, inductive reasoning (i.e., science) cannot teach us anything about the true nature of the world; the most it can do is teach us about our contingent, arbitrary social history. (Induction is, for Goodman, to borrow an ancient distinction, *nomos*, not *physis*. It is about human convention, not nature.)

The whole point of Goodman's discourse is to bring up problems that cannot be solved, to subvert the possibility of induction altogether. But this seems to be another instance of Cartesian doubt. Goodman claims that inductive reasoning cannot give us a convincing reason to prefer the scientific claim that emeralds are green over some philosopher's fancy that emeralds are grue. But closer inspection demonstrates that Goodman's argument is not merely counterintuitive; it is unfounded. What one uncovers is an adamant will to doubt rather than an evidence-based example of a deep problem with induction.

To begin with, the new riddle of induction commits the fallacy of "complex question." This is the fallacy of the trick question, "Have you stopped beating your wife yet?" Consider. The proposition, "emeralds are grue," can be unpacked into three separate claims: emeralds are green before time *t* ($proposition_1$); emeralds are blue after time *t* ($proposition_2$); and emeralds turn from green to blue at time *t* ($proposition_3$). Goodman illegitimately translates support for $proposition_1$ into support for $proposition_2$ and $proposition_3$. But the fact that we have evidence in support of $proposition_1$ does not give us any evidence in support of all three propositions taken together. If the truth of $proposition_1$ is *compatible* with the other propositions, this does not translate into positive support for them. The proposition that Barack Obama is president of the United States is compatible with the proposition that Guy LaFleur is the king of France, but the fact that we believe that Barack Obama is the president of the United States gives us no reason to believe that Guy LaFleur is the king of France.

The problem with the predicate grue is that it brings together different issues under the cover of a single concept and illicitly transforms evidence for one aspect of the predicate into support for another, different one. If we unpack the concept into its constituent parts, the problem surfaces more clearly. The colour green or blue may qualify as an objective characteristic of an object. But the predicate grue is also a reflexive predicate; it refers not merely to the colour of the object in question, but to the time when we observe it. But the time we observe something is not really a fact about the object. It is more suitably described as a fact about us. Call an emerald observed before ten o'clock tonight a ten-o'clock emerald.

Suppose I observe fourteen emeralds at nine o'clock. I make the following induction: "This emerald, this emerald, and this emerald, etc., are ten-o'clock emeralds; therefore, all (future) emeralds will be ten-o'clock emeralds." Clearly, this is an absurd inference. But it is not illegitimate because induction is flawed; it is illegitimate because we cannot assign the property of being a ten-o'clock emerald to those observed in the future without contradicting ourselves. The problem does not lie with induction. The problem here lies with the misuse of a predicate.

Goodman's problematic induction runs as follows: "This emerald, this emerald, this emerald, etc., is grue; therefore all emeralds are grue." Substituting the meaning of the term "grue," we are left with, "This emerald, this emerald, this emerald, etc., is green if first observed before *t* and blue if first observed after *t*; therefore all emeralds are green if first observed before *t* and blue if first observed after *t*." But there is absolutely no evidence that any emeralds are blue if observed after time *t*. The only emeralds that have been observed (those observed before time *t*) are always green. So why should we conclude that emeralds will be blue if first observed after *t*? This is an entirely unfounded inference. Goodman's suggestion is, in the bad sense, just a philosopher's thought experiment. It is a fanciful claim without any scientific merit. To believe in grue is to *ignore* all the evidence; it is to retreat into post-Cartesian scepticism.

But it is not simply that inductive reasoning does not provide any evidence for the grue hypothesis. Indeed, it seems to rule out this possibility altogether. Inductive reasoning produces the laws of physics, chemistry, optics, and geology. To claim that emeralds can turn blue (or be blue) at time *t* would be to claim that the scientific laws that regulate the colours of gemstones can suddenly change. But where is the evidence for any such change. There is nothing in these laws (or in their associated fields of discovery) that provides any reason for believing in the kind of mineral transformation Goodman has in mind. Time *t* is completely arbitrary. Just pulled out of thin air. If Goodman was advancing a serious scientific claim, he would have to show that the laws of chemistry, physics, optics, and geology point to this kind of temporal change. He does nothing of the sort. This is not inductive reasoning but a wilful philosophical imagination in search of a puzzling paradox that raises the spectre of this uncaused possibility. Goodman attacks the belief that emeralds will continue to be green (and never blue) without marshalling any scientific evidence in support of his radical conclusion. He advances an empty argument.

Note the basic form of Goodman's criticism. All induction is illogical because of the possibility of blue (purple, yellow, red, orange, black, etc.) emeralds after time *t*. What Goodman suggests is that we ignore all the evidence, i.e., all the findings of science, and accept a possibility for which there is no evidence. We are to smuggle this unfounded possibility into our concept grue and use it to destroy the credibility of all induction. This is Cartesian doubt at work. The laws of science were built up over a long period of time, pieced together from innumerable observations and innumerable inductions. Not only do they provide an explanation for the green colour of emeralds. They posit the necessity of certain kinds of optical behaviour.

We know why emeralds are green. Emeralds are beryls, composed of aluminum beryllium silicate (a transparent crystal lattice) containing chromium as an impurity.[115] The host crystal is associated with an electric field that fixes the energy levels of the chromium electrons so that they can only absorb certain wavelengths of light (the crystal- or ligand-field effect). These electrons remove yellow-red and blue light from sunshine, which is why the emerald looks green. Could green emeralds turn blue? Not without violating the laws of physics and chemistry. To produce blue light, the chromium electrons fixed in these orbitals by the electrical field of aluminum beryllium silicate would have to *absorb* green (red and yellow) light and *not* absorb blue light. But electrons fixed in these unoccupied orbitals cannot undergo the energy changes such chemical behaviours necessitate. Or at least, they cannot do this without a basic violation of physical laws. Of course we can use Cartesian doubt to doubt all the laws of chemistry and physics, but so what? If we are unable to protect the laws of chemistry from Cartesian doubt, this is neither surprising nor devastating. As we have seen, Cartesian doubt erodes epistemological commitment to anything and everything.[116]

Goodman is heavily influenced by Hume's argument against induction that the future may be completely different from the past. He seems to simply assume that this is an incontrovertible notion. But what evidence do we have that the future might be completely different from the past? The idea seems to be that the future is open to change because it has not happened yet. But it does not follow from this that *anything* is possible.

115 Note that we could define emeralds crudely as "green stones." But this is not a true scientific definition. The colour green is not the defining (essential) trait of emeralds; being composed of beryllium silicate and containing chromium impurities is the defining trait. The colour green is a necessary property of beryllium silicate and chromium, but it is not the essential trait; otherwise, all green stones would have to be emeralds. (More could be said.)

116 Sapphires, for example, are blue, but they have a different chemistry. They are composed of a corundum crystal lattice containing two impurities, titanium and iron.

Induction is based on past or present experience. We must move from what has happened or what is happening to a conclusion about the unknown. As Goodman indicates, any inference that emeralds will continue to be green is based on past or present evidence. But is this a weakness in the argument? All the evidence available to me on *any* question must come from the past or the present. To discount all past and present evidence is, in principle, to discount *all* evidence. And to discount all evidence is to imprison oneself in Cartesian doubt. If the post-Cartesian sceptic is impervious to correction or persuasion, this does not give us a good reason to dispute the rationality of induction. To ignore the only evidence we possess has no epistemological merit. It is, in fact, irrational.

Inductive reasoning extrapolates. In its simplest form, it attributes observed properties to unobserved events or things. What is observed in the past and present is attributed to what exists in the future. In the present circumstances, what is observed are green emeralds. This basic method of induction proposes a simple inference: "these observed emeralds are green; therefore emeralds observed in the future will be green." Goodman, through the invention of an artificial predicate grue, transforms the inference into "these observed emeralds are green; therefore emeralds first observed after *t* will be blue." This is a strange sort of inference. Whatever it is, it is not inductive reasoning. It is not applying past and present experience to the future. It is inventing a future that is completely different than what past and present experience indicate. This is, in disguise, an anti-induction. No wonder it doesn't make any sense!

If predicates such as "grue" do not make up part of our "entrenched usage," this is because they make no rational sense. To use the same word to refer (at different times) to two incompatible concepts is to purposely introduce into language the kind of ambiguity that Goodman's riddle hinges on. Why, except under exceptional circumstances, would we include a reference to the time at which we first observe an object in a description of the object's nature? At least on the Aristotelian model, induction is, first and foremost, about discovering the necessary properties of things. These properties are what they are regardless of when we observe them. To bring the time when they are first observed into the definition of a property is to complicate issues with an extraneous factor. (One could make a more sophisticated argument on the basis of quantum mechanics about the relationship between observation and necessary properties [e.g., Schrödinger's Cat], but that is clearly not what Goodman is about.)

The incredulity Goodman expresses about induction is an instance of Cartesian doubt. It does not arise from a careful examination of the evidence but from a wilful attempt to disregard it. If someone researching into the optics of gems had a scientific reason for disputing the green colour of all emeralds, if someone uncovered concrete, empirical (or even theoretical) evidence against this conclusion, this might count as an instance of epistemologically induced doubt. But this is not Goodman's method. He presents a transcendental argument. He thinks that he has found a way to throw an entire category of inference into dispute. He does it, not by appealing to evidence, but by smuggling in a possibility for which there is no evidence. We should be suspicious of such attempts.

Perhaps the apparent soundness of Goodman's riddle can be attributed to a logical confusion. It may seem, at first glance, that the following line of reasoning holds. (Call this formulation 1.) Suppose we know that *A* is true. It will follow that the proposition "*A* or *B*" is true, because (on the standard account) the claim "*A* or *B*" counts as true if one of three criteria is met: (1) if *A* is true, or (2) if *B* is true, or (3) if both *A* and *B* are true. But we already know that *A* is true (1), so "*A* or *B*" must be true. The logical step of turning "*A*" into "*A* or *B*" is known as "weakening," as there are less stringent demands for establishing the truth of "*A* or *B*." (Even if "*A*" is false, "*A* or *B*" could still be true.) Goodman formulates his riddle as follows:

(1) Define "A emeralds" as "green and first observed before *t*."
(2) Define "B emeralds" as "blue and first observed after *t*."
(3) Define "grue" as "A emeralds or B emeralds."
(4) Induction shows that the claim that "all emeralds are A emeralds" is true. (If all observed emeralds have been green, and if induction is a reliable process, any emerald observed at any time must be green.)
(5) If, however, the claim, "all emeralds are A emeralds," is true, we can conclude (by weakening) that the claim, "all emeralds are A emeralds or all emeralds are B emeralds," is true.
(6) It follows that the claim, "all emeralds are A emeralds or B emeralds," i.e., that "all emeralds are grue," is also true.

That is, except that this formulation is not, on closer inspection, exact. The predicate "grue" should be represented, not as "A emeralds *or* B emeralds," but as the conjunction "A emeralds *and* B emeralds." In order for "grue" to be true, it must be the case that (1) all emeralds first observed before *t* are green; *and* (2) all emeralds first observed after *t* are blue. In other words, two separate conditions must be met (depending on the time of observation). So the line of reasoning should be depicted as follows (call this formulation 2):

(1) Define "A emeralds" as "green and first observed before *t*."
(2) Define "B emeralds" as "blue and first observed after *t*."
(3) Define "grue" as "A emeralds and B emeralds."
(4) Induction shows that the claim that "all emeralds are A emeralds" is true, but it gives no support for the claim, "all emeralds are B emeralds."
(5) So we do not have grounds to conclude that "all emeralds are A emeralds *and* all emeralds are B emeralds."
(6) So, in direct contrast to what Goodman suggests, we do not have any grounds to claim that "all emeralds are grue."

We cannot move from the claim "*A*" to the claim "*A* and *B*" by weakening. This is an illegitimate logical move. But to claim that "all emeralds are grue" is to claim that there are A emeralds *and* B emeralds. But induction provides no support for "B emeralds."

More could be said. We need not belabour the point. Yes, we can conclude that "all emeralds are grue" if we doubt the laws of physics. But it is irrational to doubt the laws of physics. If, however, we are going to doubt the laws of physics, why not doubt the laws of logic? Why not doubt deductive reasoning? Why not doubt sense perception? Why not doubt the language Goodman uses to elucidate his argument? Why not doubt human intelligence? Goodman, like Descartes, is rather selective in his method. He uses Cartesian doubt to throw inductive reasoning into question. If we are to be consistent Cartesians, we must begin by doubting everything. And if we do that, we will dig a hole so deep, we will never get out of it.

SUBSTANCE: A METAPHYSICAL PROBLEM

Peter Millican writes, "Hume was the first to raise skeptical doubts about inductive reasoning, leaving a puzzle as to why the concerns he highlighted had earlier been so completely overlooked."[117] I will argue that the oversight does not lie with earlier thinkers such as Aristotle. Quite to the contrary, it lies with Locke and Hume and their empiricist followers, who never came to any fair understanding of earlier perspectives on the topic. Hume may mention learning Greek in his brief autobiography, but he does not display any careful knowledge of an author such as Aristotle.[118] In the *Enquiry*, Hume mentions Aristotle twice, once to emphasize his "utterly decayed" reputation, and once in a general reference to the four elements

117 Millican, "Induction," 172–6.
118 See "My Own Life" (Reproduced in most editions of Hume's works.)

of Greek science: water, fire, earth, and air.[119] Some commentators leave us with the impression that Hume understood the Aristotelian and medieval points of view on induction and refuted them. It is more plausible to suggest that he never seriously considered these doctrines in the first place.[120] Although Locke displays greater understanding of the Aristotelian heritage, he seems to be familiar with the later stages of a scholastic tradition that was uncongenial to his scientific temper. By the time later authors such as Immanuel Kant and John Stuart Mill appear on the scene, mainstream philosophy had already lost sight of the original understanding of induction.

In this section I will review Aristotle's concept of substance and then show how the empiricist account entails a misreading of this earlier one. Locke and Hume first conceived of the empiricist understanding of induction in opposition to an earlier Aristotelian-scholastic tradition. They attack the Aristotelian notion of "substance" and replace it with a new empiricist account derived from a scientific corpuscularism. While empiricist authors naturally have little respect for metaphysical notions of substance, they nevertheless misunderstand what Aristotle is about. In a genuinely Aristotelian metaphysics, the problem with induction in some sense solves itself. The empiricist account of substance is, I will argue, one more expression of Cartesian scepticism. Turn, then, to Aristotle.

Aristotle's term for substance is "οὐσία" (*ousia*), which is the abstract-noun form of the Greek verb "to be." *Ousia* means, in some sort, "being." Aristotle believes that being manifests itself in particular objects.[121] A primary substance is an individual,[122] a unity;[123] it is separable from other things;[124] it is the "thing" that possesses the properties predicated of it.[125] Aristotle refers specifically to a particular man, horse, ox, or god as primary

119 The second mention is in a reference to "earth, water and other elements" (Hume, *Enquiry* [Selby-Bigge, Nidditch], §1, para. 4, 7; §8, pt 1, para. 65, 84).

120 Whatever the merits of Hume's arguments, he cannot be called a fair historian of philosophy. The objectivity of his more important *History of England* has also been questioned. See Okie, "Ideology and Partiality."

121 See *Metaphysics*, bk 4. Aristotle claims, "substance is an individual thing" (*Metaphysics* [Tredennick], bk 3, ch. 6, 1003a5–10, in Aristotle, *Aristotle in 23 Volumes*).

122 See *Categories*, chs 3 and 5.

123 Aristotle writes, "things whose substances are numerically one are numerically one" (*Metaphysics* [Tredennick], bk 7, ch. 16, 1040b15–18). And again, "each individual thing is one" (ibid., bk 8, ch. 6, 1045b18–22).

124 *Metaphysics*, bk 7, ch. 1, 1028a35–1028b; and bk 12, ch. 1, 1069a25.

125 *Metaphysics* (Tredennick), bk 5, ch. 8, 1017a10–15.

substances.[126] "These are called substances because they are not predicated of [anything else], but other things are predicated of them."[127] A body part, a chemical element, or a physical object, insomuch as it can be separated from the larger whole, can also count, in a derivative sense, as a primary substance.[128]

Aristotle clearly distinguishes between substances and properties. A substance is that unit of being or existence, that "thing," to which the properties must be ascribed. It is not an action; it is the thing acting. Aristotle writes, "One might raise the question whether the terms 'to walk' and 'to be well' and 'to sit' signify each of these things as 'being' [substance] ... [but] not one of them by nature has an independent existence ... Rather, if anything, it is the *thing* which walks or sits or is well that is existent."[129] In other words, it is not "walking," "sitting," or "being well" that are substances, but the one who "walks" or "sits" or "is well" that is a substance.

Aristotle observes that the self-same substance may come to possess contrary or opposing properties: "It seems most distinctive of substance," he writes, "that what is numerically one and the same is able to receive contraries ... For example, an individual man – one and the same – becomes pale at one time and dark at another, and hot and cold, and bad and good."[130] If the man was only his properties, he would become a different man whenever he took on different properties, but substance retains its identity through time. It can be the same substance even when some of its properties change.

We should situate Aristotle's account within ancient Greek philosophy. The Presocratics had set out to discover the ἀρχή (*arche*), the ultimate root or origin of things. Thales seems to have identified this ultimate reality with moisture; Anaximenes, with air; Anaximander with the ἄπειρον (*apeiron*), the infinite; Leucippius and Democritus, with atoms; Empedocles, with the four elements; Anaxagoras, with mind – and so on. Aristotle, in contrast, identifies individual substance as the ultimate component of reality. He affirms, "if the universe is to be regarded as a whole, substance is

126 *Metaphysics*, bk 7, ch. 1, 1028a15–20; and *Categories*, ch. 4, 1b28; ch. 5, 2b15, 26–27.

127 *Metaphysics* (Tredennick), bk 5, ch. 8, 1017a10–15.

128 Aristotle writes, "Substance means simple bodies, e.g. earth, fire, water and the like; and in general bodies, and the things animal or divine, including their parts which are composed of bodies" (*Metaphysics* [Tredennick], bk 5, ch. 8, 1017a10–15).

129 Ibid., bk 7, ch. 1, 1028a20–25.

130 *Categories* (Ackrill), ch. 5, 4a10–20 (in Aristotle, *Complete Works*).

the first part."[131] The cosmos is, properly speaking, a collection of primary substances, of individual things. Primary substances constitute, so to speak, the bottom floor of existence. Everything stops here. We cannot delve any further. "If the primary substances did not exist it would be impossible for any of the other things to exist."[132]

While individual things are substances in the most excellent sense, Aristotle uses the term "secondary substance" to refer to entire species and to families of species or genera. Aristotle writes, "The species in which the things primarily called substances are, are called secondary substances, as also are the genera of these species. For example, the individual man belongs in a species, man, and animal is a genus of the species; so these – man and animal – are called secondary substances."[133] It follows, by extension, that we can use the word "substance" in a secondary sense to refer to natural kinds, understood as collections of individuals sharing a common nature. Still, Aristotle insists, "Of the secondary substances the species is more a substance than the genus, since it is nearer to the primary substance."[134] Primary substances are, well, primary. As we move conceptually downward from species to individual thing, we move from something that is a substance in a derivative or secondary sense to something that is a substance in the strictest, truest, and most proper sense. The primary substance is the thing that is more than anything else a substance.

We might explain the Aristotelian concept of substance logically. Logic deals with terms, propositions, and arguments. Propositions (or statements) are composed of terms, and arguments are composed of propositions. Consider the larger role an Aristotelian substance plays in a simple proposition. A *metaphysically correct* proposition joins a property to a substance. The standard Aristotelian form, "*S* is *P*" ("the subject is the predicate") takes the form "Substance *copula* [connecting link] property." Consider the proposition, "the horse is black." This sentence joins the property "blackness" to the primary substance "the horse." Or consider the proposition, "all horses are four legged." This sentence joins the property "four legged" to the secondary substance "horses." A substance is, then, an individual or collective thing that most fittingly and properly takes the place of the subject of a proposition. As we shall see, Aristotle believes that despite the occurrence of defective substances, we can posit as a general

131 *Metaphysics* (Tredennick), bk 12, ch. 1, 1069a20.
132 *Categories* (Ackrill), ch. 5, 2b5–6.
133 *Categories* (Ackrill), ch. 5, 2b15–18.
134 Ibid., ch. 5, 2b8–9.

rule that substances (primary or secondary) have natures or essences composed of certain indispensable properties making these substances what they are.

The philosophical term "essence" derives ultimately from the Greek phrase "τὸ τὶ ἔστι" (*to ti esti*), which literally means "the what is" of something. The essence of a horse is *what* a horse is; it is the unique collection of properties that combine to make a horse a horse. Aristotle emphasizes the identification of substance and essence. In the *Topics*, he replaces the term "substance" (*ousia*)[135] with the term "essence" (*to ti esti*) as if the two terms were synonyms.[136] Elsewhere he writes: "The term 'being' has several senses. … It denotes first the 'what of a thing'." And again, "Of all senses which being has, the primary sense is clearly the 'what', which denotes the *substance*."[137] Aristotle believes that being and kind, existence and nature, substance and essence, are inextricably linked. "What a substance is" and "the fact that it is" come together in the thing itself. There is no clear divide between this thing that is a horse and the nature of the horse, for this nature is what constitutes this horse.[138] Aristotle writes, "clearly, then … the individual thing and its essence are one and the same."[139] And again, "each thing is one and the same with its essence, and not merely accidentally so."[140] And again, "the thing and its essence are one."[141]

Unlike Locke and Hume, Aristotle does not conceive of substance as an occult cause or a hidden nature. Substance does not lie under, over, or behind the object; it *is* the object. When we observe it, its existence and essence are both on display; the object itself is open to being investigated by science.

135 Which he uses in the *Categories*.

136 *Topics* (Forester), bk 1, ch. 9, 108b20–25. Of course, substance is not, strictly speaking, a predicable, but Aristotle means more loosely that it is something that can be said about something.

137 *Metaphysics* (Tredennick), bk 7, ch. 1, 1028a10–15.

138 In fact, Aristotle's account is somewhat uneven. In the *Posterior Analytics*, he does distinguish between questions about essence and questions about existence. As he puts it, "*what* man is and *that* man is are two different things" (*Posterior Analytics* [Tredennick], bk 2, ch. 7, 92b10). More on this issue later.

139 *Metaphysics* (Tredennick), bk 7, ch. 6, 1032a5–7.

140 Ibid., bk 7, ch. 6, 1031b17–20.

141 Ibid., bk 7, ch. 6, 1031b25–1032a.

EMPIRICIST SUBSTANCE

Compare Aristotle's treatment of substance with the so-called empiricist account.[142] As we shall see, standard usage of the term "empiricist" is itself problematic. The word originally comes from the Greek ἐμπειρία (*empeiria*), which means experience; so empiricists would, it seems, champion the epistemological authority of experience (or sense perception). But this is not, in any straightforward way the view they champion. They do display an enthusiasm for empirical science relying on observation but quickly come to see sense perception as metaphysically deceitful or radically inconclusive. As the tradition develops, sense perception and ultimately human cognition – the way we experience the world – is seen as something separating us from what reality truly is. Substance, the ultimate metaphysical reality, is driven underground. That which truly exists, the true nature of things, comes to reside in a different realm *underneath* our perceptions. It cannot be thought or observed; it can, at best, be referred to obliquely or perhaps captured in abstract theoretical calculation.

The term "empiricism" has come to denote a focus on modern science as it surfaces in authors such as Francis Bacon (1561–1626), Galileo (1564–1642), René Descartes (1596–1650), John Locke (1632–1704), Gottfried Wilhelm Leibniz (1646–1716), David Hume (1711–1776), Immanuel Kant (1724–1804), and John Stuart Mill (1806–1873). Most of these authors display a vehement dislike of the scholastic/Aristotelian metaphysical tradition in favour of a partisan enthusiasm for modern empirical science. They tend to champion the elevation of observation and experiment over classical authority, a nominalist rejection of natural kinds, the supremacy of mathematics, and the necessity of atomism. Together these intellectual cross-currents converge to produce a new understanding of substance that persists to this day. (Note that I am using the term "empiricist" in a wider sense than usual. Early modern philosophers on both sides of the early debate between "rationalists" and "empiricists" would qualify as empiricists in the larger sense referred to here.)

Intellectual historians sometimes trace the modern division of the world into experience and things-in-themselves to Kant's influential separation of the world into phenomenon and noumenon. But this hiving off of the world of experience from true metaphysical reality appeared much

142 I would like to thank Dr Laura Byrne for valuable assistance with this section.

earlier.[143] Begin with Galileo, who argued for what can only be described as a new Pythagoreanism. Galileo claims that mathematics tells us what the world is really like. In a discussion of the metaphysical nature of "heat," he claims, perhaps surprisingly, that mathematical ideas are, whereas our perceptual experiences are not, a necessary component of physical existence. Perception is a fabrication of the observer. The sights, tastes, sounds, smells, and textures we experience do not really exist as part of the world; they come from inside us. We are tricked into thinking that they are a feature of outside existence, because we give names to them. Galileo writes as follows:

> Whenever I conceive of any material or corporeal substance, I am necessarily constrained to conceive of that substance as bounded and as possessing this or that shape, as large or small, … as in this or that place, during this or that time, as in motion or at rest, as in contact or not in contact with some other body, as being one, many, or few, – and by no stretch of the imagination can I conceive of any corporeal body apart from these conditions. But I do not at all feel myself compelled to conceive of bodies as necessarily conjoined with such further conditions as being red or white, bitter or sweet, having sound or being mute, or possessing a pleasant or unpleasant fragrance. On the contrary, were they not escorted by our physical senses, perhaps neither reason nor understanding would ever, by themselves, arrive at such notions. I think, therefore, that these tastes, odors, colors, etc., so far as their objective existence is concerned, are nothing but mere names for something which resides exclusively in our sensitive body (*corpo sensitivo*), so that if the perceiving creatures were removed all of these qualities would be annihilated and abolished from existence. But just because we have given special names to these qualities, different from the names we have given to the primary and real properties, we are tempted into believing that the former really and truly exist as well as the latter.[144]

Galileo distinguishes, for example, between two notions of heat: "true heat" and "experienced heat." True heat is caused by fire which "consist[s] of a multitude of tiny particles of such and such a shape, and having such

143 Of course, a host of earlier authors subscribed to similar notions. Think, for example, of Parmenides' notorious doctrines, of Pythagoreanism, of the ancient atomists, or of the general distrust of sense perception (as opposed to logic) one finds among the Presocratics.

144 Galileo, "Two Kinds of Properties" (Danto) (online).

and such a velocity."[145] It is a mathematical reality comprised of a *number* of particles, having a specific geometrical *shape*, in a certain *location*, traveling at a certain *speed*, in a certain *direction*, etc. *Experienced heat* is purely subjective. What we, in vulgar parlance, call "heat" is something we ourselves add to the physical phenomenon. The *sensation* of heat escapes scientific, i.e., rigorous, analysis. Galileo writes, "That there exists in fire, apart from shape, number, movement, penetration, and contact, some further quality which we call 'heat', I cannot believe ... Heat is altogether subjective, so that if the living sensitive body is removed, what we will call heat would be nothing but a simple word."[146] Of course, Galileo is no philosopher. His use of the word "subjective" is somewhat ambiguous. But already here, we can see the beginning of the familiar modern division between what we perceive and what is really out there.

Galileo effectively distinguishes between primary qualities, which are mathematical, and secondary, which are empirical. Primary qualities constitute the true reality of physical things; secondary, a mental or psychological fabrication. The latter do not exist out in the world but are only in minds and nerves. A later author, such as Locke, accepts this two-layered picture and uses it to develop an influential empiricist account of substance. Aristotle, in contrast, conceives of substance as an independent thing, as the existent subject to which predicates are attributed. The individual horse is the substance; blackness, four-leggedness, warm-bloodedness, etc., are properties of the substance. Locke, however, conceives of substance, in a radically different way, uniquely as a substratum. It is not the individual horse that is the substance, but something that lies under the horse. Substance becomes here, a sort of invisible metaphysical glue holding the horses' properties together, binding them together into a single unit. Substance is no longer what we see but the underlying, unreachable ontological stuff in which all the visible, palpable properties adhere. Locke believes that the true nature of this metaphysical "stuff" is completely unknowable. He writes,

> If any one will examine himself concerning his notion of pure substance ... he will find he has no other idea of it at all, but only a supposition of he knows not what ... If any one should be asked, what is the subject wherein colour or weight inheres, he would have nothing to say, but the solid extended parts; and if he were demanded, what is it that solidity

145 Heat is caused by fire, which "consist[s] of a multitude of tiny particles of such and such a shape, and having such and such a velocity" (ibid.).

146 Ibid.

> and extension adhere in, he would not be in a much better case than the Indian before mentioned who, saying that the world was supported by a great elephant, was asked what the elephant rested on; to which his answer was – a great tortoise: but being again pressed to know what gave support to the broad-backed tortoise, replied – something, he knew not what … The idea then we have, to which we give the general name substance, [is] nothing but the supposed, but unknown, support of those [observable] qualities we find existing … We call that support *substantia*; which, according to the true import of the word, is, in plain English, standing under or upholding.[147]

On Locke's account, secondary qualities (what we directly perceive) can be attributed to mathematical properties which, in turn, inhere in a mysterious, unknowable substratum. Ultimate reality is doubly removed from human apprehension. What we perceive is merely an epiphenomenon of a mathematical reality. Even if we can make some sense of this mathematical reality, we still cannot conceive of the nature of substance that underlies even mathematics. Substance is forever irretrievable, an untouchable, invisible substratum underlying the phenomenal appearances of things. What is the world composed of? Metaphysics is of no use here. We simply cannot know.

Even this quite straightforward reading of Locke can be contested. J.L. Mackie claims that Locke, in fact, inherits the concept of substance, viewing it with suspicion: "The doctrine of substance … is not something that Locke is himself constructing … rather it is something he found already in use, of which he was both critical and suspicious."[148] Certainly, Locke's account has precedents, but any suggestion that he rejects or even distances himself from the notion is implausible. Mackie tacitly admits as much. He continues, "Locke does not go so far as explicitly to reject this notion of substance, [by] either proposing a different notion or rejecting the term 'substance' altogether … [He expresses] the belief that there is such a thing as substance … yet admitting that neither he nor anyone else can get nearer to it than in the unsatisfactory way [he describes]."[149] In other words, even on Mackie's account, Locke believed that substance, the ultimate metaphysical category, was entirely unknowable. This is generally how he has been understood by contemporaries and succeeding generations.

147 Locke, *Essay*, bk 2, ch. 23, §2, "Of Our Complex Ideas of Substances," 295–6.
148 Mackie, *Problems from Locke*, 75.
149 Ibid., 75–6.

In the empiricist tradition, this general line of reasoning is developed, with innumerable wrinkles, by a series of authors leading up to and including Kant and Mill. Kant places substance definitively out of reach. We can only know phenomena, how the world appears to us, filtered through the structure of the human mind. We cannot know the noumenon, the true nature of things-in-themselves. Even mathematics is, in some important sense, a product of human ingenuity. (We discuss these issues in more detail in chapter 9.) Mill, in his later *Logic*, observes,

> There is not the slightest reason for believing that what we call the sensible qualities of the object ... bear any affinity to its own nature. A cause does not, as such, resemble its effects; so the east wind is not like the feeling of cold, nor heat like the steam of boiling water. Why then should [substance] resemble our sensations? Why should the innermost nature of fire and water resemble the impressions made by those objects upon our sensations? Or on what principle are we authorized to deduce from the effects, anything concerning the cause, except that it is a cause adequate to produce those effects?[150]

This is a summary of a line of reasoning from Locke, Hume, and Kant, but it puts on display a train of thought that began with authors such as Bacon and Galileo. This, then, is where modern empiricism leads: to a belief in an unknowable concept of metaphysical substance that lies underneath and apart from the world of experience. As we shall see, it is the remoteness of this ultimate metaphysical reality that undermines induction. I will argue, however, that analysis of the empiricist account of substance reveals that it is one more expression of a post-Cartesian scepticism.

TWO METAPHYSICS

According to a familiar caricature, the ancient and medieval commitment to metaphysics obscured the epistemological tenuousness of induction. Early moderns, and particularly Hume, shook off the dogmatic slumbers of previous ages, saw through the superstitious obfuscation of metaphysics and discovered the inevitable untrustworthiness of induction. But this is a self-serving view of what happened. The early moderns did not shake off metaphysics; they subscribed instead to a new metaphysics. The difference between this new metaphysics and Aristotelian metaphysics accounts for the contrast between traditional and modern attitudes toward induction.

150 Mill, *System of Logic*, bk 3, ch. 2, §7, 39.

We have, then, two metaphysics. On the Aristotelian, substance, understood as the true nature or existence of things, is open to view. The world can be observed. On the empiricist, it lies underneath perception; the true nature of reality lies within an invisible substratum forever closed to human penetration. Seen from the later empiricist perspective, the traditional claim that we can discern the true essences of things is tantamount to saying that we have x-ray vision and can see through the concrete floor on which we stand, to whatever the house is built on. Locke and colleagues claim that we cannot know what individual objects ultimately are. Induction is not a rigorous form of inference because, as Hume argues, we literally do not know what it is we are talking about. Because we lack knowledge of the secret existence of things, the best we can do is rely on appearances. But appearances are often deceiving; they may disguise the real, secret nature of things and events.

Milton attributes the empiricist scepticism about induction to an inherited medieval nominalism.[151] He explains, "Nominalism is best understood as the thesis that everything which exists is an individual or a particular … Hobbes, Locke, Berkeley and Hume were all quite unambiguously nominalists … in that they were in full agreement … that only individuals exist."[152] But this is ambiguous. After all, it could be said that Aristotle believed that only individuals exist. It is not the fact that the world is made up of individuals (and parts of individuals) but the worry that these individuals all possess different natures that drives early modern scepticism about induction. On Aristotle's account, we can see each individual substance. Its nature is open to inspection. So we can compare two individual substances to see whether they possess the same or different natures. We can observe, for example, that this apple is fundamentally like other apples. On the empiricist view, we cannot view the real substance (the metaphysical reality) that constitutes the apple; we have no way of determining what the perceptual properties that we associate with an apple inhere in. Because we cannot know what an apple really is, we cannot know whether a real apple is the same or different from other apples. Hence the worry about induction. Given the inaccessibility of whatever it is that constitutes this apple, trying to compare the apple with other superficially similar things involves at best speculation and conjecture.

151 Nominalism, this emphasis on individuals as opposed to universals, began with earlier medieval authors such as Roscellinus (c.1050–1122) and, most famously, Ockham (c.1285–c.1347). It grew out of mindset impatient with complex abstraction.

152 Milton, "Induction before Hume," 70.

Our purpose here is more critical than historical. I mean to argue that this empiricist account of substance represents, in fact, the corruption of an earlier and better doctrine. Empiricists never *proved* that substance is something hidden underneath things. Instead, they *assumed* that this is the case. They advanced this esoteric notion for at least two reasons. Firstly, they wanted to champion the new physics over the old Aristotelianism. So they contended that reality is made up of mathematical rather than perceptual objects. Secondly, and more germanely to our purposes, they needed an offensive weapon in their battle with the old metaphysics. The empiricist's doctrine of substance is not a positive argument. It is a negative argument dressed up as a positive one. It is a way of raising doubts, of disputing claims. It does not tell us anything positive about the world; it gives us a reason to question earlier ideas. As such, it is an expression of the method of systematic doubt initiated by Descartes.

Kornblith's new Locke not withstanding, the empiricism reaching back to Locke's mainstream philosophy entails an extremely deep scepticism about the truthfulness of empirical observation. Induction fails because the world, reality, or nature, is secretive. The later Mill writes, "of the outside world, we know and can know absolutely nothing, except the sensations which we experience from it."[153] It is this alienation of the observed object from its true nature that makes induction unreliable. We can never make valid generalizations about loaves of bread or lumps of gold or horses because we can *never* know what the true nature of bread, gold, or horses is. We can only access appearances, but appearances are not the cause of what really happens. Hence Locke's odd comments about men who digest stones or Hume's reference to flames that do not give off heat.

Why is the empiricist account of substance the logical extension of the Cartesian method of comprehensive scepticism? Because Locke and others in the empiricist tradition place the notion of substance out of reach. It becomes a question mark. That is all. This is substance *qua* rationale for radical doubt, not *qua* positive doctrine about the nature of the world. The unknowability of substance supplies the empiricists with a rationale for an incorrigible scepticism about *any* metaphysical claim. Whatever someone asserts, it can always be doubted. We cannot know what ultimate reality is like, so we can doubt the evidence of our senses; we can doubt induction; and most importantly for these authors, we can doubt metaphysics. If, after all, our goal is to get rid of the "old metaphysics," we could have found no better way to invalidate all previous reasoning about the depths of

153 Mill, *System of Logic*, bk 3, ch. 2, §7, 39.

existence than to simply posit the existence of an inaccessible layer of reality and in one fell swoop do away with that metaphysics. It is simply naive to accept the new metaphysics at face value without taking the historical context in which these ideas were raised into account.

Note that the empiricist understanding of substance rules out *all* inductive reasoning. Positing the existence of this second, secretive substratum of things-in-themselves does not provide us with a criterion for distinguishing between good and bad, legitimate and illegitimate, sound and unsound inductions. It invalidates all inductions indifferently. (Despite later attempts by authors such as Kant to limit the damage, this metaphysical stance arguably erodes any knowledge of the world outside ourselves.)

Cartesian doubt is not epistemological; it is not specific doubt based on positive evidence. We could have no evidence for empiricist metaphysics, that is, for the invisible-substratum account of the world, for the doctrine that the true nature of individual things is incommensurable with the one we observe. Corpuscular explanations are not the issue. The point is that if the real nature of things is unknowable (corpuscular or not), we could never know it. It is one thing to posit, for example, a corpuscular reality that can be understood in terms of cause and effect, mathematics, space and time, and so on. It is another to assume the reality of an unknowable *suppositum* sealed off from any kind of meaningful exploration. This is a far cry from an evidence-based concept. It is a device (like Descartes' evil demon) that unwittingly secures the rationale for transcendental, all-encompassing doubt. As the tradition develops, the spectre of this unsubstantiated metaphysical construct becomes the familiar ground for disposing of the older metaphysics.

ARISTOTELIAN SUBSTRATUM

Those with party ties may protest that the empiricist metaphysics was a much-needed corrective to the practices of credulous metaphysicians who naively assumed that we could see the world as it really is. Already, in the late sixteenth and early seventeenth century, Francis Bacon sketched out the kind of position later empiricist authors come to adopt. In a discussion of "the idols of the tribe," Bacon addresses the limits of human nature. It is a familiar refrain. As he explains, "The[se] idols … have their foundation in human nature itself … for it is false assertion that the sense of man is the measure of things. On the contrary, all perceptions both of the sense and of the mind are according to the measure of the individual, and not according to the measure of the universe. And the human understanding is like a false mirror, which, receiving rays irregularly, distorts and discolours the nature of things by mingling its own nature with it."[154] Bacon could not, of course, have anticipated how far later authors would take this line of reasoning, but the seed is already there. On Bacon's account, traditional philosophers simply *assumed* that the world was the way they perceived it. They did not recognize how our mind and nerves fundamentally distort our picture of what reality is. In equating truth with the human perspective, they overlooked the inherently problematic character of human cognition.

But to anyone who carefully reads the history of philosophy, this kind of argument is less than compelling. The first problem with the "naive old metaphysics argument" is that it is historically dubious. As we shall discuss in succeeding chapters, Aristotle does not think that human cognition is infallible; he is fully aware of the sceptical challenge; he does not believe that we can *prove* that scepticism is wrong; his approach is more subtle. He believes rather that educated people know when to stop asking questions. They must have a certain basic confidence in human judgement; otherwise, knowledge unravels, and scepticism is inevitable.

Aristotle and earlier philosophers, generally, were not naive realists. Aristotle does not display any simple-minded confidence in sense perception. He does not believe that the way the world appears to us is, without qualification, the way it really is. He is not insensitive to the idea that there are deeper levels of reality that must be taken into account. At the beginning of his *Physics*, Aristotle writes, "The things which are immediately obvious and clear to us are usually mixed together; their elements and principles only become clearer later, when one separates them."[155] Learning is a matter of analysis, of pulling things apart to gain a better understanding.[156] "We start with what is more intelligible and clear *to us* and move from there to what is clearer and more intelligible *in itself*."[157] Consider a specific example. How do we learn about green emeralds? We begin by noticing that certain hard, transparent crystals are green. We call these green gemstones "emeralds." This is how they appear to us. But as our study of chemistry progresses, we discover that emeralds are a mixture of "aluminum beryllium silicate and chromium." The latter definition is the true one. Green is not, on an Aristotelian account, the defining property of emeralds; emeralds are not emeralds because they are green; they are green because they have the chemical makeup of emeralds. So we move from what is clearer and more intelligible to us, that

154 Bacon, *New Organon* (Ariew and Watkins), bk 1, aphorism 41.

155 *Physics* (Waterfield), bk 1, ch. 1, 184a22–23 (in Aristotle, *Physics*).

156 This method of analysis comprises the four causes.

157 *Physics* (Waterfield), bk 1, ch. 1, 184a16–17.

"emeralds are green-coloured gemstones," to what is clearer and more intelligible in itself, that "emeralds are aluminum beryllium silicate and chromium." As it turns out, "green" is a necessary but not the defining attribute of emeralds.

Aristotle recognizes the recondite nature of knowledge. He understands the need for abstraction and conceptual sophistication. Knowledge is not a matter of lazily relying on first impressions. It *begins* in sense perception, but it requires hard, persistent analysis. Aristotle also develops an account of an underlying physical substratum.[158] In the *Metaphysics*, for example, he observes that the ὑποκείμενον (*hupokeimenon*), or substrate, of oil and wine and melted things is said to be water.[159] He uses the same term to refer to the subject that stays the same through accidental change and sometimes as a synonym for "substance."[160] So Aristotle does understand that sometimes we cannot make sense of what happens in the world without reference to some sort of support that is not immediately observable, except he nowhere subscribes to anything like the radical empiricist understanding of a substance.

We may understand Aristotle's view of the physical substratum in two ways. From the somewhat unorthodox viewpoint of Christopher Byrne, the world begins with an actual material substratum lying under the water, fire, earth, and air – the four sublunary elements. It is "the extended, divisible, and movable stuff out of which all perceptible substances are made."[161] Although it "never occurs apart from the elements," it is a *material* thing.[162] Byrne (in contrast to many other commentators) associates this material substratum with Aristotle's concept of "prime matter" or πρώτη ὕλη (*prote hule*). On a more conventional understanding, the Greek elements themselves constitute the material substratum making up, so to speak, the ground floor of existence. On either reading, we have a world ending in some kind of material stuff we can use to explain how things operate at a deeper level. Unlike the modern empiricists, however, Aristotle does not

158 See, for example, *Metaphysics*, bk 8, ch. 2, 1042a25–32.

159 "All liquids are said to be one (e.g. oil and wine), and melted things; because the ultimate substrate of them all is the same, for all these things are water or vapour" (*Metaphysics* [Tredennick], bk 5, ch. 6, 1016a20–25).

160 In the *Physics*, Aristotle speaks of the substrate as that which persists through change (*Physics*, bk 1, ch. 1, 190a–b). In *Metaphysics Z*, he talks of substance as subject or *hupokeimenon* (bk 7, ch. 3). See *Metaphysics* (Tredennick), bk 5, ch. 6, 1016a18–20.

161 Byrne, "Prime Matter and Actuality," 213.

162 Ibid., 210.

posit the existence of any *additional*, non-empirical *je ne sais quoi* lying underneath matter. There is no invisible submaterial support that grounds the world. The outside properties of things we see are a reliable reflection of what is inside these things. We can move from one level of material existence to another. To use a simple example, if the substrate underlying wine, oil, and melted things is water, this is why wine, oil, and melted things have liquid properties.

The Greek philosophers generally, appeal to more elementary levels of physical existence as an explanatory device. Things that have heat are thought to be made of fire; sour or bitter substances are assumed to be made of jagged, sharp atoms; light is thought to pass through transparent glass because it has invisible pores – and so on. Anaximenes (to cite only one example) is said to have believed that "clouds are caused by the increased thickening of air, and that when air is concentrated even more rain is squeezed out, that hail happens when the water is frozen as it is falling, and snow when a windy ingredient is included in the moisture."[163] The material element which acts as the substratum here (air) gives the physical object its perceptual properties. It is not a secret, ghostly, occult essence in the empiricist sense. It is something empirical that causes the empirical properties we perceive. A direct correspondence connects the physical properties of the substratum to those of the perceived object – there is no sense here of an invisible floor to existence tricking us into believing what is not the case. Existence is fundamentally, thoroughly empirical.

It seems ironic that modern *empiricism* champions a fundamental commitment to the *unempirical* nature of ultimate reality. Words can be misleading. The empiricist attack on induction specifically, and on metaphysics more generally, depends on an appeal to an *unempirical* metaphysical support. Aristotle, on the contrary, situates individual objects (and any substratum) squarely inside the empirical realm. The familiar modern empiricist criticism, that this is a naive way of looking at the world, is essentially an *attack* on philosophical belief in an empirical world. The "empiricists" contest Aristotle's account because it is unflinchingly empirical, because Aristotle believes that reality is, at bottom, open to empirical inspection. It is only through a strange trick of terminology that one could call this attack on the old metaphysics "empiricism." On closer inspection, the standard view that, in killing off the old metaphysics, the modern empiricists rescued the world from superstition, i.e., from unempirical belief, is little more than a caricature. A stalwart Aristotelian could argue that the reverse is almost true.

163 Anaximenes, testimonial 40, in Robin Waterfield, *The First Philosophers*, 20.

In their battle with the old metaphysics, Locke and Hume and like-minded thinkers brandished Occam's razor, the idea that the simplest explanation is to be preferred. At least that is the legend. But empiricist arguments against induction depend, in fact, on multiplying natures. In Ockham's original phrase, "a plurality is not to be posited without necessity" (*pluralitas non est ponenda sine necessitate*).[164] But the idea of substance as a separate invisible substratum that underlies existence does not simplify, it complicates metaphysics, without taking advantage of any corresponding increase in explanatory power. In other words, it posits a plurality without necessity. Aristotle proposes a simpler picture. There is no invisible second substratum underlying existence. We live in an empirical world composed of empirical objects. Substance does not lie underneath these objects. It is what these objects are and what they are made of.

Modern empiricism derided the allegedly unempirical character of the old metaphysics. But what are we to make of the new "empiricist" account of substance? Gilbert Ryle, to great applause, dismissed the Cartesian mind-in-a-body account of human nature as "a ghost in the machine." But modern empiricism could be caricatured as the ghost-in-each-substance view. Except the new "empiricists" do not merely argue that there is an unempirical metaphysical ghost inside every individual thing. Worse still, they argue that this ghost is the *true* nature of the thing. Because we have no access to this ghost, we cannot know its true nature. Aristotle, we could counter, does not believe in ghosts. Not because he is naive. (You could complain that it is the people who believe in ghosts who are naive.) Aristotle does not believe in ghosts, because he is an empiricist.

But even more could be said against this new empiricism. If believing in ghosts seems, for the most part, silly, people who actually do believe in ghosts usually point to some kind of empirical evidence: muffled screams in the middle of the night, whispy white shapes, whatever. These new empiricists, by contrast, believe in the ghost in the thing, despite a total dearth of evidence. Aristotle, we could say, does not believe in ghosts in things, because there is no evidence for them. His position squares with common-sense realism. To claim that there is no evidence for ghosts, but that we should believe in them anyway seems epistemologically irresponsible. But this is, in effect, what modern empiricism recommends.

Imagine that somewhere in the world there is a closed room. The windows are curtained and tightly shut; the doors are securely locked; the walls are completely soundproof. No one knows what is inside the room. Should worries about the room count as evidence against our ways of

164 Hyman and Walsh, *Philosophy in the Middle Ages*, 431.

thinking about the world? Suppose the realist says, "There are no unicorns in the world." The anti-realist responds, "But maybe there is a unicorn in that room." The realist counters, "There has never been a reliable eyewitness account of a unicorn; no one has ever found a dead body of a unicorn; no one has ever taken a photograph of a unicorn; no one has ever discovered a fossil of a unicorn. There are no unicorns in the world." The anti-realist replies: "I agree that there is and never will be any evidence for unicorns. But we will never know what there is inside *the room.* Perhaps *the room* contains a live or dead unicorn or a fossil of a unicorn. So we cannot claim, "there are no unicorns in the world." This seems analogous to the modern empiricist predicament, except that the empiricist position is even more radical. The empiricists concede that no one has ever seen *the room,* that no one can, in principle, ever find it. And yet they claim that the possible existence of this invisible room is a good enough reason for doubting empirical evidence. This is, in effect, Locke's and Hume's argument against induction. Such authors effectively lock up the true natures of things in the hypothetical room. Because we cannot see inside *the room,* we cannot know what is hiding there! So induction is inconclusive.

But does the possibility of the invisible room provide adequate grounds for doubting what we know about the world? Doubt may arise in two different ways. We may doubt a claim because the evidence against the claim is greater than the evidence for it: this is epistemological doubt. Or we may doubt a claim because we *can* find a way to doubt: this is Cartesian doubt. Epistemological doubt follows the evidence; Cartesian doubt disenfranchises the knower. Hume and colleagues choose the latter alternative. We can, in many ways, doubt the possibility of knowledge. We can doubt authority because we need to find out for ourselves. We can doubt sense perception because it sometimes tricks us. We can doubt our own judgement because human beings are fallible. We can doubt induction because exceptions may occur. But belief in an unknowable substance, belief in *the room,* is a particularly effective way of supporting scepticism. To place substance, ultimate existence, outside the limits of human cognition, is to leave us enough mental room to doubt anything.

The empiricist notion of substance functions, not as a meaningful addition to what we can know about the world, but as a hidden possibility that provides an invulnerable rationale for doubt. We cannot prove that *the room* exists, but neither can we prove that it does not exist. The mere possibility of *the room* is alleged to justify scepticism. The received view, that Hume destroyed the credibility of induction by pointing out an oversight by earlier philosophers, does not withstand close historical scrutiny. It is a belief in "the room" that undermined induction. Aristotle, uncovering no evidence for its existence, did not believe in it. Hume and Aristotle adopt different world views. One posits an unknowable substance; the other thinks of substance as an empirical reality. Their opposing metaphysics explains their opposing attitudes.

Hume calls himself a mitigated sceptic. But the metaphysical attitude that drives his inductive scepticism is anything but mitigated. Rationality requires that we base our beliefs on evidence. Call this the evidentiary criterion.[165] Hume and his colleagues reject the evidentiary criterion. In short, they believe in *the room* in the absence of evidence. This is, more or less, the method of Cartesian doubt.

In contemporary philosophy, the rise of modern empiricism is often tied to notions of fallibility, suggesting that the old metaphysics was somehow absolutist. As I have already argued, Aristotle is a fallibilist and entirely aware of the possibility of human error. But human fallibility is a fact about us; it is not a fact about the metaphysical furniture that makes up the world. If we cannot know everything there is to know about existence, if the possibility of error is always attendant on human judgement, it does not follow that we have no access to an underlying ontological layer of existence: "the real nature of things." The limits of human intelligence do not lead to a hidden substratum. They detract from human certainty but do not add another ontological component to the universe.

Cartesian scepticism is a powerful tool to use against all and sundry opponents, but those who rely on comprehensive doubt to defeat opposing positions are inevitably partisan: they rarely acknowledge that the same strategy could be used to explode their own arguments as well. Transcendental doubt can be turned in any direction whatsoever. Attempts to corral comprehensive doubt so that it only applies to this or that target are disingenuous, ideological, and/or naive. The mere fact of human fallibility can be used to throw into question any source of epistemological conviction: induction, deduction, sense perception, language, mathematics, introspection, science, and so on. Any consistent use of methodological doubt will end in a generalized scepticism that defeats every position, including the one you use it to defend. (The ancient sceptics, at least, wrestled with this dilemma.)

Consider Hume's philosophical method. Hume himself acknowledges that his philosophy ends ultimately in scepticism, while at the same time he subscribed to the Enlightenment view that the new science and logic (as opposed to religion and tradition) would be the correct ways of thinking about the world. But how could we reconcile these opposing points of view? If

165 This "evidentiary criterion" is perhaps the germ of truth in the so-called "verificationist principle" that the logical positivists unsuccessfully tried to articulate.

comprehensive doubt could be used to scuttle the old metaphysics, it could be used to scuttle a belief in the new science and logic as well. Graciela De Pierris discusses "the puzzle created by Hume's endorsement of both radical skepticism and informed causal reasoning in science and common sense," and argues that he compartmentalizes his philosophical approach, dividing it into two separate endeavours.[166] De Pierris explains that

> Hume's stance towards his own Pyrrhonian skepticism ... indicates that for him the rational search for the justification of our most fundamental natural beliefs is ... an independent standpoint external to those beliefs. The true novelty of [his] approach is that he takes his empirical science of human nature to be independent of the philosophical skeptical inquiry precisely because he appreciates that science and common sense are detachable from that inquiry, and thus they can be shielded from the kind of philosophical reflection that in his view leads to a theoretically unassailable form of skepticism.[167]

This seems an accurate description of Hume's attitude, but it hardly justifies what he is about (as De Pierris seems to think). More plainly put, Hume embraces two methods of philosophical inquiry – comprehensive doubt when it comes to the old metaphysics, and the criterion of ordinary human conviction when it comes to issues of the new science and common sense. But this is only a more fancy way of saying that Hume is inconsistent. He uses comprehensive doubt when it serves his ideological ends – when he wants to destroy the old metaphysics – but he refrains from comprehensive doubt when dealing with the world view he defends. It is this kind of inescapable inconsistency that renders Cartesian scepticism an ideological rather than a truly philosophical tool.

This kind of underlying inconsistency runs throughout Hume's work. Consider his attack on the "papist" doctrine of transubstantiation, the belief that the bread and wine in the Eucharist literally become the body and blood of Christ. This was a hotly debated religious issue at the time and, to Enlightenment thinkers, the epitome of religious superstition. Locke, for example, marvels at the credulity of the cradle Catholic. He writes, "Take an intelligent Romanist, that from the very first dawning of any Notions in his understanding, hath had this Principle constantly inculcated ... How is he prepared easily to swallow, not only against all probability, but even the clear evidence of his senses, the doctrine of transubstantiation? This

166 De Pierris, "Hume's Pyrrhonian Skepticism," 358.

167 Ibid., 353–4.

principle has such an influence on his mind, that he will believe that to be flesh which he sees to be bread."[168] Hume, who is even more scathing, models his argument against miracles on John Tilloston's against transubstantiation. He begins, "There is, in Dr. Tillotson's writings, an argument against the real presence, which is as concise, and elegant, and strong as any argument can possibly be supposed against a doctrine, so little worthy of a serious refutation."[169]

Hume, like Locke, argues that transubstantiation is "directly contrary to the rules of just reasoning" because "it contradicts sense."[170] He ridicules the papist who believes, in direct opposition to the evidence of his senses, that there is a secret nature of another sort hidden under the appearances of bread. But, religious motives aside, doesn't this belief almost exactly parallel Hume's own belief in the Lockean view of substance. Hume argues against induction because he believes that a secret nature of another sort hides under the appearances of bread. Granted there are theological issues to be addressed, but it is an odd spectacle to see Hume thundering against his opponents for believing in occult natures underlying the empirical appearances of things. For this is what he himself believes. It is Hume's ideological opposition to religion that fuels his thunder against Romanists, not impartial reason. The incident illustrates a general attitude: I am justified in doubting empirical appearances for my own philosophical purposes, but my opponents make a ludicrous mistake when they do the very same thing. This cannot be. If we are logically justified in using the sceptical Cartesian methodology to undermine our opponents' beliefs, they are just as justified in using that methodology to undermine our own. Any other approach would be inconsistent. A thorough Cartesian scepticism ends ultimately in an all-out scepticism that defeats all knowledge claims. If we are serious about doubting, nobody wins. We are left with a stalemate of unbelief that questions all claims to knowledge equally.

Historical issues aside, we can criticize Hume's philosophical method on another, deeper level. Hume, like any philosopher, relies on argument. That is, he presupposes the validity of logic. But logic is an expression of fallible human judgement. And we can question it. Suppose we grasp an inference, work through a proof, "see" that an argument is valid. These are

168 Locke, *Essay*, bk 5, ch. 20, "Of Wrong Assent, or Error," 713.

169 He continues, "Nothing is so convenient as a decisive argument of this kind, which must at least silence the most arrogant bigotry and superstition, and free us from their impertinent solicitations" (Hume, *Enquiry* [Selby-Bigge, Nidditch], §10, pt 1, para. 86, 109).

170 Ibid.

only human experiences. They depend ultimately on our fallible conviction. Because we have strong convictions about something, this does not prove, absolutely, that what we believe to be the case really is so. Hume, following after Descartes, felt entitled to question anything for which we have no absolute proof. Well, we have no absolute proof for logical consistency, for the first principles of reasoning, or for the ultimate soundness of human inference. So Hume, in playing the philosopher, is again restricting Cartesian doubt to the old metaphysics while refraining from such doubt when it comes to his own philosophical pronouncements.

The unshakeable Cartesian confidence in logical inference is, on closer inspection, inconsistent with comprehensive doubt. Unless we concede that the human intellect has some authority or sense of discernment, the task of building knowledge cannot get off the ground. Of course, in some specific circumstances, our trying hard to doubt our beliefs may serve a useful heuristic function. But as Peirce suggests, we cannot doubt all our beliefs all at the same time. And even if we could, this would end in nothing more edifying than uncomprehending unintelligibility.

As we shall see, Aristotle argues that we need to start with reasonable belief and be open to counter-evidence or we will end up in an unmanageable scepticism. If, however, evidence-based doubt is a necessary tool for critical inquiry, Cartesian scepticism seems philosophically superficial. Despite all the grandiose gesturing, it does little philosophical work. Goodman cites the possibility of a change in the colour of emeralds. Suppose a serious chemist were to uncover physical evidence that emeralds can change colour, that they really can be blue. This would be a remarkable achievement; it would constitute a definite advance in science, and it would invalidate the inductive claim that "all emeralds are green." But to argue (like Goodman) that that claim would not stand if we ignored all the scientific evidence we have – this is not so compelling. In the following chapters, I will argue, not that induction is foolproof, but that these kinds of transcendental gestures do little to undermine the credibility of inductive reasoning properly understood.

HISTORICAL EMPIRICISM

We can always ask a historical question: Why did authors such as Locke and Hume, Kant, and Mill embrace inductive scepticism? Divide previous metaphysics into Neoplatonist and Aristotelian traditions. Given their fondness for mathematics, authors in the modern-empiricist tradition could have turned to Neoplatonism. Or, given their confidence in the empirical method, they could have turned to Aristotelianism. They did neither. Following in the footsteps of Descartes, they embraced a new kind of scepticism so that they could win their battle with the old metaphysics. On the one hand, they could dismiss Neoplatonism as unempirical; on the other hand, they could dismiss Aristotelianism as naive. It was effective, if inconsistent, strategy.

No historical idea arrives on the scene without some kind of antecedent. Could we not then trace the early modern empiricist account of substance back to earlier philosophical notions? Two possibilities immediately come to mind: the metaphysical doctrine of prime matter and the scholastic notion of *esse* or being. But whatever the precise provenance of the empiricist account of substance, the concept can be seen as a response to a genuine metaphysical problem. The later empiricists focused on the importance of sense perception. They wanted to identify reality with whatever we can perceive. However, the existence of a thing cannot be directly perceived but only inferred. As Descartes (who is, in this sense, more of a rationalist than an empiricist) explains, "we cannot initially become aware of a substance merely through its being an existing thing, since this alone does not of itself have any effect on us. We can, however, easily come to know a substance by one of its attributes, in virtue of the common notion that nothingness possesses no attributes ... no properties or qualities. Thus if we perceive the presence of some attribute, we can infer that there must also be present an existing thing or substance to which it may be attributed."[171]

Consider the world from an empiricist point of view. We perceive the properties of things. We can see the shape and colour of say a red brick; we can pick it up and feel its weight; we can hear the sound it makes when we knock it against the wall – and so on. But we can never perceive the act of existing that carries or displays these perceptible attributes. We only perceive its qualities: "rectangular," "red," "heavy," "knockable," and so on. We assume that there is a real brick here, not a mere figment of our imaginations or a brick in a dream, but an existing brick, something substantial that is, so to speak, clothed in these qualities. It seems a small jump to the idea of an invisible, unknowable substratum that provides some kind of platform (or substance) in which these properties can inhere.

It is as if the empiricists separate out the bare existence of the brick from its perceptible manifestations and treat it as a separate, underlying thing. This is reminiscent of medieval accounts according to which every "being" (*ens*) is composed of an act of existence (*esse*) that realizes a certain nature (*essentia*).[172] But there is a crucial difference. On the medieval view,

171 Descartes, *Principles of Philosophy* (Cottingham, Stoothoff, and Murdoch), §52, 210 (in Descartes, *Philosophical Writings*).

172 See, for example, Reith, *Metaphysics of St Thomas Aquinas*, 193.

existence "is neither a substratum nor the bearer of qualities."[173] To say that something exists is not to identify a second nature that preserves the first nature in existence. The act of existence that characterizes an object coincides with the object. It *is* the object. There is no invisible platform of existence underlying the brick and maintaining it in existence. No, the brick's existence is nothing more (or less) than the realization of those attributes that make the brick what it is.

The empiricist account seems an erroneous simplification of this traditional picture. We have the brick we perceive but also have the hidden substance that is the real brick, the brick as it really is. Every object has two natures, an observable one, which is supported by a second, invisible one. But this needlessly complicates the picture. Despite all the rhetoric to the contrary, empiricist metaphysics violates Occam's razor; it needlessly multiplies natures, supplying a second occult platform with its own nature that lies underneath every object. If we resist this bifurcation of reality, if we eliminate the hiatus between the object and its own existence, the original empiricist critique of induction collapses.

Traditional metaphysicians would argue that existence is a fact about the reality of a thing's nature; it is not a separate, invisible nature. It does not lie underneath the object. The existence of the object is the act by which the object preserves itself. It is the object being the object. That is all. Existence is not another object below, above, or somehow beyond the object we see and know, holding it up.

Empiricists speak as if an object has two natures, one above and one below our range of perception. This double-nature view of objects in the world is problematic. On the traditional model, an object is made up of "existence plus nature" (*esse* + *essentia*). We can distinguish questions about an object's existence from questions about what kind of thing it is. (God is a special case we need not consider here.) But existence (*esse*) is not a second nature (*essentia*) lying underneath what the object is in the world. These are two different aspects of the very same object.

The empiricist model reifies an object's existence, turning it into a second (unknowable) nature underlying the first (knowable) one. But this is to conflate the concept of "existence" (*esse*) with that of "nature" or "kind" (*essentia*). It is to make a category mistake. Instead of an object composed of "existence plus nature," we have an object made up of "nature$_1$ plus nature$_2$" (*essentia*$_1$ + *essentia*$_2$). These are two separate but connected natures, one made up of what we see, the other of an invisible substratum. This way of thinking leads, however, to an infinite regress. An object

173 Meyer, *Philosophy of St Thomas Aquinas*, 88.

cannot exist without an act of existence. Any existent object composed of "nature_1 plus nature_2" would have to be composed of "nature_1 plus nature_2 plus existence." If, however, "existence" is "nature," any existent object composed of "nature_1 plus nature_2 plus existence" must, in fact, be composed of "nature_1 plus nature_2, plus nature_3." But any existent three-natured object must possess an act of existence. So it must, on closer inspection, be re-described as "nature_1 plus ... plus nature_n, plus existence," with n taken to infinity.

Occam's razor suggests that we distinguish between existence and nature right at the outset. Modern empiricists unwittingly avoid (or postpone) this distinction. If, however, "existence" is just another "nature," if the world is composed exclusively of however many natures, it turns out that the world must be non-existent! It does not matter how many times we multiply acts of existence. In each case, the act of existing will turn out, on closer inspection, to be another nature, which requires another act of existence (which turns out to be a nature needing another act of existence, and so on, *ad infinitum*).

Perhaps a metaphor may help. If objects in the world need a nature that holds them up – roughly, the empiricist concept of substance – we can always push our analysis further and ask, what is holding up this second nature? A third nature? But what is holding up this third nature, and so on, *ad infinitum.* Consistently applied, the empiricist approach of turning existence into a nature ends in an infinite regress; to use the familiar phrase, we end up with "turtles all the way down."

I will discuss Kant's role in the historical development of empiricist metaphysics in a later chapter.

3

A "Deductive" Account of Induction

Like all other inductive arguments, this one is not deductively valid.

Trudy Govier[1]

If you insist that the inference is made by a chain of reasoning,
I desire you to produce that reasoning.

David Hume[2]

DOUGLAS WALTON, IN A RECENT BOOK on argumentation theory, emphasizes "the Aristotelian roots of logic as an applied, practical discipline."[3] While theorists in argumentation theory and informal logic acknowledge the seminal contribution of Aristotle, I will argue that most nevertheless misconstrue his position with respect to induction. In the following chapter, I make the case that Aristotle, in contrast to mainstream modern opinion, believes that inductive arguments are deductively valid. His position resembles that view attributed to deductivists in contemporary argumentation theory. Although this seems out of step with consensus, a historical survey reveals that it is not a rarely expressed point of view in Western philosophy. Both Aristotle and his medieval commentators defend this general position. "Traditional" logicians in the modern period such as John Stuart Mill, Richard Clarke, and Jacques Maritain follow suit, as do major authors in the Continental tradition such as Bernard Bosanquet and Bernard Lonergan. I will discuss the history of this approach as a propaedeutic to Aristotle.

I go on to consider Aristotle's specific account of induction in the *Prior Analytics* and criticize the familiar but misguided suggestion that Aristotle's inductive syllogism about long-lived bileless animals is a complete or perfect

1 Govier, *Practical Study of Argument*, 293.

2 Hume, *Enquiry* (Selby-Bigge, Nidditch), §4, pt 2, para. 29, 33 (in Hume, *Enquiries*).

3 Walton, *New Dialectic*, 7.

induction. In exploring Aristotle's position, I focus especially on his use of the logical relationship of "convertibility." Deductivists have shown that we can bring to the surface the pivotal assumptions implicit in a specific line of reasoning by supplying hidden premises. I use this deductivist technique to uncover the hidden components in Aristotle's account of inductive reasoning. As I will demonstrate, Aristotle correctly identifies the kind of identity or resemblance that ties the premises to the conclusion in an inductive argument.

DEDUCTIVISM AND CONTEMPORARY LOGIC

A modern renaissance in informal logic and argumentation theory has been spearheaded by authors such as Charles Hamblin, Frans H. van Eemeren, Rob Grootendorst, Ralph Johnson and Anthony Blair, Trudy Govier, Leo Groarke and Christopher Tindale, and Michael Gilbert.[4] In the scholarly community, one sees this new orientation expressed in journals such as *Informal Logic* and *Argumentation*, in grassroots movements that propose the adoption of critical-thinking training at all levels of education,[5] and in the formation of research groups like the International Society for the Study of Argumentation, in Amsterdam.[6]

This burgeoning interest in argumentation theory and informal logic is, in part, a reaction against the perceived narrowness of formal logic. Whereas formal logic tends to investigate deductively valid arguments, using symbolic structures, informal logic concerns itself with the analysis and evaluation of natural-language arguments, often, though not exclusively, within a pedagogical context.[7] Argumentation theory links an interest in both formal and informal aspects of argumentation to a wider approach

4 See Hamblin, *Fallacies*; Toulmin, *Uses of Argument*; Kahane, *Logic and Contemporary Rhetoric*; Eemeren and Grootendorst, *Argumentation, Communication, and Fallacies*; R. Johnson and Blair, "Informal Logic"; R. Johnson, *Rise of Informal Logic*; Govier, *Problems in Argument*; Woods and Walton, *Fallacies*; Walton, *New Dialectic*; *Informal Logic*; Hansen and Pinto, *Fallacies*; Leo Groarke, Tindale, and Fisher, *Good Reasoning Matters*; and Gilbert, *Coalescent Argument*.

5 See, for example, the (American) Foundation for Critical Thinking, *Critical Thinking Community*.

6 See, for example, Eemeren, Grootendorst, Blair, and Willard, *Proceedings of the Third ISSA*, vol. 1, *Perspectives and Approaches*; vol. 2, *Analysis and Evaluation*; vol. 3, *Reconstruction and Application*; and vol. 4, *Special Fields and Case Studies*.

7 For a recent overview, see *Stanford Encyclopedia of Philosophy*, s.v. "Informal Logic" (by Leo Groarke).

used in subjects such as communication and media studies, legal reasoning, casuistry, rhetoric, and dialectic. Many argumentation theorists attack what they view as an unhealthy preoccupation with the formal, deductive aspects of reasoning. This includes an attack on deductivism.

Trudy Govier writes, "Many logicians – both formal and informal – endorse a deductivist theory of argument."[8] Govier, who uses the term pejoratively, defines deductivism as the theory that all good arguments must be logically valid. In a valid argument, the truth of the premises entails the truth of the conclusion. Rigorously expressed, it is necessarily the case that "if the premises are true, the conclusion is true." (This is the semantic conception of validity.) Consider the following example. Premise_1: All bus drivers have a class-A licence. Premise_2: George is a bus driver. Conclusion: Therefore, George has a class-A licence. This is a valid (deductive) argument. The conclusion follows *necessarily* from the premises. If George is a bus driver and all bus drivers have class-A licences, it *must* also be the case that George has a class-A licence. A valid argument may, of course, be composed of untrue premises. Perhaps George is not a bus driver, or perhaps bus drivers do not need class-A licences. This does not matter. The requirement for validity is only that *if* the premises are true, the conclusion must be true. In argumentation theory, most commentators distinguish between "sound" and "valid" arguments. Sound arguments are valid arguments with true premises.

A small group of argumentation theorists explicitly defend the idea that validity is an indispensable feature of any good argument. Authors such as Gerald Nosich, S.N. Thomas, Ron Yezzi, Leo Groarke, and Louis Groarke argue for one version or another of deductivism.[9] This may appear counterintuitive. Suppose I argue as follows. Premise: The weather network said it was going to rain tomorrow. Conclusion: Therefore, it is going to rain tomorrow. Most theorists would argue that this is not a valid argument. The truth of the conclusion does not follow necessarily from that of the premise. Even if the premise is true (if this is what the network said), the conclusion (that it is going to rain tomorrow) could be false. After all, the weather is notoriously fickle. The network could announce one thing, and the opposite could happen.

8 Govier, *Problems in Argument*, 22.

9 See Lambert and Ulrich, *Nature of Argument*, 18; Nosich, *Reasons and Arguments* ("Validity and truth of premises are all there is to a good argument," 27); S. Thomas, *Practical Reasoning in Natural Language*; Yezzi, *Practical Logic*; Leo Groarke, "In Defence of Deductivism"; Louis Groarke, "Deductive Account of Induction"; and Gerritsen, "Defense of Deductivism."

Deductivists have, however, a ready answer to this more familiar analysis. They contend that looser forms of argument are simply valid arguments in disguise. We do not realize this at first glance, because they include implicit or unspoken elements. When we articulate these hidden steps, however, a valid argument results. Consider the previous example. Suppose the person who argues that it *must* rain tomorrow because the weather network said it would rain tomorrow has an absolute (not to say, naive) confidence in the accuracy of the weather network's forecasts. Once we make explicit the role that this attitude of absolute confidence plays in this person's reasoning, the argument becomes as follows. Premise: The weather network said it was going to rain tomorrow. Hidden Premise: The weather network is never wrong. Conclusion: Therefore, it is going to rain tomorrow. This is not, of course, a sound argument. The hidden premise is just silly. Nonetheless, this is a valid argument. If it is true both that the weather network would never be wrong and that the weather network predicted rain, it would have to be the case that it would rain tomorrow. If the premises are true, the conclusion must be true as well.

Perhaps we could improve the argument. Suppose someone were to argue, "The weather network said it was going to rain tomorrow. Therefore, it is probably going to rain tomorrow." If we include the hidden element in this line of reasoning, we might end with something like the following. Premise: The weather network said it was going to rain tomorrow. Hidden premise: The weather network is usually accurate. Conclusion: Therefore, it is probably going to rain tomorrow. Probability is a complicated issue. Nonetheless, it makes sense to claim that a rational agent cannot believe in the first two premises without believing in the conclusion. If the weather network announced rain and if the network is usually accurate, then (assuming that nothing important has been left out of this rendition of the argument), it must be the case that it will probably rain. Note that what follows from the premises is not the physical fact of rain but the probability. It is the arguer's confidence in the accuracy of the network's predictions that secures the conclusion. If we embrace this attitude of confidence, we *must* accept the probable conclusion.

Our purpose here is not to investigate the nature of probability, but simply note that the use of probability, in and of itself, does not rule out deductivism. We need to distinguish between the belief that a proposition about probability follows necessarily from other propositions and the belief that we can know with 100-per-cent certainty that some physical event is going to happen. Contemporary deductivism embraces the former, not the latter, belief. This belief – that the truth of the conclusion of a good argument follows necessarily from the truth of the premises – is compatible with probabilistic reasoning.

Contemporary deductivism is not intended as a metaphysical or as an epistemological doctrine, but as a pedagogical device. In a typical textbook situation, students are asked to supply the hidden premises needed to secure the validity of the argument. This forces students to uncover the assumptions, attitudes, and prejudices of the arguer. We can, however, use this deductivist technique of articulating hidden premises to uncover the link between premises and conclusion in inductive reasoning. I will focus on inductive arguments considered as a class. I mean to show that inductive arguments, in both everyday and scholarly contexts, appeal to an unspoken premise that is taken for granted but indispensable to the reasoning process. Once we articulate this hidden step in reasoning, a valid argument results. As we shall see, this procedure would be in line with Aristotle's account of induction.

Aristotle is, in two different senses, a deductivist. To begin with, he uses the term "enthymeme" in two different ways, to refer to arguments made of only probable premises and to those with hidden or unspoken premises.[10] An enthymeme in this second sense has a conclusion "deduced from few premises, often from fewer than the regular syllogism; for if any one of these [premises] is well known, there is no need to mention it."[11] Aristotle gives the following example: "To prove that Dorieus was the victor in a contest at which the prize was a crown, it is enough to say that he won a victory at the Olympic games; there is no need to add that the prize at the Olympic games is a crown, for everybody knows it."[12] The following sets out the example more formally. Premise: Dorieus won a victory at the Olympic Games. Hidden premise: The prize at the Olympic Games is a crown. Conclusion: Therefore, Dorieus won a crown. Though this (deductive) argument has a hidden component, it is not the premise but the fact that it is hidden that seems to detract from the argument's validity. Once we fill in the missing piece of information, a valid syllogism results.

10 An enthymeme in this first sense is "concerned with things which may, generally speaking, be other than they are," with matters that are, "for the most part only generally true," or with "probabilities and signs" (*Rhetoric* [Rhys Roberts], bk 1, ch. 2, 1357a, in Aristotle, *Complete Works*). See also *Prior Analytics*, bk 2, ch. 27. An enthymeme in this sense is a rhetorical syllogism (*Rhetoric*, bk 1, ch. 2, 1356b).

11 *Rhetoric* (Rhys Roberts), bk 1, ch. 2, 1357a.

12 *Rhetoric* (Freese), bk 1, ch. 2, 1357a19–22 (in Aristotle, *Aristotle in 23 Volumes*).

Aristotle is, however, a deductivist in another, more important, sense. In the *Prior Analytics* (and elsewhere) he discusses "the syllogism that springs out of induction."[13] We discuss these passages in detail below. For the moment, simply note that authorities now translate Aristotle's word *sullogismos* (συλλογισμός) as "deduction" (including Robin Smith, John Corcoran, Terrence Irwin, Gail Fine, Timothy Smiley, A.J. Jenkinson, to name only a few.) This is accurate, for Aristotle posits three requirements every syllogism must meet: the premises and conclusion must be distinct; the conclusion must come about because of the premises; and the conclusion must follow necessarily from the premises. As he puts it, a syllogism is "an argument in which, certain things being laid down, something other than these necessarily comes about through them."[14] And again, we know that we are dealing with a syllogism whenever "it is shown that, certain propositions being true, a further and quite distinct proposition must also be true in consequence."[15] When Aristotle refers to "inductive syllogisms," he is referring, literally, to "inductive deductions," an odd-sounding phrase to modern ears, but entirely in line with Aristotle's basic mentality. He believes, as we shall see, that these "inductive deductions" are valid.

Robin Smith discusses Aristotle's definition of the syllogism. He explains, "The core of this definition is the notion of … necessity … [which] corresponds to the modern notion of logical consequence: X results of necessity from Y and Z if it would be impossible for X to be false when Y and Z are true. We could therefore take this [definition of syllogism] to be a general definition of a valid argument."[16] To talk of an "inductive syllogism" is literally to talk of an inductive "valid argument." Aristotle is, in this basic sense, a deductivist. As we discuss below, he believes that rigorous scientific induction and rhetorical (or unscientific) induction both produce valid arguments.

13 *Prior Analytics*, bk 2, chs 23–4. We discuss these passages in detail below.

14 *Topics* (Pickard-Cambridge), bk 1, ch. 1, 100a25 (in Aristotle, *Complete Works*). And again, the premises in a syllogism "involve necessarily the assertion of something other than what has been stated" (*De Sophisticis Elenchis* [Pickard-Cambridge], ch. 1, 165a1–2, in Aristotle, *Works of Aristotle*).

15 Aristotle adds "whether universally or the most part." Note that this is in the *Rhetoric*, which deals with probable or plausible rather than rigorous or scientific arguments. More discussion of this later. See *Rhetoric*, bk 1, ch. 2, 1356b15–17.

16 *Stanford Encyclopedia of Philosophy*, s.v. "Aristotle's Logic" (by Robin Smith) (online). As Smith observes, the notion of necessity is captured in the Greek, *ex ananke sumbainein*. There are differences between modern notions of validity broadly construed and Aristotle's account of syllogistic, but they need not detain us here.

ADVANTAGES OF MODIFIED DEDUCTIVISM

Critics such as David Stove,[17] Ralph Johnson,[18] Trudy Govier,[19] Carl Wellman,[20] and Walton[21] believe that deductivism overemphasizes strict logical implication at the expense of more creative and looser types of relationships that can obtain between the premises and the conclusion in an argument.[22] They view deductivism as an inordinate attempt to force all argument into a formal logic mode. Walton complains,

> It has been presumed that formal logic is the most important kind of logic, or perhaps the only important kind of logic, and that formal logic is the abstract study of certain kinds of correlations – primarily the deducibility relation characteristic of the deductively valid type of argument. [On] this conception of logic ... the only thing that matters is the relation between the set of propositions called the premises, and the single proposition designated the conclusion ... Reasoning has now become exclusively concerned with the question of how the conclusion *necessarily* comes about from the premises.[23]

17 See Stove, "Deductivism"; *Probability and Hume's Inductive Scepticism*; and *Rationality of Induction.* Stove is an interesting and admirable figure. He wants to defend common sense and induction, but he is locked inside the empiricist paradigm and the traditional approach escapes him. He (mistakenly) identifies Hume as a deductivist, the idea being that Hume's inductive scepticism stems from his realization that inductive arguments cannot be construed as deductively valid arguments (Stove, "Deductivism," 78, 94–5). As I will abundantly show, inductive arguments can be construed as deductively valid ones.

18 See R. Johnson, *Manifest Rationality.*

19 For an extended critique of deductivism see Govier, *Problems in Argument*, ch. 2, "Are All Good Arguments Deductively Valid?"; ch. 3, "The Great Divide" ; and ch. 5, "Deductivism and Missing Premises." And see R. Johnson, *Manifest Rationality.*

20 See Wellman, *Challenge and Response.*

21 See Walton, *Argument Structure*, 237–40.

22 Trudy Govier – for example, in a survey of non-deductive and non-inductive argument types – speaks of "conductive" arguments (*à la* Wellman), "convergent" arguments (*à la* Thomas), and "good-reasons" arguments (*à la* Baier) (*Problems in Argument*, 50). Douglas Walton speaks of three types of arguments: deductive, inductive, and presumptive (*Argument Structure*, 240).

23 Walton, "What Is Reasoning?" 418–19 (my italics).

Walton attributes this preoccupation with validity to "the positivist philosophy that has been the orthodox way of thinking in universities since the Enlightenment." This attitude, which became "even more dominant in the twentieth century, [takes] science, especially the hard sciences of mathematics, physics and chemistry as the models of correct reasoning ... [It views] deductive logic of the kind one would find in the reasoning of Euclidean geometry, as the model of correct reasoning."[24]

While some modern deductivists take their views to such an extreme, there is no necessary connection between the claim that all good arguments are valid and the kind of strident formal positivism Walton (correctly) critiques. Aristotle, for one, believes that deductive and inductive arguments, *although distinct*, are both valid. He is, in this sense, a deductivist. (His classification scheme is depicted in figure 3.1.) At the same time, Aristotle does not restrict logic to a single-minded obsession with issues of validity. He formulates an expansive account of logic, has plenty to say about those "unscientific" arguments that occur in a rhetorical or a dialectical context, and recognizes the importance of inductive as well as deductive reasoning.

Much of the present debate about deductivism seems to skirt around the real bone of contention. What is fundamentally at stake is a core belief about how premises connect to a conclusion in a good argument. Deductivists and anti-deductivists disagree, in a very deep way, about what an argument is. What is it that differentiates a good argument from say, a poem, a figure of speech, two declarative sentences in a row, or an aphorism? Whatever it is, it has something to do with the logical relation – the inference – that binds premises and conclusion closely together. The deductivist argues that what I will call the "inference relation" is an all-or-nothing thing. The anti-deductivist argues that this description is unnecessarily restrictive. Some well-chosen metaphors would help to elucidate the difference.

The anti-deductivist claims, so to speak, that the inference relation is like glue. But glue (including the logical variety) comes in different strengths. That is all. Sometimes premises and conclusion are glued so tightly together, the bond is almost unbreakable; sometimes the bond is extremely weak and tenuous; sometimes, somewhere in-between. On this account, the inference relation holding an argument together is a matter of variable strength or intensity.

Using another metaphor, we could say that for deductivists the inference relation is more like a bridge. To move from premises to conclusion, we

24 Walton, "New Dialectic," 71–2.

Figure 3.1
How deductivism views the relationship between induction and deduction

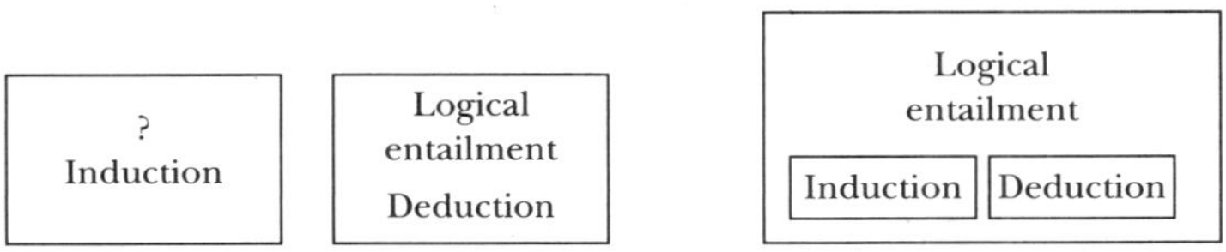

Orthodox contemporary view

Aristotle's "deductivist" view

need something under our feet *every step of the way*. If there is a gap anywhere in the bridge, we will fall into the abyss. It is an all-or-nothing affair. Either your feet are supported by something solid at all times or you fall through into logical nothingness. You cannot have a bridge that stops in mid-air and is still a bridge. A bridge is by definition a link that connects you to the other side. If it stops before getting there, it no longer counts as a bridge.

This way of putting it may seem, at first glance, to favour the anti-deductivist. Isn't it simplistic to make the inference relation an all-or-nothing affair? Surely half a bridge does some kind of logical work. To continue with the same metaphor, if only a small gap occurs in the evidence that leads us from here to there, why not consider the structure leading to and beyond the gap as a bridge with a missing plank, but still a bridge? If an argument is supposed to get us from here to there, we can leap across the gap and still get over to the other side, except that this seems to misconstrue what an argument is. Even supposing we come up with the correct answer – we would not get it through inference. It would not be logic that takes us over to the other side. It would be something else, a lucky guess, happenstance, a fit of madness, divine intervention, whatever. But even if such things can yield correct conclusions, the point is that whatever we would be left with – it would no longer be an inference.

On the deductivist view, argument is (as an historical author such as Descartes insists) about devising an uninterrupted chain of inference leading from premises to the eventual conclusion. We might say, metaphorically, that the conclusion swings from the premises by means of a logical chain. But we cannot hang a conclusion from premises unless is a continuous, link-to-link connection, all the way down. If a single link breaks, if a gap occurs in the chain, the conclusion falls to the ground. It has no support and thus there is no argument, for this is precisely what an argument entails: supporting the conclusion. (There may be something interesting in its place – some kind of lucky, free association of ideas, but not an argument.)

The difference between deductivist and anti-deductivist boils down to two contrasting accounts of the inference relation: the anti-deductivist conceives of it as a glue cementing premises and conclusions, with varying degrees of strength; the deductivists, as an uninterrupted thread, one that drives us to a conclusion we cannot avoid. On the anti-deductivist account, the inference relation is a little like fishing line: you can have a 20-, 30-, 50-pound test, and so on, implying stronger or weaker inference relations. On the deductivist account, the inference relation is like fishing line so strong that no one could break it; the inference relation pulls us irresistibly from *A* to *B*. Once we set up the logical path that takes us from *A* to *B*, we inevitably end up at *B*.

The variable-strength model of the inference relation seems enormously complicated. How, for example, could we determine how strong an inference relation is? What could we use to precisely measure whether the inference relation between two statements is extremely weak, moderately weak, of medium strength, strong, or absolute? (By the means of other arguments?) The idea gains some plausibility perhaps, considering that the amount of evidence we uncover may affect how firmly or confidently we embrace a conclusion. If we see one, three, thirty, three hundred, thirty thousand black crows, we may, each step of the way, claim with ever-increasing confidence that all crows are black. The more crows we observe, the stronger the inference relation. But this rough intuition does not survive close scrutiny. It seems to rest on a category mistake. To say that a claim is (to whatever degree) uncertain is to evaluate the conclusion not the inference relation that brought us to that conclusion. If, for example, I use the probability calculus (a kind of logical inference) to arrive at the conclusion that has a 50-per-cent chance of being true, it does not follow that I have only 50-per-cent confidence in the probability calculus that produced that conclusion or that I only have 50-per-cent confidence in the information that I started with. Deductivism is entirely consistent with the idea that we are logically compelled to believe that some conclusions are more or less probable, compared with others. Depending on the evidence, an uninterrupted thread of logical inference may bring us to the belief that a particular conclusion is, to whatever degree, certain or uncertain.

The modern notion of validity is only a more specific expression of this basic intuition that the inference relation in a properly structured argument is an unbreakable and uninterrupted logical chain. In a valid argument, we are compelled to move forward from premises to conclusion. The link is of the sort, "If you believe this, you must believe this." Walton writes, "There are many arguments commonly used in everyday language conversations that are not deductively valid and yet are structurally correct."[25] It is hard to know what to make of this claim. What could it mean to say that the premises in an argument are not logically linked to the conclusion? If we are going to tie premises to conclusion by something else – mere habit, expectation, feeling, imagination, moral intuition, or sheer willpower – we no longer have an argument, at least not in the *logical* sense of the word.

Aristotle is, in a very deep sense, a deductivist. On his account, a properly formed argument is "a discourse in which, certain things being stated, something other than what is stated follows of necessity from their being so."[26] We move in a continuous, uninterrupted logical sweep from premises to the conclusion – no gaps and no suggestion of the inferential link's being weaker in probabilistic arguments. The conclusion is weaker, but the logic that takes us to that conclusion is the same. Logical inference is just that. Aristotle realized, of course, that the conclusion in an inductive argument oversteps the evidence. We end up with more than we started with. As we shall see, he has a view about the first act of intelligence that makes this mental leap possible. He remained, nonetheless, a steadfast deductivist. Paralleling the methodology of modern deductivists, he articulates the hidden premise to be added to inductive arguments to turn them into valid deductions.

ARISTOTELIAN VERSUS PEDAGOGICAL DEDUCTIVISM

The critic might complain that the kind of deductivism I am attributing to Aristotle is very different from the pedagogical approach labelled as deductivism in contemporary argumentation theory. There is a difference in focus, to be sure. Nonetheless, both views originate in a similar intuition about logical inference. Compare Aristotle's approach to inductive reasoning with that of "pedagogical deductivism."

Contemporary logicians who advocate this approach propose filling up the gaps in natural-language arguments with hidden premises, as a method for evaluating arguments. This method has been attacked, principally for two reasons. First, how can we identify the missing components in a given argument? Colwyn Williamson remarks, "It is difficult ... to be sure the hidden premise is really there."[27] Anti-deductivists claim that any attempt to

25 Walton, *Argument Structure*, 239.

26 *Prior Analytics* (Jenkinson), bk 1, ch. 1, 24b19–20 (in Aristotle, *Complete Works*).

27 *Oxford Companion to Philosophy*, s.v. "Enthymeme" (by Colwyn Williamson).

fill out an argument with our own ideas seriously risks misrepresenting the arguer's intentions. Govier has gone so far as to suggest "that the missing premises are nowhere except in the mind of the critic."[28] Second, is the reconstructed argument really the same as the original? If I add new premises to argument *A* to produce argument *B*, are *A* and *B* the same? Some would suggest that *A* and *B* are different, though related, arguments. They are not numerically identical. If *B* is valid, that does not that make *A* so. If *B* is an inductive argument, that does not make *A* into one. Each has to be evaluated on its own terms.

We cannot sift through a wealth of attendant issues here. Suffice it to say that the complaints to the effect that we can never get behind what is implied or intended by a text seem exaggerated. We can, at least, in many cases come up with a good approximation of what someone must have been thinking. Any adamant suggestion to the contrary would make human communication close to impossible. Indeed, without this ability, we could not, among other things, do philosophy. We could not determine, for example, how to put Aristotle's scattered texts on induction back together to produce what hopefully approximates well his original theory.

We can understand a text as an expression of authorial intention, as a logical argument, or as both. But it is the text *qua* argument that must prevail in logic. While we cannot always capture exactly what a specified author intended by a written or spoken text, the point of logic is to force the issue so that we can at least examine various beliefs and see which stand up to the closest scrutiny. We demand that reasoners fill gaps in their reasoning and make their presuppositions explicit.[29] Such criticism forces all of us to improve our arguments. Pedagogical deductivism is only a more formal approach to this endeavour.

Return to the concern about whether incomplete argument *A* would be the same as completed argument *B*, composed of *A* and any of its missing premises. Seen from the deductivist perspective, *A* is not, but *B* is, an argument. However perfectly or imperfectly *B* captures the arguer's original intention, it is what we need to carry on a proper logical evaluation. Without something along the lines of *B*, we are left with an opinion, an idea, a description, an explanation, a text – whatever. Such material may be more than worthy of attention, but it is not an argument. This is why deductivists feel compelled to reconstruct *A* as *B*, so that they can apply all aspects of logical analysis to the text they are considering.

28 Govier, *Problems in Argument*, 101.

29 See Ennis's distinction between gap-fillers and presuppositions ("Identifying Implicit Assumptions").

Aristotle's analysis of inductive syllogism brings the deductivist approach to an entire category of arguments. Unlike contemporary deductivists, Aristotle is not so much interested in supplying beginning students with tools for analyzing specific arguments as in uncovering the basic pattern of inference at the very heart of inductive reasoning. He fills the gap, so to speak, that separates premises and conclusion in the usual formulation of inductive arguments. He produces the missing premise that must be added to inductive *proto-argument* A to turn it into valid inductive *argument* B. It does not follow from all this that the inductive is in no way distinct from deductive reasoning; the difference is easily identified: induction moves from specific to general, whereas deduction moves from general to specific. As we discuss in future chapters, Aristotle ultimately traces induction to a movement of the mind more properly labelled as a species of intuition or insight than as an argument – but more on these details later.

AN ABBREVIATED HISTORY OF DEDUCTIVISM

While most contemporary logicians take the invalid nature of induction for granted, we should nevertheless point out that, historically, most mainstream philosophers were deductivists. Contrary to the prevailing impression, many thinkers in the Western tradition believed that induction is a valid form of inference. It is only the ascendancy of the modern-empiricist tradition that now makes what is really a minority opinion seem so incontrovertible.

Contemporary argumentation theorist Trudy Govier identifies a "tradition going back to Aristotle, which maintains that there are two and only two broad types of argument: deductive arguments which are conclusive, and inductive arguments, which are not."[30] This is what most commentators believe. But, in fact, the modern split between valid deductive arguments and invalid inductive ones is an artefact of the modern empiricism espoused by historical authors such as John Locke and David Hume. It does not in any way derive from Aristotle or his ancient colleagues. Ancient, medieval, and early modern authors conceived of induction, at least in large part, as a valid form of inference.

J.R. Milton identifies a long tradition of scepticism about induction. But Milton (who misconstrues Aristotle's subtle position) does not distinguish between the belief that induction (or human belief, generally) is fallible and the belief that inductive arguments are invalid. As we have already argued, the belief that inductive arguments are valid does not, as Milton seems to assume, rule out the possibility that they are fallible. Even if it is

30 Govier, *Problems in Argument*, 52; see also 37.

allowed that "the most commonly held [historical] position was that … inductive arguments are inherently fallible and produce (at best) only probability and not certainty,"[31] this is not incompatible with a belief in inductive validity. Milton quotes Miles Burnyeat to the effect that, according to the ancient Stoics, "the logic of our reasoning is always deductive."[32] But whether that means that the Stoics as a group believed that inductive arguments are always invalid is very hard to tell. We know that the Epicureans were strong advocates of induction and that the Stoics, in some robust way, opposed them. But it is hard to discern precisely what these early thinkers believed about the validity question because the textual evidence is so scanty and because the necessary research still has to be done.

Move on to the medieval Schoolmen, who refer to induction as an "argument from experience" (*argumentum ad experimentum* or *argumentum ad experientia*).[33] These authors, who conceive of induction as the process of inferring universals from experience, generally believed that inductive reasoning could produce *certain* knowledge about particulars. Albert the Great (1206?–1280), for example, writes that our senses teach us an obvious truth about the nature of wine – that it intoxicates – and that the intellect grasps this truth with a certainty that cannot be doubted.[34] Duns Scotus (1274?–1308) comments that induction sets "the mind at ease"[35] so that "the expert infallibly knows [what is], and that it is always so, and in all things."[36] John Poinsot (commonly known as John of St Thomas, 1589–1644) explains that

31 Milton, "Induction before Hume," 62.

32 Ibid., 54.

33 From the Greek ἐμπειρία (*empeiria*). See, for example, Joyce, *Principles of Logic*, 227–8, 232–4; Maritain, *Introduction to Logic*, 283; and *Catholic Encyclopedia*, s.v. "Induction" (by Peter Coffey) (online).

34 Cited in Joyce, *Principles of Logic*, 234 (citing Albertus Magnus, "De demonstratione, id est, posteriorum analyticorum" ["On the Posterior Analytics"], *Opera Omnia*, vol. 2, bk 1, treatise 1, ch. 2, 5).

35 This is an echo of the Aristotelian phrase describing induction as the universal "coming to rest" in the soul (*Posterior Analytics* [Tredennick], bk 2, ch. 19, 100a5–10, 100b, in Aristotle, *Aristotle in 23 Volumes*).

36 Paraphrase by Joyce, *Principles of Logic*, 234 (of John Duns Scotus, "Quaestiones in librum primum Sententiarum," ["Commentary on the First Book of Peter Lombard's Sentences"], *Opera Omnia*, vol. 9, 174). Duns Scotus argues at some length that experience is NOT, strictly speaking, the cause of our knowledge, but only the occasion of it, and this is why we can have certain knowledge even without a perfect induction. (Helpful commentary courtesy of Jason West.)

induction "is directed to discovering and *proving* universal truths," that its "principal function is to make evident the *proof* of a universal by ascending from singulars."[37] Even William of Ockham (1285–1347), the famous nominalist, contends that inductive and deductive reasoning are of the same nature or kind.[38] We can arrive at knowledge that is known with certitude either way.

Old-school logicians knowledgeable in the medieval tradition make the point even more explicitly. Modern Thomist Jacques Maritain, not one to mince words, claims modern logicians (whom he pejoratively labels "logisticians") misunderstand the true nature of inductive argument and unwittingly reduce it to "no more ... than an *invalid* syllogism or a defective reasoning." They "reduce it to *nothing*," he complains; they "purely and simply destroy it."[39] Maritain claims, in contrast, that every properly constructed inductive argument "is valid and formal."[40] Richard Clarke, an earlier author with similar allegiances, maintained (1889) that all inductive reasoning could be reduced to a (valid) syllogism.[41]

While medieval authors and their modern descendants generally consider inductive reasoning as unproblematic, most traditional empiricist writers, not surprisingly, take a similar approach. The arguments of Locke and Hume notwithstanding, they usually conceive of induction as an enthymeme with a hidden premise. Once this hidden premise is explicitly stated, a deductively valid argument results. Milton himself suggests, for example, that Pierre Gassendi (in a c. 1658 text) teaches that "the only inductive arguments of any value are enthymemes – arguments which can be turned into regular syllogisms by the addition of a concealed premise of premises."[42] John Stuart Mill, taking a cue from Archbishop Whately, later argued that "every induction is a syllogism with the major premise suppressed."[43] Mill paraphrases the missing premise, "that the course of

37 John of St Thomas, *Outlines of Formal Logic* (Wade), bk 3, ch. 2, 104–5 (my italics).

38 See Willliam of Ockham, *Venerabilis inceptoris*, Q. 2, art. 2; *Summa logicae* [*Logical Treatise*], pt 2, ch. 11, and pt 3).

39 Maritain, *Introduction to Logic*, 268: "The only thing [left to do is] to rule [induction] out of Logic as several logisticians have done."

40 Ibid., 279.

41 R. Clarke, *Logic*, 380.

42 Milton, "Induction before Hume," 58.

43 Mill attributes this remark to Archbishop Whately (Mill, *System of Logic*, bk 3, ch. 3, §1, 202).

nature is uniform."[44] The followers of Christian Wolff (1679–1754) had earlier construed induction as an enthymeme with an unstated major premise (relating individuals to a universal).[45] All the way up into the twentieth century, authors such as George Joyce (1936) and Thomas Crumley (1947) continued to appeal to Mill's principle of uniformity as the hidden premise rendering inductive arguments valid.[46] Ralph Eaton (writing in 1931), who is on the other side of this issue, complains that most modern logicians mistakenly conceive of induction as a *valid* enthymeme. Eaten laments, "The idea that induction requires some general statement about the whole of the actual world haunted the minds of logicians in the nineteenth century. This was called the principle of determinism, or the uniformity of nature, or of causality. Mill and many others went further than merely require this principle. They thought that induction, through its aid, *could be assimilated to deduction and could prove the truth of general conclusions* on the evidence of particular instances."[47]

Although, following Hume, Eaton believes that induction is invalid, he himself explains that his own convictions are at odds with the historical consensus. He comments pointedly, "The two most important names in the history of inductive theory are Bacon [1561–1626] and Mill [1806–1873]. Both of these writers, while they analyzed certain of the central elements in inductive proof, were in error to its essential nature ... *Their aim was really to turn induction into deduction* by discovering methods which, starting with particulars, would give truth to generalizations extending beyond those particulars." Eaton argues against philosophers who seek a "Principle of Induction" "which will magically transform the slow process of accumulating evidence, of eliminating irrelevancies, of building systems piece by piece, which is induction, into [deductive] demonstration."[48] No such Holy Grail, he claims, exists. But the very fact that an author such as Eaton feels the need to rail against attempts demonstrates the pervasiveness of this other view.

44 Ibid., bk 3, ch. 3, §1, 201. Mill explains, "That there are such things as parallel cases, that what happens once, will, under a sufficient degree of similarity of circumstances, happen again, and not only again, but as often as the same circumstances recur" (ibid.).

45 See Maritain, *Introduction to Logic*, 267–8.

46 See, for example, Joyce, *Principles of Logic*, 235–51; Crumley, *Logic Deductive and Inductive*, 339–46.

47 Eaton, *General Logic*, 535.

48 Ibid., 502.

I cannot consider the Continental tradition in any detail here. One modern English-speaking Continental author who does, however, discuss induction in some detail is the idealist author Bernard Bosanquet (1848–1923). He, following Hegel, attempts to reconcile inductive and deductive reasoning.[49] In the former, we start with certainty but need to refine our conception of reality, to extend the scope and depth of our understanding. Induction is more than generalization; it is to have an insight into what is. Bosenquet attacks the variable-strength concept of the inference relation proposed by anti-deductivists. He chastises "repetition theorists" who claim that inductive inference grows stronger as more cases are examined.[50] We have no need to prop up inductive conclusions with corroborating evidence, merely repeating what went before. Bosanquet writes, "What is proved once does not need to be proved again. Every datum *proves irrefragably* the reality of the system to which it belongs, *whatever that may be.*"[51] And again, "How many observations, which experiments, how many ... conjunctions of phenomena, may be needed to establish the [conclusion] is ... theoretically indifferent."[52]

Bosanquet, in sharp contrast to contemporary analytic authors, believes that the inductive insight is rock solid. "Every fact, every sense-perception, every datum of testimony absolutely and irrevocably proves *something.*"[53] The problem is not that the inductive inference is illogical or ungrounded; it is that it needs to be augmented so that we can refine our conception of reality. Individual instances of induction, considered by themselves, provide an incomplete picture of what is going on, but when it comes to *proving* the regularity that lies behind the inductive insight, "One datum is as good as a host to prove this."[54]

Contemporary theologian and philosopher Bernard Lonergan, following in the post-Hegelian tradition, takes a similar view of induction. We will

49 See Bernard Bosanquet's influential 1883 essay, "Logic as the Science of Knowledge."

50 Induction "gains nothing from any repetition of established consequences once established to be fact" (Bosanquet, *Logic or the Morphology of Knowledge*, 171). And again, "To allege variety and range of data as contributory to this proof is to fall once more into the fallacy of generalization from number of instances" (Ibid.)

51 Ibid., 172.

52 Ibid., 171.

53 Ibid., 172.

54 Ibid., 171.

discuss Lonergan's position at length in a later chapter. For the moment, simply note that Lonergan also dismisses the alleged problem of induction. "Similars," he writes, "are similarly understood."[55] Nothing, he claims, is inherently illogical or worrisome about inductive reasoning. (His account is not entirely consistent, but leave this for later discussion.)

This is only a very incomplete survey. Suffice to say that the by now widespread view that induction is inherently problematic and that inductive arguments deal with invalid inferences is nevertheless not a universally accepted one. It only seems so because, rightly or wrongly, a particular philosophical mindset has come to the fore in the present period of intellectual history.

ARISTOTLE AND PERFECT INDUCTION

Before we can build a road, we must clear the obstacles out of the way. Before undertaking any detailed examination of Aristotle's account of induction, we must critique an erroneous but somewhat influential exegetical tradition that insists that Aristotle elaborated a theory of "perfect induction." In so-called "perfect" or "complete" induction we observe *every* member of the class being investigated. Suppose, for example, I look at *every* painting Picasso produced during his "blue period." I physically observe that every painting has some shade of blue. I conclude, "All of the paintings Picasso produced during this historical period have some shade of blue." This would be an example of a perfect induction, for the universal conclusion, "all paintings from this time period are blue," is precipitated by a complete examination of each one of the relevant set of objects. Perfect induction allegedly produces indubitable conclusions; it proves that its claims have no exceptions.[56] As such, it is sometimes considered to be an epistemologically superior form of induction. It is arguably, the mechanical ideal toward which statistical theories of induction naturally tend.

As we shall see, ancient and medieval authors did not think about induction in this way. Nonetheless, a long list of commentators have attempted to explain the Aristotelian inductive inference as a form of perfect induction. Richard Clarke, Peter Coffey, George Joyce, and many others, all

55 Lonergan, *Understanding and Being*, 289.

56 Of course, Cartesian scepticism can doubt perfect induction just as easily as regular induction.

abound in this sense.[57] Maritain (rightfully) castigates proponents of this "enumerative" approach.[58] And a group of recent commentators such as Troels Engberg-Pedersen, Lambertus Marie de Rijk, and Paolo Biondi correctly distance themselves from any such suggestion.[59] Understanding how this erroneous interpretation arose is instructive.

Adherents of the perfect-induction school base their account on an interpretation of *Prior Analytics*, book 2, chapters 23–4, probably the most important formal passage on induction in Aristotle's corpus. (We consider the passage in detail below.) The problem is that Aristotle seems to suggest here that inductive arguments (syllogisms) are deductively valid. He states, for example, that the arguer "deduces" the inductive conclusion; he points out that the conclusion follows necessarily, and he claims, more generally, that an inductive argument proves the conclusion.[60] This is all evidence for a deductivist interpretation. Indeed, the mere fact that Aristotle parses out inductive arguments in the general form of a valid syllogism indicates that he believes that inductive arguments are deductively valid. (As we have seen, the word "syllogism" [συλλογισμός] means "deduction" in Aristotle.)

To philosophers heavily influenced by modern empiricist notions, this seemed like an enormous philosophical mistake. How could Aristotle conceive of ordinary induction, which typically begins with an incomplete sample, as a valid argument? As eminent a commentator as Ross repeats the Humean dogma: "Where a statement about a whole species is based on facts about a mere selection of its members, or an inference about a whole genus on facts about a mere selection of its species, it cannot be reasonably supposed that there is a valid inference."[61] This left Aristotlean commentators in a serious bind. How could a great thinker like Aristotle overlook

57 See R. Clarke, *Logic*, 368; Coffey, *Science of Logic*, vol. 2, §207, 27–32; Joyce, *Principles of Logic*, 230 (Joyce is more reserved in his approval. He notes [indecisively] the difficulty with this reading); Crumley, *Logic Deductive and Inductive*, 314–15; Eaton, *General Logic*, 487; Guthrie, *History of Greek Philosophy*, vol. 4, ch. 10, §3, "Induction," 187–90; Ross, *Aristotle's Prior and Posterior Analytics*, 49; McKirahan, *Principles and Proofs*, 251; Peters, *Greek Philosophical Terms*, s.v. "Epagoge," §5, 58; Detel, *Aristoteles*, 251, 257, 260, 262; and Milton, "Induction before Hume," 51, 53.

58 Maritain, *Introduction to Logic*, 269–70.

59 Engberg-Perderson, "More on Aristotelian *Epagoge*," 313ff.; de Rijk, *Aristotle*, vol. 1, §2.54, 146; and Biondi, *Aristotle*, §3.3, "Enumeration of All Cases," 202–7.

60 See *Prior Analytics* (Jenkinson), bk 2, ch. 23, 68b16, 24–25, 34.

61 Ross, *Aristotle's Prior and Posterior Analytics*, 48.

such an elementary difficulty and present induction as a valid argument form? How could he claim that inductive conclusions follow necessarily?

Empiricist commentators who respected Aristotle found a way of saving face (and it could only be described as a desperate measure) by imposing a theory of perfect induction on the original text. As they point out, Aristotle does write that induction proceeds through an enumeration of *all* cases and that the middle term in an induction must be understood as being made up of *all* the particulars.[62] So they concluded that Aristotle's comments on inductive syllogism must be restricted to the highly unusual case of perfect induction. But any such suggestion seems quite seriously problematic.

We can conceive of induction as a kind of counting (what old textbook authors sometimes called "induction by enumeration"). On this account, induction is akin to an arithmetical operation; we total up, in some sort, the number of observations (with or without statistical aid). Perfect induction represents the best, most complete tabulation; we can know the conclusion with absolute certainty. When it comes to induction, however, Aristotle had very different ideas. He conceived of induction as a stroke of insight, a creative intellectual penetration into the heart of a puzzle. It involves a moment of illumination; it has little or nothing to do with counting. Robert Schmidt, who makes a similar point about Thomas' inductive logic, cites the following example.[63]

As Schmidt points out, we cannot grasp the physical principle that explains why boats float on water from mere enumeration. It does not follow that because this and that and that boat floats on water, all boats float on water. We need to be able to somehow see through individual instances of floating boats to the underlying physical principle that the phenomenon "floating" results whenever an object displaces an amount of water that is heavier than their own weight. As Schmidt explains, "From the fact that some vessels float on water we cannot judge that all vessels float on water; but if those which float on water are seen to agree in the property of displacing water of a greater weight than their own, then we can judge that every watertight vessel that displaces more water than would equal itself in weight floats on water."[64] But grasping this principle is a heady feat. It has nothing much to do with counting. We must be able (like Archimedes) to penetrate, by some creative stroke of genius, the surface appearances and discern the underlying cause of floating. This is not something we can arrive at by merely adding.

62 *Prior Analytics*, bk 2, ch. 23, 68b27–28, 69a16–17.

63 Schmidt, *Domain of Logic*, 270–301.

64 Ibid., 279.

Seen from an ancient or medieval perspective, statistical models of induction miss the point. They reduce it to the mechanical process of enumerating cases, ignoring the movement of dawning discernment that culminates in the leap to the universal. But this mental leap is ultimately what Aristotelian inductive reasoning is all about. Aristotle conceives of it as "enumeration" AND "cognitive leap." The purpose of the enumeration is only to give impetus to the leap. As contemporary commentator Biondi explains, Aristotle divides the inductive process into two distinct phases: the "adducing" (or enumerating) instances and the "leading on" from particular instances to a universal. But "the activity of enumerating [is] ... subordinate to, and merely a necessary condition of the properly inductive act of going from particular to universal."[65] Proponents of the perfect- or complete-induction reading unwittingly reduce the inductive syllogism to a mere enumeration. This is to think of the universal conclusions produced by inductive reasoning as a mechanical summary of data rather than as creative insight.

Maritain, most notably, dismisses perfect induction as "the purely verbal and sterile form which [modern commentators] have the *naivete* to regard as the only induction known to the ancients, although the latter never [even] thought of considering it in their theory of induction."[66] He is, in the main, correct. As influential a historical figure as John Stuart Mill argues that perfect induction does not even count as a logical inference at all.[67] This is clearly not what Aristotle had in mind by inductive syllogism.

OBJECTIONS TO THE PERFECT-INDUCTION INTERPRETATION

Because the "perfect-induction" interpretation represents the logical consequence of the usual way of thinking about Aristotle and induction, it is important to refute it thoroughly. Consider then, in a more structured way, the kinds of objections someone could raise against the idea that an inductive syllogism is only a valid argument because it involves the inspection of every member of the class we are considering.

To begin with, Aristotle is not an "empiricist" in the modern post-Humean sense. Modern commentators are driven to the perfect-induction interpretation, in large part because they are looking over their shoulders

65 Biondi, *Aristotle*, §3.1, 193.

66 Maritain, *Introduction to Logic*, 270.

67 Mill, *System of Logic*, bk 2, ch. 2, §1, 188–200.

at modern statistical accounts. Aristotle has an altogether different metaphysics and a different understanding of inductive logic.

Second, Aristotle's views are much closer to those of the scholastic tradition, which did consider *imperfect* induction, induction from an *incomplete* sample, to be a valid logical move. John Duns Scotus writes, "As to what is known by experience [i.e., by induction], I have this to say. Even though a person does not experience every single individual [case], but only a great many, nor does he experience them at all times, but only frequently, still he knows infallibly that it is always this way and holds for all instances. He knows this in virtue of this [universal] proposition reposing in his soul."[68] Maritain attributes the view that *incomplete* induction is valid to medieval philosophers like Albert the Great, Thomas Aquinas, and John of St Thomas.[69] As Schmidt points out, on this Aristotle-influenced account it is not the empirical inspection of every member of the specified class but "the discovery of a common nature [that] is the real basis for [inducing] the universal conclusion."[70] Valid universal conclusions derive, not from a complete sample, but "from the experience of a few instances."[71]

Third, it is a general misconception to believe that only perfect induction could be reduced to a three-term, three-statement syllogistic form. F.E. Peters writes that "the reduction of induction to syllogistic form [is] something [we] can only achieve by means of a perfect induction."[72] This is simply mistaken. All inductive arguments may be transposed into a three-term, three-statement syllogistic form, as I demonstrate below. Mill (who refers to Archbishop Whately's treatment), Clarke, and Maritain all cast incomplete inductive arguments into syllogistic form.[73]

Fourth, Aristotle points out elsewhere in his corpus that a successful induction may be precipitated by a single instance of a large class.[74] We discuss this case below.

Fifth, it would be strange to think that Aristotle, with his encyclopaedic vision, would devote his principal treatment of inductive syllogism to the rare case of perfect induction. Why not coin a special word or phrase to

68 Duns Scotus, *Philosophical Writings* (Wolter), pt 5, "Concerning Human Knowledge," art. 2, "The Rejection of Skepticism," §b, "Experimental Knowledge," 117.

69 He attributes the same view to Aristotle (Maritain, *Introduction to Logic*, 282–3).

70 Schmidt, *Domain of Logic*, 281.

71 Ibid., 277. Schmidt presents a detailed textual analysis, referring to Thomas' *Commentary on the Posterior Analytics*, bk 2, lecture 20, art. 11.

72 Peters, *Greek Philosophical Terms*, s.v. "Epagoge," §5, 58.

73 See Mill, *System of Logic*, bk 3, ch. 3, §1, 202; and R. Clarke, *Logic*, 380. See also, for example, the schema Maritain presents at *Introduction to Logic*, 263.

74 *Posterior Analytics*, bk 1, ch. 32, 88a15.

indicate that this is a special case? As Richard McKirahan observes, Aristotle uses the same word, ἐπαγωγή *(epagoge)*, in the passage from the *Prior Analytics* and in other passages.[75] This suggests that he is referring to the same procedure he discusses elsewhere.

Sixth, perfect induction is not so much a mode of insight or inference as a method of evidence gathering. It is, as we have seen, an enumerative not an illuminative procedure. Being confronted with a complete empirical fact is not the same as jumping, by a species of rational insight, to a conclusion. But Aristotelian induction is ultimately about a kind of inspiration that operates through a leap of creative insight.

Seventh, Aristotle's example of an inductive argument is about the longevity of bileless animals (those who lack any excess of choleric fluids). This is an ancient lesson in biology that presupposes the theory of the four humours: choleric, sanguine, phlegmatic, and melancholic. Aristotle argues, to paraphrase, that because some bileless animals (mankind, horse, and mule) are long lived, all bileless animals are long lived. But any attempt to turn this biological argument into a perfect induction is wholly implausible. We could understand the argument in two ways.

McKirahan claims that Aristotle intends the syllogism to be the perfect induction of species rather than of individuals.[76] Although the biological kind "mule" is not, rigorously speaking, a species,[77] scientific syllogisms generally do deal with classes rather than individuals.[78] In his syllogism, Aristotle mentions three "species": mankind, horse, and mule. Elsewhere in the *Posterior Analytics*, Aristotle identifies the broad class of quadrupeds as bileless.[79] And, in his biological works, he mentions that other animals lack a gallbladder and are therefore bileless, including roe deer, fallow deer, seals, dolphins, some kinds of pigs, and camels.[80] If this were meant to be a

75 McKirahan, *Principles and Proofs*, 251.

76 Ibid.

77 The mule is the bastard child, so to speak, of a horse and a donkey.

78 For an example of (rhetorical) induction from individuals see the argument about Dionysius taking a bodyguard (*Rhetoric*, bk 1, ch. 2, 1357b31–1358a1).

79 "The cause of longevity in quadrupeds is lack of bile" (*Analytica Posteriora* (Mure), bk 2, ch. 17, 99b5, in Aristotle, *Works of Aristotle*).

80 "Some animals have a gall bladder close to the liver, and others have not. Of viviparous quadrupeds the deer is without the organ, as also the roe, the horse, the mule, the ass, the seal, and some kinds of pigs" (*History of Animals* [Thompson], bk 2, ch. 15, 506a 22–23, in Aristotle, *Works of Aristotle*); "In some animals there is absolutely no gallbladder at all–in the horse, for instance, the mule, the ass, the deer, and the roe; and in others, as the camel, there is no distinct bladder, but merely small vessels of a biliary character. Again, there is no such organ in the seal, nor,

perfect induction of species, Aristotle would have had to possess knowledge of *every* species (and quasi-species) of bileless animal in the world. But he was a biologist involved in the pioneering task of cataloguing and recording known species. It is very doubtful that he himself could have claimed to have acquired knowledge of every single bileless species (or quasi-species). But without such knowledge, a perfect induction of species would be impossible.

And there is a deeper problem: How do we come to know that this or that species of bileless animals is long lived? We can only know that "particular long-lived [bileless] animals: such as men, horses, mules,"[81] and so on share a certain characteristic, through an initial inspection of the individual members of that species. On this second, more in-depth of reading of the bileless argument, it must include (explicitly or implicitly) some reference to the observation of individual bileless animals. As Biondi explains, "recourse to sensible particulars is inevitable in all inductions."[82] If, however, perfect induction is what Aristotle has in mind, the induction about bileless animals would have to rest ultimately on an empirical inspection of every bileless animal! As Biondi exclaims, "such a simplistic understanding borders on complete nonsense."[83] How could the scientist inspect every bileless animal? The number of such animals having existed far exceeds the scope of human observation. What about those that lived in the distant past? Or will live in the future? These must be included in any perfect induction of *all* bileless creatures. As Biondi reports, "As having recourse to sensible individuals in some way is unavoidable, the dilemma of having to actually enumerate an indefinite number of particulars cannot be avoided by this interpretation."[84]

Eighth, and more importantly, a different way of understanding this passage from the *Prior Analytics* would be more consistent with Aristotle's broader thought. On this understanding, we access the universal, not

among sea animals, in the dolphin ... There are other animals that have no gallbladder ... such as the camel and the dolphin" (*Parts of Animals* [Ogle], bk 4, ch. 2, 676b26–30, 677a34–35, in Aristotle, *Aristotle in 23 Volumes*). It seems clear from the text that Aristotle would include all these animals in the subject term of his inductive syllogism. More on this issue below.

81 *Prior Analytics* (Tredennick), bk 2, ch. 23, 58b20–22 (in Aristotle, *Aristotle in 23 Volumes*). Jenkinson translates the passage "the particular long-lived animals, e.g. man, horse, mule" (see *Analytic Priora*, in Aristotle, *Works of Aristotle*).

82 Biondi, *Aristotle*, §3.3, 204.

83 Ibid., §3.3, 203.

84 Ibid., §3.3, 204.

through an empirical inspection of every member of a class, but through some cognitive insight that apprehends the universal nature expressed through *every* case in question. Biondi explains, "an induction can be held to have gone through all particular instances, not because it has actually enumerated every single particular instance ... but because it has done so potentially by having acquired the cognition of the universal essence of the particulars being enumerated."[85] This medieval-sounding interpretation begins in Aristotle. Once we grasp the nature that is common to all bileless animals, we know something about *all* members of that class. The incomplete empirical inspection of *some* bileless animals (or of *some* species of bileless animals) is thus transformed into an intellectual understanding of the nature of *every* bileless animal. In discerning and identifying the universal, we enumerate, in principle, all cases.

Aristotelian induction presupposes our recognizing some necessary and universal nature. In the words of one contemporary scholar, the mind in the act of induction, fixes on "the universal [nature that] resides within the material confines of the individual sense data."[86] The mind does not grasp the individual *qua* individual, but the individual *qua* part of a larger whole.[87] Once we see that this individual as part of the larger group, we can attribute its characteristics to the other members of the group.

Ninth, Aristotle's induction of bileless animals is intended to be a comment on the properties of a common nature, not the contingent features of specific individuals. Although Aristotle believed, for example, that both mice and men are bileless, he makes it clear elsewhere that he considered individual exceptions associated with disease.[88] Clearly, it is plainly false that every individual human being, horse, mule, roe deer, fallow deer, seal, etc., is long lived. The existence of exceptions, of individuals who do not make it into old age for a variety of reasons, does not, in Aristotle's mind, invalidate the universal claim that bilelessness naturally tends toward longevity. Aristotle is not arguing that every single bileless animal has been long lived but, more precisely, that longevity is a necessary property of

85 Ibid., §3.3, 207.

86 Peters, *Greek Philosophical Terms*, s.v. "Epagoge," §4, 58.

87 It is the nominalist tendency to consider individuals *sui generis*, which betrays the Aristotelian insight.

88 "Even within the limits of the same genus, some animals appear to have and others to be without it. Such is the case with mice; such also with man ... Almost invariably, those who suffer from these forms of disease are persons who have no gallbladder at all" (*Parts of Animals* [Ogle], bk 4, ch. 2, 676b30–32, 677a9). More on the issue below.

bilelessness. If bileless individuals realized their natures perfectly, if they were allowed to develop fully, they would be long lived.

Off-the-cuff attempts to discredit earlier accounts of induction by pointing to unusual or exceptional instances are little more than silly (anachronistic, in fact). They misconstrue what earlier accounts of induction are about. Robin Smith (despite his generally sound views) insists that "A good inductive argument [must] suppose there are no counterexamples."[89] He proposes the following inductive syllogism: "Socrates, Plato, Aristotle have two legs. Socrates, Plato, and Aristotle are human. Therefore, all humans have two legs." Smith concludes, "A single one-legged human like Monosceles – a single counterexample – is sufficient to block the inductive inference."[90] But the fact that Monosceles is an amputee from the Peloponnesian Wars, who lost a leg in a battle somewhere, does not defeat the Aristotelian generalization, "all human beings have two legs." Induction, for Aristotle, is insight into the nature of things. It is not about numerical instances. To consider Monosceles as a definitive counter-example is to slip back into the modern mode of understanding induction as mere counting. On the statistical account, the universal affirmation "all human beings have two legs" has a numerical meaning. It means that every individual instance of humanity is two legged. In Aristotle, the same universal statement has a metaphysical meaning. It means, not that every numerical instance of humanity has two legs, but that it is of the nature of human beings to have two legs. A properly formed human being, a human being who properly actualizes human nature, will have two legs. Being without two legs is an injury, a disease, a deformity. The fact that there are "defective" human beings without two legs does not count against the genuine meaning of the generalization.

Consider a different example. Suppose a child was to crack open an egg for breakfast and find a half-developed chick inside. The child might reason, "So that's what eggs are for. They're supposed to contain baby chickens!" Clearly, most eggs do not contain baby chickens. Still, eggs are the way chickens reproduce. To claim that this is what eggs are for is not to claim that all eggs actually produce chickens. It is to say something about the nature of an egg that holds true, even if, in specific cases, this or that egg does not develop into a baby chicken. In the same way, bileless creatures may possess a long-lived nature, even though many (indeed most) individual bileless animals, due to contingent circumstances, die early.

Tenth, Aristotle's account of the inductive syllogism depends, as we shall see, on the key concept of convertibility. If an inductive syllogism is to be valid, the two terms in the minor premise must be "convertible." This is a

89 R. Smith, "Logic," 31.
90 Ibid.

formal requirement which can only be fulfilled if the middle term includes all particulars. This is why Aristotle stresses the requirement that (successful) induction rest on a comprehensive knowledge of all particular cases. It has nothing to do with an empirical examination of all cases. We discuss this point in detail below.

Finally, to conceive of Aristotle's syllogism about bileless animals as a perfect or complete syllogism is to ignore the purpose of inductive syllogism in Aristotle. The syllogism about bileless animals is intended to uncover a cause of longevity: Why are these animals long lived? Because they are bileless. A mechanical enumeration of instances is not the same as a causal explanation. It is not enough to simply notice what universally is the case; induction penetrates the effect and sees the cause. As Stephen Gaukroger comments, "A complete syllogism, if that were ever possible … could tell us that a thing is [universally] so, but not why it is so – it could not provide *aitia* [cause]."[91] There is more to the understanding of causality than a complete enumeration of instances. I discuss this aspect of Aristotle's theory in detail in the next chapter.

THE MEANING OF THE WORD "INDUCTION"

Having cleared away an enduring source of confusion, I want to elaborate a more accurate account of Aristotle's bileless-animal induction. But first, an important note about terminology. In his corpus, Aristotle generally uses the Greek word "ἐπαγωγή" (*epagoge*) to refer to induction. The noun derives from the verb "ἐπάγω" (*epago*), which one standard dictionary defines as "to set on, urge on, as hunters do dogs … to lead an army against … to lead on by persuasion, influence … to bring forward, propose a measure;"[92] and another as "to lead, bring, or drive to or on; to add, to apply; to impel, cause, instigate, seduce."[93] Induction is, then, a kind of mental movement that comes from the outside. It involves "the leading on from particulars to the universal."[94] Rational agents are urged on, driven, impelled, pushed, pulled, encouraged, seduced.[95] They are led upward and away from this

91 Gaukroger, *Explanatory Structures*, 93. He continues, "The distinction between that which is essential and that which is merely universal is a *sine qua non* of a theory of a demonstrative syllogism and hence it is crucial that Aristotle respect it" (ibid., 93–4).

92 *Liddell and Scott's Greek-English Lexicon*, s.v. "ἐπάγω."

93 *Langenscheidt's Greek-English Dictionary*, s.v. "ἐπάγω."

94 Peters, *Greek Philosophical Terms*, s.v. "Epagoge," §5, 57–8.

95 The adjective ἐπαγωγός (*epagogos*) means "attractive, tempting, alluring, seductive" (*Liddell and Scott's Greek-English Lexicon*, s.v. "ἐπαγωγός").

and that separate instance to an awareness of the universal. This process involves a gaining of mental momentum that comes, so to speak, from both a pushing and a pulling. The pushing comes from sense perception, which impels knowers, driving them forward to a greater understanding; the pulling (arguably) comes from the universal that irresistibly attracts the mind in its struggle toward understanding. Aristotle (unlike Plato) does not believe that the universal exists on its own, separate and apart from material objects. Nonetheless, it is already there, resident in physical things. And, somehow or other, it attracts the mind that strives to know.

In the *Metaphysics*, Aristotle comments that Socrates was the first to use inductive reasoning.[96] As any student of Plato would know, Socrates methodically presents examples and puzzles to his interlocutors with an eye to "inducing" an understanding in the audience.[97] Hamlyn cites his geometrical demonstration in the *Meno* as a case in point.[98] In this dialogue, geometrical knowledge is portrayed as the realization of some latent capacity within the student. The philosopher does not supply knowledge but needles and cajoles and brings to fruition something already hidden inside the mind of the learner. Hence the picturesque metaphor of the philosopher as midwife, someone who helps the pregnant knower give birth to an understanding they somehow already possess.[99]

We must place Aristotle's account of induction within the context of this Platonic background. Aristotle, like Socrates, conceives of induction as a process of the mind gaining momentum. The knower is pushed, prodded, pulled to a culminating insight. If, however, Plato presents Socrates, the embodiment of dialectical philosophy, as the midwife who induces childbirth, it is the act of sense perception that becomes the midwife in Aristotle. In Aristotle, the *observation* of particular cases replaces Dame Philosophy as the impetus of knowledge. It is no longer philosophy understood as dialectic but the scientific examination of the physical world that brings us to a deeper understanding of reality.

W.D. Ross alleges that Aristotle uses the word *epagoge* in three different ways. In the first case, it refers to perfect induction, a theory we have already

96 *Metaphysics*, bk 13, ch. 4, 1078b25–30.

97 See, for example, Plato, *Republic*, bk 1, 331e–336a. Two key concepts relating to Socratic induction are (ὁ) ἔλεγχος (*elenchus*), which means a kind of dialectical refutation, and ἀπορία (*aporia*), which means roughly, a puzzle. See *Theaetetus*, in Cornford, *Plato's Theory of Knowledge*, 184.

98 Hamlyn, "Aristotelian *Epagoge*," 168, 170–171.

99 Plato, *Theaetetus*, 149a–151d.

discounted. In the second case, it refers to "a mode of argument from particulars which merely tends to produce belief ... without proving it."[100] In the third, it is "the psychological preparation upon which knowledge ... supervenes,"[101] "the flash of insight by which we pass from knowledge of a particular fact to ... the corresponding general principle."[102] I have already criticized Ross' first definition, but the second is more helpful. As Ross suggests, the main goal of Aristotelian induction is discernment. It illuminates the mind. The goal of induction is not simply to *prove* that something is the case but to provoke an understanding of the general case. And yet, Ross' description of induction as something which tends to produce belief is much too weak. For Aristotle, induction grasps the true nature of things. It is not about producing just any belief, but the right, true, universal, necessary, scientific belief.

Ross' third definition also captures a crucial aspect of Aristotelian meaning. Present-day authors tend to overlook the creative element, the inspirational "flash" that precedes or accompanies or motivates the leap to the universal. John Venn, writing in the nineteenth century, explains that induction begins with "a stroke of insight or creative genius."[103] This is more in line with the Aristotelian model – except that this creative leap of mental insight is not, as Ross suggests, merely psychological but properly epistemological or even metaphysical. It produces knowledge, not merely a psychological state. It is not a state of excitement that precedes knowledge; it is the mental movement of cognition that grasps whatever is to be known.

Generally speaking, we might distinguish between three ways of understanding Aristotelian *epagoge*: (1) the method of empirical inspection that inductive reasoning depends on; (2) the cognitive/psychological mechanism that produces the leap of insight; or (3) the argument (syllogism) that results. The method of empirical inspection, considered in and of itself, is just careful observation. It is not an argument. It cannot be valid or invalid. The cognitive mechanism that unleashes the leap to the universal is also not an argument. It is an act of discernment, of directly apprehending the truth. It may produce a claim that is true, but only an argument can be valid or invalid. That leaves us with the inductive syllogism. As I shall demonstrate, on Aristotle's account, inductive syllogisms are valid.

100 Ross, *Aristotle's Prior and Posterior Analytics*, 50.

101 Ibid., 49.

102 Ibid., 50.

103 Venn, *Principles*, 351.

BILELESS ANIMALS

In the famous passage about bileless animals, Aristotle, in fact, compares deductive and inductive arguments.[104] His reasoning loses its force, because it depends on an outdated model of biology. Nonetheless, we can make logical sense of it. I will, in what follows, suggest ways of translating his more obscure technical vocabulary into a more contemporary idiom.

First, a word about Aristotle's biological beliefs. Aristotle claims that animals without a gallbladder, those that lack bile, are long lived. This appears puzzling to the modern reader, but a perusal of his biological works makes his rationale clear. Aristotle believes that bile cleans the blood. In *Parts of Animals* he explains "the bile is not for the sake of anything, but a purifying excretion."[105] It is mostly found in animals with dirty or "bitter" blood (which Aristotle associates with excrement).[106] Animals "whose liver is healthy in composition and supplied with none but sweet blood, are either entirely without a gallbladder … or have merely small bile-containing vessels."[107] He concludes, "It was therefore no bad saying of old writers that the absence of a gallbladder gave long life."[108] In other words, bileless (or gallbladderless) animals live long because they have good, healthy, sweet blood (that does not need to be purified). Animals with (an appreciable amount of) bile are not long lived, because their blood is impure.[109] This is why bilelessness is a physiological sign of health.

Aristotle intends the induction about bileless animals as a scientific inference, one that uncovers the physiological cause of a biological phenomenon. He is not, in his own mind, trying to prove some novel scientific discovery; he is repeating a piece of uncontroversial, proverbial wisdom and demonstrating both how knowledge of this biological fact could logically arise and how it could be formally stated in a proper scientific theory. His inductive syllogism about bileless animals must be inserted into a larger account of scientific methodology that includes both deduction and induction. As Biondi explains, science involves two "intellectual motions,

104 *Prior Analytics*, bk 2, ch. 23, 68b8–36.

105 *Parts of Animals* (Ogle), bk 4, ch. 2, 677a30–31.

106 "For the very meaning of excrement is that it is the opposite of nutriment, and of bitter that is the opposite of sweet; and healthy blood is sweet" (*Parts of Animals* [Ogle], bk 4, ch. 2, 677a28–30).

107 Ibid., bk 4, ch. 2, 677a19–21.

108 Ibid., bk 4, ch. 2, 677a32–33.

109 "When animals are formed of blood less pure in composition, the bile is the residue left by this" (ibid., bk 4, ch. 2, 677a26–27).

which ... can be respectively referred to as de-duction, leading down (or out) from a universal, and in-duction, leading up (or in) to a universal."[110] For purposes of illustration, construct first the relevant deduction about bileless animals and then go on to show how this reasoning differs, in principle, from the corresponding induction about bileless animals.

Aristotle explicitly refers to "particular long-lived [bileless] animals: such as men, horses, mules."[111] Construct, then, the corresponding deduction. According to standard usage, define the terms in the syllogism as follows: subject term (*S*), men, horses, mules, etc.; predicate term (*P*), long-lived animals; and middle term (*M*), bileless animals. In this *metaphysically correct* arrangement of a deductive syllogism, the subject term is a substance or a group of substances; the predicate, a property we attribute to that substance; and the middle, a nature or essence making that substance what it is. A proper deduction using these terms would have to run, "All bileless animals are long lived. All men, horses, mules, etc., are bileless. Therefore, all men, horses, mules, etc., are long lived." The syllogism can be represented symbolically. Major premise: All *M* is *P*. Minor premise: All *S* is *M*. Conclusion: Therefore, all *S* is *P* (Barbara).

Aristotle writes that the terms in an induction appear in a different order. Instead of having a middle term joining the two extremes, we have a subject term that allows us to join the middle to the predicate term. If the deduction runs, "All bileless animals are long lived; all men, horses, mules, etc., are bileless; therefore, all men, horses, mules, etc., are long lived" – the corresponding inductive argument runs, "All men, horses, mules, etc., are long lived; all men, horses, mules, etc., are bileless; therefore, all bileless animals are long lived." Using the same definition of terms, we are left with the following. Major premise: All *S* is *P*. Minor premise: All *S* is *M*. Conclusion: Therefore, all *M* is *P*. This arrangement of terms constitutes, then, a true inductive argument.

In a deductive argument, we prove that a property belongs to a substance because it possesses a certain nature; in an inductive one, we prove that a property belongs to a nature because it belongs to individual substances possessing that nature. Expressed formally, deduction proves that the subject is associated with a predicate by means of the middle term; induction, that the middle is associated with the predicate by means of the subject term.[112] Aristotle does not claim that the inductive syllogism is

110 Biondi, *Aristotle*, §3.1, 192.

111 *Prior Analytics* (Tredennick), bk 2, ch. 23, 58b20–22. Recall, Jenkinson translates the passage "the particular long-lived animals, e.g. man, horse, mule" (see note 81).

112 *Prior Analytics*, bk 2, ch. 23, 68b31–35.

invalid, but only that the terms in an induction have been rearranged. In deduction, the middle term joins the two extremes; in induction, one extreme, the subject term, acts as the middle term, joining the true middle term with the other extreme.

This formal account may seem problematic, for the induction outlined above is clearly invalid. This can be easily shown. Following standard usage, where "A" denotes a universal affirmation, "u" signifies an undistributed term, and "d," a distributed one, we can represent our syllogism thus: *S*d A *P*u. *S*d A *M*u. *M*d A *P*u.[113] This syllogism clearly violates, however, the second rule of syllogisms that any term distributed in the conclusion must be distributed in the premises. (The middle term is distributed in the conclusion, but it is not distributed in the premises.) And so we are left, it seems, with an invalid argument.

We may use the popular Venn-diagram method to make the same point. Where shading indicates that the designated domain is known to be empty, we can illustrate the premises and conclusion of the above argument as in figure 3.2. As the diagram makes clear, the two premises, even taken together, do not include all the information contained in the conclusion, for the conclusion makes claims about the domain of *M*-by-itself, whereas the premises do not provide any information relating to this area. So the conclusion makes a larger claim than the premises; the conclusion is not contained in the premises. It follows that the premises could be true while the conclusion is false, so the argument is invalid.

While this inductive syllogism seems, at first glance, invalid, Aristotle proposes a remedy. His solution appeals to the notion of convertible terms. In ancient logic, convertible terms possess an identical extension.[114] If, for example, we were to believe (like ancient and mediaeval thinkers) that fire is the cause of all heat, then the terms "fire" and "heat" would be convertible. Every instance of fire would be one of heat, and every instance of heat would be one of fire. Again, if we claimed that the terms "bird" and "feathered" were convertible, every instance of "bird" would have to be one of "feathered," and every instance of "feathered" would have to be one of a "bird."[115] What has this to do with our inductive syllogism?

Aristotle observes that the subject and middle terms in the minor premise (All *S* is *M*) of the inductive syllogism are "convertible" (in Greek, ἀντιστρέφω or *antistrepho*: literally, to turn to the other side). The terms "men, horses, mules, etc.," and "bileless animals" are, in effect,

113 See Leo Groarke et al., *Good Reasoning Matters*, 101–39.

114 See Maritain, *Introduction to Logic*, 258ff.

115 Icarus is not a bird, but his wings are an artificial contrivance.

Figure 3.2
Venn diagrams of premises and conclusion

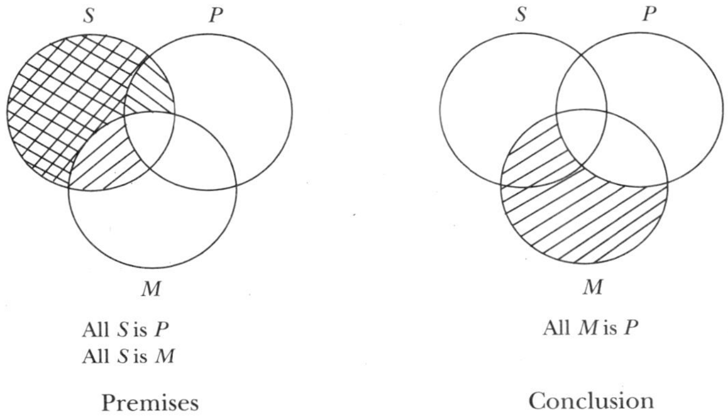

interchangeable. They possess the same extension. It follows that we can rewrite the minor premise, "All *S* is *M*" as "All *M* is *S*."[116] And we can rewrite the entire argument: All *S* is *P*. (All *S* is *M*, convertible to) All *M* is *S*. Therefore, all *M* is *P*. But this leaves us with a valid syllogism (Barbara).

The standard formalism can be extended to deal with the special case of convertible terms. Invent a new operator "AA," which will stand for a convertible universal affirmation; that is, for that special type of categorical statement "All *S* is *P*" that is to be read as both "All *S* is *P*" and as "All *P* is *S*." (The relationship of an AA statement to an A statement is analogous to that of a bi-conditional and a conditional statement in propositional logic.) In an AA statement, the universal predication runs, so to speak, in both directions. It will follow that both terms will be distributed in an AA statement, for the specified relation includes the complete extension of both terms. We may, then, formalize the above induction: *S*d A *P*u. *S*d AA *M*d. *M*d A *P*u. But this syllogism is valid, for the middle term (*M*) distributed in the conclusion is also distributed in the second (minor) premise, and the argument violates none of the other rules.

We can make the same point with a Venn diagram. Depict an *S* AA *P* statement as in figure 3.3, where the shading indicates that the area in *S* outside *P* and the area in *P* outside *S* is empty. We may, then, diagram our inductive syllogism as in figure 3.4. It is clear from the diagram that the information contained in the conclusion is already contained in the two premises.

116 See *Prior Analytics*, bk 2, ch. 23, 68b23–29.

Figure 3.3
Venn diagram of *S* AA *P* statement

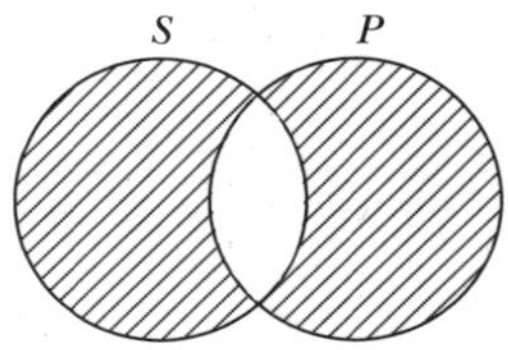

SAAP

{ All *S* is *P*
  All *P* is *S*

Note: AA, convertible universal affirmation

Figure 3.4
Venn diagram of Aristotle's inductive syllogism

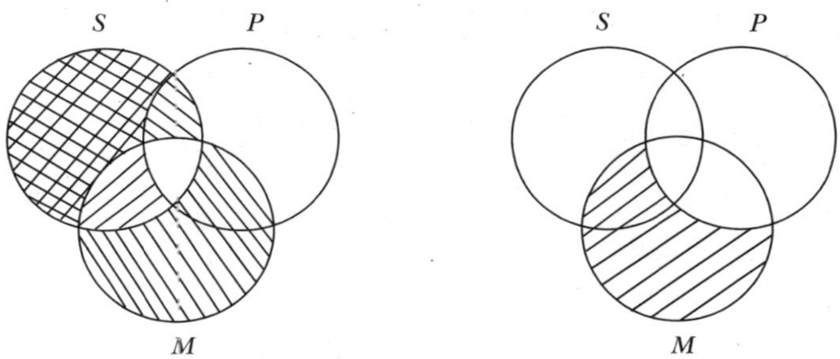

All *S* is *P*
All *S* is *M* }
All *M* is *S* }
Premises

All *M* is *P*
Conclusion

Because the empty (shaded) area in the conclusion is shaded in the premise diagram, the conclusion is guaranteed by the premises. If the premises are true, the conclusion must be true. So we have a valid syllogism.

As the preceding analysis indicates, the distinction between deductive and inductive arguments in Aristotle does not hinge on the issue of logical validity. It has to do with the arrangement of the terms. Induction is valid because the subject term and the middle term in an inductive syllogism are convertible. To say that these terms are convertible is, in effect, to place an equal sign between them; it is to say that *S* = *M*. If, however, *S* = *M*, then all *M* is *S*. Reformulating the minor premise in this way secures the validity of the argument.

CONVERTIBILITY

In *Topics,* Aristotle writes that "every predicate of a subject must be convertible with its subject or not."[117] The two conditions for convertibility (or counter-predication) are uniqueness and necessity. In the case of convertible terms "*S*" is "*P*," the extension of *S* and *P* must coincide. If the extension of the predicate term is larger than the extension of the subject term, the predicate is not *unique* to the subject and the terms are not convertible. Assume that the claim that "All fire trucks are red" is, in fact, true. Still, the subject term, "fire trucks," and the predicate term, "red," are not convertible, because redness is not a unique property of fire trucks. Not every instance of "red" is equally an instance of a "fire truck." Autumn leaves are red; songbirds are red; radishes are red – and so on. While the extension of the predicate is smaller than that of the subject term, however, the predicate is not a *necessary* property of the subject and the terms are not convertible. If, for example, I make the true claim that "Every human being is a math teacher," the subject, "human being," and the predicate, "math teacher," are not convertible, because human beings are not necessarily math teachers. Every "human being" is not an instance of a "math teacher." So the terms "human being" and "math teacher" are not interchangeable. (In this kind of case, the claim is inevitably false.)

In most propositions, subject and predicate terms are not convertible. But this is not always the case. Aristotle, for example, would claim that the term "human being" is convertible with the definition "rational animal." In other words, all the individual instances of human being added up together exactly coincide with all those of rational animals. The two groups are interchangeable for they share the very same members. This relationship of convertibility obtains because of the objective nature of things.

Aristotle writes that convertible terms are either definitions (i.e., essential traits) or properties.[118] This terminology is (as we shall see) too narrow, but it demonstrates Aristotle's basic attitude. To say that the term "mankind, horse, mule, etc.," is convertible with the term "bileless animals" is to say that all the individual instances of "mankind, horse, mule, etc.," added

117 *Topics* (Pickard-Cambridge), bk 1, ch. 8, 103b5–15. See also *Topics,* bk 1, ch. 5, 17–20.

118 "If [the predicate term] is convertible, it would be a definition or a property, for if it signifies the essence, it is the definition; if not, it is a property" (*Topics* [Pickard-Cambridge], bk 1, ch. 8, 103b5–15). Again, see also *Topics,* bk 1, ch. 5, 17–20.

together, are equivalent to (they constitute the extension of) "bileless animals." This is not to make the silly claim that we have investigated all individual instances of bileless animals. It is to say something about how the world is, not about how we discovered the way it is. Inspecting even a small group of men, horses, and mules is equivalent to inspecting all bileless animals, for all these animals share an identical constitution. Once we identify the properties of one animal with this constitution, we identify those of all animals with this constitution. The author of the inductive syllogism comes to realize that "the extensions of these terms are identical." This is what inductive reasoning is about.

This point bears repeating. Suppose we have a large collection of identical statues. To examine a small number of statues or even a single one is tantamount to examining every one, for they are all the same. Each succeeding examination will be a mere repetition of the one before. We will be doing what we have already done. This is the sense of the dependence of Aristotle's account of the inductive syllogism on "an enumeration of all cases." There is no physical, but an *in principle*, examination of all cases. We can even reconstruct the moment of biological discovery captured by the inductive syllogism about bileless animals.

Suppose the ancient biologist notices that "mankind, horse, mule, etc.," are long lived. He or she wonders why this is the case and begins dissecting specimens. In the course of the inspection, the biologist comes to see that mankind, the horse, and the mule do not have a gallbladder (or only a small gallbladder), and the biologist suddenly understands, "So this is the cause of longevity; they have clean rather than dirty blood!" This is the process of discovery the bileless syllogism parallels. In discovering the cause of longevity, the biologist is able to attribute the property of longevity to an entire class. Because bileless animals have the cause of longevity within them, they are long lived. That is, they will be long lived if they are allowed to realize their natural potential.

We moderns misconstrue Aristotle's intentions. He is not saying that every bileless animal is long lived (which is plainly false). Nor is he saying that the biologist physically inspects every bileless animal to see if it is long lived (which would be an impossible feat). He is saying that attentively observing some bileless animals can spur the leap to the understanding, "bilelessness causes longevity." The syllogism that springs out of this realization counts as a valid inference because the bileless animals we observe possess the same internal constitution and are therefore interchangeable with other bileless animals. This is the sense in which the term "mankind, horse, mule, etc.," is convertible with the term "bileless animals." Understanding why even one of these animals is long lived is the same as understanding why all of them are so.

We must be careful not to overstate the case. Aristotle's inductive syllogism about bileless animals uncovers a cause of longevity. But Aristotle is not saying that bilelessness is the *only* cause of longevity. Elsewhere in the *Posterior Analytics* he notes that bilelessness results in longevity in quadrupeds, whereas "the cause of longevity ... in birds [is] a dry constitution – or certainly something different."[119] In any inductive syllogism, the subject and the middle terms must be convertible. As we shall see, however, the subject and the predicate terms in a syllogism may also be convertible. This is not the case in Aristotle's bileless-animals syllogism. The predicate term "long lived" is not convertible with the subject term "mankind, horse, mule, etc." Although bileless animals such as "mankind, horse, mule, etc.," are all long lived, Aristotle believes that there are other non-bileless animals such as birds that are also long lived. So the terms "mankind, horse, mule, etc.," and "long lived" are not interchangeable. Their extensions do not exactly coincide.

The modern reader with queasy sensibilities may still resist the notion that inductive arguments are valid. In *An Enquiry Concerning Human Understanding*, Hume claims that although we infer (or seem to infer) the conclusion of inductive arguments, "no one has ever been able to discover any connecting proposition or intermediate step, which supports the [resulting] conclusion."[120] Aristotle adds an implicit step – in effect, a hidden premise – to his account of inductive reasoning. When we see the convertibility of subject and middle terms, this secures the validity of inductive syllogisms. The difference boils down to two different metaphysics. Aristotle accepts the reliability of an identity relation like convertibility, whereas Hume does not. Those who dispute the validity of Aristotelian induction sometimes appeal to specific passages in the *Posterior Analytics.* This is to take such comments out of context. We shall investigate these specific passages in detail in the next chapter. (Note that Eaton claims that Aristotle's "so-called inductive syllogism" is not really a true syllogism, since it contains an extra premise, the claim that the terms are convertible.[121] This seems a bit of a quibble. I will show how inductive syllogisms can be put into a structure consistent with the usual formalism in chapter 6.)

119 *Analytica Posteriora* (Mure), bk 2, ch. 17, 99b.5.

120 Hume, *Enquiry* (Selby-Bigge, Nidditch), §4, pt 2, para. 22.

121 Eaton, *General Logic*, 487.

EVERY INDUCTIVE ARGUMENT CONSIDERED AS AN INDUCTIVE SYLLOGISM

Although induction, in its most proper Aristotelian sense, is about the necessary properties of things, we could use the same syllogistic form to formulate *any* inductive argument. Clarke (writing in 1889) explains,

> Induction comes into Logic as reducible to syllogistic form … This is true of both Complete and Incomplete Induction … For instance, [suppose] I argue from the fact that I have observed on a number of separate days … [that] a gradual fall in the barometer [has] been followed by rain: [I can] state the result of my observation in the following premises:
>
> January 18th, March 4th, April 7th, October 19th were succeeded by rainy weather;
>
> January 18th, March 4th, April 7th, October 19th were days when there was a fall of the barometer;
>
> ∴ All the days on which there is a fall of the barometer are days followed by rainy weather.
>
> In order that the conclusion may hold true in strict logic, I must be able to assert that January 18th, March 4th, April 7th, October 19th were all the days when there was a fall in the barometer, and this is obviously ridiculous. But may I not … say: *What is true of January 18th etc. is true of all days when there is a fall in the barometer.* If I can, the conclusion certainly follows, and I can rearrange my syllogism in a convenient form of the first figure and argue thus:
>
> What is true of January 18th, March 4th, April 7th, October 19th is true of all days when the barometer falls;
>
> Rain near at hand is true of January 18th, March 4th, April 7th, October 19th.
>
> ∴ Rain near at hand is true of all days on which the barometer falls.[122]

We can reformulate Clarke's induction in Aristotelian form. Define our terms as follows: *S*, days such as 18 January, 4 March, 7 April, 19 October, etc.; *P*, days followed by rainy weather; and *M*, days with a falling barometer.

The induction runs, "All days such as 18 January (etc.) are those followed by rainy weather. All days such as 18 January (etc.) are those when

122 R. Clarke, *Logic*, 380–1.

the barometer falls. Therefore, all days when the barometer falls are those followed by rainy weather." In symbols, "All *S* is *P.* (All *S* is *M*, convertible to) All *M* is *S.* Therefore, all *M* is *P.*" This is a valid inductive syllogism, not because it is a perfect induction but because the *S* and *M* terms are (allegedly) convertible. The claim is that the subject term, "days such as 18 January, 4 March, 7 April, 19 October, etc.," and the middle term, "days when the barometer falls," are interchangeable. Because "days such as 18 January, etc.," possess the very same nature as "days when the barometer falls," what is true of one must be true of the other. This claim that the two terms are convertible may, of course, be false, but the argument is still valid. It follows *necessarily* that if the premises of this argument (including the claim about convertibility) are true, the conclusion must follow. That is all we need for validity.

Aristotle does not conceive of the inductive syllogism as a statistical argument. But even statistical inductions could be cast into the general form of an inductive syllogism. Suppose we set out to study premature morbidity among smokers. We study three sample populations, *A*, *B*, and *C*, and discover that more than 15 per cent of smokers in each sample die before they reach the age of fifty. We conclude that more than 15 per cent of smokers die before they reach the age of fifty. We can easily express this line of reasoning as an inductive syllogism. Define our terms: *S*, individual sample populations such as *A*, *B*, *C* (etc.); *P*, having a morbidity rate of more than 15 per cent for individuals less than fifty years old; and *M*, populations of smokers. The inductive syllogism will take the form, "All sample populations *A*, *B*, *C*, etc., have a 15-per-cent mortality rate for individuals less than fifty years old. All sample populations *A*, *B*, *C*, etc., are populations of smokers. Therefore, all populations of smokers have a 15-per-cent mortality rate for individuals under fifty years old." Symbolically, "All *S* is *P.* (All *S* is *M*, convertible to) All *M* is *S.* Therefore, all *M* is *P.*"

This argument hinges, once again, on the claim that the *S* and *M* terms are convertible. To claim that these terms are convertible is to say that the term "individual sample populations such as *A*, *B*, *C*, etc.," is interchangeable with the term "populations of smokers." But this reduces to the equivalent claim made by modern logicians that in a sound induction, sample populations must be representative of the target. To say that "individual sample populations such as *A*, *B*, *C*, etc.," are representative of "populations of smokers" is to say that these various groups possess the same nature; they must be, in the relevant sense, interchangeable with one another. Statistical inductions differ significantly from those Aristotle contemplated, but we will discuss these issues further in chapter 4.

SWANS SWIM OVER THE SEA: THE PROBLEM OF INDUCTION

Contemporary logicians have been intensely preoccupied with the "problem of induction" that arises because of the widespread view that inductive arguments are invalid. The challenge has been to somehow rescue induction from infamy by some careful tweaking of the logical form. Seen from an Aristotelian perspective, the problem with bad examples of induction is not invalidity but the falsehood of premises. Consider the ubiquitous (and admittedly tiresome) textbook example of white and black swans, used to show that inductive arguments must be invalid.[123] This trope is often accompanied by a story. Everyone (in Europe) assumed swans are white; that is, they induced the general conclusion "all swans are white." But then black swans were discovered in Australia. So induction is unreliable.[124]

But is this induction truly an invalid inference? As modern-day deductivists point out, natural-language arguments usually contain hidden elements. We need to fill in the blanks to understand what is going on. In the present instance, what Europeans were (allegedly) assuming seems clear. They were assuming that all swans possess the same colour. They reasoned, informally: These birds are white; these birds are swans; all swans are the same colour; therefore, all swans must be white. Note, however, that this is a *valid* argument. If the premises are all true, then the conclusion must be true. Of course, the premises are not all true. All swans are not the same colour. But that has no bearing on the issue of validity.

Note that the hidden premise "all swans have the same colour" is not a mere repetition of the other premises. It makes a different kind of claim. It assumes, in effect, that the term "these particular birds" and the term "swans" are, with respect to colour, convertible. This identification of the two terms is more of an assumption than an inference. (It does not require the kind of insight Aristotle associates with induction.) Still, we can try to formalize the argument in Aristotelian terms. Define our terms: *S*, these particular birds; *P*, white birds; and *M*, swans. The Europeans (allegedly) reasoned, "These particular birds are white birds. These particular birds

123 For an early reference to the "problem" of black swans, see Bowen, *Treatise on Logic*, 392: "But to Europeans, not many years ago, the proposition 'All swans are white', appeared an equally unequivocal instance of uniformity in the course of nature. Further experience proved they were mistaken."

124 Williams, for example, writes, "The inductive premise that, say, all the observed swans in an observed group, no matter how many, have been white, cannot contradict the supposition that other swans are not white" (*Ground of Induction*, 31).

are swans, convertible to all swans are (equivalent to) these particular birds. Therefore, all swans must be the same colour as these birds; i.e., all swans must be white." Despite the awkward phrasing, this is a valid argument. It fits the following form. Major premise: All *S* is *P.* Minor premise: (All *S* is *M,* convertible to) all *M* is *S.* Conclusion: Therefore, all *M* is *P.* As it turns out, the subject and middle terms are not convertible. At least when it comes to colour, the nature of these individual birds is *not* interchangeable with the nature of all swans. Whiteness is not a necessary property of swans. The argument goes astray then, because the hidden premise about convertibility is false, not because of something inherently wrong with the logical form.

The sceptic may object that we can never know whether the claim about convertibility is true. But even if we cannot know whether these white swans are interchangeable with other swans (in terms of colour), this would still be a valid argument. The argument *posits* convertibility. It assumes that these white swans are interchangeable or representative (in the relevant sense) with all other swans. If we can never know whether this is true, we will never know if the premises in the argument are true. But this does not detract from the validity of the argument. The argument only tells us that the conclusion must follow, *if* convertibility holds. Whether this is, in fact, the case is another issue.

Donald Williams writes, "If we could ... demonstrate, using deductive principles in the process, that the premise of an induction entails its conclusion in accordance with ... [the] principles of deductive logic, then we should have solved the problem of induction with supreme *éclat.*"[125] Aristotle, it would seem, has already "solved the problem of induction with supreme *éclat,*" except that modern authors do not acknowledge his achievement. As we discuss in later chapters, the problem of induction should be seen as an artefact of a certain metaphysical view. It is not that no formal solution to the problem of induction exists; it is that we have forgotten the solution proposed by Aristotle.

CONVERTIBILITY AND RESEMBLANCE

I have already argued elsewhere that Aristotelian induction makes an implicit appeal to a law of identity or resemblance.[126] In *Topics,* Aristotle declares, "The examination of likeness ... is useful for inductive arguments, because it is by means of ... cases that are alike that we claim to bring the

125 Ibid.

126 Louis Groarke, "Deductive Account of Induction," 360–1.

universal in evidence."[127] Again, in the *Posterior Analytics,* he claims that induction operates on the principle "that every case is like this, because none is otherwise."[128] Induction deals, then, with similar cases. All bileless animals are long lived because they all possess the *same* nature. Because they resemble one another, they must share the same fundamental properties.

We cannot do justice to the Aristotelian notion of resemblance, however, without making reference to essence or nature. Resemblance is more than skin deep. Despite individual differences, Aristotle believes that things can be separated into fundamental groups or kinds of things. Aristotle limits rigorous science to necessary properties, to those indispensable traits that remain the same from individual to individual in a single species. Later authors in the tradition follow suit. Medieval commentator John of St Thomas presents the following induction: "This fire warms, and this one, and this one, etc. Therefore, every fire warms."[129] The proposed line of reasoning is not simply that all fires resemble one another, so all fires produce heat. The argument is that because all fires are the same thing, they must possess the same necessary (or defining) attributes, so all fires must produce heat.[130] Heat is both an essential and a necessary property of fire. This is why the induction works. Despite superficial differences, wherever there is fire, we can confidently conclude, there must be heat.

On Aristotle's account, claims about convertibility and identity go together. To claim that these individual fires are convertible with all other fires is to claim that they all share the same fundamental nature. Because every fire is the presence of an identical nature, what is fundamentally true of one instance of fire *must* be so of all others. If producing heat is what fire is, all fires must produce heat. Nothing is incorrect or illogical about this line of thinking. It applies to all necessary properties. (Aristotle's account may be adapted to accidental attributes as well, a possibility we discuss later.)

Because Aristotle's account of induction depends crucially on a relationship of identity or resemblance, the number of specimens examined is not a central issue. If we have identical objects *A* and *B*, then what is true of *A* must be true of *B*. When we have examined *A*, we have no need to examine *B*. It is often assumed that we need large numbers of samples to come to

127 The line finishes, "for it is not easy to do this if we do not know the points of likeness" (*Topics* [Pickard-Cambridge], bk 1, ch. 18, 108b7–12).

128 This is from a discussion of definitions which we consult below. *Posterior Analytics* (Tredennick), bk 2, ch. 7, 92a25–30.

129 John of St Thomas, *Outlines of Formal Logic* (Wade), bk 3, ch. 2, 104.

130 We can already see a subtle change here from Aristotle's original position. The emphasis is on the frequency of the property, less on understanding causality.

credible inductive conclusions, but this is not always the case. Suppose object *A* is identical to several million *A* copies. Once we have examined *A*, we have in principle examined several million *A* copies. Because Aristotle believes that fundamental identity exists in the world, he believes in the possibility of inductive reasoning.

McKirahan explains, "*Epagoge* does not require a large number of cases, just enough for the individual in question to recognize the common principle or element in the cases given."[131] Indeed, Aristotle claims that a valid inductive argument may be based on a single observation. In the *Posterior Analytics,* he discusses the question, "Why is glass transparent?" He claims that if we had microscopic vision and could see the tiny pores in the glass the light passes through, we would know *in every instance* why light shines through glass. With a single observation, we would have "grasped something universal from seeing. E.g. if we saw the glass to be perforated and the light coming through it … [we would understand] at one time that it is thus in every case."[132] Aristotelian inductive reasoning is not about the enumeration of repeated instances but the understanding of the most fundamental causes of things.

The induction based on a single instance of light passing through transparent glass may, of course, be set up as an inductive syllogism. $Premise_1$: This object has pores that let light shine through. $Premise_2$: This object is transparent glass. Conclusion: Therefore, all transparent glass has pores which let light shine through. This is a valid syllogism because the subject term "this object" is convertible with the middle term "transparent glass." It is convertible because every piece of transparent glass, in order to be glass, must possess the same nature. Of course, Aristotle's explanation of the transparency of glass is inadequate, but that is another matter.

HASTY GENERALIZATION

Aristotle's account of induction stands in marked contrast to contemporary views. On the modern view, the main problem with faulty induction is not a lack of insight. It is that we do not look at enough samples. We jump to conclusions too quickly. The fundamental error is "hasty generalization." The attack on hasty generalization can be traced all the way back to

131 He continues, "The number needed will depend on the aptitude of the individual and the value of the cases, in some situations a single case will suffice" (McKirahan, *Principles and Proofs*, 251).

132 *Posterior Analytics* (Barnes), bk 1, ch. 31, 88a10–18 (in Aristotle, *Complete Works*).

Francis Bacon's impatience with glib metaphysical assumptions. When it comes to induction, Bacon privileges the steady, incremental accumulation of empirical evidence. The right way "of searching into and discovering truth," Bacon tells us, is to use a gradualist method that "derives general principles from the senses and particulars, rising gradually and continually, so that it arrives at the most general principles last of all."[133] The great mistake is jumping the gun, generalizing too quickly before accumulating sufficient evidence. Contemporary textbooks in informal logic carry on the tradition. They put on display a prominent list of errors, all stemming from the same basic oversight: the fallacy of "hasty generalization" or "appeal to anecdotal evidence,"[134] the "fallacy of generalization from too few cases";[135] "insufficient sample";[136] "fallacy of insufficient statistics";[137] "glittering generality";[138] "converse accident,"[139] and "*secundum quid.*"[140] In the specialized literature, Douglas Walton distinguishes, in a more qualified way, between universal (or absolute), inductive, and presumptive (or defeasible) generalizations.[141] Our purpose here is not to do an in-depth review of fallacy theory, but to simply note, in passing, how the basic thrust of contemporary concern is at odds with Aristotle's original mentality.

Because most modern authors tend to view induction in numerical terms, they also tend to insist that perfect or complete induction is the only certain form of inductive inference. The only way we could be sure that all swans are white is by looking at every swan. And the only way we can be sure that every fire produces heat is by examining every fire. The problem is, of course, that we must invariably rely on incomplete induction. It follows, as a matter of course, that the second-best form of inductive argument is an incomplete one approaching as closely as possible completeness. As a rough rule of thumb, the more samples the better.

133 Bacon, *New Organon*, bk 1, aphorism 19 (various documents).

134 Engel, *Analyzing Informal Fallacies*, 43; Toulmin, *Introduction to Reasoning*, 151–5, 173; Kelly, *Art of Reasoning*, 266–267; Leo Groarke et al., *Good Reasoning Matters*, 219; Conway and Munson, *Elements of Reasoning*, 129; Woods and Walton, *Argument*, 65; and Govier, *Practical Study of Argument*, 344.

135 Fearnside and Holther, *Fallacy*, 13.

136 Damer, *Attacking Faulty Reasoning*, 109–10.

137 Salmon, *Logic* (3rd ed.), 56.

138 Woods and Walton, *Argument*, 65.

139 Hurely, *Concise Introduction to Logic*, 142–4; Copi and Cohen, *Introduction to Logic* (1994), 125.

140 Hamblin, *Fallacies*, 28–9, 46–7; see also Woods and Walton, *Argument*, 65.

141 See, for example, Walton, "Rethinking"; and "Ignoring Qualifications."

The standard textbook explanation conceives of hasty generalization as a matter of "jumping to conclusions."[142] We commit a hasty generalization when we "generalize too quickly, on the basis of insufficient evidence."[143] This results in sweeping claims that have been drawn "from too small a sample."[144] Govier describes the problem in the usual fashion. Everyday generalizations are, she says, often "based on an exceedingly small number of sample cases – sometimes only one or two. A person rather carelessly assumes that the case or cases that have come to her attention are more than just episodes or isolated events; she [mistakenly] assumes, without sufficient warrant, that they indicate a general tendency or trend."[145]

Some contemporary theorists distinguish between two kinds of hasty generalization. Stephen Toulmin, for example, writes that "we commit fallacies of hasty generalization when we: (1) draw a general conclusion from too few specific instances ... or, alternatively, when we (2) draw a general conclusion from atypical examples."[146] But these do not seem to be separate mistakes. Suppose I commit mistake (1): I investigate "too few instances" of something. If I look at too few instances, I may unwittingly investigate atypical examples and be led to false conclusions. This is why this reasoning strategy is fallacious. So mistake (1) derives from the possibility of mistake (2). Suppose, however, I commit mistake (2): I investigate "exceptional rather than typical cases of something."[147] If I am confusing atypical and typical cases, this can only be because I have not looked at *enough* cases to realize that the one that I am investigating are atypical. So mistake (2) presupposes mistake (1). In both cases, the problem is the same: I have not scrutinized enough samples.[148]

In their discussion of hasty generalization, Moore and Parker cite a statistical rule of thumb: "anecdotes prove nothing."[149] In other words,

142 Leo Groarke, et al., *Good Reasoning Matters*, 219.

143 Kelly, *Art of Reasoning*, 266.

144 Damer, *Attacking Faulty Reasoning*, 109.

145 Govier, *Practical Study of Argument*, 344.

146 Toulmin, *Introduction to Reasoning*, 151.

147 Ibid., 173.

148 While many contemporary authors distinguish between reasoning from too few and from atypical examples, Woods and Walton, in a discussion of sampling methods, draw an analogous distinction between the fallacy of "insufficient statistics" and that of "biased statistics" (Woods and Walton, *Argument*, 66). This is a useful statistical distinction between the number of cases studied and the method employed for selecting them. Statistical analysis does not draw any distinction between necessary and accidental properties, as discussed below.

149 Moore and Parker, *Critical Thinking*, 396.

isolated instances based on particular personal experiences have no inductive weight. As they authors explain, “An anecdote that shows one or two Xs have feature f proves only that one or two Xs have feature f.” It “doesn’t prove anything about Xs in general.”[150] This is a standard view. We cannot move from a small number of samples to an accurate generalization. Clearly, this is not always true. I can conclude from the inspection of a single triangle that all triangles have interior angles that add up to 180 degrees (a favourite Aristotelian example). And I can conclude from the inspection of a single whale that all whales have lungs. Moore and Parker go on to concede that one can generalize from a few examples if the class being studied “is known to be very homogenous.”[151] But this is not very helpful. Triangles are not so homogenous: there are right triangles, obtuse or acute or equiangular triangles, scalene or isosceles or equilateral triangles, and so on. It is not the fact that specimens are homogenous that matters; what matters is that they happen to be homogenous in one very specific respect. S. Morris Engel more accurately explains that hasty generalizations may fail “because there is no essential connection between [the specified case] and the generalization it is called to support.”[152] But this is too strong. It is not an essential but only a necessary connection that is required. Having angles equal to 180 degrees is a necessary, not an essential, property of triangularity. What defines a triangle is the property of being a three-sided straight-line figure. It just so happens that three-sided figures inevitably have interior angles adding up to 180 degrees. If, however, we are dealing with necessary attributes, the conclusion of an inductive argument follows necessarily, *regardless of the number of cases examined.*

Walton’s specialized account of universal, inductive, and presumptive generalizations constitutes a useful enlargement of the received way of looking at the fallacy of hasty generalization. Mostly, Walton successfully shows that what he calls presumptive generalizations are not hasty after all. A presumptive generalization is a defeasible rule of thumb, with the onus on those who wish to dispute its application to particular circumstances. So, for example, the universal claim that “birds fly” is a good presumptive generalization, even though we all know that there are odd exceptions to this general rule. In other words, some few birds – ostriches, penguins, dodo birds, barnyard chickens – cannot fly. This does not defeat the presumptive generalization “birds fly.” Walton accuses those who attack presumptive generalizations of the logical error traditionally known as

150 Ibid., 396–7.

151 Ibid., 397.

152 Engel, *Analyzing Informal Fallacies*, 43.

secundum quid, the fallacy of interpreting, absolutely, something meant to be taken in one specific way, i.e., in a qualified sense.

Walton's account is useful and accurate and generally in line with the Aristotelian mentality that numerical exceptions do not always undermine an inductive generalization. Except that the diehard Aristotelian would complain that Walton does not go far enough. Presumptive generalizations report on the usual or expected case. Walton accepts that a few counterexamples do not invalidate the overall weight of the evidence. But a serious Aristotelian must go much further. He or she may have to argue that we can have true scientific generalizations *even when most or all examples run counter to the thrust of the generalization*. Consider a thought experiment.

Suppose that everyone in the world cut off the right foreleg of every dog as soon as it was born. (Not a logical impossibility.) Suppose every dog in this cruel world was a three-legged dog. A clear-thinking Aristotelian would still have to claim that the scientific generalization "dogs have four legs" is true. Why? Because the three-leggedness of all the observed examples is an artificial contrivance dependent on human intervention. It is an expression of human perversity, not a reflection on the true nature of dogs. The generalization "dogs have four legs," on the contrary, captures the true nature of dogs. Walton, like other contemporary authors, views induction as a report on numerical or statistical uniformity of samples. Aristotle views it as a report on the underlying reality.

Walton traces his account of the *secundum quid* fallacy back to Aristotle.[153] But he mostly concentrates on how we use generalizations once we have formulated them. In fact, the fallacy of hasty generalization can be traced back to a complaint about how we go about forming a universal claim in the first place. And Walton sheds no new light on this crucial issue. Indeed, he seems to embrace the usual modern view that we use valid inductive arguments to arrive at stronger or weaker generalizations, depending on the amount (i.e., the quantity) of evidence amassed in their support. Why, for example, is the presumptively universal claim, "birds fly," a good generalization? On the modern account, this is because countless observations confirm it. Aristotle goes more deeply. An inductive claim like "birds fly" would be a good generalization in his view because it captures what being a bird is all about. Flightless birds constitute a statistical violation of the all-birds-fly induction, but this is relatively unimportant, for they do not invalidate the more fundamental point that birds – even flightless birds – are winged animals because they are "designed" to fly. The induction correctly identifies a (necessary)

153 *De Sophisticis Elenchis* 16b38–167a21. He specifically mentions the Ethiopian is black fallacy.

link between flying and being a bird, a link which is not discredited by occasional or even multiple examples of flightless birds.

Aristotle views induction as a mode of discernment. Correct induction does not depend so much on multiplying examples but, more fundamentally, on the knower's discernment. It does not follow that hasty generalization is *always* wrong. Generalization on the basis of few samples may be a sign of intellectual superiority, rather than carelessness. Imagine a quick-witted and a slow-witted Archimedes. And suppose quick and slow Archimedes both come to the same "Eureka!" conclusion, that one can measure the volume of an irregular object by immersing it and measuring the water it displaces. Both come to this realization by observing their bathwater overflow. Except that quick Archimedes hits on this idea after a single bath, whereas slow Archimedes has to take three thousand baths, before the same conclusion eventually dawns on him. The truth is no different for each of these two conclusions. What differs is only that one process of intelligent discernment happens very slowly, while the other occurs very quickly. Clearly, quick Archimedes, the "hasty" reasoner, is more intelligent. He is not to be chastised because he thinks quickly.

Aristotle himself notices that some individuals are especially quick when it comes to understanding. He defines ἀγχίνοια (*anchinoïa*) – acumen, quick or sharp wit – as "a talent for hitting upon the middle term [the essence or nature of the thing] in an imperceptible time."[154] He offers some examples of *anchinoia*: the promising student of astronomy who rapidly understands that the moon's light comes from the sun and the shrewd entrepreneur, who immediately understands that someone is talking to a rich man in a certain way because he wants to borrow money from him.[155] The modern account of "quick reasoning" is too simple. It ignores the fact that insight depends, not merely on the amount of evidence, but on the mental quickness of the knower. The mathematical genius gets the point after a

154 *Posterior Analytics*, bk 1, ch. 34, 89b10–16. Mure translates "quick wit" (*Analytica Posteriora*, in Aristotle, Works of Aristotle); Apostle, "acutness" (in Aristotle, *Aristotle's Posterior Analytics*).

155 "Acumen is a talent for hitting upon the middle term [i.e. finding the essence through induction] in an imperceptible time; e.g. if someone sees that the moon always holds its bright side towards the sun and quickly grasps why this is – because it gets light from the sun; if he is aware that someone is talking to a rich man because he is borrowing money from him; or why they are friends – because they are enemies of the same man. For seeing the extremes (the subject and predicate) he becomes familiar with all the explanatory middle terms" (*Posterior Analytics* [Barnes], bk 1, ch. 34, 89b10–16).

single example; the mathematical dunce must slave mechanically over example after example before he or she understands. Faced with very little evidence, the streetwise con man knows what is going down; faced with a plethora of evidence, the foolish victim still does not understand. Some individuals are gifted with more mental quickness, more intellectual penetration than others.

Modern statistical methods of induction study accidental properties in vast populations with a rigor far beyond the scope of anything Aristotle could have imagined. They are peculiarly susceptible to the fallacy of hasty generalization. But this is because they treat induction as a mechanical algorithm rather than a process of intelligent discernment. Even Aristotle would agree that we can make mistakes in reasoning. We may reason too quickly without looking at enough examples, but Aristotelian induction depends on insight rather than the tabulation of numerical frequencies. So quick reasoning is not always a fallacy.

IDENTITY: SPECIES AND GENUS

As I have already indicated, induction presupposes sameness or resemblance. We can generalize from one case to another because both possess an identical nature. Consider more closely the concept of identity inductive reasoning presupposes.

Baruch Brody defines "identity" as "a relation that holds only between an object and itself."[156] But this is, more precisely, a definition of self-identity. This is not what we are interested in here. Most inductive arguments steer clear of applying what we have previously learned about a particular object to the very same object. More often, these arguments apply what we have learned to other objects. We need to enlarge the concept of identity to include relationships between discrete objects to account for inductive reasoning.

Inductive arguments are about objects identical in some important respects, not about those identical in every way. Robert Baum complains that induction is problematic because "no two states of affairs resemble each other exactly."[157] But this is to appeal to too strict a concept of identity. It sets too high a standard. Individual horses are not identical in every sense, yet we can make true inductive generalizations about horses. Induction has

156 *Encyclopedia of Philosophy*, s.v. "Glossary of Logical Terms" (by Baruch Brody). Is there really a relation between an object and itself? One wonders.

157 Baum, *Logic*, 322.

to do with the kind of identity that ties together the members of a single species or genus. Call this "shared identity."

Aristotle distinguishes between three kinds of identity: (1) numerical sameness, when different expressions refer to the same thing (e.g., "Socrates" and "the teacher of Plato," or "biped pedestrian animal" and "mankind"); (2) specific sameness, when we refer to different individual things that belong to the same species (e.g., "one and another instance of humanity," or "one horse and another horse"); and (3) generic sameness, when we refer to different individual things in the same genus (e.g., a horse and a human being, both being mammals).[158] We can parse out the logical form of induction in terms of kinds 2 and 3, if we appeal to a general principle of shared identity. This principle might be articulated in a variety of ways.

Joseph Gredt, in an old Thomist manual, proposes the following wording for the logical principle ultimately supportive of inductive reasoning: "a specific nature is the same in all the individuals of the same species, and a generic nature is the same in all the species of the same genus."[159] Simply put, members of the any natural category must possess the same nature or essence. Although this formulation of a principle of shared identity appeals to a certain medieval essentialism (which is hardly popular today), the precise wording of the principle is not as important as the general idea that membership in the same species or genus necessitates shared properties. We could express the same principle otherwise: members of the same natural kind possess the same natural properties; such individuals must resemble one another; they must share an identical nature – and so on. Whatever the precise wording, shared identity is a self-evident principle of logic. To claim that members of the same kind do not possess the same properties would be self-contradictory.

The role of induction is to look past individual differences to seize on fundamental similarities. Aristotle believed that because resemblance of the most fundamental sort exists in the world, this is enough to secure the usefulness of induction. The usual counter-examples to induction found in textbooks and the academic literature deal uncritically with contingent or accidental attributes. They do not defeat the principle of shared identity. If black and white swans differ in colour, this is because colour is a contingent characteristic of swans. But black and white swans are both swans: they both have feathers, webbed feet, long, slender necks, they both lay eggs, and so on.

158 *Topics*, bk 1, ch. 7, 103a–103b.

159 Gredt, *Elementa Philosophiae*, para. 77. Translation courtesy of Jason West.

Leave aside the syllogism, and recast inductions in a more familiar form as propositional arguments. Begin with a simple instance of inductive reasoning. Suppose we test a piece of copper wire and discover that it conducts electricity. We test a second, a third, and a fourth piece of copper wire and discover that they too conduct electricity. We conclude that copper wire conducts electricity. We might reason, "Premise$_1$: *a, b, c, d,* etc., are pieces of copper wire (observation). Premise$_2$: *a, b, c, d,* etc., conduct electricity (observation). Premise$_3$: anything that possesses the nature of copper wire must possess the same properties as *a, b, c, d,* etc. (principle of shared identity). Conclusion: all pieces of copper wire must conduct electricity (from premise$_1$, premise$_2$, and the hidden premise)."

The argument presupposes convertibility. Premise$_3$ tells us that the nature of *a, b, c, d,* etc., is interchangeable with the nature of copper wire generally. If, then, *a, b, c, d,* etc., conduct electricity, so must copper wire generally. This conclusion follows necessarily. If all the premises are true, the conclusion must be true. If the premises are false, the conclusion may or may not follow. The premises could be false if *a, b, c, d,* etc., are not pieces of copper wire, if *a, b, c, d,* etc., do not really conduct electricity, or if we misapply the principle of shared identity, because electrical conductivity is not a fundamental property of copper wire. Still, this is a valid argument. If the premises are true, the conclusion must be true. This is enough to secure validity.

Hume contends that the denial of the conclusion in an inductive argument "implies no contradiction."[160] But we cannot consistently deny the conclusion (that "all pieces of copper wire must conduct electricity") while asserting premise$_3$ (that "anything that possesses the nature of copper wire must have the nature of *a, b, c, d,* etc."). So the premises cannot be true and the conclusion false, which is just another way of saying that the argument is deductively valid.

Suppose, *per impossibile,* we found a piece of copper wire that did not conduct electricity. What would we do? Presumably, we would revisit our tests to make sure that this piece of copper wire really did not conduct electricity. If

160 Hume, *Enquiry* (Selby-Bigge, Nidditch), §4, pts 1–3. Hume cites several examples and employs this formula repeatedly. J.J.C. Smart tells us, "Hume showed conclusively that our belief that all past, present and future As are Bs cannot depend on a valid deductive argument from the fact that all hitherto observed As have been Bs. We cannot even deduce the much weaker proposition that the next observed A will be a B. His reason is a very simple one: there is no contradiction in asserting the proposition 'All observed As are Bs but some not yet observed As are not Bs'" (Smart, *Between Science and Philosophy,* 177).

this turned out to be the case, we would have to conclude *that we had discovered a different kind of copper.* We would have two kinds of copper, call them "copper$_C$" and "copper$_{non\text{-}C}$." Anything with the same nature as copper$_C$ would, and anything with that of copper$_{non\text{-}C}$ would not, conduct electricity. Our previous induction would, then, have to be restricted to copper$_C$ wire, not copper wire generally. The principle of shared identity would have to be applied to copper$_C$ and copper$_{non\text{-}C}$ separately.

Although science must make do with a finite set of observations, this does not invalidate the logical form of inductive reasoning. If we sometimes make mistakes adding up numbers, this does not invalidate arithmetic. Just so, if we make mistakes about shared identity, this does not invalidate the underlying idea that deep resemblance makes inductive arguments possible.

A STATISTICAL INDUCTION

This propositional account of induction could (like the inductive syllogism) be applied to any case of induction. Consider an argument from probability. Suppose someone were to argue, "Premise$_1$: You have caught one hundred fish from this lake. Premise$_2$: Seventy-five fish have stomach ulcers. Conclusion: About 75 per cent of the fish in this lake have stomach ulcers." Clearly, this is an induction. The argument moves from considering a specific subset of fish in this lake to a generalization about all fish in this lake. Although stomach ulcers are not an indispensable feature of being a fish in this lake, we can formulate this inductive inference as a valid argument.

Let us restate the argument, adding the hidden premise: "Premise$_1$: The one hundred fish you caught come from this lake (observation). Premise$_2$: Seventy-five of these fish have stomach ulcers (observation). Hidden premise: All the fish from the same lake as these fish must, in the relevant sense, possess the same properties as these one hundred fish (principle of shared identity). Conclusion: So about 75 per cent of these fish must have stomach ulcers (from premise$_1$, premise$_2$, and the hidden premise)." As the hidden premise reveals, this argument assumes the convertibility of these one hundred fish with fish in the lake generally. If the sample of one hundred fish and the entire population of fish in this lake share the same nature, the same percentage of fish will, in both cases, possess stomach ulcers. This may or may not be an accurate assumption. If, however, all the premises of this argument are true, the conclusion must follow. So this is a valid argument. If Hume and his followers discern a logical gap in inductive arguments, it is because they overlook the principle of shared identity, the hidden premise about convertibility. This is the logical step on which any induction depends.

Aristotle would not consider the inductive argument for stomach ulcers in fish to be a scientific demonstration. Stomach ulcers are not an essential or a necessary attribute of fish. Individual fish do not have stomach ulcers as a result of having the nature of fish. Nonetheless, this argument presupposes a mode of necessity. It is not that every individual fish must have stomach ulcers. It is that 75 per cent of this *population* of fish must have stomach ulcers. The necessity applies to the population rather than the individual. We will discuss the different kinds of induction in the next chapter.

MODERN SCEPTICISM ABOUT NECESSARY ATTRIBUTES

Aristotle conceives of induction as a form of inference pertaining most properly to essential or necessary properties. Contemporary authors, with notable exceptions, eschew any hint of essentialism. They reject, explicitly or implicitly, any clear distinction between essential (necessary) and accidental attributes. But frequency is not the same as necessity. To say that all observed *X*s have feature *Y* is not the same as saying that *Y* is a necessary or an essential property of *X*. To speak of the necessary or essential attributes is to provide an account of a thing's nature; to speak of frequency is to talk about how many times something happens.[161] If, for example, every adult male in the world wore a blue shirt between noon and two o'clock in the afternoon, we could induce a true generalization: anyone who is an adult male between noon and two o'clock today will be wearing a blue shirt. But wearing a blue shirt is not a necessary or an essential property of adult masculinity. It is a contingent feature of male adult human beings, even if it occurs universally.

In sharp contrast to modern Empiricists who were rattled by Cartesian scepticism, Aristotle is confident that human intelligence is able to grasp the deep nature of things. We possess a capacity for rational judgement that can, at the best of times, distinguish the contingent from the necessary, the accidental from the essential, the trivial from the momentous, or the superficial from the fundamental. Call this capacity human intelligence. Human intelligence, not argument, distinguishes between necessary (essential) and accidental attributes. As we shall see, Aristotle believes that logic is useless without intelligence.

161 This is in line with modern attitudes, which posit the primacy of epistemology over metaphysics.

Return to Schmidt's earlier example about floating objects. Whether a floating object happens to be a duck or a river otter or a motorboat or a bit of flotsam or jetsam has no importance here. Considered from the viewpoint of physics, these are accidental properties. Floating objects do, however, possess a *necessary* feature, the property "of displacing water of a greater weight than their own."[162] So we can make the appropriate induction: because these individual floating objects possess this "weight-displacement" property, all floating objects must possess 'the greater weight displacement property'." This is a sound induction. It has a valid form, and the premises are true.

But suppose we were to reason, "These floating objects are red. Therefore, all floating objects are red." This induction fails because colour is an accidental property of floating objects. It is not just that floating objects are sometimes not red. The point is that a red object does not float *because* it is red. No one in any ship-building culture ever believed that painting something red would make it float. The world just does not work that way. How do we come to know that the "redness" is an accidental property of floating things? Through intelligence and observation, through shrewdness, not through argument.

Stephen Gaukroger claims that the Aristotelian approach "can provide us with knowledge of accidents but not necessary attributes as such."[163] If, however, Aristotle did not devise any logical method for distinguishing between accidental and necessary properties, this is because he believed that intelligence, not logic, makes this distinction possible. What happened in the course of modern intellectual history is that the empiricists lost confidence in intelligence and searched instead for a logical method to differentiate in some absolute way between necessary and accidental kinds. But no such algorithm exists. Aristotle believes that we can *intuit* natural kinds. We access them through some kind of intelligent awareness. We can turn this experience into a (valid) inductive syllogism, but we cannot do this without intelligence.

Aristotle thinks of induction as an act of empirical inspection that triggers a moment of insight into the whatness of things. Understanding is what is needed; mere enumeration will not do the trick. Aristotelian induction is not a mere listing of data but the unleashing of a cognitive capacity as a reliable guide to the way the world is. Aristotle conceives of induction, not as proof, but as discernment. Induction is not so much

162 Schmidt, *Domain of Logic*, 279.

163 Gaukroger, *Explanatory Structures*, 107. Gaukroger thinks of Aristotelian induction as a kind of "abstractionism," which is only partly accurate. I discuss Aristotelian abstraction in the next chapter.

about determining how many times fire is accompanied with heat; it more about understanding what fire is and why it produces heat. Once we understand what fire is, it will become clear why it must produce heat. The idea that we can mechanically, through blind enumeration, build up knowledge – without inspiration, intuition, or discernment – is foreign to Aristotle. Human intelligence includes the ability to understand why certain things must be so. No special algorithm, no logical, mechanical, or statistical process, could replace human intelligence. We can distinguish between necessary (essential) and accidental properties, not because we have logic, but because we have intelligence.

I will not propose any developed theory of necessary properties here. Suffice it to consider a couple of examples. Suppose an ornithologist is studying the anatomy of birds. In his dissections, the ornithologist comes across the ventriculus (the gizzard). The scientist's eventual argument might be as follows: this bird has a gizzard; this bird has a gizzard; this bird has a gizzard; so all birds have a gizzard.[164] The discovery could be presented as a sound inductive argument, with a valid logical form and true premises. Because the gizzard is a necessary property of birds, the argument works so to speak. It reveals a necessary correlation between a particular natural kind and a specific property. This is good, as far as it goes. But surely, this is not what science is about. Aristotle believes that scientists investigate causality. They try to answer "the why question."

The rigorous ornithologist would want to ask, why do bird have gizzards? And why do these gizzards have bits of sand, grit, and even small stones inside them? And why are the walls of these "little stomachs" so muscular? One could imagine a perceptive mind hitting on the answer, birds have no teeth! So they need a gizzard with muscular walls and internal grit to masticate food. This is the kind of insight Aristotle associates with reasoning inductively. A gizzard is a necessary property of birds, not simply because all birds have them, but because they have no teeth. They need something to grind up food to digest it. Digestion is a necessary condition of survival, and mastication is a necessary aspect of digestion.[165]

164 We could formalize the argument as an inductive syllogism: this, this, and this organism has a gizzard; this, this, and this organism is a bird; so all birds have gizzards.

165 The situation is, of course, a bit more complex. Prehistoric birds had, it seems, teeth. Some birds have "tomia," serrated edges on their bills, used for grasping and cutting; birds that eat seeds and nuts tend to have more prominent gizzards than those that eat flesh; scientists have created mutant chicken embryos with a kind of "crocodile teeth" – etc. But the general line of reasoning still holds.

Figure 3.5
Why triangles must have internal angles equal to 180 degrees

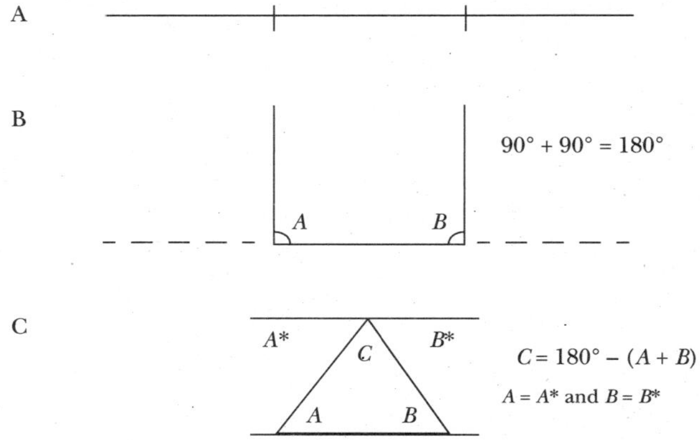

Mere logic will not provide us with this kind of insight, insight into why birds need a gizzard. Moderns mistakenly assume that knowledge about the frequency of gizzards in birds is the central point. For Aristotle, this statistical fact is only a by-product of a larger movement of human intelligence. Knowledge about the necessary correlation between gizzards and birds relies on a deeper understanding about causality. We will discuss Aristotle's understanding of science in detail in the next chapter.

It is important to point out that this kind of analysis need not be restricted to teleological explanations in biology. Suppose we want to understand why having angles adding up to 180 degrees is a necessary property of any triangle. We can demonstrate this geometrically. Draw a line and divide it into three segments as in figure 3.5A. If we want to produce a triangle, we must bend the outer segments so they meet. The resultant internal angles *A* and *B* must be less than 90 degrees; otherwise, they would not touch (figure 3.5B). But that means that angles *A* and *B*, added together, must be *less* than 180 degrees. Draw the triangle produced by joining two line segments. Draw a parallel line contingent with the apex of the triangle as in figure 3.5C. Without entering into details, simply note that angles *A** and *B** are congruent with (equal to) angles *A* and *B*. But that means that angle *C* must be equal to 180 degrees minus angles *A* and *B*. It will follow, for any triangle, that the value of angles *A* plus *B* plus *C* is equal to 180 degrees. We can thus demonstrate why having angles equal to 180 degrees is a necessary property of triangularity. (This is the kind of thing Euclid was on about.) This requires creative intelligence.

MORE ABOUT SWANS

The ubiquitous counter-example of black swans swims through modern textbooks. We all know the refrain: gullible people once thought that whiteness was a necessary property of "swanness." Then they discovered that there are black swans in Australia. So this proves that induction is not reliable. Or does it? The test case deserves a second look.

As it turns out, the commonsense intuition that familiar white swans are a natural kind is basically correct. Nothing about this cognitive leap should make us doubt induction. Biologists, to this day, distinguish between diverse species of swan, largely on the basis of the colour of their plumage. There are, as it turns out, various species of swans. Some are pure white (the mute swan, the trumpeter swan, the whooper swan, the whistling swan, etc.), some white and black (the South American black-necked swan, the coscoroba swan (with black wing tips) and some almost entirely black (the Australian black swan, with white flight feathers). When people ordinarily declare that "all swans are white" they are not making a rigorous scientific claim. What they mean presumably is that the kind of bird we call "a swan" (most likely, the mute swan or the polish mute swan) is white. And they are right. Indeed, that kind of bird is white. We might be surprised to learn of the existence of black swans in Australia, but outside of Australia people are not ordinarily talking about those kinds of birds; they are talking about the birds they know, about the birds they refer to when they use the term "swan."

The black-swan example seems more a rhetorical trope than anything else. Plain parlance is too loose to stand up to precise scrutiny. On being told that there are black swans in Australia, we would, in all likelihood, ordinarily conclude that they must be a different species of bird. And we would be right. *Black swans are a different species of bird.* They do not provide a counter-example to the carefully worded inductive claim, "the species of swans we have here in Europe are white." We could move rigorously from the particular claim, "this Polish mute swan and that Polish mute swan are white," to the universal generalization that "all mute swans are white." This would be sound inductive reasoning.

White plumage is a necessary feature of European swans (in fact, of swans in the Northern Hemisphere), but it is not a necessary feature of the genus swan. Are people who claim that all swans are white referring to the species or to the genus? We cannot really know, but it seems more sensible to suggest that they are referring to the species. They are referring to "the kind" of bird they know. They are not claiming anything about unborn birds living in habitats half a world away. If they are, they are guilty of lazy thinking. But this is to take an uncharitable view of what is actually happening.

Aristotle does not claim that human beings never make mistakes. People are often, for example, inattentive, but that should not destroy confidence in inductive science. Whatever philosophical vocabulary we settle into – notions such as genus, species, nature, essence, necessary or accidental property – will be indispensable tools for making sense of the world. I will delve into Aristotle's understanding of these issues in the following chapters.

MILL'S UNIFORMITY PRINCIPLE

Contemporary philosophers, almost unanimously, assume that inductive arguments are invalid. (They consider invalidity a necessary if not a defining feature of reasoning inductively.) But even if we leave Aristotelian syllogism behind, we can still show (as above) that inductive reasoning is a valid form of argument. By way of conclusion, consider two ways of demonstrating the validity of inductive arguments, one that derives from Hume, the other from Mill. Reformulate Aristotle's ideas in the more familiar guise of propositional logic as above.

While Hume contends that induction is never valid, he himself unwittingly supplies a hidden premise capable of rendering inductive arguments valid. "We always presume," he writes, "when we see like sensible qualities … effects similar to those which we have experienced."[166] In other words, we assume that objects that have the same perceptible qualities will produce the same effects. If, however, we add this unspoken presupposition to the other premises in an inductive argument, this will produce a valid argument. Formalize Hume's own example of nourishing bread. Premise$_1$: This, this, this physical object nourished me. Premise$_2$: This, this, this physical object has the sensible qualities we call "a slice of bread." Hidden premise: Like sensible qualities have like effects. Conclusion: All slices of bread will nourish me. This is a valid argument. If the premises are all true, the conclusion *must* be true. Humeans may, of course, dispute the truth of the hidden premise (that all slices of bread are convertible with one another), but this does not undermine the validity of the argument. Valid arguments may contain false premises. So Hume's account does not show that inductive arguments are *invalid*. In fact, it seems to demonstrate just the opposite.

166 To cite in full, "We always presume when we see like sensible qualities, that they have like secret powers, and expect that effects, similar to those which we have experienced" (Hume, *Enquiry* [Selby-Bigge, Nidditch], §4, pt 2, para. 29). And again, "similar sensible qualities will always be conjoined with similar secret powers" (ibid., §4, pt 2, para. 33). As I have already explained, Hume thinks that it is the secret powers underlying things that accounts for their causal efficacy.

Mill's appeal to the uniformity of nature is, no doubt, the most famous attempt to remedy the alleged problem of induction. Mill proposes five methods for identifying the causes behind things: agreement, difference, agreement and difference jointly, residues, and concomitant variations. I will not discuss specific methods in any detail here. They are all based on the idea that by attentively analyzing the correlations between things and events, we can come to know, in a deep sense, what causes what. Mill believed that an invariable correlation between the presence or absence of one thing and the presence or absence another signifies a relationship of cause and effect. By observing these correlations, we can advance our scientific knowledge of the world.

Mill presents the principle of the uniformity of nature as the ultimate ground of all induction. He writes, "The universal fact which is our warrant for all inferences from experience [is] that the course of nature is uniform."[167] Although Mill himself tends to interpret the principle as one of the uniformity of past and future experience, as Morris Cohen and Ernest Nagel explain, his basic idea can "be expressed in various ways: that nature is uniform, that the universe is governed by general laws, that the same case will under similar circumstances be accompanied by the same effect."[168] Consider an example. Mill believes that we can logically conclude that because bread slices have been nourishing in the past, they will be nourishing in the future. Why? Because the deep nature of things in the world does not change with the mere passing of time. Because nature stays the same, tomorrow's is interchangeable (convertible) with yesterday's bread.

Mill uncritically embraces the empiricist account of substance. Because we cannot know the real nature of things, we must simply accept on faith that nature is regular and determinate. This is somewhat unsatisfying. Modern commentators generally claim that Mill's use of the principle of the uniformity of nature is circular. But he is not trying to *prove* the reliability of induction. The uniformity of nature is an empirical fact that confronts us. It is not something we have to argue our way to. Once we accept that nature stays the same, we can go on with the scientific work of determining how the world functions.

The important point for this analysis is that Mill believes that every properly formed induction is a valid argument. We can argue as follows. $Premise_1$: Bread slices have been nourishing in the past. $Premise_2$: The nature of things is the same in the future as in the past. Conclusion: Bread

167 Mill, *System of Logic*, bk 3, ch. 3, §1, 201.

168 M. Cohen and Nagel, *Introduction to Logic*, 267.

slices will be nourishing in the future. This is a valid argument. It is necessarily the case that "if the premises are true, the conclusion must be true."

We can, of course, criticize Mill's approach. Familiar criticism focuses on $premise_2$, the uniformity principle. It is impossible to prove, absolutely, that the future will be the same as the past. Still, without entering into details, we can accept that this is a reasonable assumption. In any case, Mill never sets out to prove his uniformity principle. This is not how induction works. The goal in induction is not to prove the uniformity principle but to use it, in conjunction with accurate observation, to discover *specific* examples of cause and effect. The principle is a premise, not the conclusion of a previous argument.

Seen from an Aristotelian perspective, Mill's account is less than felicitous. Any single-minded focus on the frequency of events is inevitably problematic. We cannot distinguish between mere correlation and true causality on the basis of frequency alone. As Mill himself suggests, invariable sequence is not synonymous with the cause of something's happening. What we need is a more robust account of human intelligence as capable of grasping the deep nature of things and their necessary properties. But more on this later.

CONCLUSION

Aristotle defines an inductive argument as an uninterrupted inference that moves from particulars to a universal. He conceives of it formally as a special kind of syllogism that uses convertible or interchangeable terms to connect a necessary property to a natural kind. In propositional logic, we might conceive of induction as an argument form appealing to some version of the principle of shared identity, that things of the same kind must possess the same properties. These definitions are more or less equivalent. Every instance of convertibility is one of shared identity.

On the traditional view, to reason inductively would be to move from particular to general; deductively, from general to particular. Clearly, deductive reasoning depends on induction. We need to arrive at a universal before we can reason back down to the particular case. This dependence of deductive on inductive reasoning tends to be obscured by the contemporary focus on formal logic. Formal logicians can pluck generalizations, so to speak, out of thin air. Real-world generalizations, by contrast, depend on a prior inductive inference.

It is remarkable to hear repeated again and again the pious empiricist dogma: induction is not a valid form of argument. Hume and his heirs did not refute earlier views, however; rather, they never made any serious attempt to understand them. Earlier historical authors had more logical dexterity than we imagine. Careful examination of their work shows that they could make logical sense of induction as a valid argument form. Instead of summarily rejecting the tradition, it behoves contemporary authors to spend some time trying to understand what earlier authors were about.

4

Five Levels of Induction

It is quite likely that induction, much like syllogism, is divisible into different types of induction.

Paolo Biondi[1]

IN *A SYSTEM OF LOGIC*, JOHN STUART MILL DESCRIBES the Greek view of induction:

> The induction of the ancients has been well described by Bacon … It consists in ascribing the character of general truths to all propositions which are true in every instance that we happen to know of. This is the kind of induction which is natural to the mind when unaccustomed to scientific methods. The tendency, which some call an instinct … is simply a habit of expecting that which has been found true once or several times, and never yet found false, will be found true again. Whether the circumstances are few or many, conclusive or inconclusive, does not much affect the matter; these are conditions which occur only on reflection; the unprompted tendency of the mind is to generalize experience, provided this points in one direction; providing no other experience of a conflicting character comes unsought.[2]

Considered as an account of Greek philosophy, this passage, from no less a thinker than Mill, is almost ludicrously inaccurate. Aristotle himself suggests that anyone who uncritically assumes that what is usual is logically necessary – i.e., happens all the time – makes a silly mistake.[3] As he comments in a discussion of debating techniques, "If a necessary occurrence is asserted to be usual occurrence, it is obvious that the man who makes the assertion … is in error; and the same is true if he has stated that a usual attribute is necessary."[4]

1 *Aristotle*, §3.1, 192.

2 Mill, *System of Logic*, bk 3, ch. 3, §2, 204.

3 See *Posterior Analytics*, bk 2, ch. 12, 96a8–20.

4 *Topics* (Forester), bk 2,ch. 6, 112b3–10 (in Aristotle, *Aristotle in 23 Volumes*).

If Mill brushes off the Ancients as unsophisticated and credulous, this kind of uninformed verdict is highly partisan. Aristotle's use of the term induction or ἐπαγωγή (*epagoge*) is analogical. The precise meaning changes according to the context. This has led to many misunderstandings. As I explain at length below, Aristotle provides a complete theory of induction, one which rivals Mill's empiricist account. We can use the Aristotelian schema to differentiate between at least five distinct levels of theoretical induction. In contrast, the empiricist account tends to reduce all induction to a single type. It overlooks Aristotle's precise distinctions.

Begin, then, by distinguishing between five levels or kinds of Aristotelian induction, as in table 4.1. Our table of categories begins with the mental ability that constitutes the very origin of inductive reasoning. At this most basic of levels, Aristotle views induction as an unerring ability to arrive at a universal concept from an acquaintance with particular instances. The first level of induction produces the most fundamental concepts and principles. It does not involve argumentative reasoning but direct insight into the nature of things. It includes a mental process traditionally referred to as abstraction. Aristotle's method of definition is a particularly important form of this first level of induction.

We might call the first level of induction true, proper, or strict induction. Although Aristotle accepts that human beings are fallible, he claims that we must rely on whatever true induction tells us. As human beings, we cannot do any better. (More on this later.) If, however, true induction supplies the most basic principles of reason, we can also have general insights of a more tentative or provisional nature. Call this more tentative kind of induction "recognition." Recognition is a leap of cognition that grasps a similarity or likeness. It is the ability to "see" a plausible pattern, a likely regularity in phenomena.[5] Aristotle associates this ability with arguments by analogy. This is the second level of induction.

If these first levels involve some direct act of discernment or mental discovery, the next three require argument. We can identify three categories of inductive argument: rigorous (inductive syllogism), rhetorical (arguments by analogy), and statistical (arguments by enumeration). Rigorous induction deals with necessary properties; rhetorical, with contingent ones, and statistical inductions are, broadly speaking, numerical or mathematical in nature. Aristotle focuses on rigorous induction as the paradigm case of inductive reasoning. He presents the rhetorical as a weaker kind of inductive syllogism to be used in dialectical contexts. Statistical induction plays little role in his thinking.

5 See de Rijk, *Aristotle*, vol. 1, §2.61, 162.

Table 4.1
Five levels of induction

Level	*Kind of induction*	*Operates by means of*	*Knowledge produced*
First level	*Induction proper* (ἐπαγωγή)	*Induction as intuition* Operates through infallible exercise of νοῦς (*nous*), through the activity of intellection, understanding, comprehension, insight	Abstraction of necessary concepts, definitions, essences, necessary attributes, first principles, natural facts, moral principles
Second level	*Recognition*	*Induction as intuition* Operates through cleverness, a general power of discernment or shrewdness, referred to by terms such as ἀγχίνοια (*anchinoia*), εὐστοχία (*eustochia*), δεινότης (*deinotes*) or even μῆτις (*metis*)	Any likeness or similitude, the general notion of belonging to a class, any discernment of sameness or unity
Third level	*Rigorous induction* (Inductive syllogism: ὁ ἐξ ἐπαγωγῆς συλλογισμός)	*Induction as argument* The most rigorous form of inductive inference	Essential or necessary properties or principles (including moral knowledge)
Fourth level	*Rhetorical induction* Includes arguments by analogy, called arguments from likeness (τῶν ὁμοίων), arguments by example (παράδειγμα)	*Induction as argument* A less rigorous sort of inductive inference	What is plausible, contingent or accidental; knowledge relating to convention, human affairs
Fifth level	*Statistical induction* Induction by enumeration, modern arguments from probability	*Induction by enumeration (counting)* The probability calculus	Accidental features, frequency of properties, correlations in populations

This division of induction into five levels of insight and argument is only preliminary. Each individual category may be used in different contexts and applied to vastly different subject matters. But this fivefold Aristotelian schema provides us with a starting point for understanding the diversity and richness of inductive reasoning.

ORIGINS OF INDUCTION

As Troels Engberg-Pedersen explains, "the root idea of Aristotelian *epagoge* [induction] in its full technical sense" is "something like attending to particular cases with the consequence that insight into some universal point is acquired."[6] At this most fundamental level, Aristotelian induction is not an argument but an intellectual movement of discernment that grasps, in a non-discursive manner, the nature of particular objects. It is an instance of pure intellection or intuitive thought: νοῦς (*nous*). The mind moves from the perception of particular objects to a concept that refers to all objects that possess the same nature.

Lambertus Marie de Rijk, in his magisterial work *Aristotle: Semantics and Ontology*, neatly captures this aspect of the inductive process. He explains, "In Aristotle, the term ἐπαγωγή ... refers to a pre-argumentation procedure consisting in (A) [the] adduction of one or more particular instances, which (B) is directed toward disclosing a καθόλου [universal] element that enables us to understand the formal nature of the particular and its likes. The disclosure does not take place by a formal, discursive inference, but is, as it were, jumped upon by an intuitive act of knowledge, and it is this intuitive act which enables us to recognize the particulars of this or that formal nature."[7]

De Rijk rejects out of hand "Ross's idea that Aristotelian *epagoge* is an inferential device"[8] and concurs instead with D.W. Hamlyn's claim that Aristotelian induction "should not be taken to refer to any procedure of formal inference."[9] In other words, he claims that Aristotle did not, in the first instance, conceive of induction as an argument, a way of inferring conclusions from premises, but as a "noetic, sudden and instantaneous [act of] cognition,"[10] an "instantaneous effect of suddenly grasping,"[11] "a flash of insight into a universal point."[12] De Rijk's vocabulary thus corrects a familiar error, but his solution goes to the other extreme. While Aristotelian induction begins, as de Rijk suggests, in an intuitive flash of understanding, Aristotle also leaves a place for inductive

6 Engberg-Pedersen, "More on Aristotelian *Epagoge*," 305.

7 De Rijk, *Aristotle*, general introduction and vol. 1, §2.53, "The Works on Logic," 141–2.

8 Ibid., vol 1, §2.53, 141.

9 Ibid., vol. 1, §2.53, 144. He cites Hamlyn "Aristotelian *Epagoge*," 171.

10 De Rijk, *Aristotle*, vol. 1, §2.55, 153.

11 Ibid., vol. 1, §2.56, 153n222.

12 Ibid., vol. 1, §2.56, 155.

arguments. And any time we have an argument, we have presumably, some sort of inference. But more on this later.

Where, then, does induction begin? It begins, not with arguments, not even with words, but with concepts. Induction, of this rudimentary sort, is a response to sense perception. We look at the objects surrounding us, and we come up with corresponding ideas. In technical language, we "see" the universal concept immanent in the particular. We see individual dogs and come up with the concept "dog," see individual trees and come up with the concept "tree," see individual houses and come up with the concept "house." Traditional logicians called this process "abstraction." We can somehow abstract the idea of "dog" from the individual dogs actually living in the world and consider the form of "dog" on its own. This is an inductive process; we examine particular dogs and end up with a concept applicable to all dogs universally.

Aristotle writes that sense experience apprehends individual objects "at a definite present place and time," whereas concepts refer to "what is always and everywhere."[13] A concept is a theoretical kind. It is properly universal. Every dog in the world is contained within the classification "dog." Perception, by contrast, is inevitably particular. When we perceive, we do not perceive a universal dog, but this or that canine individual. In abstraction, the mind moves from the world of sense impressions to the theoretical world of ideas or concepts. This requires a mental leap from particular objects to a universal idea that brings together a group objects under a single rubric.

For Aristotle, induction represents the very first stage of thought. If we can differentiate between the perceptual and the conceptual, between what we perceive and what we know, inductive reasoning bridges the gap between the two.[14] It transforms or transmutes the perceived into the known, the sensible into the conceptual, the particular into the universal, the material into the theoretical. This metamorphosis necessitates *epagoge*, a running leap from the individual instances of sense perception to a universal understanding.[15]

13 *Analytica Posteriora* (Mure), bk 1, ch. 31, 87b27 ff. (in Aristotle, *Works of Aristotle*).

14 "Existing things are either sensible or thinkable; and knowledge is in a way what is knowable, and sensation is in a way what is sensible" (*On the Soul* [Smith], vol 3, ch. 8, 431b20–23, in Aristotle, *Complete Works*). Although Aristotle believes that we cannot think of a concept without a sensible mental image (technically, a "phantasm"), the concept is not equivalent to a mere image (ibid., bk 3, ch. 8, 432a2–12).

15 We could ask traditional metaphysicians whether we can have a concept of an individual, say of Socrates. This raises problems we will not examine here.

Aristotle proposes this first intuitive level of induction to solve a problem. In contrast to his teacher, Plato, Aristotle does not believe that concepts exist on their own in some immaterial realm we can access through contemplation. How, then, can we retrieve concepts? Aristotle is very clear. "Although concepts cannot exist in separation, some of them inhere in each class of objects, insofar as each class has a determinate nature."[16] Concepts do not exist on their own in heaven; they already exist here on earth. The concept "dog" exists embedded in individual dogs; the concept "tree," in particular trees; and the concept "house," in individual houses. Induction extracts or detaches the concept while leaving behind the matter. Guthrie explains, "[Aristotelian induction begins with] the familiar, all-important operation of abstracting (better 'extracting') the form (*eidos*) from particulars, separating from their matter those common qualities which mark off those particulars ... as belonging to the same species (*eidos*)."[17]

Traditionally, abstraction has been thought of as a subtractive process. When we abstract the concept "dog," we subtract the individual traits that make this dog unique, and consider only the formal residue it shares with every other dog. We remove the idiosyncratic bits – this dog's particular breed, its exact size, colour, age, who the owner is – and focus on what this dog shares with every other dog: the fact that it is a domesticated, warm-blooded, four-legged, gregarious, colour-blind animal with a keen sense of smell that wags its tail when it is happy, and so on. The mind leaps, so to speak, from the concrete reality of one dog to a mental artefact that encompasses all dogs.

Earlier textbooks in logic take a more studied approach to abstraction. Traditional logician George Joyce illustrates abstraction by means of the concept of a circle. He explains, "If I see a circle drawn on a blackboard, the concept which I form of that geometrical figure will express not merely the individual circle before me, but all circles. The figure I see is of definite size, and is in a particular place. But my mind by an act of abstraction omits these individual characteristics, and forms a concept of a

16 *Posterior Analytics* (Tredennick), vol. 1, ch. 18, 81b–5 (in Aristotle, *Aristotle in 23 Volumes*).

17 As Guthrie explains, the process involves separating out the "form" from the "matter." Because the material component is traditionally thought of as the principle of individuality, removing it from the object produces a universal concept applicable to all individual instances (of the same species). Guthrie, *History of Greek Philosophy*, vol. 6, 190.

circle as elucidated in Euclid's definition. This concept is applicable to every circle that was ever drawn."[18]

On traditional views, what differentiates one member of a species from other members is the fact that it occupies or is contained within a different bit of matter. Abstraction, then, subtracts this individual bit of matter from the form; it subtracts the matter composing this dog to expose the universal form "dog." But abstraction is not restricted to metaphysical substances. We can abstract concepts referring to predicates, qualities, or relationships, rather than individual things. Think of the concept "red." Red does not exist on its own. It is a property of a material thing. Having subtracted the matter that the red inheres in, we are left with the idea of "red" that applies equally to all red objects. The concept "red" brings together in a single mental object the colour property that all these individual objects share.

Richard Clarke, in another historical text, defines abstraction "as the drawing away of our attention from some qualities in order to fix it upon others." He continues, "I may abstract from the whiteness of a piece of sugar and fix on its sweetness. I may abstract from whiteness and sweetness and concentrate my attention on its crystallization. I may abstract from whiteness and sweetness and crystallization and mentally contemplate its wholesomeness for little children."[19] Clarke envisages four separate acts of abstraction. We can, in this way, formulate a universal concept of whiteness, sweetness, crystallization, or wholesomeness pertaining, not simply to instances of sugar, but to all instances of the specific predicate of concern to us. This process involves a movement from particular to universal; i.e., it represents a kind of inductive inference.

As we shall see, the traditional doctrine of abstraction represents the development of Aristotle's original thought taken in a certain direction. It provides a wider perspective on the alleged "problem of induction." If any "inference" from particular to universal is unreliable, it must follow that the very concepts we use are unreliable, for every concept presupposes a generalizing movement of thought. A thoroughgoing scepticism regarding inductive reasoning would undermine not only inductive arguments but also deductive ones, for they too are composed of concepts. Induction, in the most basic sense, includes any mental movement from specific to general. It includes abstraction. If any deep problem affects induction, even deductive logic would be grounded. Any attack on inductive is, then, one

18 Joyce, *Principles of Logic*, 16.

19 R. Clarke, *Logic*, 102.

on deductive reasoning as well. We will consider these epistemological problems in a later chapter.

GEACH AND GAUKROGER: ATTACKING ABSTRACTION

I have argued that Aristotelian inductive originates in abstraction. Peter Geach, in an inquiry into the origins of mental acts, traces the notion to the late Middle Ages and to a corruption of the scholastic principle *nihil in intellectu nisi prius in sensu* – there is nothing found in the mind that was not first in the senses.[20] Geach defines abstractionism "as the doctrine that a concept is acquired by a process of singling out in attention some one feature given in experience – *abstracting* it – and ignoring the other factors simultaneously given – *abstracting* from them."[21] Not one to mince words, he concludes, "the whole idea of abstractionism – of discriminative attention to some feature given in experience – is thoroughly incoherent."[22] Geach goes on to claim that no mental concepts are ever acquired by "the supposed process of abstraction."[23]

Stephen Gaukroger has argued, in a different but equally critical vein, that Aristotle himself is guilty of "abstractionism." Gaukroger claims that the modern revolution in mathematical physics, beginning with thinkers such as Galileo, was a necessary correction to "the concepts of Peripatetic physics [that] are based on an abstraction of everyday experience."[24] Gaukroger believes that contemporary physicists concern themselves with a kind of mathematical knowledge that "is clearly not the same as that derived by abstraction from individual cases." Indeed, he goes so far as to claim that true scientific knowledge, "cannot be attained, at least in [Aristotelian] physics and cosmology."[25] Consider, then, the case Geach and Gaukroger amass against the doctrine of abstractionism.

20 Geach, *Mental Acts*, 19. As Paolo Biondi points, out, "Aquinas is generally considered to be one of the first to describe νόησις as fundamentally abstractive" (who does this in his *Commentary on Aristotle's "De Anima"*) (Biondi, *Aristotle*, appendix, 266n11). Biondi points out that Alexander introduces the concept of abstraction outside a mathematical concept long before Aquinas (in his *De Anima liber cum Mantissa*; see Biondi, *Aristotle*, appendix, 266n12).

21 Geach, *Mental Acts*, 18.

22 Ibid., 19.

23 Ibid., 18.

24 Gaukroger, *Explanatory Structures*, 161.

25 Ibid., 107.

Geach argues through example. He tries to show that many concepts cannot conceivably arise from abstraction, traditionally understood. Gaukroger adds his own examples from physics and astronomy. Consider, then, some of their counter-examples.

Numbers

On a familiar account, we abstract numbers from experience. We ignore completely the question, "What kind of things are these?" and focus exclusively on, "How many things are there?" We count seven apples, seven oranges, and the like, and then ignore the kinds of thing we counted to come up with the number seven. We subtract, so to speak, the fact that these objects happen to be apples, oranges, or something else and focus exclusively on the issue of number apart from the issue of kind.

Geach argues that we cannot learn to count by dropping any reference to kind and counting in the abstract, for counting presupposes classification into kinds. "Things are numberable only as belonging to a kind." The activity of counting is inextricably linked to that of classifying. When we count, we end up with a given number depending on the *kind* of thing we are counting. As Geach points out, "The same auditory experience may [for example] give me the number 2 if what I have in mind is *heroic couplets,* 4 if it is lines of *verse,* 40 if it is *syllables,* 25 if it is *words.*" If we do not pay attention to any *kind* of thing we are concerned with, counting becomes impossible. "If I have no special kind of thing in mind, no number will suggest itself to me at all."[26]

But this seems a clear case of equivocation. In point of fact, we do just what Geach claims we cannot do, we count without reference to kind: "one, two, three, four, five, etc." Clearly, the verb "to count" has two meanings. If "counting" means ascertaining how many of some kind of thing exist at a specific place and time, then obviously we cannot count without classifying objects into kinds. But if "counting" means following consistently, coherently, step-by-step through a series of numbers, we can do that very well without classifying anything into kinds. Geach assumes that because we cannot count in the first sense without classifying into kinds, then we cannot do so in the second sense. This is simply false.

How do we learn to count? Aristotle's doctrine of abstraction is sketchy, but we can surmise what he has to say. As he himself points out, mathematical or theoretical abstractions "can only be grasped by induction."[27] We

26 Geach, *Mental Acts,* 28.

27 *Posterior Analytics* (Tredennick), bk 1, ch. 18, 81b–5.

begin with sense perception and induce numbers. We *perceive* one, two, three oranges, etc., one, two, three apples, etc., and are somehow able to drop out the reference to a particular kind of thing, extract the number or the sequence of numbers by itself, and – through a momentous insight – count. We do not see numbers out in the world; we see objects. Yet somehow we move from the empirical experience of a plurality of objects to an idea of the specific fact of this or that plurality by itself, apart from the actual objects. This is a form of abstraction. As we shall see, abstraction is a creative endeavour. Numbers are, in a sense, artefacts of human consciousness. Nonetheless, Geach has not shown that we cannot create them by abstracting from experience.

Concepts Such as "Big" and "Small"

On the familiar, commonsense account, we can derive concepts such as "big" and "small" by abstraction. If, for example, we see a big mountain, we come up with the concept "big" by ignoring the fact that it is a mountain and by focusing exclusively on its being a big mountain. The concept "big" surfaces when we ignore the question, "What kind of thing is this?" and we concentrate on, "How large is it?" In directing all our attention to the issue of size, we overlook other features: the fact the mountain is made of granite, covered with snow, located in Colorado, and so on. In this way, we can extract the concept of bigness, leaving behind the fact that we were looking at a mountain.

Geach, however, claims the classifications of "big" and "small" are inextricably linked to those of kind. "Big" objects have nothing in common to be somehow extracted, to produce a universal concept. Geach explains,

> Is there a common identifiable feature shared by a big elephant, a big rat and a big flea, and which they do not share with a small elephant, a small rat and a small flea? Can I pick out this feature by discriminative attention, abstracting from what kind of thing it is that I am calling big or small? Certainly not. I cannot rightly apply the term "big" or "small" unless I am meaning a big or small thing of a certain kind. A big flea or rat is a small animal, and a small elephant is a large animal. There can be no question of ignoring the kind of thing to which "big" or "small' is referred and forming a concept of *big* or *small* by abstraction.[28]

28 Geach, *Mental Acts*, 32.

Once again, here again, we seem to do just what Geach claims we cannot do – separate the concept of "bigness" from the notion of kind. Suppose the author of a novel were to write the following: "Ralph was preoccupied with 'bigness'. Everything had to be big to impress him: cars, trucks, women, steaks, glasses of beer, bank accounts, horses, mountains. He didn't mind if you told a lie as long as it was a big one. He was a megalomaniac at heart." This is perfectly intelligible prose. What the author is suggesting is that bigness, not bigness of a particular kind, but bigness in general, bigness applied to *any* kind, was what impressed Ralph. This kind of description would be impossible if we could not somehow separate the concept of "bigness" from the notion of kind.

We can speak of big objects. But we can also use the word "big" to refer to a type of relation. Consider an analogy. The ordinary term "pet" refers to a certain relationship between human beings and nonhuman animals. We can speak of a pet dog, cat, guinea pig. But we can also refer to pets generically; that is, we can attend to the nature of this human-nonhuman relationship, without taking into account the kinds of animals involved. I can assert, for example, that pets should be properly cared for. This is a kind of abstraction. It entails a movement from specific to general. We can, in the same way, abstract the relationship of bigness while ignoring the specific kinds of things included in this relationship. When we use the term "big" in this sense, we mean, "this is a big example of this category of thing." We can certainly focus on this kind of relationship while ignoring the kind of thing it holds of.

Logical Concepts Such as "And," "Or," or "Not"

It may seem, at first glance, that logical concepts such as conjunction ("and"), disjunction ("or"), and negation ("not") cannot be derived from abstraction. These concepts do not refer to physical objects existing out in the world. We cannot, it seems, extract them from things in the world through some kind of focused mental exercise. Geach elaborates, "Logical concepts are not to be explained as the result of performing abstraction on any sense experience. In the sensible world you will find no specimens of alternativeness or of negativeness from which you could form by abstraction the concept of *or* or of *not* ... Nowhere in the sensible world could you find anything, nor could you draw any picture, that could be suitably labeled 'or' or 'not'."[29]

29 Ibid., 22–3.

Logical concepts such as "or" or "not" clearly do not exist as things out in the world, but abstraction – in an Aristotelian sense anyway – is not limited to substances. In Aristotle everything begins in sense perception. How could such concepts arise? I am looking for my keys. I feel in my pockets, and find they are empty. I discover that something is *not* the case, that my keys are not in my pockets. I can somehow separate this state of affairs from the specific circumstances of my missing keys, and consider it on its own. Or suppose I have to make a decision – a fork in the road. I am somehow able to abstract this concept of "one or the other," to separate it out from specific circumstances of the forked path, and consider it on its own. In both cases, we have a kind of induction. There is a circumstance I experience, and I can somehow abstract one element of that circumstance and turn it into a general concept that I can apply universally. Geach can claim that this does not happen, but this seems an obvious feature of ordinary human experience.

Chromatic Colour

Geach argues that not even colour concepts can arise by abstraction. He introduces the concept of "chromatic colour," which he defines as colour "other than white, grey, and black." The concept of chromatic colour cannot be arrived at through abstraction, it seems, for it requires the simultaneous coexistence of overlapping colour concepts. Geach contends, "It is quite impossible that I should form this concept, chromatic color, by discriminative attention to a feature given in my visual experience. In looking at a red window pane I have not two sensations, one of redness and one … of chromatic color; there are not … two distinct sense-given features, one of them making … a sensation of chromatic color; the other making … a sensation of redness."[30] And yet, the mind is able to make "a distinction between redness and chromatic color, although there are not two features to be found in the red glass or in my visual sensation."[31]

But Geach's concept of "chromatic colour" can be explained in terms of a higher-level form of abstraction. We can derive a concept of a colour "other than white, grey, and black" through abstraction. And once we have primitive concepts, we can manipulate and combine them in various ways to create more complicated concepts. We can, for example, derive the concept "primary colour" from the concept "red," "blue," and "yellow." We do this by focusing on one particular aspect of these three colours: in this

30 Geach, *Mental Acts*, 28.

31 Ibid., 38.

instance, the fact that they are the colours other colours are mixed from. There is a shifting of attention from irrelevant aspects of these primary colours to a feature they all share, thus a kind of abstraction. We can explain chromatic colour likewise.

Bodies Falling Freely in a Void

Gaukroger makes the case that the concepts of modern physics cannot be retrieved through abstraction. This is a familiar enough complaint. On this reading, modern mathematical physics needed to discard the straitjacket of Aristotelian logic to get on with the work of scientific inquiry. Gaukroger develops the point that, "[abstractionism] denies evidential value to [any] situation to which we have no experiential access. Situations which we … never will perceive – such as bodies falling freely in a void – are excluded as being of no evidential relevance to physics, in particular." [32]

But no definitive obstacle stands in the way of the abstraction of these kinds of theoretical entities. How could we derive a concept of "bodies freely falling in a void"? To begin with, we might observe rocks, nails, rubber balls, missiles, falling downward and abstract a concept of "a physical body freely falling through air." That seems unproblematic. And what about the concept of a void? We cannot detach the concept of a void from those we encounter in the world, for there are no voids in the world of lived experience. (In fact, interstellar space offers a good approximation of the void, but leave that aside for the moment.) And there is a further problem. Even if voids existed in the world, we could not perceive them. A perfect void is absence. They would offer nothing to be perceived. So the fact that we can come up with the idea of a void seems to demonstrate that we do not derive all our concepts by abstracting from empirical experience. Or does it?

The point is that our ideas have to come from somewhere. At least in Aristotle, they must ultimately derive from our experience of the world. Where else would they come from? And in fact, we can arrive at the concept of a void through abstraction. Several scenarios seem possible. We might abstract a concept of "air" and one of negation – "we encounter no this, that, or that here" – and then combine these two concepts to produce the concept of "no air." Or we might observe that the quantity of something can be reduced. We might focus single-mindedly on one aspect of the circumstance – the fact of our encountering less and less of something. But once we have detached this concept of "becoming less and less" from

32 Gaukroger, *Explanatory Structures*, 125.

the world, we might apply it to the concept of "air" to produce the idea of less and less air until we arrive at the concept of a vacuum. Or again, we could abstract mechanical and mathematical concepts from the world and use them to calculate an object's velocity and acceleration without taking into account the resistance of the medium, and so on. None of this seems particularly problematic. We may, then, combine the idea of a "freely falling body" with that of "a void" to produce the concept of "a body freely falling through a void."

Neither Geach nor Gaukroger succeeds in presenting a counter-example suggesting an insuperable barrier to a thoroughgoing theory of abstraction. If Geach vehemently attacks modern notions of "abstractionism," he carefully distances himself from any criticism of the historical and, in particular, the medieval understanding of abstraction. Indeed, he acknowledges his debt to Thomas Aquinas, targeting instead a "degenerate" modern tradition of "manual" Thomism. Geach declares, "Aquinas is very often regarded as an abstractionist, and many of his professed followers are abstractionists; and of course he does use the term '*abstraction*' for the process of forming concepts. All the same it can be decisively shown that in his maturest work ... his views are opposed to what I have called abstractionism."[33] But whatever else it is, Thomas' understanding of abstraction is thoroughly Aristotelian. It represents a specific development of ideas that originated in Aristotle.

What Geach objects to in more modern theories of abstraction is the passive role of the intellect. He counters, "the mind *makes* concepts, and this concept-formulation ... is never a mere recognition or finding."[34] As Geach points out, Thomas compares the cognitive power of the mind to a light that *creates* the colours it sees. In Geach's words, "Aquinas is careful to add ... that colors are generated by [intelligence] – that the light is not just revealing colors that already existed in the dark."[35] It is not as if concepts exist preformed in the world, waiting to be unearthed by the passive mind, which simply records what is already there. The mind *brings concepts into existence; it makes* concepts as a new reality that would not be there without the operation of the mind's faculties.

33 Geach, *Mental Acts*, 130.

34 Ibid., 40.

35 Ibid., 130. Thomas is specifically referring here to the *intellectus agens*, the agent intellect (the active *nous*). The reference is to *Summa theologiae*, pt 1, Q. 79, art. 3, *ad* 2.

But Geach misses the point. Aristotle (like Aquinas) conceives of abstraction (and inductive reasoning generally) as a creative rather than a passive process. He does not conceive of the mind as a passive mirror but as a dynamic intellectual agency engaged in selectively (but accurately) comprehending the world. To formulate concepts is to actively create something that did not exist prior to or independently of the act of conceptualizing.

Geach writes, "We must resist the perennial philosophical temptation to think that if a thought is true of reality, it must copy it, feature by feature like a map."[36] But the solution is not to jettison the notion of "correspondence" entirely. To say that the proposition, "dogs have four legs," is true is to state, simply, that it corresponds to the number of legs a dog naturally has. Do concepts exist out in the world? Clearly, concepts are a mental fabrication. We induce them from experience. But we can acknowledge this without getting rid of the idea of correspondence entirely.

ARISTOTLE AND ABSTRACTION

Aristotle's rather sketchy theory of abstraction is not so important here. What Aristotle emphasizes is our ability to identify the species or genus of individual things.[37] How is the universal concept "humanity" established in the soul? We see individual human beings, Callias, Socrates, Xenophon, etc., and through repeated experience come to recognize, Aristotle tells us, "a man … not the [individual] man Callias."[38] The concept we form of "man" is what Aristotle refers to as "the one beside the many," i.e., as the one (idea) beside the many (particulars). It is, so to speak, the single unit of thought simultaneously and equally representing every member of the entire group.[39] Aristotle clearly intends these passages as a reference to induction.

One might complain that the term "abstraction" brings with it unwanted associations. Paolo Biondi writes, "Aristotle himself … never speaks of abstraction (*aphairesis* or *en aphairesei*) to describe this intellectual operation [of separating out the universal form from the individual matter] but tends, instead to restrict the term to the context of mathematics … This [mathematical] view of abstraction connotes, therefore, a separation that is a departure from reality and an intellectual or logical fabrication." In

36 Geach, *Mental Acts*, 41.

37 Dwayne Raymond at the University of Western Ontario is presently developing formal aspects of a logic of "belonging" to better account for Aristotle's modal logic.

38 *Analytica Posteriora* (Mure), bk 2, ch. 18, 100b.

39 Ibid., bk 2, ch. 18, 100a3–7.

sharp contrast to the Pythagoreans, Aristotle does not want to attribute ontological reality to numbers. Numbers are, in some inescapable sense, artificial. They are a human contrivance. As Biondi makes clear, "[a number] is an entity that cannot have a separate substantial existence outside of a physical substance but is capable of being separated out from it for consideration by the intellect."[40]

Biondi's point is well taken, but mathematical is not unlike conceptual abstraction. The difference between the concept "dog" and the concept "two" is that a dog is an independent thing (a substance), whereas a number is only a property of a thing (or a group of things). But the distinction between substance and property concepts should not be overstated. As we have already seen, we can abstract properties from their circumstances. In the case of any concept, the mind must somehow disengage the idea from the matter – numbers included.

We might speak of three degrees of disengagement. (1) Perceptions are not reality but a conscious representation of reality. The perception of a dog is not the same as a real, physical dog. (2) A concept is not the same thing as a perception. The concept "dog" is an idea about something; it has its origins in perception but it is not a sensation of something. (3) A concept of a property is not the same as a concept of a substance. The concept "brown" does not refer to any *thing* in the world. It detaches a feature of a substance and considers it on its own.

The difference between an abstraction of substance and of a property is one of degree, not one of process. In the latter case, the abstraction is carried on one step further. There is, so to speak, an additional degree of disengagement. But the same basic process applies. This separation of properties from things is not limited to mathematical concepts. Consider moral concepts (which play an important role in Aristotle). We can extract a notion of courage from a soldier's brave exploits on the battlefield. But courage does not exist on its own in the world. It only exists as a property attached to some person or group of persons. Still, we can consider the moral property on its own. This is analogous to what happens with numbers.

The difference between an abstraction of substance and of properties recalls a familiar distinction between extensional and intensional definitions.[41] In the case of an extensional definition, we may define a concept

40 Biondi, *Aristotle*, appendix, 266.

41 "[Exitensional definitions] seek to clarify the meaning of a term by identifying members of the class of things named by that term ... Intensional definitions clarify the meaning of a term by identifying the essential qualities that make something a member of the class named by that term" (Leo Groarke, Tindale, and Fisher, *Good Reasoning Matters*, 50).

by referring partially or fully to the "set of individuals that a given class term stands for." For example, we may define the term "athlete" extensionally, as in "football player, hockey player, gymnast, long-distance runner, etc." In the case of an intensional definition, we may define a concept by specifying an intension, the "properties shared by [all] these individuals."[42] For example, we may define the term "athlete" intentionally, as in "someone who engages in organized competitive activity that demands physical prowess." The first definition lists substances; the second, properties. In the case of true definitions, the extension and intension of the same concept must, of course, coincide. If, however, extensional definitions refer to substances, and intentional definitions refer to properties, both require an act of abstraction.

Consider our extensional definition of the term "athlete." Football players, hockey players, gymnasts, long distance runners, etc., are very different from one another. In formulating our definition, we must ignore these differences and focus on one common feature, the fact they all participate in sport. The same holds true for our intensional definition. In defining what an athlete is we must separate one set of properties from others in the world of sport. In both cases, we focus on one aspect of reality to the exclusion of others.

Identify abstraction with the process of concept formulation. Traditional accounts emphasize the mind's ability to separate out individual features of reality, but abstraction, it should be noted, also involves combining individual features. Human beings are rational, fallible, risible, moral, social, and so on. When we intuit the concept "human being," we apprehend a unity that brings diverse properties together within the idea "humanity."[43] Abstraction is, in this sense, a matter of both separation and union. It joins together properties and individual things within a single genus and species.

FIRST PRINCIPLES

The first level of induction (what I have called true or strict induction) includes all levels of abstraction. We might differentiate between at least three different kinds of abstraction in Aristotle: (1) of concepts; (2) of first

42 Olson, *Meaning and Argument*, 25–6. The denotation-connotation (extension-intension) distinction is also pressed into service for this purpose.

43 Biondi suggests as much. As he puts it, abstraction "is really a case of 'overlooking' the sensible to focus on its proper object, the indivisible which is intelligible" (Biondi, *Aristotle*, appendix, 268).

principles; and (3) of definitions and necessary properties. Having already considered the first level of abstraction, that of concept formulation, consider the second, the way our minds discover first principles. Define as a principle any combination of concepts, any rule, precept, fact, or judgement that covers a whole class of cases. W.K.C. Guthrie identifies as Aristotelian first principles: the basic rules of logic,[44] the axioms and definitions of geometry,[45] the starting points of the natural sciences,[46] and the ends of morality.[47] We will consider definitions below and moral principles in another chapter.

G.E.L. Owen has argued that Aristotle believes that we discover the first principles by means of dialectical argument.[48] Terence Irwin has, more recently, developed and defended this position at some length.[49] This has led to a great deal of misunderstanding. As Robin Smith has persuasively argued, the Owen-Irwin interpretation is based on a misreading of isolated texts in Aristotle.[50] According to Irwin and Owen, first principles arise from ἔνδοξα (*endoxa*), i.e., from opinions "which are accepted by everyone, by the majority or by the wise."[51] We learn about *endoxa* through dialectic, a less-than-rigorous form of argument based, not on "true and primitive" principles, but on "reputable opinion."[52] But this is only a half-truth. Yes, *endoxa* play an important role in *alerting* us to "the first principles of all disciplines."[53] It does not follow, however, that we arrive at first principles through rhetorical *argument*. First principles represent the very first steps in cognition. They cannot be argued for. If we could arrive at these principles through argument, they would not be first principles.

44 For example, the law of non-contradiction (*Metaphysics*, bk 4, ch. 3, 1005b5–34; and bk 4, ch. 6, 1011b13–14) or the law of the excluded middle (*Posterior Analytics*, bk 1, ch. 1, 71a14, 88b1).

45 For example, ibid., bk 1, ch. 9, 76a31.

46 For example, *Prior Analytics*, bk 1, ch. 30, 46a17–25.

47 For example, *Eudemian Ethics*, bk 2, ch. 11, 1227b22. See Guthrie, *History of Greek Philosophy*, vol. 6, 180ff.

48 See Owen, "Tithenai ta Phainomena."

49 See Irwin, *Aristotle's First Principles.*

50 See R. Smith, "Dialectic and Method in Aristotle."

51 *Topics* (Pickard-Cambridge), bk 1, ch. 1, 100a21–22 (in Aristotle, *Complete Works*).

52 *Topics* (Pickard-Cambridge), bk 1, ch. 1, 100a30.

53 *Topics* (Irwin), bk 1, ch. 1, 101b3–4 (cited in Irwin, *Aristotle's First Principles*, 37); and *Topics* (Pickard-Cambridge), bk 1, ch. 2, 101b3–4: "The path to the principles of all inquiries."

Owen refers to what Aristotle says in the *Nicomachean Ethics*: "We must, as in all other cases, set the phenomena before us and, after first discussing the difficulties, go on to prove, if possible, the truth of all reputable opinions ... or, failing this, of the greater number and most authoritative."[54] But this defeats the whole purpose of first principles. As Guthrie explains, first principles "must be regarded as axiomatic or self-evident." We do not arrive at these through a process of argument from more primary principles. We hit on them through a stroke of understanding or insight. "One must not ask the reason why [they are true]; each must carry conviction on its own."[55]

For Aristotle, the mental activity of formulating first principles is like the activity of concept formulation. Just as we distil concepts from sense experience, we distil the first principles of thought. There is no room here (as de Rijk insists) for argumentation or inference. As Jacques Maritain explains, "For Aristotle ... [the first level of] induction is neither an inference properly so-called, nor an argument, nor proof; it merely leads the mind to a connection of terms whose intelligible necessity it perceives immediately, without reasoning."[56]

Peter Coffey calls the mental process by which we arrive at the principles of logic "geometrical" or "mathematical" induction.[57] Ralph Eaton calls it "intuitive induction." Nomenclature aside, notice that the discovery of first principles (logical or otherwise) does not involve argument but insight. How do these principles arise? Eaton describes the origins of the principle of non-contradiction. We arrive at this principle through abstraction, by focusing on one specific feature of experience. "We observe that when the sky is dark, it is dark and not light; that when the leaves are falling, they are falling and not fixed to their stems ... and from these and many other experiences it dawns on us that a thing cannot be both P and not-P at the same time in the same respect."[58] Eaton tries to captures the inductive leap, the movement from particular to universal in the first level of induction generally. We begin with the perception of a particular situation and then abstract a principle covering *all* similar cases.

The Owen-Irwin interpretation poses a second, equally perplexing problem. In Aristotle's system, dialectical arguments deal with premises and

54 *Nicomachean Ethics* (Ross, Urmson), bk 7, ch. 1, 1145b1–7 (in Aristotle, *Complete Works*).

55 Guthrie, *History of Greek Philosophy*, vol. 6, 179.

56 Maritain, *Introduction to Logic*, 273–4 (my italics).

57 Coffey, *Science of Logic*, 25.

58 Eaton, *General Logic*, 498.

conclusions only provisionally or for the most part true. But first principles are the most certain of all. How, then, could we use an *uncertain* argument to arrive at a *certain* principle? In Aristotle's system at least, the conclusion of a properly constructed argument cannot be more certain than the premises. So we cannot use dialectical reasoning that is, in principle, restricted to less certain beliefs to establish the authority of the most certain of all.

So is there anything to the Owen-Irwin reading? Indeed, there is. Aristotle believes that universally shared (or almost universally shared) opinions must contain at least a grain of truth. This is a good place to begin reasoning. In picking through what everyone or the wise believe, we come across principles that immediately strike us as incontestable. Not every *endoxon,* of course, turns out to be a first principle. Nonetheless, dialectic provides a vast fund of good sense and received opinion alerting us to the most basic truths. In examining reputable opinions, we may uncover genuine first principles without any need for argument or proof. It takes a keen mind to separate the wheat from the chaff, but it can be done.

THREE KINDS OF PREDICATES

Aristotle places special emphasis on the third level of abstraction, definition. Aristotelian science is not so much about the formulation of rules or laws as about discovering adequate definitions for things. Without definition, we could not construct proper scientific demonstrations. The most important material on definition in Aristotle's corpus can be found in the first ten chapters of book 2 of the *Posterior Analytics,* where he, with alarming inconsistency, first declares it impossible to demonstrate definition and then turns around and argues that such a demonstration is, well, at least in some sense, possible. As Owen Goldin remarks, "Scholars have found Aristotle's arguments in [these] chapters exceedingly obscure, and there is no consensus on what Aristotle thinks he has shown and on whether his account is successful."[59]

One thing is certain. Aristotle believes that definitions arise through inductive inference. We induce definitions. If we hope to make sense of Aristotle's apparently inconsistent claims, we must sort out the different kinds of induction he (or his editors), somewhat loosely, refer to. Once we

59 Goldin, *Explaining an Eclipse,* 11. Biondi comments, "Aristotle's *Posterior* (or *Second*) *Analytics* is one of the most difficult treatises to understand. This may explain the relatively few commentaries that have been made on it throughout the history of Aristotelian commentary" (Biondi, *Aristotle,* Preface).

identify the related meanings of a notion like *epagoge*, we will be able to show that the process of induction in a sense does and in another does not produce definition.

Clarke, in a traditional text, correctly identifies the act of defining as a species of abstraction. Understood in this way, definition does not "prove" or "demonstrate" essence; that is, it does not operate by means of a series of logically entailed propositions. The mind *abstracts* out the essence of natures it encounters in the world. In Clarke's words, definition is "the intellectual act by which I draw forth (*abstrahere*) from the individual object that determinate portion of its nature which is … the essence, while I neglect all the rest."[60] As we shall see, this traditional explanation corresponds, *grosso modo*, to Aristotle's basic position.

Before investigating definition, however, we must distinguish between different kinds of predication in Aristotle. In the *Topics* Aristotle identifies definition (ὅρος), peculiar property (sometimes termed merely "property") or proprium (ἴδιον), genus (γένος), and accident (συμβεβηκός) as the four kinds of predicates.[61]

- Definition: A definition lists essential properties, the genus and differentia of something. A stock example is the definition of a "triangle" as a three-sided (differentia) figure (genus).
- Peculiar property: A peculiar property is an attribute, not the genus or differentia, which belongs exclusively to a group, i.e., which is convertible with it.[62] As Aristotle explains, "[It] is something which does not indicate the essence of a thing, but yet belongs to that thing alone and is predicated convertibly of it." Aristotle cites the example of being able to learn grammar. "For if he is a man then he is capable of learning grammar, and if he is capable of learning grammar, he is a man."[63]
- Genus: The genus is "what is predicated … of a number of things exhibiting differences in kind."[64] It is, in other words, the larger group made of a number of species. The genus of human being is "animal," a designation that applies to all other animal species such as dogs and horses and frogs and earthworms.

60 R. Clarke, *Logic*, 103.

61 *Topics*, bk 1, chs 4–6.

62 These are sometimes referred to as "essential accidents" (see Guthrie, *History of Greek Philosophy*, vol. 6, 148).

63 *Topics* (Pickard-Cambridge), bk 1, ch. 6, 102a17–23.

64 Ibid., bk 1, ch. 6, 102a32–33.

- Accident: An accident is a property that may or may not belong to the object in question. Aristotle cites the example "being seated." Clearly, a human being may or may not be seated.

Later commentators such as Porphyry added *differentia* to this list of predicates. The differentia is the unique feature that distinguishes a species. If a human being is a "rational animal," "animal" is the genus and "rational" is the differentia. Taken together, this list of five predicables came to play a major role in later ancient and medieval philosophy. If we add the notion of *necessary property* (which we have already discussed) to Porphyry's traditional list, we are left with six categories of predicables: definition, convertible property, necessary property, genus, differentia, and accident.

We can simplify this expanded list by dividing predicables into three broad categories. Every predicate can be thought of as a *definition*, as a necessary property, and/or as an *accidental property*. Traditionally understood, a definition is a composite predicate made up of the genus and the differentia of the thing taken together. A necessary property is an indispensable characteristic of a designated nature. And an accidental property is a contingent characteristic that may or may not characterize that nature.[65] Although these abbreviated categories are fairly straightforward, note that the category "necessary property" is, in traditional terms, a miscellany made up of a number of importantly different kinds of things. It includes the definition of the thing (the genus and differentia taken together), the genus or the differentia taken individually, peculiar (or convertible) properties, and necessary but non-convertible properties. Still, this threefold scheme has certain advantages. As we shall see, the major difference between Aristotelian and modern accounts of induction is that Aristotle divides it into two broad types: proper, dealing with necessary properties (including definition) and rhetorical or dialectical, dealing with accidental ones.

FOUR KINDS OF INDUCTION

Our goal here is to systematize, in the simplest manner possible, the Aristotelian account. Whereas we can divide predicates into three broad classes, we may divide induction into four such categories, which I will call ordinary, essential, necessary, and accidental. We can distinguish between these categories in the following way: Ordinary induction fixes on a universal without any consideration of whether the predicate is an essential, necessary, or

65 An accident is "an attribute which can belong to a thing and also not belong" (*Topics* [Pickard-Cambridge], bk 4, ch. 1, 120b35).

accidental property of a thing. Essential induction abstracts the essential predicate as an essential property; necessary, the necessary predicate as a necessary property; accidental, the accidental predicate as an accidental property. Essential induction includes an awareness that the identified predicates constitute a definition; necessary induction, that they belong necessarily to the thing; and accidental, that their presence is a contingent or happenstance occurrence.

Consider an example of each kind of induction:

- Ordinary induction: I notice that crows are black, that sugar tends to be sweet, that bread is nourishing, or that everyone in the room is wearing a blue shirt. It never occurs to me to consider whether these shared properties are essential, necessary, or accidental.
- Accidental induction: I notice that two people have dyed their hair the same colour, that three people happen to be eating the same item on the menu for lunch, that this rainbow trout and that rainbow trout are exactly the same size, that the first name of my next-door neighbour also begins with "A," and think, in the same breadth, what a wonderful coincidence!
- Necessary induction: I notice that all ducks have webbed feet, that human beings need oxygen, that helium is lighter than air, that two plus two (necessarily) makes four, and I realize, in the same breadth, that this must be the case.
- Essential induction: I notice, too, that all birds have wings and feathers, while realizing that this is what makes birds birds; I discover that the "s" electrons in helium have no empty orbitals and that this is what makes helium helium; I define a circle as a closed line with every point equidistant from a center and realize that this is what makes a circle a circle.

As we have seen, the very first level of induction involves a kind of direct mental discernment; it does not involve argument. Ordinary, essential, necessary, and accidental induction all begin, then, in a sort of illumination that has both a psychological and an epistemological (or noetic) aspect. The thinker grasps – without argument – that all *X*s are *Y*s, that most *X*s are *Y*s, or even that some *X*s are *Y*s. We can go on formalize this discovery in a valid inductive syllogism, but inductive *arguments* are developed inevitably after the fact. They are a discursive or deductive equivalent, a logical copy, of what is going on in the original leap of understanding. Direct insight comes first; argument follows.

Having identified four uniquely different kinds of inductive insight in Aristotle, we can now begin to make sense of his seemingly contradictory comments in the *Posterior Analytics*. As it turns out, comments on the inconclusiveness of induction as a method of defining are, more specifically, about ordinary, accidental, or even necessary inductive reasoning. His basic argument is that such reasoning is inconclusive as a method of defining anything, for it does not indicate which attributes are essential. Although it can give us some information, it does tell us which attributes are to be considered as essential predicates. Accidental induction, which only deals with temporary or contingent properties, cannot in principle yield definition. Even necessary induction fails to yield such a thing. Only essential induction yields definition. We consider Aristotle's original text more closely in the next chapter.

DEFINITION

In the *Posterior Analytics,* Aristotle ponders the problematic nature of definition. He poses what is technically an ἀπορία (*aporia*), a puzzle about definitions.[66] It seems that there is no way of coming up with definitions.[67] We cannot discover them through argument, for such things do not proceed from argument but from the first level of induction. We cannot discover definitions through induction, however, for it "proves not what the essential nature of a thing is but that it has or has not some attribute."[68] We cannot discover them by mere sense perception, for perceiving something is not the same as defining it. And finally, we cannot discover them ostensively, by merely pointing, for this only identifies what needs to be defined;

66 In the *Nicomachean Ethics,* Aristotle describes the delight sophists took in such puzzles. He reports, "Sophistic argument presents a difficulty, for … they want to produce paradoxical results to show how clever they are." *Aporia* results in mental paralysis: "when they succeed the resulting inference presents a difficulty (for thought is bound fast when it will not rest because the conclusion will not satisfy it, and cannot advance because it cannot refute the argument)" (*Nicomachean Ethics* [Ross, Urmson], bk 7, ch. 2, 1146a22–25).

67 The original passage follows intact: "How then by definition shall we prove substance or essential nature? We cannot show it as a fresh fact necessarily following from the assumption of premises admitted to be facts – the method of demonstration; we may not proceed as by induction to establish a universal on the evidence of groups of particulars which offer no exception, because induction proves not what the essential nature of a thing is but that it has or has not some attribute. Therefore, since presumably one cannot prove essential nature by an appeal to sense perception or by pointing with a finger, what other method remains?" (*Analytica Posteriora* [Mure], bk 2, ch. 7, 92a33–b3).

68 Ibid., bk 2, ch. 7, 92a38–b1.

it does not define it. And yet we regularly do come up with definitions. So how can we define something when there is no possible way to define it?

But, Aristotle thinks, the puzzle hinges on an equivocation. The term "induction" has more than one meaning. To say that we cannot arrive at definition through induction is true if by the latter we mean ordinary, accidental, or necessary induction. We can arrive at it through essential induction, however, for essential induction discovers definition. Distinguishing different kinds of induction resolves the apparent difficulty.

What I have called "essential induction" is the most important form of induction in Aristotle. Consider, then, the role of definition in Aristotle's epistemology. Aristotle distinguishes two types of definition. Nominal definitions reveal "what the name signifies," whereas real definitions reveal "what a thing is."[69] Anyone who elaborates a definition must produce either a nominal or real definition. As Aristotle puts it, "He who defines proves either the whatness of the object or what the name means."[70] Aristotle is mostly interested in real definitions. This is what science is about.

Aristotle champions a scientific method of definition by genus and differentia. Someone "who defines must put the subject into its genus and add the differentia."[71] The genus is the larger group or kind; the differentia is the distinguishing characteristic separating one special group of individuals from others of the same kind. Where the definition of mankind is "rational animal," "animal" is the genus and "rational," the differentia.[72] Human beings possess rationality – a level of intelligence that sets them apart.

We have already introduced the concept of convertibility. In a proper definition, the *definiendum* (the term defined) and the *definiens* (the expression defining it) must be convertible, possess, in other words, the exact same extension.[73] This is why Aristotle inverts the usual English order when formulating definitions. A proper Aristotelian definition has the form, "This genus and differentia are this thing." The definiens precedes the definiendum. Suppose we want to define "human being." The proper definition is not, "All human beings are rational animals," for that leaves open the possibility of other rational beings not being human. The proper definition is "All rational animals are human beings," for this wording

69 See *Posterior Analytics*, bk 2, ch. 10, 93b28–94a1 ff.

70 Aristotle, *Aristotle's Posterior Analytics* (Apostle), bk 2, ch. 7, 92b26–27.

71 See *Topics*, bk 6, ch. 1, 139a25–30.

72 *Topics* (Forester), bk 1, ch. 5, 102a32–37.

73 See *Posterior Analytics*, bk 2, ch. 4, 91a16–19; and *Topics*, bk 1, ch. 4, 101b37–102a.

conclusively demonstrates the convertibility of the two terms. Anything a rational animal must also be a human being.

A purely nominal or linguistic concept of definition would restrict the activity of definition formulation to a mere recording of the conventions of human language. Aristotle wants to investigate the empirical world. A real definition reports on natural kinds; it tells us about their features. While contemporary scientists try to formulate scientific laws understood as numerical or statistical regularities in nature, Aristotle conceives of science as a search for real definitions. Discovering "what things are" is the true business of rigorous science. (To investigate non-scientific definitions would be to move beyond the scope of the present discussion.[74])

What Aristotle means by a real definition identifies "the essence of something."[75] An essence is literally "τὸ τί ἦν εἶναι" (*to ti en einai*), "the what-it-is-to-be" of something. When I define "helium" as "the inert gas [genus] with two electrons [differentia]," I am claiming that the what-it-is-to-be of helium is the condition of being an inert gas possessing two electrons. It follows that we cannot have *a real* definition of a nonexistent being, for how could we identify the what-it-is-to-be of something that does not exist. Aristotle comes up with the example of a "goat-stag," a fictitious animal that is a cross between a deer and a goat. He writes, "You may know what … the name signifies when I say goat-stag, but it is impossible to know what a goat-stag is."[76] It is impossible to know what a goat-stag *is*, for it is *nothing* at all. To claim it is something is already a falsehood. Any real definition includes, then, an existential assumption. Definitions of goat-stags (and

74 Suppose someone were to ask for a real definition of an "all-terrain vehicle." All-terrain vehicles (ATVs) are an artificial kind. They are a human contraption. They are not natural features of the deep structure of reality. But they are also not make-believe objects like goat-stags or unicorns. So a real definition of an ATV seems possible, even in light of Aristotle's existence requirement. To define an ATV we need only identify the "essence," the genus and the differentia. An ATV is a motorized carriage (the genus) built to travel over any kind of surface (the differentia). Or suppose we were asked to define what a "substitute teacher" is. Substitute teachers are not a natural kind. Still, they actually do exist and we can formulate a real definition of a substitute teacher. A substitute teacher is a school teacher (the genus) who replaces the permanent teacher on a temporary basis (the differentia). So we can identify the definition of a substitute teacher, even though this is a social, economic, anthropological class rather than a true scientific category.

75 *Topics* (Forester), bk 1, ch. 4, 101b37–102a.

76 *Posterior Analytics* (Barnes), bk 2, ch. 7, 92b5–8 (in Aristotle, *Complete Works*).

unicorns) include a false existential implication. They are not just uninformative; they are, in any rigorous scientific sense, misleading.

APODEIXIS: DEMONSTRATION

Compare Aristotelian with modern science. Modern philosophers of science privilege the mechanistic explanations of physics. Authors such as Karl Popper, Carl Hempel, and Paul Oppenheim propose a deductive-nomological (covering-law) model of scientific explanation. They divide science into two complementary activities: (1) the discovery of scientific laws; and (2) the use of these laws to explain and make predictions. Aristotle, in contrast, explains the world, not in terms of mathematical laws, but in terms of real definitions. Nonetheless, he adopts a parallel model of scientific activity, dividing science into two complementary activities: (1) the discovery of real definitions; and (2) the use of these definitions to explain and make predictions.

Offhand attempts to discredit Aristotle's philosophy of science miss the mark. As Alexandre Koyré argues, the rejection of Aristotelian physics can be traced to the adoption of the metaphysical conviction that reality is ultimately mathematical. This numerical approach represents a return to Plato and the Pythagoreans. Koyré quotes Isaac Newton, "The business of true philosophy is to derive the nature of things … and to inquire after those laws on which the Great Creator actually chose to found this most beautiful Frame of the World."[77] Newton proposes a dual approach to science. Scientists are (1) to discover the nature of things and (2) to formulate mathematical laws. Later science has, by and large, championed the second aspiration.[78] This is somewhat misleading, for (as Nancy Cartwright indicates) modern science continues to rely on notions of natural kind. The periodic table is the most obvious example, but even physics cannot dispense with the idea that the world is made up of diverse kinds of things.

In Aristotle, we discover the deep causes of things by investigating nature. "To know a thing's nature is to know why it is."[79] Questions about cause collapse, then, into those of definition or essence. Aristotle cites a specific example. He explains, "The question 'What is an eclipse?' and its answer 'The privation of the moon's light by the interposition of the

77 Cited in Koyré, *From the Closed World*, 232, from Issac Newton, *Mathematical Principles* (Motto, Cajori), General Scholium, 543ff.

78 Some recent philosophers have challenged the nomological approach. I discuss the "new essentialism" of Brian Ellis and others in chapter 8.

79 *Analytica Posteriora* (Mure), bk 2, ch. 1, 90a32.

Earth' are identical with the question 'What is the reason [or cause] of eclipse?'" When we know what an eclipse is, we know what causes an eclipse. As it turns out, "The nature of the thing and the reason of the fact are identical."[80]

Seen from an Aristotelian perspective, the nomological view misconstrues causality. Laws report a regularity; they do not *cause* it. We may describe behaviour in mathematical terms, but the only things actually existing in the world are substances with natures. If, then, we want to identify and isolate the most fundamental causes, we must investigate real definitions to seize on the essential characteristics of the things.

As we have seen, Aristotle divides science into an inductive phase, producing a universal regularity (in Aristotle's case, a real definition), and a deductive one, applying that universal regularity to specific cases. Most past commentary focuses on Aristotle's account of *deductive* science, partly because the surviving texts display a similar emphasis. But this produces an impoverished account of scientific inquiry. It may seem as if Aristotle rushes in to consider how scientific knowledge should be displayed or demonstrated in syllogistic logic, without carefully considering how we initially generate scientific knowledge. A more patient inspection reveals, however, a scattered but thorough account of its genesis. I will consider Aristotle's description of both the deductive and inductive methods of science. Consider, first, how scientific knowledge should be put on display *after it has been produced*, and second, the inductive method by which it is produced.

In line with the usual scholarly emphasis, Aristotle (or his editors) are preoccupied with deductive science. True scientific knowledge is most perfectly expressed in the "scientific syllogism" or demonstration, in Greek, ἀπόδειξις (*apodeixis*).[81] A demonstration puts on display the reason for something. The premises in a rigorous demonstration must be "true, primary, immediate, better known than, prior to, and causative of the conclusion."[82] They must be familiar, factual, and necessarily true.[83] The conclusion must yield information about a species or secondary substance, i.e., about a class or group of individual things. And it must produce universal knowledge, ἐπιστήμη (*episteme*) or ἐπίστασθαι (*epistasthai*).[84]

80 Ibid., bk 2, ch. 1, 90a15–20.

81 He defines a demonstration as "a syllogism which produces scientific knowledge" (*Posterior Analytics* [Tredennick], bk 1, ch. 2, 71b18–20).

82 Ibid., bk 1, ch. 2, 71b20 ff.

83 See ibid., pt 1, ch. 4, 73a24–26.

84 Ibid., bk 1, ch. 31, 87b32–34.

These issues have been the subject of much scholarly discussion. I will argue that demonstration is, first and foremost, an argument from terms defined. In scientific syllogism, we begin with a real definition and deduce its consequences. Although rigorous science explains the relationships between classes, some of Aristotle's demonstrations (and inductions) seem to deal with individuals. But whether we are dealing with groups or individuals the basic structure of the deductive and inductive stages of science is, for Aristotle, the same. As we have already noted, induction has to begin, ultimately, with individuals.

In a discussion of thunderstorms (or more specifically, of different kinds of thunderstorms), Aristotle introduces the following first-figure syllogism. To paraphrase, "All extinguishing of lightning (*M*) is thunder (*P*). All storm clouds (*S*) extinguish lightning (*M*). All storm clouds (*S*) thunder (*P*)."[85] This rather bald example is intended as a demonstration. It begins (as Aristotle himself points out) with a definition of thunder.[86] In formal terms, a definition follows the logical pattern, "all *M* is *P*," where *P*, the predicate term, is what is being defined; and *M*, the middle term, is the essence or nature of the thing defined. To express the definition in correct form, "All extinction of lightning is thunder," where "thunder" is what is being defined; and "extinguishing lightning" is the essence or definition. ("Things that extinguish fire" is the genus; "things that extinguish lightning" [lightning being *heavenly* fire] is the differentia.)

Perfect demonstrations are, then, arguments from definition. We begin with a definition and deduce the necessary consequences. To set out this particular demonstration formally, "All *M* is *P*. All *S* is *M*. All *S* is *P*." (Barbara.) The conclusion links a class of subjects (storm clouds, or those of a particular type) to a necessary predicate by means of a definition.[87] Understanding what thunder is provides a causal explanation. We come to understand why storm clouds thunder – because they extinguish lightning.

Aristotle presents another example of demonstration.[88] (Clearly, a demonstration of an individual case.) Let *S* stand for moon (i.e., the only moon that orbits the earth). Let *P* stand for an eclipse. Let *M* stand for blocking

85 This is a paraphrase of ibid., bk 2, ch. 8, 93b8 ff. Again, Aristotle is not saying that every single storm cloud thunders; he is saying that he finds an inextricable link between the nature of storm clouds and thunder.

86 Ibid., bk 2, ch. 8, 93b12.

87 Thunder and clouds are, in fact, not convertible, for as it turns out – as strange as it sounds – there can be lightning (and therefore) thunder without clouds. Did Aristotle realize this?

88 Ibid., bk 2, ch. 8, 93a31 ff.

out the sun's light by the interposition of the earth. The demonstration runs: All blocking out light by the interposition of the earth is an eclipse. The moon suffers the blocking out of light by the interposition of the earth. So the moon suffers an eclipse. Translated into symbols, "All *M* is *P*. All *S* is *M*. All *S* is *P*" (again, Barbara).

As Aristotle again points out, we begin this demonstration with a real definition of an eclipse.[89] What is an eclipse? First, it is a "blocking of light" (the genus); and second, it is caused by "the interposition of the earth" (the differentia). So the proper Aristotelian definition is "All blocking of light by the interposition of the earth is an eclipse," where "eclipse" is the term being defined and "blocking of light by the interposition of the earth" is the essence or definition. Symbolically, All *M* (the essence) is *P* (the thing defined).

In both these examples, we use definition to elucidate the cause. Once we know what thunder is, we know why storm clouds thunder. Once we understand what an eclipse is, we know why the moon suffers an eclipse. In a properly formed demonstration, the middle term, the term that elucidates the essence or nature, does the work. It tells us what something is. Aristotle affirms, "everything we seek is a search for a middle term."[90] To seek out the middle term is, however, to seek a definition of something. Once we find the middle term, we know the essence of the thing in question, and we can deduce why things (events or substances) have the properties they do. This is, in Aristotle's mind, the role of science.

Perfect science operates by means of real definitions. But imperfect demonstrations are also possible. Consider the following syllogism: "All animals die. Human beings are animals. Therefore, all human beings die." This argument is valid and sound. It reveals a necessary cause of mortality. Why do human beings die? Because they are animals, not immortal gods or spirits or angels. But this is not a perfect demonstration, for it does not begin with a definition. To say "all animals die" is not to explain what animals are but to affirm the existence of a necessary property. (Note, in a proper definition, the definiendum and the definiens must be convertible. The terms "animals" and "things that die" are not convertible, for plants, which are not animals, also die. Note also that the predicate "animals" is not a composite predicate; it does not distinguish genus from differentia. But a proper definition must state the genus and

89 "But B is a definition of the other term, viz., in these examples, of the major term A" (*Analytica Posteriora* [Mure], bk 2, ch. 8, 93b7).

90 *Posterior Analytics* (Barnes), bk 2, ch. 3, 90a35.

differentia.) This perfectly valid syllogism about dying animals differs, then, from a perfect demonstration.

A perfect demonstration has the following form: "This genus and this differentia constitute this natural kind. This class (or individual) belongs to this genus and differentia. Therefore, this class (or individual) is this natural kind." The structure of the syllogism about mortal human beings is, "This genus has this necessary property. This class (or individual) belongs to this genus. Therefore, this class (or individual) has this necessary property." We might call this a "necessary-property" demonstration. It supplies us with *episteme*, with knowledge that is universal and true. But it does not discover the real definition. It is, in Aristotelian terms, less than rigorous.

I will not attempt any exhaustive classification of perfect and imperfect demonstrations here. As Aristotle himself admits, knowledge of definition is often unavailable. Still, rigorous knowledge about necessary and even accidental properties is still possible. Modern science rightfully includes such investigation within its scope.

WHY WE CANNOT PROVE DEFINITION

Given the prominence of definition in Aristotelian science, we might jump to the conclusion that definitions themselves come about through scientific demonstration. But this is impossible. As I have shown, a perfect demonstration begins with a definition. If we were to use a perfect demonstration to produce a definition, we would have to begin with the (true) definition in our first premise; that is, we would have to use the definition to prove one. This would "beg the question."[91] The conclusion, in stating the definition, would simply repeat (perhaps in new words) what the first premise said. There would be no inference; the arguer would simply assume what he or she had to prove.[92]

Aristotle cites the example of someone trying to prove through demonstration the essential nature of humanity.[93] In a perfect demonstration, we would have to prove the definition of humanity through a middle term exhibiting the nature or essence of the predicate "humanity." By stipulating this middle term in our premises, we would already have defined humanity. So we would have to know the definition in order to prove it! As Aristotle indicates, we could begin our demonstration with a different phrase, a synonym for "rational animal." But this use of "reciprocating terms" only

91 *Posterior Analytics*, bk 2, ch. 4, 91a12 ff.

92 See ibid., bk 2, ch. 4, 91a31, 91b10.

93 Ibid., bk 2, ch. 4, 91a27 ff.

disguises, and does not eliminate, the tautology. Aristotle concedes that in the curious case of something having two essences or an essence made up of two parts, you might demonstrate one essence or part through the other essence or part, but such esoteric possibilities need not detain us here.[94] The general point is clear: one cannot demonstrate, in the usual sense, a definition.

In the *Posterior Analytics*, Aristotle claims that those who try to prove (i.e., through demonstration) what the soul is, inevitably presuppose or assume a definition of the soul. Pythagoreans, for example, argue (to simplify) that the soul is life, and because life is a self-moved number the soul is a self-moved number. Aristotle claims that this demonstration proves nothing. Why? Because the definition is presupposed, not proved, by the two premises of the argument. An analogy may help. Suppose I want to argue that people should vote for Bob. I make the following argument: people should vote for the best candidate; Bob is the best candidate; so people should vote for Bob. This argument does no work. Unless we are already going to vote for Bob, we would not accept the premise that Bob is the best candidate. Something similar is going on in the Pythagorean argument. Unless we believe that souls are self-moved numbers, why should we accept that life is a self-moved number? This is to assume, rather than to prove, the Pythagorean doctrine of the soul. In the *Prior Analytics*, Aristotle defines the fallacy of "begging the question" as a failure to give a reason for something. "Begging or assuming the point consists ... in failing to demonstrate [ἀποδεικνύναι] the required proposition."[95] The argument about the soul being a self-moved number begs the question. The conclusion merely repeats what has already been assumed (not proved) in the premises. It fails to show that something follows from independent, prior, better-known reasons.

Aristotle also points out that a demonstration of a definition would have to be made up of three convertible terms.[96] In a definition, the defining expression (the definiens) picks out the essence of the term (the definiendum). They must share the same extension. All men must be rational animals, but all rational animals must also be human beings. But a demonstration of a definition would have to begin end with one. So it would have to possess the following form: "All *M* are *P* (convertible). All *S* are *M*. All *S*

94 Ibid., bk 2, ch. 8, 93a9–14. See Apostle, in Aristotle, *Aristotle's Posterior Analytics* (Apostle), 232n9.

95 *Prior Analytics* (Tredennick), bk 2, ch. 16, 64b28–30 (in Aristotle, *Aristotle in 23 Volumes*).

96 *Posterior Analytics*, bk 2, ch. 4, 91a13–27.

are *P* (convertible)." If, however, *M* has the same extension as *P*, and *S* has the same extension as *P*, *S* would have to have the same extension as *M* (transitivity). So *S* and *M* will have to be convertible. The syllogism would have to possess the following form: "All *M* is convertible with all *P*. All *S* is convertible with all *M*. All *S* is convertible with all *P*." We are left, not with a proper inference, but with a relation of simple identity, with three terms which signify the very same thing. The syllogism can be expressed: $M = P$; $S = M$; and $S = P$. The result is repetition, rather than logical inference. (Although Aristotle dismisses this logical form here, I will argue that it should, in fact, count as an inference in his system.)

IS INDUCTIVE SYLLOGISM *APODEIXIS*?

To summarize Aristotle's view, once we induce the definition, we can engage in demonstration, but we cannot use demonstration as a way of defining. That seems to be Aristotle's basic message. Except that things are not quite so simple! After arguing, adamantly and explicitly, that we cannot use demonstration to define anything, Aristotle turns around and claims that every definition requires a *demonstration* of something's nature. As he puts it, "Without demonstration [we] cannot become aware of what a thing is."[97] This cannot be a mere slip of the pen, for Aristotle repeats the point several times: even though he acknowledges that there is "no deduction or demonstration" of definition, he simultaneously claims that "what a thing is … is clear through deduction and through demonstration."[98] Again, he repeats himself,"[Although] neither a syllogism nor a demonstration of whatness can be formed, yet whatness is revealed through a syllogism and a demonstration."[99] These apparently contradictory claims, that we cannot demonstrate definition but that definition can only be revealed through demonstration, need to be reconciled.

If we hope to understand this very scrambled text, we must keep in mind that there are, as it turns out, various kinds of definition. Aristotle writes, "We conclude then that definition is (a) an indemonstrable statement of essential nature, or (b) a syllogism of essential nature differing from demonstration in grammatical form, or (c) the conclusion of a demonstration

97 *Posterior Analytics* (Barnes), bk 2, ch. 8, 93b16–20.

98 Ibid.

99 "[Although] neither a syllogism nor a demonstration of whatness can be formed, yet whatness is revealed through a syllogism and a demonstration" (*Posterior Analytics* [Apostle], bk2, ch. 8, 93b16–18).

giving essential nature.[100]" The first and most primary sort of definition Aristotle refers to depends on direct insight, rather than argument (It is a matter, so to speak, of the first level of induction.) As Aristotle puts out, it is "an *indemonstrable* statement of essential nature." But this direct insight can be formalized as an inductive syllogism. Definition, in this secondary or derivative sense, is then a kind of quasi-demonstration. So we begin with an intuition that induces the essence of something. We then construct a formal argument, an inductive syllogism, that puts this insight on display. This syllogism is what Aristotle refers to as "a syllogism of essential nature differing from demonstration in grammatical form." It differs from demonstration in grammatical form because it is an inductive syllogism, and (as we have already seen in a previous chapter) an inductive syllogism has a different arrangement of terms. The third kind of definition is merely the conclusion of this inductive syllogism, considered on its own, apart from the larger argument. This proposition, disconnected from the argument, states the genus and differentia of something. This is what Aristotle refers to as "the conclusion of a demonstration giving essential nature."

We have, then, three related ways of thinking about definitions. Human intelligence grasps what something is; the scientist parses out this illumination in the form of an inductive syllogism, and the lexicographer can then insert the conclusion of the inductive syllogism into a dictionary. Aristotle classifies the inductive syllogism that formalizing the original insight as a sort of imperfect demonstration. It does not have the strict form of a perfect demonstration but can be called a demonstration insomuch as it produces a necessarily true universal statement explaining the cause of something. It is, to use G.R.C. Mure's apt translation, a "quasi-demonstration."[101]

It must be acknowledged that my interpretation is, to put it mildly, unusual. Scholarly opinion is, for the most part, united in the belief that demonstration and induction are mutually exclusive logical procedures. De Rijk comments, "it is obvious and has never been ignored by the commentators that there is a difference between [induction] and [demonstration] in Aristotle."[102] Richard McKirahan asserts, "Demonstration is a form of teaching but it is quite different from [induction]."[103] And again, "[Induction]

100 *Analytica Posteriora* (Mure), bk 2, ch. 10, 94a11–14.

101 Aristotle elliptically refers here to his inductive syllogism about the cause of thunder (ibid., bk 2, ch. 10, 94a ff.).

102 De Rijk uses the Greek terms, ἐπαγωγή (*epagoge*); and ἀπόδειξισ (*apodeixis*) (de Rijk, Aristotle, vol.1, §2.54, 144).

103 Again, McKirahan uses the Greek *epagoge* (McKirahan, *Proofs and Principles*, 252).

has no place in achieved demonstrative sciences."[104] Similar sentiments are expressed elsewhere. Because earlier commentators have mistakenly equated inductive syllogism with the rare and logically trivial form of perfect induction, they have, in general, misunderstood its role in Aristotelian science. As Biondi remarks, "induction itself may be said to demonstrate, though it is not the strict sense of demonstrating."[105] This is what inductive syllogism is, a kind of inductive demonstration putting on display, in formal, logical dress, so to speak, the process of inductive inference that makes science possible.

As we have already seen, the inductive syllogism is deductively valid. It is necessarily the case that if the premises are true and if the logical property of convertibility properly holds, the conclusion must also be true. F.E. Peters writes, "In technical Aristotelian methodology *apodeixis* is a syllogistic demonstration that, if the premises are true and primary, will lead to *episteme*."[106] But a sound inductive syllogism is a syllogistic demonstration with true and primary premises that leads to *episteme*. (Their premises are primary in that they derive immediately from sense perception, instead of from argument; they form the ground floor of knowledge, so to speak.)

The root meaning of the word *apodeixis* or demonstration is to "show forth," or "point out."[107] Someone who demonstrates is someone who brings something to light, who puts it on display, who makes a public revelation. This is what inductive syllogism does. It makes a public spectacle of the inductive inference from particulars to universals. It gives a reason for something. The previous induction about bileless animals puts on display the reason why certain animals are long lived. (Aristotle himself affirms that "the *cause* of longevity in quadrupeds [horse, mule, etc.] is lack of bile."[108]) In this rudimentary sense then, inductive syllogism is demonstration.

For two other reasons, it could be argued that an inductive syllogism is, *in a subordinate sense*, a demonstration. First, Aristotle writes: "If we have *demonstrative* knowledge of a proposition, the predicate must apply necessarily to the subject."[109] Evaluated on this basis, however, a properly

104 Ibid.

105 Biondi, *Aristotle*, §3.2, 196.

106 Peters, *Greek Philosophical Terms*, s.v. "Apodeixis."

107 The word signifies, in English and Greek, a kind of pointing out, a showing forth, making known, exhibiting. See *Langenscheidt's Greek-English Dictionary* and *Liddell and Scott's Greek-English Lexicon*, s.v. ἀπόδειξις, *apódeixis*.

108 *Analytica Posteriora* (Mure), bk 2, 17, 99b5–6 (my italics).

109 "Otherwise we shall recognize neither the fact of the conclusion nor the reason for it as necessary" (*Posterior Analytics* [Tredennick], pt 1, ch. 6, 74b12–16; my italics).

constructed inductive syllogism produces demonstrative knowledge. (In the bileless-animals syllogism, the predicate "bileless animals" applies *necessarily* to the subject term, "long lived.") Second, Aristotle notes, "The most scientific of figures is the first figure … for it is by this figure, if not universally, at least as a general rule and in most cases, that the syllogism establishing the reason is effected."[110] Properly formed demonstrations are first-figure syllogisms. But the logical form of the inductive syllogism fits the pattern of the first figure. This is not immediately evident, but we only have to do a little work to recognize the underlying structure. If we redefine the terms in an inductive syllogism, in line with the logical role they play in the syllogism, we get, "*M P* (major); *M S* (minor); *S P*." The minor premise (with the subject term of the conclusion) is, however, convertible. When we convert the two terms, we get, "*M P* (major); *S M* (minor); *S P*. But this is a syllogism of the first figure.

THE SCIENTIFIC ROLE OF DEFINITION

We need to formulate a better explanation of the role of inductive syllogism in Aristotelian science. Aristotle believes that intellectual inquiry follows a precise path of development. We move from sense perception, to memory, to experience, to knowledge. In bringing up the example of astronomy, he observes: "It is the business of experience [i.e., induction] to give the principles which belong to each subject … Astronomical experience [i.e., observation] supplies the principles of astronomical science: for once the phenomena were adequately apprehended, the demonstrations of astronomy were discovered. Similarly with any other art or science."[111] This, then, is the role of induction/observation in science. Science begins with observation, but observation has to be somehow translated into theory. Induction provides the bridge between observation and knowledge. Understood intuitively, as a non-discursive leap of the intellect, induction brings us from immediate experience to the very first principles of scientific knowledge.

Aristotle thinks of scientific knowledge as knowledge of universals. Universals come to us through sense perception via inductive inference.[112] Aristotle remarks that the mere observation of, say, an eclipse would not constitute scientific knowledge, for it would not yield the universal that

110 *Posterior Analytics* (Tredennick), pt 1, ch. 14, 79a17–23.

111 *Prior Analytics* (Jenkinson), pt 1, ch. 30, 46a18–21 (in Aristotle, *Complete Works*).

112 Scientific knowledge "cannot be acquired by sense-perception … [for] universals cannot be perceived by the senses" (*Posterior Analytics* [Tredennick], b, 1, ch. 31, 87b28–35).

tells us why all eclipses occur. If, however, "after observing repeated instances" we succeed "in grasping the universal, we should have our [scientific] proof: because it is from the repetition of particular experiences that we obtain our view of the universal." This is plainly a reference to induction. Induction, fixing on a repetition of particular experiences, yields the knowledge that "exhibits the cause" and *proves* the point.[113]

Return to Aristotle's demonstration about thunder (or perhaps kinds of thunder). As we have already seen, Aristotle elaborates a demonstration of thunder, to wit, "All extinguishing of lightning is thunder. All storm clouds extinguish lightning. All storm clouds thunder."[114] This demonstration begins with a definition. But the question naturally arises, how do we arrive at the definition? How do we arrive at an understanding of what thunder is? Aristotle believes that this is the role of inductive reasoning. We simply intuit, from experience, *without any argument*, that thunder is the extinguishing of lightning (heavenly fire) in storm clouds (or in certain kinds of storm clouds). But we can also systematize this discovery, at the most basic level, in a kind of quasi-demonstration: "This, this, this noise is thunder. This, this, this noise is the extinguishing of lightning. Therefore (as Aristotle reverses the usual order of definitions), all extinguishing of lightning is thunder." This properly formed inductive syllogism produces the definition. It supplies us with a middle term. What is thunder? It is the extinguishing of lightning. This middle term is both the nature (and the cause) of thunder. Once we know the middle term constituting the definition, we can go on to use it to form the scientific demonstration above.

We now see what the role of inductive syllogism is in Aristotelian science. It puts on display the real definition, the convertible proposition identifying the essential attributes of something, as the basis for scientific demonstration. Inductive syllogism supplies the middle term, the real definition, we need for scientific reasoning. Scientists begin with induction, produce the real definition through a kind of direct discernment, and move on to deduce the consequences of this real definition in a proper demonstration.

Use the thunder example to illustrate the complementary role of inductive and deductive aspects of science. Define our terms (in line with the above demonstration). Let the middle term (*M*) be "extinguishing

113 Ibid., bk 1, ch. 31, 88a8–10. So we cannot use sense perception to gain demonstrative knowledge *unless* we intend the phrase "sense perception" to mean induction. Aristotle concludes, "Clearly then it is impossible to acquire knowledge of any demonstrable fact by sense-perception, *unless* by sense-perception one means the acquisition of knowledge by sense-perception" (ibid.) (my italics).

114 *Posterior Analytics*, bk 2, ch. 8, 93b8 ff.

lightning"; the predicate term (*P*), "thunder"; and the subject term (*S*), "this, this, and this noise." The inductive syllogism takes the form: All *S* is *P*; (all *S* is *M*, convertible to) all *M* is *S*; therefore, all *M* is *P* (the definition, which is also convertible).[115] But once we have this definition, we can use it to construct the corresponding scientific demonstration: All *M* is *P*; all *S* is *M*; therefore, all *S* is *P*. So we begin with sense perception, apprehend essence through induction, and are, then, able to make explanations using essence, using demonstration.

The inductive syllogism designed to produce the definition of thunder seems more of a scientific platitude than anything else. (It is not exactly clear what Aristotle has in mind. Jonathan Barnes suggests the following line of reasoning: anything hot sizzles; lightening is hot-ness in the heavens; so when there is hot-ness in the heavens, the heavens sizzle. This sizzle theory of thunder seems as good a suggestion as any other.) In any case, this inductive syllogism qualifies as a kind of demonstration, for it explains the cause of thunder. What thunder is is the cause of thunder. Thunder is the extinguishing of lightning but thunder occurs because there is an extinguishing of lightning. So the syllogism produces a necessarily true universal statement to explain the cause of something. In this sense at least, it produces scientific knowledge. It qualifies as a quasi-demonstration producing a scientific fact that turns out to be a definition.

A second, botanical example may serve to illustrate the process. Aristotle has an explanation as to why tree leaves fall in autumn. He believes that this happens because of "the coagulation of sap at the junction of the leaf-stalk and the stem."[116] (This is not completely off the mark. What happens is that as veins gradually restrict themselves and become clogged, a separate layer of cells forms at the leaf base.) How, then, do scientists in the field discover this truth about deciduous trees? They go out and observe at first-hand what happens with deciduous tree leaves in the fall. They then translate the results of their observations into language. They do not have to argue this knowledge into existence; they simply look at what happens to tree leaves and understand. This mental movement from observation to understanding might be formalized in the following inductive syllogism (to paraphrase Aristotle): "Vine, fig, etc., are deciduous. Vine, fig, etc., coagulate sap. All sap-coagulators are deciduous." The conclusion of this inductive syllogism is a definition of deciduous. What is "deciduous"?

115 If we wanted to be more exact, we could formalize the syllogism: All $\{S_1, S_2, S_3 \ldots\}$ is *P*; all $\{S_1, S_2, S_3 \ldots\}$ is *M* (convertible); therefore, all *M* is *P* (convertible, definition). But more about this next chapter.

116 *Posterior Analytics* (Apostle), bk 2, ch. 17, 99a28–29.

Figure 4.1
Aristotelian science

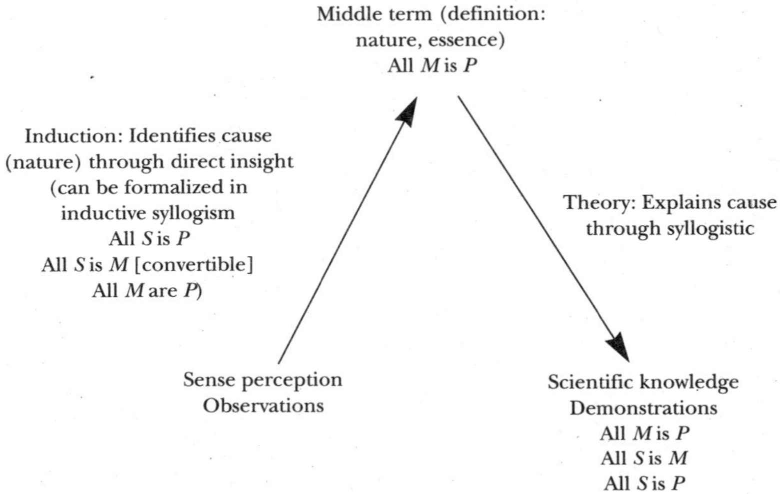

Something that has sap (genus) that coagulates (differentia). (Note, as in any definition, the terms "deciduous" and "sap-coagulator" are convertible.) But once we know what the nature of "deciduous" is, we can construct a corresponding scientific demonstration. In R.J. Hankinson's reformulation: "All sap-coagulators are deciduous. All broad-leaved trees are sap-coagulators. All broad-leaved trees are deciduous."[117] Once again, we move from the observation of nature via induction, to knowledge of real definition (essence), to a proper theoretical explanation in a rigorous (i.e., logically necessary and universal) demonstration. Induction understood, first, as intuition or insight, second, as inductive syllogism, plays a key role in this process. The practice of science can be schematically depicted as in figure 4.1.

Clearly, Aristotle is excessively restrictive when it comes to the formal structure of science. If perfect science begins with a knowledge of essence, knowledge of a necessary attribute should be enough, even on his own scheme, to secure some kind of scientific understanding. Consider the bileless-animal syllogism: "All human beings, horses, mules, etc., are long lived. All human beings, horses, mules, etc., are bileless. All bileless

117 Hankinson, "Philosophy of Science," 122.

animals are long lived." As we have already pointed out, this conclusion is not a definition. (Bileless and long lived are not convertible; other beings not bileless are long lived.) Nevertheless, we can use the conclusion to begin the following scientific demonstration: "All bileless animals are long lived. All dolphins are bileless. Therefore, all dolphins are long lived." This is clearly a scientifically informative procedure. This should count as part of rigorous science. We have a parallel movement from sense perception via induction to generalization about necessary attributes and then down, via a scientific demonstration, to an informative conclusion. The inductive syllogism explains a cause of longevity, whereas the demonstration explains why dolphins are necessarily long lived. Although the induction of necessary properties is, in some epistemological sense, a less perfect form of inductive inference, it is obviously a useful scientific procedure.

Jonathan Barnes suggests that Aristotle's account of demonstrative science "is exclusively concerned with the teaching of facts already won; it does not describe how scientists do, or ought to, *acquire* knowledge; it offers a formal model of how teachers should *present* and *impart* knowledge."[118] Guthrie, for one, disagrees (diplomatically).[119] Although Barnes' interpretation handily solves a traditional problem in Aristotelian exegesis – how Aristotle could have made so little use of his preferred method of scientific demonstration in his own scientific writing – Barnes' claim that science is almost purely pedagogical is extreme. In a general discussion of birds, Aristotle reports,

> Birds … all have a head, a neck, a back, a belly, and what is analogous to a chest. [They are] remarkable among animals as having two feet, like man, but bent backwards as quadrupeds do … [They] are furnished with a mouth, but an exceptional one, for they have neither lips nor teeth, but a beak. Neither have they ears nor nose, but only passages for the sensations connected with these organs … Like all other animals they have two eyes, and these are devoid of lashes … Further birds have neither tessellations nor hair, but feathers and the feathers are invariably furnished with quills.[120]

These generalizations about birds derive from extensive and meticulous observations of many diverse species of birds. We tend to take this kind of

118 Barnes, "Aristotle's Theory of Demonstration," 77.

119 Guthrie, *History of Greek Philosophy*, vol. 6, 170–2.

120 *History of Animals* (Thompson), bk 2, ch. 12, 593a29–594b12 (in Aristotle, *Complete Works*).

obvious generalization for granted, but the logical movement from observing experience to formulating a general principle could be cast in the form of a series of inductive syllogisms. How, for example, did Aristotle come to the conclusion that birds have feathers? He must have reasoned somewhat as follows: robins, red-tailed hawks, ducks, etc., are birds; robins, red-tailed hawks, ducks, etc., have feathers; therefore, all birds have feathers. This is an inductive syllogism. It is not that Aristotle disregards his own account of scientific methodology in his scientific work, then, but that he is preoccupied with the *inductive* rather than the deductive phase of science. (Granted, worded this way, the argument that birds have feathers represents a kind of induction that is so basic and obvious it comes precariously close to bare observation. But even in its simplest formulation, this line of reasoning requires a leap from the specific to the more general. Presumably, Aristotle would think that the insight into birds having feathers involves some issue of cause and effect. For example, perhaps they necessarily have feathers because feathers are suited to flying, and so on.)

Many contemporary commentators follow Barnes in claiming that for Aristotle scientific demonstrations are purely pedagogical. The examples Aristotle uses in his philosophical work on science are obvious illustrations of logical method rather than scientific discoveries in their own right. Still, the process is clearly useful. If, for example, we know that mammals are all warm blooded and we discover that whales are mammals (perhaps because we observe them nursing their young), we can immediately conclude that whales must also be warm blooded. This deduction is not without scientific value.

ARISTOTLE VERSUS MODERNITY

Aristotle's view of science differs in important ways from contemporary philosophical accounts. To begin with, Aristotle is not bothered by modern worries about the problematic nature of induction. He views induction as an entirely legitimate form of *rational* insight. Induction fully justifies its own conclusions. The same capacity for intelligent understanding expressing itself in deduction reveals itself in induction. Induction has epistemological authority in its own right. We discuss these issues in a future chapter.

Secondly, Aristotle is an unabashed (though qualified) realist. Contemporary philosophers take the Kantian separation of noumenon from phenomenon for granted. Aristotle does not harbour such scruples. The nature of reality is close at hand. Although induction does not, in any naive sense, copy the world, it provides a trustworthy link between real things and the life of the mind. Science is difficult; we do make mistakes. Although we cannot absolutely disprove the relentless sceptic, an exaggerated scepticism is unworkable and implausible.

Thirdly, Aristotle conceives of the activity of the perfect science as an investigation of essences. His essentialism boils down to the view that we can separate things in the world into kinds. To question the legitimacy of this ability would fly in the face of our reliance on sense perception and undermine any pretence to human knowledge. It is true that Aristotle exaggerates the importance of strictly defining things (in terms of their *essential* qualities). In the actual practice of science, it may be that necessary or even accidental properties must suffice.

Fourthly, Aristotle emphasizes nature over mathematical law. The notion of kind is prior to that of quantity, or rather, quantity is itself a kind, so Aristotle's account subsumes mathematical models of science. Seen from an Aristotelian perspective, the mathematical turn is unscientific, insomuch as it overlooks the basic causes of things happening as they do in the world.[121] Modern science investigates events, but the natures of events depend, more fundamentally, on the natures of things. The world is made up of things; science investigates the natures of those things. Once we understand what things are, we can begin to understand the ways they interact to produce events in the world.

The great advantage of the modern approach is that it widens the scope of science to include the empirical study of all necessary properties. Any natural necessity can be described in terms of a numerical law. We can go far beyond fundamental physics: the way stratocumulus clouds form is a matter of necessity – likewise the way photosynthesis operates or the way iodine kills bacteria. Insomuch as these events unfold in accordance with quantitative laws, they can be described in mathematical terms. The project of coming up mathematical descriptions opens up the world to almost limitless scientific exploration. And the modern development of sophisticated statistical techniques pushes the envelope of science even further. We can even study contingent properties with at least some claim to scientific rigour.

Aristotle writes, "We hold, not only that scientific knowledge is possible, but that there is a definite first principle of knowledge by which we recognize ultimate truths."[122] What I have called "the first level of induction" –

121 One might adopt, of course, a process metaphysics, a metaphysics of becoming, where events are more fundamental than things, but this is foreign to Aristotle.

122 *Posterior Analytics* (Tredennick), bk 1,ch. 3, 22–25.

induction understood as a direct, non-discursive insight – is the first principle of knowledge. Through a primitive but powerful movement of illumination, the mind is able to hit on concepts, universal claims, and definitions describing the world. This inductive process operates by means of the intellectual faculty of *nous*, which is always true and even more infallible than scientific demonstration.[123]

PROBLEMS OF EXEGESIS

Problems of exegesis arise because Aristotle (or his editors) use terms such as "induction," "demonstration," or "definition" in various specialized ways. If we hope to sort out the resulting imbroglio, we need to distinguish between different kinds of induction. Consider the difference between what I have called "necessary" and "essential" induction. Necessary induction proves that a property (necessarily) attaches to a subject; the essential, reveals the definition of something. Aristotle thinks these are two very different issues. (He is less interested in accidental properties, which merely distract from rigorous science.)

Aristotle repeatedly insists that it is impossible to know by definition the nature of something without knowing that it exists.[124] His vehemence derives, in part, from his focus on real rather than nominal definitions. But there is a second issue also at stake. If we do not know what properties an entity has, i.e., if we do not know which properties (necessarily) exist, how could we determine which properties are essential? For example, if I do not know that humans are rational, i.e., if I do not know that rationality is a (necessary) property of humanity, how could I know that humans are to be defined as rational animals? Logically, we must identify the (necessary) properties of a thing, before determining which of these would qualify as the essence.

Aristotle says, "we never get to know any attribute, whether essential or accidental, by defining it."[125] And again, "The degree of our knowledge of a thing's essential nature is determined by the [fact that] we are aware that it exists."[126] Knowledge of the existence of a property is *logically* prior to

123 *Posterior Analytics*, bk 2, ch. 19, 100b5 ff.

124 "In that case a man will know by definition what a thing's nature is without knowing whether it exists. But that is impossible" (*Analytica Posteriora* [Mure], bk 2, ch. 7, 92b17–18).

125 *Posterior Analytics* (Tredennick), bk 2, ch. 3, 90b16–18.

126 *Analytica Posteriora* (Mure), bk 2, ch. 8, 93a28–29. I am, in the main, agreeing with the general sense of Mure's translation.

knowledge of the same property as an essential feature.[127] We cannot know that three-sidedness is the essence of a triangle without first knowing that three-sidedness is a property of triangles. It is in this precise sense that claims about essential characteristics rely on prior knowledge about the mere existence of these essential characteristics.

While we learn whether something exists through necessary induction, necessary induction does not distinguish between essential and non-essential properties. This is why Aristotle would (correctly) deny that necessary induction could be used to arrive at definitions. "Because [necessary] induction proves not what the essential nature of a thing is but that it has or has not some attribute."[128] To arrive at definition, we need something more, that is, we need to be aware both of the property and of its essential connection to a thing. *Essential* induction is, then, the engine of definition.

Although necessary and essential inductions begin in a movement of intellectual discernment, they may also be cast into the logical form of an inductive syllogism. Suppose we express in a syllogism the basic insight that the rotation of a radius through 360 degrees is a necessary property of a circle. Induction ultimately begins with our perception of actual circles. We might formalize the inductive inference in the following way. Premise: This, this, this shape has a radius that rotates through 360 degrees. Premise: This, this, this shape is a circle (convertible). Conclusion: Therefore, all circles have a radius that rotates through 360 degrees (non-definition; non-convertible). The conclusion of this syllogism cannot be a true definition, for the terms are not convertible. (The radii of all closed figures must be characterized by rotation through 360 degrees, for that is the only way a circumference could come back around and touch itself.) So this syllogism, which I will call syllogism A, informs us of a necessary property of circles.

We might, however, use an inductive syllogism to demonstrate the definition of a circle. Consider the following syllogism, which I will call syllogism B: Premise: This, this, this shape is a circle. Premise: This, this, this shape is a closed figure with every point equidistant from a centre (convertible). Conclusion: Therefore, all closed figures with every point equidistant from a centre are circles (definition; convertible). The conclusion of syllogism B is the definition of a circle. The two terms are convertible. Every closed

127 This is not a comment about temporal sequence. Even supposing we can recognize that an attribute exists and that it is an essential attribute all-at-once, even if this awareness could happen in a single simultaneous leap of recognition, the logical priority holds.

128 Ibid., bk 2, ch. 7, 92a37–b.

figure (genus) equidistant from a centre (differentia) is a circle. The conclusion puts on display the *essential* feature that makes a circle a circle.

Compare syllogisms A and B. Both are inductive syllogisms. Both possess the same logical form, the same arrangement of terms. Nonetheless, they are different kinds of arguments because they yield different kinds of scientific information. Syllogism A identifies a necessary property; it is a logical demonstration of the *existence* of a necessary property. Syllogism B identifies an essential property; it is a logical demonstration of *definition*. Because syllogism B yields the most important kind of knowledge, it is a more perfect argument. This is why Aristotle insists that a theory of "induction ... affords sufficient grounds for holding that [demonstration of] definition and demonstration [of existence] are not the same."[129]

Aristotle comments, "what a man is and that a man is are different."[130] We cannot know essence and existence by the same argument. Aristotle differentiates between inductive arguments that produce definitions and inductive arguments producing claims about necessary (or existent) properties. "Moreover," he goes on to explain, "if one were to prove both the whatness and the existence of [the properties of] an object, how would he do it with the same argument? For a definition signifies one thing, and so does a [necessary] demonstration, but the whatness of a man is different from the fact that he exists."[131] So we are left with two kinds of inductive syllogism: one proves existence, one proves essence. (In fact, Aristotle claims that we can "demonstrate" existence through observation as well as through inductive syllogism. The geometry teacher proves that a triangle has thee sides, not by coming up with a definition, but by drawing one on the blackboard. Aristotle suggests that this exercise is, in the most rudimentary sense, a demonstration; it puts on display the existence of something.[132])

Recognizing this distinction between what we can call "existential" and "definitional" syllogisms helps resolve one remaining textual difficulty. In a very puzzling passage, Aristotle seems to assert that knowledge of essence is not to be obtained by definition! Indeed, he seems to claim that we cannot discover a thing's essence at all, either through definition or demonstration. "It appears from these considerations," Aristotle writes, "that definition

129 *Posterior Analytics* (Tredennick), bk 2, ch. 3, 90b14–16.

130 *Posterior Analytics* (Barnes), bk 2, ch. 7, 92b10–12. This forthright claim foreshadows Thomas' later distinction between *esse* and *essentia* (existence and essence), but Aristotle's preoccupations are more limited.

131 *Posterior Analytics* (Apostle), bk 2, ch. 7, 92b5–11.

132 Perhaps this is what Aristotle intimates in *Posterior Analytics*, bk 2, ch. 7, 92b14 ff.

neither demonstrates nor proves anything, and that knowledge of essential nature is not to be obtained either by definition or by demonstration."[133] If we hope to make sense of what is going on here in the text, we need to closely analyze the problematic passage, clarifying its meaning. Once we recognize the difference in kinds of induction, we can provide a reading in line with Aristotle's general thought.

Aristotle seems to be making two separate claims: (1) "definition [understood as intuition] neither demonstrates nor proves anything"; and (2) definition "is not to be obtained either by [a demonstration of] definition or by [a] demonstration [of existence]." The first claim is readily explained. To prove or demonstrate something is to come up with reasons in support of a conclusion. At the first level of induction, definition happens intuitively, without argument. No proving or demonstrating is going on, just an act of bare discernment. Because the intellectual movement of *nous* or insight does not provide reasons in support of a conclusion, it does not "prove or demonstrate" definition. It finds the definition without proof. We discover essence, then, through discernment not argument.

Aristotle's second claim can be divided into two further ones: (1) that knowledge of essence does not come from demonstrations of existence (formalizations of necessary induction); and (2) that knowledge of essence does not come from demonstrations of essence (formalizations of essential induction). Subclaim (1) goes without saying. Demonstrations of existence only show us which attributes exist, not which attributes are essential. But (2) is more puzzling. As we have seen, demonstrations of essence put on display the essential attributes of something, and yet Aristotle wants to argue that they do not produce knowledge of essence. At first glance, this seems contradictory.

But Aristotle has a legitimate point. Inductive syllogism is inconclusive as a method of definition, not because it is an invalid argument, but because it cannot demonstrate with logical necessity what the *essential* attributes are. Consider syllogisms A and B. They are both valid syllogisms, possessing exactly the same format, and displaying the very same arrangement of terms: "All *S* is *P.* (All *S* is *M,* convertible to) All *M* is *S.* All *M* is *P.*" Yet syllogism A only identifies a necessary property, whereas syllogism B yields a definition. The logical difference is that the conclusion of syllogism B is convertible to "All *P* is *M.*" The conclusion of syllogism A is not convertible. But this knowledge of convertibility is not forced on us by the arrangement of terms. It is, so to speak, before the logical fact. It is something we bring to the argument, not something proved by the argument. Hence, Aristotle's

133 *Analytica Posteriora* (Mure), bk 2, ch. 7, 92b35–37.

insistence that we can have a demonstration of definition but that we cannot demonstrate what the definition is. We must arrive at syllogisms A and B with some prior understanding of what a circle is. Otherwise we could not identify which syllogism qualifies as a proper demonstration of how we define a circle.

Aristotle is claiming "that knowledge of essential nature is not to be obtained either by [a demonstration of] definition [by itself] or by [a] demonstration [of existence by itself]." Proving that all circles have a property only demonstrates that the property is a necessary attribute. It does not prove it is the defining trait. We can only grasp that fact through the first level of induction, i.e., through direct discernment. Consider syllogisms A and B. Syllogism A links "circles" with the property of having "a radius that rotates through 360 degrees." Syllogism B links circles with the property of having "every point equidistant from a centre." The conclusion of syllogism B is convertible because it is the definition. The conclusion of syllogism A is not convertible. But how can we determine which conclusion is convertible? Not through logic. We have to add something more to the logical form of the argument if we are to end up with knowledge of convertibility. We have to add a moment of mental illumination. This is Aristotle's point. Definition depends on a non-discursive moment of insight that exists outside logic.

Logic, narrowly construed as the arrangement of terms in a demonstration, cannot produce definition. We could try to reconstruct syllogism B to render the information about essential attributes logically explicit. We might argue, "Premise$_1$: This, this, this is a circle. Premise$_2$: This, this, this has as an essential characteristic, equidistance from a centre. Conclusion: All things that have equidistance from a centre as an essential characteristic are circles." This is a valid inductive syllogism. But it does not *prove* what the essence of a circle is. It *assumes* what the essence of a circle is. Is premise$_2$, which identifies the essence of a circle, true? Only someone who already knows what a circle is can know that premise$_2$ is indeed true. It is not the argument but prior knowledge that identifies what the essential property of a circle is. This knowledge must come from insight, not from argument.

Aristotle sets up essential induction as the most rigorous and penetrating form of insight. He downplays or takes for granted the distinction between accidental and necessary properties. Human intelligence can, he believes, recognize what is necessary and what is accidental in the same way that it picks up on the more momentous distinction between essential and necessary properties. We distinguish these through intuition or insight, not through argument. Consider the following two syllogisms: "This, this, this animal is brown. This, this, this animal is a dog. All dogs are brown animals." And: "This, this, this animal has four legs. This, this, this animal is a dog. All dogs are animals that have four legs." The first syllogism reports on an accidental property of dogs; the second syllogism reports on a necessary property of dogs. Aristotle thinks that we can and regularly do distinguish between accidental and necessary properties. Everyone knows that some dogs are naturally not brown, and that dogs – baring mishap, disease, or artificial alterations – have four legs. These facts are immediately evident to anyone who thoroughly sets about learning about dogs. But we know these facts, not through argument, but through an attentive grasp of experience. Induction, understood as a kind of direct intuition, allows us to make sense of what we see. And it allows us to make sense of dogs. On some very basic level, induction includes the ability to distinguish between the accidental and the necessary.[134]

To summarize, Aristotle presents essential induction, understood as a non-discursive intuition, as the sole means of elaborating definition. His thought is remarkably complex. At a later point in the *Posterior Analytics*, he writes, "We have already said how what a thing is [the essence] is set out in the terms [i.e., in the subject, middle, and predicate terms of a syllogism], and in what way there is or is not demonstration or definition of it."[135] Inductive syllogisms of definition are possible; they serve a useful purpose but they are irredeemably after the fact. Definitions always originate in a flash of bare intelligence. This first level of induction, what I have already called true or strict induction, is the most reliable manifestation of human rationality.[136]

Modern commentaries sometimes find support for the modern view of induction from selected passages in the *Posterior Analytics* commenting on the insufficiency or inconclusiveness of inductive reasoning. They take such passages out of context. Aristotle does argue that the *necessary* would be *insufficient* for *essential* induction and that the inductive syllogism that

134 But if brownness is obviously an accidental trait of "dogginess"; and four-leggedness, a necessary trait of dogginess – identifying the essence of dogginess is a much more puzzling endeavour. Obviously, a three-legged dog, although defective, would still be a dog. So four-leggedness cannot be the essential characteristic of dogginess. Perhaps Aristotle would define a dog as a "domesticated wolf," where "wolf" is the genus; and "domesticated," the differentia. I will not pursue the matter here. We should simply note that Aristotle, rightly or wrongly, privileges essential induction as the most accomplished form of inductive inference.

135 *Posterior Analytics* (Barnes), bk 2, ch. 13, 96a20–22.

136 *Posterior Analytics*, bk 2, ch. 19, 100b5 ff.

proves *definition* is *incomplete* unless it is accompanied by an intuitive insight triggered by sense perception. Still, he believes that induction is, in the first instance, a reliable form of insight and, in the second instance, a valid syllogism. Aristotle never argues in the way of Locke and Hume that inductive syllogisms are inconclusive and therefore formally invalid.

DIVISION

In addition to discussing demonstration or inductive syllogism, Aristotle proposes a method of division or of dividing into groups, as a way of arriving at an adequate definition. We can reconstruct a somewhat simplified variant of this originally Platonic method from a passage in the *Posterior Analytics*.[137] Suppose we wish to define "humanity." Begin by noting that humanity is some kind of an animal. "Animal" serves, then, as the genus. We must then divide this group, "animal," into smaller and smaller groups until we have isolated the exact group corresponding to the differentia. So, for example, we might first divide "animal" into "aquatic" (fish) and "terrestrial," with humanity belonging in the "terrestrial" group; divide "terrestrial" into "feathered" (birds) and "featherless," with humanity in the "featherless" group; divide "featherless" into "unfooted" (or "serpentine") and "footed," with humanity in the "footed" group – and so on, finally dividing "two-footed" into "non-rational" (monkeys and apes) and "rational."[138] Humanity belongs in the "rational" group, and we have completed our definition, for "we have reached a point at which there is no further differentiation."[139] So we can conclude that humanity is a "rational animal." In this way then, we may arrive at a definition through an enumeration of the genus and differentia of "human being." This process is represented in figure 4.2.

Aristotle points out that the method of division must be carried out in a certain way. Groups must be arranged in the proper order. We must move from larger to smaller groups, and the series of divisions must be complete.[140] In our example, we divided each succeeding group into two

137 Ibid., bk 2, ch. 13. See, especially, 97a25 ff. Plato elucidates a similar method in his *Sophist*. Porphyry made the method famous.

138 See, for example, ibid., bk 2, ch. 5, 92a; and *Topics*, bk 2, ch. 5, 17–20.

139 *Posterior Analytics* (Tredennick), bk 2, ch. 13, 97b5–8.

140 The series must be read in the right direction, i.e., backward, from last to first, not from first to last. We can say that all terrestrial, wingless, footed, two-footed, rational beings are animals, but we cannot say that all animals are terrestrial, wingless, etc. We can predicate "animal" of all "terrestrial," "wingless," "footed," "two footed," and "rational," but we cannot predicate "terrestrial," "wingless," and so on, of all animals.

Figure 4.2
A definition of "human being" by the method of division

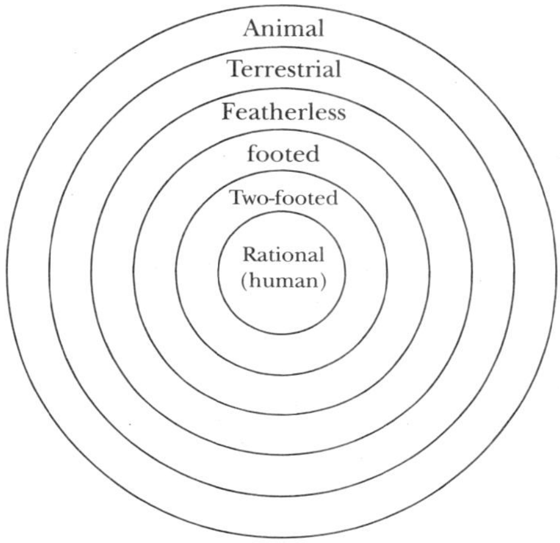

parts. But Aristotle claims that this method of "division by dichotomy" may be problematic.[141] We cannot assume that each new group being divided into differentiae should always be divided into only two parts. Perhaps some groups should be divided into three or four (etc.) different parts. Maybe we should have several lines of division, making use of many differentiae simultaneously. McKirahan elaborates a modern version of this method, based on a citation from the *Parts of Animals,* that permits such multifarious division.[142]

But an even deeper problem with division, understood as a method of definition, is that the whole procedure begs the question. How does the individual doing the defining know where to start and stop? How does he or she know which differentia denote essential properties? Aristotle writes, "Is man animal or inanimate? If he [the person defining "man"] *assumed* animal, he has not deduced it. Again, every animal is either terrestrial or aquatic: he *assumed* terrestrial. And that man is the whole [expression] – a terrestrial animal – is not necessary from what has been said, but he

141 See *Parts of Animals,* bk 1, chs 2–3; see Hankinson, "Philosophy of Science," 124–7.

142 McKirahan, *Principles and Proofs,* ch. 9, 111–21; and *Parts of Animals,* bk 1, ch. 3, 644a2–8.

assumes this too."[143] The method of division assumes the case; it does not prove it. If we already know what a human being is, everything follows. If, however, we do not know what a human being is, it is hard to see how we could ever to implement this method.

Division, Aristotle thinks, can (like inductive syllogism) reveal the necessary properties, but it cannot prove the essential properties. We could, for example, use the method of division to identify "humanity" as a "terrestrial animal," but this is not enough for the definition. As Aristotle puts it, "It is quite possible that the whole expression should be truly predicable of man, and yet not exhibit the essence or essential nature of man."[144] This is the difficulty. Even if division can inform us of the existence of necessary properties, it does not tell us which necessary properties are essential. Aristotle adds that this is not surprising, "since presumably [necessary] induction too proves nothing, but nevertheless it gives some information."[145] Division, like inductive syllogism, provides some information but does not by itself secure what is *essential.* Without *essential* induction, division is helpless to produce the definition of anything.

Division should be thought of as a heuristic device, as a way of sorting through our ideas and identifying what we already know, and not as a rigorous logical argument. On Aristotle's account, we can only come to a full understanding of an essence through a kind of mental illumination as a consequence of directly observing something in our experience. This is, in the first and most important sense, what induction is about. Science begins, then, not in argument, demonstration, or theory, but in the first, intuitive level of induction. No wonder that a contemporary scepticism about induction should inevitably lead to a more global scepticism, not merely about definition, but even about the very existence of natural kinds and about science itself.

RECOGNITION

We have been focusing on Aristotle's account of science. We are now in a better position to revisit and elucidate the different kinds or levels of induction. Begin with two fundamental distinctions. First, we must distinguish induction as intuitive discernment and as argument. Second, we must distinguish induction dealing with necessary properties and that

143 *Posterior Analytics* (Barnes), bk 2, ch. 5, 91b17–22. Aristotle (or his editors) mixes arguments about necessary and essential induction (my italics).

144 *Posterior Analytics* (Tredennick), bk 2, ch. 5, 91b25–28.

145 Ibid., bk 2, ch. 5, 91b34–35.

Table 4.2
Induction as intuition and argument

	Induction as intuition	*Induction as argument*
Induction of necessary properties	*First Level* True induction in the best epistemological sense (ἐπαγωγή)	*Third Level* Inductive syllogism strictly understood (ὁ ἐξ ἐπαγωγῆς συλλογισμός)
Induction of Non-necessary properties	*Second Level* Any recognition of likeness, belonging, unity, etc. (ἀγχίνοια)	*Fourth Level* Dialectical or rhetorical induction including: arguments by analogy (τῶν ὁμοίων), arguments by example (παράδειγμα)

dealing with non-necessary (or accidental) ones. We might represent these distinctions as in table 4.2.

Consider first induction as an intuitive movement of the mind. We have focused, to this point, on the first level of induction, a sort of immediate awareness enabling us to identify necessary and essential properties. This is in keeping with Aristotle's own metaphysical priorities. Although we can intuit what is necessarily true, we may also have insights into things that are accidental or merely plausible. This is what happens at the second level of induction. As Aristotle does not coin any special term for this less rigorous form of non-verbal induction, we will use the English term "recognition."[146] Recognition is a quite general mental ability enabling us to identify, in a non-discursive moment of understanding, some resemblance or similitude. We can extract out likenesses, discern patterns, generalize in a loose and tentative way, and divide things into classes, based on accidental attributes. This second level of inductive reasoning operates by means of a less rigorous power of mental illumination. It picks out a more superficial form of likeness or similarity.

The Greek has several terms we could use to refer to the general mental capacity for recognition: ἀγχίνοια (*anchinoia*, the readiness of mind, quick wit, ability to quickly grasp a middle term),[147] εὐστοχία (*eustochia*, quickness in guessing, happy conjecture, sagacity),[148] δεινότης (*deinotes*,

146 Thanks to Margaret Burgess for suggesting this term.

147 *Posterior Analytics*, bk 2, ch. 34, 89b10–20; and *Nicomachean Ethics*, bk 6, ch. 9, 1142b5.

148 Ibid., bk 6, ch. 9, 1142a35 ff.

cleverness, shrewdness, mental dexterity),[149] and even μῆτις (*metis*, skill, cunning, knack), a term not used by Aristotle.[150] These words all refer, in one way or another, to a kind of ready intelligence of a lesser sort, exhibiting itself in skill, shrewdness, knack, craft, wily understanding. Recognition is a kind of cleverness, a sort of mental quickness. It abstracts concepts, propositions, and principles to apply to contingent, artificial, or accidental events or things. It identifies resemblances of a looser sort; it seizes on what is probably true, what may be true, what is sometimes true. Consider, for example, the case of an approximate science.

Although the most perfect science deals with necessary properties, Aristotle realized that many natural events happen "for the most part" or "as a general rule" and that we can have scientific demonstrations of these "for the most part" predications.[151] He introduces, for example, the issue of facial hair.[152] Our daily experience may prompt us to conclude that men have beards and women are beardless. But this cannot be a case of induction proper, the first level of induction, for facial hair is neither a necessary nor an essential feature of maleness. You see beardless men and bearded women. Rigorously speaking then, we do not discern the usual relationship between facial hair and gender through true inductive reasoning but only through recognition. We *recognize* that men seem to share a certain likeness; they seem to share the common property of facial hair.

To discern an accidental property is merely to recognize. Suppose I suddenly realize that every woman in this room is wearing a red dress. I cannot do this without recognizing a feature these particular women all seem to share. But this feature – wearing a red dress – is not a necessary feature of the world. It is a matter of mere circumstance. Even if this were, in an enumerative sense, a perfect induction, even if I were to individually observe every woman in this crowd, it would not count as a rigorous insight. Because this generalization deals with accidental rather than necessary features, it only qualifies as recognition rather than as an instance of rigorous scientific induction.

In the *Rhetoric* Aristotle tells the following picturesque story about the famous fabulist Aesop:

149 Ibid., bk 6, ch. 12, 1144a23 ff.

150 See Detienne and Vernant, *Cunning Intelligence.*

151 "Teeth and all other natural things either normally or invariably come about in a given way" (*Physics* [Mure], bk 2, ch. 8, 198b34). See *Posterior Analytics*, bk 2, ch. 12, 96a8–19.

152 See ibid., bk 2, ch. 12, 96a8–11.

> Aesop, defending before the assembly at Samos a popular leader who was being tried for his life, told this story: A fox, in crossing a river, was swept into a hole in the rocks; and, not being able to get out, suffered miseries for a long time through the swarms of fleas that fastened on her. A hedgehog, while roaming around, noticed the fox; and feeling sorry for her asked if he might remove the fleas. But the fox declined the offer; and when the hedgehog asked why, she replied, "These fleas are by this time full of me and not sucking much blood; if you take them away, others will come with fresh appetites and drink up all the blood I have left." "So, men of Samos," said Aesop, "my client will do you no further harm; he is wealthy already. But if you put him to death, others will come along who are not rich, and their peculations will empty your treasury completely."[153]

The point of the fable is the implied resemblance between the fox's predicament and the situation in Samos. But the implied resemblance is hardly scientific. First, the story is a fiction, and second, it deals with contingent human affairs. Human affairs depend on mutable circumstance. What is the right or shrewd thing to do in this circumstance is the wrong or the imprudent thing to do in another. We can have no one right way of acting all the time. Politics is an approximate science. But we cannot discern the likeness between Aesop's fable and the situation in Samos without a moment of recognition. We "see" that the story and the real event are the same. This intuition of likeness is practical rather than scientific or rigorous. It does not deal with natural kinds but with our practical everyday experience. Still, it counts as a moment of recognition.[154]

Consider one other example. Suppose a baseball pitcher throws a strike. The concept "strike" is a purely human convention. There are no strikes outside the ballpark in nature. The umpire identifies strikes by recognizing them. This is a kind of induction. He or she fits this pitch into the general category "strike" and this pitch into the general category "ball." Still, this is to recognize rather than to truly induce, for it deals with a contrived rather than a natural (or scientific) category.

Summarize our findings so far. The first level of induction comes up with the most rigorous concepts and principles; the second abstracts concepts and principles of a looser or more superficial sort. In both cases,

153 *Rhetoric* (Rhys Roberts), bk 2, ch. 20, 1393b23–1394a2.

154 For example, Aesop assumes that all politicians are self-interested. This may be true for the most part, but one could disagree and still be rational. A selfless politician is possible, however unlikely!

the process operates through a moment of mental illumination that fixes on a likeness, a common feature, a causal link, or a relationship binding individuals together into a single group. Chronologically, it may be that recognition leads to true induction; we may begin with a rough awareness of some kind of likeness and move on to a more focused awareness of a necessary or an essential property. Nonetheless, true or strict induction is always more authoritative. The second level is, at best, a rough-and-ready copy of the first level of induction. It is always a less reliable form of insight.

Two final points are in order. First, although discussion of induction usually focuses on our ability to acknowledge the similarities that somehow tie things together, we could also present induction, in another light, as an awareness of difference. Understanding difference seems parasitic on our awareness of resemblance. In knowing what things are alike, we inevitably acknowledge what things are unlike. It follows that the capacity to discern accidental and/or necessary resemblance is also one of discerning accidental and/or necessary difference.

Second, the intuitive moment that produces the first two levels of inductive reasoning could be said to have a tactile or a visual aspect. We may *grasp* an insight or *see* what something entails. To grasp something is to become aware of it gradually through some dawning comprehension; to see what is the case is to understand it altogether, all at once. Biondi, who compares the intuitive mental process behind induction to our sense of sight and touch, discusses these issues in some detail.[155]

THE THIRD LEVEL: TRUE INDUCTION AS ARGUMENT

While the first and second levels of induction operate by means of a kind of immediate awareness of what is the case, the next three require argument. The third level involves arguments dealing with necessary properties; the fourth, arguments dealing with accidental properties; and the fifth, statistical arguments (which do not play a role in the original Aristotle).

De Rijk describes the first two levels of induction as pure intuition, "a mere heuristic method of procuring a universal point."[156] But this is not nearly strong enough. Aristotelian *induction* is not simply "an aid to

155 See Biondi, *Aristotle*, §4.4, "*NOESIS* as Sight and Touch," 247–50.

156 De Rijk, *Aristotle*, vol. 1, §2.54, 148. And again, "Aristotelian ἐπαγωγή by its very nature is heuristic, not inferential" (ibid., vol. 1, §2.53, 141–2); and again, "when taken by themselves both ἐπαγωγή, and παράδειγμα are just heuristic devices and do not have inferential force on their own" (ibid., vol. 1, §2.57, 159).

learning ... or problem-solving [relying on] ... trial-and-error methods."[157] We tend to psychologize mental states, but Aristotelian induction – whether intuitive or argumentative – is also an *epistemological* conviction. It is more than a psychological push in the right direction. It is an instance of knowledge. The first level of induction is the most certain way of knowing. The second is a more tentative sort of discernment but is still a way of knowing.

While tending to view the first levels of induction in purely psychological terms, some commentators also downplay the importance of argumentative induction. Traditional logician, Joyce, writes, "Induction is not a syllogistic, but a purely abstractive process."[158] His comment is both correct and incorrect. Induction begins as a purely abstractive process, but (as we have seen) Aristotle also believes we can formalize inductive insight as a valid syllogism. It is not as if we are faced with a choice between inductive reasoning *qua* intuition or *qua* argument. Aristotle makes room for both options. The term "induction" may refer to a non-discursive moment of immediate illumination or to an argument expressing this original insight. Such arguments cash out, in properly ordered sequential propositions, the leap of understanding represented by the corresponding level of intuition. They are a verbal expression of some deeper level of insight. Thus, our intuitions often find expression in words, but this need not always be the case.

Imagine that Lily, a mentally handicapped adult who loves cats, is bitten by a dog. Lily is afraid of dogs but not afraid of cats. She can distinguish between dogs and cats. Her behaviour presupposes some intuitive understanding.[159] Lily has somehow induced the two natural categories "dog" and "cat" and is able to distinguish them in her head. Yet she may have no or very limited language abilities. She does not think in inductive syllogisms. So we can have induction without inductive arguments.

157 *Merriam-Webster Dictionary.*

158 Joyce, *Principles of Logic,* 227. De Rijk writes that modern scholarship, *pace* Ross, "rejects the idea that Aristotelian induction has any formal inferential force." This seems an exaggeration. See de Rijk, *Aristotle,* vol. 1, §2.56, 148.

159 You might claim that George has (incorrectly) realized that "all dogs are dangerous." They might be said, in some latent sense, to possess propositional, as well as conceptual, knowledge. Geach cites the curious example of someone who suffers from aphasia, an inability to use language properly. He comments, "If a man struck with aphasia can still play bridge or chess, I certainly wish to say he still has the concepts involved in the game, although he can no longer exercise them verbally" (*Mental Acts,* 13).

We cannot have inductive arguments without inductive discernment, but we can have inductive discernment without inductive arguments. Arguments require language proficiency. Aristotle intends inductive arguments as a "demonstration in words" of what goes on inside the head of a reasoner who induces a rigorous conclusion. Arguments move, not from observation to understanding, but from verbal premises to a verbal conclusion. They are not the only form of knowledge, but they are a conspicuously subtle and sophisticated sort of knowledge.

Broadly speaking, we can distinguish two levels of inductive argument in Aristotle. The third level of induction is made up of the inductive syllogism used in science. This is, for Aristotle, the most rigorous inductive argument. It puts on display the knowledge that derives from the very first level of induction. It provides a verbal counterpart to true or strict induction. Inductive syllogisms are composed of premises that summarize or report on some process of observation. They end in conclusions imparting necessary knowledge of causality; they explain why something is the way it is. They are valid arguments that rely on an added element of immediate discernment to recognize convertibility.

The fourth level of induction is composed of argument by analogy and what Aristotle calls "argument by example." This merely rhetorical form of induction is a less rigorous type of inference. It produces merely contingent, plausible, or probable claims. For Aristotle, certain subject matters do not lend themselves to rigorous, scientific analysis. Rhetorical induction possesses a valid logical form, but it produces a lesser form of knowledge. It verbally expresses the exercise of intuition I have called "recognition."

De Rijk incorrectly presents the inductive syllogism as a "dialectical argument" and contrasts it with the rigorous syllogisms discussed in the *Prior Analytics*.[160] This is to turn "rigorous" into "rhetorical" induction, collapsing the third and fourth levels into a single category. The inductive syllogism about the longevity of bileless animals is in the *Posterior Analytics*, which is a work on science not on dialectic. Aristotle's editors properly included that discussion of rhetorical and dialectical argument forms in treatises such as the *Topics*, and in the *Rhetoric*. I will discuss arguments by analogy and by example below.

THE MODERN REJECTION OF RIGOROUS INDUCTION

Most contemporary authors do not even recognize the third level of inductive reasoning. We have been so impressed by the alleged problem of

160 De Rijk, *Aristotle*, vol. 1, §2.54, 145.

induction that the possibility of a logically necessary and metaphysically rigorous form of inductive argument escapes us. Contemporary authors typically bolster belief in the unreliability of inductive arguments by carefully selected examples focusing on accidental rather than necessary properties. Trudy Govier introduces the following textbook example of inductive reasoning: "Suppose that you have seen 1000 students who have graduated from a particular high school with 1500 students, and every single one has been blind. You infer that the school is a school for the blind ... Such arguments are usually called inductive ... The connection between what we experience and what we expect to experience is ... not that of deductive entailment. There would be no logical impossibility in the 1001st student being sighted; it could happen."[161]

Seen from an Aristotelian perspective, such examples miss the point. Blindness is not an essential feature of human nature. Indeed, blindness is a defect. There may be blind students and there may be able-sighted students. No *physical* impossibility attaches to either circumstance. That is why this argument is only tentative, not because of anything having to do with the deep nature of induction, but because it deals with accidental properties.

Morris Engel offers the following stock example of hasty generalization: "The welfare program is totally unnecessary. Why, I know a guy who runs a very lucrative gambling operation and who drives his new Cadillac downtown every week to collect his welfare check."[162] David Kelly warns, "A single bad experience while traveling can prejudice our view of an entire city or country. Most of us have stereotypes about ethnic groups, professions, or people from different regions of the country based on our exposure to a few individuals. Even a judgement about the character or personality of a particular individual is a generalization drawn from our observation of that individual on specific occasions."[163] If, however, such didactic tales have their place in moral philosophy, they hardly constitute a sound basis for a fair assessment of the essential nature of inductive inference.

The ancient Epicureans, it appears, made a case for the reliability of induction, using the arguments that "all men who have been beheaded ... die at once."[164] Suppose, then, we were to apply the form of Govier's argument to this issue. Suppose you have met 1,000 students who have

161 Govier, *Practical Study of Argument*, 71.

162 Engel, *Analyzing Informal Fallacies*, 43–4.

163 Kelly, *Art of Reasoning*, 266.

164 Philodemus, *On Signs*, para. 18, quoted in Milton, "Induction before Hume," 55.

graduated from a given high school with 1,500 students, and you find that every one has a head. You infer that all students in the school have heads. Does it follow, given the incomplete sample size, given the fact that you have not examined every student, that the next student could be headless? Clearly not. This conclusion, "all students have heads," follows necessarily.[165] So the uncertainty Govier attributes to inductive reasoning does not derive from the logical form of her argument but from the contingent nature of the subject matter.

When we make arguments about students having heads, we sound silly. There is nothing to dispute. The conclusion is so certain apparently no one could argue against it. Logic textbooks (and academic papers generally) tend to focus on arguments designed to address controversial issues. The point is to convince an adversary to accept a contentious conclusion. If, however, we hope to understand the deep nature of reasoning, we must not restrict logic to the study of eristic. Any inductive inference that moves from premises to a conclusion is logically an argument. So the line of reasoning about all students having heads is an argument. The fact that the conclusion is so uncontroversial is a testimony to our belief in the inductive method.

To restrict examples of inductive arguments to those dealing with accidental properties is a case of special pleading. Contemporary authors emphasize an epistemologically vulnerable mode of inductive inference and conclude that all inductive reasoning is invalid. They establish, in short, the plausibility of the standard Humean dogma through an exclusive appeal to fourth-level induction.[166] They overlook the third level completely. This omission can be traced to two separate causes.

Firstly, a pervasive distaste for metaphysics has made us squeamish about distinctions between necessary and accidental attributes. But these are important *logical* issues. Consider the following two arguments: (1) some citizens vote Conservative, therefore all citizens vote Conservative; and (2) some students have heads, therefore all students have heads. Voting Conservative is not a *necessary* property of citizens. So the conclusion does not follow. Heads are, by contrast, a necessary property of students. So the second argument is both valid and sound.

Secondly, a prevalent focus on symbolic logic can lead to an impoverished account of necessary inference. Consider the propositional argument form

165 The post-Cartesian sceptic could doubt the conclusion, but this sceptic could then doubt anything.

166 Hume adopted a similar strategy, hence his examples about eggs and notoriously fickle weather.

called *modus ponens.* "If Tom is a human being, then Tom votes Conservative. Tom is a human being; therefore, Tom votes Conservative." Or, to repeat the same formal pattern with different content, "If Tom is a human being, Tom has a head. Tom is a human being; therefore, Tom has a head." These arguments possess the same logical form. But they are not, on an Aristotelian view, equivalent. In the second, the conclusion follows necessarily. In the first, it is mere conjecture. It does not follow necessarily. The difference is that having a head is a necessary attribute of "human being," whereas voting Conservative is not. The first argument is an example of fourth-level induction; it is merely a rhetorical argument. The second is a more rigorous case of third-level induction. (The first argument is, in Aristotelian terms, only an enthymeme; the second is a proper inductive syllogism.)[167]

Aristotle does not consider logical form in isolation from the content of an argument. In Aristotle, the idea that something "follows necessarily" follows from a nature; it is the nature that produces the necessity, not the logic. Logic follows after metaphysics, not the other way around.[168]

THE FOURTH LEVEL: ARGUMENTS BY ANALOGY

While the inductive syllogism is the most perfect kind of inductive argument, Aristotle recognizes that less rigorous forms of induction that are also persuasive. The fourth level of induction is made up of arguments τῶν ὁμοίων (*ton homoion*) – "from likeness" – in modern terminology, arguments by analogy. Arguments by analogy are a weaker type of inductive inference employed to secure opinion, instead of scientific fact. They produce general conclusions admitting of exceptions. They yield a fallible grasp of some contingent or accidental likeness. As we shall see, Aristotle places particular emphasis on arguments made from examples which he considers to be a specialized form of analogy. Call this fourth level of induction "rhetorical," as opposed to "scientific."

167 Authors in the Thomist tradition distinguish between metaphysical and physical necessity (see Joyce, *Principles of Logic*, ch. 15, 235–51). Aristotle does not develop his theory in this way. Necessity arises because of the principle of identity. To be itself, a nature must possess its necessary properties. If it lacked any of these attributes, this would be a contradiction in terms. A (human) student without a brain would be such a contradiction in terms. It would be inconceivable, for having a brain is a necessary attribute of humanness.

168 We might try to differentiate between these two arguments by introducing a more sophisticated notion of modality, some account of *a priori* and *a posteriori* necessity perhaps. We discuss this possibility in chapter 9.

We will, first, investigate arguments by analogy and move on to consider those by example. The rhetorical form is the argumentative analogue of the mental capacity I have called "recognition." Thus, in a discussion of debating techniques, Aristotle advises the student, "Try to secure admissions by means of likeness; for such admissions are plausible and the universal involved is less patent ... This argument resembles induction, but it is not the same thing; for in induction it is the universal whose admission is secured from the particulars, whereas in arguments from likeness, what is secured is not the universal under which all the like cases fall."[169]

Aristotle provides an example of what seems to be an argument by analogy: "If the skilled pilot is the best pilot and the skilled charioteer the best charioteer, then, in general, the skilled man is the best man in any particular sphere."[170] Joyce is at great pains to point out that Aristotle does not intend this argument "as a typical instance of the [inductive] argument in its perfect form." It is instead "given as an example of dialectical argument, in which demonstrative certitude being unattainable, we must be content with probabilities."[171] In other words, it represents an instance of rhetorical rather than scientific induction.

We can cast this argument in the form of an inductive syllogism: "The skilled pilot, the skilled charioteer, etc., are the best in their particular sphere. The skilled pilot, the skilled charioteer, etc., are experts. Therefore, the experts are best in their particular spheres." Clearly, this conclusion is generally but not universally true. We may encounter exceptional individuals who, without any training, by daunt of sheer natural aptitude, excel at this or that area of expertise. This conclusion is, then, a generally reliable but not a rigorously exact inference; i.e., it is rhetorical rather than scientific.

Aristotle's analogy about experts is (like most of his scientific examples) a truism. It does not depend on any momentous insight or leap of creative discernment. Still, even this trivial analogy requires, at the very least, an attentive observation of human life. Analogy, like inductive syllogism, requires some sort of penetrating gaze, a moment of immediate intelligence. One sees, one notices, one picks up on some significant similarity. This exercise of recognition may require great ingenuity or it may require little more than focused, patient observation. One way or the other, it is an indispensable aspect of the logical process precipitating an argument.

169 *Topics* (Pickard-Cambridge), bk 8, ch. 1, 156b10–19.

170 *Topics* (Forester), bk 1, ch. 12, 105a10–16.

171 Joyce, *Principles of Logic*, 230.

In the *Rhetoric*, Aristotle lists several inductive arguments that are, to borrow the terminology of the *Topics*, arguments by analogy, as they deal with a conspicuously weaker, less-exacting form of inference. Consider the following passage, which Aristotle attributes to Alcidamas: "Everyone honors the wise. Thus the Parians have honored Archilochus, in spite of his bitter tongue; the Chians Homer, though he was not their countryman; the Mytilenaeans Sappho, though she was a woman; the Lacedaemonians actually made Chilon a member of their senate, though they are the least literary of men; the Italian Greeks honored Pythagoras; the inhabitants of Lampsacus gave public burial to Anaxagoras, though he was an alien, and honor him even to this day."[172] This is another argument by analogy. The conclusion is that human societies resemble one another in a specific way: they all honour the wise. The evidence is that the Parians, Chians, Mytilenaeans, Lacedaemonians (etc.) honoured the wise, *despite negative factors.* Formally, we can cast the argument as an inductive syllogism. Define the terms: *S*, "Parians, Chians, Mytilenaeans, Lacedaemonians, Italian Greeks, inhabitants of Lampsacus, etc."; *P*, "honoring the wise"; and *M*, human societies. The argument can be represented as, All *S* is *P*; (all *S* is *M*, convertible to) all *M* is *S*; all *M* is *P*.

While Alcidamas' argument has, thus, the form of an inductive syllogism, it nevertheless deals with the contingent affairs of history. Having societies honouring the wise is not a law of nature. Clearly, some human societies might not, in fact, honour the wise. (Indeed, Aristotle was well aware of the tragic fate that befell the wise Socrates at the hands of the Athenians.) Still, this counts as a highly plausible general principle. Arguments by analogy are rhetorically sound rather than metaphysically (or scientifically) true. They do not secure a necessary conclusion.

Arguments by analogy depend, like inductive syllogisms, on the convertibility of the middle and subject terms. This is what secures the valid inference. Alcidamas' argument is successful to the extent that the subject term – "Parians, Chians, Mytilenaeans, Lacedaemonians, Italian Greeks, inhabitants of Lampsacus, etc." – is convertible or interchangeable with the middle term, "human societies." In other words, the argument hinges on the idea that these specific societies each possessed the same nature. In scientific inductive reasoning, we infer that because two or more things have the same nature, they must have identical properties. In argument by analogy, we infer that because two or more things have a similar (not quite identical) nature, they must have similar properties. We use a similarity to establish a

172 *Rhetoric* (Roberts), bk 2, ch. 23, 1398b10–16.

Table 4.3
Argument by example (παράδειγμα)

Ordinal sequence	*Kind of argument*	*Logical structure of argument*
First step	Argument from likeness	Inductive movement from particular to general
Second step	Enthymeme	Deductive movement from general to particular

similarity. The inference pattern is, more or less, an imperfect copy of the more robust inference of rigorous inductive syllogism.

Move on to the more specialized case of what Aristotle calls arguments by example (παράδειγμα, *paradeigma*). Aristotle writes, "When we base the proof of a proposition on a number of similar cases, this is … example in rhetoric."[173] De Rijk claims that what Aristotle calls "example" is "merely a weaker form of argument by induction," but the circumstance is somewhat more complicated.[174] "Argument by example" is, on closer inspection, a compound argument made up of two separate arguments: an argument by analogy followed by an enthymeme (not an incomplete syllogism but a rhetorical deduction). When we use this logical strategy, we first induce a general principle and then deduce a particular conclusion from this general principle as demonstrated in table 4.3.

An example will help. In the *Prior Analytics*, Aristotle sets out the logical structure of argument by example using the following instance of rhetorical induction.[175] Suppose that we want to prove that if Athens goes to war against Thebes, this military aggression would harm Athens. Aristotle recommends that we secure this conclusion by pointing out that when Thebes waged war against its neighbour Phocis, it did not turn out well for Thebes. He proposes a two-stage strategy. We must first establish the general principle "that war against neighbours is ruinous." We can do this by arguing that Thebes waging war against Phocis was ruinous and that Thebes making war against Phocis was war against neighbours, so that all war against neighbours is ruinous. This is an argument by analogy. But once we have established that all war against neighbours is ruinous, we can deduce that Athens going to war against Thebes would be ruinous. That is, we can make the following deduction. "War against neighbours is ruinous; a war by Athens against Thebes would be war against a neighbour; so a war

173 Ibid., bk 1, ch. 3, 1356b14–15.

174 "And … is built on discovering (or stating at least) a common characteristic" (de Rijk, *Aristotle*, vol. 1, §2.59, 159).

175 *Prior Analytics*, bk 2, ch. 24.

between Athens and Thebes would be ruinous." This is how argument by example works. We first use the Thebes example to *induce* the general principle that waging war on neighbours is ruinous and then deduce the conclusion we want, that a war of Athens against its neighbour would be ruinous. This rhetorical procedure parallels the inductive-deductive structure of Aristotelian science, but it deals with political matters impossible to scientifically demonstrate.

Aristotle considers the following example in the *Rhetoric*.[176] Suppose we wish to argue that Dionysus, in asking for a bodyguard, is scheming to set himself up as a despot. We may establish this by arguing as follows: Peisistratus, Theagenes, etc., were scheming to make themselves despots; Peisistratus, Theagenes, etc., asked for a bodyguard; so everyone who asks for a bodyguard is scheming to make themselves despots. Thus, if all people asking for a bodyguard are scheming to make themselves despots and Dionysius is asking for a bodyguard, Dionysius must be scheming to make himself despot. This argument follows the same strategy. We induce a probable conclusion and then deduce a probable consequence. The argument is intended to be persuasive or plausible rather than rigorous. Waging war on one's neighbours is not necessarily ruinous. Nor does it necessarily follow that someone who asks for a bodyguard *must* be scheming to make himself a despot.

Aristotle's conception of argument by example differs in an important way from modern accounts of argument by analogy that typically compare particular cases without any reference to an overarching generalization. In Aristotle, the movement is always from a particular up to a general class and then down to another particular. The reasoner uses analogy to establish some general principle, then constructs a plausible syllogism so as to deduce an individual instance from this general principle.[177]

Traditional logician Jacques Maritain, in criticising modern treatments of analogy, insists, "There is no inference from the particular to the particular. We never find a direct union of the particular to the particular in reasoning."[178] This is Aristotle's attitude as well. To compare particular cases

176 *Rhetoric* (Roberts), bk 1, ch. 2, 1357b31–1358a1.

177 Francis Bowen writes, "Mr. Mill's doctrine is, that "we much oftener conclude from particulars to particulars directly, than through the immediate agency of any general proposition" (Bowen, *Treatise on logic*, 232). But Aristotle could respond that the movement to the general principle is implicit in this sort of immediate induction. It is a logically necessary, if unstated, part of the argument.

178 The inference from particular to particular only happens "in the order of images and of sense knowledge" (Maritain, *Introduction to Logic*, 285–6).

Figure 4.3
Aristotelian argument by example

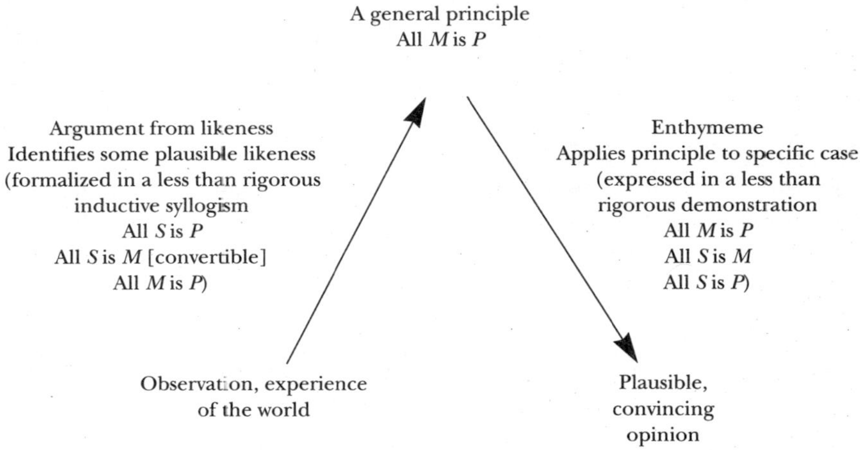

is a mere figure of speech, not logic. Logically construed, two particular cases are alike only because they belong to some larger class. Any rigorous inference from analogy must move from the particular up to the universal and back down to another particular. We secure a properly *logical* conclusion, not from the bare fact that particular cases resemble one another but from the inclusion of each case in the larger group.[179]

It is worth noting that, in Aristotle, rhetorical induction follows the same inductive-deductive model as scientific induction. We use rhetorical induction or analogy to move up to a general principle and then use rhetorical induction or enthymeme to infer a conclusion regarding a particular, as in figure 4.3.

VALIDITY REVISITED

Aristotle's modal logic is, as specialists maintain, obscurely expressed and less than adequate as a solution to time-honoured problems.[180] Hugh

179 Robert Olson recognizes the initial step in the case of argument from particulars to the universal but makes a further distinction between argument from analogy and "argument from an analogical model." The latter is, in essence, abduction (Olson, *Meaning and Argument*, 274–9).

180 See *Prior Analytics*, bk 1, chs 7–22.

Tredennick goes so far as to suggest that relevant sections in the *Prior Analytics* may have been composed largely by the Philosopher's students.[181] We cannot undertake any careful analysis of these issues here. Simply note that Aristotle does have a general strategy for dealing with probabilistic argument.

Return to the example of bearded men. Aristotle comments, "Not every male human being grows hair on the chin, but it happens usually."[182] He suggests a deduction of the type, "All men grow beards. Socrates is a man. Therefore, Socrates grows a beard." But how can we understand this inference when we know that the universal premise is only *usually* true? Aristotle suggests that we only accept the conclusion as "usually true." We are to believe the conclusion to the same degree we believe the premises. We should, he recommends, attribute the same degree of probability to the conclusion of a rhetorical argument to the premises. As he explains, "Every syllogism proceeds through premises which are either necessary or usual; if the premises are necessary, the conclusion is necessary too; and if the premises are usual, so is the conclusion."[183]

This may seem like a primitive way of dealing with modal logic, but the important point is that even here, when we are dealing with for-the-most-part generalizations, Aristotle does not disavow proper syllogistic form. He considers rhetorical, like scientific, induction to be a valid form of argument. Insomuch as a rhetorical syllogism is a syllogism, it has a conclusion that "necessarily follows."[184] The rhetorical syllogism is not less rigorous than the scientific when it comes to inferential or implicational strength. It does not follow, of course, that the conclusion is invariably true. The difference between rhetorical and scientific induction (i.e., between the third and fourth levels of induction) is the degree of conviction warranted by the premises. The difference does not hinge on the notion of logical validity. It is merely that rigorous induction employs premises that must be accepted as true, whereas analogy depends on premises that are only, to

181 Tredennick, introduction to *Prior Analytics*, 189 (in Aristotle, *Aristotle in 23 Volumes*).

182 *Posterior Analytics* (Tredennick), bk 2, ch. 12, 96a8 ff.

183 Ibid., bk 1, ch. 30, 87b25–29.

184 Aristotle defines a syllogism as "a form of words in which, when certain assumptions are made, something other than what has been assumed necessarily follows from the fact that the assumptions are such … There is no need of any further term to render the conclusion necessary" (*Prior Analytics* [Tredennick], bk 1, ch. 2, 24b19–23).

whatever degree, plausible. In the case of scientific induction, things could not be otherwise. In the case of analogy, the reported generality only holds more or less.

We have already considered Aristotle's formalization of rigorous induction in the inductive syllogism. The same analysis applies to analogy. Rhetorical inductions presuppose convertibility. Revisit Govier's induction about blind students. To express her argument in syllogistic form, "All Mary, Betty, John, George, etc., are blind. All Mary, Betty, John, George, etc., are students at school *X*. Therefore, all students at school *X* are blind." Represent our terms: *S*, Mary, Betty, John, George, etc.; *M*, students at school *X*; and *P*, blind students. The syllogism is, "All *S* is *P*. (All *S* is *M*, *convertible* to) all *M* is *S*. All *M* is *P*."

Govier's argument is an argument by analogy because it deals with an accidental rather than a necessary attribute. The argument is valid, but the conclusion does not follow with any necessity, because the hidden assumption of convertibility may or may not hold. The conclusion is not about what it means to be a human being; it is about what is means to be a student at school *X*. But school requirements vary, depending on human decision-making and local circumstance. We cannot use this example to show that all inductions are invalid. The example only succeeds in showing that some inductions are, as it turns out, arguments by analogy. This does not undermine in the least Aristotle's views.

THE FIFTH LEVEL: NUMERICAL OR STATISTICAL INDUCTIONS

Contemporary accounts presuppose a statistical or probabilistic model of inductive reasoning. Although Aristotle does not offer any serious account of statistical arguments, they can be incorporated into his system.[185] Let us call statistical inductions the fifth, and final, level of induction.

As we have seen, statistical analysis depends on a kind of convertibility, the convertibility of the samples with the population in general, in the sense of sharing the same nature. We may, then, represent statistical induction (which deals with contingent characteristics) as a rhetorical syllogism. One might envision a generalized formula: "Sample *x, y, z*, etc., has characteristic *A*. Sample *x, y, z*, etc., is convertible with the population at large. Therefore the population at large has characteristic *A*." The subject term is "*x, y, z*, etc."; the middle term is "population at large"; the predicate term is

185 "There can be no demonstrative knowledge of the fortuitous" (ibid., bk 1, ch. 30, 87b19 ff.).

"things with characteristic *A*." So formally, "All *S* is *P*; All *S* is *M* convertible to all *M* is *S*; All *M* is *P*." This is a valid syllogism. The crucial step is, of course, the implicit claim about convertibility. To say that the samples are convertible with the population at large is, in Aristotelian terms, to claim that they possess the same nature. This is the crucial assumption made by statistical arguments. Because the samples and the population possess the same nature, it will follow that anything that is true about the samples will be true about the population as a whole.

The basic rationale behind statistical induction is already expressed in Aristotle. Induction is not an issue of inspecting every individual case, but of examining individual cases of a representative nature. We may, then, transfer the properties of the individual cases to the genus as a whole. In statistical induction, we transfer the properties of the selected samples to the entire population. The underlying assumption is that the samples are representative of the target population. This assumption may, of course, be false. If it is true, however, the conclusion must be true. As it turns out, even statistical induction is deductively valid.

The statistical mode of inductive reasoning depends, like any other form of induction, on convertibility. Still, there is a key difference between statistical and Aristotelian accounts of inductive inference. Aristotelian induction always depends on a leap of creative insight. It involves some element of direct discernment or understanding. Statistical induction turns the inductive inference into a "counting procedure." It is the *number* of examples (and counter-examples) that establishes convertibility. Once we know how to calculate using the correct technical procedure, we can get by without the intellectual leap of discernment that is at the heart of Aristotelian induction. Of course, we could not master statistics or mathematics without intellectual insight, but that is another story. Human ingenuity may design the statistical tools we employ, but once the algorithm has been set in motion, the mathematical operations journey toward their necessary end devoid of human insight.[186]

Although numerical induction is susceptible to syllogistic treatment, we could only speculate as to what Aristotle would say about such a procedure. In his own scientific research, he played the role of the field biologist, a naturalist who relies on his own and others' observations. Suppose I go out into the field and discover a snapping turtle. How many snapping turtles do I have to observe before I come to realize that this species of turtles has

186 One could complain that this gives a false appearance of objectivity. After all the way the problem is set up influences the results, and the science of statistics, however skilfully used, is still a human contrivance.

shells? One? Two? It does not take much to realize that a shell is a necessary property of a snapping turtle. (A snapping turtle without a shell would be a defective or an injured turtle or a different species altogether.) Probability calculations are largely beside the point. We readily arrive at the proposition "all snapping turtles have shells" through understanding, through *nous*, not by calculating.

It must be granted that the science of probability extends the range of induction in a brilliant way.[187] But Aristotelian insight is something different than statistics. For Aristotle, we do not make sense of the world through a tabulating of raw frequencies but through an understanding of natures. A nature is more than a frequency. It is a unity, a pattern, an intelligible form that cements properties together into a distinctive, necessary whole. When we reinterpret the world in terms of frequencies, something gets lost in the exchange. If natures are the cause of frequencies, to focus on mere frequencies is to focus on the effects and overlook the causes. This would be, for Aristotle, a less rigorous scientific procedure.

We can compare the three levels of inductive argument. In the case of the scientific, we infer something about the necessary properties of things; in the case of the rhetorical, something about accidental, contingent properties; and in that of the statistical, something about the frequency of these properties. We might illustrate the three types of inductive argument, using parallel examples. Begin with the statistical form of inductive reasoning.

Suppose, to use a favourite textbook example, we are presented with a large urn and told that it is full of coloured marbles. We reach in and randomly pull out a number of marbles. All the marbles we pull out are blue. We then calculate the probability of all the marbles in the urn being blue. This would be an example of statistical, fifth-level, induction.

Suppose we know that all the marbles in the urn belong to George who is absolutely mad about blue. He paints his house blue, collects paintings from Picasso's blue period, always wears a blue suit, owns a blue car, and so on. We pull out a number of marbles and see that they are blue. We immediately realize that all the marbles are blue, because George simply loves blue. This would be a rhetorical induction. It depends on a flash of understanding supplying a probable conclusion. This is a plausible prediction, but we could be mistaken.

Finally, suppose we pull out a number of marbles and see that they are made of lapis lazuli. We have heard that all the marbles are made of the same material, and immediately conclude that all the marbles must be

187 Despite some deep problems surrounding issues of epistemological justification.

coloured blue, because we know that lapis lazuli is blue. This would be a scientific induction. All the marbles *must* be blue, for this blue is a necessary property of lapis lazuli.

Many contemporary logicians simply assume that statistics is rigorous and that all other inductions are but rough-and-ready approximations of the statistical model. But for each of these three kinds of induction, a different rationale secures the conclusion. In the first case, the analysis is mathematical. In the second, it depends on some knowledge of the collector's habits. In the third, we rely on scientific knowledge. We have, then, three separate arguments. To evaluate them as if they were all statistical inductions is to collapse three categories of argument into one. It is to make a "straw man" of ancient and medieval accounts. (In fact, the marbles-in-a-jar scenario is flawed for an arrangement of marbles in an urn is an artificial, contrived circumstance. An arrangement of marbles in a vase could always be different. On Aristotle's account, scientific induction tells us about true things that cannot conceivably be different. Aristotle might have dismissed the statistical inference as too weak to be contemplated.)

To treat all inductions as statistical is to treat all properties as contingent and accidental. It is to divest the world of natural kinds. This clashes, not just with Aristotle, but with practical and scientific experience. As some recent philosophers argue, the enormous success of science demonstrates that the human mind is capable of identifying and describing natural kinds. We will consider their arguments in a future chapter.

5

Moral Induction

It is needless to push our researches so far as to ask, Why we have humanity or fellow-feeling with others? It is sufficient that this is experienced to be a principle in human nature. We must stop somewhere in our examination of causes; and there are, in every science, some general principles beyond which we cannot hope to find any principle more general. No man is absolutely indifferent to the happiness and misery of others. The first has a natural tendency to give pleasure, the second pain. This everyone may find in himself. It is not probable that these principles can be resolved into principles more simple and universal.

David Hume[1]

CONTEMPORARY THINKERS TEND TO ASSOCIATE INDUCTION with science, but Ancient philosophers proposed induction as a solution to the problem of identity, more globally construed. In Plato's last dialogue, he imagines a conversation between a Cretan, a Spartan, and an Athenian about the relationship between the various virtues. The Athenian poses a problem: "Take our language about the four types of virtue [: courage, purity, justice, and wisdom]. If there are four of them, obviously we must hold that each type by itself is one … And yet we give one name to all of them … and this implies that they are … just one thing … It is easy enough to point out [how they differ and have] distinct names. It is not so light a matter to show why we have given [them] the one common name, virtue."[2] Plato poses a fundamental problem. How can four different things – courage, purity, justice, and wisdom – be the same thing? After further discussion, the Athenian continues, "[Students of philosophy] must be constrained, first and foremost, to see what exactly is the identity permeating all the four [virtues], the unity to be found … alike in courage, in purity, in rectitude, in wisdom, and entitling them all to be called by the same name,

1 *Inquiry*, §5, pt 2, 47–8 (various editions).

2 *Laws* (Taylor), 963c–e (in Plato, *Collected Dialogues*).

virtue."[3] The goal here is an inductive insight into what makes different virtues all one. In the ancient world, induction, the ability to see the one in the many, had a moral as well as a scientific function. In this chapter, I will briefly consider Aristotle's account of moral reasoning, leaving aside much of the moral content, and focusing on epistemological and logical issues.

Aristotle presents morality as a practical as well as an epistemological achievement. I begin, then, by considering an Aristotelian response to the "is-ought fallacy," the logical challenge to morality most often raised by modern authors. As we shall see, Aristotle situates the capacity for moral ideas in human reason. Morality starts in a kind of "connatural knowledge" that has its origins in a non-verbal knowing how. Moral induction accounts for this first level of moral awareness. Although I only propose a rudimentary summary, we can easily see how one could develop these basic insights into a more complete theory of moral reasoning.

Next, I show how moral induction (like other forms of inductive reasoning) presupposes a leap from particular to general, defend Aristotle's theory of virtue ethics, and construct an inductive-deductive model of moral reasoning. Although moral induction may be formalized, it is most fundamentally a species of direct insight rather than of logic. But once we secure first principles, we can use the "practical syllogism" (the moral equivalent of scientific syllogism) to apply these first principles to the specific circumstances of our lives. As we will see, Aristotle's inductive-deductive method of moral reasoning closely parallels his inductive-deductive model of science.

After considering Aristotle's general attitude toward moral reasoning, I go on to explain what a fully developed Aristotelian account of moral *theory* might entail. I then consider four moral mistakes: brutishness, viciousness, incontinence, and self-indulgence. In each case, the underlying problem can be traced to faulty moral inductive reasoning. An epistemic failure is inevitably compounded by a character flaw. I finish the chapter by comparing the epistemological status of science and morality from an Aristotelian point of view. Although Aristotle believed that science is more rigorous than morality, he secures a rational basis for ethics. Suitably refined and expanded, his account of morality provides a sophisticated answer to contemporary epistemological worries about the rational foundations of moral reasoning.

3 Ibid., 965b, 965d.

THE IS-OUGHT "FALLACY"

Does moral reasoning rest on a logical fallacy? Ignore the moral repercussions here. Focus on the logic. David Hume observed that moral arguments seem to move from *descriptive* premises to *prescriptive* conclusions.[4] On this well-received account, moral reasoning unwittingly jumps from premises about what *is* the case to a conclusion about what we *ought* to do. It illegitimately moves from one side of the "is-ought" divide to the other. G.E. Moore baptized this alleged mistake the "naturalistic fallacy."[5]

Traditional authors such as Aristotle elaborate an account of moral reasoning that eliminates the problem. We do not derive an "ought" from an "is." We derive an "ought" from an "ought." Simply put, an "ought" already resides in human nature. This human propensity for the good supplies the normative premise leading to a normative conclusion in a moral argument. Moral reasoning moves, not from an absence of all morality to a moral conclusion; it moves from a general (if implicit) moral stance to a more specific (explicit) moral conclusion. Despite a lot of philosophical posturing to the contrary, a closer inspection reveals no is-ought gap between premises and conclusions in a moral argument.

Aristotle believed that morality begins in human nature, in some kind of rational inclination. He writes, "We are adapted by nature to receive [the virtues]."[6] Suppose, then, I reason, "Gloria needs help. Therefore, we ought to help Gloria." I seem to move here from a descriptive claim about Gloria to a prescriptive one recommending a specific course of action. But the argument is really an enthymeme. If we rewrite the argument, elucidating the hidden premise, we are left with, "Premise$_1$: Gloria needs help. Hidden premise: We ought to do what we can to help. Conclusion: Therefore, we ought to help Gloria." Observation supplies the first premise: "Gloria needs help." Human nature supplies the hidden premise: "We ought to do what we can to help." Because the argument is addressed to human beings, the normative principle that we ought to help others is understood rather than explicitly stated.

To posit an is-ought gap between premises and conclusions in a moral argument is to reason as if people had no natures. Because people have

4 In truth, Hume says very little about the is-ought distinction. His comments are restricted to one paragraph added as an afterthought. See Hume, *Treatise* (Norton and Norton), §3, pt 1, para. 27, 302.

5 See Moore, *Principia Ethica.*

6 *Nicomachean Ethics* (Ross, Urmson), bk 2, ch. 1, 1103a24–25 (in Aristotle, *Complete Works*).

natures, they have an "ought" inside them that predisposes them to act in certain way. Aristotle writes, "one must be born with an eye, as it were, by which to judge rightly and choose what is truly good, and he is well endowed by nature who is endowed with this. For it is what is greatest and most noble, and what we cannot get or learn from another, but must have just such as it was when given at birth."[7] Healthy human beings can *see* right and wrong. This translates into an original inclination toward what is right. When we act immorally, it is always because we have, somehow, lost touch with our deepest inclination.

Aristotle recognizes the practical inefficacy of bare theoretical reason. He writes, "Thought by itself ... moves nothing, but only thought directed to an end, and dealing with action."[8] Practical reason, or φρόνησις (*phronesis*), includes a desire component. It is not enough to have sound moral opinions; the moral person must be motivated to act on those opinions. In moral endeavour, "both the reasoning must be true and the desire right."[9] Correct practical reasoning results in *practical* syllogisms.[10] In the above example, the conclusion of this line of thought is an action, not a proposition. We reason, Gloria needs help; we ought to do what we can to help; and, by way of conclusion, we go help Gloria. We end up doing something. This is, in Aristotle, what moral reasoning is about: action, not theory.

As demonstrated below, we can draw a direct parallel between moral and scientific reasoning. In the case of science, we come to know first principles through the first two levels of induction – that is, through true or strict induction or through recognition – and the same holds true, roughly, for morality. We come to know morality through a discernment that is either completely reliable, what we could call "strict" moral inductive reasoning, or through a more tentative sort of awareness, what we could call "moral recognition." The difference is that practical reasoning comprises a strong motivational component. "Practical wisdom issues commands."[11] It tells us what to do. Still, it operates in sequence; when we reason morally we move from moral induction to moral deduction, from the initial formation of moral ideas to their application in a specific context.

7 Ibid., bk 3, ch. 5, 1114b6–13.

8 Ibid., bk 6, ch. 2, 1139a35–1139b1.

9 Ibid., bk 6, ch. 2, 1139a24–25.

10 See *Movement of Animals*, ch. 7, 701a6 ff.

11 *Nicomachean Ethics* (Ross, Urmson), bk 6, ch. 10, 1143a8–1143a9.

KNOWING HOW

All thought, theoretical or practical, begins in induction. To elucidate induction is to understand the origin of our ideas. How, then, does the mind come to have its very first moral ideas? How does a child first arrive at morality? Although Aristotle does not explicitly tackle the issue, his inductive schema provides a sophisticated answer to the difficult question of first moral development.

Anyone who acts morally must have some sense of right and wrong. What, then, are we to make of linguistically inarticulate child at the very beginning of moral development? Do they have a concept of morality? Modern analytic philosopher Peter Geach claims that conceptual knowledge is possible, even in the absence of language. He cites the example of someone with aphasia (a clinical verbal incapacity) who can still play bridge. According to Geach, we should grant that the bridge player "still has the concepts involved in the game although he can no longer exercise them verbally."[12] So long as he can make the right moves and participates intelligently, he must have conceptual knowledge of bridge playing. The question arises, is a child (or handicapped adult) with very limited verbal competency capable of morality? Could the moral beginner, who has yet to master language, possess conceptual knowledge of morality? Could moral agents engage in *wordless* moral induction and, in general, act morally with little if any mastery of moral vocabulary?

Aristotle does not answer (to my knowledge) this question in the surviving texts. But my goal here is to provide a complete account of moral induction *ad mentum* Aristotle. We can borrow a few ideas, to fill in the blanks, from some surprising modern allies. Gilbert Ryle, hardly a sympathetic reader of Aristotle, provides nonetheless an account of mental activity seemingly Aristotelian at heart.[13] Ryle disputes what he calls "intellectualism," the idea that alert human agents must "think things through inside their heads" while they are acting. Ryle writes, "To do something … is, according to this [intellectualist] legend, always to do two things; namely to consider certain appropriate propositions, or prescriptions, and to put into practice what these propositions or prescriptions enjoin. It is to do a bit of theory and then to do a bit of practice."[14] On this intellectualist account, "the chef must recite his recipes to himself before he can cook … the hero must lend his inner ear to some appropriate moral imperative

12 Geach, *Mental Acts*, 13.

13 Ryle, *Concept of Mind*, ch. 2, "Knowing How and Knowing That," 25–61.

14 Ryle, *Concept of Mind*, 29.

before swimming out to save the drowning man; the chess-player must run over in his head all the relevant rules and tactical maxims of the game before he can make correct and skillful moves."[15] But simple introspection demonstrates that we usually act without relying on words.

Ryle responds to intellectualist exaggerations by developing a distinction he borrows from American pragmatist John Dewey. Dewey observes, "We walk and read aloud, we get off and on street cars, we dress and undress, and do a thousand useful acts without thinking of them. We know something, namely, how to do them."[16] Dewey distinguishes between *knowing how* to perform specific tasks and *knowing that* certain facts are true.[17] Whereas Dewey's comments are rather brief and somewhat dismissive, Ryle applies the concept of knowing how to a much wider cross-section of human behaviour.

Consider knitting. Knitting is an intelligent, if repetitive, activity. It is a kind of knowing how. But knitters just knit. For the most part, their hands go on, making the required movements without them having to think about it. And yet knitting has to be learned. It requires skill. Expressing in words what knitting consists of (over the phone, say) would be no mean task! As it turns out, the vast majority of knitters, even the most excellent knitters, are more or less inarticulate ones. Making arguments about knitting and knitting are not equivalent tasks. If we want to find out whether you are a good knitter, we look at the results of your work. Knowing how is a matter of performance, not verbal skills. The same can be said about morality.

The moral individual is not someone who talks the talk but someone who walks the walk. They are moral because of what they do, not because of any ability to explain their decisions in words. Aristotle views practical wisdom in these terms. A properly formed practical syllogism ends in an act, not a verbal proposition. Moral agents do not have to argue about morality inside their heads. Ryle asks, "What is involved in our descriptions of people as *knowing how* to make and appreciate jokes, to talk grammatically, to play chess, to fish, to argue?" And he immediately responds, "Part of what is meant is that, when they perform these operations, they tend to perform them well, i.e., correctly or efficiently or successfully. These performances come up to certain standards, or satisfy certain criteria."[18] The same holds true for morality. People who know how to be moral, act morally. Their behaviour meets a certain standard of excellence. We judge

15 Ibid.

16 Dewey, *Human Nature and Conduct*, 177–8.

17 Ibid., 178.

18 Ryle, *Concept of Mind*, 28–9.

how moral they are, not by asking them questions, but by observing and evaluating their actions.

It would seem that, on an Aristotelian account, morality begins as a form of knowing how. Most people do not learn how to knit by reading books. They learn by imitation, by *mimesis*, by doing. Knitting teachers, showing someone how to knit, knit in front of them; they make students imitate their own actions; they reach over and manually guide their student's hands. Likewise, we do not teach young children to be moral by arguing with them but by giving a good example, by encouraging them to imitate virtuous behaviour, and by continually correcting their performance. Good example allows for the transmission of moral wisdom without any theoretical focus on moral theory. Just as the person who knits has a natural dexterity that can be developed, a child has a moral propensity that can be developed. An intellectual formation in morality accompanies this *apprentissage*. Morality requires mental alertness, sensitivity to feedback, an exercise of will, and conceptual knowledge of right and wrong. It entails the continual exercise of judgement. It is a skill that we learn over time.

This is presumably how morality first develops in childhood. Given the right upbringing, children are somehow able to insert things into the right moral categories, to discern, at the most basic level, the difference between right and wrong. The moral life does not start with words, but with moral discernment. In the morally receptive child, this meeting of inclination with example produces moral knowledge. As children progress in verbal proficiency, they begin to express this moral knowledge verbally, in concepts, principles, and ultimately, arguments. This movement from moral intuition to moral argument directly parallels the movement in science from strict induction to inductive syllogism and from recognition to argument from analogy. I shall not enter into the details here. Note, however, that we can postulate a movement in moral reasoning from strict moral induction to a kind of inductive moral syllogism and from moral recognition to a more tentative kind of moral argument from analogy.

CONNATURAL KNOWLEDGE

If morality begins in a wordless knowing how, some traditionalist philosophers would make the point in a more Aristotelian manner. Jacques Maritain situates the origins of morality in connatural knowledge. We can use his gloss on Thomas Aquinas' concept of moral wisdom as a resource for understanding Aristotle.[19]

19 Maritain, *Introduction to Logic*, 33–4.

Thomas' own account of "natural law" is open to two divergent interpretations. On the intellectualist reading, moral knowledge comes to us in propositions. We make moral decisions by reasoning syllogistically. We add together the rules of natural law and propositions about individual circumstances and infer conclusions about how we should act in a particular situation. On Maritain's connatural interpretation, morality begins in a nonverbal skill that pushes us inwardly toward a certain way of behaving. The first principles of morality are "discovered in an indemonstrable manner, *and in a non-conceptual, non-rational way*."[20] Morality has its source in rational inclinations which may exist even in the absence of linguistic utterance.

The accuracy of this exegesis of Thomas is not the issue here. What is important for our purposes is that this second reading seems to resemble what Aristotle would have thought. Maritain is inspired by Thomas' observation that moral wisdom "can come about in two ways, through the prefect use of reason or through a certain natural kinship with the things one is judging."[21] "In matters of chastity," Thomas writes, "one who is versed in moral science will come to a right judgement through rational investigation, another who possesses the virtue of chastity will be right through a kind of natural affinity."[22] In the first case, we learn about chastity by doing moral theory. In the second, we learn about chastity by being chaste. The chaste person comes to know chastity, not through argument, but from the inside-out, through a direct experience of this virtue. In the first case, the knower has theoretical, and in the second case, connatural, knowledge of chastity. Even if the second knower cannot explain in words what chastity is, he or she can act in a chaste way. He or she *knows how* to be chaste.

Maritain situates the origins of morality in a kind of knowing how. Connatural knowledge, does "not proceed from any conceptual, discursive, rational exercise of reason,"[23] but from "the experience [the subject] has of himself."[24] Maritain, like Aristotle, locates the ability to tell the difference between right and wrong in human nature. We learn what is right or wrong through self-knowledge. What is good is congruent with, what is bad is inimical to, our rational natures. Moral arguments may serve a useful moral purpose, but they are not the original source for

20 Ibid., 22 (my italics).

21 Thomas Aquinas, *Summa theologiae* (Heath), pt 2 of pt 2, Q. 45, art. 2.

22 Ibid.

23 Maritain, *Introduction to Logic*, 20.

24 Ibid., 34–5.

moral knowledge. "The moral law was discovered by men before the existence of any moral philosophy."[25]

In the modern age, we tend to separate reason and morality. Being a good reasoner means being a proficient arguer; being moral means doing good acts. In Aristotle, these two aspirations come together. Someone who acts generously, courageously, truthfully, compassionately, patiently (etc.), is already, by that very fact, being a good moral reasoner. Moral *behaviour* is a kind of successful intelligence. This is the point of the practical syllogism. It is not as if we have to resort to arguments if we want to reason about morality. When we make moral decisions, when we decide to yield to one desire and to resist another desire, we are already reasoning morally. Practical reason and moral action are one seamless whole of aspiration. Modern accounts of "knowing how" and "connatural knowledge" provide an accurate analogue of Aristotle's meaning, because they situate moral *knowledge* in the actual performance of successful moral action, not outside moral behaviour in the discursive thought that may or may not accompany it.

Could individuals with limited language proficiency act morally? It seems, on this kind of model, they could. It is hard to get inside the minds of those without language skills. If, however, like Geach's bridge player, they make the right moves, if they deliberately do what is right and avoid what is wrong, we should attribute moral agency to them. If they are capable of the right kind of knowing how, then even though they cannot explain morality in words, they should be considered, on Aristotle's account, to be moral reasoners. We accept that they are moral reasoners, not because they have mastered important moral arguments, but because they have, in Maritain's terminology, connatural knowledge of morality. They know, for example, how to care for someone else, not because they have thought it through, but because they have experienced, from the inside out, what it means to care for others.

St Augustine cites the opposite possibility. He writes, "I have personally watched and studied a jealous baby. He could not yet speak and pale with jealousy and bitterness, glared at his brother sharing his mother's milk."[26] This is, no doubt, to overestimate the intellectual capacities of the child. Note, however, that the possibility of inarticulate morality brings with it, of course, the possibility of inarticulate immorality. Goodness and wickedness are, so to speak, two sides of the same coin.

25 Ibid., 22.

26 Augustine, *Confessions* (Chadwick), bk 1, § 7 (para. 11), 9.

THE MORAL LEAP FROM PARTICULAR TO GENERAL

In the *Nicomachean Ethics*, Aristotle divides the soul into a theoretical and practical part.[27] "The function of both the [rational] parts ... is truth."[28] But there is a crucial difference. If the theoretical part distinguishes truth from falsehood, the practical one discerns "truth in agreement with right desire."[29] Aristotle comments, "What affirmation and negation are in thinking, pursuit and avoidance are in desire."[30] Moral discernment is, for Aristotle, a kind of knowledge, but it is knowledge with an affective component. It is both impulse and judgement. It must not only inform us as to what is right or wrong; it must, at the same time, *motivate* us to do what is right.

What I have called strict moral induction and moral recognition must have affective, as well epistemological, aspects. In contemporary thought we tend to overlook the role of induction in ethics. Morality originates in an intelligent impulse to pursue good and avoid evil. This attitude is both feeling and intellectual leap to a new understanding of the world. If some intelligent agents are without moral capacity – psychopaths, sociopaths (what Aristotle calls "brutes") – this is actually an epistemological problem, not just a psychological one. Those who lack all morality are intellectually deficient, not because they argue illogically, but because they are unable to *induce* the first principles of human behaviour. But this is a defect in rational understanding, not merely one of feeling.

On Aristotle's account, inductive inference moves from the particular to the general. In the case of scientific inference, we leap from a particular case to a universal principle. In the case of morality, we leap from self-interest to selflessness, from a highly individualized point of view to some universal moral principle. Moral induction establishes a new way of looking at things. It divides up the world according to a new set of *universal* categories that transcend self-concern. The agent discerns the universal significance of something like truthfulness, courage, loyalty, or love.

Objectivity is an epistemological virtue, but it is also moral virtue. John Finnis, who traces philosophical suspicions about morality back to Thomas Hobbes and David Hume, quotes contemporary philosopher Philippa

27 *Nicomachean Ethics*, bk 6, ch. 1, 1139a ff. The theoretical part deals with what is necessary; the practical, with what is contingent – for, as Aristotle, says, "no one deliberates about what cannot be otherwise" (ibid., bk 6, ch. 1, 1139a14–15).

28 Ibid.

29 Ibid.

30 Aristotle comments, "What affirmation and negation are in thinking, pursuit and avoidance are in desire" (ibid., bk 6, ch. 2, 1139a21–22).

Foot: "there is no such thing as *an objectively good state of affairs.* [Moral judgements] are used subjectively, to mark what fits in with the aims or interests of a particular individual or group."[31] Foot has changed her views in the meantime, but this earlier statement summarizes an entrenched attitude.[32]

Aristotle believed that morality is an objective viewpoint. Moral inductive reasoning moves then from subjectivity to objectivity. When we move from, "I want," "this is what I feel," "this is what is good for me," to "this is what a good human being should want or feel right now," "this is what is good for human beings (in this circumstance)," we ascend to a moral perspective. Moral induction enables the transition from one level to the next. It produces a movement beyond instinctive egoism to grasp a universal point of view.[33] The modern concern about convincing amoral agents, such as "brutes," to be moral is misconceived. While such "philosophical brutes" can use language to construct moral arguments, this is not enough for morality. Their problem has to do with inductive reasoning. They are incapable of strict moral induction or perhaps even moral recognition. They have not made the necessary leap of insight to a higher way of viewing things. So they are, not surprisingly, incapable of morality.

VIRTUE ETHICS

Aristotle views morality from the perspective of virtue ethics. What matters is developing positive character traits like generosity, courage, honesty, loyalty, and so on. Gilbert Harman has recently argued that virtue ethics rests on an outdated folk psychology: the routine but mistaken assumption that people have fixed character traits, regular patterns of thought, attitude, or personality that predetermine the way they act.[34] Harman insists that *scientific* evidence from social psychology demonstrates that the determinate influence in behaviour is external circumstance, rather than individual character.[35] He writes, "It is very hard to do studies that might indicate whether or not people differ in character traits, but the few studies [undertaken] do not support this idea. We must conclude that, despite appearances, there is no

31 Finnis, *Of Ethics*, see especially ch. 2, "Desire, Understanding, Human Goods," 26–55; and Foot, *Virtues and Vices*, 154.

32 See Foot, *Natural Goodness.*

33 It does not follow from this, as authors such as Thomas Nagel wish to argue, that no room is left for individuality or particular affections.

34 See Harman, "Moral Philosophy Meets Social Psychology" and "Non-Existence of Character Traits."

35 See Ross and Nisbett, *Person and the Situation.*

empirical support for the existence of character traits."[36] Harman compares the belief in character traits to the obviously erroneous if "commonsense" belief that an object dropped from a plane will fall straight down and hit the ground at a point directly below the point of release. This is clearly false. The forward velocity of the plane will be transferred to the object, so that it will fall in a parabolic curve and land a good distance away from the original point of release. Harman claims that virtue ethics is based on an equivalent kind of uncritical belief.

It is hard to take Harman's epistemological concerns seriously. First, as Julia Annas points out, Harman appeals to psychological "situationalism" without fairly or rigorously reporting on the diversity of psychological views.[37] Textbooks in social psychology distinguish between three competing views or models of human behaviour: "situationalism" focuses on the role of external circumstances; "dispositionalism," on personality; and "interactionism," on the way circumstance and personality combine to affect human behaviour. Harman brandishes situationalism as a foolproof argument against virtue ethics, but most social psychologists view human behaviour as a function of circumstance and character, not exclusively as of one or the other. Some may focus on the situation and ignore issues of individual personality, but this is an issue of methodology, not a definitive conclusion about the existence or non-existence of individual human virtue.[38]

Second, Harman compares our belief in the existence of character traits with the naive view someone might have that an object falling from a plane drops straight down. But the two cases are not equivalent. Someone who was fond of dropping objects from planes would quickly learn (indeed, after even a single attempt) that the object did not fall straight down relative to the ground but gained forward momentum in the direction of the plane's movement.[39] Their mistaken belief would be quickly corrected by ordinary experience. Virtue ethics, on the other hand, is routinely

36 Harman, "Moral Philosophy Meets Social Psychology," 330.

37 See Annas, "Virtue Ethics and Social Psychology."

38 Situationalists originally set about vindicating the methodology of social psychology. This doctrine is not quite the neutral theoretical instrument Harman suggests, but part of an academic strategy. In eliminating individual agency, extreme situationalism would undermine all ethics insomuch as ethics presupposes individual responsibility.

39 More rigorously put, seen from the viewpoint of someone in the moving plane it drops straight down; seen from the viewpoint of someone on the ground it drops in a diagonal. Measured within the inertial frame of the plane, it drops straight down; measured with the inertial frame of the ground, it drops in a diagonal.

confirmed, not disproved, by ordinary evidence. Keen observation of the world seems to indicate that some of us are *consistently* lazy, dishonest, timid, patient, generous, and so on. This is what countless intelligent, keen observers from all cultures continue to report.

Thirdly, Harman cites experiments in social psychology recording solely the behaviour of a subject on a single extraordinary occasion. But such experiments are not finely grained enough to meaningfully test sophisticated notions of virtue (and vice). Aristotle defines virtue as a habit. To investigate habit, we would have to study a string of successes or failures and the individual circumstances that occasioned them. Simply recording how many people acted in this or that way is not enough. Careful analysis of such situations would require sustained analysis. One would have to investigate, for example, whether these individuals felt ashamed or proud, guilty or sorry, after performing such actions.

Fourthly, Harman refers to experiments placing individuals in situations of great duress. Duress may be a matter of perceived threat or positive reward. Clearly, if we put a gun to someone's head and order them to do something immoral, even usually moral individuals may do what they are told. Again, if we offered them a reward of $10 million, many (or most) might again comply. Extreme duress only masks the influence of individual character. It does not demonstrate its non-existence. But let us move on to more serious issues.

A MODEL OF MORAL INDUCTION, DEDUCTION

We can now construct a general model of moral reasoning in line with Aristotle's conception of virtue ethics. Divide the activity of morality into two separate stages. Call the first stage moral *induction*, and the second moral *deduction*. On Aristotle's account, moral induction first grasps what virtue is. Moral deduction determines the best means of achieving this goal.

Aristotle analyzes human behaviour from the perspective of means and ends. The end is what we aim at; the means is how we accomplish that goal. The goal of human behaviour is, of course, virtue. We do not argue our way to virtue. Virtue "is not a matter of logical inference or rational principle, [it] must be assumed as a starting-point."[40] Once we induce a concept of virtue, we deduce the specific means for achieving it. So, for example,

40 *Eudemian Ethics* (Rackman), bk 2, ch. 12, 1227b29–20 (in Aristotle, *Aristotle in 23 Volumes*). Again, Aristotle writes, "as in the theoretic sciences the assumptions are the first principles, so in the productive sciences the End is a starting point and assumption" (ibid., bk 2, ch. 12, 1227b29–20).

Figure 5.1
Aristotle's account of medicine

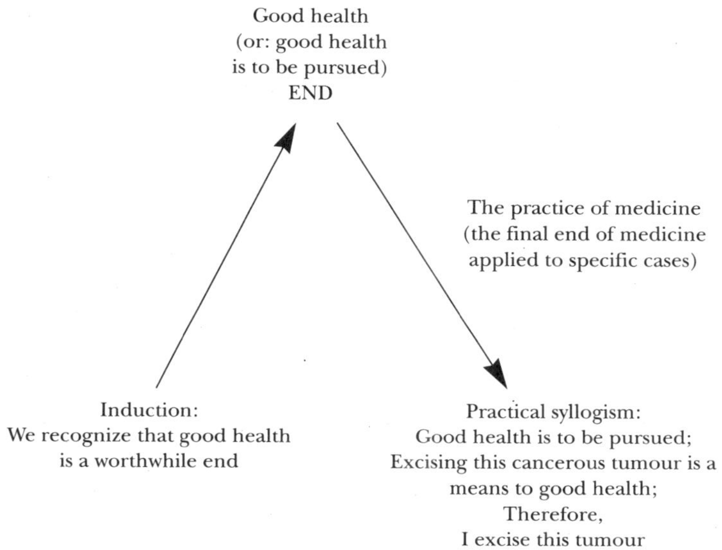

we induce the concept of courage, which is a good thing to aspire to, and then, in the individual circumstances of our own life, we deduce a means of being courageous. A general example will help.

Aristotle compares moral behaviour to medicine. In medicine, the aim of human health is induced. "The doctor does not ask whether one ought to be in good health or not."[41] The doctor posits good health as the end and tries, in the specific case he or she is dealing with, to realize this aim. Likewise in morality. The moral person induces that virtue is the end and tries, in the specific situation that presents itself, to realize this aim. We can, then, erect a model of moral reasoning by drawing an analogy with medicine. Suppose someone has a cancerous tumour. And suppose that excising it would restore that person to good health. The competent doctor would excise the tumour. We can express the behaviour in a practical syllogism: "Good health is something to be promoted; excising the cancerous tumour promotes good health; therefore I excise the tumour." And we can schematically represent what is going on here, as in figure 5.1.

41 *Eudemian Ethics* (Solomon), bk 2, ch. 12, 1227b26 (in Aristotle, *Complete Works*).

Medicine is, like morality, practical activity. Medical practice involves doing something. Whereas in theoretical reasoning, we induce a middle term, in practical, we induce a goal. In theoretical reasoning the middle term is (most perfectly) a definition identifying a nature, but in practical reasoning the goal is a virtue (or a good) to be realized. Whereas theoretical reasoning demonstrates the "reason" or cause behind something, moral reasoning directs our striving. Both require an induction of first principles and the subsequent application of these to specific cases. Once we have *induced* our goal, we *deduce* a practical means of achieving it. That is, we choose a course of action.

We can, then, establish a formal model for moral reasoning. Consider the virtue of courage. Growing up in a courageous society, we come to see courage as a noble ideal. We hear courage praised; we are told stories about it, see examples of it; we are punished when we are cowardly – and so on. We develop a habit of courage and abstract the idea of it. In short, we induce the concept "courage." This process of concept formulation can be formalized in an inductive syllogism: "This, this, and this instance of human behaviour is good fearlessness. This, this, and this instance of human behaviour is an example of courage. Therefore, courage is good fearlessness." To express all this more technically (where *S* is "this act"; *P* is "what is good fearlessness"; and *M* is "courage"): "All S_1, S_2, S_3, etc., is *P.* (All S_1, S_2, S_3, etc., is *M,* convertible to) All *M* is *S.* Therefore, all *M* is *P* (definition, convertible to all *P* is *M*)."

But once we know (through induction) that courage is the aim – in other words, that courage *ought* to be pursued – we can, then, deduce ways of being courageous. For example, the brave soldier can reason, "Courage ought to be pursued. Standing my ground in the pitch of battle is courageous. Therefore, I stand my ground!" This practical syllogism, which ends in an action, is a valid deduction. More technically (where *M* is "courage"; *P* is "good fearlessness"; and *S* is "standing my ground in battle"): "All *M* is *P.* All *S* is *M.* Therefore, all *S* is *P.*"[42] (Note that the final active premise, "I stand my ground in battle," is equivalent to "standing my ground in battle is *good* fearlessness.")

This is the formal mechanism of moral reasoning. In short, moral inductive reasoning identifies goals; moral deductive reasoning identifies the means of achieving those goals. We first induce a goal, "courage." We then devise a means for achieving this goal: "standing our ground in the pitch of battle." We can schematically depict the rational structure of morality, as in figures 5.2 and 5.3.

42 My account agrees, in the main, with David DeMoss, as expressed in "Acquiring Ethical Ends." See also DeMoss, "Aristotle." But DeMoss wants to sharply distinguish inductive reasoning, *nous*, and habit, whereas I argue that *nous* is the engine of inductive reasoning and that the developed inclination of habit facilitates it.

Figure 5.2
Aristotelian ethics

Virtue
(the mean)

Moral induction
(what Aristotle *sometimes*
call virtue) determines
the end to be aimed at

Moral deduction
(what Aristotle *sometimes* calls
practical wisdom) determines
the means to the end

We begin with human nature and
a proper upbringing

Practical syllogism leading to
practical conclusion:
I do this!

Figure 5.3
Courage example

Virtue
(the mean)

Moral induction:
This, this, and this instance of
human behavior is good fearlessness;
This, this, and this instance of human
behavior is courage;
Therefore, courage is good
fearlessness

S: This act
P: Good
M: Courage

All S_1, S_2, S_3, etc., is *P*
All S_1, S_2, S_3, etc., is *M*
(convertible to All *M* is *S*)
Therefore, all *M* is *P* (convertible)

Moral deduction:
Courage is good fearlessness;
Standing my ground in the pitch
of battle is courageous;
Therefore standing my ground in the
pitch of battle is good fearlessness;
which is equivalent to:
This is a good thing to do
(so, practical syllogism);
Therefore, I stand my ground

S: Standing my ground in battle
P: Good fearlessness
M: Courage

All *M* is *P* (convertible)
All *S* is *M*
Therefore, all *S* is *P*

While this general picture is sound, some further details of Aristotelian exegesis should nevertheless be mentioned. Guthrie (among others) argues that Aristotle sharply distinguishes virtue (ἀρετή, *arete*), the mental capacity of selecting a good end, from φρόνησις (*phronesis*), the mental capacity of selecting the means to that end.[43] One can give textual evidence for this reading. Guthrie cites Aristotle: "Virtue [referring to *arete*] ensures that the aim is right, and *phronesis* [practical wisdom] the means to that aim."[44] And again, "Virtue [*arete*] points out the end, and *phronesis* [practical wisdom] makes us do what is conducive to it."[45] But we should not insist too much on this distinction. Aristotle is not referring here to two independent activities that are accidentally connected. He is referring to two logical stages that follow one after another in the very same process of moral decision-making. (Aristotle does mention the possibility of correct moral judgement that exists apart from virtuous behaviour [*sunesis*] but that is not what he is talking about here.)

Aristotle himself writes, we cannot be "practically wise without moral excellence [i.e., without virtue]."[46] And again, "it is impossible to be practically wise without being good."[47] In other words, we cannot be moral without both mental capacities. We cannot separate the activity of choosing ends ("virtue") from that of choosing our means ("practical wisdom"), for morality requires that we do not choose evil means to a good end. It might be better to say that practical wisdom includes virtue or that virtue is a necessary but not a sufficient condition for practical wisdom. Or again, that virtue is prior to practical wisdom.

We should note, in passing, that Aristotle also makes a number of finer distinctions in his discussion of practical wisdom. Most importantly, he distinguishes "cleverness," "deliberation," "moral understanding," and "moral judgement." Cleverness, or quickness of mind (δεινότης, *deinotes*), is a natural intelligence allowing us to fit means to ends.[48] But cleverness can be used for good or for evil. If clever people efficiently do whatever they set out to do, they are not always moral. Deliberation or βούλευσις (*bouleusis*)

43 See Guthrie, *History of Greek Philosophy*, vol. 6, 347n3. Guthrie cites E. Zeller, W. Jaeger, and J. Burnet in favour; D.J. Allan, R.A. Gauthier, and E.M. Michelakis, opposed.

44 *Nicomachean Ethics*, bk 6, ch. 12, 1144a6–9, translated by Guthrie, *History of Greek Philosophy*, vol. 6, 347.

45 Ibid., bk 6, ch. 13, 1145a5–6.

46 *Nicomachean Ethics* (Ross, Urmson), bk 6, ch. 13, 1144b30–31.

47 Ibid., bk 6, ch. 12, 1144a336–37.

48 See *Nicomachean Ethics*, bk 6, ch. 12, 1144a23 ff.; and bk 6, ch. 13, 1144b1 ff.

has to do with the activity of choosing (from a number of options) the right means, i.e., the right course of action (one that leads to the right end).[49] Moral understanding or σύνεσισ (*sunesis*) is the mental ability to know which moral opinions are right. It is not the same as practical wisdom, for practical wisdom expresses itself in moral activity. We can mentally know which moral opinions are right, without putting them into practice.[50] Finally, moral judgement or γνώμη (*gnome*) is a kind of moral intuition that good people naturally develop over a long period of time. They are able to intuitively determine (without argument) what is right or wrong. So, for example, Aristotle advises, "we ought to attend to the undemonstrated [i.e., unargued for] sayings and opinions of experienced and older people ... not less than to demonstrations [i.e., to arguments]; because experience has given them an eye they see aright."[51]

Although we will not belabour the point here, note that this model of moral reasoning closely parallels Aristotle's one of scientific reasoning. Aristotle would presumably consider this line of reasoning about the prominent virtue of courage to be a case of strict moral inductive reasoning transformed, through verbalization, into a moral inductive syllogism. Once we know that courage is good, we can proceed with the proper moral deduction. We could look at other cases involving moral recognition and moral arguments from analogy. But I will leave such matters to the reader.

MORAL REASONING, THEORETICAL REASONING

Aristotle considers moral reasoning as analogous to but different from theoretical or scientific reasoning. The moral involves the same up-and-down movement, through induction to a generalization and through deduction to a particular conclusion. But practical wisdom is not *theoretical* knowledge, in part because it lacks precision and rigour. It is more approximate than theoretical reasoning. As Aristotle explains, "fine and just actions ...

49 "Excellence in deliberation will be correctness in assessing what is conducive to the end, concerning which practical wisdom gives a true conviction" (*Nicomachean Ethics* [Ostwald], bk 6, ch. 9, 1142b34–35). And again, "A person deliberates when he is engaged in investigating and calculating (things not yet decided)" (ibid., bk 6, ch. 9, 1142b2).

50 "So (we use understanding) when it implies the use of one's faculty of opinion in judging statements made by another person about matters which belong to the realm of practical wisdom – and in judging such statements rightly, for good understanding means that the judgement is right" (ibid., bk 6, ch. 9, 1143a13–16).

51 *Nicomachean Ethics* (Ross, Ackrill, Urmson), bk 6, ch. 11, 1143b8–13.

admit of much variety and fluctuation of opinion." This is why "we must be content," when we speak of morality, "to indicate the truth roughly and in outline."[52] Because morality has to adapt to contingent human circumstance, to matters which "are capable of being otherwise,"[53] we must use moral principles "which are only for the most part true," and accept "to reach conclusions that are no better."[54]

Although we will not investigate the issue in any detail here, it is common knowledge that Aristotle defines virtue as a mean between "too little" and "too much" of a character trait. So, for example, the virtue "courage" is a mean between the dispositions of those who are too fearful (cowards) and those who are too fearless (the reckless). The point is not to *prove* what courage is. The mean is a rule of thumb for those who are *already* moral. It is not a recipe for the moral ignoramus, who has no idea of what virtue is. If virtue is a mean, it is one we still need to adjust in dealing with particular circumstances. Good actions are preformed "at the right times, with reference to the right objects, toward the right people, with the right aim, and in the right way."[55]

Even formally, moral reasoning is, for Aristotle, less rigorous than theoretical reasoning. In the best theoretical reasoning, we induce a universal from particulars and use it to predicate something of an entire class of similar instances. But moral reasoning ends ideally in the practical syllogism and the practical syllogism applies the concept of a virtue to one given case. For example, I am confronted by this homeless man asking me for money; generosity is a virtue: I realize that giving him money is an instance of generosity; so I give him money. Given that moral deduction applies a general principle to a single instance rather than to a universal class, it is (for Aristotle) inevitably a less rigorous form of reasoning.

Although Aristotle focuses on virtue, reasoning about moral rules or laws follows the same inductive-deductive pattern. We *induce* a moral law and *deduce* a practical application. For example, we induce the universal moral law, "Don't tell lies," and then apply this law to the present circumstance: "Saying I did not chop down the cherry tree would be a lie; I must not tell a lie; therefore, I must own up to chopping down the cherry tree." The underlying logical structure of moral reasoning is always the same. We move up from individual experiences to a general claim and then down to an application of moral ideas to the specific circumstances in our lives.

52 *Nicomachean Ethics* (Ross, Urmson), bk 1, ch. 3, 1094b19–23.

53 See *Nicomachean Ethics*, bk 6, ch. 5, 1140a24 ff.

54 Ibid., bk 1, ch. 3, 1094b19–23.

55 Ibid., bk 2, ch. 6, 1106b22–23.

Note that Aristotle's theory of moral reasoning can also be applied to inarticulate agents. Imagine an inarticulate agent, who, without having recourse to words, comes to see benevolence as good and then strives to realize benevolence through a specific act of kindness. This agent tries to express a moral value in a particular action. As long as this process of applying a general principle to a specific situation is free and deliberate, their benevolent behaviour counts as moral activity.

ARISTOTELIAN MORAL THEORY

We can distinguish between two kinds of moral knowledge. Aristotle writes, "[moral understanding] is about the same objects as practical wisdom, but [moral] understanding and practical wisdom are not the same. For practical wisdom issues commands, since its end is what ought to be done, but [moral] understanding only judges."[56] We can have correct opinions about morality – as we have seen, this is moral understanding (σύνεσισ, *sunesis*). We can act morally – this is practical wisdom. For Aristotle, morality is primarily about making good decisions, as opposed to constructing a theory of morality.

While Aristotle thus focuses on moral practice, we can, however, construct a parallel Aristotelian model of moral theory. The practical syllogism runs as follows: Friendliness is good relationship; helping my neighbour is friendliness; therefore, I help my neighbour! The theoretical syllogism runs like this: Friendliness is a type of good relationship; helping my neighbour is friendliness; therefore, helping my neighbour is a type of good relationship. As Aristotle recognizes, these arguments are not precisely equivalent.[57] In the case of moral practice, we act. In the case of moral theory, we use formal arguments to arrive at some understanding of a moral issue. Whether we actually act on these evaluations is another matter.

The possibility of moral theory opens up alternative avenues for moral philosophy only explored by later moral philosophers. Thomas, for instance, formulates deductive instead of inductive arguments for virtue. Consider his argument for fortitude.[58] His reasoning may be expressed as an example of a sorites: a logical chain composed of two or more syllogisms leading to the requisite conclusion. The first syllogism runs, "Acting

56 Ibid., bk 6, ch. 10, 1143a7–1143a10.

57 Hence his account of σύνεσισ (*sunesis*), discussed above. See *Nicomachean Ethics*, bk 6, ch. 9.

58 Thomas, *Summa theologiae*, "Whether Fortitude Is a Virtue?" pt 2 of pt 2, Q. 123, art. 1.

in accordance with reason is (the ultimate) virtue. Fortitude enables us to act in accordance with reason. So fortitude enables virtue." The second syllogism runs, "Anything which helps us to be virtuous is virtuous. Fortitude helps us to be virtuous. So fortitude is virtuous."

Thomas uses deductive instead of inductive argument to arrive at the conclusion that fortitude is a virtue. But this in no way eliminates the need for induction. Thomas' argument about fortitude relies on two unstated inductions. First, we have to know that acting in accordance with reason is virtuous. This (self-evident) knowledge comes to us through an inductive inference. Second, we have to induce the concept of fortitude. Someone may learn what fortitude is through a verbal definition, but any such definition has to ultimately derive from our experience of the world.

MISTAKES IN MORAL REASONING

Modern instrumental accounts of rationality eliminate moral induction, replacing it with moral deduction. Rational agents maximize their preferences. Reason is about calculating the best means of satisfying these preferences. On this model, it is no longer moral induction understood as a species of reason, but bare emotion, considered preference, or radical free choice that selects the ends we pursue. Reason only comes into play *after* these ends have been chosen. The deductive side of the moral-reasoning model is all that matters. However, any such suggestion is, seen from an Aristotelian perspective, deeply troubling. Once we eliminate inductive moral reasoning, we eliminate all possibility of moral error. On Aristotle's account, all genuinely moral mistakes can be traced, in one way or another, to errors in of inductive moral reasoning.

Aristotle isolates two kinds of mistakes in moral reasoning. We may incorrectly *induce* the goals of moral action or incorrectly *deduce* the means needed to realize those goals. As he puts it, "It is possible to have one's aim right but to be entirely wrong in one's means to the end aimed at; and it is possible for the aim to have been wrongly chosen but the means conducing to it to be right; and for neither to be right."[59] Although either means- and/or ends-reasoning can be deficient, only mistakes in ends-reasoning truly count as moral errors. Through no fault of our own, we may choose the wrong means to effectuate good ends, but this is a lack of information or stupidity, not moral error. Moral error only occurs when we deliberately pursue wrong ends; that is, when the inductive stage of moral reasoning somehow misfires.

59 *Eudemian Ethics* (Rackman), bk 3, ch. 11, 1227b20–23.

We may, of course, fail to choose the right means to a good end because of an underlying moral problem, say laziness, or anger, or lack of education, or carelessness. The moral problem in such cases is, however, on closer inspection, one with ends-reasoning; it is an inductive error. This situation comes about because we have not been *aiming* at the right ends, at virtues such as industry, patience, education, or conscientiousness. At one point Aristotle goes so far as to identify deductive moral inference as a form of "perceptual knowledge," which seems a little strong, for deductive moral reasoning has, more rigorously, to do with fitting means to ends.[60] Still, his point surely is that this means-to-end function is more aptly described as a form of practical efficiency, not as a form of moral insight. My goal here is not to provide a detailed exegesis of Aristotle's sometimes confusing moral distinctions. We can, however, differentiate between four basic mistakes in moral reasoning: (1) brutishness; (2) vice; (3) incontinence (or weak-willedness); and (4) self-indulgence. Consider them in order.

(1) Brutishness: Aristotle believes that extremely immoral people, such as psychopaths, sociopaths, pedophiles, cannibals, serial killers, the types of criminally insane (etc.) are, effectively, subhuman animals. He calls them "brutish." They are brutish because they lack all power of moral inductive reasoning. They cannot induce the first principles (the ends) of morality. For whatever reason, they are unable to adequately conceive of virtue. It is not so much that they are intentionally vicious; they are vicious in the way a lion or a tiger might be vicious; because they lack a moral (i.e., a human) nature. Brutish people lack moral knowledge (or the capacity for moral knowledge) to such an extent that they are not participants in the "moral game."

Aristotle lists examples such as tribes who "have gone savage [and] delight – in raw meat or in human flesh, or in lending their children to one another to feast upon," or again, "the man who sacrificed and ate his mother," or "the slave who ate the liver of his fellow," or those afflicted with the compulsive "habit of plucking out the hair or gnawing the nails, or even coals or earth," and those involved in "pederasty."[61] He attributes these problems to a deficiency or deformity in nature, to madness or disease, to childhood sexual abuse, to active participation in surpassing evil, and again, to individual habit.

60 *Nicomachean Ethics* (Ross, Urmson), bk 7, ch. 3, 1147a26, 1147b17.

61 Ibid., bk 7, ch. 5, 1148b20 ff.

(2) Vice: Vice is a lesser degree of moral ignorance. The brutish have no inkling of morality – "What is the fuss all about?" they ask – whereas the vicious begin with moral insight that they undermine by their seriously immoral lives. Vicious people are fully human, but they corrupt their sense of moral discernment through their evil choices. They lose sight of moral principles. Aristotle believes that a good life preserves our sense of right and wrong, a bad one destroys it.[62] After many murders, the mafia enforcer is so callous as to no longer feel the wrongness of murder. If we spend all our time pursuing excessive wealth, we come to see it as a virtue. We become accustomed to seeing it as a worthy goal.

Aristotle thinks that seriously immoral lives make us morally ignorant. Qualified teachers of ethics must lead ethical lives, for immoral behaviour erodes our sense of moral judgement. It makes even the conspicuously immoral act seem routine, familiar, acceptable, legitimate. This is why disputing with the depraved and the immature is a waste of time. Aristotle advises, "To examine all the views about happiness is superfluous, for children, sick people, and the insane all have views, but no sane person would dispute over them, for such persons need not argument but years in which they may change, or else medical or political correction – for medicine, no less than whipping is a correction."[63] Indeed Aristotle goes even further, dismissing even the views of the morally mediocre masses swayed by the vagaries of popular opinion. "Similarly," he continues, "we have not to consider the views of the multitude (for they talk without consideration about almost everything ...); for it is absurd to apply argument to those who need not argument but experience."[64]

Refuting false opinions may a useful heuristic to shed light on the truth.[65] But when it comes to morality, the vicious no longer know what they are talking about. Intelligence, understood as a capacity for logical argument, is beside the point. If we start with the wrong first principles, logic does no good. When we reason from false premises, we will in all likelihood find our way to false conclusions.

(3) Incontinence: Aristotle introduces a third type of moral error that he calls ἀκρασία (*akrasia*) or weakness of will, a mistake in moral reasoning traditionally referred to as "incontinence." Whereas the vicious individual

62 "[Virtue] and vice respectively preserve and destroy the first principle" (ibid., bk 7, ch. 8, 1151a15).

63 *Eudemian Ethics* (Soloman), bk 1, ch. 3, 1214b28–33.

64 Ibid., bk 1, ch. 3, 1214b33–1215a2.

65 Ibid., bk 1, ch. 3, 1215a3–7.

leads such a bad life that he or she fails to recognize the difference between right and wrong, the incontinent are unable to resist temptation. They know the difference between right and wrong but are unable to make their actions conform to the right. They know what they should do but are unable to muster the necessary willpower.

Aristotle writes, "vice is unconscious of itself; incontinence is not."[66] And again, "vice is in accordance with choice," whereas "incontinence is contrary to choice."[67] Vicious agents choose what is wrong thinking it right. Because they have been corrupted, they do evil thinking it good. They no longer realize they are doing evil. They are happy with their choice. Incontinent agents, by contrast, choose what is right but end up doing evil. They know the difference between right and wrong, but are unable to turn their good intentions into action. They fail to live up to their own expectations. They lead lives fraught with disappointment and internal tension.

Incontinence may seem, at first glance, to be a problem of deductive moral reasoning. A practical syllogism ends in some specific action. Incontinent people see what moral conclusion follows, but something gets in the way. They are unable to put this ideal into practice. It is as if they cannot master the *means* to achieve virtue. But it is not really an issue of means-reasoning. It is a matter of will. And issues of willing the wrong things are inevitably those of moral induction. Aristotle thought of incontinence as a temporary, short-lived failure of moral induction. He reduces incontinence to an intermittent or instantaneous kind of viciousness, describing it as a bout of temporary forgetfulness brought on by passion or emotion, akin to drunkenness or sleep or madness. He explains, "outbursts of anger and sexual appetites and some other such passions ... actually alter our bodily condition, and in some men even produce fits of madness"[68] Incontinence is then a case of "having knowledge in a sense and yet not having it, as in the instance of a man asleep, mad, or drunk."[69] Passion blinds us, making us forget or lose sight of moral principles. When the emotional intensity dissipates, we recover our moral vision and discover what we've done, feeling remorse or guilt.

Incontinent agents act on appetite rather than on universal right opinion. Aristotle brings up the example of "sweetness."[70] I know I am overweight. I know I should restrain myself from eating that piece of chocolate

66 *Nicomachean Ethics* (Ross, Urmson), bk 7, ch. 8, 1150b36.

67 Ibid., bk 7, ch. 8, 1151a7.

68 Ibid., bk 7, ch. 3, 1147a14–17.

69 Ibid., bk 7, ch. 3, 1147a11–12.

70 Ibid., bk 7, ch. 3, 1147a29 ff.

cake. Why? Because both health and self-restraint are worthwhile goods. But I am overcome by appetite. I reason, "This chocolate cake is sweet; sweetness is pleasant; so I eat the chocolate cake." This is a practical syllogism. It ends in an action. As Aristotle points out, this line of reasoning is consistent. The problem is that appetite has replaced reason as the thing choosing ends. The problem has to do with choosing the wrong ends, not with reasoning about means. The error, that is, is one of moral inductive, not deductive, reasoning.

We should note that appetite can change the way we view something. When I become angry (which is a kind of appetite), I may *temporarily* come to view moral evil as an attractive option. Suppose I become very angry at my friend, punch him in the nose and then, realizing what I have done, recoil in horror. What has happened here? My anger *temporarily* changed my perception of this violent act. For a brief moment, punching my friend seemed like a good thing. In the immediate aftermath, my anger dissipated, I regained my moral vision, realized my mistake, felt shame for my action. Aristotle comments that the knowledge I had of the wrongness of this act either disappeared in the heat of action or was retained but in an ineffectual way.[71]

In the case of agents who retain an idea of what is right as they give in to temptation, Aristotle claims that they only have knowledge of morality in the way that "a drunken man may utter the verses of Empedocles."[72] Those who memorize Empedocles' poetry might be able to recite it when drunk, but they would be unable, given their addled state, to explain and retain in their minds the difficult scientific content of the verses. Likewise, the incontinent have, at most, only "word knowledge" of morality. As we explained above, morality begins in a sense of discernment that pushes us in a certain direction. Incontinent people do not experience the push. They lack the essential connative element of morality. They lack, that is, one key aspect of morality; they fail, at least momentarily, at moral inductive reasoning.

Aristotle believes that incontinence is better than vice, for it is possible to rehabilitate the incontinent. When they come to their sense, they know they have done wrong. They feel guilty. A sense of bitter remorse drives them to reform.[73] The vicious, however, are quite content with their evil ways. Ignorance is bliss. Why should they change? Given their

71 Ibid., bk 7, ch. 3, 1147b6 ff.

72 Ibid., bk 7, ch. 3, 1147b12.

73 Modern liberalism fails precisely to envisage this possibility: that agents who do what they want may, in some genuine sense, be acting against their own will.

corrupted state, they approve of their own immoral actions and so experience no impetus for change.[74]

(4) Self-indulgence: Aristotle also identifies self-indulgence or ἀκολασία (*akolasia*), sometimes translated as "licentiousness," as a moral fault.[75] Self-indulgent people are pleasure-seekers who possess an *uncorrected* sensibility. This type of individual "has no regrets; for he stands by his choice."[76] Self-indulgent agents *rationalize* their wayward activities. They practice *self-deception.*

The excessive pursuit of carnal pleasure is a paradigmatic case of self-indulgence. Consider, then, the self-indulgent man cheating on his wife. What does he do? He makes excuses: everybody does it; that's what I am; consent is all that matters; fidelity is hypocritical; it's all her fault; you only live once; it's in our genes; morality is only subjective – and so on. These kinds of arguments do not constitute a serious attempt to explore the moral status of such acts; they are used to cover up the fact that this person is greedily seeking his own sexual pleasure. Self-indulgent people do not honestly explore their moral predicaments. Instead, they spend their time trying to convince themselves they are really acting morally, until they come, at least at some level, to believe it.

The incontinent is torn apart by inner conflict and guilt. The self-indulgent, on contrary, argues away this guilt. He or she eliminates the "cognitive dissonance" that comes from a guilty conscience by eliminating the guilty conscience. Instead of striving to make his or her actions conform to true moral beliefs, the incontinent make their beliefs conform to their immoral actions.[77] Superficially, they seem better off. Yet Aristotle thinks that self-indulgence is, like vice, an incurable disease. Where incontinence is temporary, like "epilepsy," self-indulgence is a permanent condition, like "dropsy or consumption."[78] Self-indulgence makes genuine

74 Aristotle is too quick. Clearly we encounter many kinds of moral ignorance, not all of them invincible.

75 The meaning of Aristotle's brief remarks here is open to some latitude of interpretation. I provide what I think is one plausible reading.

76 Aristotle continues, "any incontinent man is subject to regrets" (ibid., bk 7, ch. 8, 1150b29–30).

77 See Leon Festinger, *Theory of Cognitive Dissonance.*

78 "The self-indulgent man is incurable and the incontinent man curable, for wickedness is like a disease such as dropsy or consumption, while incontinence is like epilepsy; the former is permanent; the latter an intermittent badness" (*Nicomachean Ethics* [Ross, Urmson], bk 7, ch. 8, 1150b32–34).

moral discernment impossible. At the very worst, moral theory, itself, teaches us how to use arguments to rationalize our behaviour, becoming nothing more than a cover for self-indulgence.

On Aristotle's account, immorality represents an inevitable failure of intelligence. Immoral agents are incapable of the very first levels of moral reasoning. They lose sight in various ways of the first principles of morality. These first principles have both an epistemological and a psychological effect. They inform us and motivate us all at once. Like the scientific, moral inductive reasoning requires a stroke or leap of understanding. We seize the universal through a creative illumination. The morally ignorant suffer from a sort of obtuseness, from a kind of practical stupidity.

SCIENTIFIC AND MORAL INDUCTION COMPARED

Contemporary authors in epistemology often champion science and devalue morality. On a familiar account, scientific judgements are factual, objective, empirical, epistemologically authoritative, and universal – moral judgements are inevitably emotional, subjective, unempirical, a matter of personal opinion, and inescapably relative. You have right and wrong answers in science, but no right or wrong answers in morality. You cannot be intelligent without believing in science, but you can be intelligent without morality.

Seen from an Aristotelian perspective, science produces explanations, whereas morality produces acts. Science produces formal demonstrations to account for the causality of events. Morality produces good behaviour. If science supplies us with true universal propositions, moral wisdom supplies us with specific virtuous acts. Both science and morality begin with inductive reasoning; both depend ultimately on the same fundamental human capacity for discernment and insight that lies behind all human concepts, claims, arguments, and theories. It is the same mind that produces both scientific and moral principles. If we cannot trust inductive reasoning in science, then we cannot trust it in morality. And *vice versa* – if induction goes, everything goes, both science and morality.

In Aristotle, we experience a basic symmetry about first principles. We know that murder is wrong with the same degree of certainty as we know the first principles of science. Theoretical and practical knowledge have absolutely same source. Both originate in rationality, not as argument or inference, but in its purest sense, as a capacity for the immediate illumination or intelligent understanding that precedes deduction and makes it possible. If the sceptic refuses to acknowledge the first principles of science, this does not mean that something is disastrously wrong with these principles. And if the sceptic refuses to acknowledge the first principles of morality, this again does not mean that something is disastrously wrong with these principles. Seemingly tireless attempts to disprove radical scepticism are a purely intellectual distraction. Just as we cannot prove the first principles of science, we cannot prove those of morality. But we cannot have knowledge of any kind unless we place some confidence in human inductive reasoning.

On Aristotle's account, we do not choose moral principles. We discover them. Moral principles are forced on us by our experience of the world. We do not arbitrarily *decide* that murder is wrong, just as we do not arbitrarily *decide* that whales are mammals. Only the morally immature or the self-indulgent would think that something becomes a virtue because we *decide* it is one. Morality is a kind of consistency; it is not a radical choice. Why should moral principles be more open to scepticism than scientific ones? In both cases, we abstract from experience. We seize on the universal underlying the particular. Why should our ability to locate a universal in individual experience be any less perfect when it comes to moral questions? Both science and morality originate in the very same capacity for human intelligence.

In sharp contrast to modern authors, Aristotle views ethics as an empirical science. The observation of the human behaviour, our own and others, is the foundation for moral ideas. The morally wise do moral theory the way a scientist does physical theory; they painstakingly and rigorously observe diverse human behaviours and seize on concepts or principles to unify and elucidate what they see. Without morality, we could not make any sense of how we ourselves or other people act. The same capacity for universal insight makes possible both science and morality.

6

Complete Syllogistic: The Hamiltonian Notation

I am inclined to admit that the credit, if there be any credit, in the thorough quantification of the predicate belongs to Hamilton. But I set no value on the proposed improvement … Nothing is saved by requiring us to put every proposition in a form so different from that which it assumes in spontaneous thought.

James McCosh[1]

Sir W. Hamilton … by substituting for it his own theory of the thoroughgoing quantification of the predicate, has revolutionized the whole science of Logic.

Francis Bowen[2]

IN THIS CHAPTER, WE WILL EXPLORE A HISTORICAL DISPUTE over the proper notation for syllogistic reasoning and use a modified version of a historical method to produce an exceptionally simple formal model capable of testing the validity of both inductive and deductive syllogisms.

The historical episode in question centres on the claim of Scottish Enlightenment figure Sir William Hamilton, that the predicate term in a categorical statement should be quantified, like the subject term.[3] Hamilton points out that the canonical notation is too vague to precisely distinguish the various categorical propositions. Consider the expression "All *S* is *P*." (Loosely, all instances of the subject are also those of the predicate term.) This expression seems ambiguous. It may mean "All *S* is *all P*," or "All *S* is *some P*." Hamilton (correctly) argues that in the traditional notation, one has no way of distinguishing between these two predications. He explains,

1 *Scottish Philosophy*, 450–1.

2 *Treatise on Logic*, 27.

3 Hamilton, *Lectures on Metaphysics and Logic*, 251ff.

> In a proposition, the two terms, the Subject and the Predicate, have each their quantity of thought. This quantity is not always expressed in language, for language tends to abbreviation; but it is always understood. For example, in the proposition, *Men are animals*, what do we mean? We do not mean that *some men*, to the exclusion of others are animals, but we use the abbreviated expression *men* for the thought *all men*. Logic, therefore ... warrants, nay requires, us to state this explicitly. Let us, therefore, overtly quantify the subject and say, *All men are animals*. So far we have dealt with the proposition, – we have quantified in language the subject, as it was quantified in thought.
>
> But the predicate still remains. We have said – *All men are animals*. But what do we mean by *animals*? Do we mean *all animals* or *some animals*? Not the former: for dogs, horses, oxen &c., are animals as well as men and dogs, horses, oxen &c., are not men ... *All men*, therefore, are not equivalent to *all animals*; that is, we cannot say, as we cannot think, that *all men are all animals*. But we can say, for in thought we do affirm, that *all men are some animals*.[4]

Hamilton was certainly not the first person to make this suggestion. Augustus De Morgan (1806–1871) and Friedrich Eduard Beneke (1798–1854) made similar proposals at about the same time, and earlier eighteenth-century authors such as Leonard Euler (1707–1783), Gottfried Ploucquet (1716–1790), and Johann Heinrich Lambert (1728–1777) proposed methods for diagramming syllogisms which, at the very least, presupposed the quantification of the predicate.[5] William Stanley Jevons attributes the discovery to George Bentham (1800–1884),[6] while another reputable source traces the idea all the way back to the Catholic ecclesiastic Juan Caramuel y Lobkowitz (1606–1682).[7] Still, Hamilton and his student Thomas Spence Baynes brought this view to hotly contested prominence. In the late nineteenth and early twentieth century, the issue became the focus of a raging scholarly debate between traditional logicians and proponents of what was to become the new symbolic logic.[8]

We may be struck with a mixture of alarm, admiration, and even awe at the vehemence of forgotten scholarly debates of bygone eras. If Jevons, in 1872, identifies the quantification of the predicate as "undoubtedly the

4 Ibid., 272–3.

5 See de Morgan, *On the Syllogism*, 17; and Beneke, *Syllogismorum Analyticorum*.

6 See George Bentham, *Outline of a New System* (1827).

7 *Catholic Encyclopedia*, s.v. "Logic" (by William Turner).

8 See Baynes, *Essay*.

most fruitful [discovery] made in abstract logical science since the time of Aristotle,"[9] Richard Clarke, in his 1889 *Logic*, affirms that "it is strange that a man of W. Hamilton's ability could be led astray by so wild a theory."[10] An only slightly more reserved John Stuart Mill claims, in 1894, that Hamilton's "new forms" are not only "difficult to learn" and "intolerably tiresome," but also have "no practical advantage which can countervail the objection of their entire psychological irrelevancy; and the invention and acquisition of them [has] little value, except as one among many other feats of mental gymnastic."[11] John Venn, in turn, concludes that although Hamilton's system has "a specious look of completeness" about it, this seeming completeness "is merely verbal, and objectively speaking illusory … merely the outcome of an exaggerated love of verbal symmetry."[12]

Twentieth-century Thomist Jacques Maritain heaps opprobrium on Hamilton's views, dismissing them as "*absolutely illegitimate*,"[13] but the triumph of set theory in mainstream symbolic logic has made all this scholarly fuss seem obsolete. In 1936, George Joyce asserted that Hamilton's theory is "quite untenable," "has nothing to recommend it," and "possesses only historic interest."[14] More recently (1959), Ralph Eaton writes that Hamilton's theory is only "a cumbersome and unnecessarily complex way of treating classes."[15] While Hamilton's precise formulation of his syllogistic notation is unfortunate, his basic approach remedies an oversight in Aristotle, simplifies notions of immediate inference, and most importantly for our purposes provides an efficient formalism for inductive "convertibility."

Historically, Hamilton was less than temperate in his sallies, and his slogan "to state explicitly what has been thought implicitly"[16] turned attention to a side issue. Disputants focused on a psychological question. "What do ordinary people think about when they make a universal statement?" Academics commenting on his works launched into vociferous disagreements about the meaning and import of ordinary-language statements. (There is some overlap here with contemporary debates about deductivism.) James McCosh, the great chronicler of Scottish philosophy, complains, "When we say 'the dog barks', we make the predication, without

9 Jevons, "Who Discovered," 823.
10 R. Clarke, *Logic*, 287.
11 Mill, *Examination*, 444–5.
12 Venn, *Symbolic Logic*, 14–5.
13 Maritain, *Formal Logic*, 216 (his italics).
14 Joyce, *Principles of Logic*, 108.
15 Eaton, *General Logic*, 140.
16 Hamilton, *Lectures on Metaphysics and Logic*, 166, 252, 254.

inquiring ... whether dogs are all or only some barking animals ... As the predicate is not always or even commonly quantified in spontaneous thought, so we do not require always to quantify it in the logical enunciation."[17] But surely, what happens in plain discourse is not logically decisive. As Hamilton insists, everyday language is imprecise and fraught with abbreviation. In formal syllogistic, the issue is, "What is the best way to make perfectly clear the logical relationship between the subject and predicate in a categorical statement?" Hamilton's method, once simplified, serves this purpose admirably.

Commentators sometimes suggest that Aristotle explicitly rules out quantification of the predicate in his work *De Interpretatione*. But careful perusal of the cited text shows that this is not the case.[18] Aristotle notes that whenever two universal terms are distributed, no affirmation will be true.[19] His point is that if we universally quantify the subject and predicate simultaneously, this will end in nonsense. Consider his example: "every human being is every animal." This claim *must* be false for, literally interpreted, it would mean that every instance of a human being would have to be every instance of animal; that is, every human being would have to (simultaneously) be a horse, dog, lion, rabbit, hen, and so on. But this is impossible. Given that the predicate term "animal" is a universal, referring to a plurality of individual animals, it is logically impossible that a single human being could be every animal.

Thomas Aquinas, who discusses Aristotle's meaning at some length, proposes two examples of well-formulated propositions with quantified predicates: "Every man is no stone" and "Every man is some animal."[20] Thomas also points out that Aristotle himself quantifies the predicate when he says that the soul is a particular act so as to differentiate it from other kinds of acts.[21]

17 McCosh, *Scottish Philosophy*, 450.

18 In the passage Aristotle distinguishes between universal kinds and universal propositions. He points out that claims such as "mankind is white" or "mankind is black" are true, because the universal "mankind" is sometimes white and sometimes black. These are *particular* affirmations. They mean, "some people are white" or "some people are black." The corresponding universal affirmations would be "*everyone* is white" or "*everyone* is black." We cannot assume, then, that any statement about a universal kind is universal. Only claims about *every* instance of a universal are properly universal.

19 Aristotle, *On Interpretation* (Cook), ch. 8, 17b13–15 (in Aristotle, *Aristotle in 23 Volumes*).

20 Thomas Aquinas, *Aristotle* (Oesterle), bk 10, lectures 23–4, 86–8.

21 Aristotle, *On the Soul*, bk 2, ch. 1, 412a22.

Neither Aristotle nor Thomas definitively rule out quantification of the predicate. To begin with, the affirmation they use "every man is every animal" is not inevitably false. Imagine a world in which the only living thing is a single human being. In this world, the proposition "every human being is every animal" would be true. Thomas writes, "In rejecting the enunciation 'Every man is every animal', the Philosopher meant it to be understood that all similar enunciations are to be rejected."[22] But this does not follow. Consider the proposition, "every God is every omnipotent being." If Thomas' monotheism is sound, there must be a single omnipotent God. But this would mean that this *is* a true proposition. To assume that the predicate class always refers to a plurality of individuals is to make a metaphysical, not a logical assumption.

In any case, this reading of the issue is uncharitable. In a spirited attack on Hamilton, Maritain uses a different example. He writes, "The proposition 'all man is all rational being' necessarily infers that 'Peter is all rational' and that 'Peter is all rational beings', which is absurd."[23] This is only to repeat Thomas' earlier point, but surely, there is a more charitable way to read a claim like "all human being is all rational being." If we understand the claim to mean that all human beings *taken together* comprise every rational being – i.e., that there are no rational beings other than these – we are left with a perfectly reasonable (though not necessarily true) assertion. Maritain assumes that the subject of the proposition is "all human beings taken individually" but it makes more sense to understand the subject as "all human beings taken together." Understood in this way, the statement would be a universal of the kind "every God is every omnipotent being," except that in this case we are making a claim about two groups of individuals. We are asserting that the extension of one group, "rational being," is completely contained in the extension of the other group, "human being." We discuss the issue further below.

Maritain (like Hamilton) overstates his case. Although Thomas does accept that double quantification can sometimes be valid, there are reasons why a medieval logician would be reluctant to embrace any such practice. On Thomas' account, a proposition is intended to give us information about the subject. The status of the predicate, which plays a *formal* role in describing the subject, is, generally speaking, a secondary matter. Thomas writes, "It is more appropriate to say 'No man is a donkey' than 'Every man is no donkey'."[24] Why? Because these propositions are about the subject

22 Thomas Aquinas, *Aristotle* (Oesterle), bk 10, lecture 24, 88.

23 Maritain, *Introduction to Logic,* 217.

24 Thomas Aquinas, *Aristotle* (Oesterle), bk 10, lecture 23, 86.

matter "man." The intended claim is about "man," not about "donkey," and so the second enunciation is not wrong, but unnecessarily indirect. Thomas continues, "It is more appropriate to say ... likewise ... 'Some man is white' than, 'Man is some white'."[25] The first formulation is more appropriate because "man" is the subject matter of the proposition. A properly formed proposition quantifies the subject matter; it tells us how many people are white. It will begin with the expression "*some* human being" or "*every* human being." How many white things are human beings is a subordinate issue.

Medieval authors such as Thomas distinguished between *significatio* or meaning and *suppositio* or reference. Seen from one perspective, the terms in a proposition may be said to have the same supposition, to stand for the same thing. Consider the proposition "Socrates is sitting." The subject term "Socrates" and the predicate term "sitting" may be said to refer, in this instance, to the same *ens* or being – they both point to the same thing, namely, sitting Socrates. If, however, we look at the proposition from this perspective, the predicate term, considered by itself, has no quantity. It too refers (in a different way) to the subject matter of the proposition. Seen in this way, any reference to the quantity of the predicate is misguided. The subject and predicate terms have the same quantity, as they both stand for the same object or group of objects in the world. The vast medieval (and secondary) literature on this subject will not detain us here.

Hamilton vigorously attacked the views of the ancients and Schoolmen on this issue. Never one to mince words, he writes,

> The whole doctrine of the non-quantification of the predicate is only another example of the passive sequacity of the logicians. They follow obediently in the footsteps of their great master. We owe this doctrine and its prevalence to the precept and authority of Aristotle. He prohibits once and again the annexation of the universal predesignation of the predicate ... giving as his only example and proof of this, the judgement – "All man is all animal." This is, however, only valid as a refutation of the ridiculous doctrine, held by no one, that any predicate may be universally quantified ... This nonsense (be it spoken with all reverence of the Stagirite) has imposed the precept on systems of logic down to the present day. Nevertheless, it could be shown by a cloud of instances from the Aristotelic writings themselves, that this rule is invalid; nay Aristotle's own doctrine of induction, which is far more correct than that usually

25 Ibid., bk 10, lecture 23, 86. In fact these propositions are not precisely equivalent, although the ambiguity of the quantifier "some" renders the meaning the same.

> taught, proceeds on a silent abolition of the erroneous cannon. The doctrine of the logicians is therefore founded on a blunder.[26]

As it turns out, however hot headed, Hamilton is in the main correct. Although Aristotle's commentators (rather than Aristotle himself) denounced quantification of the predicate as anathema, his own understanding of induction does, as we shall see, presuppose this practice.

The rancour of the ensuing debate did little to elucidate matters. So-called traditional logicians (of *Aristotelian* bent) insisted that logic could not be separated from metaphysics, whereas Hamilton and his followers insisted on a creeping formalism. Hamilton declares, "it is a matter of indifference from a logical point of view … which of the two terms be made subject or predicate of the proposition."[27] Consider the proposition, "some houses are red." This is, on the traditional view, to predicate the property "redness" of some things, "houses." But suppose we were to say "some redness is houses." Hamilton declares both formulations logically equivalent. In the first case, however, we have a property, "redness," predicated of a thing, a "house"; in the second case, we have a thing, a "house," predicated of a property, "redness." This second formulation lacks metaphysical decorum. Any logical usage which confuses the metaphysical identity of subject and predicate would have seemed monstrous to metaphysically minded traditional philosophers. There is some truth to Bert Mosselman's claim that "the quest for quantification of the predicate can only be achieved by stripping the syllogism of its metaphysical heritage."[28]

Aristotelian logic is about things that exist. If we adopt Hamilton's metaphysically empty formalism, it would inevitably blur the distinction between what does and does not exist. Mermaids, unicorns, golden mountains, the present (non-existent) bald king of France may play a logical role in an argument. Or consider the case of a proposition that links two terms that refer to the same thing, for example, "Tully is Cicero." This statement is metaphysically empty. It tells us that this particular thing is this particular thing. If, however, we invent a logic that is purely formal and emptied of substantive content, these two terms can arguably play a role in the same proposition.

In the proposition "Tully is Cicero," the relationship between the two terms is one of identity rather than of predicating. We are not predicating "Cicero" of Tully; we are saying that Tully is the same person as Cicero. Traditional logicians complained that Hamilton's system misunderstood

26 Hamilton, *Lectures on Metaphysics and Logic*, 264–5.

27 Ibid., 273.

28 Mosselman, "Aristotle's Logic," 198.

the subject-predicate relation, reducing syllogistic logic to a study of the identity relations of diverse classes. John Venn observes that in Hamilton's system "the import of the proposition must be shifted from ... the relation of subject and predicate ... [to] the relation of inclusion and exclusion of two classes."[29] Maritain, for one, distinguishes between extensivists (Hamilton, Leibniz, Segner), who see categorical statements as affirming a relation of identity (or non-identity) between the members (or extension) of diverse classes, and comprehensivists (Lambert, Hamelin, Rodier), who see categorical statements as identifying a relation between the intension (or meaning) of concepts.[30] But traditional logicians overlooked the fact that Aristotle's syllogistic (which is a bit muddled in this respect) appeals to both predication and identity. The former holds pride of place in Aristotle, but (as we have already discussed), inductive syllogism depends crucially on an identity of the subject and middle terms.[31] Aristotle communicates this identity by means of the concept of convertibility. Hamilton's method of quantification of the predicate allows us to express convertibility in simple formal terms, something Aristotle himself couldn't do.

Traditionally, syllogistic reasoning rests on a fundamental principle, the *dictum de omni et nullo* – in George Englebretsen's way of formulating it, "Whatever is affirmed of all of something is likewise affirmed of what that something is affirmed of."[32] Clarke, however, adds a second principle: "Whenever two objects of thought are identical with a third, they are also identical with each other."[33] As we shall see, this emphasis on the notion of identity is fecund, at least from the viewpoint of formalizing logic.

QUANTITY

Let us set up some kind of formal Hamiltonian method. This will reinforce earlier arguments about the validity of inductive reasoning. We can represent various categorical statements, using the symbolism associated with the traditional rule-method, Euler's circles, Venn diagrams, Hamilton's own idiosyncratic notation, or a quasi-mathematical notation inspired by

29 Venn, *Symbolic Logic*, 10.

30 Maritain, *Introduction to Logic*, 172.

31 Joyce, *Principles of Logic*, 100; and Maritain, *Introduction to Logic*, 172.

32 Englebretsen, *Three Logicians*, 23.

33 R. Clarke, *Logic*, 315, 380. This principle regulates affirmative syllogisms. Clarke also introduces a principle for negative syllogisms: "When of two things, one is identical with and the other different from some third thing, these two things are different from each other" (ibid.).

Hamilton. I will use an exceptionally sparse arithmetical notation. (The point is to capture the spirit not the letter of Hamilton's proposal.)

Hamilton's schedule of eight possible propositions is based on traditional logic and is unnecessarily cumbersome.[34] We only need to use three quantifiers:

(1) "All" will mean every instance of a concept. It signifies the whole class. When I say, "All *S* is *P*," I mean, "everything that is *S* is *P*." This is standard usage.
(2) "Some" will mean some but *not* every instance of a concept. Traditional logic accepts subalternation as an immediate inference. If we have "All *S* is *P*," we can infer that "Some *S* is *P*." In this Hamiltonian notation, subalternation is illegitimate. When I say, "Some *S* is *P*," I mean, simultaneously, "Some *S* is P" and "Some *S* is not *P*." This excludes the possibility that all *S* is *P*. Because a "some" statement represents a particular affirmation *and* a particular negation, we only need three quantifiers here instead of the usual four.
(3) "No" means no instances of the concept. This is like standard usage. When I say "No *S* is *P*," I mean "nothing that is an *S* is a *P*."

Hamilton claims that "a proposition is simply an equation, an identification, a bringing into congruence of two notions in respect to their Extension."[35] We can easily capture this notion of relationship between two classes using the following five arithmetical symbols, "$=$, $\neq$, $\leq$, $\geq$, $^1/_x$." To say, for example, that "All *S* is all P" is to say that the extension of *S* is identical with the extension of *P* which can be easily expressed as "$S = P$." I will call this somewhat odd manner of logical expression Hamiltonian notation. As eccentric as such notation may appear to modern eyes, it captures succinctly what Hamilton was about.

Maritain criticizes Hamiltonian notation because it reduces logic to algebra. He writes that when "the proposition 'Man is mortal' is reduced to the expression 'Man = some mortal' [this] is no longer a logical enunciation and no longer functions as a proposition to be thought, but rather as an

34 Here is Hamilton's original catalogue of eight categorical statements: All *S* is all *P*. All *S* is some *P*. Some *S* is all *P*. Some *S* is some *P*. Any *S* is not any *P*. Any *S* is not some *P*. Some *S* is not any *P*. Some *S* is not some *P*. See Hamilton, *Lectures*, 279–80. Jacques Maritain's criticism misses the point insomuch as it focuses on Hamilton's precise formulation, which is less than felicitous (*Introduction to Logic*, 214–21ff.). George Joyce's critique, though sometimes perceptive, suffers from the same fault (*Principles of Logic*, 108).

35 Hamilton, *Lectures on Metaphysics and Logic*, 273.

algorithm to be used without thinking."[36] But the equal sign here obviously does not function, in the mathematical sense, as a marker of quantity. It must be interpreted as a marker of identity. To assert "all S = all P" is simply to claim that the extension S and that of P are identical.[37] There is no need to read more into this usage. Hamiltonian notation is economical, intuitive, and simple. The precise choice of notation is, in any case, a secondary issue.

CATEGORICAL STATEMENTS

We may now make an inventory of all possible categorical statements. We need to set up the statements such that there is one possible meaning (and one possible diagram) for each statement. Invoke, then, a law of minimal interpretation. According to this principle, nothing can be assumed. What is not explicitly stated is *never* assumed to be the case.

We have three quantifiers, "all," "some," "no." If we quantify both subject and predicate terms in a proposition, it will follow that there are nine possible categorical statements:

(1) All *S* is all *P*
(2) All *S* is some *P*
(3) All *S* is no *P*
(4) Some *S* is all *P*
(5) Some *S* is some *P*
(6) Some *S* is no *P*
(7) No *S* is all *P*
(8) No *S* is some *P*
(9) No *S* is no *P*.

Traditional logicians, George Joyce, John Venn, Thomas Crumely, and Lewis Carroll, point out that two terms (or classes) can be related to one another in only five basic ways.[38] These authors use Euler's circles to illustrate all possible relations between two terms. Figures 6.1 to 6.5 map these five relationships onto our nine categorical statements.

36 Maritain, *Introduction to Logic*, 220.

37 George Joyce criticizes "Professor Jevons" for his use of mathematical notation. He writes, "It is manifest, however, that in the great majority of our judgements we are not concerned with a relation of equality but of identity" (*Principles of Logic*, 109). Indeed, but this only shows that such notation should not be misinterpreted, not that it is useless. Again, the notation Joyce criticizes here is less than felicitous.

38 Joyce, *Principles of Logic*, 77–81; Venn, *Principles*, 229–30; Crumely, *Logic*, 129–33; and Carroll, *Symbolic Logic*, 240–2, 247–9.

Figure 6.1
All *S* is all *P*; no *S* is no *P*

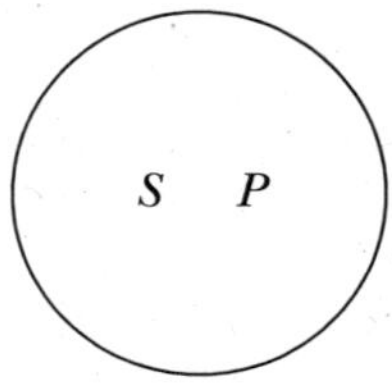

Figure 6.2
Some *S* is all *P*

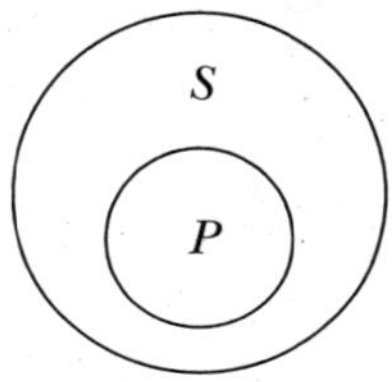

Figure 6.3
All *S* is some *P*

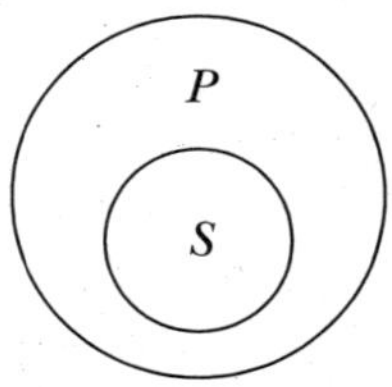

Figure 6.4
All *S* is no *P*; no *S* is all *P*

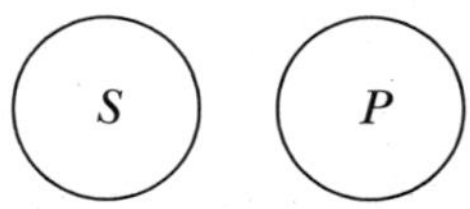

Figure 6.5
Some *S* is some *P*; some *S* is no *P*; no *S* is some *P*

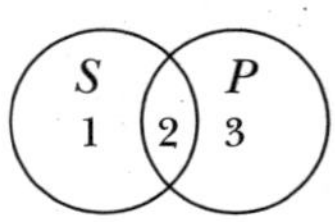

The extensions of the two terms are identical in figure 6.1. This relationship is designated by categorical statements (1) and (9). The meaning of (1), "All *S* is all *P*," is self-evident. Expression (9) is more awkward. Take "No *S* is no *P*," to mean, "there are no members of *S* that are not members of *P*." Or again (which reduces to the same thing), that the total absence of *S* must be the total absence of *P* (because they always occur together). Symbolically, $S = P$.

In figure 6.2, part of the extension of *S* includes the whole extension of *P*. This relationship is designated by categorical statement (4), "Some *S* is all *P*." This means that every member of *P* is a member of *S* but that only some members of *S* are members of *P*. Symbolically, $S \geq P$. We use a "greater than or equal to" symbol to show, first, that some of *S* is equal to (or identical with) all *P*; and second, that some of *S* is "greater than" (or outside of) all *P*. (Note that we are not saying that *S* is equal to *or* greater than *P*, but that some of *S* is greater than *and* some of *S* is equal (in the intended sense) to *P*. This is not arithmetic but logic.)

As we see in figure 6.3, part of the extension of *P* includes the whole extension of *S*. This is the reverse of the previous relationship. It is designated by categorical statement (2), "All *S* is some *P*." This means that every member of *S* is a member of *P* but that only some members of *P* are members of *S*. Symbolically, $S \leq P$. We will use a "less than or equal to" symbol to show, first, that all of *S* is equal to (or identical with) some *P*; and second, that all of *S* is "less than" (or has a smaller extension than) all *P*. (Again, note that we are not saying that *S* is less than *or* greater than *P*, but that some of *S* is less than *and* some of *S* is equal [in the intended sense] to *P*.)

The extension of *S* and *P* completely exclude one another in figure 6.4. This relationship is designated by categorical statements (3) and (7). Take (3), "All *S* is no *P*," to mean that the presence of the whole class of *S* will not include any of *P*. Take (7), "No *S* is all *P*," to mean that the entire absence of *S* does not detract, in any way, from the presence of *P* (because the occurrence of *P* is in no way linked to the occurrence of *S*). Even if there is no *S*, this leaves room for *all* of *P*. Symbolically, $S \neq P$. Keep in mind that this logical (not arithmetical) notation does not suggest anything about *S* being lesser or greater than *P*. It means that *S excludes P* (and *P excludes* S). This is a different (and much stronger) claim.

The terms *S* and *P* share only part of the same extension in figure 6.5. This relationship is designated by categorical statements (5), (6), and (8). Take (5), "Some *S* is some *P*," to mean that some but not all of *S* is *P* (and vice versa). Take (6), "Some *S* is no *P*," to mean that *only* some *S* is not *P*. (And thus, that some *S* is *P*.) Finally, take (8), "No *S* is some *P*," to mean that some part of *P* excludes all of *S* and that some other part of *P* includes *some* of S. (This awkward, but we are interested in logical form.) If we number the different regions of figure 6.5, we can see that statement (5) is a comment on region 2; statement (6), on region 1; and statement (8), on region 3. Assume that each statement presupposes the others. Symbolically, this final possibility can be rendered: $^1/_x S = {^1/_x} P$. Again, the fraction "$^1/_x$" is not an issue of precise quantity. The "x" in the denominator can be taken as a marker of variable quantity. It does not indicate what proportion of *S* is *P* or what proportion of *P* is *S*. It means (as in standard logics) that at least one member of *S* is also *P* and that at least one member of *P* is also S. But it also means (in contrast to standard logic) that at least one member of *S* is not *P* and that at least one member of *P* is not *S*.

CONVENTIONAL QUANTIFICATION

Hamilton was trying to eliminate all ambiguity from logical relationships. We could have tried to represent what he was doing using modern quantification theory, in the following way.[39] The point here is not to provide an exactly equivalent analogue to Hamilton's arithmetical notation but to bring home the deeper issue of what he was trying to do. Symbolize the traditional schedule of Aristotle propositions in such a way as to capture Hamilton's basic idea that every categorical proposition expresses a relationship between two quantified classes. (So we need two variables.) For purposes of illustration, begin with a set of traditional examples – "all human are animals," "some humans are animals," and so on – where these statements are taken to describe a completely quantified relationship between the classes "human" (H) and "animal" (A). Leave aside issues of existential import. As we shall see, even if we quantify the predicate, we cannot excise a certain ambiguity in traditional notation without implementing a stricter formalism.

- Universal affirmation: All H is A. This means, "Every human is identical to some animal." (In Hamiltonian notation, every human = some animal, where the equals sign means "identical to.") This might be quantified as, $(\forall x)\ (\exists y)\ [Hx \supset (Ay\ \&\ x = y)]$, which can be read as "it is the case that for any *x*, there exists some *y*, such that if *x* is human, then that *y* is animal and *x* is identical with *y*."
- Universal negation: No H is A. This means, "Every human is non-identical with every animal." (In Hamiltonian notation, every human ≠ some animal, where the slashed equals sign means "not identical to.") This can be quantified as, $(\forall x)\ (\forall y)\ [Hx \supset (Ay \supset x \neq y)]$, which can be read as, "it is

39 Thanks to anonymous referee for raising this issue.

the case that for any x and for any y, if x is human, then if y is animal, x is not identical to y."

- Particular affirmation: Some H is A. This means, "Some human is identical to some animal." Or again, "there is at least one human who is identical to at least one animal." (In Hamiltonian notation, some human = some animal.) This can be formally expressed as, $(\exists x)\ (\exists y)\ [Hx \;\&\; (Ay \;\&\; x = y)]$, which can be read as, "it is the case that there exists some x and there exists some y such that x is human and y is animal and x is identical to that y."
- Particular negation: Some H is not A. This means "Some human is non-identical with any animal." Or again, there is at least one human that is not identical with any animal. (In Hamilton-like notation, some human ≠ every animal.) This can be formally expressed as: $(\exists x)\ (\forall y)\ [Hx \;\&\; (Ay \supset x \neq y)]$, which can be read as, "it is the case that there exists some x such that x is human and for any y, if y is animal, x is not identical to y."

If, however, these quantified expressions capture the meaning of the four categorical statements (while quantifying the predicate term), an imprecision remains, for the existential quantifier, ∃, refers to "some" of a class without specifying whether the "some" in question constitutes *only* a part of that class or may include the whole of that class. This is, in a Hamiltonian spirit, something we should be worried about. An element of ambiguity results every time we use this existential quantifier. Suppose, then, we invent a strict existential quantifier, *∃, which rigorously means "some but not all." Using *∃, we could express our categorical statements in more precise form.

- Universal negation: No H is A. The meaning of this statement is always unequivocal; this is because universal negation is made up of two *universal* quantifiers. There is no existential quantifier.
- Universal affirmation: All H is A. This can be expressed more precisely as follows:

  $(\forall x)\ ({*}\exists y)\ [Hx \supset (Ay \;\&\; x = y)]$ or
  $(\forall x)\ (\forall y)\ [Hx \supset (Ay \supset x = y)]$.
- Particular negation: Some *A* is not *B*. This could be more precisely expressed as follows:

  $({*}\exists x)\ (\forall y)\ [Hx \;\&\; (Ay \supset x \neq y)]$ or
  $(\forall x)\ (\forall y)\ [Hx \supset (Ay \supset x \neq y)]$.
- Particular affirmation: Some A is B. This could be more precisely expressed as follows:

$(^*\exists x)\ (^*\exists y)\ [\mathrm{H}x\ \&\ (\mathrm{A}y\ \&\ x = y)]$,
$(^*\exists x)\ (\forall y)\ [\mathrm{H}x\ \&\ (\mathrm{A}y \supset x = y)]$,
$(\forall x)\ (^*\exists y)\ [\mathrm{H}x \supset (\mathrm{A}y\ \&\ x = y)]$, or
$(\forall x)\ (\forall y)\ [\mathrm{H}x \supset (\mathrm{A}y \supset x = y)]$.

Every time we use an existential quantifier, some sort of (exclusive) disjunction results. An ambiguity is perpetrated. Which one of the disjuncts holds true? Traditional notation is too coarse grained to distinguish between them.

In addition, contemporary conventional predicate notation cannot express strict partial exclusion from a class: $(^*\exists x)\ (^*\exists y)\ [\mathrm{H}x\ \&\ (\mathrm{A}y\ \&\ x \neq y)]$. Hamiltonian notation is succinct: ${}^1\!/_x S = {}^1\!/_x P$. (In such notation, partial exclusion is the same as partial inclusion.) But there is no room for this precise expression of partial exclusion in the above schedule of rigorously quantified categorical statements. At best, it requires an immediate inference to move from the first rigorously quantified disjunct of particular affirmation, $(^*\exists x)\ (^*\exists y)\ [\mathrm{H}x\ \&\ (\mathrm{A}y\ \&\ x = y)]$, to any formal acknowledgment of particular exclusion.

More could be said, but the lesson of this short aside is that familiar forms of notation are inevitably imprecise. Hamilton wanted to eliminate imprecision. He wanted a formulation that was perfectly rigorous and clear. That is what his odd arithmetical notation is about. At least for the purposes of precision, it represents an advance over earlier systems.

V OF OPPOSITION

In our Hamiltonian notation, all categorical statements are contradictories. If one statement or diagram is true or correct, all the other statements or diagrams must be false or incorrect. Aristotle proposes the square of opposition as a way of mapping out relationships such as contradiction, contrariness, subcontrariness and subalternation. Modern logicians have modified his original schema to produce what is commonly referred to as the modern square of opposition.[40] Using the Hamiltonian notation, we can map out these kinds of relationships using a new schema I will call the V of opposition. This V-shaped diagram divides the five possible relationships described in our schedule of propositions into "principal opposites" and "sub-opposites," as in figure 6.6.

40 See *Stanford Encyclopedia of Philosophy*, s.v. "Traditional Square of Opposition" (by Terence Parson).

Figure 6.6
V of opposition

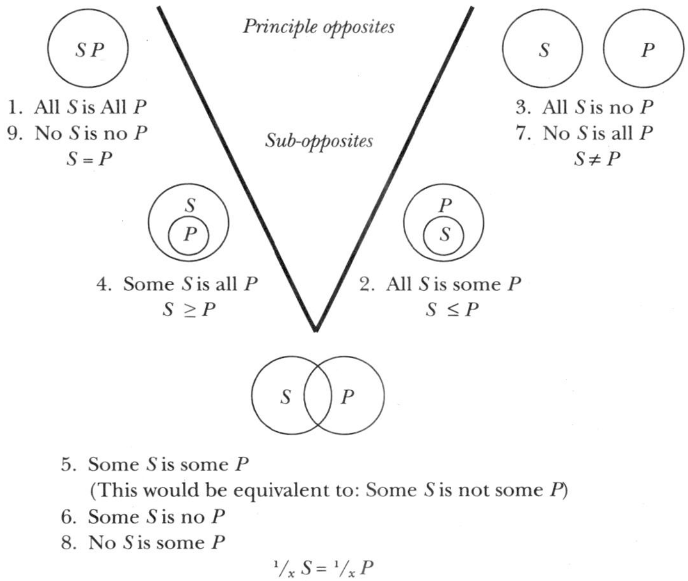

As the diagrams indicate, opposition is not the same thing as contradiction. At the level of principal opposites, total inclusion of the two terms within each other is the contrary of their complete exclusion outside one another. At the level of sub-opposites, in one subcontrary S contains P, whereas in the other P contain S. In the case of partial inclusion and exclusion of both classes, there is only one possibility and so, no opposite.[41]

CONVERSION

In this economical notation, all categorical propositions convert. We might distinguish, however, between perfect conversion and imperfect conversion. In perfect conversion, the order of the terms cannot change the meaning of the proposition. The terms S and P may change positions

41 In his attack on Hamilton, Maritain misconstrues the nature of contradictories with respect to double quantification. This undermines his criticism. See Maritain, *Introduction to Logic*, 218.

Table 6.1
Perfect conversion

Original statement	*Notation*	*Convert*	*Convert notation*
All *S* is all *P*	$S = P$	All *P* is all *S*	$P = S$
No *S* is no *P*	$S = P$	No *P* is no *S*	$P = S$
All *S* is no *P*	$S \neq P$	All *P* is no *S*	$P \neq S$
No *S* is all *P*	$S \neq P$	No *P* is all *S*	$P \neq S$
Some *S* is some *P*		Some *P* is some *S*	
Some *S* is no *P*	$^1/_xS = {^1/_x}P$	Some *P* is no *S*	$^1/_xP = {^1/_x}S$
No *S* is some *P*		No *P* is some *S*	

Table 6.2
Imperfect conversion

Original statement	*Notation*	*Convert*	*Convert notation*
Some *S* is all *P*	$S \geq P$	All *P* is some *S*	$P \leq S$
All *S* is some *P*	$S \leq P$	Some *P* is all *S*	$P \geq S$

without any modification of meaning. Three of the five possible relationships are characterized by perfect conversion, as in table 6.1.

In imperfect conversion, the order of the terms matters. One may still convert as long as one does not separate each term from its original quantifier. Table 6.2 depicts imperfect conversion.

When we change the position of the terms, we must change the direction of the sign. Clearly, $S \geq P$ is equivalent to $P \leq$ S, just as $S \leq P$ is equivalent to $P \geq S$. In a statement denoting complete inclusion within a larger class, any change in the order of terms must preserve the respective identities of "the contained" and "the containing" class.

SOME SYLLOGISMS

Now that we have a "formalism" for designating categorical statements, we can use this formalism to test individual syllogisms. Consider the following example: "All human beings are mortal. Rugby players are human beings. Therefore, rugby players are mortal." Rewrite the argument quantifying the predicate: "All human beings are some mortal things. All rugby players are some human beings. Therefore, all rugby players are some mortal things." Define our terms, according to their (formal) function: subject term (*S*), rugby players; predicate term (*P*), mortal things; and middle term (*M*), human beings. We may, then, translate as follows. Premise$_1$: All *M* is some *P*.

Figure 6.7
"Rugby" syllogism

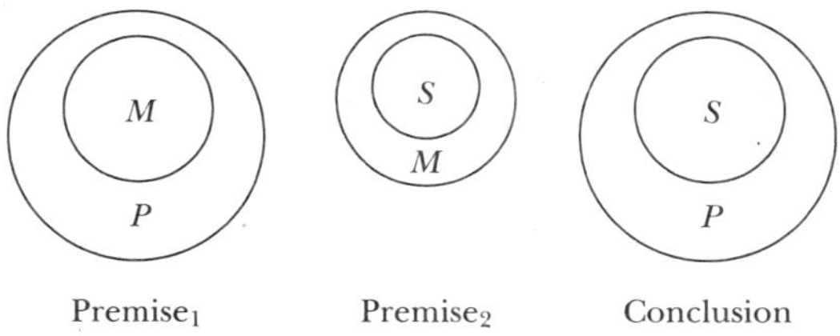

Figure 6.8
Camestres

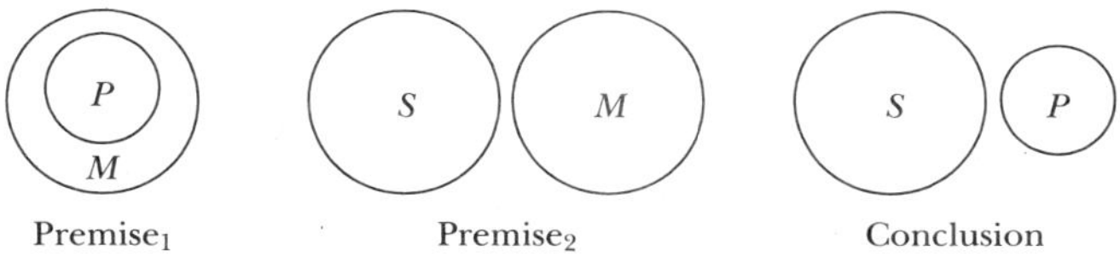

Premise$_2$: All *S* is some *M*. Conclusion: Therefore, all *S* is some *P*. If the English seems awkward, the formal version follows more smoothly: "$M \leq P$; $S \leq M$; therefore, $S \leq P$." Clearly, this is a valid syllogism. If *M* is contained in *P* and *S* is contained in *M*, then *S* must be contained in *P*. Figure 6.7 makes this immediately evident.

Or consider this example of Camestres, taken from a monograph on logic: "Socrates is mortal. Zeus is immortal. Therefore, Zeus is not Socrates."[42] Treat singular terms such as "Socrates" and "Zeus" as classes with one member. To say "Socrates is mortal" is to say that all members of the class "Socrates" are mortal. To say "Zeus is immortal" is to say that all members of the class "Zeus" are immortal. Rewrite, then, our syllogism. "All Socrates is some mortal. All Zeus is no mortal. Therefore, all Zeus is no Socrates." If we define our terms – *S*, Zeus; *P*, Socrates; and *M*, mortal things – we can translate as follows. Premise$_1$: All *P* is some *M*. Premise$_2$: All *S* is no *M*. Conclusion: Therefore, all *S* is No *P*. This, again, seems to follow more easily in Hamiltonian notation: $P \leq M$; $S \neq M$; therefore, $S \neq P$. Or, if that fails, figure 6.8 shows immediately that if *P* is (wholly) contained in *M*, and *S* is excluded from *M*, then *S* must also be (wholly) excluded from *P*.

Not all examples follow so readily. Consider an invalid syllogism adapted from a textbook: "Some cats are not troublesome. All cats are pets. So no

42 Englebretsen, *Three Logicians*, 49.

Figure 6.9
Example of an invalid syllogism

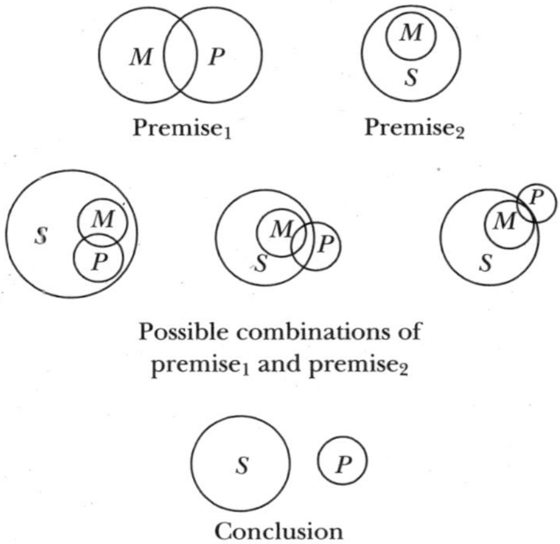

pets are troublesome."[43] Define our terms: *S*, pets; *P*, troublesome; and *M*, cats. To say that "some cats are not troublesome" is to imply that some cats are troublesome: symbolically, $^1/_x M = {}^1/_x P$. To say "All cats are pets" is to claim, $M \leq S$. And to say, "No pets are troublesome," is to claim $S \neq P$. But the sequence, "$^1/_x M = {}^1/_x P$; $M \leq S$; therefore, $S \neq P$" does not follow. Why? Look at the second premise. It tells us that *all* of *M* is contained within *S*. But if *S* includes all of *M* as part of itself, and if *M* and *P* overlap, some part of *S* must also overlap with *P*. The conclusion claims that they do not overlap. This is patently false. Figure 6.9 makes this immediately obvious.

VALIDITY

But enough of this. We can very quickly determine the validity of all primitive syllogisms, as in table 6.3. (A conclusion with a number means that this specific conclusion *must* follow from these premises, hence validity. A question mark means that it is not clear which conclusion follows from these premises, hence invalidity.) Traditional concerns about syllogistic figures are not important here, because all our propositions are perfectly or imperfectly convertible.

43 Leo Groarke, Tindale, Fisher, *Good Reasoning Matters*, 126, 331–2, exercise 6.Ma.

Table 6.3
Table of valid and invalid syllogisms

	Major premise				
Minor premise	$M = P$ $(P = M)$	$M \geq P$ $(P \leq M)$	$M \leq P$ $(P \geq M)$	$M \neq P$ $(P \neq M)$	$^1/_xM = {}^1/_xP$ $({}^1/_xP = {}^1/_xM)$
$M = S$ $(S = M)$	$M = P$ $M = S$ $S = P$ (1)	$M \geq P$ $M = S$ $S \geq P$ (2)	$M \leq P$ $M = S$ $S \leq P$ (3)	$M \neq P$ $M = S$ $S \neq P$ (4)	$^1/_xM = {}^1/_xP$ $M = S$ $^1/_xS = {}^1/_xP$ (5)
$M \geq S$ $(S \leq M)$	$M = P$ $M \geq S$ $P \geq S$ (6)	$M \geq P$ $M \geq S$?	$M \leq P$ $M \geq S$ $P \geq S$ (7)	$M \neq P$ $M \geq S$ $\mathrm{S} \neq P$ (8)	$^1/_xM = {}^1/_xP$ $M \geq S$?
$M \leq S$ $(S \geq M)$	$M = P$ $M \leq S$ $P \leq S$ (9)	$M \geq P$ $M \leq S$ $S \geq \mathrm{P}$ (10)	$M \leq P$ $M \leq S$?	$M \neq P$ $M \leq S$?	$^1/_xM = {}^1/_xP$ $M \leq S$?
$M \neq S$ $(S \neq M)$	$M = P$ $M \neq S$ $S \neq P$ (11)	$M \geq P$ $M \neq S$ $S \neq P$ (12)	$M \leq P$ $M \neq S$?	$M \neq P$ $M \neq S$?	$^1/_xM = {}^1/_xP$ $M \neq S$?
$^1/_xM = {}^1/_xS$ $({}^1/_xS = {}^1/_xM)$	$M = P$ $^1/_x M = {}^1/_x S$ $^1/_xS = {}^1/_xP$ (13)	$M \geq P$ $^1/_x M = {}^1/_x S$?	$M \leq P$ $^1/_x M = {}^1/_x S$?	$M \neq P$ $^1/_x M = {}^1/_x S$?	$^1/_x M = {}^1/_x P$ $^1/_x M = {}^1/_x S$?

Note: (1)–(13) refer to the valid forms of the syllogism

If we restrict our formal vocabulary to these five statements without allowing for any kind of compound premise or conclusion, we will be left with only thirteen valid syllogisms. We can prove these results, using traditional diagrams or rules.

AMBIGUITY AND VALIDITY

Our Hamiltonian notation modifies the practice of logic in two ways. Modern logic focuses on the question of validity. (Think of the way truth tables can be used to show that the conclusion is true in every instance in which the premises are true.) This approach often turns logic into a kind of back-checking. The Hamiltonian method is more like calculation. If we use the formalism correctly, we can use it to figure out which conclusion follows from these premises. It will follow, as a matter of course, that the resulting sequence is valid. But the focus is on determining the correct answer, not on the assertion of validity.

This does represent a difference in method. Take a simple example from arithmetic. Suppose I assert that "5 things plus 5 things = 10 things." Call the sequence before the equals sign, the antecedent; call the sequence after the equals sign, the consequent. And express what is going on by saying the antecedent implies or entails the consequent. We might say that this formula is *valid* insomuch as whenever the antecedent is true, the consequent is true. But the important thing is that the expression yields the correct answer. Validity follows as a matter of course, but it is not the point of the exercise. If logic really is (as Aristotle suggests) a kind of calculation, deductive arguments *succeed*, in the best sense of the term, when they give us the right answer. They are, of course, valid, but it is the correct answer that we are after.

The second innovation has to do with the way Hamiltonian notation, at the most basic level, reduces ambiguity to invalidity. In a primitive syllogism, there are no compound propositions. The conclusion is composed of a single categorical statement. Because each categorical statement precisely expresses one possibility, this leaves no logical room for a conclusion encompassing more than one possibility. We can, however, expand our notation to include the more complicated possibility of compound premises and conclusions. Consider the traditional syllogism Barbara, "All *M* is P. All *S* is *M*. Therefore, all *S* is *P*."

We can disambiguate the traditional formalism, using strict Hamiltonian notation. Begin with the conclusion. The quantity of the predicate in the "All *S* is *P*" statement is equivocal. "All *S* is *P*" might be interpreted to mean that all members of *S* are *some P* or that all members of *S* are *all P*. Rewrite the conclusion more precisely as a disjunction, "All *S* is some *P*" or "All *S* is all *P*." To maintain that Barbara is a correct syllogism is to claim that this conclusion must follow from the premises "All *M* is *P*" and "All *S* is *M*." Each premise is, however, also equivocal. "All *M* is *P*" may be rewritten "All *M* is some *P*" or "All *M* is all *P*." "All *S* is *M*" may be rewritten "All *S* is some *M*" or "All *S* is all *M*." Having expressed the propositions more precisely, we may now test the syllogism using a modified tree method as in figure 6.10.

As the diagram indicates, the conclusion of the syllogism will be either "All *S* is some *P*" or "All *S* is all *P*," however we interpret the premises. So the original syllogism gives us the right answer. It follows (as a matter of course) that it is valid. What this shows is that although traditional syllogistic may be imprecise, it may still be logically sound.

We can represent Barbara in strict Hamiltonian notation: Premise$_1$: "All *S* is some *M*" or "All *S* is all *M*." Premise$_2$: "All *M* is some *P*" or "All *M* is all *P*." Conclusion: Therefore, "all *S* is some *P*" or "all *S* is all *P*." More tersely, "Premise$_1$: $S \leq M$ or $S = M$. Premise$_2$: $M \leq P$ or $M = P$. Conclusion: Therefore, $S \leq P$ or $S = P$."

Figure 6.10
Tree method applied to Barbara

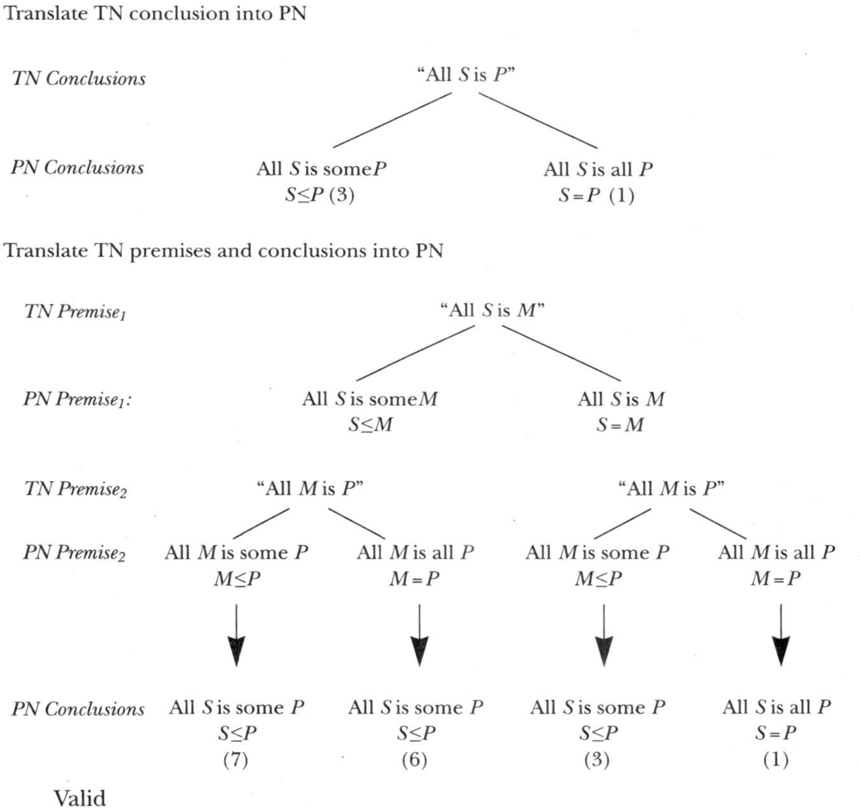

Note: Parenthetical numbering refers to valid forms of the syllogism (Table 6.3); PN, precise notation; TN, traditional notation

We might distinguish between perfect syllogisms ending in a single categorical statement and imperfect ones using compound categorical statements. Traditional Barbara is an example of an imperfect syllogism. An example of a perfect syllogism would be, All *M* is all *P*; all *S* is all *M*; therefore, all *S* is all *P* ($M = P$; $S = M$; therefore, $S = P$). We could call this "strict Barbara." The traditional formalism has no way of expressing strict Barbara. All syllogisms listed in table 6.3 are perfect syllogisms. The reader may explore further examples.

Figure 6.11
Some M is all P; some S is all M; some S is all P

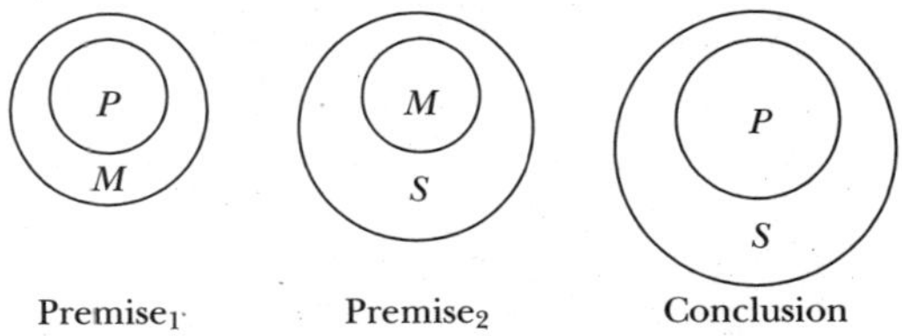

ARISTOTELIAN OVERSIGHT?

Traditional syllogistic, which developed out of Aristotle, is not equipped to deal with the quantity of the predicate. This may not make any difference in many cases, but will in some, where the validity of an argument depends crucially on the quantity of the predicate. Consider the following argument. "Premise$_1$: Some varsity athletes are on the football team. Premise$_2$: Some students are varsity athletes. Conclusion: Therefore, some students are on the football team." On the traditional model, this syllogism commits the fallacy of undistributed middle. It is an error in reasoning. But this is misleading. The problem is that the traditional notation is unable to precisely capture the intended logical inference. Why? Because it does not display the quantity of each predicate. Define our terms: S, students; P, individuals on the football team; and M, varsity athletes. In complete notation, premise$_1$, "Some varsity athletes (M) are on the football team (P)," becomes "Some M is all P" (the whole football team is made up of varsity athletes). Premise$_2$, "Some students (S) are varsity athletes (M)," becomes "Some S is all M" (all varsity athletes are students). The conclusion, "Some students (S) are on the football team (P)," becomes "Some S is all P" (the intended claim is that the whole football team is composed of students). Symbolically, "$M \geq P$; $S \geq M$; therefore, $S \geq P$." Figure 6.11 depicts this relationship.

But this is a valid syllogism (syllogism 10, table 6.3). The conclusion necessarily follows. It gives us the right answer because of the quantity of the predicates. (It does not commit the fallacy of undistributed middle, because the middle term *is* distributed in the second premise, which states, Some S is *all M*. Because traditional notation does not quantify predicates, this distribution is, so to speak, hidden from view.) The reader may explore other cases.

INDUCTIVE SYLLOGISMS

Our principal purpose here is the formal expression of inductive syllogisms. If induction moves from particular to universal, it can also be construed as a movement from a knowledge of concrete individuals to that of universal concepts. In rigorous Aristotelian science, we begin with a knowledge of some of the individuals making up a class and end with a definition, a composite universal concept that succinctly expresses the properties of the entire class. Put another way, to reason inductively involves a movement from (partial) extension to intension. We begin by observing individuals and produce general concepts expressing knowledge of individual properties (or groups of properties).

Consider again Aristotle's bileless-animals induction. Premise$_1$: All mankind, horse, mule, etc., are long-lived animals. Premise$_2$: All mankind, horse, mule, etc., are bileless animals. Conclusion: Therefore, all bileless animals are long-lived animals. Define our terms, according to their logical function (*not according to their metaphysical status*): *S*, bileless animals; *P*, long-lived animals; and *M*, mankind, horse, mule, etc. As the middle term denotes a representative sample of the individual animals under consideration, it must be understood in its extension. (Use the subscript "e" to indicate this: M_e). We can, then, translate Aristotle's inductive syllogism into strict Hamiltonian notation as follows. Premise$_1$: All M_e is some *P*. Premise$_2$: All M_e is all *S* (convertible). Conclusion: Therefore, all *S* is some *P*. Symbolically, "Premise$_1$: $M_e \leq P$. Premise$_2$: $M_e = S$. Conclusion: Therefore, $S \leq P$." This, then, is the basic form of the inductive syllogism. (It is valid syllogism 3, table 6.3.) The crucial step is premise$_2$, the claim that the middle term (M_e) and the subject term (*S*) are convertible, that is, $M_e = S$. The claim is not that these two terms are numerically identical (as in perfect induction), but that they are *identical in nature*. It takes a moment of insight to recognize this identity.

The form of the inductive syllogism also fits arguments from likeness. Consider Aristotle's previous induction about human societies honouring the wise. Premise$_1$: All the Parians, the Chians, the Mytilenaeans, etc., honour the wise. Premise$_2$: All the Parians, the Chians, the Mytilenaeans, etc., are human societies. Conclusion: Therefore, every human society honours the wise. Define our terms: *S*, human societies; *P*, whatever honours the wise; and M_e, the Parians, the Chians, the Mytilenaeans, etc. In complete notation, the argument is as follows. Premise$_1$: All M_e is some *P* (it is not just human societies that honour the wise; human individuals and the gods presumably honour the wise). Premise$_2$: All M_e is all *S* (the middle term and the subject term are convertible). Premise$_3$: All *S* is some *P.* Symbolically, "Premise$_1$: $M_e \leq P$. Premise$_2$: $M_e = S$. Conclusion: Therefore, $S \leq P$." Here again, the crucial move is the claim about convertibility. Because this is only an argument from likeness, premise$_2$ is plausible rather than necessary. So we must accept the conclusion as merely plausible.

Medieval logicians distinguished between an inductive *ascensus* and *descensus.* An inductive *ascensus* moves from particular instances to universal principles, as in the preceding two examples. Maritain gives the following example of an inductive *descensus*: Premise$_1$: Metal conducts electricity. Premise$_2$: To say metal is to say iron, copper, and gold, and silver, etc. Premise$_3$: Therefore, iron (etc.) conducts electricity.[44] This may strike the modern reader as a deduction, for the movement is from general ("metal") to more specific ("iron," "copper," etc.). Still, Maritain claims that this is a disguised induction, because it is an inference about parts of a whole. We can show that except for one important difference, this argument shares the same form as the inductive syllogism. Define our terms: *S,* iron, copper, gold, etc.; *P,* that which conducts electricity; and *M,* metal. Translate into pure form: Premise$_1$: All *M* is some *P* (some things other than metal conduct electricity, for example, air when there is lightening). Premise$_2$: All *M* is all S_e. Conclusion: Therefore, all S_e is some *P.* Symbolically, "Premise$_1$: $M \leq P$. Premise$_2$: $M = S_e$. Conclusion: $S_e \leq P$." As we can see, this argument shares the same basic form as the previous two, except we understand the subject rather than the middle term, with respect to its extension. (This is because the subject term is conceived of in terms of the *individual* groups of things that make up the middle term. We could define "metal" extensionally, i.e., "metal" means iron, copper, gold, etc.) Otherwise, the argument has the same form as an ordinary inductive syllogism and qualifies as a valid inference. Whereas in a regular induction (what Maritain calls the inductive *ascensus*), we move from *extension* to *intension* by means of a convertible premise, in inductive *descensus* we move from *intension* to *extension* by means of such a premise.

The role of extension in logic is not limited to inductive inference. Consider the proverbial form of deductive reasoning. Premise$_1$: All men are mortal. Premise$_2$: Socrates is a man. Conclusion: Therefore, Socrates is mortal. Define out terms: *S,* Socrates; *P,* mortal; and *M,* men. In this deduction, the subject term "Socrates" must be understood in terms of its extension. (Socrates is an individual, a concrete particular, not a concept.) One moves, then, from knowledge of concrete individuals to conceptual knowledge. So the deduction runs as follows. Premise$_1$: All *M* is some *P.* Premise$_2$: All S_e is

44 Maritain, *Introduction to Logic,* 265.

some *M*. Conclusion: Therefore, all S_e is some *P*. Symbolically, "Premise$_1$: $M \leq P$. Premise$_2$: $S_e \leq M$. Conclusion: Therefore, $S_e \leq P$." This is a valid inference (syllogism 7, table 6.3). It involves a movement from universal to particular, but it does not depend on any crucial claim about convertibility. So it differs, in an important sense, from the inductive arguments above.

Maritain criticizes the "ever-increasing tendency to reduce all reasoning to the mere establishment of the relations of extension."[45] But the Hamiltonian notation does not force us to accept that particular reading of the terms. Consider the proposition "all human beings are mortal." Define our subject term, *S*, as "human being"; our predicate term, *P*, as "whatever is mortal." We can understand the resulting claim either extensionally or intentionally. We can write, "All *S* is some *P*" ("$S \leq P$"). Or we can write, "All S_e is some P_e" ("$S_e \leq P_e$"). Understood intentionally, it signifies that the *idea* "humanity" must include the *idea* "mortality." Understood extensionally, it signifies that all *individuals* who make up humanity are *individuals* who are mortal. We are free to accept whichever of these readings we choose. Hamiltonian notation presents these relationships in as complete and as unambiguous a way as possible.

45 Ibid., 207.

7

A History of Intuitive Understanding

When a man *reasoneth,* he does nothing else but conceive a sum total, from *addition* of parcels; or conceive a remainder, from *substraction* of one sum from another.

Thomas Hobbes[1]

As a matter of fact, the very order of reasoning requires that the chain has a beginning.

James B. Sullivan[2]

It must be the case that we are capable of knowing at least one proposition to be true, without knowing any other proposition from which it follows.

G.E. Moore[3]

We could never arrive at any knowledge by reasoning, unless something could be known antecedently to all reasoning.

John Stuart Mill[4]

I refer to "intellect" here in a rather special sense which will be familiar to those who are students of the great patristic and medieval traditions but has otherwise been very nearly completely lost within our own. For us today, the word "intellect" has become so narrowed in meaning – reduced to a capacity for those attenuated forms of ratiocination whose paradigms are those of mathematical argument, or else of empirical justification – that we are scarcely able to read about intellect or reason in our earlier traditions of [thought] without grossly misreading them … For Thomas, as for the long tradition he inherits, you begin to occupy the place of intellect when reason asks the sorts of question the answers to which you know are beyond the power of reason to comprehend. They are questions, therefore, which

1 *Leviathan,* pt 5, para. 1, 27 (in Hobbes, various documents).

2 *An Examination of First Principles,* 25.

3 Cited in Guthrie, *History of Greek Philosophy,* vol. 6, 178.

4 Cited in ibid.

have a double character: for they arise … out of our human experience of the world; but the answers, we know, must lie beyond our comprehension, and therefore beyond the experience out of which they arise.

Denys Turner[5]

A POPULAR AND VENERABLE VIEW SHARPLY distinguishes Aristotle's system from that of his teacher, Plato. On this account, Aristotle is a man of scientific, worldly bent, whereas Plato is the mystic straining skyward. The dichotomy is most memorably expressed, not in literature, but in Raphael's famous painting, *The School of Athens*, in the Vatican. At the vanishing point of the perspective plane, among the assembled thinkers of ancient Greece, we see an aged Plato conversing with a youthful Aristotle. The old man, immobile, points upward toward the heavens, while the young man, one foot turned in a horizontal direction, gestures with an open hand toward Earth. Plato holds his theological work the *Timaeus* in a vertical position at his side, whereas Aristotle rests his *Ethics* in a horizontal position against one leg. The fresco is an impressive testimony to the humanistic revival of the southern Renaissance, and the viewpoint it presents was (and is) historically influential.

One finds similar sentiments echoed in academic prose. In a 1924 text on Greek philosophy, Margaret Taylor tells us that "Plato sought reality in the spiritual order … [whereas] Aristotle sought reality in the world itself."[6] Norman Cantor and Peter Klein remind students that "Platonism is the foundation of all purely intellectual and mystical traditions in Western thought," whereas "Aristotelianism is the beginning of empiricism and … scientific inquiry."[7] Jonathan Barnes introduces Aristotle with the quip that "Aristotle was no Platonist,"[8] while Marjorie Grene (who develops a point of view similar to those of F.M. Cornford and Joseph Owens) explains that the philosophies of Plato and Aristotle represent "two deeply divergent attitudes to experience, to man, and the world."[9] Whereas Plato turns away from the "kaleidoscope" of sensation,[10] Aristotle conceives of sensation as "the first step to knowledge."[11] Plato believes that reality is ineffable and

5 *Faith, Reason and the Existence of God*, xv.

6 Taylor, *Greek Philosophy*, 111–4.

7 Cantor and Klein, *Ancient Thought*, 15.

8 Barnes, *Aristotle*, 35.

9 Grene, *Portrait of Aristotle*, 41.

10 Ibid., 45.

11 Ibid., 46.

"written speech is second-rate,"[12] whereas Aristotle is just as confident "that men can delimit in speech the essential attributes of kinds of things."[13] Plato throws himself into an "unending" struggle "to rise beyond the merely apparent,"[14] while Aristotle seeks out philosophical standards "present on the very face of experience itself."[15] Grene concludes with a paean to Aristotle, who "found form, intelligibility, definiteness, where Plato never found it: in the limited, recurrent but orderly processes of nature itself. And [who] ... built a cosmos such as Plato and the Platonists had never known."[16]

But there is also a competing voice in the tradition. Cicero, for one, claims that Platonism and Aristotelianism represent a "single uniform system" with "two appellations," which "while agreeing in doctrine [are] differing only in name."[17] Boethius goes so far as to claim that "the Aristotelian and Platonic conceptions ... are in agreement with one another at the philosophically decisive points." Indeed, he tells his readers that he plans translations of Aristotle in which he will "not shrink from proving that the Aristotelian and Platonic conceptions in every way harmonize, and do not, as is widely supposed, completely contradict each other." [18] Although one scholar (Loyd Gerson) has published a recent volume provocatively entitled *Aristotle and Other Platonists*, this seems a little extreme. Although Aristotle does not set out to overthrow everything Platonic, there are important differences between Aristotelianism and Platonism. I will argue that Aristotle reworked the Platonic synthesis to his own ends without, however, eliminating the transcendental element traditionally associated with Plato. In Aristotle's philosophy, Plato's dependence on the divine power of contemplation is pushed into the background and becomes instead the ultimate source of the inductive insight that makes science possible.

In this chapter we investigate the kind of cognitive leap or mental inspiration that makes induction possible. I will argue that Aristotle's account of ἐπαγωγή or *epagoge* borrows heavily from Plato's theory of *noesis*. As the eminently sensible Copleston puts it, "Aristotelianism, historically speaking, is

12 Ibid., 48.

13 Ibid., 50.

14 Ibid., 51.

15 Ibid., 55.

16 Ibid., 65.

17 Cicero, *De Natura Deorum* (Rackham), bk 1, ch. 4, para. 17 (in Cicero, *De natura deorum; Academica*).

18 Cited in Watts, introduction to *Consolation of Philosophy* (Watts), xvi. The original passage is from Campenhausen, *Fathers of the Latin Church* (Hoffman), 285–6.

not the opposite of Platonism, but its development."[19] Although of course the pupil of Plato, Aristotle was an original student who modifies the master's teaching. Aristotle's originality makes us lose sight of the underlying agreement. As Clement Webb explains, Aristotle "starts from the position of a Platonist, and proceeds to develop his own … criticism of those Platonic doctrines with which he found himself unable to agree. Hence, the first impression made upon a student is that of a perpetual opposition to Plato; the fundamental agreement in many respects between the pupil and his master is less observed, because it is, naturally, less insisted upon."[20]

THE BEGINNINGS OF THOUGHT

Despite obvious differences of opinion between Plato and Aristotle, we find a Platonic residue in Aristotle. Indeed, Aristotle's theory of induction, properly understood, is a radical rereading of the mystical Platonic doctrine of *anamnesis* or recollection. The Aristotelian emphasis on science does not eliminate the need for direct mental illumination as a source of knowing.

Aristotle believes that we access the first principles of knowledge, not through argument, but through immediate enlightenment. We need, then, to investigate the mental capacity that yields the first inductive insight. This chapter places the Aristotelian account of this mental faculty within a short historical overview of contributing and competing philosophical conceptions. I begin by examining Plato's account of *nous* and *noesis* and go on to show how Aristotle adapts the Platonic understanding to his scientific world view. In both Plato and Aristotle, we can make a useful distinction between *noesis* and *dianoia*, between mental illumination and discursive reasoning. I will briefly consider the role of mental illumination in Plotinus and move on to the account of *intellectus* and *ratio* found in Thomas Aquinas. Thomas provides a sophisticated development of Aristotle's seminal ideas. In the early modern era, there is a major shift in perspective.

I will compare René Descartes' account of intuition as the source of the first principles of reason with the more traditional account of Blaise Pascal. Some contemporary commentary notwithstanding, the Cartesian position displays a radical new emphasis on the discursive aspects of reasoning. I conclude the chapter by considering Bernard Lonergan's account of "insight." In contrast to many contemporary philosophers, Lonergan displays an openness to the creative, heuristic aspects of human cognition.

19 Copleston, *Greece and Rome*, pt 2, 18.

20 C. Webb, *History of Philosophy*, 49.

Learning depends on insight, a moment of sudden mental discovery, not unlike Aristotelian *noesis.* However, irreconcilable differences divide the Lonerganian and Aristotelian accounts. As we shall see, Lonergan's understanding of insight actually restricts the role of mental discovery and privileges discursive reasoning.

Investigating how we first come to know seems particularly important in light of a new rationalism that motivates and orients much of contemporary philosophical discourse. This is not the old rationalism of innate ideas rejected by empiricists such as Locke. The new rationalism stridently champions discursive reasoning, reasoning by language and argument, and overlooks, understates, or eliminates the illuminative or heuristic aspects of cognition. It is not so much a point of view explicitly argued for as a silent assumption, an underlying attitude pervading contemporary philosophical practice. It can lead to an almost exclusive focus in philosophy on constructing and evaluating arguments.

The contemporary focus on *argument* as the paradigm of inductive method is only one conspicuous symptom of this prevailing mindset. The basic assumption that every belief needs to be justified through argument expresses itself, more globally, in the unspoken assumption that every time someone advances a claim, we have the right to question it. Whenever someone affirms that something is true, we can come right back and demand that they give reasons for it. If they question our right to press them further, if at any point they refuse or are unable to respond, they are conceding that their beliefs cannot be rationally defended and have lost the debate.

An irate author of a contemporary textbook reports,

> On a recent trip to Chicago I browsed through the section labeled "philosophy" in a popular bookstore. The only philosophical works in the entire section were selections from Plato and Aristotle. The rest were mystical writings by Kahil Gibran and books on astrology, yoga, and the occult. No wonder then, that the public thinks that philosophers are given to uttering profound-sounding verbiage that no one can understand. In fact, most philosophers are sane, level-headed men and women who try to express themselves clearly and give persuasive reasons for what they believe.[21]

Of course, we can understand the author's chagrin. But notice carefully how he defines philosophers. Philosophers are primarily "people who give

21 Curd, *Argument and Analysis*, xvii.

persuasive reasons for what they believe." In other words, philosophers are, above all, arguers. They are not so much (as an earlier tradition would have said) wise people. Philosophers are first and foremost masters of verbal dispute; they are people who are good at constructing persuasive arguments; they are skilled at rhetoric and logic; they know how to draw conclusions from premises, how to wield the tools of deductive and inductive inference.

There is nothing surprising or esoteric here. This is the general approach one encounters today. On one department website, we read, "To study philosophy you have to engage in philosophical argument (reasons or evidence leading to a conclusion) ... The analysis of reasons and arguments is a special province of philosophy. In fact, inasmuch as philosophy has a distinctive method, it is this: the construction, criticism and analysis of arguments."[22]

Colin McGinn, in a philosophical autobiography, puts on display a similar attitude. Describing his attraction to philosophy as a young man, he explains, "The idea of axioms and deductions, systematically laid out, [is] immensely appealing, and [one takes] great pleasure in seeing what follow[s] logically from what ... The power of one idea to lead to another is a never-ending source of fascination for me ... It is always a damning moment when one philosopher says to another, 'hang on, that doesn't really follow'. Since philosophy is largely about the construction of arguments, the philosopher needs to be finely tuned to what follows from what. 'Non-sequitur' is the ultimate put-down."[23]

We have no need to enter into details here. Philosophy, on this familiar account, is mostly about giving clear, persuasive reasons for our beliefs. It has to do with proving or establishing a point. It is all about arguing. Inference or entailment – the power of one idea to lead to another – is what matters. The biggest mistake is not seeing what follows from what. But this cannot be all there is to philosophy. At the very origins of thought, at the very margins of knowledge, we come to insights that we cannot secure by argument. As earlier philosophers such as Aristotle recognized, we induce first principles through some kind of non-discursive intuition or immediate awareness. Our account of reason would be incomplete without adequately recognizing this feature of human experience.

22 Nigel Warburton, "What Is Philosophy," from the website of the Philosophy Department, Open University, UK.

23 McGinn, *Making of a Philosopher*, 44.

PLATO'S DOCTRINE OF *NOESIS*: SEEING THE TRUTH

The ancient Greek philosophers believed that we can learn about the world in two radically different ways: through *perception* or *thinking*. We can use physical senses such as sight and hearing to *perceive* reality or we can use thought or mind to *understand* it. The very first philosophers, generally known as the Presocratics, came to believe that we should distrust sense perception and focus on mental understanding if we want to penetrate appearances and grasp the deep truth about things. Anaxagoras, for one, praises mind as "the finest of all things and the purest," attributing to it "all judgement about everything and the greatest power."[24]

This superiority of logic or reason over sense perception is a constant theme in early philosophy. The Pythagoreans situated reality in abstract numbers, which are thought rather than perceived, whereas the atomists divided the world into material atoms much too small to see.[25]

Heraclitus warns us that "[the faculty of] sight tells falsehoods"[26] and that "eyes and ears are bad witnesses to people if they have barbarian souls."[27] Parmenides, we are told, "made reason standard and pronounced sensation to be inexact."[28] Whereas Sextus Empiricus reports that Democritus "calls [knowledge] that comes through thinking 'genuine', and … [knowledge] that comes through the senses … 'bastard'." In Democritus' own words, "To the bastard kind [of knowledge] belong the following: sight, hearing, smell, taste, touch."[29]

24 Anaxagoras, in McKirahan, *Philosophy before Socrates*, §13.12(9) (Diels and Kranz [DK] number 59B12). Anaxagoras' appraisal of sense perception is less enthusiastic. Sextus Empiricus relates that "he offers as evidence of [the senses'] untrustworthiness the gradual change of colors. For if we take two colors, black and white, and then pour out one into the other a drop at a time, our vision will not be able to distinguish the gradual changes, even though they exist in reality" (Anaxagoras, in McKirahan, *Philosophy before Socrates*, §13.33 [DK59B23; from Sextus Empiricus, *Against the Mathematicians*, bk 7, §90]).

25 "So small they escape our senses" (Democritus, in McKirahan, *Philosophy before Socrates*, §16.3 [DK68A37]); from Aristotle, *On Democritus*, quoted by Simplicius, *Commentary on Aristotle's "On the Heavens,"* lecture 295, arts. 1–22).

26 Heraclitus, in McKirahan, *Philosophy before Socrates*, §10.19 (DK22B46).

27 Ibid., §10.21 (DK22B107).

28 Laertius, "Parmenides," in *Lives of the Philosophers*, bk 9, ch. 22, 431.

29 Cited in Waterfield, "The Atomists," *First Philosophers*, 176 (from Sextus Empiricus, *Against the Professors*, bk 7, ch. 135, §1 to ch. 139, §4).

The Greeks associated understanding with sight. The Greek verb εἴδω (*eido*), "to see, perceive, behold," was used in the present perfect form οἶδα (*oida*) to indicate the present tense of the verb "to know." Literally, "I have seen" came to mean "I know." Again, the verb νοέω (*noeo*), which originally meant "to perceive by the eyes, observe, notice," also came to mean, in an unqualified sense, "to think, to suppose," "to think out," "to conceive of." The Greek noun νοῦς (*nous*) was used to refer to both "mind" and "perception," and terms associated with thought and intelligent understanding such as νοῦς (*nous*) and νόησις (*noesis*) carried the implication, as W.K.C. Guthrie explains, of "seeing and recognizing through an act of sensation, the realities of a situation."[30]

The analogy between "seeing" and "thinking" seems natural. Thought illuminates. It discerns, examines, probes, identifies, and resolves. Like an extra sense, it adds a new perspective on reality. It is as if human beings had two sets of eyes, physical eyes to see outside appearances and mental eyes to see what is the case.

Logic has to do with arguments, sequences that move from claim to claim in a step-by-step manner until they impel us to accept a final conclusion. But the ancients did not equate philosophy exclusively with logic. They viewed philosophy as a search for wisdom that oftentimes reveals itself in a matter of inspiration, of direct insight, of suddenly *seeing* the truth behind appearances. On the ancient mindset, philosophers were unusually shrewd and insightful people. They revealed their philosophical intelligence not merely (or even chiefly) in argument, but in a spirit of quick repartee and incisive, brief, unpredictable, and illuminating elocution.

Written philosophy, in the widest sense, began with the urge to record and collect examples of these brilliant flashes of inspiration. This resulted in collections of *logoi*, insightful, witty, or simply colourful expressions or remarks made in specific situations by an acknowledged sage. Hence the notoriously unreliable stories (or *chreia*) of an author such as Diogenes Laertius in *The Lives of the Eminent Philosophers*. Although Diogenes relates the principles of this or that philosophy baldly, without any great subtlety, his love for the picturesque, the wonderful, and the memorable leads him, for the most part, to emphasize the piquant sayings (and actions) of a heterogenous collection of famous names. The worth of his text does not lie in its factual accuracy but in its record of the probing, questioning spirit that first animated philosophy. The goal here was largely edification. Philosophy was mostly about how to live a good life; it was often closer to moral inspiration than to logic.

30 Guthrie, *History of Greek Philosophy*, vol. 6, 193.

We find the same impulse to collect, remember, and disseminate such verbal displays of wit or wisdom in other diverse sources such as Heraclitus' aphorisms, Parmenides' poem, the so-called fables (really the *logoi*) of Aesop, and in Aristotle's own records of numerous passages from the Presocratics. When Socrates and Plato turn to the question-and-answer method of dialectic, it may seem that they are self-consciously turning their backs on this earlier tradition of philosophy, systematizing the discipline and leaving behind inspiration for discursive reason and logic. But this is misleading. Socrates' originality is that he proposes a method for achieving (or at least encouraging) immediate insight. Dialectic does not displace the experience of being inspired; it is a prelude to it. It works as a kind of propaedeutic that stimulates the mind; it primes students so that they can experience the tell-tale flash of sudden understanding.

In the *Theaetetus*, Socrates describes himself as a philosophical midwife who assists in the delivery of propositions and concepts. He and the young Theaetetus converse as doctor and patient:

> *Theaet.* I can assure you, Socrates, that ... I cannot shake off a feeling of anxiety.
> *Soc.* These are the pangs of labor, my dear Theaetetus; you have something within you which you are bringing to birth.
> *Theaet.* I do not know, Socrates; I only say what I feel.
> *Soc.* And have you never heard, simpleton, that I am the son of a midwife, brave and burly, whose name was Phaenarete?
> *Theaet.* Yes, I have.
> *Soc.* And that I myself practise midwifery? [...] And I dare say too ... that the mid-wives know better than others who is pregnant and who is not?
> *Theaet.* Very true.
> *Soc.* And by the use of potions and incantations they are able to arouse the pangs and to soothe them at will; they can make those bear who have a difficulty in bearing, and if they think fit they can smother the embryo in the womb.[31]

Birthing is a metaphor for immediate inspiration. Birthing is creative – it brings something new into the world in a sudden, momentous instance. We *induce* labour. Just so, Socratic philosophy is intended to incite and trigger the mental travail and then harvest and cull the new ideas an interlocutor immediately discerns.

31 Plato, *Theaetetus* (Jowett), 148e–149d.

Some commentators overlook this inspirational side of Plato's philosophy, because they want to clearly distinguish Platonic dialectic from the art of poetry and theatre. Socrates argues that poets and performers (*rhapsodes*) do their work and achieve their effects by being inspired rather than through reasoning. As Socrates tells Ion,

> the epic poets, all the good ones, have their excellence, not from art but are inspired, possessed, and thus utter all these admirable poems. So it is also with the good lyric poets ... [they] are not in their senses when they make these lovely lyric poems. No, when once they launch into harmony and rhythm, they are seized with Bacchic transport and are possessed ... The deity has bereft them of their senses and uses them as ministers ... it is not they who utter these precious revelations while their mind is not within them, but [rather] the god himself who speaks, and through them becomes articulate to us."[32]

Plato deftly manages to praise poetry without really praising poets. He does not claim that poets and performers are engaged in art and therefore rely on inspiration; he makes the more unusual claim that poets and performers must rely on it *because they write without art.* An art – a *techne* – is a skill, a technique, a knowing how to do or make something. Plato argues that poetry does not rely on skill but on some kind of direct communication with the divine. The difference between philosophy and poetry is that philosophy, unlike poetry, *is* an art. Socrates is *skilled* in the art of dialectic; he has mastered a "technique," the method of intellectual midwifery. He knows the "potions and incantations," how to induce and retard labour, and even how to smother "the embryo in the womb." He shares in that private store of knowledge restricted to philosophical midwives.

Plato, in the *Ion*, argues that poetry is a divine gift or θείᾳ μοίρᾳ (*theia moira*) rather than an art. Philosophy, by contrast, is a maieutic art that ideally produces a direct illumination, a stroke of insight, in the mind. In *Letter VII*, Plato describes five stages of knowledge: knowing names, knowing descriptions, knowing images, knowing about the object, and finally grasping the idea itself. The first four levels of knowing cannot, by themselves, bring us to knowledge of ideas in themselves. Plato explains, "After ... detailed comparisons of names and definitions and visual and other sense perceptions, after scrutinizing them in benevolent disputation by the use of question and answer without jealousy, at last in a flash, understanding of

32 Plato, *Ion* (Cooper), 533e–534d (in Plato, *Complete Works*).

each blazes up, and the mind … is flooded with light."[33] After benevolent disputation – i.e., after dialogue – inspiration blazes up. Philosophy should *induce* a burst of understanding; dialectic is preamble, but it is inspiration that is the prize. Only "after a long period of attendance on instruction … like a blaze kindled by a leaping spark, [knowledge] is generated in the soul and at once becomes self-sustaining"[34]

Understood in this Platonic sense, the noun *noesis,* which denotes the activity of pure thought or intelligent understanding, comes to represent a form of immediate illumination providing direct access to the forms.[35] As we see in the analogy of the divided line, *noesis* transcends language. In this final stage of learning, "the soul passes out of hypotheses, and goes up to a principle which is above hypotheses, making no use of images … but proceeding only in and through the ideas themselves."[36] Plato situates, then, the highest form of knowledge in some sort of wordless, immediate illumination. He places dialectic or διάλεκτος (*dialektos*) at the service of inspiration, not inspiration at the service of dialectic.

On Plato's account, we move from individual experience through discursive reasoning, to universal principles through immediate illumination, to a direct awareness of universal ideas. If, however, *noesis* is the experience of being illuminated, it is also an instance of inductive reasoning. It counts as such, for it requires a movement from particular to universal. Beginning with ideas of particular things, we ultimately arrive at a knowledge of the most universal ideas of all. Consider what happens in geometry. The ultimate aim of geometry is not, for Plato, knowledge about this or that particular square. It is not even knowledge of the general principles of squareness. The ultimate goal is to "see" squareness itself. Socrates sets it out as follows: "Although [geometers] use visible figures and make claims about them, their thought isn't directed to them but to those other things that they are like. They make their claims for the sake of the square itself … [which] one cannot see except by means of thought."[37] This, then, is the ultimate goal of geometry, to contemplate the idea of the square-in-itself that every square participates in. *Noesis* brings us, then, into intellectual contact with the universal essence all individual squares share. It waits at the end of a learning process beginning in the world, in knowledge of individual physical objects. It is, in this sense, an instance of inductive reasoning.

33 Plato *Letter VII* (Post) 343e–344b.
34 Ibid., 341c–d.
35 See Peters, *Greek Philosophical Terms,* s.v. "Noesis."
36 Plato, *Republic,* bk 6, 510b.
37 Plato, *Republic* (Grube, Reeve), 510d–e (in Plato, *Complete Works*).

Plato's account depends, of course, on his famous doctrine of reasoning through recollection or ἀνάμνησις (*anamnesis*). It is not as if we invent the idea of squareness. Our experience of individual squares brings to mind an awareness of what we already know. The immortal soul *remembers* the idea of squareness, already possessed by the soul in a previous existence. As Socrates recounts to Meno, "The soul ... having been born again many times, and having seen all things that exist ... has knowledge of them all; and ... there is no difficulty in her eliciting, or as men say 'learning' [anything] ... for all inquiry and learning is but recollection."[38] We come, then, to know the idea of the square itself through recollection. Teachers awaken lost memories that lie sleeping within. The student must be badgered into reminiscence. They must strain and labour until they give birth to an understanding that, paradoxically, they already possess.

J. Moravcsik describes the sudden nature of intellectual discovery in Plato's account of learning. "We can go over and over the same [problem] many times, and then, without anything new being added, we are suddenly able to see it in a new light ... The new understanding is not a result of new information. No new facts or beliefs are added; we simply keep going over the same structure repeatedly ... until 'it all makes sense'."[39] *Until it all makes sense.* Platonic dialectic supplies a jolt of intellectual electricity that turns a light on inside the mind. It does not rely on a mechanical summary of data. What we need is to discern, not to calculate.

ARISTOTLE AND PLATO COMPARED: BEYOND RECOLLECTION

One might imagine that the worldly Aristotle would have little use for a quasi-mystical activity like *noesis*. In fact, it plays a crucial role in his system. Aristotle does not jettison this Platonic concept of understanding so much as redefine its role. In effect, he turns Plato's account on its head. Whereas Plato claims that learning *ends* in inspiration, Aristotle countered that this is where knowledge *begins*. Platonic *noesis* becomes, in effect, the engine for Aristotelian *epagoge*.

Aristotle inverts both the chronological and logical order of the learning process. In Plato, discursive reason precedes *noesis*; in Aristotle, *noesis* precedes discursive reason. In Plato, reasoning discursively leads us up the divided line to the verge of a culminating, intuitive insight; in Aristotle, a logically prior intuitive insight "kicks off" the process of discursive

38 Plato, *Meno* (Jowett), 81c–d.

39 Moravcsik, *Plato and Platonism*, 18.

reasoning. In Plato, theory ends in *noesis*; in Aristotle, the activity of *noesis* gives the initial impetus to the absolutely first principles of theory.

In both Aristotle and Plato, *noesis*, the power of pure thought, answers the most basic question of all. It tells us what something is. To say that this is a square is to turn an individual object into a universal concept. Understanding "squareness" is, for Plato, an act of recollection; for Aristotle, an act of induction. In Plato, recollection – in Aristotle, induction – communicates the basic form or essence of a thing.[40]

Aristotle's conception of inductive reasoning (or *epagoge*) can be seen as a response to the Platonic doctrine of recollective reasoning.[41] Aristotle concedes that "in the process of induction we acquire knowledge of particular things just as though we could remember them."[42] But there is a fundamental difference. On Aristotle's account, we can intelligently analyze our experience and grasp the way things are. We do not remember something from another world; we see what must be the case through an intelligent appraisal of human experience. This happens non-discursively and in the absence of argument.[43] As F.E. Peters explains, "[Aristotelian] *epagoge* is not a discursive process ... [but] an intuitive grasp of the mind, which Aristotle terms *nous* and which is as trustworthy as demonstration itself."[44] Modern philosophers think of induction as a kind of argument, but Aristotelian inductive reasoning does not begin in logic. We derive the very first concepts and principles through immediate experience. The inductive syllogism is an odd sort of discursive reasoning that replicates, but does not replace, the original inductive leap of *noesis*. In Aristotle's epistemology,

40 "Induction [is] the way in which general concepts are conveyed by sense perception" (*Posterior Analytics* [Tredennick], bk 2, ch. 19, 100b2–5, Aristotle, *Aristotle in 23 Volumes*).

41 Aristotle suggests that the passive *nous* and thus the capacity for individual memory is destroyed at death. Because he does not subscribe to the Platonic notion of recollection, he is forced to elaborate a new explanation of the mechanism of induction.

42 *Prior Analytics* (Tredennick), pt 2, ch. 21, 67a21–27 (Aristotle, *Aristotle in 23 Volumes*).

43 Maritain captures this aspect of the Aristotelian schema where he writes that this form of *epagoge* "is neither an inference properly so-called, nor an argument, nor a proof; it merely leads the mind to a connection of terms whose intelligible necessity it perceives immediately, *without reasoning*." But this mental illumination does involve "reason"; it is only that it does not involve *discursive* reasoning (Maritain, *Introduction Logic*, 273–4).

44 Peters, *Greek Philosophical Terms*, s.v. "Epagoge" (definition 3).

this first, intuitive movement of induction yields a type of knowledge even *more certain* than science.[45]

As we have seen, Aristotelian syllogism operates by means of a middle term. In induction (rigorously understood) we do not reason through a middle term to a conclusion. We discover through sheer insight. Syllogism is, then, "middled" knowledge; induction is "unmiddled" knowledge. Syllogism operates by logical inference; pure inductive reasoning operates by *noesis*, through some kind of immediate discovery. Even "the syllogism that springs out of induction" is not quite "middled knowledge." We use the *subject* term to connect the middle to the predicate term in the inductive syllogism.[46] We do not reason, in other words, through the middle term but *to* it.

Aristotle believed that we cannot prove (i.e., logically demonstrate) the very first starting points of reason. Knowledge begins, not with proof but with an intuition "more infallible"[47] and "more accurate"[48] than argument. Aristotle does not deem it a weakness that knowledge must begin somewhere. To ask for a defence of starting points is epistemological overkill. If starting points could be proved by some other form of reasoning, they would not be starting points.

As Ralph Eaton explains, "intuitive induction is not proof."[49] We cannot prove or demonstrate everything. Aristotle insists, "All problems of this kind amount to the same thing. [Radical sceptics] demand a reason for everything ... They require a reason for things which have no reason, since the starting point of demonstration is not a matter of demonstration."[50] Attempts to furnish a complete proof of belief lead to problems of infinite regress. Aristotle observes, "it is impossible that there should be a demonstration of absolutely everything: [for] there would be an infinite regress, so that there would still be no demonstration." We simply have to accept that knowledge begins in discernment, not argument. "Not to know of what things one may demand a demonstration, and of what things one may not" is, for Aristotle, to lack education.[51]

45 See *Posterior Analytics*, bk 2, ch. 19.

46 *Prior Analytics*, bk 2, ch. 23, 68b31–35.

47 *Posterior Analytics* (Tredennick), bk 2, ch. 19, 100b11–12 (Aristotle, *Aristotle in 23 Volumes*).

48 Ibid., bk 2, ch. 19, 100b6–8.

49 Eaton, *General Logic*, 500.

50 *Metaphysics* (Tredennick), bk 4, ch. 6, 1011a3–15 (Aristotle, *Aristotle in 23 Volumes*).

51 *Metaphysics* (Ross), bk 4, ch. 4, 1006a5–10 (in Aristotle, *Complete Works*).

Figure 7.1
Aristotelian "arch of learning"

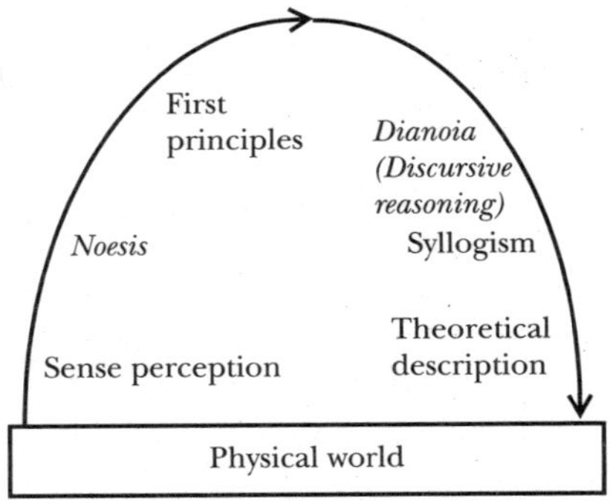

Where Plato depicts the various stages of learning as a vertical line, pointing skyward, we could depict the Aristotelian doctrine as a sort of "divided line" bent so the upper end touches the earth. We are left with an arch of learning, as in figure 7.1.[52] Plato's divided line points upward, leaving the material world of sense perception behind, but Aristotle's "arch of learning" turns around and returns to earth. Knowledge is no longer an escape from but a commentary on the world.[53]

The traditional account correctly views Aristotle as a scientist. Whereas Plato, who has little regard for sense perception, focuses on dialectic as the engine of understanding, Aristotle substitutes sense perception for language. In Plato, philosophical conversation – in Aristotle, sense perception – triggers *noesis*. Plato presents Socrates as the personification of philosophy, the midwife who induces labour by his persistent questioning. In Aristotle, nature herself is the midwife stimulating the mind to a new understanding. Thought does not provoke itself. Observation, rather, induces understanding. We discover the nature of things, not by talking about them, but by physically examining them. This is to adopt the methodology of empirical science.[54]

52 For a somewhat similar diagram, which I saw after completing mine, see Kelley L. Ross, "The Arch of Aristotelian Logic: The Doctrine of the *Prior* and *Posterior* Analytic."

53 Hence Raphael's depiction of an aged Plato gesturing vertically next to a youthful Aristotle gesturing horizontally.

54 The focus on experiments involving our deliberately manipulating nature, forcing her to yield her secrets, comes later.

Aristotle is best understood as a *revised* Plato. As Taylor explains, "while professing to build up the structure of knowledge on a foundation of perceived facts, [Aristotle] really comes back to a position very much like Plato's and admits that the knowledge of the highest principles of reason is a matter of direct intuition. We cannot prove the reality of these principles ... Through the repetition of similar experiences, [we come to recognize] a principle which was there all the time."[55] Where do our ideas come from? Plato claims that the immortal soul remembers them from a previous existence. What is Aristotle's explanation? We have to posit the existence of some mental capacity that transforms sense perception into thought. This is the role of *nous* or mind. Aristotelian science may not aim skyward in the Platonic sense, but it is divine reason that makes progress in knowledge possible.

We may express this otherwise. Any system has to begin with first principles: with concepts, definitions, universal propositions. Where do these come from? In Plato, we revisit memories. On Aristotle's account, the mind creates entirely new knowledge. Deprived of Plato's otherworldly memories, the mind "invents" an understanding that explains phenomena. But this "invention" provides a snapshot of reality. It does not separate us from what is really out there; it grasps, in a non-arbitrary way, what follows from natural necessity. We discuss these issues further in the next chapter.

ARISTOTELIAN INDUCTION AND TRUTH

In a famous but puzzling passage, Aristotle writes that knowledge "come[s] about from perception – as in a battle when a rout occurs, if one man takes a stand [then] another does and then another, until a position of strength is reached."[56] It is not surprising that the battle metaphor would suggest itself to Aristotle, for the term he coins for induction, *epagoge*, is derived from the verb ἐπάγω (*epago*), which means (in part) "to lead an army on as against an enemy."[57] Commentators generally interpret the battle metaphor metaphysically. On this account, inductive reasoning begins with the species. The mind moves from one individual species to another and another, until it comes to grasp a common genus tying all these species together. This is often depicted as a movement from scientific to metaphysical categories. As Guthrie explains, the student "continues, from the definable species dog, elephant, man to the genus animal, upwards until

55 Taylor, *Greek Philosophy*, 116.

56 *Posterior Analytics* (Barnes), bk 2, ch. 19, 100a10–15 (in Aristotle, *Complete Works*).

57 *Liddell and Scott's Greek-English Lexicon*, s.v. ἐπάγω, *epago*.

he reaches the *summa genera* common to all sciences, the ultimate categories of substance, quality and the rest."[58]

But this can hardly stand as a complete account of induction, for Aristotle conceives of it as the process by which theory gets off the ground. It does not begin with concepts but with sensory stimuli. We perceive this individual dog, cat, or horse and *induce* the universal species "dog," "cat," or "horse." To conceive of induction (or of inductive syllogism) as a movement from universal concept to universal concept is to overlook what induction, in the most fundamental sense, is about. How, then, are we to understand the battle metaphor?

Overpowered by error and misunderstanding, the mind is like an army in retreat. Once, however, the mind understands a single case, it is immediately able to apply the same understanding to another case and another and another, until it hits on the universal principle that explains every case. By this point, the mind is now in a position of strength and can stand firm against the onslaught of its traditional enemy, ignorance.

The battle analogy captures the precipitous nature of induction. The thinker is brought to the verge of an understanding by way of a consecutive examination of cases, but it begins with a single case. One soldier holds a position, the soldier's neighbour does likewise, as does that one's neighbour, and so on, until the whole army resists. It is through a multiplication of individual cases that the understanding suddenly crystallizes in the soul. As Aristotle explains, each individual case "comes to a halt" or "takes a stand" in the soul until, after successive halts or stands, the whole universal comes to reside in the soul.[59] An understanding of this or that case expands, perhaps precipitously, into an understanding of all relevant cases.

As we have seen, Aristotle claims that *noesis*, the faculty of mental illumination that produces the first inductive insight, is more certain than argument. Aristotle writes, "The thinking of the definition in the sense of what it is for something to be is never in error."[60] Aristotle believes that *scientific*

58 Guthrie, *History of Greek Philosophy*, vol. 6, 183 (the citation is from *Metaphysics*, bk 4, ch. 3, 1005b10). But someone might argue that thought goes in the opposite direction, not from specific to general but from general to specific. We first notice that this is a thing (a substance), then that it moves and is living, that it is covered in fur and is a mammal, that it can walk upright and is a bear. Hence the method of definition by division I discussed in chapter 4.

59 *Posterior Analytics* (Tredennick), bk 2, ch. 19, 100a16; *Posterior Analytics* (Barnes), bk 2, ch. 19, 100a16; cf. Plato, *Phaedo*, 96b. See also *Posterior Analytics* (Tredennick) 100a5–10, note a.

60 *On the Soul* (Smith), bk 3, ch. 6, 26–28 (in Aristotle, *Complete Works*).

definitions (not nominal definitions), if properly arrived at, are "always true."[61] We can make definitions by throwing words around the way we might make a tossed salad. That is not what Aristotle has in mind. He believes that induction makes true claims about the world. If we can distinguish between species, this is because inductive insight provides a true picture of reality. Truth is conformity to what exists. If we do not assume the truth of the most fundamental distinctions, knowledge will unravel. More on this later.

THOMAS' DOCTRINE OF *INTELLECTUS*: STILLNESS AND MOTION

Aristotle's theory of induction was not universally acclaimed in ancient thought. In later antiquity, Neoplatonists such as Plotinus and his diverse followers developed a rival notion of *noesis* that harkens back to Plato. This Neoplatonic synthesis provides a historical bridge, in some sort, between the ancient and mediaeval accounts of induction. Plotinus describes two ways of thinking about the world. *Noesis* (or intuition) takes in the whole truth instantaneously, altogether. As Kevin Corrigan explains, it "is not the sort [of thing] that has to work things out ... bit by bit. [It] is more like a complete grasp of the whole at one glance."[62] *Dianoia* (or discursive reasoning) operates by argument. It moves from premise, to premise, to a conclusion. Later thinkers such as Thomas come to see this division between instantaneous understanding and logic as equivalent to that between inductive and deductive reasoning.

Although a late medieval thinker like Thomas Aquinas is thoroughly Aristotelian, he is deeply influenced by Neoplatonic accounts of *noesis*. Following after Boethius, Thomas distinguishes between *intellectus* (or *intelligentia*) and *ratio*.[63] *Intellectus* is usually designated by the English term "understanding" (less frequently by "intellection"); *ratio*, by the English term "reasoning."[64] Thomas fully intends that these terms be taken in a Neoplatonic

61 See *Posterior Analytics* (Tredennick), bk 2, ch. 19, 100b6–8.

62 Corrigan, *Reading Plotinus*, §1.5, 34.

63 Boethius, *Consolation of Philosophy*, verse 4. In fact, Boethius distinguishes sense perception, imagination, reason, and intelligence (*intelligentia*), but the details of his account will not concern us here.

64 In the *Posterior Analytics*, Barnes translates *noesis* as "comprehension" and *apodeixis* as "understanding," but this reverses the traditional usage, which identifies "understanding" with *noesis*. See *Posterior Analytics* (Barnes), bk 2, ch. 19, 100b6 ff.

sense. *Intellectus* is what Plotinus refers to by the Greek *noesis* – an instantaneous mental operation that provides a holistic grasp of what is the case. *Ratio* is what Plotinus refers to as *dianoia.* We engage in *ratio* when we reason discursively, when we advance, one by one, from premise to premise to conclusion.[65]

If modern philosophers have generally focused on logic and deduction as the most authoritative source of knowledge, Thomas, following after Plotinus, considers *intellectus* or "understanding" to be a higher form of knowing. This doctrine of the superiority of *intellectus* over *ratio* informs his religious metaphysics. Thomas believes that the angels, who are higher intellectual beings, naturally know by *intellectus*; human beings know naturally, but not exclusively, through *ratio.* Angels know everything effortlessly, through a species of immediate, instantaneous illumination. Human beings, by contrast, have to reason their way laboriously to true conclusions. Most of their knowledge comes through *ratio.* Unlike angels, we have to figure out what is true; we have to use arguments, working slowly and sequentially through true premises to true conclusions. Except that human beings know first principles by means of *intellectus.*

Thomas compares the difference between *intellectus* and *ratio* with that of stillness and movement. Thomas claims that angels, who are heavenly beings like the planets and stars, do not need to move intellectually to achieve perfection.[66] Angels know in an instant: "Simply without intellectual process, [they] grasp the truth of things."[67] They do not have to "think things out." They grasp "conclusions" instantaneously. They do not have to reason, bit by bit, step by step, in stages.[68] Angelic knowledge is knowledge in the absence of movement, knowledge accompanied by rest or stillness. Thomas believes that the souls of angels are filled with such an abundance of intellectual light that they immediately intuit, not just first principles, but all the consequences that follow from first principles: "In the truths

65 See, for example, Thomas Aquinas, *Summa theologiae*, pt 1, Q. 79.

66 In fact, Thomas knew that planets and stars move. The point is they do not need to move to actualize their own natures to perfection, because they are heavenly and therefore already perfect.

67 Thomas Aquinas, *Summa theologiae* (Suttor), pt 1, Q. 79, art. 8. Note that knowledge is the natural act of an immaterial being.

68 Thomas compares *intellectus* to looking in a mirror. "If in a thing perceived something else is perceived at the same time, as an object and its image are seen simultaneously in a mirror, this is not discursive knowledge. And it is thus that angels know things in the world" (Thomas Aquinas, *Summa theologiae* [Foster], pt 1, Q. 58, art. 3, "Does An Angel Know by Discursive Thinking?").

which their nature enables them to know [angels] apprehend immediately all that such truths can possibly imply for them."[69]

On Thomas' account, what we call reasoning is, in fact, an inferior form of knowing. We do not immediately grasp the implications of the facts that we know. We are not intelligent enough for that! Because we lack intelligence, we must reason through a middle term. Discovering the truth requires effort. We need an aid, a crutch. This is what logic provides. Because "of the dimness of the intellectual light in [our] souls," we must reason things out, moving step by step from premise, to premise, to conclusion.[70] As Thomas explains, *ratio* "goes to its perfection ... by a kind of movement ... advancing from one thing known to another."[71] We see part of the truth and use it to logically calculate another part of it. Although Thomas could be said to devote his whole theological and philosophical career to logical argument, he himself recognized that this form of insight is *inferior.*

Where Thomas distinguishes between angelic *intellectus* and human reasoning, he also recognizes that human beings are not completely fallen. We are capable of a more limited type of *intellectus.* Human beings have the angel-like ability to intuit some of the first principles of thought as well as the essences of certain things.[72] This distinctly human capacity for *intellectus* provides an instantaneous grasp of the starting points of reason. Thomas observes, "The indemonstrable first principles of thought belong to the habit called understanding."[73] Once human beings have grasped first principles through this immediate understanding, they can, then, use *ratio* to deduce further truths about themselves and the world.

Thomas does not believe that the angelic and human understandings are, in every respect, identical. Angels have no physical bodies and no sense organs. Their knowledge does not originate in physical appearances. They know by a kind of pure intellectual activity of grasping the quiddity or essence of things.[74] Human knowledge, on the contrary, originates in our perceiving sensory objects. Hence, the familiar Thomist dictum, *nihil in intellectu quod prius non fuerit in sensu.* ("there is nothing in the mind that was not first in the senses") Thomas, following Aristotle, anchors human

69 Ibid.

70 Ibid., pt 1, Q. 58, art. 4.

71 Ibid., pt 1, Q. 58, art. 3.

72 Thomas Aquinas, *Summa theologiae* (Suttor), pt 1, Q. 79, art. 8.

73 Ibid., pt 1, Q. 79, art. 9.

74 Thomas comments that they know by some form of connatural knowledge. See *Summa theologiae,* pt 1, Q. 55, art. 2.

knowledge in a mental capacity for instantaneous understanding as triggered by observation. In this precise sense, Aquinas carries on the Aristotelian understanding of inductive reasoning. We discover first principles by illumination, not by reasoning. Sense perception triggers a moment of immediate cognition that reveals the truth in a simple act of intellectual apprehension, like Aristotelian *epagoge*.

Thomas distinguishes between three types of inductive inference: abstraction, formulating propositions, and *argumentum ad experimentum* or argument from experience. Only abstraction involves *intellectus* in any pure form. In abstraction, the soul leaves out the individual features of an object and extracts the universal nature that is the same for all similar individuals. Abstraction tells us "what a thing is."[75] It "brings one to the essence of the thing."[76] It is a way of thinking "according to the reason of the species."[77] It operates through *intellectus*, through a kind of intellectual vision. We persist in our contemplation of specific objects until "the soul ... arrives at something invisible in them, which is universal."[78] In sense perception we "see" physical individuals; in abstraction we "see" invisible ideas.

75 See Thomas Aquinas, *Summa theologiae*, pt 2 of pt 2, Q. 8, art. 1, "Whether understanding is a gift of the Holy Ghost?" Again, Thomas writes that induction is the mysterious way sense perception "brings about the universal within the soul" (Thomas Aquinas, *Exposition of the "Posterior Analytics"* [Conway], bk 2, lecture 20, art. 14).

76 Thomas Aquinas, *Commentary on the Sentences* (Gilby), bk 3, distinction 35, Q. 2, art. 2, *ad* 1. Thomas derives the word *intellectus* from *intelligere* (to understand), which is, as he puts it, "the same as '*intus legere*' [to read inwardly]" (*Summa theologiae*, pt 2 of pt 2, Q. 8, art. 1). *Intellectus* is, then, a kind of mental vision which allows us to see "the inside of things." To see the inside of something is to understand its nature.

77 "The universal is said to come to rest in the soul, inasmuch as it is considered beyond the singulars, in which there is motion. He calls it, one outside of many, not according to being, but according to the consideration of the intellect, which considers nature, e.g. that of man without considering Socrates or Plato. Which, even though according to the consideration of the intellect it is the one outside the many, nevertheless according to being, it is in all the singulars, one and the same, not in number, as though there were the same humanity as to number of all men, but according to the reason of species" (Thomas Aquinas, *Exposition of the "Posterior Analytics"* [Conway], bk 2, lecture 20, art. 11).

78 This is from a commentary on Aristotle. The extended passage is as follows: "In those things, namely in man and horse, the soul persists in its consideration until it arrives at something invisible in them, which is the universal ... Since therefore we

Abstraction is a form of inductive inference insomuch as it moves from the particular to the universal. In perceiving sensory objects, we encounter the particular and the contingent; in abstracting, we come to know the universal and the necessary. The individual physical objects we perceive change through time. Although individual human beings like Socrates, Plato, and Aristotle grow and move and perish, the idea "human being" never changes. So abstracting is a window on eternal, unchanging truths. It communicates, through a simple movement of understanding the permanent natures or essences of things.

The second kind of induction Thomas refers to yields universal propositions. This form of induction has a discursive aspect. Remember that for Thomas *intellectus* is understanding without movement, without plurality, without internal or temporal parts. *Intellectus* is, at its origins, without method, without process, without any kind of internal ordering, or grammar, or logic. It is simply inspiration. We know, so to speak, in one fell swoop. *Ratio*, however, has to do with combining individual parts into a larger whole. The formulation of universal propositions or compound definitions is, then, for Thomas, a derivative or impure form of *intellectus*. It requires *intellectus*, an insight into the way things are, but once we express this insight in words, we need *ratio* so as to properly organize these parts into a truthful whole.

Thomas tells us that angels do not think in propositions but intuit essences by a simple, self-contained movement of the mind. As Boethius had earlier expressed the idea, they "behold the simple form itself."[79] If, however, we hit on definitions in a simple moment of understanding, we then have to express these definitions in words. Consider Boethius' definition of "man" as "a biped rational animal."[80] This definition joins together different parts of human nature – "biped," "rational," "animal" – in a single expression. It is an expression of unity. But it is also an expression of plurality, as it explains human nature in terms of a compound truth. As

attain knowledge of universals from singulars, he concludes that it is plain that it is necessary for the first universal principles to be known through induction. For thus, namely, by the way of induction, sense brings about the universal within the soul" (ibid., bk 2, lecture 20, art. 14). Thomas also describes the movement from lower- to higher-level concepts as a kind of induction. He writes, "we consider this animal and that, e.g. man and horse, until we arrive at some common animal, which is the genus, and in this we do the same until we arrive at some superior genus" (ibid.).

79 Thomas Aquinas, *Summa theologiae* (Foster), pt 1, Q. 58, art. 4; see also Boethius, *Consolation of Philosophy* (Watts), verse 4, 159.

80 Ibid.

Plotinus might observe, the claim "humanity is a biped, rational animal" cuts the world up into four parts: the part made up of "humanity," the part made up of "being," and the part made up of "bipedness," and the part made up of "rational." It then joins these parts together. The resultant unity expresses a seamless insight into the nature of things by means of grammar, by a proper ordering of internal parts. So we have here a kind of *intellectus* that ends up requiring some exercise of *ratio*.

The third form of inductive reasoning in Thomas is *argumentum ad experimentum* or argument from experience. In Thomas, as in Aristotle, inductive arguments provide a logical analogue to the illuminative or inspirational process of true induction. Thomas, like Aristotle, distinguishes contingent resemblances and the law-like universals arising from inductive reasoning proper. Suppose a doctor discovers that a certain herb cures a particular fever. Thomas comments, "As long as the doctor considered that this herb cured Socrates when in a fever, and Plato and many other singular men, it is [mere] experience." This does not count as true induction. Only the affirmation that "this species of herb cured a feverish man absolutely" counts as true induction.[81] Induction, strictly construed, reveals a necessary, universal rule or regularity in nature.

We might formally express the syllogism associated with this line of reasoning as follows. Premise$_1$: Socrates, Plato, and these other individuals were feverish men. Premise$_2$: Socrates, Plato, and these other individuals were cured by this herb. Conclusion: So, we can take it as a "rule of medicine" that this herb cures feverish men. The inductive syllogism leads us to a law of medicine that this specific herb should be administered in case of fever. We have already discussed the logical form of this argument at length.

To summarize, we find three kinds of induction in Thomas. At the first level, we abstract concepts; at the second, we combine (and separate) concepts to elaborate propositions; at the third, we add propositions together to arrive at a universal conclusion. Take the products of abstraction, in its widest sense, to mean the intuition of essences, necessary properties, and even merely usual or common properties; take those of proposition formulation to include not only descriptive general statements but also those expressing logical axioms such as the law of non-contradiction or that of identity; take syllogistic to include all arguments moving from premises regarding individuals to general conclusions – and we have a Thomistic account of inductive reasoning in its widest sense.

81 Thomas Aquinas, *Exposition of the "Posterior Analytics"* (Conway), bk 2, lecture 20, art. 11.

Many present-day authors view "reasoning" and "intuition" (the closest thing to Thomistic *intellectus* modern authors are familiar with) as opposing categories. Reason is what people do when they "give persuasive reasons for what they believe." Intuitive understanding, which happens without argument, is at best uncanny, even irrational. But Thomas sees things quite differently. *Intellectus* is not an odd or irregular movement of the mind, a mere hunch, a feeling, or a guess. It is a *higher* form of reason. It is an expression of the same intelligence expressing itself in argument. In the first case, truth is immediately discovered; in the second, it is arrived at through a middle term. The process differs. However, in both cases we end up with knowledge.

Thomas believes that reasoning (*ratio*) and understanding (*intellectus*) are expressions of the same cognitive power. Human intelligence moves by reasoning and rests in understanding. But it is always the same power of intelligence. "The relation of reasoning to understanding is that of motion to rest, or of acquiring to having." Just as "it is by the same natural thrust that a thing goes where it goes and stays when it gets there," so "we understand and reason with one same power." [82] "Higher and lower reason," *intellectus* and *ratio*, "are one and the same [mental] faculty."[83]

Although the modern world has little use for non-discursive understanding, it played a prominent role in earlier philosophy. Plato proposes *noesis* as the culmination of rationality. Aristotle claims that *noesis*, understood as the faculty of illumination that yields first principles, is more certain than science. Plotinus claims that *noesis* yields supreme understanding. And Thomas, in line with this earlier tradition, extends the Aristotelian position, reconciling it, in some sort, with the earlier Platonist conception of *noesis* as the most important and authoritative source of knowledge. Indeed, not only claiming, like Aristotle, that *intellectus* supplies the starting points of reasoning, Thomas goes further and claims that we know the *conclusion* of an argument through *intellectus*. In effect, we start with *intellectus* and we end with it. He writes, "The discourse of reason always begins from an *understanding* and ends at an *understanding* … and the discourse of reason is perfected when we come to *understand* what hitherto we ignored."[84]

Taken with the new rationalism, modern Thomists themselves overlook his original meaning. It is *intellectus* that provides for a capacity for inference allowing us to see what follows from what. Logic is only an issue of

82 Thomas Aquinas, *Summa theologiae* (Suttor), pt 1, q. 79, art. 8.

83 Ibid., pt 1, Q. 79, art. 9.

84 Thomas Aquinas, *Summa Theologica* (English Dominican Province), pt 2 of pt 2, Q. 8, art. 1, *ad* 2, "Whether Understanding Is a Gift of the Holy Ghost" (my italics).

strategy. It leads us, step by step, to a new mental discovery. But it could not operate without the basic capacity for simple understanding. Thomas abounds in the spirit of Plato's account of dialectic. When we order the premises of an argument in a certain way, we come to "see" that the conclusion must be true. While reasoning provides a mechanical structure for knowledge, understanding, so to speak, brings us to the verge of a realization and pushes us over the edge. It is like cocking a rifle. *Ratio* is well-oiled mechanism, but *intellectus* pulls the trigger.

Thomas does not claim that we can *prove* the truth of the starting points of reason.[85] He repeats Aristotle's disclaimer that any attempt to produce absolute proof "would proceed in demonstrations to infinity."[86] The human quest for epistemological comfort must come to rest in understanding. This is the secure foundation we are given. If the most basic principles of human reasoning are false, everything else collapses. So we must accept the most basic principles of human reasoning as true.

On Thomas' account, error is a discursive failing. Human beings can directly intuit the simplest truths. They do not err "as regards simple objects, not subject to composite definitions."[87] But once they begin to combine the simplest thoughts to devise definitions, propositions, or arguments, they may make mistakes. If we human beings reasoned rigorously from true starting points, we would always arrive at true conclusions.[88] But, of course, we make all sorts of mistakes. Thomas identifies three main types of error: (1) We are sometimes blind to the true nature of things.[89] (2) We sometimes join together incompatible concepts. And (3) we make mistakes when we try to apply concepts to real things in the world.

Thomas' account of *intellectus* and *ratio* brings together diverse threads from earlier philosophy. As we have already seen, the first philosophers associated the power of rational thought with inspiration as much as with argument. Plato distinguishes more specifically between pure thought (*noesis*) and discursive reason (*dianoia*). Aristotle adapts Plato's doctrines,

85 Angels cannot make mistakes except in relation to the ways of God's supernatural providence, for everything they know, they know through *intellectus*. Human judgement, when it relies exclusively on *intellectus*, is likewise infallible.

86 Thomas Aquinas, *Exposition of the "Posterior Analytics"* (Conway), bk 2, lecture, 20, art. 15.

87 See Thomas Aquinas, *Summa theologiae*, pt 1, Q. 85, art. 6, "Whether the Intellect Can Err."

88 This is the sense in which science is "always true" (Thomas Aquinas, *Exposition of the "Posterior Analytics"* [Conway], bk 2, lecture 20, art. 15).

89 *Metaphysics* (Ross), bk 9, ch. 10, 1052a2–3 (in Aristotle, *Complete Works*).

elaborating a more rigorous account of discursive reason (*dianoia*) as syllogistic and envisaging a new role for pure thought (*noesis*) as the mental faculty that produces the starting points of reason. Plotinus then returns to Plato, distinguishing understanding (*noesis*), as an awareness of unity, and discursive reason (*dianoia*) as an inferior form of thinking leading to a compound expression of truth. Finally, Thomas distinguishes "understanding" (*intellectus*), as an instantaneous form of insight, and "reason" (*ratio*) as logic. In the Thomistic account, understanding is the most basic form of intelligence. It grasps first principles and motivates the ordering process of reasoning.

Thomas' account of induction borrows from all these traditions. Thomas follows Plato in his explanation of the syllogism as a discursive movement of reason that precipitates an understanding; and Aristotle, in linking understanding to sense perception. And Thomas follows the Neoplatonic tradition in describing understanding as an utterly unified act; and reasoning, as one of organizing a plurality.

DESCARTES: *LUMINE NATURALI*

But turn now to the modern period. As we shall see, Enlightenment authors lose sight of the earlier historical understanding of induction and propose a mechanical replacement wholly inadequate to the task. These misunderstandings prevail to this day.

While Descartes makes a great display of breaking with tradition, he must, like earlier philosophers, posit a faculty of intuition to provide first principles. The term "intuition," derives from the Latin *intuitus*, which means to look at or inspect. In contemporary parlance, it has come to suggest a vague feeling of something. Descartes, in a way opposed to contemporary usage, points to "intuition" as the clearest and most distinct form of cognition. Using language reminiscent of earlier thinkers, he defines intuition as "the conception of a clear and attentive mind which is so easy and distinct that there can be no room for doubt about what we are understanding."[90] Like Thomas, Descartes believed that, when not distracted by sensory stimuli, the rational mind can somehow "see," without any obstruction or hesitation, the most basic truths.

If Thomas observes that we acquire first principles, "not through reasoning," but "by the natural light of the active intellect itself," the idea that we can somehow *see* what is true by the light of the mind is a common trope in

90 Descartes, *Philosophical Writings of Descartes* (Cottingham, Stoothoff, and Murdoch), vol. 1, 14. See *Oeuvres de Descartes* (Adams and Tannery), vol. 10, 368.

medieval philosophy. Augustine, for one, claims that "the intellectual mind is so formed … as to see [natural] things … by a sort of incorporeal light … as the eye of the flesh sees things … [by a] bodily light."[91] Boethius, in turn, refers to the "exalted eye of intelligence which … behold[s] the simple form … with the pure vision of the mind."[92] Descartes, in proposing his own account of intuitive understanding, returns to this basic conception of intelligence as light. He locates fundamental understanding in something he calls "the natural light of reason" or *lumine naturali.* This natural light operates through an introspective mechanism – it comes from *inside* the individual. Descartes has great confidence in this innate faculty for correct discernment. He writes, "whatever is shown me by the light of nature … cannot in any way be doubtful."[93] And again, "there can be no other faculty that [we] can trust as much as this light."[94] By this light of reason, "everyone can mentally intuit that he exists, that he is thinking, that a triangle is bounded by just three sides and a sphere by a single surface, and the like"[95]

Descartes writes, "We shall comply with [proper method] exactly if we reduce involved and obscure propositions step by step to those that are simpler, and then starting with the intuitive apprehension of all those that are absolutely simple, attempt to ascend to knowledge of all others by precisely similar steps."[96] The Cartesian method operates through analysis and synthesis. We can divide knowledge into simpler components until we arrive at the simplest truths and/or we can combine simpler truths into larger wholes. These two processes should ideally meet. Whether we proceed by analysis or synthesis, or by both together, we should be able to reduce complex propositions to the first principles of reason, and/or build up from these first principles of reason to the most complex propositions.

91 Augustine is here denying the Platonic doctrine of recollection. Augustine, *On the Holy Trinity* (Haddan), bk 12, ch. 15, para. 24, 48 (in Augustine, *St Augustine*).

92 Boethius, *Consolation of Philosophy* (Watts), verse 4, 158.

93 "[In contrast,] as far as my natural impulses are concerned, … I have often judged myself to have been driven by them to make a poorer choice when it was a question of choosing a good; and I fail to see why I should place any greater faith in them than in other matters" (Descartes, *Meditations* [Cress], Meditaton 3, 72, in *Discourse on Method and Meditations*).

94 Ibid.

95 Descartes, *Philosophical Writings of Descartes* (Cottingham, Stoothoff, and Murdoch), vol. 1, 14. See *Oeuvres de Descartes* (Adams and Tannery), vol. 10, 368.

96 René Descartes, *Rules for the Direction of the Mind,* rule 5, p. 14 (in *Philosophical Works of Descartes* [Haldane and Ross]).

Although Descartes' debt to the tradition is immediately obvious, his account of intuition differs in two important ways from earlier ones of induction. First, as we have seen, Descartes replaces the Aristotelian emphasis on sense perception with an introspective methodology. He is, in the familiar sense, a modern rationalist. What matters is the role and power of interior reason. We need, as a general rule, to disengage from the distractions of sense perception and focus inward on the "treasure house of the mind."[97] We do not derive the first principles from observation but from an inward awareness of self. The emphasis is squarely on self-discovery and on the incorrigibility of introspective awareness.

Leaving aside his opponents' critiques of "innate ideas," the inward Cartesian turn is problematic. Descartes believes that the unmistakable clarity of this interior vision he calls the light of reason guarantees its truthfulness. If the individual subject can see a truth so clearly, it must be true. This is just what earlier authors had argued, except they did not (for reasons they in fact elaborate) begin with any kind of comprehensive scepticism. Older philosophers began by asserting some kind of secular faith in human intelligence. Descartes began by *questioning* human intelligence. He started with the most radical scepticism possible. But the radical sceptic will not accept as an *indubitable* warrant for truth the mere fact that a *fallible* creature feels or thinks (however vehemently) that something is *clearly* true. If human reason is questionable, the natural light of reason is an unreliable guide to truth. Descartes' project deconstructs. It falls prey to a criticism that is only a natural extension of its own internal principles.

Introspection is, in any case, a metaphysically hazardous philosophical method, for it inevitably introduces a sharp division between the introspecting subject and the world. Aristotle and Thomas claim that observers arrive at a mental illumination by fixing their attention on the external world. In Descartes' system, on the contrary, we begin by ignoring the world and looking inside ourselves. But once we have lost the world, we cannot argue it back into existence, especially while taking the possibility of radical scepticism seriously.

A second way Descartes' approach differs from traditional accounts is that he begins epistemology with an *argument*: "I think, *therefore* I am." But how could the *cogito* be a truly primitive insight? It is, in the words of one commentator, "a complex between the elements of which there is an implication."[98] We have here a plurality of simpler elements ordered into a

97 Cited in Cottingham, *Descartes Dictionary*, s.v. "Innateness." (The expression is from *Meditations*, Meditation 5.)

98 Beck, *Metaphysics of Descartes*, 86.

Figure 7.2
Complex syllogism, "I think, therefore, I am"

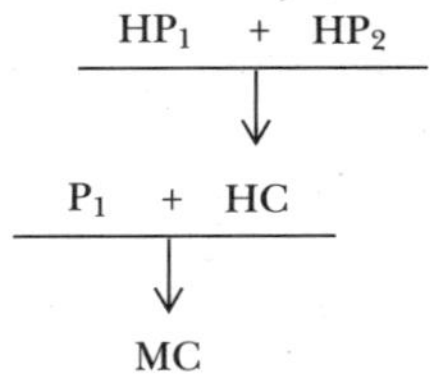

Note: premise$_1$ (P_1), "I think"; hidden premise$_1$ (HP_1), "To think is to act"; hidden premise$_2$ (HP_2), "Anything that acts exists"; hidden conclusion (HC), "Anything that thinks exists"; main conclusion (MC), "I exist"

larger whole. Before we can get the entire sequence off the ground, we need to induce a series of general concepts: "thinking," "existing," and "individual self." Indeed, we need to properly arrange these concepts into two separate propositions, and we need to make the necessary inference from the first proposition, "I think," to the second, "I am." We cannot even articulate this "first principle" without proposing prior conditions that produce concepts, propositions, and inferences.

Where Descartes insists that the *cogito* is not an argument, he may mean that we grasp the inference all at once; the reasoner instantaneously recognizes its truth. But the sequence, as Descartes presents it, can be put into standard form. Premise$_1$: I think. Conclusion: Therefore, I exist. Once the argument is formalized, it is immediately evident that it is, in fact, an enthymene with hidden or implicit components. As other authors have indicated, Descartes overlooks (or suppresses) at least one hidden premise. Clearly, I cannot move from the premise, "I think," to the conclusion, "I exist," unless I believe something else, namely, that "anything that thinks must exist." And even this general principle seems but a more basic application of a more general metaphysical principle that "any acting thing must exist." We might represent the structure of Descartes' inference informally as figure 7.2. (Descartes still thinks of arguments as syllogistic.)

I will not parse the logical structure of the *cogito* any further here. Simply note, for our purposes, that this implication also presupposes certain principles of logic: for example, the *dictum de omni* of the classical syllogism, that what is true of a class must be true of each member of that class; and the idea of validity, that if the premises in a properly constructed argument are true, what necessarily follows from those premises must also be true. As it turns out then, the *cogito* is a somewhat sophisticated argument that presupposes a substantial series of simpler, more basic insights.

Ian Hacking writes, "Some Cartesian scholars have recently debated whether the *cogito ergo sum* is inference or intuition or something else again ... It is completely immaterial to [Descartes] whether one man needs to infer where another intuits directly. The point of the cogito, as the *Discourse* informs us, is to display a truth one cannot doubt."[99] But this is too easy. Descartes himself writes, "He who says, 'I think, hence I am, or exist', does not deduce existence from thought by a syllogism, but, by a simple act or mental vision, recognizes it as if it were a thing known *per se*."[100] Descartes cannot construct a logical demonstration of the *cogito*, for at the point in the *Meditations* where the argument appears, he does not know anything but the *cogito*. There is nothing logically prior to base a syllogism on. How, then, could we know the *cogito*? Only through "intuition," through a capacity of mental illumination akin to what traditional philosophers called *intellectus* or *noesis*, which, in this case, grasps an entire argument, a compound sequence, all at once, in a single leap, so to speak.

DESCARTES: INSPIRATION OR LOGIC?

One may criticize the Cartesian account of the natural light of reason. But, in fact, the deeper problem with Descartes method is the rhetorical emphasis on deductive reasoning. Descartes tries to show that we can come up with a deductive line of argument that establishes a complete system of human knowledge. In a work like the *Meditations*, his account of the natural light of reason fades into the background. It is reasoning, logic, that he advances as the principal engine of knowledge. He believed that we can use logic to climb up (or down) a lattice work of logically necessary ideas until we arrive at the most distant conclusions. This is the central theme in all of Descartes' epistemological work. He writes, "ideas that do not surpass the limits of human intelligence are all enchained with such a marvelous link, and can be drawn one from another by consequences that are so necessary, that we do not need too much skill or capacity to find them, provided that having begun with the simplest notions, we know how to lead ourselves by degree until we reach the most elevated ideas of all."[101]

The Cartesian method is, principally, the method of deductive argument. What comes to the fore here is *dianoia* or *ratio* as the authoritative source of belief. This is what Descartes champions: a method of serial

99 Hacking, "Leibniz and Descartes," 53–4.

100 Descartes, "Replies to Objections," in *Philosophical Works* (Haldane, Ross), vol. 2, 38.

101 Descartes, *Recherche de la vérité*, 1106–7 (my translation throughout).

inference that begins with the natural light of reason but operates according to a properly logical mode of mental movement. We begin with the simplest truths of all and pull ourselves up, individual inference by individual inference, from premises to conclusion, from premises to conclusion, until we arrive at comprehensive knowledge. In Descartes' unfinished dialogue *La recherche de la vérité par la lumière naturelle* (*The Search for Truth by the Natural Light [or Reason]*), the protagonist Eudoxe reassures his interlocutors that discovering truths "is not as difficult as one might believe … The whole secret is to begin with the first and simplest and to then elevate ourselves little by little and as if by degrees until we arrive at the most distant and sophisticated truths."[102]

The Cartesian method privileges logic as the science of drawing out necessary implications. In the *Regulae* (*Rules for the Direction of Our Native Intelligence*), Descartes proposes a definition of deduction: "By *deduction*, we mean everything that is necessarily concluded from certain other things known with certainty … Even if by themselves these things are not self-evident, it is sufficient that they are deduced from true principles that are already known, by a continuous uninterrupted movement of thought." Descartes compares deductive inference to the way we physically observe the connection between individual links on a long chain. "We know that the last ring of some long chain is attached to the first, even if we cannot take in the whole string of intermediate rings on which this connection depends in a single glance; it is sufficient if we have examined the individual rings one after another, and we remember that from the first to last, each one is attached to its immediate neighbours"[103] This is how we deduce truth, step by step, down the length of a connected sequence of individual inferences.

Descartes distinguishes the cognitive operations of intuitive and deductive reasoning in a manner reminiscent of Thomas. Intuition is knowledge at rest; deduction is mental movement toward knowledge. Although we can come to know the same truths, "sometimes from intuition, sometimes by deduction," these methods differ sharply.[104] Intuition is an instantaneous, all-at-once illumination.[105] Deduction is "a sort of movement or succession." Intuition does not rely on memory. It is a simple matter of seeing clearly. "It is the memory that … endows [deduction] with certitude."[106]

102 Ibid., 1140.

103 Descartes, *Régles*, rule 3, 88–9 (here and henceforth, all English translations of this work are my own of Brunschwig's French).

104 Ibid., rule 3, 89–90. Hence Hacking's point above (see "Leibniz and Descartes," 51–2).

105 Descartes, *Régles*, rule 3, 89–90.

106 Ibid., rule 3, 89.

Descartes observes, "It only takes a single link, however insignificant, but once forgotten – there you go! The chain is immediately broken and all the certitude of the conclusion collapses."[107]

Descartes' protagonist, Eudoxe, promises to teach his listeners the method of certain knowledge. Eudoxe comments, "I believe I will have fulfilled my promise rather well, if in explaining truths which can be *deduced* from ordinary things known by everyone, I make you able to find by yourself all the others, whenever it pleases you to take the trouble to search them out."[108] It does not matter much where we end up. We start somewhere, and we end somewhere. We grasp first truths by intuition, and we grasp the final truths through deduction. "First principles are only known by intuition, while distant conclusions can only be known by deduction."[109] In this way, Descartes thinks, we can come to know the world.

Although recent historians, such as John Cottingham, Stephen Gaukroger, and Jacques Brunschwig, claim that Descartes reduces deduction to intuition, this is an exaggeration.[110] In some cases, a primitive deduction is so obvious, so "inference-less," it becomes, roughly speaking, an intuition.[111] The *cogito* is a case in point. But *inference* is not generally considered to be an intuition. Although Descartes does propose a technique of accelerated deduction as a mental exercise so that the reasoner can "heal a certain mental slowness, and increase by a certain measure his mental capacity," logic implies movement, a transition from premises to conclusion. Think of logical argument (in the traditional sense) as a *step-by-step* process up a flight of stairs to a higher understanding. What Descartes proposes as "accelerated deduction" involves a rapid movement up a chain of premises and subsidiary conclusions to the top of stairway. But moving very fast – furious stride by furious stride – up a long series of steps is not the same as reaching the top through some telepathic leap of insight.[112] For Descartes, intuitions, so to speak, dwell in the mind. We do not have to argue our way to them. We do not have to move *step by step* from premise to conclusion; we simply need to pull ourselves away from our distractions and attend to them. They do not involve *movement* at all. They are already there, motionless inside us. We just have to concentrate and we will discover them. These first principles are a product of "looking," not reason.

107 Ibid., rule 7, 110.

108 Descartes, *Recherche de la vérité*, 1112.

109 Descartes, *Régles*, rule 3, 89–90.

110 Cottingham, *Descartes Dictionary*, s.v. "Intuition"; Gaukroger, *Cartesian Logic*, 50; and Brunschwig, in Descartes, *Régles*, rule 3, 89n1.

111 Ibid., rule 7, 111.

112 Gaukroger, *Cartesian Logic*, 27; and Descartes, *Régles*, rule 7, 111.

We cannot overstate Descartes' confidence in the process of deductive reasoning. He writes, "our experience of things is often erroneous, but deduction, that is, the pure and simple inference of one thing from another ... can never be improperly drawn by an understanding endowed with reason, even to the slightest degree ... Of all the errors into which men fall ... none ever derives from a false inference, but only from the fact that we accept certain misunderstood experiences and that we make judgements lightly and without any foundation."[113] The contemporary, sentimentalist account of intuition has obscured Descartes' original understanding of the natural light of reason. With time his deductive method morphed into a rationalism with a focus on logical argument as the most authoritative and reliable expression of rationality, leaving his modern heirs with feeling as the original source of belief and conviction.

We should add that Descartes also recognizes the scientific importance of "induction" or "enumeration."[114] He claims that when we induce a generalization from particulars, "we arrive at a truth with more certainty than by any other type of proof, with the exception of simple intuition.[115] Proper inductive reasoning requires a sufficient, but not a complete, enumeration.[116]

PASCAL: KNOWLEDGE FROM THE HEART

It is important to point out that many of Descartes' contemporaries understood the limitations of his approach. In his famous *Les Pensées*, Blaise Pascal makes a brief and unforgiving comment: "Descartes useless and uncertain."[117] Pascal, a literary figure often overlooked by philosophers, opposes the Cartesian project because it tries to produce certain knowledge through argument. In elaborating a theory of "knowledge from the heart," Pascal recuperates, in effect, a more traditional understanding of human cognition. Heartfelt knowledge is not knowledge that arises through any sentimental excess, but through a mental illumination that

113 Ibid., rule 2, 83–4.

114 Descartes writes that "enumeration is necessary to perfect science" (Descartes, *Régles*, rule 7, 110).

115 Descartes, *Régles*, rule 7, 111.

116 For example, he writes, "If finally, I want to show by enumeration that the surface of the circle is larger than that of all the other figures with an equal circumference, it is not necessary to review every figure, but it suffices to make this demonstration on some particular shapes, in order to draw, by induction, the same conclusion with respect to all the rest" (ibid.).

117 Pascal, *Pensées and Other Writings* (H. Levi), 445.

allows us to glimpse the deep nature of things. The rational faculty that Pascal associates with the human heart is more or less equivalent to the faculty of non-discursive reason that historical authors variously refer to as inspiration, *noesis*, *intellectus*, understanding, or even intuition.

Allan Bloom writes, "Every Frenchman is born, or at least early on becomes, Cartesian or Pascalian."[118] He intends this statement as an exclusive disjunction. One is either a follower of Pascal or of Descartes, and not of both men, for they represent incompatible approaches to philosophy. Consider, then, Pascal's doctrine of heartfelt knowledge and how it differs from Cartesian rationalism.

Pascal distinguishes between knowledge coming from the mind and from the heart. He associates the mind with discursive and the heart with intuitive reasoning. Discursive reasoning is the deductive method of logic that reaches its apogee in the rigorous proofs of geometry and mathematics. Intuition instantaneously, creatively confronts experience to induce basic truths. Although Pascal does look at the role of the human mind, the originality of his account lies in its treatment of the heart.

Pascal observes, "We know the truth not only by means of reason but also by means of the heart."[119] The heart does not operate by logic, but by inspiration, by intuition, by immediate awareness. When the heart knows something, "the truth must be seen right straightaway, at a glance, and not through a process of reasoning."[120] "It is through the heart that we know the first principles,"[121] not only those of mathematics and science, but also those of morality and religion.

Steering clear of a common misunderstanding, Pascal does not conceive of intuitive reasoning as a type of mere feeling. Pascalian intuitive reasoning is not fully devoid of feeling but is also not *mere* emotion.[122] It is an intellectual event; it is like a light coming on inside the mind in response to experience. Honor Levi translates Pascal as follows: "[The] principles [that come from the heart] can hardly be seen; they are *felt* rather than seen;

118 Bloom, *Closing of the American Mind*, 52.

119 Pascal, *Pensées and Other Writings* (H. Levi), 142.

120 Ibid., 670.

121 Ibid., 142.

122 Pascal uses the noun *sentiment* which can indeed be used to refer to "affections, passions, and all the movements of the heart." A metaphorical sense of *sentir* is "hav[ing] the heart touched; the soul moved by something." See L'Académie française, *Le dictionnaire* (1694): "Sentiment: Il se dit aussi, Des affections, des passions, & de tous les mouvemens de l'ame." Also, "Sentir: Avoir le coeur touché, l'ame émeuë de quelque chose. Il sent comme il doit le bien qu'on luy fait. il ne sent point les affronts. il ne sent point la perte qu'il a faite."

enormous care has to be taken to make them *felt* by people who cannot *feel* them themselves."[123] While Pascal uses French terms like *sentiment* and *sentir* to describe intuition, the *Dictionnaire de l'Académie française* (1694) defines the noun *sentiment* as the "impression that objects make on the senses"[124] and the verb *sentir* as the activity of "receiv[ing] an impression in the senses."[125] Pascal means to suggest that intuitive reasoning is like sense perception. The heart *senses* first principles. They are immediately grasped; we are aware of them the way we are aware of physical objects; we do not reason our way to them.

The French words *sentir* and even *sentiment* also have a more specialized meaning. They refer, especially, to the sense of smell.[126] If conventional translations affirm that the heart "feels" first principles, we could just as easily say, it *smells* them. We might translate the previous passage: "We *smell* [the] principles [that come from the heart] instead of seeing them, and we must go to infinite pains to make their odors apparent to those who cannot smell them on their own." Odour is an invisible quantity. That is the point. If logic shines a light on things, intuiting them is like enjoying a sixth sense; it "sniffs out" what is true, instead of demonstrating it. We can smell these principles even in the dark.

123 Pascal, *Pensées and Other Writings* (H. Levi), 670 (my italics). The original runs, "On les voit à peine, on les sent plutôt qu'on les voit; on a des peines infinies à faire sentir à ceux qui ne les sentent pas d'eux-mêmes."

124 "Sentiment: Impression que font les objets sur les sens: sentiment picquant, aigu. douloureux, agreable, exquis, delicat. La fonction des sens: Il y a encore quelque sentiment dans cette partie. Il n'y a plus de sentiment dans son bras. il semble qu'il soit mort. il n'a plus de mouvement ni de sentiment. il est privé de tout sentiment" (L'Académie française, *Le dictionnaire* [1694]).

125 "Sentir: Recevoir quelque impression dans les sens" (ibid.).

126 "Sentiment: ... En parlant des chiens, signifie, Odorat. Ces chiens n'ont point de sentiment [Referring to dogs, indicates the sense of smell]." "Sentir: Il ne se dit guere que de l'odorat, de l'attouchement & du goust [It is hardly ever used except for the sense of smell, touch, and taste]. Sentir le froid. sentir du froid. sentir le chaud. sentir du chaud. sentir des fleurs. dés que j'ay gousté de ce pasté, j'ay senti le sel, le poivre. j'ay senti de l'amertume. sentir du mal. sentir de la douleur au bras, à la teste. le feu se fait bien sentir. il se sent la teste pesante. il sent une pesanteur dans le bras. il ne sent plus son pied tant il est engourdy. il sent je ne sçay quoy qui le picque. il va neiger je le sens bien. ces chiens ont le nez bon, ils sentent de loin. ils sentent par où la beste a passé. quand les chevaux sentent l'avoine." Sentir: "Se dit plus particulierement de l'odorat [It is more specifically said about the sense of smell]. Sentir une rose. sentir une tubereuse. quand il sent des parfums, ils luy font mal. il est enrhumé, il ne sent rien" (ibid.).

One may approach Pascal's concept of heartfelt knowledge as if it was only a more poetic version of Cartesian intuition – a sort of romantic re-reading of the natural light of reason. But there are important differences. Pascal's account of heartfelt knowledge is much closer to traditional accounts of induction. First, unlike Descartes, Pascal associates intuitive reasoning with sense perception. Second, he has little patience for radical doubt. Whereas commentators do *mistakenly* classify Pascal as a comprehensive sceptic, he did not believe that knowledge is impossible. He believed rather that a one-sided reliance on logical reasoning alone leads to scepticism. Pascal critiques modern rationalist thinking. We need something more than logical inference or argument. We cannot make adequate sense of the world without knowledge from the heart.

A comparison of Descartes' most widely read work, the *Meditations*, with Pascal's, *Les Pensées* is illuminating. In the *Meditations* Descartes goes to great lengths to present his philosophical system as one long, continuous argument. Chronology and logical order prevail. We are impelled, driven, through a series of inferences, step by step, necessarily, to a certain conclusion. Pascal's text reads like a jumble of isolated thoughts, jotted down in a breathless hurry, then collected and catalogued after the fact. The disjointed aphorisms are terse and untidy. It is as if the connecting prose passages are missing, leaving exposed the bare bones of inspired thinking on which his theory stands.

Descartes' polished prose reads like dinner theatre: every word and gesture in its proper place, leading logically and smoothly (and artificially) to a sensational conclusion. Pascal, the writer, *induces* aphorisms. The movement is from particular experience to a principle applicable to human life generally. The process here is creative; it is like giving birth. It happens in a single stroke of inductive insight. The style of composition is not method but genius. This is to revert to the Socratic understanding of philosophy. The point is to break out of the mental straightjacket of *aporia*, to solve the riddle of human life itself through the birth of new ideas.

Pascal's aphorisms are naked inspiration, illuminated truths arrived at without process of any kind. He gives us flashes of brilliance, sudden thoughts that enlighten in a twist of irony or a memorable phrase. The movement is from particular experience to general statement, but the stroke of understanding is utterly simple. It happens non-discursively, without argument. The mind lights up in a flash of understanding. This is *noesis*, *intellectus*, angelic knowledge, knowledge acquired instantaneously, through a kind of immediate, effortless discernment. Whereas Descartes places his hope in a type of serial inference expanding ever outward, Pascal looks to intuitive understanding, as a creative grasp of the world, to be the engine of discovery.

A consummate mathematician and leading scientist, Pascal nowhere denigrated the role of discursive reason. Indeed, *most* of our knowledge comes through argument. Pascal writes, "Would to God that we never needed [argument] and that we knew everything through instinct and feeling! But nature has denied us this benefit: on the contrary it has given us very little [intuitive] knowledge." Like Thomas, Pascal believed that human beings must, for the most part, rely on discursive argument. Knowledge of the heart, non-discursive knowledge coming to us only through intuition is a rare commodity. "All the other kinds [of knowledge] can only be acquired through [discursive] reason."[127]

In comparison with thinkers like Descartes, Pascal had no patience for the great Enlightenment project in philosophy: the elaboration of an all-encompassing logical system to be used rigorously and mechanically to deduce all truths about reality. Although poor health hampered his scientific and philosophical endeavours, the issue is deeper than that. A religious man, Pascal scoffs at such hubris. The problem is not that we cannot have knowledge but that modern secularism has lost faith in one necessary source of certain knowledge, the heart.

Descartes began with methodological scepticism he tried to overcome with argument. Pascal disapproves. The lesson we should draw from Cartesian scepticism is not that knowledge is uncertain but that discursive reason is incomplete. While logic or argument is powerless to prove the principles of science, mathematics, morality, or even the dogmas of religion, "this powerlessness should only serve to humiliate reason, which would be the judge of everything, not to attack our certainty." Pascal argues *against* any systematic scepticism. He comments, "The Pyrrhonists [i.e., the radical sceptics] who have only reason as the object of their attack are working ineffectually. We know we are not dreaming, however powerless we are to prove it by reason. This powerlessness proves only the weakness of reason, not the uncertainty of our entire knowledge as they claim."

Pascal, like traditional authors, believes that intuitive understanding is a reliable source of knowledge. He writes, "[our] knowledge of first principles such as space, time, movement, numbers, is as certain as any that our reasoning can give us, and it is on this knowledge by means of the heart and instinct that reason must rely, and must base all its argument. The heart [senses] there are three dimensions in space and that there is an infinite series of numbers … The principles are [sensed,] the propositions are proved, both conclusively, although in different ways."[128] Pascal's solution

127 Pascal, *Pensées and Other Writings* (H. Levi), 142.

128 Ibid.

to scepticism is faith in the human heart. We are inspired. The heart can sense what is true. Largely unaware of the complications of earlier philosophy, he effectively recuperates the traditional doctrine of inspiration, understanding, *noesis*, and *intellectus* as a legitimate category of knowledge. A recognition of this non-discursive way of knowing is at the very *heart* of the Western tradition.

It is instructive to briefly compare the legacies of Pascal and Descartes. The idea that Descartes is the father of modern philosophy and that modern philosophy is an improvement over the "old philosophy" that uncritically assumed things were true without proving them is a mainstay of received wisdom. *The Stanford Encyclopedia of Philosophy* contains eight separate entries for "Descartes."[129] There is no general entry for Pascal, who is only mentioned under a single heading: "Pascal's Wager." Every philosophy major in a mainstream university will, at some point in his or her studies, critically examine Descartes' *Meditations* in detail. Students will sample a wide range of his seminal ideas in a host of introductory courses, and graduate departments will offer higher-level courses focusing, in large part or exclusively, on Descartes' individual texts and arguments. Pascal might be mentioned, in passing, in a course on Continental philosophy, as one of the forerunners of modern existentialism. Lecturers might discuss the "wager" in courses about religion or game theory. In most cases, however, any serious study of Pascal's thought will be relegated to courses in French literature dispensed by a modern-languages department.

LONERGAN'S "INSIGHT"

Canadian theologian and philosopher Bernard Lonergan has proposed a contemporary account of knowledge based on a species of direct insight. He seems, at first glance, to provide a much-needed correction to a rationalism that conceives of philosophy solely or largely as a game of argument or logical demonstration. Some commentators suggest that Lonergan's account of insight is fundamentally Aristotelian. Closer examination belies, however, these first impressions.

Lonergan situates his account of insight within a larger epistemological framework not unlike the theory of logical abduction, developed by Charles Sanders Peirce (which I will discuss in the last chapter). Lonergan's description of creativity bears a striking resemblance to Arthur Koestler's more popular account of the "aha! experience." In his major work *Insight*, Lonergan

129 These deal, in turn, with his mathematics, epistemology, ethics, life and works, modal metaphysics, ontological argument, physics, and the pineal gland.

begins with the well-known story of Archimedes' *eureka* experience. As legend would have it, Archimedes noticed the water-level rise in his bath and suddenly realized that he could measure the volume of a solid by immersing it in water. He was so elated at this discovery, he jumped out and ran naked through the streets shouting, "Eureka!" Lonergan points to this type of spontaneous puzzle-solving as the ultimate source of all knowledge. Knowing begins, as it turns out, not in an incremental, mechanical process, but in a creative illumination or discovery.

Terry Tekippe describes various aspects of Lonerganian insight. It represents "a high pitch of creative activity."[130] It "is often experienced as a sudden breakthrough"[131] and is "sometimes referred to as the 'Aha!' experience."[132] "[It] collates, it puts together, it connects."[133] "Before the insight occurs, no pattern is discerned, the materials jostle one another without being connected; one scratches one's head in complete amazement. But once the insight has occurred, [the resultant explanation] may seem the simplest thing in the world; one only wonders why it took so long to catch on."[134] Lonergan himself identifies five characteristics of insight. Insight (1) provides "a release to the tension of inquiry"; (2) happens "suddenly and unexpectedly"; (3) is a function not of exterior circumstances but of mental readiness; (4) links "the concrete and the abstract"; and (5) introduces an understanding that becomes "habitual."[135]

Seen from this general perspective, Lonergan seems to provide a modern reworking of traditional doctrines of inspiration, *noesis, intellectus,* or knowledge of the heart. His focus on mental discovery seems to provide an alternative to the usual one on evidence or logical argument. But Lonergan's account is fundamentally different from traditional accounts, for he divides the activity of insight into a series of steps or stages that he tellingly refers to as "experiencing, understanding, and judging."[136] His

130 Tekippe, *What Is Lonergan Up to in Insight?*, 50.

131 Ibid.

132 Ibid.

133 Ibid., 18.

134 Ibid., 19.

135 Lonergan, *Insight,* 3–4ff.

136 Lonergan, *Understanding and Being,* 33ff. (see index entry on 444). Lonergan also uses the longer phrase "inquiry, understanding, conception, reflecting, reflective insight, and judging" (ibid., 33ff.). Elsewhere he refers to the activity of insight as "experience-understanding-reflection" (*Insight,* 759). The differences between these specific designations have no bearing on the present discussion.

followers further divide this activity of mental illumination.[137] But all these schema share one important feature. What carries the epistemological weight in Lonergan's account is not any kind of intuitive understanding but discursive reasoning.

On Lonergan's account, we move from illumination, to a moment of understanding, to discernment. The middle stage of this sequence most closely resembles Aristotelian *noesis.* This is "the click, the grasp, what is added to our knowledge when you see the *must* in the data."[138] But once we have this original "bright idea," we need to test its truthfulness. Judgement, corroboration, is what separates truth from "airy speculation."[139] It is what allows us to say Yes or No to the original insight.[140] Without this final step, we do not have knowledge. We have to be able to produce reasons to show that the content of the original insight is true. Non-discursive understanding has to be buttressed by demonstration, i.e., by *argument.* At the end of the day, knowledge requires this final act of judgement and "judging is discursive and not intuitive."[141]

Appearances can be deceiving. Lonergan is a modern rationalist; he believes in the authority of logic, not in that of any kind of intuitive understanding. Non-logical knowing is never decisive. By itself, it never counts as knowledge. There is no room in Lonergan's account for the immediate apprehension of knowledge. Only judgement, understood as logical inference, as the giving of reasons, is decisive. As Michael Vertin maintains, "Only after judgment can we say that we have discovered knowledge, something true."[142]

Lonergan presents a thought experiment designed to illustrate the kind of justification required for knowing:

137 Marc Smith has identified four principal stages of insight: (1) experiencing involves our first immediate awareness of ourselves and the world; (2) understanding (or direct insight) tells us in a sudden enlightenment what something is; (3) judging (or reflective understanding) affirms or denies the resultant insight; and finally (4) deciding translates that knowledge into action (see Marc Smith, "Educating the Human Subject"; and "Essential and Effective Freedom"). Michael Vertin divides Lonergan's account of insight into six separate stages: (1) experiencing, (2) transcendental intending (asking questions), (3) direct insight, (4) conceiving, (5) reflective insight, and (6) affirmation (see Vertin, "Maréchal, Lonergan," 415–8).

138 Lonergan, *Understanding and Being,* L.2, 36.

139 Lonergan, *Insight,* 270.

140 Ibid., 275ff.

141 Vertin, "Maréchal, Lonergan," 419.

142 Ibid.

> Let us suppose two spheres of exactly the same size. One of them is an aluminum shell, and the other solid lead. You are seated at a table and there is a curtain between your face and your arm … In the first instance, someone places the lead sphere in the palm of your hand; and in the second instance, he places your hand on the aluminum shell, not all by itself, but with a spring above it that gives you exactly the same pressure you would feel from the lead sphere. Then it is true that one sphere is heavy, and it is true that the other is light; but the pressure on the palm of your hand in both cases is exactly the same. You can say, "I feel pressure"; you can say "It appears to be heavy"; but you cannot say, "It is heavy" or "It is light." The appearances are deceptive. How do you make that step? When do you come to the point where you have objective knowledge, when you can say, "It is heavy?" It is judgement, insofar as you introduce data that settle the issue. If you are allowed to take either of the spheres successively in your hand, all by itself, and put your whole hand around it, then you can determine that there is no spring attached. Or you can move your hand quickly; when you move the lead sphere you will encounter considerable resistance, and when you move the aluminum sphere you will encounter hardly any. Then you will know which one is the heavy one, and you will be able to say, "This is heavy." That point is reached in judgement.

In his discussion of this thought experiment, Lonergan distinguishes three levels of cognition. "On the first level we have sensations, perceptions, images. On the second level we understand, and understanding yields objects of thought – it may be heavy, and it may be light; if I could only get my hand around it and move it quickly, I would know which it is. [On the third level] one performs the experiment, makes the judgement and [having arrived at the third level] says, 'This is heavy'."[143] We only arrive at knowledge in this final stage. As Smith explains, "Knowing … is not just seeing; it is experiencing, understanding, [*and*] judging."[144]

Lonergan's account of the "metal sphere experiment" recalls familiar accounts of the experimental method. Confronted with a new physical object, insight supplies a hypothesis: "this is a lead sphere." We test the hypothesis to see whether it is true. We use our hands to explore the surface of the sphere. We finally realize that there is a spring attached and we *infer* a conclusion: "this is a fake lead sphere." This, then, is what Lonergan means by insight. We move from perception, to insight, to empirical verification, to a

143 Lonergan, *Insight*, 117.

144 See M. Smith, "Educating the Human Subject" (online).

weighing of evidence, to knowledge. The last step requires logic. We use reason to construct a case to justify eventually believing a conclusion.

In his account of insight, Lonergan focuses on the spontaneous nature of thought, on the fact that we often find the mental solution to puzzles or problems all at once. In all sorts of circumstances, we do not reason incrementally, step by step, to the right answer; we have an illumination. This *is* an important fact about human cognition, but it does not offer much of a perspective on the more detailed epistemological accounts of traditional philosophers. What they were interested in was laying a solid foundation for logical argument. Where earlier authors discussed non-discursive understanding, they were investigating the way the mind recovers the most fundamental truths of all. If human thought operates in leaps and bounds, if a successful awareness comes on us suddenly, then not every state of sudden awareness counts as universal knowledge or as a first principle. Not every state of inspiration, intuition, or illumination is the same. To use the vocabulary of an earlier chapter, mere recognition of similarity differs entirely from true inductive reasoning. Lonergan's account is not finely grained enough to pick up on such important differences.

TWO DESCRIPTIONS OF MENTAL ILLUMINATION: INDUCTION AND BRAINSTORMING

We might distinguish traditional and modern theories of intuitive reasoning, what I will call "the inductive view" and "the brainstorming view." On the inductive view, we inspect the physical evidence and a light comes on. Intelligence discerns in the evidence what is inescapably true. So-called proof is after the fact. On the brainstorming view, the mind throws out ideas in a provisional way. These hypotheses must be tested. It is not the process of discernment but that of empirical (or logical) verification that has epistemological weight. Knowledge only supervenes when we prove (or disprove) the hypothesis.

Brainstorming is not discernment. It is the activity of free creativity, that is all. Brainstorming produces ideas indiscriminately. We cannot recognize whether these ideas are true until after empirical corroboration. This is, on the modern account, when understanding occurs. Where Lonergan opts for the new, brainstorming model of intuitive understanding, his position reflects larger trends. Iconoclast Henry Veatch criticizes a pervasive belief "among contemporary scientists and philosophers of science that (1) it being impossible to derive scientific theories either inductively or by any other logical means from the facts of observation, (2) the only alternative would seem to be to regard such theories as being on the order of things which the mind freely creates from its own design."[145] Veatch complains that "it is not unusual for current writers ... to compare the devising of explanatory theories in science to the inventing of 'musical themes', of 'dramatic conflicts', and even of 'fairy tales'."[146] He cites Albert Einstein's claim that "the fundamental concepts and postulates of physics [are] in the logical sense free inventions of the mind, [and not] deduced from experience by 'abstraction' [or any] logical means."[147] On the brainstorming model, the source of scientific ideas is not discernment but the free play of creativity. It is not as if we could espy something that somehow exists in the data. We do not infer, i.e. extract "logically," what necessarily follows from what we see. We invent ideas that happen to turn out, on verification, to be true. But this is an impoverished notion of human rationality.

Clearly, experiment plays an important role in modern science. But Lonergan's brainstorming or "hypothesis-formation" model of insight is problematic. On his account, the act of insight is separated from the moment of epistemological justification. *Human understanding, taken by itself, counts for nothing.* It is the fact that the hypothesis is confirmed by evidence that provides epistemological basis. Consider the universal law of gravity. On the inductive model, intelligence "sees" something in the phenomena. Newton's mind views a falling apple and comes to a sudden understanding: "This is why objects fall." We can, then, verify that this understanding holds true in this or that observed case, but the original insight already counts as knowledge. On the brainstorming model, the original mental discovery cannot even count as knowing. The law of gravity begins as an unproven possibility, a wild idea perhaps – that is all. Understanding only takes place after we collect evidence and confirm the hypothesis. But we can only collect an exceedingly limited amount of the evidence. We cannot examine the behaviour of every mass in the universe to see if it obeys the law of gravity. Proof – and therefore justification – remains irreparably incomplete, hence the modern problem of induction.[148]

As we have seen, traditional authors recognize a species of knowledge operating as an immediate awareness of something. Whether we call this faculty the natural light of reason, immediate inference, *intellectus*, *epagoge*,

145 Veatch, *Two Logics*, 165–6.

146 Ibid., 166. The "fairy tale" analogy comes from Campbell, *What Is Science?* 106–7.

147 Veatch, *Two Logics*, 166.

148 Lonergan's position is, in fact, inconsistent, for he himself dismisses the problem of induction. See Lonargan, "Similars Are Similarily Understood," *Understanding and Being*, 289.

or *noesis*, it plays an indispensable role in human cognition. On the traditional account, human intelligence has epistemological authority. Why? Simply because it is what it is. Intelligence has authority because, well, it is intelligent. Because it possesses a basic power of discrimination capable of recognizing what is true, accurate, consistent, and so on. Human intelligence is not a purely psychological operation. It is not an eccentric and unreliable creative capacity. It is not arbitrary or tentative, standing in need of some outside correction or proof. The judgements of human intelligence are properly and authoritatively epistemological. Thomas believes that angels who know through *intellectus* know without error. Human *intellectus* is a more limited but equally incorrigible process.

Lonergan seems embarrassed by historical claims that intuitive understanding is infallible.[149] Aristotle describes induction as a state of mind "by which we have truth and are never deceived about things invariable or even variable."[150] Thomas claims that our ability to intuit first concepts is "always true."[151] Clearly, both Aristotle and Thomas believe that human beings make mistakes. At the same time, they both believe that we must *assume* that human intelligence is, at the deepest level, reliable. If we do not begin by acknowledging the epistemological authority of human intelligence, knowledge of any sort will always be questionable.

Lonergan unwittingly removes the justification for insight. Even true insight cannot count as knowledge. It must be justified *after the fact* by empirical confirmation. In placing justification outside understanding in the act of empirical confirmation, Lonergan effectively strips human judgement of its epistemological authority – hence the inevitable slide into scepticism. Lonergan responds to the sceptical challenge in two distinct ways. First, he makes understanding dependent on discursive reasoning. We have to back up our ideas with evidence. Second, he emphasizes the importance of empirical confirmation. We can only believe in our ideas because empirical verification proves they "correspond" to the world.

As authors such as Aristotle and Thomas recognized, the appeal to discursive reason leads to an infinite regress. If we have to back up our beliefs with arguments, any argument presupposes beliefs that must be backed up

149 Lonergan claims that Thomas only believes that human understanding is "infallible" in the sense that it produces concepts that *may* be used in a truthful way (Lonergan, *Insight*, 406–7).

150 *Nicomachean Ethics* (Ross, Urmson), bk 6, ch. 6, 1141a3–5 (in Aristotle, *Complete Works*).

151 Thomas Aquinas, *Exposition of the "Posterior Analytics"* (Conway), bk 2, lecture 20, art. 15.

by further arguments, and those by others, and so on, with the resulting infinite regress. The appeal to empirical confirmation is equally inadequate. It is not only that our observation of nature is inevitably incomplete – perception (like intelligence) manifests human nature. The radical sceptic will not be satisfied by appeal to empirical observations made from a fallible human perspective.

As we have seen, Lonergan appears to base his account of understanding on the experimental method.[152] But he misconstrues the chronology of the method. On his brainstorming account, it is as if discernment is postponed until after the proof. We are blind and empirical corroboration makes us see. But this is not how successful science proceeds. In successful cases, the scientist discerns what must be the case and then proceeds to prove it. Confirmation plays an important role but it is logically *a posteriori*. It is not, initially, what makes us understand anything.

The modern scientific method has its place. The testing and formation of hypotheses is, of course, a legitimate heuristic device in human inquiry. The mind may *induce* a hypothesis that must be verified *after the fact* by a consideration of evidence. But to suggest that *all* knowledge or that all knowledge of *universals* or that knowledge of *first* principles comes to us in this way is to exaggerate.

152 The experimental method has, of course, an important role in science. Note, however, that much scientific practice is observation, simply finding out what the facts are, or again, working out the ramifications of an accepted theory, and not strictly speaking the experimental method of forming and testing hypotheses.

8

Creativity: The Art of Induction

Thought is held to be the most divine of things observed by us.

Aristotle[1]

No block of marble but it does not hide
the concept living in the artist's mind –
pursuing it inside that form, he'll guide
his hand to shape what reason has defined.

Michelangelo[2]

IN THIS CHAPTER I WILL ARGUE that the mental operation of induction is, in the most fundamental sense, a creative endeavour and that even on Aristotle's account true creativity must entail "the creation of something from nothing." This may strike the careful reader as extreme, absurd, or even dangerous. It is important to avoid a misunderstanding. Though I argue for a kind of "creation of something from nothing," this is not to make any kind of metaphysical claim about existent things somehow springing out of non-existence. It is to claim, more modestly, that induction produces more knowledge from less. Output exceeds input. In the most familiar case, inductive arguments are ampliative. The conclusion states more than the premises. This expanding movement from less to more knowledge is the identifying feature of all modes of induction, both intuitive and argumentative. Whenever we engage in induction, we end up with more than what we started with. We begin with sense perception and are somehow able to transform our experience into a larger understanding. We begin with a few examples and are somehow able to know something about the universal case. We do this kind of thing so frequently, we take it for granted. But there is something important to be explored here.

1 *Metaphysics* (Ross), bk 12, ch. 9, 1074b15 (in Aristotle, *Complete Works*).

2 "Non ha l'ottimo artista alcun concetto," in *Michelangelo*, Sonnet 153 (Girardi no. 151).

Consider an uncontroversial example of creativity. You want to paint the next great painting. You visit an art class and ask the teacher, "How do I paint the next great painting?" What you want is a recipe, an algorithm. You want to be told, in forty easy steps, here is how you hold the brush; here is how you mix the paint; here is how you draw a tree (etc.). Memorize this routine, and you will end up with a great work of art. You can imagine the instructor scratching his or her head in amazement. What is one to tell you? There is no recipe, no algorithm, no surefire method. Truly great art results from an unaccountable epiphany. You can go to art school and learn how to paint trees and techniques of watercolour and gouache, but you cannot go to art school to learn how to be a great artist. No secret, step-by-step protocol could secure artistic vision.

The search for the hidden mechanism of creativity would reduce the production of the next great painting to a very complicated paint-by-number project, that is all. Those who want to turn the world into one great machine, the reductionists, the rationalists, the inheritors of the great Enlightenment project, those who are suspicious of anything unaccountable or mysterious or transcendent, have always worried about creativity. Traditional accounts, which often view intelligence as quasi-divine, have fewer problems accepting the notion of real creativity. Consider the process of induction. On the traditional account, the mind goes in a single stroke from incomplete experience to a universal understanding, from a mere collection of properties to a definition of the essence of a thing, from the practicality of everyday life to a transcendent moral aspiration. How do we manage this? All this happens through a kind of inspiration. How do we explain it? Explaining this inspiration is impossible. To explain something is to account for it by reference to something more fundamental. But nothing is more fundamental than induction. (In a way, perceptual experience itself is more fundamental, but this type of experience is not knowledge. When we say that induction is the first step, we mean that we cannot explain the knowledge inductive inference yields from the point of view of prior knowledge; nor can we explain it as a form of sense perception, which is, unlike conceptual knowledge, inevitably individual and limited.)

Induction gives us the very first principles. We cannot explain first principles by reference to those prior to these principles, for these are the very first principles. On the traditional account, this is where our abilities begin, in an inexplicable leap of creativity. The human mind brings into existence something remarkably new. This involves a quantum leap to a new possibility that includes much more than we find in sense experience. This is the very edge of our understanding; once we have retreated to this lonely frontier, we have no place else to go. This is the end of the road; we can go no further.[3]

In this chapter, I will argue that the mental process that precipitates induction operates by a radical leap of creativity that closely resembles artistic inspiration. Perhaps not surprisingly, Michelangelo Buonarroti's theory of artistic inspiration, having been deeply influenced by medieval theories of induction, provides a close analogue of Aristotle's account of inductive reasoning. I will use Michelangelo's account of the creative mechanism behind the art of sculpture to demonstrate the parallels between the creativity of art and of inductive science. In explicating the nature of the latter, I will examine and compare four mental operations: perception, imagination, artistic inspiration, and induction.

CREATIVITY AND INDUCTION

The contemporary approach tends to overlook the creative element in the inductive process. Complete, perfect induction is the only valid induction. Why? Because the number of specimens included in the conclusion is equal to the number of specimens examined. Input equals output. Everything is accounted for. On the usual account, induction looks like a *mistake* in reasoning. The jump from the premise "this is true for some cases" to the conclusion "this is true for all cases" seems unwarranted. Why? This is because modern philosophy has no resources to account for such an enlargement in the scope of the predicate. Intuition has been reduced to a mere hunch or feeling; deductive logic is unavailable at this first level of cognition, and Cartesian scepticism has undermined any generalized confidence in human reason. If, however, induction does not operate through some credible leap of understanding, if it is a mere mechanical expansion of terms, it is, of course, problematic – hence the modern obsession with the alleged problem of induction.

The only way to "rescue" induction as a credible source of knowledge is through some account of creativity. An earlier generation of logicians did acknowledge the fundamentally *creative* nature of the inductive process. Daniel Robinson, writing in the early twentieth century, illustrates the process of induction by means of William Harvey's "great discovery of the circulation of the blood."[4] As it turns out, Harvey *inferred* the existence of

3 We might, of course, try to explain induction by reference to some larger metaphysical or theological perspective. Such ruminations are beyond the scope of the present inquiry.

4 D. Robinson, *Principles of Reasoning*, 211.

"capillary channels connecting the arteries and veins … from his [incomplete] knowledge of the rest of the system."[5] This instance of inductive reasoning did not involve a mechanical summary of previous data but a creative insight pushing the bounds of understanding further than the available evidence. The real connection between veins and arteries was only verified at a *later* date, after the invention of the compound microscope.

Idealist Henry Tappan, in a nineteenth-century text, comments at some length on the creative element of the inductive process. Tappan criticizes John Stuart Mill's attempt to identify a method for inductive reasoning. According to Tappan, the process of such reasoning cannot be expressed in a series of steps or rules to be memorized or learned by rote. As he explains, "[in] the discovery of [scientific] laws there is so much that appears like inspiration, and indeed so much that really is inspiration … that to lay down exact rules and formulae designed to represent and govern the process of discovery, would appear puerile … and impractical." Induction hinges, according to Tappan, on a spontaneous moment of mental illumination, arriving in a single stroke or realization. Because induction is a simple rather than a discursive act, it escapes logical elucidation.

Tappan provides an enthusiastic description of the creative *élan* that characterizes the inductive process. "By a sudden and wonderful leap [those of genius] are seen to pass … to a stupendous conclusion. With a prophetic power they seem to foretell the law which, before ordinary minds, lies only as a result of an immense and laborious observation." Tappan conceives of successful science as the union of induction and observation. "The mere experimenter and observer collects facts, but does not gain laws. On the other hand, a mind of high intuitive energy cannot make itself independent of experiment and observation … It is the union of the two which makes the true [scientist], for it is the union of the two which makes the true inductive logic."[6] Whereas induction supplies the creative intuition that begets universal laws of nature, observation or experiment triggers and confirms this universal understanding.

Even a sworn enemy of induction such as Karl Popper acknowledges the *nonlogical* origin of successful scientific ideas. He affirms, "there is no such thing as a logical method for having new ideas, or a logical reconstruction of this process … Every discovery contains 'an irrational element' or a 'creative intuition'."[7] Popper quotes Albert Einstein, "There is

5 Ibid., 213.

6 Tappan, *Elements of Logic*, 307.

7 Popper, *Logic of Scientific Discovery*, 32.

no logical path … leading to [scientific] laws. They can only be reached by intuition, [by] something like intellectual love [*Einfühlung*] of the objects of experience'."[8]

Popper views scientific discovery as an irrational, even a "crazy" act. But this seems lame. On the traditional account, induction is the most reliable form of reason. It operates through pure cognition. The most basic concepts and principles have to be grasped through an epistemologically authoritative but creative leap of reason. There is no point trying to explain away the jump by something that is not a jump. This obscures what is really going on. There is a jump, but it is not a random or a mechanical leap to something obtuse or unreliable. Not even Popper can explain how we arrive at successful scientific ideas without backhandedly acknowledging the need for intelligent creativity.

Hilary Kornblith, in discussing the atomic theory of matter, cites chemist Wilhelm Oswald, who writes in a 1908 textbook of chemistry, "I have become convinced that we recently came into possession of experimental proofs of the discrete or particulate nature of matter, proofs which the atomic hypothesis sought for centuries, indeed for millennia."[9] But this poses a serious epistemological puzzle. How is it that so many thinkers could have come up with the atomic hypothesis long before any proof of the theory occurred to anyone? Unless we are willing to dismiss such episodes as lucky guesses, we have some explaining to do.

Popper's rejection of induction is really a denial of creativity. To ignore or overlook the creative capacity of such reasoning is to misconstrue the history of science. We are capable of an intelligent discernment that anticipates scientific proof. This has been repeatedly demonstrated in the history of science. However much this possibility offends the reductionist, it seems a regular feature of day-to-day scientific practice.

CREATION FROM NOTHING

In line with Tappan's view of induction as an inspirational leap, I will argue that a similar account of induction is implicit in Aristotle. In Plato, concepts arise out of "recollection." We retrieve what already exists hidden in our minds. Thinking is the repetition of what came before – no birth, no genesis of what is truly new and unprecedented brings something from out of nothing. In Aristotle, the mind gives birth to a new intellectual object.

8 Cited in Ibid.

9 Kornblith, *Inductive Inference*, 32.

The mind does not remember the past but somehow transforms the present data of sense perception into the first principles of thought. This requires a leap, a creation of more from less.

Parmenides quipped that "the force of conviction" would not "permit anything to come to be from what is not."[10] This is a constant theme among early Greek philosophers who tend to view the generation and corruption we see around us as second-level phenomena. Because things in the world are aggregate entities, they can be created or destroyed by the union or separation of their constituent parts. But fundamental things (like atoms) that are not made up of anything else cannot be created or destroyed, for that would necessitate the creation of something out of nothing or the equally impossible destruction of something into nothing. Empedocles writes, "There is no coming-to-be of anything, but only a mingling [of elements] and a divorce of what has been mingled."[11] Again, Anaxagoras claims that "no thing comes to be, nor does it perish, but they are mixed together from things that are and they are separated apart."[12]

In the *Metaphysics*, Aristotle stipulates that everything comes from something else. Indeed, he posits a universal rule of transformation: "Everything ... comes to be by the agency of something and from something and comes to be something."[13] I will call this principle the transformation rule. The transformation rule can be applied to both nature and art. Consider a human baby. It had to be made *through the agency* of something – the parents. It had to be made *from something* – a human egg and sperm. And it had to be made *into something* – a newborn baby. Or consider a statue of Hercules. The statue had to be made *through the agency* of something – the sculptor. It had to be made from *something* – a block of marble. And it had to be made *into something* – a statue of Hercules.

Although induction is genuinely creative and does, in a certain sense, entail a kind of creation out of nothing, it does not violate Aristotle's transformation rule. Induction produces first principles, but first principles have to be made *through the agency* of something – the mind. They have to be made *from something* – from the contents of sense perception. And they

10 Parmenides, in McKirahan, *Philosophy before Socrates*, §11.8 (Diels and Kranz [DK] number 28B8).

11 *On Generation and Corruption* (Joachim), bk 1, ch. 1, 314b8 (in Aristotle, *Complete Works*).

12 Anaxagoras, in McKirahan, *Philosophy before Socrates*, §13.17 (DK59B17).

13 *Metaphysics* (Ross), bk 7, ch. 7, 1032a13 (in Aristotle, *Complete Works*). Aristotle considers the creative processes of both nature and art. See *Metaphysics*, bk 7, ch. 8, 1033b23.

have to be made into *something* – concepts and universal propositions and even arguments. And yet induction is, at the same time, a more radical form of creativity than first appears. Suppose we were to add three to three and get seven. This would, of course, be impossible for three plus three can only give us six. Still, if, *per impossibile*, we were to add three to three and get seven, the extra "one" would have to come from nothing. Something similar happens in the case of induction. In the most obvious case, the conclusion of an inductive argument includes more than the premises. We end up with more than we started with. This is why contemporary philosophers worry about inductive arguments. They seem less than logical, for extra knowledge is, it seems, created out of nothing.

But induction is not just about arguments. It is also about concept formulation. Consider the concept "triangle." We begin with an *awareness* of a few individual triangles and end with knowledge of all triangles. René Descartes, in many ways the defining figure of modern philosophy, declares, "if we assume that something is found in the idea that was not in the cause, then the idea gets that something from nothing."[14] In the case of inductive reasoning we move from human experience to concepts. But human experience is inevitably individual, whereas concepts are universal. So induction involves a kind of creation from nothing.

The same thing happens with moral induction. Morality "forces" us to move outside our selfish concerns and care about other people as much as ourselves. This requires a leap, a creative jump to another person's point of view. We cannot rationally access this perspective without a mental enlargement of self-concern. We overlook the novelty of what is going on because we are so used to it. Every moral concept, proposition, and argument contains more than the particular experiences that produced it. Indeed, anytime we assume an objective point of view, we move beyond the confines of our own individuality and adopt a transcendent perspective.

We could find other examples. The important point is that the products of induction cannot be accounted for entirely on grounds of what went before. Induction, seen on from an Aristotelian viewpoint, hinges on a hidden premise, that the subject and middle terms are convertible. There is a kind of identification that must be seen, discerned, grasped, rather than argued to. Knowledge of this hidden premise presupposes an ability to see the universal in the individual. We must posit the existence of a creative power that is somehow able to move us from an awareness of the here and now to one of totality.

14 Descartes, *Meditations on First Philosophy* (Cress), Meditation 3, 74 (in Descartes, *Discourse on Method and Meditations*).

COGNITIVE SCIENCE AND INDUCTION

The guardians and watchdogs of rationality may dismiss radical creativity as mere superstition, a metaphysical or mystical hocus-pocus. But rationalist explanations of induction fundamentally miss the point. Holland et al. (John Holland, Keith Holyoak, Richard Nisbett, and Paul Thagard) propose a cognitive science model of induction.[15] Thagard (in a separate work) identifies as the "central hypothesis" of cognitive science, the idea "that thought can be understood in terms of computational procedure on mental representation." He enthusiastically assures us that this idea has "had enormous empirical success, providing explanations of numerous phenomena of human problem solving, learning, and language use."[16] But this seems a bit of hyperbole.

Cognitive scientists such as Thagard and Holland and colleagues eschew narrowly formalistic approaches to human thought and examine the practical, epistemological, emotional, and even the moral aspects of human cognition. Still, the expansive nature of the enterprise cannot disguise the underlying reductionism. Holland et al. warn the reader, "Whether we are describing organisms or prescribing for machines, it is our intent that all assertions ultimately be rendered computational. Our description of the behavior of organisms is always in terms that we believe capable of being translated eventually into computational procedures on machines."[17] The goal, then, is to develop a model of induction to program, without alteration or distortion, into a mechanical agent such as a computer.

How are we to turn inductive reasoning into an algorithm? How can we turn a creative leap of mind into a computational method? Simply put, we cannot. The traditional model simply accepts that creativity is possible. It does not try to explain it away through some kind of reductionist logic. Holland and his colleagues, by contrast, go to heroic but ultimately fruitless lengths to produce a computational analogue of inductive reasoning. They recast it as a rule-obeying procedure. Universal knowledge is to be represented by condition-action rules: "If such-and-such, Then so-and-so."[18] So the universal affirmation, "All birds have feathers," can be recast as "If *x* is a bird, *x* has feathers." Or again, the universal affirmation, "All hungry crocodiles must be avoided," can be recast as "If *x* is a hungry crocodile, avoid *x*!" In one case, we end up with a theoretical principle; in the

15 See Holland et al., *Induction*.

16 Thagard, *Coherence in Thought and Action*, 9–10.

17 Holland et al., *Induction*, 2.

18 Ibid., 21, 14.

other, a practical rule. (This whole procedure merely revisits the old mistaken idea that conditional statements in propositional logic can adequately replace universal statements in syllogistic logic.)

If we think of universal knowledge as taking the form of condition-action rules, we can easily come up with a procedure for amending and improving rules we already have. Suppose rule B is "If *x* is a piece of bread, *x* is edible." Rule W is "If *x* is a female human being, *x* will have long hair." As life progresses, rule B is verified over and over again. And so it gains more authority. As we encounter female human beings, however, we come to realize that some women have short hair and so rule W is weakened, modified, or even discarded. In this way, we can corroborate or discredit or modify specific condition-action rules, eliminating over time the inaccurate and retaining the accurate ones. Human behaviour can, then, be depicted as an attempt to obey those condition-action rules that stand the test of time. Holland and colleagues identify this mechanism of after-the-fact verification with inductive reasoning.[19]

Holland and colleagues develop an algorithmic model that distinguishes, after the fact, between lucky and unlucky guesses. But this is just the brainstorming model rehashed and reiterated in computational form. If a computer produces random generalizations, exhaustive validation occasionally transforms what began as a random conjecture into what seems to be a true generalization. But this is to reduce inductive reasoning to the process of validating claims *after the induction has already occurred.* As with Lonergan, we only recognize truthful (or almost truthful) inductive generalizations *in retrospect.* This kind of model fails to explain how we are to come up with the correct idea in the first place.

Holland and colleagues – like Popper, Bernard Lonergan, and others – reduce the true act of induction to the art of the lucky guess. They place knowledge at the end, not the beginning of the verification process. Philosophical attention is focused, not on the process of coming up with an insightful generalization, but on the subsequent activity of empirical corroboration. In effect, Holland and colleagues solve the problem of creativity by ignoring it. Their approach offers no place for induction as it is traditionally understood.

As it turns out, this implausible account runs into technical problems. Holland and colleagues even run into technical difficulties. Too many random generalizations can be made; the process of testing and validating all

19 The authors continue, "A rule that leads to a successful prediction should be strengthened in some way, increasing the likelihood of its use in the future; one that leads to error should be modified or discarded" (ibid., 16).

of them is just too time-consuming, even with the largest computer resources. As these authors themselves explain, their computational models quickly accumulate "mud." They leap to all sorts of generalizations and then "clog up their gears" trying to differentiate between meaningful and meaningless. But the solution is not a bigger computer or more clever programming. The solution is an account of intelligence that more closely resembles what actually happens in intellectual inquiry.

Lonergan gives joke-telling as an example of mental insight. We do not usually associate joke-telling with induction, but we do in a sense *induce* the punchline of a joke. We create a mental twist that brings to an unexpected but fitting end the information that went before. The punchline of a funny joke is not a natural extension of previous discourse. If it were, we would find no source of amusement, only a continuous stream of prosaic experience. The punchline must bring to light something new and unexpected that naturally completes the original thought. We might imagine two ways of writing jokes. We could complete our jokes with random punchlines and then wade through the results until we found something that made us laugh. But the scriptwriter who has a facility for writing jokes does not write jokes this way. They do not produce thousands of mostly unfunny punchlines and then try them all out to identify the ones people laugh at. Really talented scriptwriters *see* in advance what will be funny. They choose punchlines *because* they will be laughed at. This ability to grasp what is unexpectedly pertinent and appropriate is a kind of intelligence. And it is raw intelligence that is the ultimate power behind inductive reasoning.

Telling jokes is not so much a matter of moving from the general to the specific as one of determining what fits. But induction likewise involves determining what fits. Spurred on by particular observations, the mind grasps what follows. The brainstorming model developed by Holland and colleagues ignores the starting point of human learning: a sense of intelligent discernment that includes some creative power of recognizing patterns and penetrating issues intellectually. As Hilary Kornblith points out, young children develop an ability to recognize patterns and distinguish between essential and accidental properties early on.[20] Not even immature human beings think with random guesses; they size up what must be the case and act accordingly. Traditional accounts accept this human

20 "The current evidence," he observes, "supports the innateness of psychological essentialism" (psychological essentialism being the ability to identify natural kinds). See Kornblith, *Inductive Inference*, 78.

intelligence for what it is: a mental power capable of hitting on the correct and fundamental answer to questions that cannot be solved except through some leap of understanding.

The contemporary explanations of induction that focus on abduction (or inference to the best explanation) are taken up in the next chapter. For the moment, simply recall that we can understand abduction in two separate ways: as a form of brainstorming or as a form of insight. If we opt for the brainstorming model, we will be unable to explain how the original leap to the best explanation arises. The only alternative is to posit abduction as a form of insight or inspiration. If, however, abduction is insight, it requires a creative leap of the kind referred to in traditional accounts. The kind of leap elucidated here.

INDUCTION AND *TECHNE*

I mean to argue that the mechanism behind Aristotelian induction is best understood as art; in more precise technical terms, that *epagoge* is a kind of τέχνη (*techne*). This line of argument may seem irresponsible, for Aristotle himself clearly distinguishes creative art and induction. Still, I will argue that we should amend and develop his account in this direction.

Aristotle pinpoints six differences between *techne*, the intellectual and physical skill to produce art, and *nous*, the mental activity behind induction: (1) *Nous* is infallible, whereas *techne* is fallible.[21] (2) *Nous* deals with concepts and propositions that follow necessarily,[22] whereas *techne* deals "with things that can be otherwise."[23] (3) *Nous* operates by understanding, whereas *techne* works independently of the understanding.[24] (4) *Nous* gives birth to intellectual objects (concepts and propositions), whereas *techne* produces physical ones.[25] (5) *Nous* discovers first principles, whereas

21 Aristotle excludes art from his list of "those states of mind by which we have truth and are never deceived" (*Nicomachean Ethics* [Ross, Urmson], bk 6, ch. 6, 1141a2–5, in Aristotle, *Complete Works*).

22 See *Topics* (Pickard-Cambridge), bk 8, ch. 1, 155b35–36 (in Aristotle, *Complete Works*): "One must secure the necessary propositions either by deduction or induction."

23 *Nicomachean Ethics* (Ross, Urmson), bk 6, ch. 6, 1140a1–2.

24 Ibid., bk 6, ch. 3, 1139b15–18.

25 "All things that come to be either by nature or art have matter; for each is capable of being or not being, and this capacity is the matter in each" (*Metaphysics* [Ross], bk 7, ch. 7, 1032a20).

techne is incapable of such discovery.[26] And finally (6), *nous* operates by a simple movement of the mind, whereas Aristotle thinks of *techne* as a fundamentally discursive activity.

Much of what Aristotle says is obviously true. Still, I will argue that inductive reasoning involves a kind of art or *techne*. Aristotle himself defines art as "making."[27] The artist makes something – a painting, a poem, a vase. But as Peter Geach points out, "the mind *makes* concepts."[28] Aristotle himself presents inductive reasoning as the process of *making* concepts, universals, definitions, moral ideas, first principles, and even certain types of arguments. Induction is, properly speaking, "poetic" activity; indeed, the English word "poetic" is derived from the Greek verb "ποιέω" (*poieo*), which means "to make, produce, create."[29] We should then regard induction as a kind of *techne* or art, as an activity that creates something entirely new, something that could not exist in the absence of induction.

We identify art with being inspired. The artist is capable of expressing his or her self felicitously. This happens, not mechanically, but through some kind of an uncanny knack; the artist hits, in a single stroke, on the right answer to an artistic problem. But at the deepest levels, inductive reasoning follows a similar pattern. In Aristotelian *epagoge*, non-discursive

26 See *Nicomachean Ethics* (Ross, Urmson), bk 6, ch. 3, 1139b28; Aristotle claims that "the first principle[s] of what can be known cannot be an object … of art" (ibid., bk 6, ch. 6, 1140b33–35).

27 In the *Nicomachean Ethics*, Aristotle defines *techne* as the act of expert making. "[If] building is essentially a reasoned capacity to make … there is neither any art that is not such a state nor any such state which is not an art" (Ross, Urmson, bk 6, ch. 4, 1140a5–9). Again, "Making and acting being different, art must be a matter of making not acting" (ibid., bk 6, ch. 4, 1140a16). And again, "The reasoned state of capacity to act is different from the reasoned state of capacity to make. Nor are they included in one another, for neither is acting making nor is making acting. Now since building is an art and is essentially a reasoned capacity to make, and there is neither any art that is not such a state nor any state that is not such an art, art is identical with a state of capacity to make, involving a true course of reasoning … Making and acting being different, art must be a matter of making not acting" (ibid., bk 6, ch. 4, 1140a4–10). He points out that ethical wisdom is not a form of art, because it is directed toward the completion of (right) actions rather than producing artefacts. "Practical wisdom cannot be scientific knowledge nor art … not art because action and making are different kinds of things" (ibid., bk 4, ch. 4, 1140b2–3).

28 Geach, *Mental Acts*, 40.

29 The derivation comes through the Latin word *poiesis* (*Liddell and Scott's Greek-English Lexicon*, s.v. "ΠΟΙΈΩ").

reason produces the mental object. Induction begins in intuition, in direct insight. The reasoner does not argue his or her way to a conclusion but hits on the right answer to an epistemological problem through sheer intelligence. The inspirational side of art compares, then, with the first two levels of induction. If there is an element of creative discovery that unleashes the artistic impetus, this element of sudden disclosure is a conspicuous feature of inductive thought. It is not surprising that a later author such as Thomas should identify induction with angelic understanding.

Art is an evident manifestation of real creativity. It is not so much that an artwork has to distinguish itself from all others. It is that artists are able to create something more than what they started with. There is a leap across a gap to something more felicitous than before. The artist transforms human experience into a momentous physical object that captures something compelling and universal. Induction involves a similar leap, across a gap, to a concept or claim containing more than the reasoner started with. Where the artist expresses an artistic idea in a material medium, the inductive reasoner transforms particular human experience into something more general through the sensible medium of language. In exemplary cases, the resultant mode of expression captures and communicates something equally momentous and universal.

Art also has evident differences with induction. In the mainstream Western tradition, artists try to create works that are momentously unique. We have only one Sistine Chapel ceiling. Induction, in contrast, often produces universal ideas we all share. We tend to reason from the *same* basic concepts and first principles. But this is only to demonstrate that the same capacity for creativity can be turned to different ends. Art is specialized production directed to the end of aesthetic appreciation; inductive reason is about producing the common building blocks of human thought. Still, inductive reasoners are "artists" insomuch as they engage in a kind of expert *making*. They individually create the mental objects we all think with. As I intend to show, this requires a radical creativity we can usefully compare with artistic activity.

ARISTOTLE AND PERCEPTION

Aristotle's comments about mental life are scattered and obscure, but we can sketch out a basic model of human thought that may, at the very least, provide a general overview of his system. He distinguishes between three forms of mental representation: perception, imagination, and thought. In perception, the mind is aware of phantasms (sensible images) proceeding directly from the outside world. In imagination, the mind is aware of phantasms arising inside the mind independently of any immediate stimulus. And in thought, the mind, it would appear, uses language. Language is, however, composed of phantasms – ordered sequences of sensuous stimuli – sights or sounds or even textures that have a symbolic function conveying designated meanings.[30] The activity of thought involves actively manipulating these symbols.[31]

Because thought depends on the phantasms produced by sense perception, we need to begin any Aristotelian theory of mind by investigating what happens inside the mind when the organs of perception receive stimuli from the outside world. I shall not focus on the physiology of perception here. Clearly, Aristotle, who had an interest in biology, did not overlook the importance of the physical processes of perception. Perception begins in the physical organs. It is the mental side of perception, however, that concerns us here. As I will show, the intuitive intellectual capacity for human creativity that expresses itself both in inductive reasoning and in art functions at a more fundamental level in perception. The capacity for the creation of phantasms inside the mind is a prior condition for human thought. Knowledge depends on thought; thought, on perception; and perception, in a genuine sense, on a kind of creation from nothing.

Aristotle clearly distinguishes between actual perception and mere physical alteration.[32] In *De Anima*, he cites two examples of material change involving no conscious awareness. Although plants become hot or cold, they do not *perceive* hot or cold: they lack the requisite sensibility.[33] Again, although the air may be altered by the odorous, air does not "smell," for "smelling is an observing of the result produced."[34] The activity of

30 Aristotle writes, "The soul never thinks without an image" (*On the Soul* [Smith], bk 3, ch. 7, 431a17, in Aristotle, *Complete Works*).

31 *On the Soul* (Smith), bk 3, ch. 8, 431a17 (in Aristotle, *Complete Works*). Aristotle writes, "No one can learn or understand anything in the absence of sense, and when the mind is actively aware of anything it is necessarily aware of it along with an image" (*On the Soul* [Smith], bk 3, ch. 8, 432a7–9).

32 For materialist (or materialistic-like) interpretations, see Slakey, "Aristotle on Sense Perception"; P. Webb, "Bodily Structure"; Bynum, "A New Look"; Sorabji, "Body and Soul in Aristotle" and "Intentionality and Physiological Processes"; Everson, *Aristotle on Perception*, ch. 5, especially 203; and Hamlyn, *Aristotle's "De Anima,"* 104, 113. For anti-materialist interpretations, see Silverman, "Colour and Colour-Perception"; Modrak, *Aristotle*; and Ward, "Perception and Logos."

33 *On the Soul*, bk 2, ch. 12, 424a32–b3.

34 Ibid., bk 2, ch. 12, 424b15.

perception is like the activity of thinking, "for in one as well as the other the soul discriminates and is cognizant of something."[35]

Perception is a matterless transaction between observer and object. When we perceive a physical object, the matter remains outside, while the sensible form – the shape, colour, texture, etc. – enters into the soul. "The sense organ [receives] the sensible object without its matter."[36] Perception is, then, the transfer of sensible forms. The form of the object enters the mind without the matter. Aristotle quips, "It is not the stone which is present in the soul but its form[!]"[37] When the mind perceives a stone, it receives the appearances of the stone: the material mineral that is the stone is left outside, but the shape, size, colour, texture, etc., enter into the mind. We are left with an intellectual copy minus the original matter, as the copy takes up residence in the mind.

Aristotle compares the perceiving mind to a wax seal that takes on the shape of a ring without the metal.[38] He defines perception as an equivocal phenomenon.[39] Equivocal terms have more than one (related) meaning. Suppose someone is perceiving the colour red. There are in fact two kinds of the colour red: "red-in-the-mind" and "red-in-the-world." Redness-in-the-mind is an intellectual replica or copy of physical redness-in-the-world. The colour-in-the-mind and the colour-in-the-world are analogous but distinct phenomena. They are, in technical terms, "analogous equivocals."[40]

Aristotle uses the Greek mathematical concept of an extended ratio to explain the relationship obtaining between these colour terms. Euclid defines the ratio (or *logos*) of *A* to *B* (symbolically *A*:*B*) as "a sort of relation in respect of size between two magnitudes of the same kind."[41] A proportion or extended ratio is a four-term relationship between a pair of ratios (or *logoi*). As Fowler explains, it "is a condition that ... hold[s] between four objects. It may appear as a question: 'Are A, B, C and D proportional?' [Or again] 'Is A to B as C is to D?' or 'Is the ratio of A to B equal to the ratio of C to D'."[42] Aristotle uses the notion to explain the concept of analogy or likeness. He writes, "Analogy is possible whenever there are four terms so related that the second [B] is to the first [A] as the fourth [D] is to the

35 *On the Soul* (Smith), bk 3, ch. 2, 427a21–22.

36 Ibid., bk 3, ch. 2, 425b23–24.

37 Ibid., bk 3, ch. 8, 431b29–30.

38 *On the Soul*, bk 2, ch. 12, 424a18–23.

39 See Louis Groarke, "Looking at Aristotle."

40 Owens, *Doctrine of Being*, 111. See also *Categories*, ch. 1, 1a1–6.

41 Euclid, *Elements* (Heath), bk 5, def. 3.

42 Fowler, *Mathematics of Plato's Academy*, 16.

third [C]."[43] Elsewhere, he comments, "Likeness should be studied … the formulae being 'A:B::C:D' … and 'As A is in B, so is C in D'."[44] His account of perception is modeled on this kind of relation.

In describing the activity of perception, Aristotle writes that "sense is a ratio."[45] Colour is a ratio of light to dark; sound, of sharp to flat; texture, of warm to chilled, or dull to sharp;[46] odours and tastes, of sweet to bitter (saline).[47] Perception occurs when the mind, through the sense organ, receives the correct ratio from the object in the world. Consider the way we see colour.[48]

Setting aside Aristotle's antiquated knowledge of physics and physiology, transpose his original schema into a contemporary idiom. Colour can conceivably exist as (1) a physical state in the world; (2) a "disturbance in the transparent" (i.e., a photon); (3) a physiological state in the organ; or (4) a phenomenal feature (or conscious state) in the mind. We might say, for example, this apple is "red"; this photon is "red"; this brain state corresponds to "red"; or this phenomenal experience is "red." Assume, then, that red is characterized (to borrow Aristotle's terminology) by a ratio of three parts light (L) to two parts dark (D).[49] The colour "red" could, then, be instantiated in four different ways: (1) in the physical object (O) ($3L_O{:}2D_O$); (2) as a certain kind of wavelength (W) ($3L_W{:}2D_W$); (3) as a physiological state in the body (B) ($3L_B{:}2D_B$); and (4) finally, as a conscious event (C) ($3L_C{:}2D_C$). Each instantiation of red is characterized by the same ratio or *logos*. And so the perception of the colour red could be designated as a fourfold analogous equivocal:

$$3L_O{:}2D_O{::}3L_W{:}2D_W{::}3L_B{:}2D_B{::}3L_C{:}2D_C.$$

The perception of red is, then, the transmission of this specific ratio of light and dark from the object, through photons, to the body, to produce the phenomenal experience of red. This is the precise sense in which a colour term like "red" is an equivocal term. It refers simultaneously to four different things: an object in the world, a photon, a brain state, and an experience in the conscious mind. These four separate states are all red, for

43 *Poetics* (Bywater), ch. 22, 1457b16–18.
44 *Topics* (Pickard-Cambridge), bk 1, ch. 17, 108a6–12.
45 *On the Soul* (Smith), bk 3, ch. 2, 426b3.
46 Ibid., bk 3, ch. 2, 426a27–426b9.
47 *Sense and Sensibilia* (Beare), ch. 4, 442a13 ff.
48 For more details, see Louis Groarke, "Looking at Aristotle."
49 See *Sense and Sensibilia* (Beare), ch. 3, 439b20 ff.

they all embody the same ratio of light to dark. When we perceive the "red," this ratio is somehow transferred from the red object in the world to the conscious mind. The mind *sees* red. A similar analysis could be used to explain the perception of sounds, tastes, textures, and smells.

Aristotle uses the mathematical notion of proportion as an explanatory device allowing us to conceive of perception as an equivocal event. We might argue that the perception of colour is, in the final instance, a qualitative rather than a quantitative experience. But no ideological point is intended here. Aristotle uses arithmetical proportion to establish the equivalence of series of states. To say that the mind sees red is to say that two distinct phenomena, the "red-in-the-mind" and the "red-in-the-world," are in the relevant sense "identical." Aristotle expresses this identity-in-difference in terms of the relevant analogous equivocal.

We are interested here in the conscious aspects of perception. Modern authors in philosophy of mind largely overlook the phenomenological concerns of someone like Aristotle who wants to elaborate the features of conscious experience. What happens inside the mind when we perceive? What do we experience? What is the basic structure of the phantasm that enters the mind? Aristotle comes up with a vivid description and explanation of internal consciousness. He divides the mind, as is well known, into two separate components: the active and passive *nous*. The active mind is pure actuality; the passive is pure potentiality. The active rules over the passive mind. It is, so to speak, the ultimate source of all conscious understanding.[50] The active mind is constituted by the intelligent creativity that, in some sort, *makes* sense impressions. Unlike the passive intellect, the active is divine and immortal.[51]

Aristotle elaborates a precise explanation of the way the mind conjures up sensations and thoughts.[52] Consider, for example, visual perception. I see a tricycle, an old man, a cathedral, and so on. What happens inside the mind? How is it that it can have within itself all these different images? How can the mind, so to speak, turn itself into the image of a tricycle, an old man, a cathedral, and so on. The mind can, it seems, embody

50 *On the Soul* (Hett), bk 3, ch. 5, 430b10–18 (in Aristotle, *Aristotle in 23 Volumes*).

51 Aristotle writes, "When isolated [the active *nous*] is its true self and nothing more, and this alone is immortal or everlasting … and without this nothing thinks" (ibid., bk 3, ch. 5, 430b18–25).

52 It is little less than remarkable to see how these issues have been ignored by contemporary "philosophy of mind" and even psychology. Aristotle's mental literalism is perhaps an embarrassment for scientific reductionists and their allies.

or represent any kind of image, indeed, any kind of sensation. How could this be possible?

Aristotle uses the distinction between the active and passive mind to explain what is going on. The active mind is pure awareness. It is consciousness and nothing else. If, however, the act of being consciousness has no intrinsic colour or shape or taste or smell, how can an awareness of these kinds of things dwell inside the mind? Only, thinks Aristotle, if something foreign has a way of getting inside the mind. Aristotle points to the passive intellect as the locus of transmission.

The active has an actual nature, but the passive mind is pure potentiality. Left to itself, it is a *complete* absence of features; it is a blank slate, a void, entirely uncontaminated and separate from the body.[53] It has "no characteristic except its capacity to receive."[54] This is why we are left with no residue in the mind after perception or thought; the passive mind disappears when we are no longer perceiving or thinking, for without a borrowed form, the passive mind is an just this absence of features. It is an empty capacity to receive form and is by itself imperceptible.

Aristotle writes, "since everything is a possible object of thought," the passive mind "can have no nature of its own, other than having a certain capacity."[55] Because it has no fixed features of its own, this mind does not interfere with the content of perception. If, for example, the passive mind happened to be green, all our perceptions and thoughts, in passing into the mind through the passive mind, would have to be green. But mental images can be any colour. To become any colour whatsoever, the passive mind must lack all colour. It must be the absence of all formal features so that it takes on any form whatsoever.[56]

The role of the passive mind is essential to our ability to both perceive and imagine. Without the movie screen, we cannot see the movie. The passive mind is like a blank movie screen. It becomes the image projected onto it. In perception, the ratio constitutive of red-in-the-world is as if reflected inside ourselves on the blank screen of the passive mind. The passive mind, so to speak, becomes red. The form of red comes to dwell inside us. It is as if we had a lens (the sense organ, e.g., the eye, the brain) that gathers the red-in-the-world and deposits it in the mind so that we see red.

53 "For this reason it [the passive *nous*] cannot be regarded as being blended with the body; if so, it would … even have an organ like the sensitive faculty; as it is, it has none" (*On the Soul* [Smith], bk 3, ch. 4, 429a25–28).

54 *On the Soul* (Hett), bk 3, ch. 4, 17–28.

55 Ibid., bk 3, ch. 4, 429a18–23.

56 *On the Soul*, bk 3, ch. 4, 429a20.

Figure 8.1
Active and active/passive mind

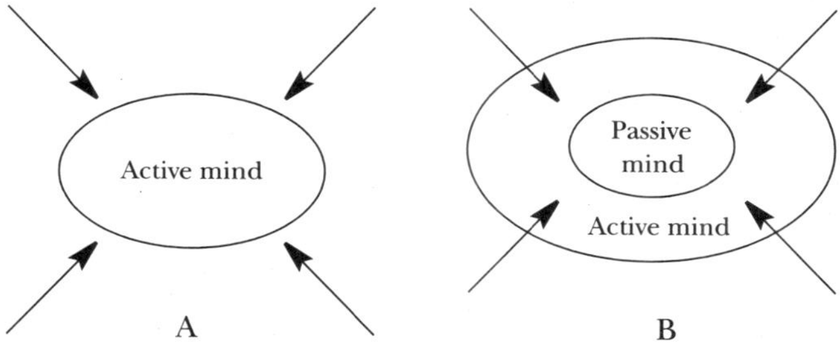

We might distinguish two possible models of consciousness, as in figure 8.1. Model A represents a mind composed of a single component: the active mind. Model B represents the mind composed of the active and passive minds. In model A, consciousness happens at the interface between the active mind and the outside world. In model B, it happens at the interface between the active and passive minds. Model A may, at first glance, appear to be an economical alternative, but any attempt to eliminate the passive mind is problematic.

To begin with, model B cannot account for the actual operation of consciousness. To produce an awareness of the outside world, the active mind would have to take on the nature of the outside world. But this is impossible. The active mind has a fixed nature; it is pure consciousness, pure actuality. It cannot become something other than what it is. We are left with the confrontation of one fixed nature with another. For us to perceive, something must be subject to change inside the mind. The mind has to have something to assume the forms of things in the outside world. This is the role of the passive mind. Eliminate the passive mind and perception is no longer possible. This is what perception is: it is aptly compared with a mirroring of formal aspects of the world inside the mind.

And we have a second problem. Model A leaves no room for imagination. In model A, consciousness occurs at the interface of the mind with the external world. Our sense organs mediate this interface. In imagination, however, we close our eyes; the sense organs shut down; and the mind has no access to the external world. But the forms of the outside world still exist inside our mind. How is this possible? Only through the presence of the passive mind.

Consider dreaming (technically, a form of imagination). I dream of a rose. My eyes are closed. There is no rose for miles around. Yet I see inside my mind a rose. Where does the rose exist? It cannot exist in my sense organs; my eyes are shut. If someone were to cut open my skull, they would discover no rose in the grey matter of my brain! Where, then, is the rose? It must exist somewhere. Aristotle offers an explanation for this astonishing phenomenon. The rose is, so to speak, inside the passive mind. It is the passive mind that receives the sensible form of the rose. The active mind projects the image of the rose onto the blank movie screen of the passive mind, and this accomplishes the awareness. This is how the image of a non-existent rose can be inside my consciousness. It is because, as in model B, the passive mind is there. Because the mind has a featureless, passive substrate, we can imagine a rose – or anything else conceivable.[57]

Aristotle adopts a "two-tier" account of the mind because it better explains our ability to perceive, imagine, and think. When we dream, think, and imagine, phantasms appear inside the mind. Aristotle's theory of the passive mind explains, so to speak, how they got there. On Aristotle's account, it is always the active mind doing the work of consciousness. But the passive mind plays an indispensable role in our perceiving, imagining, and thinking. The existence within the mind of a featureless potentiality capable of taking on the characteristics of anything, explains how we can see all sorts of images "inside our heads" when we dream, when we daydream, when we imagine, and even when we hallucinate.

ARISTOTLE AND THOUGHT

If Aristotle equates thought with the use of language, we can draw a parallel with the purely mental and overtly physical means of communication. We can use language publicly or privately. We can think "out loud" in physical acts of speaking or writing, or we can think inside our heads, using the sensible forms of language. When we speak out loud, we order sounds with our voice. Using the imagination, however, we can make the same sounds "inside our heads."[58] When we write in letters, we make visual signs. Using the imagination, however, we can make the same *signs* "inside our heads." How, then, does mental thought occur? Through the power of our imaginations, we can conjure up and order sounds, signs,

57 Dr Wilder Penfield, the famous Canadian brain surgeon, had a patient with seizures who, when her brain was activated at a particular point, uttered the phrase, "I smell burnt toast." The question *philosophical* remains, where do we locate the sensible form of this imagined smell?

58 Aristotle defines imagination as "that in virtue of which an image arises for us" (*On the Soul* [Smith], bk 3, ch. 3, 428a1).

textures into meaningful sequences. In this way, the mind can think without overt physical acts of speaking or writing.

Aristotle compares the passive mind to an empty writing tablet that lies inside the active-passive mind, waiting to be written on.[59] When we think, we, in effect, write words on this internal blackboard and erase or rearrange them at will. We tend to take our capacity for thought for granted. We tend to overlook how absolutely momentous it is. Mental thought requires a radical kind of creativity. The active mind, as the ultimate source of intelligent thought, must create something from nothing, on at least three distinct levels. This requires a kind of creation from nothing, first, in the mental representation of a phantasm; second, in the imagination; and third, in knowledge. Consider these mental processes in turn.

Mental representation is the mechanism through which the active bestows a sensible form on the passive mind. It is the *modus operandi* of perceiving and imagining. Consider imagination. How does this occur? When we conjure up a mental representation, the mind seems to call a form out of nothingness. Nothing is in the mind, and suddenly something is there. We accomplish this by a mere act of will. The phantasm simply appears, as if commanded into existence. When I think of a rose, the passive mind in its formlessness suddenly takes on the form of a rose. When I stop thinking of the rose, the image disappears.

Aristotle calls the active mind "νοῦς ποιητικός" (*nous poietikos*), which means, literally, "the thinking principle that makes." The active mind *makes* something; it makes phantasms. It makes them out of the passive mind. To use an apt metaphor, the active mind is the artist; the passive, is the clay. The active mind shapes the clay inside itself into a likeness of something in the world. This is how the mind brings the sensible form of something from the outside world into itself.

On Aristotle's account, mental representation is not the creation of something physical. No "thing," no substance, is created. The movement is not metaphysical either. It is purely intellectual. Aristotle writes that the images in the mind "are like sensuous contents except in that they contain no matter."[60] In mental representation, a purely intellectual form, a phantasm fills our consciousness. Something with colour, shape, sound, smell, taste

59 "Mind is in a sense potentially whatever is thinkable, though actually it is nothing until it has thought? What it thinks must be in it just as characters may be said to be on a writing-tablet on which as yet nothing actually stands written: this is exactly what happens with mind" (ibid., bk 3, ch. 4, 430a1).

60 Ibid., bk 3, ch 8, 432a7–9.

(etc.), suddenly materializes out of nothing (and then disappears again). This is a purely phenomenal event.

To compare the activity of the active mind in mental representation to that of an artist shaping the clay of the passive mind is to describe, however, a radical form of creativity. The artist models a material medium; he or she rearranges its form. In mental representation, the active mind brings something out of nothing. Aristotle writes, "[the passive intellect] is nothing until it has thought."[61] The passive mind is pure potentiality. Without the borrowed form imposed on it by the active mind, it has no features. It is, so to speak, a featureless void. This is the sense in which mental representation is literally a kind of creation from nothing. In this mental transformation, the thinker conjures up a sensible form from the nothingness of the passive mind. Out of the mental void, a form appears. The absence of features suddenly becomes something else. Our familiarity with these mental processes obscures how remarkable it is. (The artist working in clay converts one actuality into another. The active mind, on the contrary, converts something that has no actuality into something that has the purely mental actuality of a sensible form – a far more momentous feat.)

The second way thought involves creation from nothing concerns the power of imagination. Perception proceeds from the outside world through the sense organs. When I *dream* of a rose, nothing in the outside world imposes the image on my mind. Instead of a form-in-the-world creating a form-in-the-mind, we have a form-in-the-mind arising by itself in the absence of any external stimulus. That is, we have a self-creation of the mind, literally arising out of nothing. Instead of a rose in the world producing a phantasm of one in the mind, we have a phantasm of a rose arising out of an absence of a rose in the external world.

Presumably, I can only imagine a rose because I have seen roses in my previous awareness. The phantasm in my mind depends, then, on the operation of memory. But we cannot see into the past in any literal sense. The past no longer exists. There is no longer anything to see. When we remember an image, a sound, a smell, we re-create the sensible form, *without the original stimulus.* The form does not come into the mind through the agency of the sense organs – not transmitted from something "out there." It is a re-creation of what no longer exits, and thus, it is a construction of the phantasm from nothing. When the active mind conjures up a memory, it brings a *non-existent* thing back into existence without the assistance of the outside world.

61 Ibid., bk 3, ch. 4, 429a32.

When we perceive, an external stimulus somehow stamps the sensible form on the mind. When we imagine, the active mind generates the sensible form through its own devices. In perception, it is as if the mirror in the mind reflects back the image of whatever is placed in front it. In imagination, it is as if the mirror reflects back an image of something not there. It is as if the mirror develops a capacity for producing images of things no longer present – adopting the precise form of the reflection in the absence of the "reflectee." This is why dreaming is so astounding. Or, consider the ability of the mind to hallucinate. The schizophrenic who hallucinates, literally "sees" what is not there. The mind produces a phantasm so distinct that the sufferer mistakes it for reality. Imagining is like perceiving, except that the imagined phantasm is a creation from nothing.

The third way thought involves a creation from nothing has to do with the achievement of knowledge. Language makes knowledge possible. Language is made up of symbols conveying meaning. This meaning has to come from somewhere. It comes, for Aristotle, from the mind. The mind adds the conceptual content to particular sensible forms. This is the fundamental role of induction in Aristotle's philosophy of mind. Using the intermediary of language, inductive reasoning devises concepts and definitions, rules of syntax and logical order, and ultimately propositions and arguments. When it comes to arguments, inductive inference comes first; deductive, second. Inductive reasoning gives us universal knowledge; deductive reasoning uses that universal knowledge to produce science.

Aristotle views the cognitive process of induction as a bridge between sense perception and language. Its role is, first and foremost, creative. It opens up a new possibility, one of the indefinite extension of understanding. Interpretations of Aristotle's inductive reasoning as mechanical miss the point. Aristotle is a champion of creativity. In Plato, knowledge has gone to sleep in the soul, and we only need to reawaken it. In Aristotle's model, this is never an option. Because the passive intellect is destroyed at death, recollection is impossible.[62] The mind has to create knowledge anew through induction. This process begins with sense perception. It involves the abstraction of concepts, definitions, universal propositions, and the most basic principles. This typically necessitates a movement from less to more. We leap from limited experience to universal concepts; we leap from universal concepts to properly formulated definitions, to universal propositions, to valid arguments. Each step in this process adds something more to what went before. What results cannot be fully explained or accounted for in anything but a radical, intelligent creativity.

62 *On the Soul*, bk 3, ch. 5, 430a25.

As already explained, induction is a creation from nothing in the sense that something is inexplicably added along the way. The mind creates knowledge by taking what it has (sense perception) and reorganizing it to produce something greater. Creativity rankles. Positivists and rationalists cling fast to the idea of a complete theory of everything. These modern champions of mechanism think that explaining rationality means accounting in full for every increase in knowledge. They want to fill up all the gaps, to reduce what looks like a leap to a mere routine of enumerating – hence their befuddlement and their dismay at the seemingly intractable problem of induction. This seems to be accounting gone astray. This seems to warrant an inescapable scepticism, hence the inevitable collapse of modernism into radical postmodernism.

Post-Cartesian scepticism, in undermining confidence in human intelligence, doubts the possibility of creative intelligence. An earlier author such as Aristotle locates reason in creativity. Reason is not, strictly speaking, a mechanism. The maieutic metaphor is not to be taken lightly. The mind is fertile. It gives birth. For whatever reason (or for no reason at all), we possess an active sense of discernment to enable us to pull more out of less. We can create meaning from nothing, induce universal conclusions, understand the world morally, and so on. We can do all these things because we have intelligence. But we cannot explain intelligence. That is the end of the line. We have nothing more to say, once we travel backward in our theories to the active mind that, as Aristotle insisted, is the beginning of everything.

MICHELANGELO'S TWOFOLD THEORY OF ARTISTIC CREATION

Induction is only a more specialized manifestation of the power of radical human creativity designated by the general term intelligence. As we have already mentioned, in chapter 3, the Greek verb "to induce" (ἐπάγω or *epago*) means "to bring upon, to set on, urge on, as hunters do dogs, to lead on an army … to lead on by persuasion [or] influence; to bring in, invite … to bring forward, propose a measure;"[63] or again, "to lead, bring … drive … impel, cause, instigate."[64] The constant theme here is a sense of movement, of picking up speed or momentum, of pulling, pushing or drawing forward along some natural path to an inevitable climax. The activity of induction drives, impels, instigates, unleashes, causes, precipitates the moment of intellectual realization. This movement of understanding

63 *Liddell and Scott's Greek-English Lexicon*, s.v. "ἐπάγω."

64 *Langenscheidt's Greek-English Dictionary*, s.v. "ἐπάγω."

could also be said to inspire. When we think of being inspired, we naturally think of art. Consider, then, a theory of visual art that comes close to presenting it as a form of inductive reasoning.

Renaissance sculptor Michelangelo Buonarroti (1475–1564) devises a description of artistic creation that provides a remarkable parallel to Aristotle's account of induction. I will focus on the basic philosophical content of Michelangelo's theory rather than its historical origins. Still, we may well wonder how Aristotle's theory of induction could have influenced a sculptor such as Michelangelo.[65] But one can trace a line of influence through Albert the Great, Thomas Aquinas, and the late Middle Ages. Ian Maclean, in a paper criticizing Michel Foucault's characterization of the Renaissance as a Platonic age, affirms that "Aristotelianism, not Platonism [was] the dominant universe of discourse of the day."[66] Again, Paul Oscar Kristeller confirms that "the tradition of Aristotelianism continued to be very strong throughout the Renaissance period, and in some ways, it even increased rather than declined."[67] As Nicholas Jardine explains, "There was a fair amount of discussion of the various types of *inductio* [ἐπαγωγή] that figure in Aristotle, discussion that generally distinguished sharply between the 'demonstrative' induction which leads from sense-perception to universals and other forms of induction, including induction by enumeration."[68]

Whatever the precise providence of Michelangelo's ideas, what is important for our purposes is his understanding of artistic creativity. On this Renaissance account, true art is more of an intellectual than a physical activity. Michelangelo, who (along with his Italian colleagues) views sculpture as the creation of idealized human forms in stone, thinks of art as a two-step process. The inspired artist possesses a kind of x-ray vision, first, seeing, in a flash, a human figure hidden inside the rough marble block, second, working with the chisel to liberate the hidden figure. "The less the stone remains, the more [the image] grows."[69] What matters is the initial act of seeing, the intellectual leap of creative discernment that initiates the process. The activity of carving only serves to expose and display the original idea. The finished art object possesses only as much (or as little) artistic worth as the idea that inspired the process.

65 Thanks to Renaissance historian Richard Raisewell for helpful comments in this respect.

66 Maclean, "Foucault's Renaissance Episteme," 149.

67 Kristeller, *Renaissance Thought*, 24.

68 Jardine, "Epistemology of the Sciences," 703.

69 Michelangelo, *Complete Poems* (Tusiani), Sonnet 84.

Michelangelo uses two key concepts in his comments on art. First, he uses the term *intelletto*, the Italian word for "intellect or understanding," to refer to the faculty of inspiration needed to "see" the hidden figure lurking in the marble. Second, he uses the term *concetto*, the Italian for "concept or idea," to refer to the three-dimensional image the artist "liberates" from the stone. Consider first, Michelangelo's account of *intelletto* and second, his account of *concetto*.

Intelletto

Renaissance architect and theorist Leon Battista Alberti explains how sculptors remove "that which is superfluous ... making a form appear in the marble, as a man's figure which was hidden there from the first and *in potenza*."[70] In one of his sonnets, Michelangelo writes, "There exist in marbles rich and base images, insofar as our genius can *draw them out*."[71] And again, "one already sees, in the hard marble of the North, the living figure one has to bring forth."[72]

On this Renaissance account, the artist sees the hidden human form in the marble *via* a leap of creative intelligence or *intelletto*. *Intelletto* is not the imagination; it not brainstorming; it is not trial and error. *Intelletto* is a flash of insight. Art begins, then, in a momentous act of intelligent understanding. By a kind of inspired vision, the artist is able to penetrate the rough exterior of the raw block and extract an image. While it is true the physical work of the chisel reveals what lay beneath, it is the power of artistic genius or *intelletto* that lay bare the artistic possibility. "Only the hand which obeys *intelletto*" can produce real art.[73]

Michelangelo, perhaps unwittingly, borrows a standard medieval account of *intellectus* or understanding and applies it to art. Thomas Aquinas describes *intellectus* as a kind of x-ray vision, a rational power to penetrate, to see inside the nature of things. He traces the etymology of the word to the Latin verb *intelligere*, – to understand – which derives, he suggests, from *intus*

70 Cited in Clements, *Michelangelo's Theory of Art*, 22 (from *Della Pittura e della Statua*).

71 Cited in Clements, *Michelangelo's Theory of Art*, 17 (Sonnet 65 [Clements]) (my italics).

72 Michelangelo, *Complete Poems* (Tusiani), Sonnet 84. This recalls Leonardo's advice to the apprentice painter looking for a way to begin a new composition, that one can see horses and battles in ink spots and stains.

73 Clements, *Michelangelo's Theory of Art*, 16 (Sonnet 83 [Clements]).

legere, meaning "to read inwardly."[74] But we can go even further back. As Robert Clements explains, "in the deliberations of the Italian humanists," the Greek word *nous* (νοῦς) "became universally *intellectus* or *intelletto*."[75] This, then, is the source of Michelangelo's explanation of artistic genius. The power of non-discursive understanding – what Aristotle calls *nous* (or *noesis*) and Thomas, *intellectus* (or *intelligentia*) – is what produces great art. But this is also the same mental faculty that makes induction possible.

In Aristotle, *nous* – in Thomas, *intellectus* – is the engine of inductive reasoning. In Michelangelo, *intelletto* is the engine of art. This is no coincidence. Thomas writes,

> [perception] is concerned with external sensible qualities, whereas intellective knowledge penetrates into the very essence of a thing, because the object of the intellect is "what a thing is" ... Now there are many kinds of things that are hidden within, to find which human knowledge has to penetrate within so to speak. Thus, under the accidents lies hidden the nature of the substantial reality, under words lies hidden their meaning; under likenesses and figures the truth they denote lies hidden (because the intelligible world is enclosed within as compared with the sensible world, which is perceived externally), and effects lie hidden in their causes, and vice versa. Hence we may speak of understanding with regard to all these things. Since, however, human knowledge begins with the outside of things as it were, it is evident that the stronger the light of the understanding, the further it can penetrate into the heart of things. Now the natural light of our understanding is of finite power; wherefore it can reach to a certain fixed point. Consequently man needs a supernatural light in order to penetrate further still so as to know what it cannot know by its natural light: and this supernatural light which is bestowed on man is called the gift of understanding.[76]

This God-given ability to see inside things, to view the reality underneath the surface appearances is precisely the mental faculty Michelangelo identifies with artistic inspiration. It is as if we only need to add an addendum to Thomas' text: that underneath the surfaces of stones great works of art lie hidden and that we need a supernatural light of understanding (which Michelangelo associates with artistic genius) to see them.

74 Thomas Aquinas, *Summa Theologica* (English Dominican Province), pt 2 of pt 2, Q. 8, art. 1, "Whether Understanding Is a Gift of the Holy Ghost?"

75 Clements, *Michelangelo's Theory of Art*, 15.

76 Thomas Aquinas, *Summa Theologica* (English Dominican Province), pt 2 of pt 2, Q. 8, art. 1.

To Michelangelo, art is a product of intelligence, not craft. "This is not achieved by skill."[77] Art springs from a creative power of understanding. In a flash of insight, artistic genius penetrates the exterior shape of the marble block and reads the figure hidden inside the marble. The sculptor hits on the image in a stroke of inspiration, in a fit of mental discovery. There is no method, only a manner of seeing.

Perhaps it is not so surprising, then, that someone like Michelangelo would identify art with the cognitive process of induction. He was part of a larger artistic movement with others who conceived of art as a kind of natural science.[78] Giorgio Vasari tells the well-known story of how the artistic talents of Giotto, the progenitor of the new naturalism, were first discovered when he was found without any artistic training, as a young shepherd drawing sheep with a rock made of chalk in a field. This was the artist as "wolf-boy," as "bon sauvage," taught only by Nature herself. Vasari claims, "Apart from Nature he had no other teacher."[79] As Frederick Hartt comments, "the virtue of Giotto's style for his contemporaries and successors lay in its fidelity to the human, natural, Italian world they knew, as against the artificial, [Byzantine] manner imported from Greece."[80]

Michelangelo and others like him in this era rejected the "Neoplatonism" of Byzantine art and embraced instead an "Aristotelian" realism.[81] Vasari relates that Michelangelo "very often used to flay dead bodies to

77 Michelangelo, *Complete Poems* (Tusiani), Sonnet 134.

78 See Louis Groarke, "Art of History."

79 Vasari, *Lives* (Hinds), vol 1, 66.

80 Hartt, *History of Italian Renaissance Art,* 51.

81 Renaissance artists display, at times, an unflinching realism, aptly expressed in Domenico del Ghirlandio's portrait of the old gentleman with the diseased nose, in (Tommaso) Masaccio's earthy treatment of the Expulsion of Adam and Eve, and in Pisanello's grisly but realistic sketches of the dangling corpses of hanged men. This penchant for realism also surfaces in the new craze for scientific systems of perspective (an invention attributed to Filippo Brunelleschi) (see Field, Lunard, and Settle, "Perspective Scheme"). Alberti produced the most famous treatise on perspective (*Della Pittura*), but Piero della Francesca produced his own private manuscript (*De Prospectiva Pingnedi*). And examples of the laborious, elaborate application of scientific systems of perspective proliferate as the Renaissance advances. Paolo Uccello meticulously plots out the three-dimensional shape of a chalice; such diverse artists as Andrea Mantegna and Michelangelo delight in the rendering of foreshortened figures, as in Michelangelo's own Sistine Chapel figures; and even sculptors such as Lorenzo Ghiberti and Donatello incorporate the new optical discoveries into their reliefs.

discover the secrets of anatomy."[82] Leonardo da Vinci tells the apprentice painter that he must collect specimens in the field, bring them back to his studio and practice drawing them from life. The student is not to "take the [art]works of others as his standard," but "apply himself to learn from the objects of nature."[83] This is not to claim, of course, that Renaissance artists believed that careful observation is all there is to art. We need observation, but observation triggers inspiration. Without inspiration, there is no true art. Michelangelo writes, "After the divine part [*intelletto*] has well conceived / Man's face and gesture, soon both mind and hand / Give life to stone, but this is not achieved / By skill. In painting too ... / Only after the intellect [*intelletto*] has planned, / ... can the ready hand / Take up the brush and try all things received."[84]

What happens in sculpture is not very different from inductive inference. On the traditional account of latter, the reasoner begins with close observation. Observation then triggers, in a stroke of understanding, universal knowledge. On Michelangelo's account of sculpture, art begins in observation. Observation then triggers, in a stroke of inspiration, the artistic idea. This leap of *intelletto* brings the artist to another level. As we shall see, it produces a visual image that is more universal than the depicted things themselves. The successful artistic image functions as an archetype;

82 Vasari, *Lives* (Bull), pt 3, vol. 1, 333. Leonardo, who frequently engaged the secretive practice of dissection, created a system of anatomical illustration based on real-life observation, fourfold vantage points, cross-sectional representations, and the addition of explanatory notes. See the drawings, *Male Nude* (1503–7), *Studies of a Left Leg* (1508), in Hartt, *History of Italian Renaissance Art*, 391, or *Embryo in the Womb* (1510), in Janson, *History of Art*, 352. Note that the dissection of cadavers was a common practice. Renaissance artwork is often a visual exhibition of this kind of intimate anatomical knowledge. We can point to many examples such as Antonio del Pollaiuolo's (strangely static) engraving *Battle of the Ten Nudes*; his small but remarkably effective bronze statue of *Hercules and Antaeus*, and Luca Signorelli's crowded, turbulent frescos, *The Resurrection of the Dead* and *The Damned Consigned to Hell.* Michelangelo's own work displays a similar versimilutude, as in his youthful relief depicting the battle between the Lapiths and Centaurs, his cartoon of the projected fresco *The Battle of Cascina*, and, of course, his Sistine Chapel frescos.

83 Leonardo da Vinci, *Notebooks*, 164. Leonardo exhorts his colleagues, "Look to it, O painter, that when you go into the fields you give your attention to the various objects and look carefully in turn first at one thing and then at another, making a bundle of things selected" (ibid., 163).

84 Michelangelo, *Complete Poems* (Tusiani), Sonnet 134.

it synthesizes and brings together, in a single visual reference, an entire class of objects or experiences.[85]

Concetto

Turn now to Michelangelo's account of the idea or the *concetto* (concept) the sculptor discovers in the stone. Renaissance artists thought of their nude figures as universal types, representations of the ideal human form, of which our own physical bodies are inevitably defective copies.[86] Artists seized on the opportunity presented by religious iconography for expounding and putting into practice theories about human proportion, physiognomy, and anatomy.

Leonardo captures this general Renaissance attitude when he claims that painting is more *universal* than literature. What does the painter do? Like the inductive reasoner, he or she produces universal forms. Leonardo asks a rhetorical question, "Consider, then, which is more fundamental to man, the name of man or his image? The name changes with change of country; the form is unchanged except by death ... Since painting embraces within itself all the forms of nature, [the artist has] omitted [nothing] except the names, and these are not universal like the forms."[87] The Renaissance nude is not merely a representation of this or that individual model; it is the universal type: "humanity." Art, then, produces in pictorial terms a *universal* concept.

Seen from this Renaissance perspective, the artist does not simply depict human beings, battle scenes, horses, crucifixions, distant mountains, and so on. The artist expresses the idea of a human being, the idea of a battle, the idea of a horse, and so on. Leonardo explains how one should paint a storm:

85 In fact, other factors are at work, but we will not explore them here.

86 The examples of sculpture and painting are endless. Consider del Pollaiuolo's *St Sebastian* (1475) (in Hartt, *History of Italian Renaissance Art*, 265) (colour illustration [col. illus.]); Antonello da Messina's version of *St Sebastian* (c. 1475) (p. 367) (black-and-white illustration [b/w illus.]); Donatello's *Crucifix for S. Antonio* (c. 1444–47) (p. 204) (b/w illus.); Andrea del Castagno's *Crucifixion with Four Saints* (c. 1445) (p. 221) (b/w illus.); Masaccio's *Crucifixion* (1426) (p. 153) (col. illus.); Michelangelo's wooden Crucifix (1492–93) (p. 616) (b/w illus.) and *David* (1501–04) (p. 420) (b/w illus.) (also in Goldscheider, *Michelangelo*, xix–xxv [b/w illus.]); Donatello's *David* (c. 1430s), in Hartt, *History of Italian Renaissance Art*, 202 (b/w illus.); and Andrea Mantegna's *St Sebastian* (1455–60), in Janson, *History of Art*, 315.

87 Leonardo da Vinci, *Notebooks*, 157.

> The trees and shrubs should be bent to the ground, as though showing their desire to follow the direction of the wind, with their branches twisted out of their natural growth and their leaves tossed and inverted. Of the men who are there, some should have fallen and be lying wrapped round by their garments and almost indistinguishable on account of the dust, and those who are left standing should be behind some tree with their arms thrown around it to prevent the wind from dragging them away; others should be shown crouching on the ground, their hands over their eyes because of the dust, their garments and hair streaming in the wind.[88]

A painting of a storm is not a snapshot of one particular storm but depicts the essence of a storm; it is a visual image of what an "ideal" storm would be like. But the exercise in representing the universal does not end there.

Renaissance artists also try to express some universal aspects of the human condition. Leonardo explains how one should represent an angry figure: "An angry figure should be represented seizing someone by the hair and twisting his head down to the ground, with one knee on his ribs, and with right arm and fist raised high up; let him have his hair disheveled, his eyebrows low and knit together, his teeth clenched, the two corners of his mouth arched, and the neck which is all swollen and extended as he bends over the foe, should be full of furrows."

Again, Leonardo explains the painter's best way of depicting someone in despair: "A man who is in despair you should make turning his knife against himself, and rending his garments with his hands, and one of his hands should be in the act of tearing open his wound. Make him with feet apart, his legs somewhat bent, and the whole body likewise bending to the ground, and with his hair torn and streaming."[89]

The suggested depictions are intended as the universal archetypes of specific emotions. They describe, in the most pronounced way possible, the emotions they represent. This is the *idea* of anger, the *idea* of despair. Renaissance art is, then, more than the mere representation of physical things. In a fit of inspiration, artists hit on concepts to capture the underlying reality of an entire class of events or things. Like the inductive reasoner, artists pull out of the ordinary experience a perceptible token to capture and put on display a universal reality.

The inductive reasoner *creates* the first principles of thought in an intuitive leap. The Renaissance artist creates a universal image, one operating

88 Ibid., 196.

89 Ibid., 891.

on many different levels. What Michelangelo calls the "concept" in the stone may be intended as a universal, an archetype, the definition of an emotion, a symbol, a comment on human nature, a solution to a theological problem. Michelangelo conceives of art, not as a product of the imagination, but of the understanding. Art tells the truth about something. Sculpture is language. It imparts a meaning that we can and must read into the visual image.

Michelangelo's statutes serve an explicit symbolical function. Consider an incident surrounding the famous *Pietà* in St Peter's Basilica.[90] Contemporary observers wondered why Michelangelo had depicted such a youthful Mary. Vasari, basing his view on a quip by the artist, explains that the Virgin Mary retained the bloom of youth into old age because she escaped the servitude of physical lust. Vasari complains, "There are some critics … who say that he made Our Lady look too young. They fail to see that those who keep their virginity unspotted stay for a long time fresh and youthful."[91]

Contemporary scholar Hartt proposes a different interpretation. He points out that Michelangelo's friend Giovanni Strozzi composed a poem for a copy of the statue based on Dante's line, "Virgin Mother, Daughter of thy Son." Hartt comments, "Michelangelo represented not an incident but a timeless doctrine. The Virgin is shown according to the Catholic belief, as the mortal vessel of Divine Grace, the body through which divinity took on man's flesh. The question of age is thus irrelevant. Any attempt to translate a painting or sculpture by Michelangelo in terms of literal reality arrives at absurdity, because throughout his life the artist was interested in the inner meaning conveyed by his works, not in the literal illustration of anecdotes."[92]

Michelangelo intends his *Pietà* as an expression of a timeless theological idea, that a mother could be the daughter of her son. As such, the image is intended as the affirmation of a theological doctrine, not as a mere picture. It does not matter if the real individual Mary was much older than depicted at the actual physical event of the crucifixion. It is not the literal but the symbolic content which has priority. This is what determines the final design of the work.

We need not enter into any detailed exegesis of individual works here. The point is that Michelangelo sees art as the creation of symbols with meanings. His twin statues *The Dying Slave* and *The Rebellious Slave* depict

90 Michelangelo's *Pietà*, in Hartt, *History of Italian Renaissance Art*, 202 (b/w illus.) (also in Goldscheider, *Michelangelo*, xiii–xviii [b/w illus.]).

91 Vasari, *Lives* (Bull), vol. 1, 337.

92 Hartt, *History of Italian Renaissance Art*, 417.

heroic, muscular figures bearing all the signs of interior struggle. What do these figures represent? What is their meaning? According to Hartt, "the prisoners ... twisting and writhing in their bonds, are held by sin."[93] Sin is the universal human condition. These conflicted figures are physical metaphors of enslavement to sin. This is the essence of the human predicament. The sculptor, who first discerns these figures hidden in the marble, sees more than an image. The artist hits on a concept that illustrates and communicates the universal human condition.

As Clements explains, "In Michelangelo's theory, the intellect-principle [i.e., *intelletto*] which enabled the artist to create great works also enabled the spectator to appreciate them."[94] Michelangelo believes that the informed spectator who views an artwork will experience the same flash of understanding that produced the artwork in the first place. We have here a kind of communication between artist and spectator. The artist hits on an image that allows the spectator to experience the same stroke of inspiration. What begins as a private experience is turned into a public understanding. Art serves a language-like function. It communicates conceptual content.

Compare Michelangelo's account of artistic inspiration with Aristotle's understanding of induction. In both cases, we have a movement that begins in observation and ends in a universal idea. In both cases, an intuitive act of understanding makes an idea, a concept, that encloses some sort of universal meaning. But the analogy can be pushed even further. Michelangelo claims that the sculptor arrives at an idea that God had previously placed in the marble block. As Clements explains, "[these] art-forms ... existed before the artist and will survive him."[95] The sculptor does not superimpose an idea on the stone. He discovers, through *intellectus*, something that is already there, hidden under the surface appearances. Aristotelian induction operates according to a similar principle. We do not impose concepts on the world. We extract them out of ordinary experience. The mind of the inductive reasoner does not create concepts in any arbitrary or artificial way. Creation here means seeing, unearthing, what is actually out there, bringing into full view what is already hiding underneath empirical appearances. It is the discovery of ideas existing prior to the knower's awareness of them, but going unnoticed until someone comes along with the power of acknowledging what is already there.

93 Ibid., 459 (originally intended for Pope Julius II's tomb). See also *Dying Slave* and *Rebellious Slave* (both before 1513), in ibid. (b/w illus.) (also Goldscheider, *Michelangelo*, cil–cliv [b/w illus. plates]).

94 Clements, *Michelangelo's Theory of Art*, 19. See Sonnets 109, 68.

95 Ibid., 21.

Implicit in Michelangelo's thought is a distinction between art-as-manual-craft and art-as-inspiration. Art-as-craft would be an expression of manual dexterity without inspiration. Nothing would be added on; there would be no creative leap of understanding. Michelangelo presents art as an induction-like process. The artist *makes* something, a sculpture, a painting, a poem; the inductive reasoner *makes* something, a concept, a definition, a universal principle. The artist and the inductive reasoner both begin by observing. Both use some kind of sensible medium. In both cases, we see a widening of meaning; an artist or scientist moves from something particular to something universal. And most importantly, in both cases, the product issues from a moment of mental illumination, of grasping something in a single stroke through non-discursive reasoning.

Art is not science. Science is not quite art. Still, science begins in creativity. It begins in something akin to art. The inductive reasoner, like Michelangelo's artist, pulls the necessary concepts, principles, and universal claims out of the world, to make explanation possible. To draw an analogy, nature is the rough-hewn block of marble. Through some inspired vision, the student of nature, the scientist, the physicist, the metaphysician (etc.) catches a glimpse of what is already hidden underneath the marble block's rough surfaces. The story of science is a story of creative discovery. Induction is the scientific counterpart of artistic inspiration.

THE SCANDAL OF CREATIVITY

Modern philosophers, harassed by a fashionable Cartesian scepticism, embrace deductive argument as the hallmark of rationality. Aristotle, by contrast, believed that knowledge begins in the creative power of inductive inference. Creativity of this precise sort is not irrational; it is the highest pinnacle of rationality. Art historian H.W. Janson writes, "The concept of genius as divine inspiration, as a superhuman power granted to a few rare individuals and acting through them, is nowhere exemplified more fully than in the life and work of Michelangelo. Not only his admirers viewed him in this light; [but] he himself … accepted the idea of his genius as a living reality."[96] Although we naturally associate artistic genius with a towering figure like Michelangelo, the Aristotelian account of inductive reason is more democratic. We all possess, on some deep level, a capacity for radical creativity. We are all, so to speak, artists. We all create first principles the way Michelangelo's sculptor creates a statue – through a moment of illumination or inspiration. We could not even begin to think unless we

96 Janson, *History of Art*, 357.

could formulate first concepts. This is what it means, on Aristotle's account, to be a human being, a "rational animal."

Rationality begins in induction. Induction is a form of creativity. We can distinguish between two understandings of creativity: "free creativity" and "representational creativity." Free creativity is nothing more and nothing less than self-expression. It means doing whatever one feels like doing, whatever one *wants* to do. The nature of the created thing is the reified will of the agent. The criterion of success is his or her disposition. In representational creativity, the criterion of success is outside the agent. There is an objective measure of creative efficiency. The nature of the created thing is intended to convey something true about the object of such representation.

In one isolated passage, Michelangelo does invoke a concept of free creativity. Describing his own artistic vocation, he ventures so far as to claim, "[I work] in stone or on candid paper. Which has naught within, and now has what I wish."[97] Clements observes that Michelangelo, a pious Christian, could only have expressed such uncharacteristic sentiments "in an exalted moment when feeling like God himself."[98] This is artistic creation as *creatio ex nihilo*. But this creation from nothing is, in a Christian context, reserved for God. Hence Michelangelo's more habitual description of art as representational creativity.

As Clements explains, Michelangelo endorses a representational account of aesthetics. He consistently conceives of artistic inspiration as a power to penetrate and to describe, rather than to impose one's will on something else. While human understanding (*intelletto*) is the divine part (*la diuina parte*) of human nature, it is not a power of will but of discernment. The artist peers inside things to discover their true nature – to see as God sees. The art object is the embodiment of this intellectual vision.

We tend to associate creativity and subjectivity. (Contemporary art, in its worst examples, sufficiently illustrates this tendency.) In Michelangelo's system, art is not "subjective." Artists do not project an image onto the stone. They recover objective ideas God has already embedded in the world. They extract out a universal form that is already there.

97 Cited in Clements, *Michelangelo's Theory of Art*, 63, Sonnet 107.

98 Ibid. Saslow translates the same verse, "[I work] on a blank sheet or in stone/ That has nothing within, and then what I want is there" (in Michelangelo, *Poetry of Michelangelo*, Sonnet 111 [Saslow]). Taken literally, such sentiments would have been, from Michelangelo's devout outlook, blasphemous. Cf. "The Creator, who from nothingness could make all Time and every creature in the void" ("Cholui che fece, e non di cosa alcuna," in Michelangelo, *Michelangelo* [Porter, Bull], Sonnet 151, Girardi no. 104).

Representational creativity is description. Good description is the product of a creative process. But it also provides an accurate reading of the world. Michelangelo's sculptor penetrates the nature of things and seizes on archetypes to accurately express and explain whole classes of phenomena. Aristotle's inductive reasoner does likewise. Induction extracts ideas out of reality that are already there. But these abstract ideas accurately reflect the world. The fact that they arise in an act of radical creativity does not negate their epistemological authority.

On Aristotle's account, induction is not logical proof; it is the discovery of a true, universal idea. First principles are necessary; they are forced on us by the world; but they are, just the same, human creations. Induction is not an exercise in free creativity, but in representational creativity. On Aristotle's account, first principles are not, as some contemporary authors would suggest, merely a reflection of one's self. The movement is not from inside the self into the created object, but from the world, to the self, to the created object. Induction is a power of making that also supplies an accurate account of something. The reasoner looks at the world and, like Michelangelo's sculptor, pulls out of particular experience concepts and principles that have universal significance.

Michelangelo's theory of art insists on the need for artistic genius. Induction, like art, depends on genius. We need to be able to see "inside" of things; we need a kind of x-ray vision. Theories of inductive reasoning as a mechanical process abound. They reduce such reasoning to a summing up of data. This would be like reducing artistic genius to an act of literal copying. Suppose we could invent a sculpture machine that would carve, in exact detail, whatever object we put before it. And suppose we were to describe our copying machine as an artist. This would be, on Michelangelo's theory, artistic blasphemy! It would be to miss altogether what art is about. Likewise, to confuse enumerating with insight would be, on Aristotle's theory, to miss what induction is about.

A rationalistic age that prides itself on scientific accomplishment regards the scandal of creativity with suspicion. But creativity precedes all knowledge. Without creativity, we would have no language, no science, no logic, no philosophy. Without creativity, there would be nothing to say, nothing to argue, nothing to understand. We could see the world physically, but we would be, in a deeper sense, blind.

DEDUCTION AND INDUCTION

The contemporary literature on the so-called problem of induction reveals as much about the modern mindset as it does about induction. This seems to be the age of deduction. In the modern philosophy, deductive arguments are held up as logically exemplary, as the acme of reason. Aristotle's enthusiasm for the syllogism, especially for the scientific or demonstrative syllogism, may give the causal reader the false impression that philosophers have always believed that anything other than strict deduction, including induction (and inductive syllogism) is an imperfect copy or an inferior form of rational thought. There is, however, no suggestion in Aristotle that induction is somehow flawed.

As Descartes demonstrated, we can question anything. Deduction is as open to questioning as induction. What, for example, about the perennial charge that deduction is a *petitio principii?* Karl Popper and John Eccles restate a truism: "the *informative content* of [a deductive] conclusion can never exceed the premises."[99] It seems, then, that the conclusion of a deductive argument is only the repetition of what is contained in the premises. In R.W. Newell's words, "to reason deductively 'is to repeat laboriously what one already knows'."[100] Suppose I argue, "Every member of the Smith family has red hair; Julie is a member of the Smith family; so Julie has red hair."[101] What does the conclusion in this argument accomplish? It makes an observation about information that is already there, for to say that Julie belongs to a family of red-haired people is to already know that Julie has red hair. So the conclusion merely states, in more explicit terms, what I already know. It does not add anything to the knowledge I already possess.

The point here is only to show that to criticize inductive reasoning exclusively would be to take a partisan approach. Deductive reasoning is equally open to question. Not to underestimate the value of deduction. There is, in fact, a more challenging form of deduction that resembles induction. Consider proofs in mathematics and formal logic. It takes great ingenuity, in some cases, to discern what follows. In such cases, deduction may require a leap of insight. This is like the inductive inference: the reasoner hits on the correct inference in a single stroke, through a kind of mental illumination. The elaboration of such reasoning reveals it to be as much a display of creativity as one of rigorous inference. The whole process relies, not on mechanically enumerating data, but on creative intelligence.

99 Popper and Eccles, *Self and Its Brain,* 80 (italics in the original).

100 Guthrie, *History of Greek Philosophy,* vol. 6, 163. He is citing from Newell, *Concept of Philosophy,* 2, who argues *against* this critique of deduction.

101 This is a deductive argument in the modern sense because the conclusion follows necessarily, and in the traditional sense because the movement is from universal to particular.

Philosophers motivated by an indefatigable drive to account for all knowledge may find it disturbing to admit the implication that human knowing begins with a leap of creativity. The idea that some things cannot be accounted for by anything other than an intuitive creativity may seem repugnant to the overly cautious mind. Still, the way Aristotle goes about explaining the inductive syllogism, the rhetorical example, definition, *nous*, perception, and imagination is helpful in that it captures, however imperfectly, the gist of what needs to be said. I have tried to draw out, in a systematic fashion, the wider implications of his position here.

In the order of knowing, induction precedes deduction. Understanding precedes discursive reasoning. The modern belief in argument has its comforts and its obligations. We ensconce ourselves in deductive reasoning, retreating, we think, from the perils of a comprehensive scepticism. If we do not investigate the issues too closely, we may think our logic is proof against assault when, in actual fact, it rests on a deeper foundation only creativity can account for.

9

Where Science Comes to an End

A fairly characteristic view of Aristotle is given by the physicist J. D. Bernal in his book *Science in History* (1969 Penguin). "Bruno had to be burnt and Galileo condemned before doctrines which were derived from Aristotle ... could be overthrown ... The subsequent history of science is largely, in fact, the story of how Aristotle was overthrown in one field after another. Indeed [Pierre] Ramus was not far from the mark when he maintained in his famous thesis of 1536 'that everything Aristotle taught is false'."

Michael Rowan Robinson[1]

For induction, as we all know, has fallen into some disrepute nowadays, at least so far as the logic of scientific discovery is concerned. Nor would it be amiss, perhaps, were we to look into some of the reasons for this currently fashionable tendency to dismiss induction out of hand, as being both incompetent and irrelevant to the matter of scientific discovery.

Henry Veatch[2]

The distinction between the Form and Matter of Thought – that is, between Logic and Metaphysics – is but very imperfectly preserved by Aristotle.

Francis Bowen[3]

IN THIS FINAL CHAPTER I WANT TO COMPARE THE ACCOUNT I have developed of Aristotelian induction with contemporary views largely taken for granted in philosophy, science, metaphysics, and argumentation theory. A proper canvassing of issues calls for a somewhat disjointed treatment. This chapter falls roughly into three sections. The first section deals with a historical account of first principles; the second, with a recent attempt to insert a slightly reworked essentialism into the framework of

1 "Was Aristotle the First Physicist?" (online).

2 *Two Logics*, 164–5.

3 *Treatise on Logic*, 119.

modern analytic philosophy; and the third, with whether any room can be had for Aristotle's essentialism in contemporary biology.

I begin by defending the traditional account of infallible first belief against claims that it is naive. I reject the suggestion that first principles are only "probably" true and then go on to explain how mainstream historical authors account for mistakes that arise at the level of first principles, discuss the traditional use of the "qua locution" as a solution to apparent difficulties, and revisit the problem of induction. I argue that traditional philosophers were well aware of the reflexive nature of human knowledge and that Kant's attack on traditional metaphysics does not undermine the metaphysical realism that motivated earlier accounts of induction. The familiar scepticism about first principles depends crucially on a realism about the phenomenon-noumenon distinction.

I go on to examine recent claims that first principles are not universal. Whereas authors such as Weinberg et al. (Jonathan M. Weinberg, Shaun Nichols, and Stephen Stich) suggest that diverse cultures do not share fundamental intuitions, I argue, in part, that the concept of "intuition" they invoke is too ambiguous to be of much use. I investigate the controversy, fuelled in part by the elaboration of dialethic logics, surrounding one very prominent first principle, that of non-contradiction. I examine briefly the traditional liar's paradox, the strengthened liar, and Saul Kripke's revamped version with "Dean and Nixon." I claim (with Brian Huss) that we have no evidence to show that any cultures reject the traditional principle of non-contradiction.

In the second main section of the chapter, I discuss the "new essentialism" proposed by authors such as Brian Ellis, Hilary Kornblith, Saul Kripke, and Hilary Putnam, to mention a few. These authors reinvent, so to speak, the traditional notion of "essence," or natural kind. They argue that any coherent account of science requires a conception of *a posteriori* necessity. Most of these authors have been trained in analytical philosophy and generally take modern empiricism for granted. I argue, in contrast, that the modern empiricism that grew out of Locke, Hume, Kant, and Mill leaves no room for *a posteriori* necessity, that any reintroduction of the notion of natural kind into a philosophy without metaphysics would be inconsistent, and that the usual appeal to abduction or inference to the best explanation is not, on key issues, different from traditional appeals to infallible first principles.

In the third section, I compare the Aristotelian with contemporary accounts of the "species problem" in biology, and argue that Aristotle (correctly) conceived of species as first principles and that he (correctly) proposed a formal criterion for species differentiation. Contemporary accounts, in contrast, propose a species criterion appealing to the notions of material or efficient cause. The almost universal condemnation of Aristotle's "biological essentialism" (a misnomer, really) derives from a metaphysical and a textual misunderstanding. Although Aristotle could not have conceived of the possibility of evolution, his account of species is philosophically independent of, not incompatible with, such a possibility.

FIRST PRINCIPLES

Examples of First Principles

Because we may legitimately argue about many things, it does not follow that it is rationally compelling to argue about everything or anything. Aristotle and earlier thinkers in general argue that the first truths discovered by induction must be infallible. (Keep in mind, when we are speaking about infallible first principles, we are referring to "true" or "rigorous" induction, not mere arguments from resemblance.) Historical thinkers are frustratingly vague when it comes to pinning down exactly what the very first truths are. To refer to the principle of non-contradiction or the logical law of identity as a case in point seems of little help. What then are the first principles of human thought that cannot be doubted?

There are at least obvious candidates. For example, we can *induce* logical principles such as the law of non-contradiction (the same proposition cannot be true and false) or the *dictum de omni et nullo* of traditional syllogistic (whatever is affirmed or denied of a whole may be affirmed or denied of a part); we can *induce* logical relations such as identity (if $a = b$ and $b = c$, $a = c$) or transitivity (if $a > b$ and $b > c$, then $a > c$); we can *induce* mathematical or geometrical axioms such as Euclid's law (that the shortest distance between two points is a straight line) or Peano's second axiom (that for each natural number there exists only one successor natural number); we can *induce* metaphysical laws (the *metaphysical* version of principle of non-contradiction [that the same thing cannot exist and not exist], that every effect must have a cause, that the past cannot be changed, that there is an external world); we can *induce* scientific laws (that there are various chemical elements, that energy must be conserved, that there is a universal law of gravitation); we can *induce* moral principles (that dishonesty is a vice, that murder is wrong, that promise-keeping is a duty). We can *induce* concepts, the essential or necessary properties of things, and so on.

Foundationalists of various stripes have tried to elaborate comprehensive formal systems of the first principles of human knowledge. We will leave such an intellectual tour de force to more powerful minds. We can assert the importance of first principles without taking a particular stance on these issues. Suffice it to say that any investigation into the origins of knowledge is bound to hit on certain starting points. Traditional authors argue that we must rely on these starting points, otherwise knowledge would be impossible.

Infallible First Belief?

Why do we need first principles? Begin with a parable. Suppose you are lost in a blank world with a compass. The compass always points in the same direction, but you have nothing else to indicate direction, no north star, no rising or setting of the sun, no moss on the north side of trees, no birds flying south. You are alone in the darkness of these featureless barrens. The compass points north. Or does it? Can we meaningfully question this reading? The compass is all we have. Nothing else indicates direction. This is the only evidence. Such is our predicament with respect to first principles. They are the internal compass that guides rational inquiry. We have no other compass. This is the only compass we have. To give up on this one is to give up on the only evidence we have.

Someone will invariably object, "Don't simply *assume*. Prove the compass points in the right direction and I will believe." But earlier philosophers did not believe that one could *prove* first principles. Quite to the contrary, they argued that no such proof is *available*. Aristotle, for example, never claimed that philosophy provides an *absolute* proof for anything. As he insists, "it is impossible that there should be a demonstration of absolutely everything: [for] there would be an infinite regress, so that there would still be no demonstration."[4] Assume that I can prove *A* by showing that it follows necessarily from *B*. And assume that I can prove *B* by showing that it follows necessarily from *C*. And assume that I can prove *C* by showing that it necessarily follows from *D*. At a certain point, this kind of exercise must come to an end. To say that we know first principles infallibly is not to say that we can prove they are true. It is to say that they are the most basic ideas we have. We *must* accept them. They force themselves on us. Seen from a human point of view, they cannot be meaningfully contested.

Traditional thinkers generally understood that an absolute proof of anything is an impossibility. We cannot prove everything there is to prove. On the traditional Aristotelian account, induction is not a matter of proof but of discernment. We observe this or that instance and come to *see* the underlying principle at work. We come to this realization, not through discursive proof,

4 *Metaphysics* (Ross), pt 4, ch. 4, 1006a5–1010 (in Aristotle, *Complete Works*).

but through *epagoge*, through the sudden grasping of a necessary insight. We do not *prove* through tabulation; we recognize, in a flash of illumination, what *must* always be the case. Further confirmation, after the fact, may be a useful, even necessary tool; in complex cases, it confirms that we really know. But we already know first principles through induction.

Suppose I add up a long list of numbers. And suppose I do this correctly. I find out that the total is 33,456. But it is a long list so I check it again. The total is 33,456. But to be sure, I check it again. The total is 33,456. How many times do I have to do this before I can be sure that the total is 33,456? If I did it correctly the first time, is it not the case that I knew this already? We could imagine an inductive argument along these lines: "James added up this list and discovered the total is 33,456. Mary-Jo added up this list and discovered the total is 33,456. Therese added up this list and discovered the total is 33,456. Therefore, the total is 33,456." This could be set up as an inductive syllogism: "James' total, Mary-Jo's total, and Therese's total are each 33,456. James' total, Mary-Jo's total, and Therese's total are each interchangeable with the true total. Therefore, the true total is 33,456."

This is a sound (though silly) argument. Why? Because deriving the number 33,456 from the list of added numbers is logically necessary. Anyone adding up this list correctly must arrive at the 33,456. This is how earlier authors thought of induction. If true induction is properly carried out, it will result in conclusions that must be accepted as true. Although unlikely, it is at least possible that James, Mary-Jo, and Therese all made the same mistake in addition. If, however, they added the numbers correctly, they must arrive at the right answer. No other answer can be arrived at by any human being – anywhere, anytime – who follows the correct procedure. Adding new instances of this process of addition will not change the result in the slightest. It will not turn what is not knowledge into knowledge. It will only confirm that yes, indeed, we had knowledge in the first place.

On Aristotle's account, induction is an interaction between the mind and the world. The *world* possesses a definite nature; the human *mind* possesses a definite nature; and the interaction of the two results in principles that follow necessarily. It is not as if *we* alone project our categories on the world, and it is not as if the *world* alone projects its categories on the mind. The mind and the world impose on each other. Given that the world has a particular nature and the mind has a particular nature, what results is a matter of necessity. This is why induction is reliable. Things are they way they have to be. First principles follow necessarily.

Traditional philosophers did not, in general, try to prove first principles. They *accepted* first principles as the necessary starting points for the human conversation. To ask for a defence of starting points is to ask the wrong question. The person who does not produce the requested proof does not err; it is the one who requests the proof who errs. If the starting points had to be proved by some other form of reasoning, they would not be first principles. First principles represent the limits of rational inquiry. In following the thread of reason backward, this is where inquiry comes to an end.

First Probability?

If historical authors claim that we can infallibly know first principles, a contemporary reader might immediately respond that if first principles are probably true, this should be enough to build a secure foundation for human knowledge. But any such suggestion is problematic.

To begin with, it is not entirely clear what a word like "probably" could mean in this context. What could it mean to say, for example, that the principle of non-contradiction has a 60-per-cent probability of being true? That it is only valid six times out of ten? Suppose we want to calculate the probability that a randomly tossed coin comes up heads five times in a row. Given that we already know that there is a 50-per-cent probability that the coin will turn up heads on each toss, we can calculate the probability that this will happen five times in a row. But this is not the case with first principles. First principles are the most basic criteria of all. There is nothing we already know, no prior criterion of anything on which to calculate a probability. So it would make no sense to say that we could calculate the probability that first principles are true.

The claim that first principles are only probably true seems a meaningless statement. First, it cannot be expressed in any rigorous way. Second, it is, in principle, unverifiable. We have no way of evaluating human belief, except on the basis of other human belief. We can never move outside a human perspective; we have no way of getting a second opinion on the issue. If something is necessarily true from a human perspective, as far as we are concerned, that is an end to it. We cannot access first principles from a supra-human point of view so as to evaluate the belief in terms of other supra-human criteria.

And there is a third issue. When authors talk about first principles being probably true, this boils down to the claim that the future will *probably* be the same as the past. But we have absolutely no evidence to indicate that the future will be different than the past in any fundamental way. The fundamental laws of physics do not, for example, change like the weather. What could it mean to say that the future will be *fundamentally* different?

That logic will come to an end? That numbers will add up differently? That time will stop? That the universal law of gravitation will expire? That evil will become good? If we go by the evidence we are presented with, we will have to consider such suggestions as extravagant hypotheses.

Perhaps, if someone says that first principles are probably true, they only mean to suggest that as human beings are fallible creatures, their beliefs are, in some inescapable sense, fallible. This suggestion is not at odds with the traditional position. When traditional authors claim that first principles are infallible, they are claiming that these principles are infallible, *considered from a human point of view.* Contrary to a popular but highly misleading caricature, traditional authors never claimed that we could look at the world from a God's-eye point of view. They would, in most cases, have considered any such suggestion as blasphemous. As rational beings, we must conform to the evidence we are presented with. Certain beliefs impress themselves on us as necessarily true. We cannot doubt them. This is what it means to say that first principles are (considered from a human point of view) infallible. What these first principles look like from say a God's-eye point of view is not something we, as human beings, have access to. It is the growth of scientific positivism – not careful, traditional philosophy – that explains such exaggerated epistemological aspirations.

Qua*lification*

In the *Meditations*, Descartes argues that we cannot make mistakes if we use our intelligence properly.[5] Mistakes arise when the *will* overextends itself. Descartes explains, "Whence then do my errors arise? Only from the fact that the will is [much] more … far-reaching than the understanding, so that I … extend it even to those things which I do not understand … And thus it happens that I make mistakes."[6] Descartes concludes that we can

5 Because God, who is morally perfect, would not equip us with an intelligence that would deceive us. Descartes writes, "I recognize that it is impossible for God ever to deceive me, since in all fraud and deception there is some kind of imperfection … Then, by my own experience [I know] that I have some ability to judge, [or to distinguish the true from the false] an ability which I have no doubt received from God … Furthermore since it is impossible that God wishes to deceive me, it is also certain that he has not given me an ability of such a sort that I could ever go wrong when I use it properly." René Descartes, *Discourse on Method and Meditations* (Lafleur), Meditation 4, "Of the True and the False," 109.

6 Ibid., Meditation 4, 114.

avoid error if we "abstain from making a judgement upon a topic when [we] do not conceive it sufficiently clearly and distinctly."[7]

Descartes claims that error arises, not from any innate defect in human understanding, but from the misuse of our understanding by an unruly will. His basic position (minus the pronounced emphasis on voluntarism) can be traced all the way back to traditional philosophers like Thomas and Aristotle. These earlier philosophers believe that nothing is wrong with human intelligence. If, however, we cannot fall into error when we use intelligence correctly, we do, on occasion, insufficiently or inadequately exercise the inductive faculty.

As we have already seen, historical authors distinguish between understanding (*nous, intellectus*) and reasoning (*dianoia, ratio*). Understanding is the immediate awareness behind induction. Reasoning is the discursive awareness behind argument. In general then, traditional philosophers divide human error into two broad categories. Errors in understanding involve "sins of omission"; errors in reasoning, "sins of commission." Understanding is inevitably hampered by some kind of blindness, whereas reasoning fails when we put premises together in the wrong order. In the case of faulty *understanding*, error is like a dirty window. We cannot see through it. Something is obstructing our vision. Errors in *reasoning* are inevitably structural problems. They are akin to cases of faulty engineering. An argument is like a bridge; it collapses if it has not been constructed in the right way.

Contemporary courses and texts in argumentation theory focus – almost exclusively – on errors in reasoning. If, however, there is confusion over fundamental issues, learning how to construct proper arguments will not solve this sort of problem. Aristotle, by contrast, describes a process of conceptual clarification that we can use to move backward to the most basic principles of all. Aristotle claims that "by advancing from true but obscure judgements [we can] arrive at clear ones, always exchanging the usual confused statement for more real knowledge."[8] The goal here is not the discovery of something new but the clear identification of principles we

7 Ibid., Meditation 4, 115. Descartes concludes this meditation, "I have not only learned today what I must do to in order not to err, but also what I ought to do to arrive at knowledge of the truth, for I shall certainly achieve this goal if I hold my attention sufficiently fixed upon those things which I conceive perfectly and if I distinguish these from the others which I conceive only confusedly and obscurely" (ibid., Meditation 4, 118).

8 *Eudemian Ethics* (Solomon), pt 1, ch. 6, 1216b31–35 (in Aristotle, *Complete Works*).

already take for granted. The proposed methodology moves from confusion to clarity, from commonsense judgements we accept as true to a more probing and careful dissection of beliefs into their ultimate, incontrovertible components. We can, in this way, clean the window of the mind and recuperate the first principles we already possess.

We could also explain this process of conceptual clarification through Aristotle's use of the "*qua* locution." As de Rijk points out, "the adverbial '*qua*', which is the literal Latin translation of the Greek ᾗ, is used [by Aristotle] to single out a specific property or function of something and means something like 'insomuch as'."[9] The *qua* locution allows us to focus on one particular aspect of the subject matter. We can, by this means, disentangle various aspects of reality and resolve the ambiguities that obscure the most fundamental axioms. Consider a specific example from physics. Why does a cat fall to earth? A cat falls to the Earth, not because it is a cat, not because it is composed of DNA and carbon, not because it is coloured black, not because it is three o'clock in the afternoon, not because the person throwing it has just committed a crime, not because it is my cat, and not because it is named Leo. It falls to the earth because it possesses a certain weight. It does not fall to the earth *qua* biological species, *qua* chemical agent, *qua* afternoon event, *qua* criminal responsibility, *qua* property considerations, or *qua* proper name. It falls to the earth *qua* physical mass. The characteristics of the cat *qua* physical mass determine the nature of the event. By paring down the event to its most basic elements and disregarding the accumulated aspects that distract us, we can eventually arrive at one of the first principles of physics, the law of gravity.

Aristotle proposes the *qua* locution, in part, as a method for resolving puzzles or *aporiai*. We can, for example, use the *qua* locution to resolve apparent contradictions. Suppose I claim that Plato is both mortal and immortal. The contradiction dissolves once we use the *qua* locution to separate out the different senses in which Plato is mortal and immortal. Like other human beings, Plato died. So Plato is mortal *qua* human being. But Plato is immortal *qua* philosopher; i.e., insomuch as his reputation as a great philosopher continues on today, he gains immortal status. So we can assert the original proposition that Plato is mortal and immortal without jettisoning the law of non-contradiction.

On Aristotle's account, we can use the *qua* locution to clarify our ideas. Clarifying our ideas is not arguing. It is not building arguments, attaching premises to premises to arrive at a conclusion. Clarification of belief

9 De Rijk, *Aristotle*, vol. 1, §2.73, 172. See *Posterior Analytics*, pt 1, ch. 4, 74a25–32; and *On the Soul*, pt 1, ch. 1, 402b25–403a2.

requires a kind of intelligent attention. Our reason, properly applied to what we *know* is true, can dig down to the very foundations of knowledge, to those implicit principles on which everything else depends. In dwelling on what we already believe, we can sort through our beliefs until we get to what cannot be questioned. Aristotle is willing to accept conceptual clarification as a legitimate methodology because he believes in human intelligence. If, of course, we are deeply distrustful of human intelligence, we have no reason to accept the results of conceptual clarification. But then, we also have no reason to accept human claims to knowledge either.

First Mistakes

On the traditional view, induction relies on understanding. Mistakes about induction are then errors of omission. Aristotle and Thomas cite three mistakes that can mar induction. First, we can suffer from mental blindness; second, we can ignore understanding; and thirdly, we can misapply first principles (which are, nonetheless, true). Consider briefly these three types of errors in turn.

Begin with mental blindness. Aristotle describes a defect in thought which is "an ignorance ... like blindness; for [it] is akin to a total absence of the faculty of thinking."[10] Thomas writes, "Just as bodily blindness is the privation of the principle of bodily sight, so blindness of mind is the privation of the principle of mental or intellectual sight."[11] Mental blindness is a localized inability. It is a kind of specialized ignorance. It may involve a permanent, constitutional defect or a temporary lapse of rational capacity. Thomas mentions that it is evident "in the case of imbeciles and madmen."[12]

Suppose a patient suffers damage to a particular area of the brain and loses the ability to distinguish between right and wrong. (Such things do happen.) Everything else is normal. The patient is, in one very specialized respect, ignorant. He or she cannot grasp the basic idea of right and wrong. Their access to these first principles has been obstructed. This localized inability is akin to what Aristotle and Thomas refer to as mental blindness. (If, of course, this individual can no longer tell the difference

10 *Metaphysics* (Ross), pt 9, ch. 10, 1052a2–3.

11 Thomas Aquinas, *Summa Theologica* (English Dominican Province), pt 2 of pt 2, Q. 75, "Of the Vices Opposed to Knowledge and Understanding," art. 1, "Whether Blindness of Mind Is a Sin." See also pt 1, Q. 85, "Of the Mode and Order of Understanding," art. 6, "Whether the Intellect Can Be False"; and pt 1 of pt 2, Q. 76, "Of the Causes of Sin, In Particular," art. 2, "Whether Ignorance Is a Sin."

12 Ibid., pt 2 of pt 2, Q. 75, art. 1.

between right and wrong, this does not undermine the epistemological status of morality; it is the individual, not the idea of morality that is defective. Again, if we were to discover an entire planet of damaged humanoids who were unable to conceive of the difference between right and wrong, this would not subvert the authority of morality.[13] It would only mean that everyone on this planet suffered from mental blindness.) This problem is not restricted to moral examples. If I lost the ability to think in numbers, or to spatially understand certain geometrical patterns, or to pick out (say, in certain circumstances) the relationship of past to present or cause to effect (etc.), this conceptual inability would be a form of mental blindness.

Thomas describes two further mistakes that arise with respect to first principles. As we have seen, mental blindness is a constitutive or clinical problem. The individual in question has lost the ability to see the concept. In cases of deliberate or unstudied ignorance, by contrast, he or she neglects basic ideas, either through deliberate inattention or through rash and hasty thinking.[14] In this kind of case, the error does not arise through mental defect but through inattention, lack of evidence, presumption, carelessness, laziness, or distraction.[15] We all have the capacity to know that the interior angles of a triangle add up to 180 degrees. We *induce* this fact about triangles. If, however, we do not take the trouble to inform ourselves, if I believe my new-age mystical cult leader who says that the interior angles of a triangle add up to 114 degrees, I make a mistake at a very basic level with respect to what a triangle is, not because I am incapable of understanding the idea of a triangle, but because I have not given the matter the necessary attention. Again, we are all capable of grasping (through induction) the principle of non-contradiction, that the same proposition cannot be both true and false. If, however, I reject the principle of non-contradiction because my new-age mystical cult leader tells me not to believe in it, this again, is a case of deliberate or unstudied ignorance. The conceptual knowledge is available if only I would stop hiding the principle from myself. The problem is not with my faculty of understanding but with my refusal to consult this faculty.

13 Again, if we discovered an entire planet of psychopaths who could not grasp the wrongness of killing, this would not subvert the epistemological authority of the interdiction against murder (see chapter 5).

14 Ibid.

15 While Thomas cites the case of someone who purposely ignores the first principles of morality to pursue wickedness, this kind of mistake is not restricted to morality.

On Aristotle's account, we know the specialized first principles of each scientific field through induction. Take it then as a basic principle of biology that whales are not fish. And suppose someone observes several whales swimming in the ocean and immediately concludes that whales are, in fact, large fish. What is the origin of this mistake? Presumably the agent is confused by a superficial similarity – that whales and fish both live in the sea. But this is lazy thinking, for it overlooks conspicuous differences: Whales have lungs; fish, gills. Whales are warm blooded; fish, cold blooded. Whales have true skin and even hair; fish, hairless scales. Whales suckle their young; fish do not suckle their young. This mistake arises from a lack of serious study; it cannot be attributed to the mental faculties themselves. If we fairly and thoroughly consult the evidence, we will be forced to conclude that whales are mammals, not fish. In this case, our rational powers do not lead us astray; the problem is that they have not been carefully exercised.

The third mistake associated with induction occurs when an agent misapplies first principles to concrete cases in the world.[16] Thomas cites two examples: someone may misapply the definition of a circle to a triangle, or again, one may join incompatible concepts in a false definition as when we describe something as "a rational winged animal." (Rational winged creatures are for Thomas angels, which are not animals.) To turn to a scientific example, if I were to define a duck-billed platypus as a "mammal-bird" (because it has a beak), this would be a mistake, for mammals and birds are distinct natural kinds. But this is not, rigorously speaking, a mistake in understanding. I can correctly *induce* the concept "mammal" and the concept "bird" from my study of the natural world. The problem here (as in the previous whale example) is that I have joined these incompatible concepts into one definition, presumably because I did not investigate the matter with sufficient care. (In fact, Thomas claims that this kind of error is not a mistake of *intellectus* or understanding (which involves an immediate all-at-once intuition). It is a mistake of *ratio* or reason (because it results from adding two or more things together incorrectly.)

In a discussion of natural law, Thomas argues we can add, but we cannot subtract, from the first principles of morality.[17] This basic principle that we can always discover new first principles but can never invalidate previously discovered first principles could be expanded across the board. On the traditional view, advances in logic, mathematics, the natural, and even the moral sciences are possible. But these advances can never contradict

16 Ibid., pt 1, Q. 85, art. 6.

17 Ibid., pt 1–2, Q. 95, art. 5, "Whether the Natural Law Can Be Changed."

what was true in what went before. If we were to discover that something we previously took to be a first principle was false, that would only show that it was never a first principle in the first place. We would know, in hindsight, that we had, through confusion or haste, presented something that is not a first principle as a first principle. The point is that we must accept that human understanding is, at the most basic levels, true. Otherwise, knowledge would be impossible. (Every cognitive process is ultimately, a function of human understanding. Once human understanding goes, so does everything else.)

The Problem of Induction Revisited

The traditional account solves the problem of induction in the following way. First, it accepts the legitimacy of human intelligence. Second, it divides the world into natural kinds. Modern authors repudiate (and caricature) notions of essence and rebel against traditional notions of metaphysical necessity. This strategy dissolves, in effect, the glue that holds things together, turning the world into an accidental combination of properties, where reliable prediction is impossible. But we have no reason to believe that the world is like this; both ordinary experience and scientific inquiry demonstrate that it has deep, abiding regularity. As far as we can tell, there *are* fundamentally different kinds of things in the world. Nature must submit to various kinds of necessity. This solves the problem of induction. If we can know what kind of thing something is, if we can know what must necessarily be, we can reliably know something about the future.

As we have seen, an author such as Aristotle does not view induction as an enumerative process. Our confidence in the inductive claim that "all triangles having interior angles totalling 180 degrees" does not depend on the number of triangles we see. If this was the case, our confidence in the truth of the proposition would increase as we inspect more and more triangles. Elementary school teachers who have spent years adding up the interior angles of triangles would presumably be the expert authorities on such matters. But this is not what happens. Old geometers are no more certain than young ones of the truth of this proposition. Once we understand that the interior angles of a triangle *must* add up to 180 degrees, we have arrived at our insight and further examples are genuinely redundant.

Traditional induction does not operate by means of an algorithm or a probability calculus. Induction arises in non-discursive reason. It is revelation, an intelligent leap, a matter of seeing, not calculating. In describing the mechanism of induction, we might emphasize the role of the external world and downplay the role of the mind; we might emphasize the role of the mind and downplay the role of the external world; or we might try to highlight the role of the mind and the external world taken together.

The first view represents, roughly speaking, the extreme empiricism that evolved into a dogmatic positivism. On such an account, knowledge would correspond to exactly what is out there; the mind would in no way intervene, in no way creatively interpret or reconstruct incoming stimuli. The second view represents, roughly speaking, an extreme idealism that evolved into a dogmatic postmodernism. On such an account, there is, for all intents and purposes, only the mind. The external world is a construction of the mind. It possesses no independent, extra-mental existence. Knowledge reduces to the way the mind thinks. The third view represents, more or less, the mature thought of Aristotle. On such an account, the creative intelligence of the mind *makes* knowledge that "corresponds" to the way the world is. Two principles are at play. Knowledge is, in some important sense, a kind of human self-expression and an *accurate* replica of the world. We are left with a theory of knowledge that respects both the objective influence of the world and the creative contribution of the mind.

The extreme empiricist account is ultimately an attempt to eliminate mind, for the mind is a creative, transcendent reality that cannot be explained by anything else. It champions an unqualified objectivity beyond human aspiration. The extreme idealist account is an assault on objective truth; it lurches toward extreme subjectivity and solipsism. Surely, we need to aim at something between these extremes. Aristotle's account of induction, as outlined in this book, seems a sophisticated response to such theoretical extremism.

Kant's Attack on Traditional Metaphysics

It must be admitted that the historical influence of Kant's metaphysical views played a large role in the rejection of the earlier Aristotelian world view. But the familiar understanding that Kant's measured response to Hume exploded traditional metaphysics and put an end to centuries of "dogmatic certainty" misconstrues both Kant and traditional philosophy. It is generally taken for granted that Kant pointed out, if not a mistake in earlier metaphysics, at least something that had been overlooked. I will argue that the difference between traditional and Kantian metaphysics is, on closer inspection, mostly a difference in emphasis. If anything, the Kantian turn misconstrues the epistemological predicament by focusing on the role of mind to the exclusion of the external world.

Kant, of course, distinguishes between the phenomenon, the world as it appears to us, and the noumenon, things as they are in themselves. The distance between the phenomenon and the noumenon opens up the possibility of unlimited scepticism. We can never be sure that the world-as-we-see-it corresponds in any adequate sense to the world-as-it-really-is. It does not matter if our most basic ideas about the world seem absolutely compelling. For all we know, these ideas may be completely erroneous. Although we shall not review the historical evidence here, Kant and his followers stress this point relentlessly.

On the Kantian view, first principles are entirely fallible. To claim that they are infallible, even from a human perspective, is to overlook the way the human mind shapes experience. Traditional authors mistakenly assumed they were seeing the world as it really is. In fact, the human mind structures and processes information so as to present the world consistently with the mind's own nature. It is not merely that metaphysical and scientific knowledge is of appearances; these appearances are themselves a product of our own cognitive apparatus. As such, they provide an inadequate account of the world-as-it-really-is. On this Kantian account, investigating the nature of the world turns into an investigation of ourselves.

Overlook, for our purposes, that various objections can be raised against this account. What I want to show is that this new way of looking at the world does not constitute an advance over previous theories. Consider the concept of the noumenon. It is hard to know exactly what Kant means by the term. The noumenon is something so different from mental experience that we cannot access it through the basic categories of human thought. It is that aspect of reality that escapes human comprehension. Call this aspect of the world "the unthinkable." On the received account, metaphysical realism is philosophically naive because traditional philosophers overlook the possibility of the unthinkable. They assume that human thought conforms to what-really-is. In overlooking the role of the unthinkable, they embrace a theoretically unsophisticated naive realism. Although this trope is repeated over and over again in the philosophical literature, we could counter that it is, in fact, the Kantian turn that is theoretically unsophisticated.

Two ways offer themselves of our understanding the unthinkable. On a nominalist interpretation, the unthinkable is merely a name. On a realist, the unthinkable exists as an objectively existent realm of things-in-themselves that escapes human detection. In the first case, the unthinkable is an empty concept. Like the mathematical symbol "zero," it stands for what lacks reality or existence. It has no referent. In the second case, the unthinkable has ontological reality. The term denotes a real kind. It has a referent.

Nominal interpretations of the unthinkable present no obstacle to traditional metaphysics. On such accounts, the unthinkable is not a real object;

it is simply a word that points to a possibility that is literally unthinkable (like a square-circle) and which therefore does not actually exist. If, in contrast, the unthinkable does exist, indeed if it is the central feature making up the real world, then the human cognitive categories could in no way count as a reliable guide to ultimate reality. This is the gist of the line of reasoning driving modern "anti-realism." Because the unthinkable is what exists out in the world, the old metaphysics, assuming the validity of human mental categories, is naive and misleading.

On a widespread account, traditional metaphysics innocently embraces realism; Kantians see beyond the imposture. But this is not a fair description of what is going on. It is not as if modern anti-realists reject realism; they embrace, more precisely, a different kind of realism. They give up on a realist interpretation of the world (which we have good evidence for) for a realist interpretation of the unthinkable (which we have no evidence for). Traditional metaphysicians do the exact opposite. They give up on a realist interpretation of the unthinkable (which we have no evidence for) for a realist interpretation of the world (which we have good evidence for). The argument here does not pit unmitigated realists against unmitigated anti-realists. It pits one kind of realism against another. Traditionalists focus on evidence; moderns focus on possibility. It could be argued that the modern focus on possibility inevitably reduces to scepticism.

There are two alternatives. The "unthinkable" may be a non-denoting name that literally stands for nothing. If this is the case, the fact that metaphysics excludes the unthinkable cannot be properly construed as a limit on understanding. This is a mark of discernment, not of misunderstanding. Of course, we cannot know the nature of the unthinkable. There is nothing to know! Or it may be that the "unthinkable" exists (or possibly exists). But we have no evidence to show that this is the case. If the unthinkable is, by definition, beyond human cognition, any evidence as to its existence is *in principle* unobtainable. Most contemporary interpretations reify the unthinkable; they turn it into an invisible object. If, however, we can come up with a word that refers to unthinkable objects, it does not follow that unthinkable objects really exist. The fact that we can refer to "square-circles" does not prove that square-circles actually exist somewhere, underneath the limits of human consciousness. We could do worse than heed Wittgenstein's advice that an uncritical literalism about language leads to metaphysical error. If we cannot prove, in any absolute sense, that the unthinkable does not exist (indeed, we cannot) this does not give us any good reason to believe in it. Why should we give any more credence to this unfalsifiable hypothesis than we do to any other? The transcendental possibility of things surpassing human understanding should be noted. If, however, rationality requires that we only believe what we have evidence for, and if we have (in principle) no evidence for the unthinkable, belief in anything like the unthinkable is nothing short of irrational.

Philosophical opponents will complain that the mere *possibility* of something like the noumenon is enough to justify a deep scepticism about knowledge. But again, we have no evidence for this possibility. Anything the human mind can think of is, to that degree and by that very fact, thinkable. If the unthinkable were a real possibility, it would have to be a possibility outside the human ken. There is plenty of evidence that human knowledge is incomplete and imperfect and in need of improvement but none that it is fundamentally flawed. To argue that we should believe in a possibility we never have evidence for is to slip into a facile scepticism.

We need to distinguish between individual errors in judgement and a generalized belief that human judgement is fundamentally flawed. It is one thing to say that we make mistakes, and quite another, to claim that human judgement is *in principle* flawed. When earlier authors claimed that first principles were infallible, they were claiming that we cannot have knowledge unless we begin with the idea that human reason is, in some fundamental sense, reliable. Seen from within the realm of human possibility (the only realm open to us), first principles must be accepted as unconditionally true. Modern anti-realism raises the spectre of worlds beyond reason. Although most traditional philosophers believed in a realm of the divine above human reckoning, the full nature of such a possibility was, they believed, beyond human trespass. (They based such belief on a religious Revelation that anti-realism generally ignores or overlooks.)

First principles are nothing more and nothing less than an expression of the most fundamental features of reality as we can know it. Human fallibility cannot be excised; the possibility of the transcendental is always there. But from the perspective of reason, it makes no sense to argue against the only reality we can know. Any judgement we make is made from a human perspective. Seen from the only perspective available to us, first principles are not an arbitrary invention. They are inexorable, implacable; they cannot be eliminated or doubted. In this universe of discourse, they pose the limits and constraints on intelligent discourse.

Contesting Intuition?

As we have seen, Aristotle believed that we know first principles through the reflective movement of *noesis.* St Augustine called this faculty, "the interior teacher"; Thomas (following a long tradition), "*intellectus*"; René Descartes, the natural light of reason; Blaise Pascal, "heartfelt knowledge"

– and so on. According to all these authors, human beings have intuitive access to first principles. We all share the same set of first assumptions, which are transcultural, pan-historical, objective, universal, immutable. This view has, however, been contested.

Contemporary psychologists such as Weinberg et al. beg to differ. These modern authors do not pay much heed to a historical figure like Aristotle. Their arguments must be seen against the background of externalist versus internalist debates in contemporary analytical philosophy of mind. They attack, in particular, a contemporary view they provocatively label as "Epistemic Romanticism," which seems to be a contemporary version of the old rationalist idea that inborn reason provides the ultimate criterion for truth and that knowledge is largely a matter of introspection. Weinberg et al. deride, in particular, the idea that an internal sense of conviction is the key feature of knowledge.[18] (They dismiss this kind of internalism as "Intuition Driven Romanticism.") If earlier authors contended that reason is universal, these authors claim rigorously collected social data undermine belief in any universal or transcultural set of epistemic standards. As evidence, they point to their own social psychology experiments, as well as to cutting-edge research by social psychologist Richard Nisbett and his colleagues.[19]

Insomuch as the arguments of Weinberg et al. represent a certain impatience with a kind of epistemological narcissism – it is true because it seems right to me – they have serious merit. But they do not explode more thoughtful claims made by traditional philosophers about the fixed nature of first principles. In some important way, Weinberg and his colleagues miss the point, in large part because contemporary philosophy does not adequately distinguish between different kinds of intuitions. They throw (so to speak) all stones heedlessly into the same bag, when in fact there are many kinds of stones, most of them just ordinary ones no doubt, but a few which may turn out to be diamonds, once you rub the dirt off. Before evaluating their position, consider their methodology more closely.

Weinberg et al. try to answer philosophical questions, using methods from social psychology. (This approach is sometimes called "experimental philosophy.") In one study, they survey two equal groups of about one

18 Weinberg, Nichols, and Stich focus on theories which presuppose a reflective equilibrium process as the final arbiter of right or justified belief. They mention several examples of questionable epistemologies, including those of Goodman, *Fact, Fiction and Forecast*, L. Cohen, "Can Human Irrationality Be Experimentally Demonstrated?" and Goldman, *Epistemology and Cognition.*

19 See Stich, *Fragmentation of Reason*, §4.6. See also Nisbett, *Geography of Thought*, and Nisbett, Peng, Choi, and Norenzayan, "Culture and Systems of Thought."

hundred undergraduate students of Western and East Asian descent. They claim that their results demonstrate that Western and Eastern students think differently. The students in the survey were presented with the following puzzle:

> One day Charles is suddenly knocked out by a falling rock, and his brain becomes rewired so that he is always absolutely right whenever he estimates the temperature where he is. Charles is completely unaware that his brain has been altered in this way. A few weeks later, this brain rewiring leads him to believe that it is 71 degrees in his room. Apart from his estimation, he has no other reasons to think that it is 71 degrees. In fact, it is at that time 71 degrees in his room. Does Charles really know that it was 71 degrees in the room, or does he only believe it?[20]

As it turns out, a higher number of East Asian students (about twenty more) reject the claim that Charles *really knows* the temperature. Weinberg et al. want to conclude then that different ethnic and cultural groups may have different epistemic intuitions. They think about knowledge in different ways.

Weinberg and colleagues raise the possibility that Westerners and Easterners have different base intuitions about the nature of knowledge. But there is nothing in such evidence to indicate that the traditional position is flawed. It is not merely that such quantitative evidence seems remarkably slim. (In the experiment cited, most students in *both* groups rejected the claim that Charles knows what the temperature is.) If we want to discover whether there is a universal grounding for knowledge in some sort of shared human intuition, we need to start, not with strange epistemological puzzles, but with obvious, non-controversial examples. These authors seem to overlook the easily verifiable fact that Westerners and Easterners share all sorts of obvious beliefs. They both believe, for example, that fire burns, that three apples minus one leaves two apples, that we hear sound with our ears and not with our eyes, that the future comes after the past, that human beings eat food, breathe, and eventually die, that some actions are morally wrong, that fairness is different from unfairness, and so on. It does not follow from the fact that individuals from different cultures disagree about fantastic stories that human beings have, at the intuitive level, no shared beliefs. It only follows that a puzzle is, well, a puzzle, a case for which we have no clear answer.

Academic philosophers (and social psychologists) obviously disagree with respect to specialized epistemological issues. But most human beings

20 Weinberg et al., "Normativity and Epistemic Intuitions," 15 (online).

do not spend their time puzzling over precise issues of epistemic warrant, or counterfactual predication, or modal logic. If we can concoct fanciful predicaments that divide the thorough-thinking philosophical community, it is hardly surprising that similar disagreements will separate groups of individuals. Clearly, ordinary people have intuitions about what they consider to be true or plausible, right or wrong, certain or uncertain (etc.). But do they have well-formed intuitions about technical issues in contemporary epistemology? This seems like special trade for philosophers. Clearly, cultural, historical, religious factors influence ordinary belief. Religious and aggressively non-religious people may approach judgements about the world in fundamentally different ways. Still, theists and atheists can communicate with one another. They live in the same world. They share basic beliefs, despite their religious differences. This kind of disagreement does not undermine traditional belief in first principles.

And there is a deeper problem with "experimental philosophy." The problem is not that Weinberg et al. collect opinions in support of their epistemological hypothesis. Aristotle himself suggests that we collect *endoxa*, the opinions of the many or the wise, and use them as a foundation for dialectic or rhetoric.[21] The difference is that Aristotle has a carefully elaborated epistemological position on intuition, whereas authors such as Weinberg et al. use the term "intuition" so loosely that it can refer to almost any kind of unsubstantiated opinion. They write, "As we use the notion, an epistemic intuition is simply a spontaneous judgment about the epistemic properties of some specific case – a judgment for which the person making the judgment may be able to offer no plausible justification."[22] But this seems little more than the fallacy of "persuasive definition." Why should it follow that epistemic intuitions are, in any deep sense, implausible? These authors display little historical knowledge of the major role of intuition in the Western tradition.

Weinberg and his colleagues appeal to a familiar distinction between those beliefs that are and those that are not backed up by reasons; i.e., between those that are and those that are not argued for. They seem to dismiss beliefs not argued for as somehow inferior or insubstantial. But, to repeat a refrain taken from the history of philosophy, knowledge must begin in unargued intuitions that are neither arbitrary nor implausible. When authors such as Weinberg et al. define intuitions as "spontaneous judgements likely with no plausible justification," they seem to equate intuition with the most flimsy kind of utterance. Suppose you ask me if the Montreal Canadiens are going to beat the Boston Bruins in the hockey

21 See *Topics*, pt 1, ch. 1, 100a20 ff.

22 Weinberg et al. "Normativity and Epistemic Intuitions," 5 (online).

game tonight. I – a ferocious fan of the Montreal Canadiens – say spontaneously, without reflection, "Yes, of course, they are going to win! I am sure of it!" You, who happen to be a ferocious fan of the Boston Bruins, have the opposite "intuition": "No way! Montreal is going to lose! I am sure of it!" This would count as an intuition on the contemporary definition. But this is clearly not what traditional authors are talking about when they refer to infallible first principles.

Does it follow that all spontaneous judgements are subject to serious disagreement? Suppose a child contemplating the death of a beloved pet was to ask a parent, "am I going to die?" The parent *spontaneously* responds, *without any prolonged reflection*, "Yes, we are all going to die." Can we legitimately disagree with the claim that all human beings eventually die the way we disagree about the outcome of a hockey game? This is where we need to look for transcultural belief. Not in hunches about who is going to win hockey games or in implausible or contrived thought experiments, but in universal principles, which most academic researchers ignore because the agreement is so obvious, so predictable, so unexciting. Insomuch as ordinary people have epistemic intuitions, we need to start, not with puzzles, but with those things that are the blindingly, brazenly, boringly obvious. (I have listed a number of such beliefs above.)

The Law of Non-Contradiction

In their attack on shard intuitions, Weinberg et al. appeal to Nisbett's claims about systematic differences in patterns of thought in East Asia and the Western world. Nisbett ventures to claim that Eastern cultures do not accept what is often (inaccurately) cited as the first of first principles, the law of non-contradiction. This logical rule or law is a universally acknowledged first principle in traditional thought. Consider seriously whether this first principle is rejected by some cultures.

I will argue, along with Brian Huss, that claims by Nisbett and others that Eastern cultures do not accept the principle of non-contradiction are exaggerated and that these researchers have in fact misinterpreted the attitudes of non-Western groups. Huss claims, *pace* Nisbett, that the principle of non-contradiction is a universal feature of "folk psychology."[23] That is, it is a transcultural, pan-historic belief that all (or almost all) human beings accept.[24] The general consensus is that we cannot believe both "*p* and not

23 Huss, "Cultural Differences." We could criticize the term "folk psychology," but leave aside that issue, here.

24 Of course, a few recalcitrant individuals may not concur, but there is a general consensus, even if we choose to overlook it.

p" (or at the very least, that the proposition "*p* and not *p*" is necessarily false and that anyone who believes that "*p* and not *p*" is true will soon run into logical trouble). I will argue that a brief inspection of the relevant issues reveals that Huss is, in the main, correct.

Popular belief in what *seems* to be a contradiction offers some support for Nisbett's general position. But what seems to be a contradiction often turns out, on closer inspection, to be little more than a rhetorical flourish. Sundry forms of literary expression – proverbs, aphorisms, maxims, epigrams – readily avail themselves, for stylistic reasons, of the conceptual tension that accompanies contradiction. Consider the adage, "one's closest friends are one's most dangerous enemies." This *seems* like a contradiction. Assuming that "enemy" is the negation of "friend," the dictum seems to assert that our friends are not our friends. The modifiers "closest" and "most dangerous" only serve to highlight the tension. We seem to be left with a paradox: "those who are, to the greatest degree, our friends are, to the greatest degree, not our friends." But this would be a peculiarly uninsightful reading of this adage. What the saying suggests is, rather, that the trust we place in our closest friends makes us extremely vulnerable to betrayal or trickery if they should turn against us. It may be intended as a warning that we should pick our closest friends with the greatest care. Or it may be a comment on the universal perfidy of human nature. And so on. When we unpack these associated meanings, the logical contradiction disappears.

Graham Priest cites a famous example from Heraclitus: "We step and do not step into the same rivers; we are and we are not."[25] Doubtless, the cryptic Heraclitus loved contradiction as a manner of expression, in large part because he wanted to emphasize his own metaphysical belief in a struggle or war between complementary properties. But whether or not he really *believed in* contradiction is at least debatable. Aristotle weighs in on the issue: "it is impossible for anyone to believe the same thing to be and not to be, as some think Heraclitus says."[26] If, after all, contradictions are true, why

25 *Stanford Encyclopedia of Philosophy*, s.v. "Dialetheism" (by Graham Priest) (online). The translation is from T. Robinson, *Heraclitus*, 35.

26 *Metaphysics* (Ross), pt 4, ch. 3, 1005b24–25. Aristotle has an excessively literal interpretation of Heraclitus or perhaps is castigating that philosopher's followers for their own literalism. See *Metaphysics*, bk 3, ch. 2; and bk 4, chs 1–4. "And perhaps if we had questioned Heraclitus himself in this way we might have forced him to confess that opposite statements can never be true of the same subjects. But, as it is, he adopted his opinion without understanding what his statement involves" (ibid. [Ross], pt 11, ch. 5, 1062a31–34).

would Heraclitus believe in a *necessary* war between opposites. Why would he believe that the advance of one contrary requires the retreat of the other? Why, for example, would he claim the increase of the wet element, "wet," necessitates the decrease of the dry element, "not wet?" If contradiction is unproblematic, "wet" and "not wet" should be compatible with one another. Something could still be "wet" and "not wet" at the very same time. But this is not what Heraclitus believed.

We can elucidate Heraclitus' cryptic way of expressing himself, without any appeal to literal contradictions. He champions becoming over being, flux over stasis. If, however, change is a puzzling phenomenon, it need not entail a contradiction. To say that we are and are not *in the very same sense* would be contradictory, but to say that *we are* "what we are now" and that *we are not* "what we were an instant ago" is not contradictory. Aristotle and others elucidate these issues in their metaphysics. They do so without violating the law of non-contradiction.

The Liar's Paradox

In discussing possible types of belief commitment, Huss borrows a distinction between "belief" and "acceptance" from Jonathan Cohen.[27] Huss argues that although individuals may *accept* "*p* and not *p*" they do not, as a rule, *believe* "*p* and not *p*." Acceptance is an act of will; one deems something true, perhaps for some pragmatic reason. Belief is an involuntary disposition, a spontaneous conviction that something is true. Huss cites the example of a criminal lawyer who *believes* that her client is guilty but *accepts* that he is not guilty for the sake of judicial process. The lawyer does not believe that the client is both guilty and not guilty. Rather she *believes* that he is guilty and *accepts* that he is not guilty. Despite her belief in his guilt, her professional capacity requires her to act *as if* she believed the opposite. Huss concedes that "you usually accept what you believe and believe what you accept ... especially ... when your goal is to arrive at true beliefs."[28] But belief and acceptance do not invariably go hand in hand. As Huss explains, what appears to be a belief in two contradictory claims may, in fact, turn out to be an acceptance of one claim and a belief in another.

Huss' argument is directed, in part, against modern dialethism (or dialetheism), which claims that there can be true contradictions.[29] (Modern

27 See J. Cohen, *Essay on Belief and Acceptance.*

28 Huss "Cultural Differences," 380.

29 See Priest, *In Contradiction*; and Priest, Routley, and Norman, *Paraconsistent Logic.*

dialethists have devised "non-explosive" paraconsistent logics, which admit of some contradiction.) But does it follow from the fact that we can create such systems that we should *believe* in real contradictions? Devising a formal system that allows one to use the claim "*p* and not *p*" as a premise in an argument that may be an unusual accomplishment, but it does not follow from this that the statement "*p* and not *p*" corresponds to anything in the world, that it actually refers to some property of reality.

The rationale behind paraconsistent logics is, in part, a desire to solve long-standing logical puzzles such as the famous liar's paradox, first recorded by Eubulides of Miletus (in the fourth century BC). Consider briefly what modern logicians refer to as the strengthened liar: the proposition, "This statement is false." It seems to follow that if this statement is true, it must be false. If, however, this is a false statement, it must be true. We are obliged, it seems, to believe that the same statement must be true and false at the same time, a clear contradiction. Except that such logical tricks as the strengthened liar do not, on a closer inspection, seem to pose any serious threat to the traditional position.

We cannot comment here, in any detail, on the modern liar's-paradox industry. A resulting tangle of puzzles and complications has preoccupied logicians and epistemologists to varying degrees over the last two-thousand years. I only want to show that such puzzles can be plausibly dealt without appeal to paraconsistent logics. The point here is not to definitively investigate all the ramifications of the liar's paradox, but merely to show that it does not provide a definitive obstacle to an "old-fashioned" belief in first principles. The paradox does not offer any insuperable obstacle to ordinary beliefs about the law of non-contradiction.

Aristotle does not say much about the liar's paradox. However, one very brief passage in *The Sophistical Refutations* appeared to medieval scholars to be a reference to the liar's paradox. In a discussion of the fallacy *secundum quid et simpliciter* (confusing what is true in a certain respect with what is true absolutely), Aristotle refers to the argument "whether the same man can at the same time say what is false and what is true."[30] Aristotle claims that a man who is a liar without qualification (i.e., absolutely) can still say things which are, in some sense, true. Imagine, to illustrate, an inveterate liar who says, "My brother is dead." He says it in such a way that the person he addresses thinks that his first brother is dead, whereas in fact his second brother is the one who is dead. Is this man's statement, "My brother is dead," true? We want to say that it is true in one respect but false in another. It is literally true: he has a brother who is dead. But the implication

30 *Sophistical Refutations* (Pickard-Cambridge), ch. 25, 180b2–3.

he encourages is false, for he means to imply that his first brother is dead when it is really his second brother who is dead. So the liar, in some sense, tells a lie while saying something that is true.

Aristotle's paradox of the liar does not seem to be a case of the liar's paradox as we understand it. (It is more like the modern Gettier paradox.) The assertion, "This statement is false," is problematic in a different way. It has a problematic kind of grammatical structure that needs to be elucidated. I will argue that the problem here is not a fallacy of *secundum quid et simpliciter* but a kind of conceptual emptiness that has no material equivalent in the real world.

Consider the strengthened liar as a natural-language argument of the sort we regularly deal with in informal logic. This "naive" approach is more promising than may at first appear. Surely, one thing that strikes the careful reader is the strange emptiness of the sentence, "This statement is false." It just does not seem to say anything. Suppose I say, "The statement 'geese have gallbladders' is false." There is something here outside the statement which makes it true or false. If geese do not have gallbladders, then the statement "geese have gallbladders" is false; if they do have gallbladders, then the statement is true. But what possible circumstance or conditions in the world could make a sentence like "This statement is false," true? The sentence does not refer to anything outside itself. As earlier twentieth-century authors such as Henry Veatch and Alexandre Koyré indicate, it is not clear how anything could prove or establish the truth of such an empty sentence.[31] The liar's paradox is then problematic, in the first instance because it is an empty statement. It is as if we are saying, "This blank statement is false." Without our filling in the blank, the statement does not seem to mean anything. It is an empty trick with words. It cannot be true or false. It is not, in a meaningful sense, asserting anything.

Note that the problem with the strengthened liar is not simply that it refers to itself. We can have meaningful sentences which refer to themselves, such as, "This statement is not written in French." Or, "This statement is composed of seven words." In these cases, we deny or affirm a property of the sentence itself. This is unproblematic. If we know French or we can count, we know how to determine whether the statement is true. In sharp contrast, it seems meaningless to ask whether the strengthened liar is true. Even if we pay close attention to the meaning of the words, this is no help. We are left with an empty formalism. If, like Aristotle, we conceive of logic as a scientific tool for dealing with existent things, the absurdity of the statement comes into sharp focus. Ultimately, the problem with the liar's

31 See Koyré, "Liar"; and Veatch, *Intentional Logic*, 149–53.

paradox is that it looks like something is being said, but, in fact, nothing is being said. The strengthened liar is like a cipher; it has nothing behind it. It fails to be intelligible discourse because, as Parmenides argues, we cannot make sense of nothing.

What the liar's paradox demonstrates is not that the principle of noncontradiction is false or inadequate or optional. It shows that we cannot separate the formalism of language from the material meaning of words, without running into problems. On this Aristotelian-like account, it is the lack of reference that subverts the liar's paradox. Because the strengthened liar has the form of a sentence, it looks like something is being said, while nothing is said at all. The liar's paradox seems to ascribe a property to a statement. But, in fact, there is no meaningful statement (only what looks like one); there is no content, only grammatical assertion.

One variant of the liar's paradox (from Epimenides) cites an apparent real-life situation. Suppose the one man who is the only Cretan speaks once in his life and says, "Cretans always lie."[32] This scenario has contradictory implications. If what he says is true, he must be telling a lie, which means that what he is saying must be false. But if what he is saying is false, then the statement, "Cretans always lie," must be true. So he cannot be a liar. And so on. We seem to be left with a statement (with real-world significance) that is true if it is false; and false, if it is true. What are we to make of this perplexing circumstance?

The first thing to notice is that lying, unlike truth-telling, is epistemologically handicapped. Suppose we try to create a truth-telling paradox: The man who is the only Cretan speaks once in his life and says, "Cretans always tell the truth." This statement is unproblematic. What is the problem with lying? The lying Cretan who says that he is lying is, in fact, an impossible construct. If he admits he is lying, he is telling the truth and so he is not lying. If, by contrast, he is lying, he cannot say that he is lying; he must say he tells the truth. In both cases, the paradox dissolves.

Language cannot render the impossible possible. The liar's paradox presupposes the impossible: a complete liar who says that he lies. Once we admit this contradiction, anything follows. Consider the amusing Stoic tale about the crocodile. You are walking alongside the Nile one fine morning when a crocodile grabs your dear child between its teeth. It is, however, a philosophical crocodile. "I am wondering if I should eat your child," says

32 Hence St Paul's excessively literal report: "A prophet from their own people said of them 'Cretans are always liars, wicked brutes, lazy gluttons'. This testimony is true" (Titus 1:12–14). This is a strengthened version of Epiminedes' reported conundrum.

the crocodile, "but I am a merciful creature. I will let her go if you correctly tell me what I am going to do." If you tell the crocodile it is not going to eat the child that will be false, and the crocodile can eat the child. But what if you tell the crocodile that it is going to eat the child? What then? If the crocodile eats the child, your prediction will be correct, and it will have to refrain from eating it. If, however, the crocodile does not eat the child, your prediction will be wrong, so it can eat the child. In short, the crocodile can eat the child if it refrains from eating it, and it cannot eat it if it eats it! Very puzzling! But does any of this subvert the principle of non-contradiction? It only shows that the crocodile has promised something impossible. The fact that the world is structured in such a way as to make such promises unfulfillable only shows that the principle of non-contradiction has a basis in reality. (Aristotle, of course, supplied both metaphysical and logical versions of the principle.)

Saul Kripke: Howard Dean and Richard Nixon

Saul Kripke introduces a specifically modern, natural-language version of the liar's paradox (which is intended as a comment on Alfred Tarski's proposed "types solution").[33] Consider this contemporary attack on the law of non-contradiction.

Return to the historical era of the Watergate scandal, with Howard Dean and Richard Nixon as the two antagonists. Imagine the following situation. Dean makes a number of true statements about Watergate; Nixon makes a number of false statements about Watergate. Dean also states proposition$_1$, "All of Nixon's utterances about Watergate are false!" Nixon states proposition$_2$, "Everything that Dean says about Watergate is true." This results in a paradox. If proposition$_2$ ("Everything that Dean says about Watergate is true") is true, then proposition$_1$ ("All of Nixon's utterances about Watergate are false") must be true, so proposition$_2$ (Nixon's statement, "Everything Dean says about Watergate is true") must be false. So it seems that if proposition$_2$ is true, then proposition$_2$ is false, which is, of course, a contradiction.

There is a sense in which Kripke's version might be seen as an improvement on the standard liar's paradox, for it eliminates the problem of self-referentiality. "This statement is false" is problematic because it has no referent. It only refers to itself. But Nixon's statement does not refer to itself; it refers to a different statement made by a different speaker. So, it

33 Kripke, "Outline of a Theory of Truth."

seems that any logical problems that arise cannot be attributed to the reflexive nature of the assertion.

What is the problem here? Standard practice in informal logic renders explicit the hidden premises in an argument. This is the method of deductivism. Every assertion may then be said to include an implicit truth claim. When I assert, "It is raining outside," I am claiming, "It is true that it is raining outside." When Nixon affirms that the claims Dean makes are all true he is, in effect, affirming that "*it is true* that the claims Dean makes are all true." So Nixon contradicts himself. He claims, on the one hand, that his own statement is true, and, on the other hand, that it is false (for he affirms Dean's statement, "Everything Nixon says is false"). So Nixon declares both that his statement is true and that it is false. But again, this is a contradiction. And anything follows from a contradiction.

The Dean-Nixon paradox is the liar's paradox with a twist. Dean, the truth-teller, tells us that Nixon is a complete liar (that everything he says is false). But Nixon cannot be lying, at least not when he truthfully declares that what Dean says is true. A lying Nixon who says that what Dean says is true is an impossible construct. If Nixon is a complete liar, he would have to say that everything Dean says is false. But then these logical problems would dissipate of their own accord.

The Dean-Nixon paradox leads to contradictory conclusions because it begins with contradictory premises. It could be the case that neither Dean nor Nixon is aware of the contradictory nature of their assertions, either because they do not know the exact content of the other's statements or because they are not astute enough to recognize the logical implications of their own assertions. But these issues are irrelevant. If fallible individuals make contradictory statements that result in an unsolvable logical imbroglio, this does not undermine the law of non-contradiction. It only shows that violations of this law lead us into absurdity.

Suppose an elementary-school math teacher tells the students 2 + 2 = 4, and then goes out that night and gets so drunk as to tell someone at the bar that 2 + 2 = 5. Is this a logical problem? The math teacher has unwittingly embraced a belief in two contradictory statements, but this is mere oversight, not a conscious decision. Presumably, Nixon's assertion is not a genuine paradox. It is only an oversight. If, however, he claims that all of Dean's statements are true, knowing that Dean says that all Nixon's own statements are false, he would be no better than the original liar, who says that it is true that all his own statements are false. This is equivalent to asserting "*p*" and "not *p*" in the same way and at the same time. The resultant logical problems can be traced, once again, to a vicious self-referentiality (that is merely obscured by the story).

The ancient liar's paradox, the strengthened liar, the crocodile conundrum, and Kripke's Dean and Nixon paradox misuse language. As Ludwig Wittgenstein suggests, those who believe in such possibilities have unwittingly constructed a trap and they cannot escape. They are the authors of their own misfortune. If you build a house from the outside-in, with no doors or windows, you will find yourself trapped inside. This does not show that we should expand our definition of houses to include those without doors or windows. It only shows that it is a mistake to build houses without doors and windows.

Wittgenstein writes as follows: "Is there harm in the contradiction that arises when someone says: I am lying. – So I am not lying. – So I am lying. – etc.? I mean does it make our language less usable if in this case, according to the ordinary rules, a proposition yields its contradictory, and vice versa? – the proposition itself is unusable, and these inferences equally; but why should they not be made? – It is a profitless performance! – It is a language game with some similarity to the game of thumb-catching."[34] The liar's paradox is like thumb-catching; i.e., it is a trick, a trivial pursuit, a pointless performance; it is not epistemologically momentous. Wittgenstein adds, "Such a contradiction is of interest only because it has tormented people, and because this shews both how tormenting problems can grow out of language, and what kind of things torment us."[35]

We should not take fright at logical apparitions. These apparent paradoxes do not seriously threaten first principles. Contemporary philosophers focus on logic. Consider, however, an alternative version of the liar's paradox, with an ethical focus. Assume promise-keeping is good; promise-breaking, bad. And suppose some wily ethicist says, "I promise not to keep this promise." If this ethicist keeps this promise then he or she must break it; so the ethicist is good just when he or she is bad. If, however, the ethicist breaks this promise then he or she keeps this promise, so the ethicist is bad just when he or she is good. (This is much like Aristotle's oath-taker.)[36] What are we to make of this odd state of affairs? Does it follow that being good is equivalent to being bad? Surely not. These are incompatible states. The proper response to the wily ethicist is as follows: What an absurd thing to say! Such philosopher's puzzles are linguistic games; they need not occasion any fundamental revision to our epistemological, metaphysical, or moral beliefs.

34 Wittgenstein, *Remarks*, ch. 3, §12, 120.
35 Ibid., ch. 3, §13, 120.
36 *Sophistical Refutations*, ch. 25, 180a34 ff.

Real-World Contradictions?

Modern dialethists attempt to undermine the law of non-contradiction by appealing, for example, to modern scientific theories such as quantum mechanics. But however odd, strange, or unintuitive microscopic reality seems when viewed from a macroscopic perspective, it does not follow that the physical world admits of contradictions. The presumed wave-particle duality, for example, is not a contradiction. It specifies that light acts in specific circumstances as a wave and in other circumstances as a particle. This happens in a rule-like, orderly manner. This is not a contradiction. Modern physical theories are, in any case, highly abstract and open to radically different metaphysical interpretations.

As Huss suggests, the mere existence of paraconsistent logics does not disprove the principle of non-contradiction. The issue is whether the utterance "*p* and not *p*" corresponds to an actual state of affairs in the world. Can we have a real object which has and does not have property *p* understood in the same way at the same time? If we *accept* contradictions for logical purposes to see what follows, it does not follow that we *believe* that contradictions are logical. To believe in a contradiction in this sense would be to believe that the person who always tells lies can tell the truth or that the Stoic's crocodile can give back the baby after eating it. The present author at least finds no evidence for such possibilities.

As we have already seen, Aristotle believed that a first principle like that of non-contradiction is discovered through induction rather than argued for deductively. We induce the principle of non-contradiction, and in so doing, we recognize that it *must* be true. We do not prove it is true; we *see* – through insight – that it must be true. We can produce a valid inductive argument in favour of the law of non-contradiction, but proof in the modern sense of a complete enumeration of cases is clearly impossible.

On the ancient view, contradiction has a role in philosophy. It supplies the problems that philosophers set out to resolve. Socrates tells young Theaetetus that philosophy begins in a state of *aporia* brought on by the contemplation of questions with contradictory answers.[37] Aristotle claims that philosophy begins in wonder at apparent contradictions.[38] Is philosophical

37 Plato, *Theaetetus*, 148e ff.

38 See *Metaphysics* (Tredennick), pt 3, ch. 1, 995a24–995b1 (in Aristotle, *Aristotle in 23 Volumes*): "It is necessary, with a view to the science which we are investigating, that we first describe the questions which should first be discussed. These consist of all the divergent views which are held about the first principles; and also of any other view apart from these which happens to have been overlooked. Now for those who

inquiry always successful? Clearly not. Some contradictions resist solution, at least for the time being and perhaps forever. But the existence of unsolved philosophical problems does not disprove the law of non-contradiction.

Eastern societies may privilege wonder over explanation. This attitude to life does not invalidate this logical law. The fact that apparent contradictions are a source of wonder only illustrates how strongly they defy the first principles of human understanding. To accept "*p* and not *p*" is to propose a mystery, a wonder, a miracle. A mystery is something which surpasses rational human understanding.

Contrary to what Weinberg et al. suggest, the most basic intuitions of all are not a variable, local phenomenon. Presumably, all human beings share the same mental powers of intelligence. Presumably, we all live in a world that is *fundamentally* the same. Diverse ethnic, cultural, religious, and historical differences play an important role in human disagreement. But they do not change the basic reality of the human condition: we are all going to die; two plus two equals four; the colour red is not the colour green; dogs walk on four legs; pain hurts; some people tell lies – and so on. Modern discontent or suspicion about first principles does not derive from radically divergent intuitions about the basic reality of the world; it derives instead from another source: the fact that these principles cannot be proved. This epistemic discontent is, in point of fact, what motivates the specific work of Weinberg et al. But as I have already argued, and as careful perusal of the Western tradition makes abundantly clear, we cannot limit reason to argument, to what can be proved. We need a place in our theories for non-discursive reason, the intuitive faculty behind induction.

Weinberg et al. attribute earlier notions of non-discursive reason to a "black-box" theory of mind. But the metaphor is seriously misleading. Ancients and medievals did not view the human mind as a black box closed off from the world. First principles arise from experience. They derive from sense perception. The mind is not a black box but an open eye which confronts reality. We look out into the world and *see* that this or that *must*

wish to get rid of perplexities it is a good plan to go into them thoroughly; for the subsequent certainty is a release from the previous perplexities, and release is impossible when we do not know the knot. The perplexity of the mind shows that there is a 'knot' in the subject; for in its perplexity it is in much the same condition as men who are fettered: in both cases it is impossible to make any progress. Hence we should first have studied all the difficulties, both for the reasons given and also because those who start an inquiry without first considering the difficulties are like people who do not know where they are going; besides, one does not even know whether the thing required has been found or not."

be the case. It is the structure of the world imposing itself on the sensitive structure of the mind that produces infallible first principles.

Knowing That We Know

If traditional authors (including Descartes) believe that first principles are infallibly true, their position was more complicated than is commonly understood. Duns Scotus quotes from Augustine's original account of the *cogito*: "If anyone should say 'I know ... that I live ... he cannot be deceived, no matter how often he reflects on this first knowledge'."[39] Scotus includes "knowledge that we live" within "those things which are known in such a way that they can never slip from the mind."[40] On this mainstream account, this first principle will have two components. (1) We apprehend that we exist; and (2) at the same time, we know that we know that we exist. We know that this knowledge cannot be false. Traditional philosophers view our belief in first principles as a two-tiered awareness: we are aware of the meaning of the words "we exist," but we are also aware of the indubitable nature of this assertion. If the inductive movement that produces the first principle only provides specific content, we would be left with having to prove that this content is true, an impossible task that would lead to a vicious regress. First principles must include then an awareness of the necessary nature of the principle. This awareness is a kind of intelligent discernment. The act of discernment that discovers a principle must include some awareness of its certainty (or uncertainty).

Knowledge presupposes that we know that we know. If we could not know that we know, we could not distinguish belief in truth from belief in error. Here again, no explanation can be given for this reflexive capacity of knowledge. It is a non-discursive capacity. It is a feature of pure intelligence. In some non-vicious way, it must be assumed, taken for granted. The usual allegation that traditional authors were naive is tiresome and misleading. Traditional authors correctly believed that we had to assume that human judgement would be, at least at the most basic levels, indefeasible. Otherwise, knowledge, of any sort, would be impossible. It was later authors who were naive for trying to prove everything.

We cannot understand what earlier authors propose as infallible first principles as mere propositions in any reductionist sense. It is only when the content of the principle is unbuckled from the act of intelligent

39 Duns Scotus, *Philosophical Writings* (Wolter), ch. 5, art. 2, §b, 113. He is quoting from Augustine's *De Trinitate*, bk 15, ch. 12.

40 Duns Scotus, *Philosophical Writings* (Wolter), ch. 5, art. 2, §b, 113.

discernment that problems arise. Taken by itself, treated as a disputable assertion, as something that stands in need of corroboration, the content of any concept or principle is open to Cartesian suspicion. First principles are more than information. They are, first and foremost, acts of intelligent discernment. It is not the content of the proposition by itself but the content and the judgement taken together that carries the epistemological warrant. A fashionable scepticism is overly suspicious of human judgement. But human judgement is all we can rely on. If human judgement is *fundamentally* flawed, all our assertions and arguments are problematic, including those made by philosophers who dispute first principles.

It is ironic that a wide range of modern authors use human intelligence to argue against human intelligence. These authors rely on first principles to argue against first principles. Their arguments could easily be construed as an attack on their own credibility. (Ancient sceptics seemed more aware of the limitations of scepticism.) Human intelligence is not a black box; it is discernment turned toward something. Our ability to know that we know, which cannot be explained by anything logically prior, must be final court of appeal in epistemological issues. But this capacity does not exercise itself arbitrarily but through a careful consideration of evidence.

THE NEW ESSENTIALISM

Water is H_2O

Brian Ellis has identified a general philosophical orientation he terms the "new essentialism." We can associate this new movement in logic, epistemology, and philosophy of science with diverse authors such as Kornblith, Sankey, Freeman, Kripke, and Putnam. These authors defend a theory of induction resembling, more or less, the traditional account. There are, however, important differences. Examine, in particular, the influential defence of induction Kornblith elaborates in a perspicacious book, entitled *Inductive Inference and Its Natural Ground.*

The new essentialism is, in large part, a reaction to Thomas Kuhn's famous work, *The Structure of Scientific Revolutions.* Members of the group took issue with Kuhn's basic thesis that scientific theories are incommensurable. According to Kuhn, we cannot translate claims from one theory into another. No theory is reducible to another. Science does not, strictly speaking, progress. Different theories may overlap, but they cannot be rigorously evaluated in terms of one another. Newtonian mechanics and relativistic physics are not competing but alternative, incommensurable theories. Relativity is not, strictly speaking, an improvement on or a refutation of Newton; it is a different way of looking at the world. Science does not move from a worse to a better theory but from one paradigm to another.

This sort of scientific "relativism" raised the ire of those who conceive of modern science as making inevitable progress toward a more successful and a more authoritative description of reality. Philosophers such as Putnam and Kripke, in responding to Kuhn, reintroduced a modern notion of natural kind. These authors argue that scientific theories describe natures or essences that possess real existence in the physical world. We can, for example, discuss our present chemical concept of gold, or Richard Boyle's, or the alchemist's, or Aristotle's concept of gold, but gold exists, not merely as a linguistic term in a theory, but as a natural kind "out there" in the world. The natural kind "gold" possesses certain necessary properties. Every instance of it must possess these properties. Otherwise, it would not be gold. Scientific progress is possible, for successive descriptions of what gold is may better account for the objective reality of gold. We can reasonably claim, for example, that contemporary chemistry better articulates the chemical properties of gold than, say, Richard Boyle's, the alchemist's, or Aristotle's concept of gold.

Authors supportive of the new essentialism cash out the notion of a necessary property in terms of possible worlds. Suppose, for example, I was to claim that gold is necessarily malleable. In possible-worlds terminology, this is to claim that gold must be malleable in every possible world. According to authors such as Putnam and Kripke, if the natural kind "gold" possessed different properties, it would no longer be gold. It follows that "gold" must possess the same properties in every possible world.

This new concept of natural kinds opens the door to metaphysical realism. Essence is no longer nominal, conventional, or linguistic in the traditional Lockean sense. The true nature of a thing exists on its own outside our conceptions. It provides an independent criterion of scientific truth that has to be discovered by empirical investigation. As Brian Ellis argues, "The real essence of a thing … is independent of our conceptualization of reality, and also of the language we use to describe it, for the real essences of things refer to their natural classifications, and these have to be discovered by scientific investigation."

Ellis claims, like Aristotle, that the world is composed of substances, of individual things. We can divide these individual things into natural kinds. Ellis uses the example of water to explain his concept of natural kinds:

> Consider the proposition that water is H_2O. The fact that water is essentially a compound of hydrogen and oxygen was discovered in the eighteenth century, and its molecular form was worked out in the

> nineteenth. But these are not the facts on which the distinction between water and other substances initially depended, and water would still be H_2O even if these facts had never been discovered. So the proposition that water is H_2O is not simply true in virtue of the conventions of language. It is, in fact, true independently of these conventions, since its truth is independent of whether anyone has the language to express it. Moreover, if it is true, it is necessarily true, for the molecular structure of water is essential to its nature. The substance in the glass before me would not be water if it were not H_2O, however like water it may be in appearance, savour, function, and so on.

As Ellis suggests, the existence of different natural kinds poses specific constraints on things. When chemists claim that water is H_2O, they propose a necessary (and sufficient) condition that must be fulfilled by anything that qualifies as water. We may legitimately claim, not just that water is H_2O, but that water is *necessarily* H_2O. As Ellis explains, "If water is H_2O, and this is its essential nature, then not even God could create a world in which water is not H_2O. God might conceivably create a world in which some substance other than water has a functionally similar role to the one water has on earth. But ... this stuff is not water."[41]

Critics object that practicing scientists do not appeal to notions of metaphysical necessity. Chemists assert that water *is* H_2O, not that water *is necessarily* H_2O. Still, one can counter that this notion of metaphysical necessity is implicit in scientific practice. Imagine that Mary, a student in a first-year chemistry class, is asked to determine the chemical composition of pure water. And suppose she announces to the class that pure water is, in fact, made up of nitrogen and chlorine. Mary's answer is wrong; it *must* be wrong; pure water *cannot* be nitrogen and chlorine, because water *must* be H_2O. So there is an implicit sense of necessity that accompanies the mundane claim that water is H_2O. It does not matter where or when the analysis is performed, what the particular circumstances are or what apparatus is used, modern chemistry informs us that water *must* be H_2O. This description can only be used as an objective criterion for scientific success because the description of water as H_2O *necessarily* follows.

Is there any way in which the claim that water is H_2O could turn out to be wrong? If the claim, "Water is H_2O," is a first principle of chemistry, it cannot be incorrect. In light of the overwhelming evidence collected over centuries of laborious, careful chemical research, we can confidently assert that water is H_2O, although it may, of course, be the case that this description of

41 Ellis, *Philosophy of Nature*, 16.

water could be improved on. Perhaps more sophisticated physical theories will supersede the theories of contemporary chemistry. Perhaps we can be more informative about the natural properties of water, but whatever we learn in the future about water cannot contradict what has already been shown to be true. The statement, "Water is H_2O," is, in the sense intended by traditional authors, infallibly true.

The new essentialists' belief in natural kinds solves the alleged problem of induction.[42] Physical possibility is divided into discrete substances that display necessary features. In this kind of physical world, generalization and prediction are, more or less, unproblematic. New essentialist Howard Sankey elaborates the correct response to Hume's attack on induction.[43] As Sankey explains,

> We are rational to employ induction when we form our beliefs about the future because nature is, in fact, uniform. It is uniform in the sense that the fundamental kinds of things which exist … possess essential sets of properties … Unobserved members of a kind will possess the same properties as members of the kind which have already been observed. This is why, when we infer that an unobserved object will have [the same properties], we turn out to be right. For having such a property is just what it is to be an object of the same kind … What makes it rational to make inductive predictions … is simply that it is part of the nature of objects of a given kind to have certain properties.[44]

This response to the problem of induction closely parallels the Aristotelian account of induction already outlined in this text. There are, however, some important differences. Aristotelian natural philosophy is not narrowly physicalist but heavily influenced by biology. Aristotle believed that metaphysics precedes epistemology; the new essentialists, by contrast, tend to regard metaphysics with inevitable suspicion and believe that epistemology is logically prior to metaphysics. On Aristotle's account, science considers formal and even final causes, whereas the new essentialists champion a modern account of science focusing on the material or efficient cause.

42 "Were it not for the existence of natural kinds and the causal structure they require … reliable inductive inference would be impossible. The causal structure of the world as exhibited in natural kinds thus provides the ground of inductive inference" (Kornblith, *Inductive Inference*, 7).

43 Sankey is respectfully cautious in presenting his result, but his argument is an intended response to Hume (Sankey, "Induction and Natural Kinds").

44 Ibid., 5 (online).

Aristotle claims that scientific induction depends on mental illumination (*noesis*), whereas the new essentialists believe that the epistemological authority of induction derives ultimately from abduction or inference to the best explanation. And finally, Aristotle viewed logic as a tool regulating commentary about what happens in the world, whereas the new essentialists tend to think of logic, in modern terms, as a largely formal endeavour.

The new essentialists situate themselves within analytical philosophy, and more broadly within the empiricist tradition. Their own account of natural kinds can be traced back to a causal theory of reference that associates natural kinds with proper names. But the ramifications of their views extend beyond the usual analytical paradigm. As I intend to show, if we take the new essentialism seriously, we must break decisively with contemporary attitudes. No middle ground is possible. The doctrines championed by the new essentialists subvert the strict empiricism of authors such as Locke, Hume, and Kant and *require* a return to Aristotle.

Kornblith and Locke

If the new essentialism moves resolutely forward in the right direction, it displays, nonetheless, an inner tension. Kornblith's hopeful account of induction is a case in point. Kornblith does not look to Aristotle for inspiration but to Locke.[45] This is deeply problematic. As we have already seen in an earlier chapter, Locke himself argues that induction is conclusively unreliable. If we hope to rescue it, we must move beyond the Lockean-Humean tradition. We cannot solve the problem by adding new wrinkles to the old empiricist theory.

Kornblith is attracted to Locke because of his corpuscularism, viewing him as the philosophical precursor to modern atomic and subatomic theory. This is an important aspect of Locke's metaphysics. Deeply impressed by Boyle's work in chemistry, Locke believed that observable physical natures are a surface manifestation of the hidden interactions of a world of invisible particles. In his metaphysics, he effectively splits the world in two. The macroscopic world is made up of observable objects and events; the microscopic one, of an unknowable, inaccessible substance, composed (presumably) of shadowy, invisible particles. As Kornblith himself suggests, this bifurcated picture of physical reality is not unlike the subatomic model of physical reality favoured by modern physicists – except that there is one very important difference. On the modern scientific account, ingenious

45 See, especially, Kornblith, *Inductive Inference*, ch. 2, "Locke and Natural Kinds," 13–34.

experiments using instruments such as diffraction apparatuses, spectroscopes, high-speed particle accelerators, electron microscopes, and lasers teach us, however indirectly, about the empirical properties of underlying things. On the Lockean view, atomic substance is utterly unknowable. It is forever a *je ne sais quoi.* We cannot access it in any empirical manner. It is this Lockean split between the visible and invisible that provides the rationale for his scepticism and undermines the reliability of induction.

As already mentioned, Kornblith proposes a new reading of Locke. Although he admits that Locke is "insistent that the real kinds in nature are entirely unknowable by us … a theme he repeats many times, and quite emphatically,"[46] Kornblith spies a second Locke who seems to suggest that chemists can sort substances into elements through a negative method of "severe examination."[47] According to this second Locke, chemists can attain "highly nontrivial knowledge of real kinds, so long as [they] are both careful and fortunate."[48] Kornblith champions the second Locke over the first but does not fairly acknowledge the radical nature of these amendments to Locke's original philosophy. If science can investigate real essence, the Lockean account of unknowable substance, which grew into Kant's account of the noumenon, is irretrievably wrong. Aristotle's division of the world into natural kinds, the emphasis he places on sense perception, and his carefully qualified confidence in induction provides a much closer parallel to the views of the new essentialists.

Kant: Synthetic A Priori?

Kornblith traces the modern scientific view to Locke, but the developed philosophy of Immanuel Kant is more influential. As we have seen, Kant divides the world into phenomenon and noumenon. Phenomena are a product of the way the human mind structures the world. The noumenon is the Kantian equivalent of Locke's substance, a *je ne sais quoi* which, in the course of historical development, comes to be seen as an unknowable, inaccessible object. On the orthodox (realist) interpretation of Kant, the nature of things-in-themselves is a metaphysical mystery we can never penetrate. This leaves open the possibility that our claims about the nature of

46 Ibid., 24.

47 As Locke himself writes, physical bodies which appear to be the same "upon severe ways of examination, betray qualities so different from one another, as to frustrate the Expectation and Labor of very wary Chymists" (Locke, *Essay,* bk 3, ch. 3, §17, cited in Kornblith, *Inductive Inference,* 26).

48 Kornblith, *Inductive Inference,* 28.

the world are, in one way or the other, wholly inaccurate. Induction is irredeemably unreliable, because knowledge of real essence escapes us.

Kant's epistemology builds on the Humean division of knowledge claims into "relations of ideas" and "matters of fact."[49] Relations of ideas are purely linguistic or logical; matters of fact are a product of observation. We could claim, for example, "that three times five is equal to half of thirty," which is really a claim something about how the ideas of three, five, and thirty are related to one another. Or again, we could claim that we have discovered that gold is a soft yellow metal, which is to claim something about a physical nature in the world. On Hume's account, we are faced with an exclusive disjunction. A truthful claim must be a comment about relations of ideas or about matters of fact. It must be a matter of pure definition, or it must be a matter of pure observation. It cannot be both: it must be one or the other. And what if a book or treatise or argument conflates these distinctly separate categories? What then? Hume is adamant, "Commit it to the flames, for it can contain nothing but sophistry and illusion."[50]

On Hume's account, the problem of induction subverts future prediction. Relations of ideas follow necessarily; matters of fact are contingent. We cannot know beforehand what future facts will be true of the world. But this seems problematic. As new essentialists indicate, modern science has discovered "necessary facts" about the physical world. For example, the claim that "Water is H_2O" is a necessary fact. Scientists came to know water is H_2O, through experiments and observations, but, as we have seen, they also claim that water is *necessarily* H_2O. The nature of water follows necessarily from its molecular structure. We can legitimately say, "all future water will be H_2O." There is, however, no room in the Humean scheme of things for this kind of necessary physical claim. Kant, in reworking Hume's reworking of Locke, does not resolve the problem.

Kant invokes two sets of epistemological criteria. First he distinguishes between *a priori* and *a posteriori* knowledge. *A priori* knowledge is "knowledge absolutely independent of all experience." *A posteriori* knowledge is "knowledge possible only … through experience."[51] *A priori* knowledge is necessary and universal; *a posteriori* knowledge, which comes to us through observation, is contingent. If, however, these opposing categories of judgement parallel Hume's division of knowledge claims into relations of ideas

49 Hume, *Enquiry* (Selby-Bigge, Nidditch), §4, pt 1, paras 20–1 (in Hume, *Enquiries*).

50 Ibid., §12, pt 3, para. 132, 165.

51 Kant, *Critique of Pure Reason* (Kemp Smith), intro., §1, B3, 43.

Table 9.1
Kant's account of judgement

	A priori *(independent of experience)*	A posteriori *(through experience)*
Analytic	Relations of ideas	–
Synthetic	Metaphysical necessity	Matters of fact

and matters of fact, Kant nevertheless adds a further distinction between analytic and synthetic judgements. Analytic judgements divide a subject into its constituent parts; synthetic add something new to the subject.[52] This leaves room for three forms of judgement, as illustrated in Table 9.1. Because analytic judgements are true by definition, they cannot depend on observation. So there are no analytic *a posteriori* judgements. We can divide all truthful claims into three categories: analytic *a priori*, synthetic *a priori*, and synthetic *a posteriori*.

Without focusing on these individual categories in any detail, consider the place of the necessary fact "Water is H_2O." This is *a posteriori* knowledge. Chemists learned that water is H_2O, by experiment and observation. But, on Kant's schema, all *a posteriori* knowledge is contingent. Kant leaves no place for any *a posteriori* claim that is necessarily true. So Kant's model only replicates, it does not solve, the problem inherent in Hume's original dichotomy.

Scientific claims do not fit into any of Kant's categories. The underlying problem is that he, like Locke and Hume, disputes the validity of induction. "Experience," he writes, "never confers on its judgements true or strict,

52 Kant: "Either the predicate B belongs to the subject A, as something … (covertly) contained in this concept A; or B lies outside the concept A, although it does indeed stand in connection with it. In the one case I entitle the judgment analytic, in the other synthetic. Analytic judgments (affirmative) are therefore those in which the connection of the predicate with the subject is thought through identity; those in which this connection is thought without identity should be entitled synthetic. The former, as adding nothing through the predicate to the concept of the subject, but merely breaking it up into those constituent concepts that have all along been thought in it, although confusedly, can also be entitled explicative. The latter, on the other hand, add to the concept of the subject a predicate which has not been in any wise thought in it, and which no analysis could possibly extract from it; and they may therefore be entitled ampliative" (ibid., intro., §4, B10–11, 48).

but only assumed and comparative *universality*, through induction."[53] In other words, induction supplies more or less expansive generalizations, not laws of nature. It always leaves room for exceptions. Kant continues, "If then, a judgement is thought with strict universality, that is, in such a manner that no exception is allowed possible, it is not derived from [our experience of] existence."[54] But, as the new essentialists correctly point out, this clashes with scientific practice. When chemists assert that "Water is H_2O," this statement follows with "strict universality." No exceptions are allowed. So Kant's account leaves no room for the claims of modern science.

Hume, in some sense Kant's inspiration, points to the Pythagorean theorem, "that the square of the hypotenuse is equal to the square of the two sides," as an example of a proposition involving relations of ideas.[55] But this is incorrect. The Pythagorean definition is not true by definition. It is not true *because* we decide to organize our ideas in a certain way. It is true because that is, *in fact*, what we *discover* when we study the nature of triangles. Suppose I was to devise an "un-Pythagorean theorem" that the square of the hypotenuse is equal to the cube of the two sides divided by fourteen minus four. This is just silly. I can decide to relate my ideas to each other in any way I want but this is not what the Pythagorean theorem is about. We can "prove" what the Pythagorean theorem is by constructing the triangles and measuring them.

Kant's metaphysical account of the world as an objective construction of our cognitive powers provides a more sophisticated reading of Hume, but he still relegates necessary truths to relations between ideas. These relations are forced on us by the cognitive structure of our minds; because we possess minds, we cannot reorganize these relations at will. As it turns out, the Pythagorean theorem is true because that is how we are forced to think, not because it corresponds to the way real things in the world actually are. In the final analysis, the Pythagorean theorem tells us more about

53 As Kant goes on to say in this passage, "We can properly only say, therefore, that so far as we have hitherto observed, there is no exception to this or that rule. If then, a judgement is thought with strict universality, that is, in such a manner that no exception is allowed possible, it is not derived from existence" (ibid., intro. §2, B3, 43).

54 Ibid. Kant further comments, "Experience never confers on its judgements true or strict, but only assumed and comparative *universality*, through induction. We can properly only say, therefore, that, so far as we have hitherto observed, there is no exception to this or that rule. If then, a judgement is thought with strict universality, that is, in such a manner that no exception is allowed possible, it is not derived from existence" (ibid.).

55 Hume, *Enquiry* (Selby-Bigge, Nidditch), §4, pt 1, para. 20, 25.

our minds than the world. The world is reduced to our ideas. We have discussed at length the problems with this kind of account.

The new essentialists, in contrast, distinguish "metaphysical necessity" from formal, logical, linguistic, or analytical necessity. Ellis explains, "Metaphysical necessities are propositions that are true in virtue of the essences of things … Metaphysical necessities have to be discovered by scientific investigation. They are not discoverable, as other necessities are, just by considering meanings. On the contrary, they depend on what there is in the world, and how the world is structured. In philosophers' jargon, metaphysical necessities are *a posteriori*."[56] The claim that water is H_2O is not true because we choose to a certain way of defining the term "water." This fact derives from observation. It is an *a posteriori* statement. At the same time, it follows necessarily. To posit the existence of necessary scientific truth is, however, to return to the metaphysical realism of earlier authors such as Aristotle and Thomas.

The doctrines of the new essentialism are, strictly speaking, incompatible with the general metaphysical orientation of modern authors such Locke, Hume, Kant, and Mill. More recent work has not improved things.[57] If anything, a generalized suspicion of induction has made matters worse. The eminent W.V.O. Quine, no friend of Kant, goes so far as to dismiss belief in the *a priori* as "an article of faith."[58] But this only exacerbates the predicament. On the usual post-Kantian account, the *a priori* is the only source of necessary truth. When we eliminate the *a priori*, we eliminate necessary truth. It will follow that all truths must be contingent.[59] If, however, all truths must be contingent, the findings of modern science must be, in some definitive and irremediable sense, inconclusive. But this clashes with the central tenet of the empiricist creed, an unshakable confidence in the inevitable progress and validity of empirical science.

The new essentialism proposes the recovery of what has been lost. In some salutary sense, they turn back the clock. They rescue induction by invoking the notion of logically necessary, *a posteriori* truth. But surely, this is to forsake Kant and Hume and to return to Aristotle. In Aristotle, all

56 Ellis, *Philosophy of Nature*, 17.

57 Notably, Hilary Putnam has increasingly distanced himself from any narrow interpretation of analytical philosophy.

58 Of course, one wonders whether belief in science is not equally a naturalistic article of faith, but that issue will not detain us here. See Quine, "Two Dogmas of Empiricism," 37.

59 They are *necessarily* contingent. This truth about non-analytical truths does not seem, however, to be an analytical truth.

knowledge is, in some important sense, *a posteriori*. All knowledge begins in sense perception. In Aristotle, induction produces synthetic *a posteriori* truths, truths which come to us through observation, but which follow necessarily from the deep structure of the world.

Contemporary analytical philosophy focuses on language. Aristotle is not interested in linguistic definitions; he is interested in scientific definitions, in definitions that exhibit the objective nature of things.[60] If we grasp definitions through induction, induction hinges on observation. Water is H_2O, not because of the structure of grammar, but because careful observation has revealed that this is the case. Aristotle proposes a middle way.[61] On the one hand, he is through-and-through an empiricist. We learn through experience (ἐμπειρία, *empeiria*). There is *no such thing* as *a priori* knowledge. On the other hand, he also avoids an extreme empiricism. The mind is not a passive recipient of sense impressions but a creative, dynamic power that can make knowledge. Knowledge is born of an interaction between the mind and the empirical world. The creative, organizing power of understanding and the outside world come together through the faculty of sense perception to produce knowledge. Without this meeting of understanding and perception, knowledge would be impossible.

Aristotle avoids a crude correspondence theory. Concepts are not imprinted on the "blank slate" of the mind. They are created. But he also avoids extreme idealism. Knowledge conforms to an objective reality. Concepts are not a mere human fabrication. They tell us something true about the world. On Aristotle's account, scientific knowledge begins in observation, but mere observation is not enough. It needs to be penetrated by insight. We see right-angled triangles, but we never "see" the Pythagorean theorem. The theorem itself is a relationship that is intellectually grasped but not, strictly speaking, seen. This is, for Aristotle, how scientific discovery operates. Observation elicits the necessary leap of understanding that transforms the empirical data into knowledge.

Anti-metaphysics

Some of the new essentialists, who tend to see themselves as analytical philosophers, enthusiastically endorse the modern empiricist attack on metaphysics. They contrast *a priori* metaphysics with *a posteriori* science while

60 See chapter 4, for an in-depth analysis.

61 A description he would have gladly embraced. See *Nicomachean Ethics*, bk 2, ch. 6, 1106a24ff; and *Politics*, bk 4, ch. 11, 1295a34 ff.

championing the epistemological authority and precedence of the latter. Kornblith's position is a case in point. Following in the footsteps of his teacher, W.V.O. Quine, Kornblith explains,

> Successful science is the best judge of what exists. Attempts by philosophers to dictate *a priori* to scientists on metaphysical matters have had a very bad track record. If a metaphysical claim would have us reject some piece of successful science as improper … this is evidence against the metaphysical claim. Similarly, that a face-value interpretation of some successful science commits to the existence of a certain kind of entity … counts in favor of the existence of that kind of entity. The face-value interpretation of scientific theories should be, as it were, the default interpretation.[62]

If, however, new essentialists such as Kornblith evince a familiar modern hostility to metaphysics, this basic attitude is unwarranted and even contradictory. Kornblith's naturalism can be traced back to Quine. Like Quine, Kornblith champions science over traditional metaphysics. But there are serious problems with this perspective. First, Kornblith seems to equate traditional metaphysics with something like innate ideas, a favourite whipping boy of empiricists. But this is a straw man. Traditional metaphysics is *a posteriori*, not *a priori*. Aristotle, Thomas, and other mainstream historical authors do not subscribe to a single-minded *apriorism*. Criticism of innate ideas by analytical philosophers does not invalidate all metaphysics. (Even the Neoplatonists do not believe, in any simplistic way, that metaphysics is *a priori*.)

Second, Kornblith's claim that science provides a successful guide to metaphysics seems ideological rather than descriptive. Kornblith writes, "When a successful scientific theory quantifies over some sort of object, that is the most powerful evidence we may have that those objects genuinely exist."[63] But the situation is more complex. Consider an actual episode from the history of science, the triumph of the wave over the corpuscular theory of light. Thomas Young (1773–1829) is generally credited with securing the victory of the wave model with his widely acclaimed double-slit experiment. Young (and his contemporaries) believed, however, in the existence of the ether. The resulting wave formalism (as later developed by Fresnel and others) involved "quantifying over the ether." Does it follow that ether exists? Later science jettisoned the ether concept

62 Kornblith, *Inductive Inference*, 48.

63 Ibid., 55.

completely, while retaining (and reworking) wave formalism.[64] So scientists themselves do not believe that the positing of a mathematically useful object invariably proves the existence of that object.

We can sketch out the reasoning of historical scientists such as Young and Fresnel in a simple argument: Premise$_1$: Believing in ether allows us to quantify interference and diffraction phenomena. Premise$_2$: "When a successful scientific theory quantifies over some sort of object that is the most powerful evidence ... that those objects genuinely exist" (Kornblith's existential principle). Conclusion: So ether exists. But most contemporary physicists reject this conclusion as false. So there must be something wrong with the argument. Premise$_1$ is incontestably true, so premise$_2$ must be, if not entirely false, at least unreliable. Because a theoretical concept serves a useful role, it need not follow that it is part of the ontological stuff that composes the universe. The hypostatization of the merely theoretical is an ever-present possibility.[65]

Kornblith claims that we should believe in the existence of physical kinds posited by scientific theory, even if they are unobservable, because science provides the best explanation of the world. But this is too quick. Modern mathematical physics contains abstract entities (like the ψ function of quantum mechanics) that are, at best, ambiguous. We need a more

64 Later scientists, such as Maxwell and Schrödinger, retained a wave formalism for light but eliminated the physical presence of the ether altogether. In the first case, light was reinterpreted as disturbances in an electromagnetic field; in the second case, it became a probability function. Note that, in point of fact, a very small minority of contemporary physicists (those on the fringe so to speak) want to bring back the concept of ether. This should serve as a healthy reminder to us that the case is not quite closed.

65 Kornblith justifies his scientific literalism through an appeal to abduction or inference to the best explanation (which we discuss below). He explains his logical strategy as follows: "What one postulates is that there are genuine unobservable properties which are bound together by nature. Now the mere fact one performs such a postulation does not, of course, guarantee that there are such unobservables in nature answering to the act of postulation. Nonetheless, if one does postulate such unobservables, and this act of postulation proves successful in explanation, prediction and technological application, then one surely has extraordinarily good evidence that the structure postulated does genuinely exist" (Kornblith, *Inductive Inference*, 42–3). In short, we should believe in the existence of unobservable physical kinds because they provide the best explanation of the world. The point is that the existence of ether *did* provide the best explanation of the light but it was still discarded by later scientists.

sophisticated account of scientific realism than mere literalism can provide. The point is that the existence of ether did provide the best explanation of the light but it was still discarded by later scientists (even though the mathematical approach it spawned was retained). Yes, science plays an important role in metaphysics. But it is not the entire story. Science itself has to be interpreted, as I explain below.

And further objections can be made to this way of thinking. The third problem with Kornblith's scientific literalism is its logical circularity. We cannot use science to prove the validity of science. This would beg the question. It would mean assuming the validity of the scientific method to prove the validity of that very method. Kornblith is rightly impressed with the epistemological authority of science. If, however, we want to defend that authority, we must move beyond science to larger considerations, which must include a careful investigation of logically prior beliefs about the nature of the world and the mind. But to trace out these views in any detail is to do metaphysics.

The choice is never between "metaphysics" or "no metaphysics" but between a metaphysics explicitly argued for and one that is simply assumed. Kornblith himself proclaims, "Everything which exists, I assume, is ultimately composed of physical stuff ... To believe otherwise, it seems, is to accept the existence of some sort of nonphysical thing; and this is sheer silliness."[66] But physicalist bravado is only that. It cannot replace argument. Perhaps there are good arguments for comprehensive physicalism (of some qualified sort), but to explicitly formulate and defend them would be to do metaphysics. The art of repartee is no substitute for rigorous philosophical inquiry.

The fourth problem with Kornblith's literalism is that it does not fairly acknowledge the narrow scope of the modern scientific endeavour. We live in a macroscopic, commonsense world. The enormous gap that separates this world we experience from the front edge of microphysical research leaves room for multifarious interpretation. If science is a search for causes, our belief in causality does not derive from science. It derives from ordinary experience. Everyday experience, properly understood, is logically and practically prior to science. It can serve as a basis for many different schools of metaphysics.

Science is deep but incomplete. Specialization provides a localized explanation of things. But it does not explain how everything fits together. Metaphysics, however, is a general inquiry into reality understood as totality. It addresses questions science cannot answer: Does God exist? Do humans

66 Ibid., 53.

possess free will? Is reality an idea? Is the mind immaterial? Are we being tricked by a Cartesian demon? What happens after we die? Is there purpose to history? And so on. It is not clear how science could answer these larger questions, which are not subject to experimental verification.

Finally, Kornblith does not fairly acknowledge the theoretical complexity of modern science. To claim that the "face-value interpretation" of scientific theories should be our metaphysical guide is not very helpful. What is the face-value of an abstract theory like quantum mechanics? The many-worlds interpretation? The Copenhagen? The hidden variable? The superstring? The instrumentalist? Contemporary physics, particularly, has become so complicated by issues of mathematical formalism that to say its meaning is less than plain is to indulge in understatement. Its degree of specialization fosters a sometimes discordant pluralism. What, in the final analysis, does science mean? This is a big question, but whatever the answer is, it can only be answered from the perspective of some kind of larger metaphysics.

Abduction: Inference to the Best Explanation

The new essentialists attempt to secure belief in the existence of real natural kinds through abduction. Charles Sanders Pierce originally proposed abduction as the engine of new ideas in science.[67] On Pierce's original account, it is the mental movement that supplies the researcher with a bright idea to be tested. As K.T. Fann explains, "Abduction invents or proposes a hypothesis; it is the initial proposal of a hypothesis on probation to account for the facts."[68] But this is only the brainstorming model described in a previous chapter. The new essentialists push abduction further. They conceive of it as a form of rational justification. Abduction does not propose a hypothesis; it confirms it. This is an important shift in logical strategy.

Sankey formulates an argument for natural kinds: "Science is successful. The existence of natural kinds is the best explanation of the success of science. Therefore, there are natural kinds."[69] His formulation is elegantly expressed and perhaps persuasive, but it leaves out a hidden premise that needs to be examined. We might make this assumption explicit by rewriting the argument: Premise_1: Science is successful. Premise_2: The existence

67 Note that Pierce's account of abduction closely resembles Lonergan's account of induction. One cannot help but surmise that Lonergan knew of Pierce (or Popper) (Peirce, "On Pragmatism and Abduction").

68 Fann, *Pierce's Theory of Induction*, 10.

69 Sankey, "Induction and Natural Kinds," 6 (online).

of natural kinds is the best explanation for the success of science. Hidden premise: Our ability to discern which explanation is the best one is reliable. Conclusion: Therefore, there are natural kinds. This line of reasoning only works if the hidden premise is true. Sankey simply assumes that our ability to discern best explanations cannot be mistaken. But this seems to be nothing less than an assertion of infallibility. If our ability to distinguish between better and worse explanations were infallible, we could embrace the conclusion that natural kinds exist. But how would this approach be substantially different from the traditional one? As we have seen, the mainstream metaphysical tradition recognized that we must accept that the infallibility of the process of induction that produces first principles. As it turns out, abduction hinges on a similar assumption.

We might try to avoid this potentially embarrassing state of affairs by reformulating Sankey's argument in more qualified terms: $Premise_1$: Science seems to be successful. $Premise_2$: The existence of natural kinds is the best explanation for the success of science. Hidden premise: Our ability to tell which explanation is the best one is *probably* reliable. Conclusion: Therefore, we have probably a good reason for believing that there are natural kinds. But this will not do. We have no way of determining the probable reliability of our ability to tell which explanation is best. Just how reliable is it? Is it reliable eight times out of ten? Most or some of the time? Rarely or usually? How could anyone determine this? How could we differentiate between times when our judgement is or is not reliable? We have no way to get outside of our human judgement so as to evaluate its reliability from a higher, more reliable point of view.

Suppose it were the case that human judgement is probably reliable. Then our judgement that "human judgement is probably reliable" would itself be probably reliable. And our judgement that this judgement is probably reliable would be probably reliable, and so on, *ad infinitum.* But any infinite series of probabilities arranged in this manner will tend to zero. A probably reliable judgement of a probably reliable (to infinity) judgement will be so unreliable as to be epistemologically worthless. Human finitude requires, in any case, that we stop the chain somewhere. At some point, we simply have to accept, without further justification, that human judgement is reliable. To make a longer story short, we simply have to believe that human judgement is reliably truthful, or our claims to knowledge would collapse.

As it turns out, the appeal to abduction is not that different than the traditional appeal to infallible intuition. If anything, the traditional argument seems more direct. Authors in this new school of essentialism do not fully acknowledge the break they are proposing with mainstream philosophy.

Clearly, we do not, in any absolute sense, have the final word. What extends beyond the limits of human knowability is beyond comment. Still, what the new essentialists are proposing is, in effect, a return to the sophisticated metaphysical realism of a historical author such as Aristotle.

ARISTOTLE AND CONTEMPORARY BIOLOGY

Biological Species: The Received View

The new essentialists, in line with contemporary attitudes, privilege physics as the queen of the science. Aristotle, in many ways, viewed the world as a biologist. This has led to some serious misunderstandings. Without entering into any exhaustive treatment of these issues, I will argue that Aristotle's account of induction and natural kinds can be adapted and applied to physics or biology or to other scientific disciplines and that this shift in emphasis does not subvert the metaphysical integrity of Aristotle's theory.

Historically, much of the empiricist wrath directed against traditional metaphysics stemmed from a post-Newtonian impatience with Aristotle's biocentric world view. More recently, the widespread acceptance of Darwin's theory of evolution has undermined Aristotle's reputation as a biologist. If Aristotle conceived of species as fixed, eternal, ungenerated biological forms, most modern-day biologists believe that species are subject to genetic mutation and natural selection and have evolved over an extended period of time. Bertrand Russell, not one to worry about historical details, goes so far as to (mistakenly) identify Aristotle as a literal creationist. "Each species corresponds to a different idea in the Divine mind, and therefore there [could] be no transition from one species to another, since each species resulted from a separate act of creation."[70]

Russell describes a position more Platonic than Aristotelian. Its influence can be traced back to the famous Swedish taxonomist Carolus Linnaeus (1707–1778) and ultimately to a medieval realism that took universals to be real ideas in the mind of God. It is, in part, the overtly religious element introduced by the Schoolmen that has led to vehement public debates between creationists and evolutionists, as they are commonly called. I will not investigate such overlapping issues here. As we shall see, Russell's account is a wholesale caricature and does not fairly represent the complexity of Aristotle's essentialism. Let us turn then to a more rigorous, contemporary source.

70 Russell, *Scientific Outlook*, 43.

David Stamos, in a recent book on the species problem, presents a meticulous critique of Aristotle and modern essentialism. As Stamos points out, contemporary biologists and philosophers define species in divergent ways. Stamos, for example, argues that species are horizontal (not vertical) relations in biological time;[71] David Hull, that species are individuals rather than classes;[72] new essentialist Richard Boyd, that they are homeostatic-property-cluster kinds;[73] Leigh Van Valen and David Johnson, that they are teleological responses to specific environmental niches;[74] Ernst Mayr, that they are reproductively isolated populations;[75] Philip Kitcher and John Dupré, that they are pragmatic classifications imposed on living things by biologists;[76] and Benjamin Burma, that they are fictional constructs without any real-world existence.[77] We need not definitively choose between these (and other) alternatives here. I only mean to show that the standard dismissal of Aristotle's ancient account is hasty and ill informed.

It seems ironic that the metaphysical essentialism, which originated in Aristotle's biological interests, has been largely discredited within modern biology. According to Stamos, to the extent that "the influence of Aristotle and Linnaeus in terms of species as essentialistic classes continues into the present day," it is a live issue "only in the heads of philosophers," and even there it has been "shorn of many of its Aristotelian and Christian trappings."[78] Stamos pulls no punches. Strict essentialism is, he claims, "an untenable view and should be rightly thought of, as it is among virtually all biologists today, as a dead issue."[79] Although his appraisal is more than a little hasty, it captures a prevalent attitude.[80]

71 Stamos, "Species, languages, and the horizontal/vertical distinction."

72 Hull, "Are Species Really Individuals?"

73 Boyd, "Homeostasis, Species and Higher Taxa."

74 Van Valen, "New Evolutionary Law"; and D. Johnson, "Can Abstractions Be Causes?"

75 Mayr, *Growth of Biological Thought*, 273.

76 Kitcher, "Species"; and Dupré, *Disorder of Things.*

77 Species "exist in precisely the same sense that the class of unicorns may be said to exist" (Burma, "Reality, Existence and Classification," 205.

78 Stamos, *Species Problem*, 113.

79 Ibid., 122.

80 The comments about "no living essentialists" are a bit strong. To begin with, there are even biologists who believe in literal creationism. They may exist outside the ambit of mainstream academic society, but they are alive! Secondly, practicing biologists (and even philosophers of biology) cannot be expected to be experts in Aristotle, and they are not in a position to ascertain whether or not they agree with Aristotle.

If, however, Aristotle has been roundly and vociferously criticized in biological circles for his "species essentialism," I will argue, quite to the contrary, that nothing in modern biology shows that the Aristotelian picture is irretrievably wrong. If modern theorists dispute the Aristotelian account, the disagreement is not due to a clash of opposing alternatives a shift of emphasis. Aristotle equates species with the formal cause, whereas most modern biologists focus on the efficient or material cause. Modern critiques of Aristotle are, in fact, anachronistic. They read into Aristotle what is not, in fact, there. We can do better.

Species as First Principles

Before we investigate Aristotle's notion of species, we must resolve a methodological problem clouding the usual understanding of Aristotle. Stamos, who surveys a broad sweep of literature, is adamant, "there are no species essentialists alive today in biology."[81] But it is not even clear that Aristotle was, in this modern sense, a "species essentialist."[82] Balme explains, "The traditional interpretation assumed that Aristotle did actually classify animals into genera and species, but the assumption is not supported by the evidence. [Aristotle] accepts as data the animal kinds that are presented to him by common parlance, but does not try to group them further by finding similarities ... There is no classification scheme in the background, and all attempts to construct one for Aristotle have failed."[83] Pierre Pellegrin goes so far as to observe that Aristotle "never gives even a single example of a definition of any species of animal."[84] This is not quite true, for Aristotle does provide a definition of the species human beings (as rational or social animals), but the general point is well taken. In his biological work, Aristotle does not propose any close account of the concept "species." He uses the terms genus (γένος) and species (εἶδος) loosely and interchangeably, referring both to dogs and to specific breeds of dogs as different kinds (genera) of animals.[85] Although he is clearly motivated by the idea that living things can be divided into different kinds, he never proposes any specific answer to the modern species problem. For the remainder of this discussion, I will use the term

81 Stamos, *Species Problem*, 22–3.

82 Pellegrin, *Classification des Animaux chez Aristote*; Balme, "Aristotle's Biology Was Not Essentialist"; and "ΓΕΝΟΣ and ΕΙΔΟΣ."

83 Balme, "ΓΕΝΟΣ and ΕΙΔΟΣ," 85, cited in Stamous, *Species Problem*, 107–8.

84 Pellegrin, "Zoology without Species," 99, cited in Stamos, *Species Problem*, 110.

85 Balme, "ΓΕΝΟΣ and ΕΙΔΟΣ," 85. See *History of Animals*, pt 6, ch. 20, 574a16.

"species" loosely to refer to a biological kind of an unspecified sort, as this seems more in line with Aristotle.

If Aristotle the working biologist is not an essentialist, how did the conventional account arise? Broadly speaking, a certain basic rationale is at work.[86] Early Greek philosophers strive to discern the unchanging logical order – the λόγος – beneath a shifting, confusing world of appearances. Science is about what remains the same, about what necessarily follows. Biology provides a challenge to any such view, for the individual organisms we observe are precariously contingent, constantly changing, and inevitably mortal, subject to generation and corruption. In a stroke of genus, Aristotle (along with other Greek thinkers) discovered order and permanence, not in the individual animal, but in the species. If individual organisms display accidental variety and obvious imperfections, species retain their formal integrity through time. Aristotle writes, "It is impossible for [an organism] to be eternal as an individual ... But it is possible for it as a species. This is why there is always a class of men and animals."[87] Aristotle fixes then on species as a manifestation of the necessary order of things. This is why biological science (i.e., *episteme*), properly speaking, deals with species rather than individuals.

Aristotle's account can be seen as a reworking of Plato's idealist scheme. The Greek word for species is εἶδος which means both "idea" and "form." Biological species are, for Aristotle, Platonic forms come down to Earth. Individual members represent a concrete instantiation of an underlying theme. Although species only exist insofar as they are exemplified in physical organisms, we can conceive of each species as the embodiment of a fixed and imperishable idea.[88] If this conflicts with the modern view of species as changing "units of evolution," I will argue that the conflict is, in fact, only skin deep. Contemporary philosophy of biology does not undermine Aristotle's more metaphysical account.

Although Aristotle does not come up with a precise definition of the concept of species in his biological work, this is not surprising. He is a working biologist; he gets his hands dirty. His attitude resembles that of contemporary biologist Ernst Mayr, who writes, "Modern biologists are almost unanimously agreed that there are real discontinuities in organic nature, which delimit natural entities designated as species."[89] Aristotle

86 Although wider attention should be paid to the context of Aristotle's remarks, Stamos annotates the issue in competent detail; see Stamos, *Species Problem*, 99–113.

87 *On the Generation of Animals* (Platt), pt 2, ch. 1, 731b31–732a1 (in Aristotle, *Complete Works*).

88 See *Nicomachean Ethics*, pt 6, ch. 3, 1139b23–25.

89 Mayr, *Toward a New Philosophy of Biology*, 331.

does not try to prove the existence of species; he does not try to argue species into existence; he looks out at the animate world and *sees* that they exist. In Aristotle's epistemology, species are first principles.[90] We induce first principles; we discover them through observation, not through argument and theory.

To require a philosophical proof for the existence of species is to put the cart before the horse. Species are real, not because we can provide logical arguments for them, but because attentive observation reveals they are out there. Aristotle's attitude contrasts sharply with the standard caricature. In Aristotle, we move from observation to induction to scientific explanation. We begin with the *observation* that there are various kinds of things in nature; we do not have to prove that this is the case, for this is plainly obvious to anyone who seriously investigates nature.

Aristotle's essentialism is not, in the first instance, a theory about explanation; it is a theory about what needs to be explained. We might distinguish between two levels of induction. At the non-conceptual level, at the level of ἐμπειρία (*empeiria*) or experience, we simply distinguish between different things, between bees and ants, birds and fish, dogs and cats, apples and oranges. At the level of ἐπιστήμη (*episteme*) or science, we explain these classifications in scientific demonstration or ἀπόδειξις (*apodeixis*). Biological science converts experience into theory. This is the challenge. Even if science remains forever incomplete, our ability to initiate and move forward with this project of classification and explanation is enough to establish essentialism as a valid scientific methodology.

Although distinguishing between biological kinds is, at times, a subtle and remarkably perplexing task, this does not detract from Aristotle's "species essentialism." Two conditions must be met to get essentialism off the ground. (1) There must be biological kinds. (2) We must be able to distinguish between biological kinds. Aristotle embraces both requirements. He believes that biological kinds really exist, and he believes that we can recognize them. Just as we can grasp the pattern "triangle," so we can the pattern "grizzly bear." Explaining precisely what a grizzly bear is, its anatomy, its behaviour, how it reproduces, is a serious scientific accomplishment. But it is after the fact. We first induce the idea "grizzly bear" and then, with more or less success, explain what a bear is.

Contemporary authors seem to imply that essentialism requires an exhaustive or conclusive description of membership conditions, necessary and sufficient attributes, family resemblance traits, genotype, phenotype, and so on. This is simply untrue. If I look at the colour red, I may be unable to explain this colour scientifically (in terms of the wavelength of

90 For example, *Prior Analytics*, pt 1, ch. 30, 46a17–25.

light), but red still exists. I do not have to prove that red is a different colour than blue; I can see that this is the case. I only have to explain why this is so. In biological science, observation reveals real differences that are open to explanation. This is all we need for essentialism.

It is true that Aristotle, following Plato, views a species as an ideal type. Induction selects out traits that exemplify the form of a healthy, mature specimen. But such traits do not have to be present in each individual. Aristotle was too much of a biologist to have overlooked the fact of contingent difference. If I claim that dogs have four legs, but my dog loses a leg in a car accident – this does not impugn the validity of this generalization. That some dogs are defective three-legged ones, dogs who fail to fully meet the criterion of biological success, is not surprising. Insomuch as a dog lacks four legs, it imperfectly embodies the idea of what a dog is. If, however, "dog nature" may be inadequately expressed in individual cases, such counter-examples do not alter the true nature of a species.

Aristotle the biologist is not really interested in "heavenly types." His criterion of species identification is biological, not theological. Aristotle is fundamentally a naturalist. Biological knowledge begins with familiarity (in French, *connaitre*), not with factual knowing (*savoir*). Someone who lives with lions on the savanna comes to grasp what a lion is. Someone who raises chickens comes to grasp what a chicken is. Someone who fishes for lake trout comes to grasp what a lake trout is. On Aristotle's account, the idea of a species arises out of experience. Familiarity with the natural world is where biology begins. Induction is insight into experienced reality.

Aristotle's biological works are filled with reports, reliable or not, from people who have close familiarity with animals: shepherds, breeders, hunters, farmers, travelers. In a discussion of sexual reproduction, he reports that "Scythians use pregnant mares for riding as soon as the embryo has turned in the womb, and they assert that thereby the mothers have an easier delivery."[91] He informs us that "Male elephants get savage around pairing time, [so] men who have charge of elephants in India never allow the males to have intercourse with females; on the ground that the males go wild at this time and turn topsy-turvy the dwellings of their keepers."[92] Again, he tells us that "trainers [of horses and donkeys] always allow of intervals between breeding times," so that the female will not go sterile,[93]

91 *History of Animals* (Thompson), pt 6, ch. 22, 576a21–24 (in Aristotle, *Complete Works*).

92 Ibid., pt 6, ch. 18, 571b31–572b3.

93 Ibid., pt 6, ch. 23, 577b14–15.

that "shepherds [who tend goats] appoint no bellwether as the animal is not of a stable nature but frisky and apt to ramble,"[94] and again, that "in a stable in Opus there was a stallion that used to serve mares when forty-years old."[95] This is where Aristotelian biology starts. Not up in heaven, in some abstract realm of eternal ideas but in close familiarity with nature. Species distinctions do not arise out of *a priori* philosophical conceptions; our experience of nature drives home the reality of biological kinds. Acquaintance with biological difference is a first principle of biology.

Although Aristotle believed that species are fixed or static, he could not have thought this of individual organisms. He describes, for example, the life cycle and metamorphosis of butterflies: "The so-called psyche or butterfly is generated from caterpillars which grow on green leaves ... At first it is less than a grain of millet; it then grows into a small grub; and in three days it is a tiny caterpillar. After this it grows on and on, and becomes quiescent and changes its shape, and is now called a chrysalis. The outer shell is hard, and the chrysalis moves if you touch it. It attaches itself by cobweb-like filaments, and is unfurnished with mouth or any other apparent organ. After a little while the outer covering bursts asunder, and out flies the winged creature that we call the psyche or butterfly."[96] Aristotle did not conceive of an individual organism such as a butterfly as a fixed, static physical thing, but as something moving toward a goal or aim, something with entelechy (ἐντελέχεια). The aim of a butterfly's life is the mature adult form, which then lays eggs to secure the survival of the species.

Formal Accounts of Biological Species

Assuming species (loosely understood as biological kinds) exist, we must now ask a basic question. How would someone using an Aristotelian approach explain what a species is? Aristotle is a formalist. It is the overall structure of the organism that determines what it is. It is the way that the individual parts are arranged so as to form a distinctive whole that defines each species. Aristotle claims that if we could recombine all the different kinds of animal parts in every possible way, we would, in theory, produce all possible species of animals. He explains, "If we were going to speak of the different species of animals, we should first of all determine the organs which are indispensable to every animal ... Assuming ... that there are only so many different kinds of organs, but that there may be differences in

94 Ibid., pt 6, ch. 19, 574a12–15.
95 Ibid., pt 6, ch. 18, 576b26–28.
96 Ibid., pt 5, ch. 19, 551a14–26.

them – I mean different kinds of mouths, and stomachs, and perceptive and locomotive organs – the possible combinations of these differences will necessarily furnish many varieties of animals ... And when all the combinations are exhausted, there will be as many sorts of animals as there are combinations of the necessary organs."[97] There are then as many different species of possible animal as there are possible combinations of the parts of animals.

A biological species is, then, a biological form. Imagine a universe inhabited by a single horse and a single cow. And imagine these animals somehow came suddenly into existence. Are these animals members of the same or different species? Clearly, they belong to different species. Why? Because the horse and the cow are characterized by a different arrangement of parts. This is all that is required to have different species.

Modern biological theories focus on evolution, on how individual species came to be. But to ask "how a species came to be" and "what a species is" is to ask two different questions. Consider an example from geometry. Suppose we took a wire triangle and bent it into a circle. What was the wire formerly? A triangle. What is the wire now? A circle. To consider how we bent the wire to turn it into a circle is to discuss an efficient rather than a formal cause. It is to discuss how this circle came into being. This is not to say what a circle is. We can produce circles in various ways. But the final metal shape would be a circle, even if made in a different way.

An efficient cause is not a formal cause. How a species comes to be is not what it is. This is not to deny the importance of this information. But familiar criticisms of Aristotelian essentialism miss the point. Aristotelian essentialism is not a doctrine about how things came to be; it is a doctrine about what they are. Essentialism only presupposes that there are discrete forms in nature, that we can identify these forms, and that we can describe them in words. However the horse or the cow got into our imaginary universe – they are clearly different kinds of things. This is enough for species essentialism. The real enemy of essentialism is not evolution but a perennial reductionism that would divest the world of real difference.

When Aristotle refers to species or kinds he is making a formal distinction. So his own terminology does not translate easily into the contemporary idiom. The present enthusiasm for evolutionary theory posits biological species as populations undergoing some kind of constant or punctuated change. Consider, then, from an Aristotelian perspective, whether species understood as formal causes can undergo evolutionary change. I will argue that nothing in evolutionary theory shows that Aristotle was wrong.

97 *Politics* (Jowett), pt 4, ch. 4, 1290b25–36 (in Aristotle, *Complete Works*).

Can the same species change? In one sense, yes; in another, no. Return to the example of the wire triangle bent into a circle and consider three interrelated questions:

(1) Can the same metal wire take on a different shape? Clearly it can. We can, in this sense, turn a metal triangle into a circle. This is to consider a formal change from the viewpoint of the material cause.
(2) Can we discover a method for changing the shape of the triangular wire? Clearly we can. We can bend the wire into a new circular shape in various ways. This is to consider a formal change from the viewpoint of the efficient cause.
(3) Can we come up with a reason, a purpose, for changing the shape of this wire? Clearly, we can. We can change the shape of the wire to serve some practical aim or merely for the sake of illustration. This is to consider a formal change from the viewpoint of the final cause.

Aristotle would agree that change is possible in all three cases. But can the notion of species, considered as a formal distinction, undergo change? Can, for instance, the triangle become a circle and remain a triangle? Clearly not, for once something becomes a circle, it is no longer a triangle. What happens is not that the triangle becomes a circle, for that would mean that a straight-sided figure would become a round one. This is impossible. In the case of species change, one form is destroyed and replaced by a new form different from the first. In other words, one species is destroyed and a new species comes into existence. The species "triangle" cannot and does not change into the species "circle." Formal notions of species are then, as Aristotle assumed, incapable of change.

Elliot Sober writes, "One often hears that evolution undermined essentialism because the essentialist held that species are static but … this comment makes a straw man of essentialism … Notice that the discovery of the transmutation of elements has not in the slightest degree undermined the periodic table. The fact that nitrogen can be changed into oxygen does not show in any way that nitrogen and oxygen lack essences … The mere fact of evolution does not show that species lack essence."[98] Exactly. Contemporary authors refute Aristotle by turning his account of species into one of efficient causation and then arguing that he mistakenly claimed (or implied) that efficient causes are static. It is fair to say that Aristotle overlooked the evolutionary possibility, but his account of species immutability

98 Sober, "Evolution, Population Thinking and Essentialism," 356, cited in Stamos, *Species Problem*, 122.

is one of the immutability of form, not of process. Aristotle is not preoccupied with questions of origins; that is a later development. As Aristotle intimates, a species, understood as a biological form, cannot change into a different form and remain the same species.

The concept of a changing kind, understood from a formal point of view, is incoherent. Evolution does not and cannot require changing forms that remain what they are while becoming something different. The very notion entails a contradiction. Suppose that every nitrogen molecule in the universe was changed into oxygen. It would not follow that nitrogen or oxygen lacked essences. The species "nitrogen" would become extinct and the species "oxygen" would be more prevalent than it was before. But nitrogen cannot and could not become oxygen. It cannot become oxygen because if it did it would no longer be nitrogen. The same holds for biological kinds.

On Aristotle's account, species seek to replicate their form. Reproduction is the way a species achieves immortality and preserves its formal integrity.[99] Despite appearances to the contrary, this is not, in fact, at odds with orthodox theories of evolution. On standard (non-Lamarckian) models of evolution, organisms do not initiate change. Genetic mutation and natural selection are imposed by outside forces. Reproduction (asexual or sexual) is not an attempt to create a new species; it is an attempt to preserve what went before. Evolution results from outside pressure that thwarts the propensity for formal replication. Evolutionary change occurs when something outside of form intervenes and frustrates its propagation.

Species as Similarity Relations

But there is more to say. It is not simply that Aristotle's formal account of species is consistent. In fact, it provides a clear advantage over the modern alternatives. The contemporary focus on efficient causation seriously complicates philosophical attempts at species definition. No one thing causes evolutionary change. When our wire triangle is transformed into a circle, it makes sense to say the same thing went from being a triangle to being a circle, because the very same piece of metal changed shapes. The underlying material cause is still the same. In the case of evolution, however, the material cause does not remain the same. Successive generations of animals are not composed of the same matter. Final cause (with its teleological overtones) is

99 Aristotle argues that organisms reproduce so that they "may partake in the eternal and the divine" (*On the Soul* [Smith], pt 2, ch. 4, 415a30, in Aristotle, *Complete Works*).

generally excluded from consideration.[100] What then is a species? If no material, formal, or final cause remains the same, what could serve as the marker of common identity? What could supply a thread of continuity or sameness. Modern biologists tend to conclude that it could only be the efficient cause, the ongoing process, that authors these changes. Enthusiasm for Darwinian evolution makes this an attractive alternative. But any such suggestion is, as we shall see, deeply problematic.

The present focus on the efficient cause produces the modern species problem. Contemporary responses to the species problem identify the species with something other than the form of the organisms themselves. If form is always changing, we need an "identity carrier" (something other than form) that can stay the same while the form changes. Consider briefly two responses to the problem: Stamos' account of species as similarity relations; and a more familiar account of species as historical individuals. Both accounts end up associating species with something outside the organisms themselves.

Stamos devises a relational account of species. He "conceive[s] of species as similarity complexes, composed of their member organisms and all the various similarity relations between them."[101] This sounds rather straightforward, but Stamos reifies relations; he turns them into metaphysical objects. A "similarity relation" is "the relata themselves plus something more about them in virtue of which the whole is called a relation."[102] This "something more" is an immaterial ontological object that somehow links the members of the species to one another.[103] As it turns out, these invisible links actually exist, bridging the spatial gaps between organisms of the same species. A species is the existence of a network of these reified, immaterial links.

Stamos goes on to describe similarity relations as "constituents of facts," as "more basic than classes," as "part of the physical world," and (in the case of evolution) as "spatiotemporally unrestricted."[104] A species is then an extra-mental relational object, composed of invisible ontological threads that link individual organisms together within a coherent group. These

100 The biological aim of "survival" is too general a notion to particularize a specific line of ancestry.

101 Stamos, *Species Problem*, 296.

102 Ibid., 338.

103 This "something more" that relates the organisms to one another "is both abstract and yet particular and is just as much a part of the relation as the relata" (ibid., 337).

104 Ibid., 338, 340, 349.

relations become the ontological carrier of identity that presumably remains the same as the species changes. But how is this kind of Neoplatonic alternative better than Aristotle?

While rejecting Aristotle, Stamos nevertheless adopts a kind of species realism. He is driven to what can only be called an extreme solution. To conceive of relationships in terms of invisible ontological links is to give up on empiricism. Why should we grant any ontological status to the *relation* between animals? We cannot observe anything that connects individual specimens to one another; we only observe individual organisms. To say that specimen *A* is like specimen *B* is to say something about the specimens. It is not to identify a new ontological object. Stamos' account bears a disturbing similarity to G.E. Moore's very strange moral theory about goodness as a simple, non-natural property. Although Stamos identifies with modern analytic philosophy, he (along with Moore) manages to propose some very unintuitive doctrines. Surely, Occam's razor means we should be cautious about introducing new ontological entities into the world when we have much simpler ways to describe what is going on.

Stamos does not sufficiently consider the metaphysical ramifications of his account. He claims that relationships between individual organisms are ontological objects. There are, however, relationships between organisms of the same species, as well as between organisms of different species, for example, relationships between prey and predator, parasite and host, human beings and domesticated animals – not to mention those between animate and inanimate objects. And if we reify inter-organism relationships, why should we not reify inanimate relationships. Why not allow that all volcanoes, all rubies, all instances of lightening and thunder, are "held together" by an invisible ontological thread, making them the same kind of thing? Needless to say, this exercise in consistency would result in a hopelessly complicated metaphysics.

Stamos confuses the role of a relationship with that of identity. It is not the relationship that determines the form but the form that determines the relationship. If this dog is related to that dog, it is not the relationship between them that turns them into dogs; rather it is the fact that they both possess the form "dog" that creates the special relationship between them. Stamos points to the relationship between individual organisms as the carrier of species identity. He wants to propose an account of species as remaining the same through evolutionary change. But this cannot be. The relationship between dogs is different than that between cats. If "dogs" were to evolve into a new kind of animal, the relationship between these new animals would have to be different than that between dogs; that is, these "new dogs" would end up being a completely different species. So it is hard to see how Stamos' model is any improvement on the formal account. It seems much simpler to equate species with form and to accept that as the form changes, so does the species.

Species as Individuals

The widespread notion in contemporary philosophy of biology that species can be "historical individuals" represents another attempt to identify the species concept with evolution understood *qua* efficient cause.[105] New essentialist Richard Boyd claims that species can be individuals and individuals, species.[106] Boyd and colleagues restrict the term "species" to an individual episode in evolutionary history. To be a member of the same species is to participate in the same event. In this way, it seems, we can have a species that changes its form while remaining the same. But can we?

Suppose I draw a triangle on the back of an envelope. This triangle remains a triangle whether I send the envelope to Alabama, China, Egypt, or Montreal. And it will still be a triangle if someone preserves it in a time capsule and looks at it a thousand years in the future. Location in space and time is not form. What something is is not where or when it is found. The fact that an individual organism participates in an evolutionary episode may determine what it is, but its location in time-space is not what it is. We should not confuse cause and effect with identity. It is true that I would be killed if my present spatiotemporal location placed me in front of a speeding cement truck. Allowing that my death might be caused, thus, by my spatiotemporal location, it would not by that fact *be* this location.

105 My concern here is not to provide any detailed critique of one or more authors but only to show how the species-as-individuals view fits into a general trend that is, I have argued, problematic.

106 Boyd, "Homeostasis, Species and Higher Taxa," 163. Some historical authors also consider the idea of "individuals as species." Boethius attributes an incommunicable essence to every individual. He claims, for example, that Plato has two essences: "humanity" and "Platonity." If other human beings share the property "humanity," Plato alone possesses "Platonity." See Boethius, *Commentary on* De Interpretatione, 64, 462–4, cited and translated in Gracia, *Introduction,* 91. Gracia also discusses Porphyry's more traditional view of Aristotle's categories (pp. 67–70). Although Thomas Aquinas does not favour this approach to individuality, he, analogously, cites the example of Socrates as being constituted by his Socrate-ity (*On the Power of God* [*Quaestiones disputatae de potentia*], Q. 8, art. 3, *contra*). See Thomas Aquinas, *On the Power of God* (Shapcote).

Whereas Stamos reifies relations, "individualists" reify a spatiotemporal episode, which becomes the identity carrier that is the species. But this is problematic. A historical episode is made up of numberless individual events that are contiguous with one another. A historical event is not one thing. Historical eras are academic or pragmatic distinctions, drawn up for our own convenience and utility. They are not substances. In opting for a historical criterion of species, philosophers fall back on a conventionalist criterion of biological kind. Species are something we project onto the world for our own purposes or convenience. They do not "really exist" in the world as fundamental constituents of reality. This point of view clashes with the biological realism of an author such as Mayr.

Philosophers who propose a historical definition of species do not, however, recognize their own dependence on formal criteria. If form is caused by episodes in evolutionary history, we define episodes according to form. If we consider "horses" a single event in evolutionary history, this is because horses possess the same form. We do not consider horses and racoons as a single episode in evolutionary history, because they possess different forms. Each species is a historical event insomuch as it happens at a specific time and place, but to associate it with this event is to overlook the formal similarity that binds all these individuals into a single species. Suppose that at a future moment in biological history sabre-toothed tigers reappeared on earth. And suppose these new sabre-toothed tigers possessed an identical form to that of extinct sabre-toothed tigers. (Suppose they could interbreed.) On the formalist account, these new sabre-toothed tigers would be the same species. On the species-as-individuals account, they would be different species. If, however, these new sabre-toothed tigers and the old ones were indistinguishable, classifying them differently would be to appeal to something other than the science of biology.

The species-as-individuals view identifies species with the historical context. Suppose we were to define "football" as a family of events that took place in American history in the twentieth and twenty-first centuries. It is true that football is a family of events that has taken place in America in those centuries, but surely, this would not be what makes football what it is. What makes football what it is is the way it is played, the rules of the game, the way the ball is shaped, and so on. The fact that something happened at a specific time and place does not tell us, in any deeper sense, what it is.

Seen from an Aristotelian perspective, these "evolutionary approaches" to the species problem are misguided. We cannot have a biological kind that stays the same while becoming something different and so any attempt to come up with a definition of species that changes while remaining the same species is doomed to fail. It will collapse into contradiction. We can still account for evolutionary change, but evolution must be understood as a matter of the efficient rather than the formal cause. We must not confuse process with form. What an organism is is its form, not the way it got that form.

Extension and Intension: Conflating Terms

Familiar misinterpretations of Aristotle conflate two senses of the term "species." Understood in the sense of extension, a species is made up of the individual organisms that share the same form; understood in the sense of intension, a species is the form itself. On the conventional view, Aristotle's account is incompatible with evolution, for Aristotle believed that species are static. But this is too simple. Aristotle believed that species, in the sense of formal distinctions, are static. This leaves open the possibility of the extension of a species changing. This is all we need for evolution.

Stamos cites Aristotle's example of the bronze sphere discussed in the *Metaphysics*.[107] Aristotle's claim is that we can make particular bronze spheres but cannot make the form or essence of a "sphere."[108] The shape "sphere" is a first principle. Individual spheres can change. But the spatial possibility we call "sphere" cannot do so. I can turn this individual sphere into a cube. But this does not turn the shape "sphere" into the shape "cube." In the process of transformation, the shape "sphere" is left behind, and a new form "cube" comes into existence. The matter that used to be "sphere" becomes something else. Although we can make a particular instance of matter conform to this or that set of formal specifications, the shape "sphere" is an objective possibility somehow imposed on us by the world.

Aristotle writes, "the form ... is not produced, nor does production relate to it, – the essence is not produced."[109] The same comment applies to biological species. To say that species are metaphysically fixed is not to say that this or that specimen or population cannot undergo genetic mutation or be transformed by happenstance or even divine agency into another thing. It is to say that when a new species is created, it is a new species. One species does not, in a metaphysical sense, become another one. It becomes

107 "Eg. we make a bronze sphere ... out of this, which is bronze, we make the other, which is a sphere. If then, we make the sphere itself, clearly we must make it in the same way, and the process of making will regress to infinity" (*Metaphysics* [Ross], 1033b2–10, cited in Stamos, *Species Problem*, 105).

108 His argument is from the implied infinite regress. If we were to make the shape "sphere," we would have to make it out of a previous shape that was made out of a previous one again, and so on, *ad infinitum*.

109 *Metaphysics* (Ross), 1033b2–10, cited in Stamos, *Species Problem*, 105.

a *different* one. The old species is left behind, and a new one comes into being. If wolf dogs were to evolve under evolutionary pressure into horse dogs, they would no longer be wolf dogs. They would be a different kind of animal. This sort of transition does not entail one formal possibility becoming another one; it involves the appearance of a new form arising out of something different.

We may, in the sense of the extension of a species, have one made up of a historical group of individuals. We may even have a species made up of one individual, say, the last dodo bird or the last passenger pigeon. And we may "have" an extinct species, a species which no longer exists. But these considerations do not undermine Aristotle's account. If *Triceratops horridus* (a rhinoceros-like dinosaur) is now extinct, this does not change what *T. horridus* was. What *T. horridus* was is a formal possibility that was realized (or instantiated) at a particular moment in time. The intension of the term *T. horridus* is the same yesterday, today, and tomorrow. This is the thing that, for Aristotle, does not change. It cannot change, because as soon as we begin changing this form, we end up with a different formal possibility, with a different kind of thing. It is perhaps the modern neglect of metaphysics that misconstrues these issues.

Aristotle and Evolution

Aristotle's biological thought is ahistorical. He situates the efficient cause of species in male and female principles.[110] He does not envision any evolutionary factors playing a role as a determinant of biological form. If, however, Aristotle does not present a theory of biological evolution, we can get some idea of how he might respond to such a possibility. In his *Politics*, Aristotle comments on Plato's earlier political masterpiece, *The Republic*. In books 8 and 9 of *The Republic*, Plato had chronicled the decay of an aristocracy into a tyranny. Seen from an Aristotelian perspective, this downward process of political de-evolution moves from the species aristocracy, to the species timocracy (rule by the honourable), to that of oligarchy, to democracy, to tyranny. It is the same population that undergoes each of these changes. Although the matter remains more or less the same, the form (i.e., the manner of government) changes. In the case of biological evolution, we could envisage a similar procedure.

Assume then that an Aristotelian account of biological evolution would largely resemble this Platonic account of the de-evolution of the political,

110 Aristotle goes on to argue that the male is the dominant principle. See *On the Generation of Animals*, pt 2, ch. 1, 732a1–11.

moving, not from best to worst, but from best in these circumstances to best in these other circumstances. (This is a bit of a stretch, but it is not unthinkable.) On an Aristotelian account, then, the species would be formal possibilities. These possibilities may be realized or not, depending on precise historical circumstances. Some formal possibilities would be felicitous; they would thrive. The vast majority would perish. A living species would be a successful formal possibility. When one species developed into another, there would be a (successful) change in form. Evolution would have to entail a movement through successful forms, like movement up the rungs of a ladder or up the steps of a staircase. It would be the efficient (and not the formal) cause that would bring about change in form. When species became extinct, that formal possibility would no longer be instantiated in existent individuals. But the formal possibility would remain the same as before. If rhinoceroses became extinct, this would not change what a rhinoceros is (or was). It would only mean that all the rhinoceroses would have disappeared.

On Aristotle's account, species would not come in degrees like concentrations of a soluble chemical in water. They would come in leaps and bounds. The individual members of a species would embody (to whatever successful degree) a recognizable essence. An essence would be a successful formal possibility that resulted from evolutionary change. Think of a man standing on a tightrope. If he leans too far to the right or left, too far frontward or backward, he perishes. Species would be like this. The essence would be the point of equilibrium, the model, pattern, or form that succeeded. It would not be the case (contrary to Aristotle's own apparent suggestion) that any selection of living attributes or properties could coexist in any order. Nature would be parsimonious; it would only tolerate very specific possibilities, and so life would manifest itself in distinct natural kinds, in discrete bundles of idiosyncrasy. This would leave open the possibility of sibling species and hybrid species and other complications.

An Aristotelian concept of evolution would resemble most closely the modern niche concept. On niche theories of evolution, successful adaptations are purposeful, not in the sense that they represent a deliberate, conscious attempt to adapt to changing circumstances, but in the sense that they inevitably promote a precise end – i.e., species survival. Successful formal possibilities exploit the resources available in specific environments. Nature responds to and fills up the spaces available for life. Whether this or other accounts are compatible with a higher purpose is not an issue I will consider here.

I have not tried to articulate any technical answer to biological questions. How can we best distinguish in the field between diverse biological kinds? It is not for philosophers to dictate to practicing biologists. Biology is as much practical and pragmatic as it is theoretical. We do not decide beforehand what the appropriate divisions and distinctions are. We go out and observe what is out there. This is in line with the Aristotelian emphasis on observation. It will be enough if we have shown that mainstream biology can be inscribed within the general metaphysical orientation Aristotle provides.

CONCLUSION TO THE BOOK

Moving beyond evolution, let us return to Aristotle's account of induction. The term "natural kind" is usefully ambiguous. We might claim that an elephant is a natural kind, so too an electron, and a volcano – that even an angel is a natural kind. We can extend the term to non-substances, to activities, properties, and dispositions. An irrational number is, in this secondary sense, a natural kind, also sexual reproduction, gender, courage, and so on. I will not attempt any taxonomy of natural kinds here; nor shall I try to distinguish, in any comprehensive way, genuine from counterfeit natural kinds. Suffice it to say that our ability to recognize natural kinds is the root source of induction.

As we have seen, induction presupposes the logical principle that things that possess the same nature must have the same properties. Logically, this does not seem momentous. (Logic is not intended to be momentous.) The new essentialist refers to natural kinds as "homeostatic clusters of properties." The important point is that if the world is inhabited by natural kinds (and all the evidence indicates that it is), our knowledge of the properties of one instance of a natural kind can be transferred to all other such instances. This is how induction works. We see patterns, connections, identify properties, grasp the fundamental natures of things, discover order in the world – not mechanically, not through mere enumeration, but through the kind of creative inductive insight Aristotle champions.

I have argued that Aristotle's basic understanding of induction provides a philosophical framework to solve contemporary philosophical problems. One could complain that any return to Aristotle is just too old-fashioned to countenance. This *argmentum ad populum* has more influence among working scholars than one might admit. But trends aside, Aristotle's thought represents a perennial resource. His ancient empiricism solves seemingly intractable problems posed by the reigning orthodoxy willed to us by such influential authors as Descartes, Locke, Hume, and Kant. It avoids the complication of comprehensive Cartesian doubt. It proposes a mitigated metaphysical realism that acknowledges the limits of human knowledge without descending into the chaos of an unanswerable scepticism.

The new, modern rationalism demands that we prove the first principles of both science and morality. Any such request is misguided. The whole edifice of human intellectual inquiry derives ultimately from a power of intelligent discernment understood not as a feeling but as an intelligent mental penetration. We cannot prove the first principles of human knowledge, for there is nothing we can use to prove them. There is nothing prior to first principles. We have to create them out of nothing. That is to say, we have to bring something more out of something that is less. Induction is more than an argument form, more than the inductive syllogism. It is the expression of a creative capacity to discern universal concepts and principles in the raw data of particular sense experience. First principles come into existence by a stroke of cognitive insight.

The human mind is like Michelangelo's sculptor. It can hit on the form hidden in the particular sense-datum. It does this through a leap of inspiration, through a movement of non-discursive reason. To disallow this cognitive movement, to treat it as unjustified or problematic or inappropriate, is to undermine both science and morality. Hume's modern followers vastly underrate the impact of inductive scepticism. Taken seriously, the apparent problem of induction subverts all pretensions to human knowledge.

Everything ultimately springs from and depends on the initial movements of human understanding. We cannot explain the most fundamental intelligence by means of anything else. At times in philosophical argument, we arrive at an assertion or a belief that is so certain there is nothing more certain we can use to support it. These are the starting points, the first principles of human reason. We can question the precise way an author formulates or describes or accounts for individual claims or conclusions. But we cannot eliminate the starting points. Philosophy may teach us how to argue, but philosophical acumen also means knowing when justification must come to an end, i.e., when to stop arguing.

Induction is prior to science and morality. It makes morality and science possible, but it also sets impenetrable limits on human understanding. The space we live in has walls, walls we cannot go around, cannot tunnel through. Science, by itself, is powerless to move beyond those walls. Morality, widely construed, perhaps comes closer, but even morality fails at the edges. All human knowledge comes to an end. As an old colleague used to insist, there is no complete explanation of everything. Understanding eventually falters and the light goes dim.

All knowledge begins in induction. This is where the door shuts, where the map ends. Philosophy can go no further. The only thing that can get us beyond this closed door is mysticism and her blind sister, faith. Faith believes without seeing. Mysticism – if it is a genuine possibility – sees the ineffable. But there is nothing else. And if faith and mysticism fail, well, then we must humbly accept our predicament.

This is a book about Aristotle, but Aristotle is only important insomuch as he is an aid to understanding. As Aristotle indicates, all knowledge can be traced back to the intelligent operation of the intellect. At the very beginning of knowledge, at the point where sense perception is somehow transmuted into thought proper, we must all rely on that condition of immediate enlightenment that philosophers in the Western tradition variously term *nous, noesis, intellectus, intelligentia,* the light of nature, natural law, creativity, insight, and so on. On this, and on nothing else, everything depends.

I have tried to investigate at length the beginnings of human knowledge. Perhaps T.S. Eliot best captures the human predicament in "Little Gidding" (No. 4 of *Four Quartets*). Let his eloquent words stand as a hopeful metaphor for what I have tried to accomplish here:

> We shall not cease from exploration
> And the end of all our exploring
> Will be to arrive where we started
> And know the place for the first time.

Bibliography

L'Académie Française, *Le dictionnaire de l'Académie française.* Paris: Jean Baptiste Coignard, 1694. http://dictionnaires.atilf.fr/dictionnaires/ACADEMIE/PREMIERE/premiere.fr.html

Alberti, Leon Battista. *Della pittura e della statua.* Milan: Società Tipografica de'Classici Italiani, 1804.

Albertus, Magnus. *Opera omnia.* Vol. 2. Edited by Augustus Borgnet. Paris: Vives, 1890.

Ammonius Hermeiou. *Pars I: Ammonius in Aristotelis categorias commentarium.* Edited by Adolfus Busse and Maximilianus Wallies. Berlin: G. Reimeri, 1895.

Annas, Julia. "Virtue Ethics and Egoism." *A Priori* 2 (January 2003): 20–31. http://www.apriori.canterbury.nz

– "Virtue Ethics and Social Psychology." *A Priori* 2 (January 2003): 20–34. http://www.apriori.canterbury.nz

Anscombe, G.E.M. "Modern Moral Philosophy." *Philosophy* 33 (Spring 1958): 1–19.

Aristotle. *Aristotle in 23 Volumes.* Cambridge, MA: Harvard University Press; London: William Heinemann, 1944 and 1960. Includes *Categories* (Harold Cook), *Eudemian Ethics* (H. Rackman), *Metaphysics* (Hugh Tredennick), *On Breadth* (W.S. Hett), *On Interpretation* (Harold Cook), *On the Soul* (W.S. Hett), *Parva Naturalia* (W.S. Hett), *Parts of Animals* (W. Ogle); *Politics* (H. Rackham), *Posterior Analytics* (Hugh Tredennick), *Prior Analytics* (Hugh Tredennick), *Rhetoric* (J.H. Freese), and *Topics* (E.S. Forester).

– *Aristotle's Posterior Analytics.* Translation with commentaries and glossary by Hippocrates G. Apostle. Grinnell, IA: Peripatetic Press, 1981.

– *Aristotle's Posterior Analytics.* Translated by Jonathan Barnes. Oxford: Clarendon Press, 1975.

– *Aristotle's Prior and Posterior Analytics.* Translated by W.D. Ross. London: Everyman's, 1949.

– *The Complete Works of Aristotle.* Edited by Jonathan Barnes. Princeton, NJ: Princeton University Press, 1984. Includes *Categories* (J.L. Ackrill), *De Interpretatione* (J.L. Ackrill), *Eudemian Ethics* (J. Solomon), *History of Animals* (d'A.W. Thompson), *Metaphysics* (W.D. Ross), *Movement of Animals* (A.S.L. Farquharson), *Nicomachean Ethics* (W.D. Ross, revised by J.O. Urmson), *On Generation and Corruption* (H.H. Joachim), *On the Generation of Animals* (A. Platt), *On the Soul* (J.A. Smith), *Physics* (R.P. Hardie and R.K. Gaye), *Politics* (B. Jowett), *Posterior Analytics* (Jonathan Barnes), *Prior Analytics* (A.J. Jenkinson), *Rhetoric* (W. Rhys Roberts), *Topics* (W.A. Pickard-Cambridge), and *Sense and Sensibilia* (J.I. Beare).

– *Nicomachean Ethics.* Translated by Martin Ostwald. Indianapolis, IN: Bobbs-Merrill, 1962.

– *Nicomachean Ethics.* Translated by W.D. Ross. Revised by J.L. Ackrill and J.O. Urmson. Oxford: Oxford University Press, 1998.

– *The Philosophy of Aristotle.* Edited by Renford Bambrough. Translated by A.J. Wardman and J.L. Creed. New York: Mentor, 1995. Includes *Categories, Metaphysics, Nicomachean Ethics, On Interpretation, Physics, Poetics, Politics, Posterior Analytics,* and *Psychology.*

– *Physics.* Translated by Robin Waterfield. Introduction and notes by David Bostock. Oxford: Oxford University Press, 1999.

– *Works of Aristotle.* Vol. 1. Edited by W.D. Ross. London: Oxford University Press, 1928. Includes *Analytica Posteriora* (G.R.C. Mure), *Analytica Priora* (A.J. Jenkinson), *Categoriae* and *De Interpretatione* (E.M. Edghill), *De Sophisticis Elenchis* (W.A. Pickard-Cambridge), and *Topica* (W.A. Pickard-Cambridge).

Asimov, Isaac. *The Intelligent Man's Guide to Science.* New York: Basic Books, 1960.

Augustine. *Tractates on the First Epistle of John.* Translated by John Rettig. Washington, DC: Catholic University of America Press, 1995. Includes vol. 92, *The Fathers of the Church.*

– *The City of God Against the Pagans.* Translated by Marcus Dodds. New York: Modern Library, 1993.

– *Confessions.* Translated by Henry Chadwick. Oxford: Oxford University Press, 1998.

– *On The Holy Trinity; Doctrinal Treatises; Moral Treatises.* Translated by A.W. Haddan. In *A Select Library of the Nicene and Post-Nicene Fathers of The Christian Church.* Vol. 3. Edited by Philip Schaff. Edinburgh; Grand Rapids, MI: Eerdmans, 1989.

Bacon, Francis. *Advancement of Learning; Novum Organum; New Atlantis.* Chicago, IL: Encyclopedia Britannica Inc., 1952.

– *New Organon.* In *Modern Philosophy: An Anthology of Primary Sources.* Edited by Roger Ariew and Eric Watkins. Indianapolis; Cambridge, MA: Hackett, 1998.

– *The New Organon.* Edited by Lisa Jardine and Michael Silverthorne. Cambridge; New York: Cambridge University Press, 2000.

– *The New Organon*. In *The Works of Francis Bacon*. Edited by J. Spedding. London: Longmans, 1857–74. Reprint, *The Oxford Bacon* (Oxford: Clarendon Press, 1996).

– *Valerius Terminus: Of the Interpretation of Nature*. University of Adelaide Library, Electronic Texts Collection. http://ebooks.adelaide.edu.au/b/bacon/francis/valerius/

Balme, D.M. "Aristotle's Biology Was Not Essentialist." In *Philosophical Issues in Aristotle's Biology*, edited by Allan Gotthelf and James G. Lennox, 291–302. Cambridge: Cambridge University Press, 1987.

– "Aristotle's Reform of Paideia." In *The Paideia Project ON-LINE*. Twentieth World Congress of Philosophy, Boston, MA, 10–15 August 1998. http://www.bu.edu/wcp/Papers/Anci/AnciBark.htm

– "ΓΕΝΟΣ and ΕΙΔΟΣ in Aristotle's Biology." *Classical Quarterly* 12 (1962): 81–98.

Barker, Evelyn M. "Aristotle's Logic: Techne or Episteme?" In *The Philosophy of Logos*. Vol. 1, edited by K.I. Boudouris, 38–50. Athens: International Centre for Greek Philosophy, 1996.

Barker, S.F. *Induction and Hypothesis*. Ithaca, NY: Cornell, 1957.

Barnes, Jonathan. *Aristotle: A Very Short Introduction*. Oxford: Oxford University Press, 2000.

– "Aristotle's Theory of Demonstration." *Phronesis* 14 (1969): 123–52. Revised in Jonathan Barnes, Malcolm Schofield, and Richard Sorabji, eds, *Articles on Aristotle* (London: Gerald Duckworth & Co., 1975), 65–87.

– ed. *The Cambridge Companion to Aristotle*. Cambridge: Cambridge University Press, 1995.

– "Life and Work." In Barnes, *Cambridge Companion to Aristotle*, 1–26.

Baum, Robert. *Logic*. New York: Holt, Rinehart & Winston, 1975.

Baynes, Thomas Spencer. *An Essay in the New Analytic of Forms*. New York: B. Franklin, 1971. Reprint of 1850 ed.

Beck, J.L. *The Metaphysics of Descartes: A Study of the* Meditations. Oxford: Clarendon Press, 1965.

Beneke, Friedrich Eduard. *Syllogismorum Analyticorum Origines et Ordinem Naturalem*. Berlin: Mittler, 1839.

– *System der Logik als Kunstlehre des Denkens*. Berlin: F. Dümmler, 1842.

Bentham, George. *Outline of a New System of Logic: With a Critical Examination of Dr Whately's Elements of Logic*. London: Hunt & Clarke, 1827.

Bergmann, Merrie, James Moor, and Jack Nelson. *The Logic Book*. New York: Random House, 1980.

Biondi, Paolo. *Aristotle: Posterior Analytics II.19*. St Foy, PQ: Laval University Press, 2004.

Bloom, Allen. *The Closing of the American Mind*. New York: Simon & Schuster, 1987.

Blumberg, Albert. *Logic*. New York: Alfred Knopf, 1976.

Boethius, *Anicii Manlii Severini Boetii commentarii in librum* Peri Hermeneias *[recensuit Carolus Meiser]* [*Commentaries on Aristotle's* De Interpretatione, edited by Carolus Meiser. Reprint, New York: Garland, 1987. Originally published by Teubner, 1877–80.

– *In Categorias Aristotelis Libri Quattuor.* In *Patrologiae Cursus Completus: Series Latina.* Vol. 64. Edited by J.-P. Migne. Paris: Garnier, 1844–64.

– *The Consolation of Philosophy.* Translated by V.E. Watts. London: Penguin, 1969.

Bosanquet, Bernard. "Logic as the Science of Knowledge." In *Essays in Philosophical Criticism.* Edited by A. Seth and R.B. Haldane, 67–101. London: Longmans, 1883.

– *Logic or the Morphology of Knowledge.* Edited by William Sweet. Bristol: Thoemmes Press, 1999. Reprint of Oxford: Clarendon Press, 1911.

Bourgey, Louis. *Observation et expérience chez Aristote.* Paris: Vrin, 1955.

Bowen, Francis. *A Treatise on Logic, or The Laws of Pure Thought.* Boston: Allyn & Bacon, 1895.

Boyd, Richard. "Homeostasis, Species and Higher Taxa." In *Species: New Interdisciplinary Essays,* edited by R.A. Wilson, 141–85. Cambridge, MA: MIT Press, 1999.

– "Realism, Anti-Foundationalism and the Enthusiasm for Natural Kinds." *Philosophical Studies* 61 (1991): 127–48.

Brentano, Franz. *Psychology from an Empirical Standpoint.* Edited by Linda L. MacAlister. Translated by A. Rancurello, D.B. Terrell, and Linda L. McAlister. London: Routledge & Kegan Paul, 1973.

Burma, Benjamin. "Reality, Existence and Classification: A Discussion of the Species Problem." *Madrono* 12 (1954): 193–209.

Burnet, John. *Platonism.* Westport, CT: Greenwood Press, 1928.

Bynum, Terrell Ward. "A New Look at Aristotle's Theory of Perception." *History of Philosophy Quarterly* 4 (1987): 163–78.

Byrne, Christopher. "Prime Matter and Actuality." *Journal of the History of Philosophy* 33, no. 2 (April 1995): 197–224.

Campbell, Norman. *Foundations of Science.* New York: Dover, 1957.

– *What Is Science?* New York: Dover, 1952.

Campenhausen, Hans Freiherr von. *The Fathers of the Latin Church.* Translated by Manfred Hoffman. Stanford, CA: Stanford University Press, 1964. Translation of *Lateinische Kirchenväter.*

Cantor, Norman, and Peter Klein. *Ancient Thought: Plato and Aristotle.* Waltham, MA: Blaisdell, 1969.

Carnap, Rudolf. *The Logical Syntax of Language.* London: Routledge & Kegan Paul, 1949.

Carroll, Lewis [Charles Lutwidge Dodgson]. *Symbolic Logic.* Edited by William Bartley. New York: Clarkson N. Potter, 1977.

– "What the Tortoise Said to Achilles." *Mind,* n.s., 4, no. 14 (April 1895): 278–89.

Catholic Encyclopedia. Edited by Charles Herbermann, Edward Pace, Condé Benoist Pallen, Thomas Joseph Shahan, John Wynne. New York: Robert Appleton, 1910. http://www.newadvent.org/cathen/

Chaffee, John. *Thinking Critically.* Boston, MA: Houghton Mifflin, 1994.

Cicero, Marcus Tullius. *De natura deorum; Academica.* Translated by H. Rackham. London: W. Heinemann; New York: G.P. Putnam's Sons, 1933.

Clarke, Desmond. *Descartes' Philosophy of Science.* Manchester, UK: University of Manchester Press, 1982.

Clarke, Richard. *Logic.* London: Longmans, Green & Co., 1889.

Clements, Robert. *Michelangelo's Theory of Art.* New York: New York University Press, 1961.

– *The Poetry of Michelangelo.* New York: New York University Press, 1965.

Coffey, Peter. *The Science of Logic: An Inquiry into the Principles of Accurate Thought and Scientific Method.* Vols. 1–2. London: Longmans, Green & Co., 1918.

Cohen, Jonathan. *An Essay on Belief and Acceptance.* Oxford: Clarendon Press, 1992.

Cohen, L. "Can Human Irrationality Be Experimentally Demonstrated?" *Behavioral and Brain Sciences* 4 (1981): 317–70.

Cohen, Morris, and Ernest Nagel. *An Introduction to Logic and Scientific Method.* New York: Harcourt, Brace & Co., 1934.

Conway, David, and Ronald Munson. *The Elements of Reasoning.* Belmont, CA: Wadsworth, 1997.

Copi, Irving. *An Introduction to Logic.* 2nd ed. New York: Macmillan, 1961.

Copi, Irving, and Carl Cohen. *An Introduction to Logic.* 9th ed. New York: Macmillan, 1994.

Copleston, Frederick. *Greece and Rome.* Vol. 1 of *A History of Philosophy.* Garden City, NY: Image, 1962.

– *Aquinas.* Middlesex, UK: Penguin, 1955.

Cornford, Francis. *Plato's Theory of Knowledge: The Theaetetus and the Sophist.* London: Routledge & Kegan Paul, 1933.

Corrigan, Kevin. *Reading Plotinus: A Practical Introduction to Neoplatonism.* West Lafayette, IN: Purdue University Press, 2005.

Cottingham, John. *A Descartes Dictionary.* Oxford: Blackwell, 1993.

Crumley, Thomas. *Logic: Deductive and Inductive.* New York: Macmillan, 1947.

Curd, Martin. *Argument and Analysis: An Introduction to Philosophy.* St Paul, MN: West Group, January 1992.

Curley, Edwin. "Rationalism." In *A Companion to Epistemology,* edited by Jonathan Dancy and Ernest Sosa, 411–15. Oxford: Blackwell Publishing, 1991.

Damer, Edward T. *Attacking Faulty Reasoning.* Belmont, CA: Wadsworth, 1980.

de Morgan, Augustus. *On the Syllogism and Other Logical Writings.* Edited by Peter Heath. New Haven, CT: Yale University Press, 1966.

DeMoss, David. "Acquiring Ethical Ends." *Ancient Philosophy* 10 (1990): 63–79.

– "Aristotle, Connectionism, and the Morally Excellent Brain." Paper presented at the Twentieth World Congress of Philosophy, Boston, MA, 10–15 August 1998. In *Paideia.* http://www.bu.edu/wcp/Papers/Cogn/CognDemo.htm

De Pierris, Graciela. "Hume's Pyrrhonian Skepticism and the Belief in Causal Laws." *Journal of the History of Philosophy* 39, no. 3 (2001): 351–83.

de Rijk, Lambertus Marie. *Aristotle: Semantics and Ontology.* 2 vols. Boston, MA: Brill, 2002.

Descartes, René. *Discourse on Method and Meditations.* Translated by Laurence J. Lafleur. Indianapolis, IN: Bobbs-Merrill, 1960.

– *Discourse on Method and Meditations on First Philosophy.* Translated by Donald Cress. Indianapolis, IN: Hackett, 1998.

– *Oeuvres de Descartes.* 12 vols. Translated by Charles Adams and Paul Tannery. Paris: J. Vrin, 1996. Includes vol. 6, *Discours de la Methode and Essais*; vol. 7, *Meditationes de Prima Philosophia*; vol. 8: *Principia Philosophiae*; vol. 9, *Meditations et principes* (French translation of *Principia Philosophiae* by L.C. d'Albert).

– *The Philosophical Works of Descartes.* 2 vols. Translated by Elizabeth Haldane and G.E.T. Ross. Cambridge: Cambridge University Press, 1968. Includes *Rules* and *Replies to Objections II.*

– *The Philosophical Writings of Descartes.* 2 vols. Translated by John Cottingham, Robert Stoothoff, and Dugald Murdoch. Cambridge; New York: Cambridge University Press, 1984–1991.

– *La recherche de la vérité par la lumière naturelle.* Pp. 1100–41 in *Oeuvres Philosophiques.* Vol. 2 (1638–42). Paris: Classiques Garnier, 1999.

– *Régles pour la direction de l'esprit.* Translated and annotated by Jacques Brunschwig. Pp. 66–204 in *Oeuvres Philosophiques.* Vol. 1 (1618–37). Paris: Classiques Garnier, 1999.

Detel, Wolfgang. *Aristoteles: Analytica Posteriora.* Berlin: Akademie-Verlag, 1993.

Detienne, Marcel, and Jean-Pierre Vernant. *Cunning Intelligence in Greek Culture and Society.* Translated by Janet Lloyd. Chicago: University of Chicago Press, 1991.

Dewey, John. *Human Nature and Conduct: An Introduction to Social Psychology.* London: George Allen & Unwin, 1922.

Dictionary of Latin and Greek Theological Terms: Drawn Principally from Protestant Scholastic Theology. Edited by Richard A. Muller. Grand Rapids, MI: Baker Book House, 1985.

Duns Scotus, John. *Opera omnia.* Edited by L. Wadding. Paris: Vives, 1893.

– *Philosophical Writings: A Selection.* Edited and translated by Alan Wolter. Indianapolis, IN: Bobbs-Merrill, 1962.

Dupré, John. *The Disorder of Things: Metaphysical Foundations of the Disunity of Science.* Cambridge, MA: Harvard University Press, 1993.

Eaton, Ralph. *General Logic.* New York: Charles Scribner's Sons, 1931.

Eemeren, Frans van, and Rob Grootendorst, eds. *Argumentation, Communication, and Fallacies: A Pragma-Dialectical Perspective.* Hillsdale, NJ: Lawrence Erlbaum Associates, 1992.

Eemeren, Frans van, Rob Grootendorst, J. Anthony Blair, and Charles Willard, eds. *Proceedings of the Third ISSA Conference on Argumentation.* Amsterdam: International Centre for the Study of Argumentation, 1995.

Eliot, Thomas Stearns. *Four Quartets.* London: Folio Society, 1968. http://www.tristan.icom43.net/quartets/gidding.html.

Ellis, Brian. *The Philosophy of Nature: A Guide to the New Essentialism.* Montreal: McGill-Queen's University Press, 2002.

Encyclopedia of Philosophy. Edited by Paul Edwards. New York: Macmillan, 1967.

Engberg-Pedersen, Troels. "More on Aristotelian *Epagoge.*" *Phronesis* 24 (1979): 301–19.

Engel, S. Morris. *Analyzing Informal Fallacies.* Englewood Cliffs, NJ: Prentice Hall, 1980.

Englebretsen, George. *Three Logicians: Aristotle, Leibniz, and Sommers and the Syllogistic.* Assen, Netherlands: Van Gorcum, 1981.

Ennis, Robert H. "Identifying Implicit Assumptions." *Synthese* 51 (1982): 61–86.

Etzioni, Amitai. *The New Golden Rule.* New York: Basic Books, 1996.

Euclid, *Thirteen Books of Euclid's Elements.* Translated, with introduction, by Thomas L. Heath from the text of Heiberg. New York: Dover, 1956.

Everson, Stephen. *Aristotle on Perception.* Oxford: Oxford University Press, 1997.

Fann, K.T. *Pierce's Theory of Induction.* The Hague: Martinus Nijhoff, 1970.

Fearnside, W. Ward, and William Holther. *Fallacy: The Counterfeit of Argument.* Englewood Cliffs, NJ: Prentice Hall, 1959.

Feldman, Richard. *Reason and Argument.* Saddle River, NJ: Prentice Hall, 1999.

Festinger, Leon. *A Theory of Cognitive Dissonance.* Stanford, CA: Stanford University Press, 1957.

Field, J.V., R. Lunard, and T.B. Settle. "The Perspective Scheme of Masaccio's Trinity Fresco." *Nuncius Annali di Storia della Scienza* 4 (1989): 31–118.

Finnis, John. *Of Ethics.* Washington, DC: Georgetown University Press.

Foot, Phillippa. *Natural Goodness.* Oxford: Clarendon Press, 2001.

– *Virtues and Vices, and Other Essays in Moral Philosophy.* Oxford: Basil Blackwell, 1978.

Foundation for Critical Thinking. *The Critical Thinking Community.* Dillon Beach, CA: Foundation for Critical Thinking, n.d. http://www.criticalthinking.org/

Fowler, David. *The Mathematics of Plato's Academy.* Oxford: Clarendon Press, 1987.

Galileo Galilei, "Two Kinds of Properties: From *Il Saggitore* (The Assayer)" [1623], trans. A.C. Danto. In *Introduction to Contemporary Civilization in the West.* 2nd ed. New York: Columbia University Press, 1954, vol. 1, 719–24. http://evans-experientialism.freewebspace.com/galileo.htm

Gaukroger, Stephen. *Cartesian Logic.* Oxford: Clarendon Press, 1989.

– *Explanatory Structures: A Study of Concepts of Explanation in Early Physics and Philosophy.* Atlantic Highlands, NJ: Humanities Press, 1978.

Geach, Peter. *Mental Acts: Their Content and Their Objects.* London: Routledge & Kegan Paul, 1956.

Gerritsen, Suzanna. "A Defense of Deductivism in Reconstructing Unexpressed Premises." In *Studies in Pragma-Dialectics,* edited by F.H. van Eemeren and R. Grootendorst, 41–7. Amsterdam: International Centre for the Study of Argumentation, 1994.

Gilbert, Michael. *Coalescent Argument.* Mahwah, NJ: Erlbaum, 1997.

Gilligan, Carol. *In a Different Voice: Psychological Theory and Women's Development.* Cambridge, MA: Harvard University Press, 1982.

Gilson, Etienne. *The Philosophy of St Thomas.* Translated by Edward Bullough. St Louis: Herder, 1937.

Goldin, Owen. *Explaining an Eclipse: Aristotle's Posterior Analytics II.1–10.* Ann Arbor, MI: University of Michigan Press, 1996.

Goldman, Alvin. *Epistemology and Cognition.* Cambridge, MA: Harvard University Press, 1986.

Goldscheider, Ludwig. *Michelangelo: Paintings-Sculptures-Architecture.* London: Phaidon Press, 1962.

Goodman, Nelson. *Fact, Fiction, and Forecast.* 2nd ed. Indianapolis, IN: Bob-Merrill, 1965.

Govier, Trudy. *A Practical Study of Argument.* 3rd ed. Belmont, CA: Wadsworth, 1992.

– *Problems in Argument Analysis and Evaluation.* Providence, RI: Floris, 1987.

Gracia, Jorge. *Introduction to the Problem of Individuation in the Early Middle Ages.* Washington, DC: Catholic University of America Press, 1984.

Graham, D.W. *Aristotle's Two Systems.* Oxford: Clarendon Press, 1987.

Gredt, Joseph. *Elementa Philosophiae Aristotelico-Thomisticae.* Barcelona: Herder, 1951.

Grene, Marjorie. *A Portrait of Aristotle.* Chicago: University of Chicago Press, 1963.

Groarke, Leo. "Deductivism within Pragma-Dialectics." *Argumentation* 13 (1999): 1–16.

– "In Defence of Deductivism: Replying to Govier." In *Argumentation Illuminated,* edited by Frans van Eemeren, Rob Grootendorst, J. Anthony Blair, and Charles Willard, 113–21. Amsterdam: International Society for the Study of Argument, 1992.

Groarke, Leo, Christopher Tindale, and Linda Fisher. *Good Reasoning Matters.* Toronto: Oxford University Press, 1997.

Groarke, Louis. "A Deductive Account of Induction." *Science et Esprit* 52 (December 2000): 353–69.

– *The Good Rebel.* Madison, NJ: Fairleigh Dickinson University; London: Associated University Presses, 2002.

– "The Art of History: History and the History-Painting Tradition." In *The Philosophy of History: A Re-Examination.* Edited by William Sweet, 63–78. Aldershot, UK: Ashgate, 2004.

– "Looking at Aristotle Through a Prism: The Meaning of Colour." *Kinesis* 20 (Spring 1994): 16–33.

– "Philosophy as Inspiration: Blaise Pascal and the Epistemology of Aphorisms." *Poetics Today* 28(3) (2007): 393–441.

Guthrie, W.K.C. *A History of Greek Philosophy.* Cambridge: Cambridge University Press, 1981.

Hacking, Ian. "Leibniz and Descartes: Proof and Eternal Truths." In *Rationalism, Empiricism, and Idealism,* edited by Anthony Kenny, 47–60. Clarendon Press: Oxford, 1986.

Haldane, John. "Insight, Inference, and Intellection." *American Catholic Philosophical Quarterly* 73 (Annu. Suppl. 1999): 31–45.

Hamblin, Charles Leonard. *Fallacies.* London: Methuen, 1970.

Hamilton, William. *Lectures on Metaphysics and Logic.* Stuttgart-Bad Cannstatt: Friedrich Frommann, 1969. Facs. ed. Edinburgh; London: William Blackwood & Sons, 1864.

Hamlyn, D.W. *Aristotle's "De Anima" Books II and III.* Oxford: Clarendon Press, 1974.

– "Aristotelian *Epagoge.*" *Phronesis* 21 (1976): 167–84.

Hankinson, R.J. "Philosophy of Science." In Barnes, *Cambridge Companion to Aristotle,* 109–18.

Hansen, Hans, and Robert Pinto, eds. *Fallacies: Classical and Contemporary Readings.* University Park, PA: Penn State University Press, 1995.

Harman, G. "Moral Philosophy Meets Social Psychology: Virtue Ethics and the Fundamental Attribution Error." *Proceeding of the Aristotelian Society* (1999): 315–31. http://www.princeton.edu/-harman/Papers/Virtue.html

– "The Non-Existence of Character Traits." *Proceeding of the Aristotelian Society* (1999): 223–6. http://www.princeton.edu/~harman/Papers/Virresp.html

Hartt, Frederick. *The History of Italian Renaissance Art.* Englewood Cliffs, NJ: Prentice Hall; New York: Harry N. Abrams, 1969.

Hempel, Carl. "Studies in the Logic of Confirmation I," *Mind,* n.s., 54, no. 213 (1945): 1–26.

– "Studies in the Logic of Confirmation II," *Mind,* n.s., 54, no. 214 (1945): 97–121.

Hillar, Marian. "The Problem of the Soul in Aristotle's *De Anima.*" In *Essays in the Philosophy of Humanism.* Vol. 3, edited by M. Hillar and F. Prahl, 51–82. Houston: Humanists of Houston, 1994.

Hobbes, Thomas. *Leviathan.* Indianapolis, IN: Hackett, 1994.

– *Leviathan.* Edited with introduction and notes by J.C.A. Gaskin. Oxford: Oxford University Press, 1996.

Holland, Joan, Keith Holyoak, Richard Nisbett, and Paul Thagard. *Induction: Process of Inference, Learning and Discovery.* Cambridge, MA: MIT Press, 1989.

Hospers, John. *An Introduction to Philosophical Analysis.* Upper Saddle River, NJ: Prentice Hall, 1997.

Hull, David. "Are Species Really Individuals?" *Systematic Zoology* 25 (1976): 174–91.

Hume, David. *An Enquiry Concerning Human Understanding.* Edited by E. Steinberg. Indianapolis, IN: Hackett, 1977.

– *An Inquiry Concerning the Principles of Morals.* Edited by Charles W. Hendel. Indianapolis: IN: Hackett, 1957.

– *Enquiries Concerning Human Understanding and Concerning the Principles of Morals.* Edited by L.A. Selby-Bigge. Text revised and notes by P.D. Nidditch. Oxford: Clarendon Press, 1975.

– *Treatise of Human Nature.* 2nd ed. Edited by L.A. Selby-Bigge. Text revised by P.H. Nidditch. Oxford: Clarendon Press, 1978.

– *Treatise of Human Nature.* Edited by David Fate Norton, Mary J. Norton. Oxford: Oxford University Press, 2000.

Hurka, Thomas. *Virtue, Vice and Value.* Oxford: Oxford University Press, 2001.

Hurely, Patrick. *A Concise Introduction to Logic.* 6th ed. Belmont, CA: Wadsworth, 1997.

Huss, Brian. "Cultural Differences and the Law of Noncontradiction: Some Criteria for Further Research." *Philosophical Psychology* 17, no. 3 (September 2004): 375–89.

Hyman, A., and J. Walsh. *Philosophy in the Middle Ages.* Indianapolis, IN: Hackett, 1984.

Irwin, Terence. *Aristotle's First Principles.* Oxford: Clarendon Press, 1988.

Jaeger, Werner. *Aristotle: Fundamentals of the History of His Development.* Translated by R. Robinson. Oxford: Oxford University Press, 1962.

James, William. *The Principles of Psychology.* Cambridge, MA: Harvard University Press, 1981.

Jardine, Nicholas. "Epistemology of the Sciences." In *Cambridge History of Renaissance Philosophy,* edited by Charles Schmitt, 685–711. Cambridge: Cambridge University Press, 1988.

Janson, H.W. *History of Art: A Survey of the Major Visual Arts from the Dawn of History to the Present Day.* Englewood Cliffs, NJ; Prentice Hall; New York: Harry N. Abrams, 1969.

Jevons, William Stanley, "Who Discovered the Quantification of the Predicate?" *Contemporary Review* 21 (1873): 821–4.

John of St Thomas [John Poinsot]. *Outlines of Formal Logic.* Translated by Francis Wade. Milwaukee, WI: Marquette University Press, 1955.

Johnson, David. "Can Abstractions Be Causes?" *Biology & Philosophy* 5 (1990): 63–77.

Johnson, Ralph J. *The Rise of Informal Logic.* Newport News, VA: Vale Press, 1996.
– *Manifest Rationality: A Pragmatic Theory of Argument.* Mahwah, NJ: Lawrence Erlbaum Assoc., 2000.
Johnson, Ralph J., and J. Anthony Blair. *Logical Self-Defense.* 3rd ed. Toronto: McGraw Hill-Ryerson, 1995.
– "Informal Logic: Past and Present." In *New Essays in Informal Logic.* Edited by Ralph Johnson and J. Anthony Blair, 1–19. Windsor, Ontario: Informal Logic, 1994.
Joyce, George. *Principles of Logic.* London: Longmans, Green & Co., 1936.
Kahane, Howard. *Logic and Contemporary Rhetoric.* 7th ed. Belmont, CA: Wadsworth, 1995.
Kant, Immanuel. *Critique of Pure Reason.* Translated by Norman Kemp Smith. London: Macmillan Education, 1933.
Kelly, David. *The Art of Reasoning.* New York: W.W. Norton, 1988.
Kemeny, John. *A Philosopher Looks at Science.* Princeton, NJ: D. van Nostrand, 1959.
Kierkegaard, Søren. *Fear and Trembling / Repetition.* Vol. 6 of *Kierkegaard's Writings.* Edited and translated by Howard and Edna Hong. Princeton, NJ: Princeton University Press, 1985.
– *Sickness unto Death.* Vol. 19 of *Kierkegaard's Writings.* Edited and translated by Howard and Edna Hong. Princeton, NJ: Princeton University Press, 1980.
Kitcher, Philip. "Species." *Philosophy of Science* 51 (1984): 308–33.
Kohlberg, Lawrence. *Essays on Moral Development.* Vol. 1: *The Philosophy of Moral Development.* San Francisco: Harper & Row, 1981.
– *Essays on Moral Development.* Vol. 2: *The Psychology of Moral Development.* San Francisco: Harper & Row, 1984.
Kornblith, Hilary. *Inductive Inference and Its Natural Ground: An Essay in Naturalistic Epistemology.* Cambridge, MA: MIT Press, 1993.
Kripke, Saul. "Outline of a Theory of Truth." In *Recent Essays on Truth and the Liar Paradox,* edited by R.L Martin, 55–81. Oxford: Oxford University Press, 1984.
Koyré, Alexandre. *From the Closed World to the Infinite Universe.* Baltimore; London: Johns Hopkins University Press, 1957.
– "The Liar." *Philosophical and Phenomenological Research* 4, no. 3 (March 1946): 344–62.
Kristeller, Paul Oskar. *Renaissance Thought: The Classic, Scholastic, and Humanist Strains.* New York: Harper & Row, 1961.
Laertius, Diogenes. *Lives of the Eminent Philosophers.* Translated by R.D. Hickes. Cambridge, MA: Harvard University Press, 1931.
Lambert, Karl, and William Ulrich. *The Nature of Argument.* New York: MacMillan, 1980.
Langenscheidt's Greek-English Dictionary. 3rd ed. Edited by Karl Feyerabend. Berlin: Langenscheidt; London: Methuen, 1955.
LaPlace, P.S. *A Philosophical Essay on Probabilities.* Translated by F.W. Truscott and F.L. Emory. New York: Dover, 1951.

Leonardo da Vinci. *The Notebooks of Leonardo da Vinci.* Edited by Edward MacCurley. New York; Garden City: Garden City Publishing, 1941.

Liddell and Scott's Greek-English Lexicon. 7th ed. Oxford: Clarendon Press, 2002.

Locke, John. *An Essay Concerning Human Understanding.* Edited by P. Nidditch. Oxford: Clarendon Press, 1975.

Lonergan, Bernard. *Understanding and Being.* Edited by Elizabeth Morelli and Mark Morelli. Toronto: University of Toronto Press, 1990.

– *Insight: A Study of Human Understanding* New York: Harper & Row, 1978.

Lukasiewicz, J. *Aristotle's Syllogistic from the Standpoint of Modern Formal Logic.* Oxford: Oxford University Press, 1958.

MacKenna, Stephen. "Extracts from the Explanatory Matter in the First Edition." In *Plotinus: The Enneads.* London: Faber & Faber, 1962.

Mackie, J.L. *Problems from Locke.* Oxford: Clarendon Press, 1976.

Maclean, Ian. "Foucault's Renaissance Episteme Reassessed: An Aristotelian Counterblast." *Journal of the History of Ideas* 59, no.1 (1998): 149–166.

Maritain, Jacques. *An Introduction to Logic.* London: Sheed & Ward, 1937.

– *Formal Logic.* New York: Sheed & Ward, 1946.

Martin, Robert. *The Philosopher's Dictionary.* Peterborough, ON: Broadview, 1991.

Mayr, Ernst. *The Growth of Biological Thought.* Cambridge, MA: Harvard University Press, 1982.

– *Toward a New Philosophy of Biology.* Cambridge MA: Harvard University Press, 1988.

McCosh, James. *The Scottish Philosophy, Biographical, Expository, Critical, from Hutcheson to Hamilton.* London: Macmillan & Co., 1875.

McGinn, Colin. *The Making of a Philosopher.* New York: HarperCollins, 2002.

McInerny, Ralph. *Ethica Thomistica: The Moral Philosophy of Thomas Aquinas.* Washington, DC: Catholic University of America Press, 1997.

McKirahan, Richard, Jr. *Philosophy before Socrates.* Indianapolis, IN: Hackett, 1994.

– "Principles and Proofs." *Journal of the History of Philosophy* 32, 2 (April, 1994): 294–296.

– *Principles and Proofs: Aristotle's Theory of Demonstrative Species.* Princeton, NJ: Princeton University Press, 1992.

Meyer, Hans. *The Philosophy of St Thomas Aquinas.* Translated by F. Eckhoff. St Louis, MO: B. Herder, 1944.

McGowan, Kevin, "White Crows?" Cornell Lab of Ornithology website, 2008. http://www.birds.cornell.edu/crows/whitecrows.htm

Michelangelo, Buonarroti, *The Complete Poems of Michelangelo.* Translated by Joseph Tusiani. New York: Noonday Press, 1960.

– *Michelangelo: Life, Letters, and Poetry.* Selected, translated, with an introduction and notes by by George Bull; poems translated by George Bull and Peter Porter. Oxford: Oxford University Press, 1987.

– *The Poetry of Michelangelo.* Translated and annotated by James M. Saslow. New Haven, CT: Yale University Press, 1991.

Mill, John Stuart. *An Examination of Sir William Hamilton's Philosophy.* London: Longmans, Green, Reader & Dyer, 1872.

– *A System of Logic Ratiocinative and Inductive.* London: Longmans, Green & Co., 1952.

– *On Liberty.* In *The Harvard Classics.* Vol. 25, 2. New York: P.F. Collier & Son, 1909–14. http://www.bartleby.com/25/2/2.html

– *On Liberty.* 4th ed. London: Longman, Roberts & Green, 1869.

Millican, Peter. "Induction." In *Encyclopedia of Empiricism,* edited by Dan Garrett and Edward Barbanell. Westport, CT: Greenwood Press, 1997. http://www.davidhume.org/documents/1997InductionEEmp.pdf

Milton, J.R., "Induction before Hume," *British Journal for the Philosophy of Science* 38 (March 1987): 49–74.

Modrak, Deborah. *Aristotle: The Power of Perception.* Chicago: University of Chicago Press, 1987.

Moline, Jon. *Plato's Theory of Understanding.* Madison, WI: University of Wisconsin Press, 1981.

Moore, Brooke, and Richard Parker. *Critical Thinking.* Mountain View, CA: Mayfield, 2001.

Moore, G.E. *Principia Ethica.* Mineola, NY: Dover, 2004.

Moravcsik, J. *Plato and Platonism: Plato's Conception of Appearance and Reality in Ontology, Epistemology, and Ethics, and Its Modern Echoes.* Oxford: Blackwell, 1992.

Mosselman, Bert. "Aristotle's Logic and the Search for Quantification of the Predicate," *Foundations of Science* 13, nos 3–4 (November 2008), 195–8.

Munson, Ronald. *The Way of Words: An Informal Logic.* Boston, MA: Houghton Mifflin, 1976.

Newell, R.W. *The Concept of Philosophy.* London: Methuen, 1967.

Newton, Issac. *The Mathematical Principles of Natural Philosophy.* Translated by Andrew Motto, revised by Florian Cajori. Berkeley, CA: University of California Press, 1934.

Nietzsche, Friedrich. *The Will to Power.* Translated by Walter Kaufmann and R.J. Hollingdale. Edited with commentary by Walter Kaufmann. New York: Vintage Books, 1968.

Nisbett, Richard E. *The Geography of Thought: How Asians and Westerners Think Differently – and Why.* New York: Free Press, 2003.

Nisbett, Richard E., K. Peng, I. Choi, and A. Norenzayan. "Culture and Systems of Thought: Holistic v. Analytic Cognition." *Psychological Review* 108 (April 2001): 291–310.

Nosich, Gerald. *Reasons and Arguments.* Belmont, CA: Wadsworth, 1982.

Ockham, William. *Summa logicae*. St Bonaventure, NY: Franciscan Institute, 1951.

– *Opera philosophica et theologica*. Edited by Gál Gedeon. St Bonaventure, NY: Editiones Instituti Franciscani Universitatis S. Bonaventurae, 1967–85.

– *Philosophical Writings: A Selection*. Translated by Philotheus Boehner, revised by Stephen F. Brown. Indianapolis, IN: Hackett, 1990. Includes *Summa totius logicae*. Vol. 1, ch. 15.

– *Ordinatio*, I, "Prologus." In *Opera theologica*. Edited by Gál Gedeon, 1–324. St Bonaventure, NY: Editiones Instituti Franciscani Universitatis S. Bonaventurae, 1967–85.

Okie, Laird. "Ideology and Partiality in David Hume's *History of England*." *Hume Studies* 11 (April 1985): 1–32.

Olson, Robert. *Meaning and Argument: Elements of Logic*. New York: Harcourt, Brace & World, 1969.

Owen, G.E.L. *Logic, Science and Dialectic: Collected Papers in Ancient Greek Philosophy*. Ithaca, NY: Cornell University Press, 1986.

– "Tithenai ta Phainomena." In *Aristote et les problèmes de méthode*, edited by S. Mansion, 83–103. Louvain: Nauwelaerts, 1961.

Owens, Joseph. *The Doctrine of Being in Aristotelian Metaphysics*. 3rd ed. Toronto: Pontifical Institute of Medieval Studies, 1978.

Oxford Companion to Philosophy. Edited by Ted Honderich. Oxford: Oxford University Press, 1995.

Oxford Dictionary of Philosophy. Edited by Simon Blackburn. New York: Oxford University Press, 1996.

Pascal, Blaise. *De l'esprit géométrique; De l'art de persuader; De l'autorité en matière de philosophie*. Paris: L. Hachette et Cie, 1864.

– *Les Pensées and Other Writings*. Translated by Honor Levi. Edited with introduction and notes by Anthony Levi. Oxford: Oxford University Press, 1999. Includes *The Art of Persuasion*.

– *Les pensées*. Edited with annotations and introduction by Philippe Sellier. Paris: Classiques Garnier Multimédia, 1999.

Peirce, Charles Sanders. "On Pragmatism and Abduction." Harvard Lecture 7, in vol. 5 of *Collected Papers of Charles Sanders Peirce*. Edited by Charles Hartshorne and Paul Weiss, 180–212. Cambridge, MA: Harvard University Press, 1958.

– "Some Consequences of Four Incapacities." In *The Writings of Charles S. Peirce: A Chronological Edition*. Vol. 2, edited by Max H. Fisch, 211–42. Bloomington, IN: Indiana University Press, 1984. Originally published in *Journal of Speculative Philosophy* 2 (1868): 140–57. http://www.peirce.org/writings/p27.html

Pellegrin, Pierre. "A Zoology without Species." In *Aristotle on Nature and Living Things*. Edited by Allan Gotthelf, 95–115. Pittsburgh, PA: Mathesis, 1985.

– *La classification des animaux chez Aristote*. Paris: Belles Lettres, 1986.

Perelman, Chaim, and L. O'lbrecht-Tyteca. *The New Rhetoric: A Treatise on Argumentation.* Translated by J. Wilkinson and P. Weaver. Notre Dame, IN: University of Notre Dame Press, 1969.

Peters, F.E., *Greek Philosophical Terms: A Historical Lexicon.* New York: New York University Press, 1967.

Pieper, Josef. *Scholasticism: Personalities and Problems of Medieval Philosophy.* New York: McGraw-Hill, 1960.

Plato. *The Collected Dialogues of Plato, Including the Letters.* Edited by Edith Hamilton and Huntington Cairns. Princeton: Princeton University Press, 1963. Includes *Laws* (A.E. Taylor), *Letter VII* (L.A. Post), *Meno* (W.K.C. Guthrie), *Republic* (Paul Shorey), *Theaetetus* (F.M. Cornford).

– *The Complete Works.* Edited by John Cooper. Indianapolis, IN: Hackett, 1997. Includes *Republic* (G.M.A. Grube, revised by C.D.C. Reeve).

– *Meno.* Translated by Benjamin Jowett. Upper Saddle River, NJ: Prentice Hall, 1949.

– *Theaetetus / Plato.* Translated by Benjamin Jowett, with intro. by Irving M. Copi. New York: Macmillan, 1949.

– *Timaeus.* Translated by Benjamin Jowett. New York: Macmillan, 1985.

Plotinus. *The Enneads.* Translated by Stephen MacKenna. London: Faber & Faber, 1956.

Popper, Karl. *The Logic of Scientific Discovery.* New York: Routledge, 1980.

Popper, Karl, and John C. Eccles. *The Self and Its Brain: An Argument for Interactionism.* London: Springer, 1977.

Priest, Graham. *In Contradiction.* Dordrecht: Martinus Nijhoff, 1987.

Priest, Graham, and R. Routley, and J. Norman, eds. *Paraconsistent Logic: Essays on the Inconsistent.* Munich: Philosophia, 1989.

Quine, W.V.O. "Two Dogmas of Empiricism." Pp. 20–46 in *From a Logical Point of View.* Cambridge, MA: Harvard University Press, 1953.

Rappe, Sara. *Reading Neo-Platonism: Non-Discursive Thinking in the Texts of Plotinus, Proclus, and Damascius.* Cambridge, MA: Cambridge University Press, 2000.

Reith, Herman. *The Metaphysics of St Thomas Aquinas.* Milwaukee: Bruce Publishing Co., 1958.

Rescher, Nicholas. *Kant's Theory of Knowledge and Reality.* Washington, DC: University Press of America, 1983.

Robinson, Daniel. *Principles of Reasoning.* New York: Appleton, 1927.

Robinson, Michael Rowan. "Was Aristotle the First Physicist?" *Physics Web* (7 January 2002). http://physicsworld.com/cws/article/print/3494

Robinson, T.M. *Heraclitus: Fragments.* Toronto: University of Toronto Press, 1987.

Rosenberg, Alexander. *The Structure of Biological Science.* Cambridge: Cambridge University Press, 1985.

Ross, L., and R. Nisbett. *The Person and the Situation: Perspectives of Social Psychology.* New York: McGraw-Hill, 1991.

Ross, W.D. *Aristotle's Prior and Posterior Analytics*. Oxford: Clarendon Press, 1965.

Routledge Encyclopedia of Philosophy. London; New York: Routledge, 1998.

Ruggiero, Vincent Ryan. *Becoming a Critical Thinker*. 2nd ed. Rapid City, SD: Houghton Mifflin, 1992.

Russell, Bertrand. *My Philosophical Development*. London: George Allen & Unwin, 1959.

– *The Problems of Philosophy*. New York: Oxford, 1959.

– *The Scientific Outlook*. London: George Allen & Unwin, 1931.

Ryle, Gilbert. *The Concept of Mind*. New York: Barnes & Noble, 1949.

Sadovnikov, Slava. "Escape, Fromm, Freedom: The Refutation of Historical Explanations in the Popperian Perspective." *Dialogue* 43 (2004): 239–80.

Salmon, Merilee, John Earman, Clark Glymour, James G. Lennox, Peter Machamer, J.E. McGuire, John D. Norton, Wesley C. Salmon, and Kenneth H. Schaffner, *Introduction to the Philosophy of Science*. Englewood Cliffs, NJ: Prentice Hall, 1992.

Salmon, Wesley. *Four Decades of Scientific Explanation*. Minneapolis, MN: University of Minnesota Press, 1989.

– *Logic*. Englewood Cliffs, NJ: Prentice Hall, 1963.

– *Logic*. 3rd ed. New York: Prentice Hall, 1984.

Sankey, Howard. "Induction and Natural Kinds." *Principia* 1, no. 2 (1997): 239–54. http://www.philosophy.unimelb.edu.au/staff/Sankey/howard/howardpaper3.PDF

Sartre, Jean-Paul. *Being and Nothingness*. Translated by Hazel Barnes. New York: Philosophical Library, 1956. Translation of *L'Être et le néant*.

– "Intuition." In *Classics in Logic*, edited by Dagobert Runes, 693–703. New York: Philosophical Library, 1962.

Schmidt, Robert. *The Domain of Logic According to St Thomas Aquinas*. The Hague: Martinus Nijhof, 1966.

Sextus Empiricus. "Outlines of Pyrrhonism." In *Sextus Empiricus*. Vol. 1. Translated by R.G. Bury. London: W. Heinemann; New York: Putnam, 1933–49.

Shklar, Judith. *Ordinary Vice*. Cambridge MA: Belknap Press of Harvard University Press, 1984.

Shorter Routledge Encyclopedia of Philosophy, The. Edited by Edward Craig. London; New York: Routledge, 2005.

Silverman, Allan. "Colour and Colour-Perception in Aristotle's *De Anima*." *Ancient Philosophy* 9 (Fall 1989): 271–92.

Skyrms, Brian. *Choice and Chance*. Belmont CA: Dickenson, 1966.

Slakey, Thomas. "Aristotle on Sense Perception." *The Philosophical Review* 70 (1961): 470–84.

Smart, J.J.C. *Between Science and Philosophy*. New York: Random House, 1968.

Smith, Marc. "Educating the Human Subject." Paper presented at the Twentieth World Congress of Philosophy, Boston, MA, 10–15 August 1998. In *Paideia*. http://www.bu.edu/wcp/Papers/Educ/EducSmit.htm

– "Essential and Effective Freedom: Reflections Based on the Work of Bernard Lonergan." Paper presented at the Twentieth World Congress of Philosophy, Boston, MA, 10–15 August 1998. In *Paideia.* http://www.bu. edu/wcp/Papers/Acti/ActiSmit.htm

Smith, Robin. "Logic." In Barnes, *Cambridge Companion to Aristotle,* 27–65.

– "Dialectic and Method in Aristotle." Paper presented at the 1996 APA Central Division conference, Section I, Chicago, IL, 27 April. http://aristotle.tamu.edu/Robin/APA-Central-1996.html; reprinted as "Dialectic and Method in Aristotle," pp. 39–56 in May Sim, ed., *From Puzzles to Principles? Essays on Aristotle's Dialectic* (Lexington Books, 1999).

Sober, Elliot. "Evolution, Population Thinking and Essentialism." *Philosophy of Science* 47 (1980): 350–83.

Sorabji, Richard. "Body and Soul in Aristotle." *Philosophy* 49 (1974): 63–89.

– "Intentionality and Physiological Processes: Aristotle's Theory of Sense-Perception." In *Essays on Aristotle's "De Anima,"* edited by M.C. Nussbaum and A. Oksenberg Rorty, 195–227. Oxford: Oxford University Press, 1992.

Stace, W.T. *A Critical History of Greek Philosophy.* London: Macmillan & Co., 1928.

Stamos, David. "Species, Languages, and the Horizontal/Vertical Distinction." *Biology and Philosophy* 17 (2002): 171–98.

– *The Species Problem: Biological Species, Ontology, and the Metaphysics of Biology.* Lanham, MD: Lexington, 2003.

Stanford Encyclopedia of Philosophy. Edited by Edward N. Zalta. Stanford, CA: The Metaphysics Research Lab, various years. http://plato.stanford.edu/

Stanley, Jason. "Philosophy of Language in the Twentieth Century." *Routledge Companion to Twentieth Century Philosophy.* New York: Routledge, 2008. Online preprint. http://www.rci.rutgers.edu/~jasoncs/routledge.pdf

Stich, Stephen. *The Fragmentation of Reason.* Cambridge, MA: MIT Press, 1990.

Stove, D. *Darwinian Fairy Tales.* Aldershot: Ashgate, 1995.

– "Deductivism." *Australasian Journal of Philosophy* 48 (May 1970): 76–98.

– *Probability and Hume's Inductive Scepticism.* Oxford: Clarendon Press, 1973.

– *Rationality of Induction.* Oxford: Clarendon Press, 1986.

– "So You Think You Are a Darwinian?" Royal Institute of Philosophy website. http://www.royalinstitutephilosophy.org/articles/article.php?id=26

Strawson, P.F. *Introduction to Logical Theory.* London: Methuen, 1952.

Sullivan, James Bacon. *An Examination of First Principles in Thought and Being in the Light of Aristotle and Aquinas.* Washington DC: Catholic University of America Press, 1939.

Tappan, Henry. *Elements of Logic.* New York: D. Appleton & Co., 1856.

Taylor, Margaret. *Greek Philosophy*. London: Geoffrey Cumberlege; Oxford University Press, 1924.

Tekippe, Terry. *What Is Lonergan Up To in "Insight"?* Collegeville, MN: Liturgical Press, 1996.

Thagard, Paul. *Coherence in Thought and Action.* Cambridge, MA: MIT Press, 2000.

Thomas Aquinas. *Aristotle,* On Interpretation*: Commentary by St Thomas and Cajetan.* Translated by Jean Oesterle. Milwaukee, WI: Marquette, 1962.

– *Commentarium in libros metaphysicorum.* Vol. 25 of *Opera Omnia.* 34 vols. Edited by E. Fretté and P. Maré. Paris: Vivès, 1871–80.

– *Commentary on the Sentences.* In *St Thomas Aquinas: Philosophical Texts.* Translated by T. Gilby. Oxford: Oxford University Press, 1951.

– *Exposition of the* Posterior Analytics *of Aristotle.* Translated by Pierre Conway. Québec, PQ: La Librairie Philosophique M. Doyon, 1956.

– *On Being and Essence.* Translated by A. Maurer. Toronto: Pontifical Institute, 1949.

– *On the Power of God.* 3 vols. Translated by Laurence Shapcote. London: Burns, Oates & Washbourne, 1932–4. Reprint,Westminster, MD: Newman, 1952.

– *On the Power of God* [*Quaestiones disputatae de potentia Dei*]. Translated by the English Dominican Fathers (revised by L. Shapcote). Westminster, MD: Newman Press, 1952; reprint of 1932. Online ed., edited by Joseph Kenny. http://www.op-stjoseph.org/Students/study/thomas/QDdePotentia.htm

– *Summa theologiae.* 60 vols. Translated by Thomas Gilby et al. London: Eyre & Spottiswoode; New York: McGraw-Hill, 1964–73. Includes vol. 9, *Angels* (K. Foster); vol. 11, *Man* (Timothy Suttor); vol. 23, *An Enquiry Concerning the Principles of Morals* (W.D. Hughes); vol. 28, *Law and Political Theory* (Thomas Gilby); and vol. 35, *Consequences of Charity* (Thomas Heath).

– *Summa Theologica.* 2nd and rev. ed. Translated by Fathers of the English Dominican Province. New York: Benziger, 1947.

Thomas, S.N. *Practical Reasoning in Natural Language.* Englewood Cliffs, NJ: Prentice Hall, 1981.

Toulmin, Stephen. *An Introduction to Reasoning.* New York: Macmillian; London: Collier Macmillian, 1984.

– *The Uses of Argument.* Cambridge: Cambridge University Press, 1964.

Toulmin, Stephen, and Albert Jonsen. *The Abuse of Casuistry.* Berkeley, CA: University of California Press, 1988.

Turner, Denys. *Faith, Reason and the Existence of God.* Cambridge: Cambridge University Press, 2004.

Tymoczko, Tom, and Jim Henle. *Sweet Reason: A Field Guide to Modern Logic.* New York: W.H. Freeman & Co., 1995.

Van Valen, Leigh. "A New Evolutionary Law." *Evolutionary Theory* 1 (1973): 1–30.

Vasari, Giorgio. *The Lives of the Artists: A Selection.* 2 vols. Translated by George Bull. Baltimore, MD: Penguin, 1987.

– *The Lives of the Painters, Sculptors, and Architects.* Vols. 1–4. Translated by A.B. Hinds. London: J.M. Dent & Sons, 1927.

Veatch, Henry B. *Intentional Logic.* New Haven, CT: Yale University Press, 1952.

– *Two Logics: The Conflict between Classical and Neo-Analytic Philosophy.* Evanston, IL: Northwestern University Press, 1969.

Venn, John. *The Principles of Empirical or Inductive Logic.* London: Macmillan & Co., 1889.

– *Symbolic Logic.* 2nd ed. New York: Burt Franklin, 1971.

Vertin, Michael. "Maréchal, Lonergan, and the Phenomenology of Knowing." In *Creativity and Method: Essays in Honour of Bernard Lonergan,* edited by Michael Lamb, 411–22. Milwaukee, WI: Marquette University Press, 1981.

Vickers, John. "The Problem of Induction." In *Stanford Encyclopedia of Philosophy* (2006). http://plato.stanford.edu/entries/induction-problem/

Walton, Douglas. *Argument Structure: A Pragmatic Theory.* Toronto: University of Toronto Press, 1996.

– "Ignoring Qualifications (*Secundum Quid*) as a Subfallacy of Hasty Generalization." *Logique et Analyse* 129–130 (1990): 113–154.

– *Informal Logic: A Handbook for Critical Argumentation.* New York: Cambridge University Press, 1989.

– *The New Dialectic.* Toronto: University of Toronto Press, 1998.

– "The New Dialectic: A Method of Evaluating an Argument Used for Some Purposes in a Given Case." *ProtoSociology* 13 (1999): 70–91.

– "Rethinking the Fallacy of Hasty Generalization," *Argumentation* 13 (1991): 161–82.

– "What Is Reasoning? What Is an Argument?" *Journal of Philosophy* 87 (1990): 399–419.

Warburton, Nigel. "What Is Philosophy." Philosophy Department website, Open University, UK. http://www.open.ac.uk/Arts/philos/whatis.htm

Ward, Julie. "Perception and Logos in *De Anima* II.xii." *Ancient Philosophy* 7 (Fall 1988): 271–92.

Waterfield, Robin. *The First Philosophers: The Presocratics and Sophists.* Translated with commentary by Robin Waterfield. Oxford: Oxford University Press, 2000.

Watts, V.E. Introduction to *The Consolation of Philosophy,* by Boethius. London: Penguin, 1969.

Webb, Clement C. *A History of Philosophy.* London: Thornton Butterworth, 1915.

Webb, Philip. "Bodily Structure and Psychic Faculties in Aristotle's Theory of Perception." *Hermes* 110 (1982): 25–50.

Weinberg, Jonathan, Shaun Nichols, and Stephen Stich. "Normativity and Epistemic Intuitions." *Philosophical Topics* 29 (2001): 429–60. http://www.rci.rutgers.edu/~stich/Publications/Papers/NormativityAndEpistemicIntuitions.pdf

Wellman, Carl. *Challenge and Response: Justification in Ethics.* Carbondale, IL: Southern Illinois University Press, 1971.

Whitehead, Alfred North. *Science and the Modern World.* New York: Macmillan, 1925.

William of Ockham, *Venerabilis inceptoris Guillelmi de Ockham scriptum in librum primum Sententiarum.* Edited by Girardus I. Etzkorn. St Bonaventure, NY: St Bonaventure University, 1977–9.

Williams, Donald Carey. *The Ground of Induction.* New York: Russell & Russell, 1963.

Wittgenstein, Ludwig. *On Certainty.* Edited by G.E.M. Anscombe and G.H. von Wright. Translated by Denis Paul and G.E.M. Anscombe. New York: Harper & Row, 1969.

– *Remarks on the Foundations of Mathematics.* Edited by G.H. Von Wright, R. Rhees, and G.E.M. Anscombe. Translated by G.E.M. Anscombe. Rev. ed. Cambridge MA: The MIT Press: 1983.

– *Tractatus Logico-Philosophicus.* Translated by D.F. Pears and B.F. McGuinness. London: Routledge & Kegan Paul, 1961.

Woods, John, and Douglas Walton. *Argument: The Logic of Fallacies.* Toronto: McGraw-Hill Ryerson, 1982.

– *Fallacies: Selected Papers 1972–1982.* Providence, RI: Foris, 1989.

– "Fearful Symmetry." In *Fallacies: Classical and Contemporary Readings*, edited by H.V. Hansen and R.C. Pinto, 240–50. University Park, PA: Penn State University Press, 1995.

Yezzi, Ron. *Practical Logic.* Mankato, MN: G. Bruno & Co., 1992.

Index